Advanced Applications and Structures in XML Processing:
Label Streams, Semantics Utilization and Data Query Technologies

Changqing Li
Duke University, USA

Tok Wang Ling
National University of Singapore, Singapore

Information Science
REFERENCE

INFORMATION SCIENCE REFERENCE

Hershey · New York

Director of Editorial Content:	Kristin Klinger
Director of Book Publications:	Julia Mosemann
Acquisitions Editor:	Lindsay Johnston
Development Editor:	Joel Gamon
Publishing Assistant:	Carole Coulson, Deanna Zombro
Typesetter:	Michael Brehm
Quality control:	Jamie Snavely
Cover Design:	Lisa Tosheff
Printed at:	Yurchak Printing Inc.

Published in the United States of America by
Information Science Reference (an imprint of IGI Global)
701 E. Chocolate Avenue
Hershey PA 17033
Tel: 717-533-8845
Fax: 717-533-8661
E-mail: cust@igi-global.com
Web site: http://www.igi-global.com/reference

Library of Congress Cataloging-in-Publication Data

Advanced applications and structures in XML processing : label streams, semantics utilization, and data query technologies / Changqing Li and Tok Wang Ling, editors.
    p. cm.
  Includes bibliographical references and index.
  Summary: "This book is for professionals and researchers working in the field of XML in various disciplines who want to improve their understanding of the XML data management technologies, such as XML models, XML query and update processing, XML query languages and their implementations, keywords search in XML documents, database, web service, publish/subscribe, medical information science, and e-business"--Provided by publisher.
  ISBN 978-1-61520-727-5 (hardcover) -- ISBN 978-1-61520-728-2 (ebook) 1. XML (Document markup language) I. Li, Changqing, 1975- II. Ling, Tok Wang.
  QA76.76.H94A387 2010
  006.7'4--dc22
                              2009046730

British Cataloguing in Publication Data
A Cataloguing in Publication record for this book is available from the British Library.

All work contributed to this book is new, previously-unpublished material. The views expressed in this book are those of the authors, but not necessarily of the publisher.

Table of Contents

Section 1
XML Data Management

Detailed Table of Contents

Section 1
XML Data Management

This section discusses different XML data management techniques, including XML native storage, management in object relational database systems, compression, and benchmark.

Chapter 1
    Ning Zhang, Facebook, USA
    M. Tamer Özsu, University of Waterloo, Canada

This chapter reviews different native storage formats and query processing techniques that have been developed in both academia and industry. Among the XML data management issues, storage and query processing are the most critical ones with respect to system performance. Different storage schemes have their own pros and cons. Therefore, based on their own requirements, different systems adopt different storage schemes to tradeoff one set of features over the others. Various XML indexing techniques are also presented since they can be treated as specialized storage and query processing tools.

Chapter 2
    Zhen Hua Liu, Oracle Corporation, USA
    Anguel Novoselsky, Oracle Corporation, USA
    Vikas Arora, Oracle Corporation, USA

This chapter describes the XML data management capabilities in Object Relational DBMS (ORDBMS), various design approaches and implementation techniques to support these capabilities, as well as the pros and cons of each design and implementation approach. Key topics such as XML storage, XML

Indexing, XQuery and SQL/XML processing, are discussed in depth presenting both academic and industrial research work in these areas.

Chapter 3

Chin-Wan Chung, Korea Advanced Institute of Science and Technology (KAIST), Republic of Korea
Myung-Jae Park, Korea Advanced Institute of Science and Technology (KAIST), Republic of Korea
Jihyun Lee, Korea Advanced Institute of Science and Technology (KAIST), Republic of Korea

This chapter provides a better understanding on relevant theoretical frameworks and an up-to-date research trend of the XML compression. Existing XML compression techniques are classified and examined based on their characteristics and experimental evaluations. Also, according to the comprehensive analysis, appropriate XML compression techniques for different environments are recommended. Furthermore, some future research directions on the XML compression are presented.

Chapter 4

Ke Geng, University of Auckland, New Zealand
Gillian Dobbie, University of Auckland, New Zealand

Benchmarks are widely used in database-related research, helping users choose suitable database management systems and helping researchers evaluate their new methods. Recently benchmarks for XML have been designed to support the development of XML tools and systems. In this chapter, XML benchmarks are categorized into four groups: application benchmark, micro benchmark, XML generator and real dataset. Characteristics of each benchmark are discussed and compared. Finally, the future direction of XML benchmarks are discussed.

Section 2
XML Index and Query

This section presents the XML index and query techniques, including XML index structures, labeling, keyword search, and query optimization.

Chapter 5

Samir Mohammad, Queen's University, Canada
Patrick Martin, Queen's University, Canada

This chapter gives a brief history of the creation and the development of the XML data model. Then it discusses the three main categories of indexes proposed in the literature to handle the XML semi-structured data model. Finally, it discusses limitations and open problems related to the major existing indexing schemes.

This chapter shows how to extend the traditional prefix labeling scheme to speedup XML query processing. In addition, for XML documents that are updated frequently, many labeling schemes require relabeling which can be very expensive. A lot of research interest has been generated on designing dynamic XML labeling schemes. Making labeling schemes dynamic turns out to be a challenging problem and many of the approaches proposed only partially avoid relabeling. This chapter describes some recently emerged dynamic labeling schemes that can completely avoid relabeling, making efficient update processing in XML database management systems possible.

This chapter describes the importance, challenges and future directions for supporting XML keyword search. It presents and compares representative state-of-the-art techniques from multiple aspects, including identifying relevant keyword matches and an axiomatic framework to evaluate different strategies, identifying other relevant data nodes, ranking schemes, indexes and materialized views, and result snippet generation. These studies enable casual users to easily access XML data without the need to learn XPath/XQuery and data schemas, and yet to obtain high-quality results. It also summarizes the possible future research directions of XML keyword search.

This chapter introduces an extensible and rule-based framework for cost-based native XML query optimization, which supports a large fragment of XQuery 1.0—the predominant query language in XML databases. For the evaluation of XQuery expressions, the framework can exploit around 50 physical operators. It can be configured in such a way, that different types of query optimization techniques can be compared with respect to their sufficiency for cost-based XQuery optimization under equal and fair conditions. Therefore, it relies on the native XML database management system XTC (XML Transaction Coordinator). In combination with a cost model for constraining the search space, the framework can be turned into a full-fledged XQuery optimizer in the future.

Section 3
XML Stream Processing, Publish/Subscribe, and P2P

This section is about some advanced topics of XML, including XML stream processing, publish/subscribe system, and P2P system.

Description: This chapter reviews recent advances on stream XML query evaluation algorithms with stack-based encoding of intermediary data. Originally proposed for disk-resident XML, the stack-based architecture has been extended for streaming algorithms for both single and multiple query processing, ranging from XPath filtering to more complex XQuery. The key benefit of this architecture is its succinct encoding of partial query results to avoid exponential enumeration. In addition, the chapter discusses opportunities to integrate benefits demonstrated in the reviewed work.

This chapter focuses on the content-based publish/subscribe system for XML data. Firstly, the fundamental concepts, i.e. publisher, subscriber and XML routers, in the content-based publish/subscribe system for XML data is introduced. After that, the chapter presents two important issues, i.e. the efficiency of the system and the functionalities that are supported by this system, to consider in content-based publish/subscribe for XML data, and discussed the approaches that address these problems. Finally, the chapter pointed out some potential directions in the content-based publish/subscribe for XML data.

This chapter describes the XML-based data dissemination networks. In these networks XML content is routed from data producers to data consumers throughout an overlay network of content-based routers. Routing decisions are based on XPath expressions (XPEs) stored at each router. To enable efficient routing, while keeping the routing state small, this chapter introduces advertisement-based routing algorithms for XML content, presents a novel data structure for managing XPEs, especially apt for the hierarchical nature of XPEs and XML, and develops several optimizations for reducing the number of XPEs required to manage the routing state. The experimental evaluation shows that the algorithms and optimizations reduce the routing table size by up to 90%, improve the routing time by roughly 85%, and reduce overall network traffic by about 35%. Experiments running on PlanetLab show the scalability of this approach.

This chapter presents XP2P, a framework for fragmenting and managing XML data over structured peer-to-peer networks. XP2P is characterized by an innovative mechanism for fragmenting XML documents based on meaningful XPath queries, and novel fingerprinting techniques for indexing and looking-up distributed fragments based on Chord's DHT. Efficient algorithms for querying distributed fragments over peer-to-peer networks are also presented and experimentally assessed against both synthetic and real XML data sets. A comprehensive analysis of future research directions on XML data management over peer-to-peer networks completes the contribution of the chapter.

Section 4
XML Query Translation and Data Integration

This section describes how to normalize and translate XML queries and how to do XML data integration.

This chapter argues for an algebraic optimization and evaluation technique for XQuery as it allows people to benefit from experience gained with relational databases. An algebraic XQuery processing method requires a translation into an algebra representation. While many publications already exist on algebraic optimizations and evaluation techniques for XQuery, an assessment of translation techniques is required. Consequently, the chapter gives a comprehensive survey for translating XQuery into various query representations. The chapter relates these approaches to the way normalization and translation is implemented in Natix and discusses these two steps in detail.

This chapter discusses the challenges and techniques in XML Data Integration. It first presents a four step outline, illustrating the steps involved in the integration of XML data. This chapter, then, focuses on the first two of these steps: schema extraction and data/schema mapping; the next chapter focuses on the remaining steps: merging, query processing and conflict resolution.

Chapter 15

Yan Qi, Arizona State University, USA

Huiping Cao, Arizona State University, USA

K. Selcuk Candan, Arizona State University, USA

Maria Luisa Sapino, University of Torino, Italy

This chapter continues from the previous chapter to discuss the merging, query processing and conflict resolution steps in XML data integration. Specifically, merging integrates multiple disparate (heterogeneous and autonomous) input data sources together for further usage, while query processing is one main reason why the data need to be integrated in the first place. Besides, when supported with appropriate user feedback techniques, queries can also provide contexts in which conflicts among the input sources can be interpreted and resolved. This chapter also discusses two alternative ways XML data/schema can be integrated: conflict-eliminating (where the result is cleaned from any conflicts that the different sources might have with each other) and conflict-preserving (where the resulting XML data or XML schema captures the alternative interpretations of the data).

Section 5
XML Semantics Utilization and Advanced Application

This section includes how to utilize semantics to process XML update and query, as well as XML application on web service.

Chapter 16

Dario Colazzo, Laboratoire de Recherche en Informatique (LRI-CNRS), Université de Paris-Sud, France

Giovanna Guerrini, DISI – Università degli Studi di Genova, Italy

Marco Mesiti, DICo – Università degli Studi di Milano, Italy

Barbara Oliboni, DI – Università degli Studi di Verona, Italy

Emmanuel Waller, Laboratoire de Recherche en Informatique (LRI-CNRS), Universite de Paris-Sud, France

This chapter starts from the update primitives supported by current language proposals, and deals with the data management issues that arise when documents and schema are updated and new versions created. Specifically, the chapter will provide a review of various proposals for XML document updates, their different semantics and their handling of update sequences, with a focus on the XQuery Update proposal. Approaches and specific issues concerned with schema updates are then reviewed. Document and schema versioning is considered and a review of the degree and limitations of update support in existing DBMSs is discussed.

This chapter proposes a hybrid approach which integrates the two classes of exiting XML query processing approaches, i.e. the relational approach and the native approach (inverted lists), and it wants to inherit the advantages and solve the problems in the two approaches. By performing content search using relational tables before structural pattern matching, this approach not only properly solves the value constraints, but also simplifies the pattern matching process, thus improves the query processing efficiency. The chapter also proposes three optimizations based on semantic information of object. Once more object information is known in a given XML document, the approach can use such semantics to improve relational tables, and to get a better performance.

Chapter 18

This chapter describes that web applications communicate with web services through the exchange of sequences of XML messages representing requests and responses for specific operations. The available documentation for a service constitutes what is called an interface contract, which specifies the acceptable messages and sequences of messages that can be exchanged with this service. By capturing incoming and outgoing messages during an actual execution of an application and aligning them into an XML document, it is possible to determine whether a specific execution trace satisfies an interface contract. In particular, the chapter shows how sequential constraints expressed in an extension of Linear Temporal Logic with first-order quantification on data can be verified by translating them into equivalent XQuery expressions on XML trace documents.

Foreword

Dr. Changqing Li and Dr. Tok Wang Ling have edited a very important XML book in *Advanced Applications and Structures in XML Processing: Label Streams, Semantics Utilization and Data Query Technologies*. Its purpose is to provide relevant theoretical frameworks and the latest empirical research findings in the area. It is written for professionals and researchers working in the field of XML in various disciplines who want to improve their understanding of the advanced applications and structures in XML processing, that is, XML Data Management, XML Index and Query, XML Stream Processing, Publish/ Subscribe, and P2P, XML Query Translation and Data Integration, and XML Semantics Utilization and Advanced Application.

Advanced Applications and Structures in XML Processing is not just for experts who work in a very specific field of XML processing to improve their research basing on the latest important findings in this book. It is also a very good book to broaden the readers' XML processing knowledge since this book comprehensively covers different XML processing techniques like XML storage, compression, index, keywords search, stream processing, integration etc.

This book won't replace one of those huge books about XML tutorial or manual. That's not its point. The point of *Advanced Applications and Structures in XML Processing* is for advanced XML users who want to make deep understanding about XML processing techniques and build their work/research on top of the important research results by excellent researchers around the world. Integrated the important findings of researchers from both academia and industry, this book can be a reference book for XML engineers, a must-reading book for graduate students who want to select XML as their research direction, or a text book for a course like advanced topics in XML.

The book starts right off with XML native storage and XML data management in object relational database systems, and then the XML compression. It helps if you want to know how to effectively manage XML data.

Keyword search is a very important application of XML. By reading further, you will find the important research results about XML keyword search as well as the XML indexing techniques like index structures and XML document labeling.

XML Stream Processing, Publish/Subscribe, and P2P have become hot research topics in recent years, therefore you must continue to read this book if you want to know more about these hot XML topics.

XML natively is a good tool to integrate heterogeneous data, so if you are working on data integration, how can you skip the next important part of this book, in which XQuery translation is also included?

If you are interested in XML semantics utilization and web service or you want to know more about XML, you need to complete the reading of the last section of this book.

In summary, *Advanced Applications and Structures in XML Processing* is a very important book in the XML research field, thus it must be read by researchers, engineers, and students who want to understand advanced XML processing topics in depth!

Philip S. Yu
Professor and Wexler Chair in Information Technology
Department of Computer Science
University of Illinois at Chicago, USA

Philip S. Yu *is a Professor in the Department of Computer Science at the University of Illinois at Chicago and also holds the Wexler Chair in Information Technology. He was manager of the Software Tools and Techniques group at IBM Watson Research Center. Dr. Yu is a Fellow of the ACM and the IEEE. He served as the Editor-in-Chief of IEEE Transactions on Knowledge and Data Engineering (2001-2004). He is an associate editor of ACM Transactions on Knowledge Discovery from Data and also ACM Transactions of the Internet Technology. He serves on the steering committee of IEEE Int. Conference on Data Mining. Dr. Yu received a Research Contributions Award from IEEE Intl. Conference on Data Mining in 2003. His research interests include data mining, and database systems. He has published more than 540 papers in refereed journals and conferences. He holds or has applied for more than 300 US patents.*

Preface

INTRODUCTION

The eXtensible Markup Language (XML) has become a de facto standard for data exchange and representation on the World Wide Web and elsewhere. It has played and is still playing an important role in our daily life. Different advanced applications like publish/subscribe, web services, medical information storage, etc., have acknowledged the significance of the role of XML. Therefore, it is important to understand different XML processing technologies like labeling, query and update processing, keyword searching, stream processing, semantics utilizing, etc. In this, the connection of both advanced applications and latest XML processing technologies is of primary importance. In the fields of database, information system, web service, etc., there exists a need for an edited collection of articles in the XML area.

In the past years, different XML research topics have been thoroughly studied by researchers around the world. The authors of the chapters of this book are important researchers from different countries like USA, Canada, Germany, Italy, France, Singapore, China, South Korea, New Zealand etc., and the authors are from both academy and industry. This book reflects their significant research results and latest findings.

This book is organized into five sections covering different aspects of XML research. These five sections are: (1) XML Data Management, (2) XML Index and Query, (3) XML Stream Processing, Publish/Subscribe, and P2P, (4) XML Query Translation and Data Integration, and (5) XML Semantics Utilization and Advanced Application. Each section contains 3 or 4 chapters and the book contains total 18 chapters.

The scholarly value of this book and its contribution will be to the literature in the XML research discipline. It fills the gap between reading an XML tutorial and reading a research paper; with this book, not only can readers understand a specific topic in detail, but they can know other related XML research topics at a comprehensive level.

The audience of this book is any one who wants to know in-depth the different and important XML techniques provided by top researchers around the world. In more detail, the audience could be XML researchers/professors, IT professionals, or the graduate students or seniors in undergraduate for computer science related programs or advanced XML topic courses.

CHAPTER OVERVIEW

Section 1, XML Data Management, discusses different XML data management techniques, including XML native storage, management in object relational database systems, compression, and benchmark.

Chapter 1, XML Native Storage and Query Processing, reviews different native storage formats and query processing techniques that have been developed in both academia and industry. Among the XML data management issues, storage and query processing are the most critical ones with respect to system performance. Different storage schemes have their own pros and cons. Therefore, based on their own requirements, different systems adopt different storage schemes to tradeoff one set of features over the others. Various XML indexing techniques are also presented since they can be treated as specialized storage and query processing tools.

Chapter 2, XML Data Management in Object Relational Database Systems, describes the XML data management capabilities in Object Relational DBMS (ORDBMS), various design approaches and implementation techniques to support these capabilities, as well as the pros and cons of each design and implementation approach. Key topics such as XML storage, XML Indexing, XQuery and SQL/XML processing, are discussed in depth presenting both academic and industrial research work in these areas.

Chapter 3, XML Compression, provides a better understanding on relevant theoretical frameworks and an up-to-date research trend of the XML compression. Existing XML compression techniques are classified and examined based on their characteristics and experimental evaluations. Also, according to the comprehensive analysis, appropriate XML compression techniques for different environments are recommended. Furthermore, some future research directions on the XML compression are presented.

Chapter 4 introduces the XML benchmarks, typically standard sets of data with queries enabling users to evaluate system performance that are designed specifically for XML applications. The chapter describes and compares not only the characteristics of each benchmark, but also data generators and real data sets designed for evaluating XML systems. The major contributions of the chapter are the tables for choosing the benchmark to use for a specific purpose. Possible extensions to current XML benchmarks are also discussed.

Section 2, XML Index and Query, presents the XML index and query techniques, including XML index structures, labeling, keyword search, and query optimization.

Chapter 5 gives a brief history of the creation and the development of the XML data model. Then it discusses the three main categories of indexes proposed in the literature to handle the XML semistructured data model. Finally, it discusses limitations and open problems related to the major existing indexing schemes.

Chapter 6, Labeling XML Documents, shows how to extend the traditional prefix labeling scheme to speedup XML query processing. In addition, for XML documents that are updated frequently, many labeling schemes require relabeling which can be very expensive. A lot of research interest has been generated on designing dynamic XML labeling schemes. Making labeling schemes dynamic turns out to be a challenging problem and many of the approaches proposed only partially avoid relabeling. This chapter describes some recently emerged dynamic labeling schemes that can completely avoid relabeling, making efficient update processing in XML database management systems possible.

Chapter 7, Keyword Search on XML Data, describes the importance, challenges and future directions for supporting XML keyword search. It presents and compares representative state-of-the-art techniques from multiple aspects, including identifying relevant keyword matches and an axiomatic framework to evaluate different strategies, identifying other relevant data nodes, ranking schemes, indexes and materialized views, and result snippet generation. These studies enable casual users to easily access XML data without the need to learn XPath/XQuery and data schemas, and yet to obtain high-quality results. It also summarizes the possible future research directions of XML keyword search.

Chapter 8 introduces an extensible and rule-based framework for cost-based native XML query optimization, which supports a large fragment of XQuery 1.0—the predominant query language in XML databases. For the evaluation of XQuery expressions, the framework can exploit around 50 physical operators. It can be configured in such a way, that different types of query optimization techniques can be compared with respect to their sufficiency for cost-based XQuery optimization under equal and fair conditions. Therefore, it relies on the native XML database management system XTC (XML Transaction Coordinator). In combination with a cost model for constraining the search space, the framework can be turned into a full-fledged XQuery optimizer in the future.

Section 3 entitled "XML Stream Processing, Publish/Subscribe, and P2P", is about some advanced topics of XML.

Chapter 9, XML Stream Processing: Stack-based Algorithms, reviews recent advances on stream XML query evaluation algorithms with stack-based encoding of intermediary data. Originally proposed for disk-resident XML, the stack-based architecture has been extended for streaming algorithms for both single and multiple query processing, ranging from XPath filtering to more complex XQuery. The key benefit of this architecture is its succinct encoding of partial query results to avoid exponential enumeration. In addition, the chapter discusses opportunities to integrate benefits demonstrated in the reviewed work.

Chapter 10 focuses on the content-based publish/subscribe system for XML data. Firstly, the fundamental concepts, i.e. publisher, subscriber and XML routers, in the content-based publish/subscribe system for XML data is introduced. After that, the chapter presents two important issues, i.e. the efficiency of the system and the functionalities that are supported by this system, to consider in content-based publish/subscribe for XML data, and discussed the approaches that address these problems. Finally, the chapter pointed out some potential directions in the content-based publish/subscribe for XML data.

Chapter 11 describes the XML-based data dissemination networks. In these networks XML content is routed from data producers to data consumers throughout an overlay network of content-based routers. Routing decisions are based on XPath expressions (XPEs) stored at each router. To enable efficient routing, while keeping the routing state small, this chapter introduces advertisement-based routing algorithms for XML content, presents a novel data structure for managing XPEs, especially apt for the hierarchical nature of XPEs and XML, and develops several optimizations for reducing the number of XPEs required to manage the routing state. The experimental evaluation shows that the algorithms and optimizations reduce the routing table size by up to 90%, improve the routing time by roughly 85%, and reduce overall network traffic by about 35%. Experiments running on PlanetLab show the scalability of this approach.

Chapter 12 presents XP2P, a framework for fragmenting and managing XML data over structured peer-to-peer networks. XP2P is characterized by an innovative mechanism for fragmenting XML documents based on meaningful XPath queries, and novel fingerprinting techniques for indexing and looking-up distributed fragments based on Chord's DHT. Efficient algorithms for querying distributed fragments over peer-to-peer networks are also presented and experimentally assessed against both synthetic and real XML data sets. A comprehensive analysis of future research directions on XML data management over peer-to-peer networks completes the contribution of the chapter.

Section 4, XML Query Translation and Data Integration, describes how to normalize and translate XML queries and how to do XML data integration.

Chapter 13, Normalization and Translation of XQuery, argues for an algebraic optimization and evaluation technique for XQuery as it allows people to benefit from experience gained with relational databases. An algebraic XQuery processing method requires a translation into an algebra representation. While many publications already exist on algebraic optimizations and evaluation techniques for XQuery, an assessment of translation techniques is required. Consequently, the chapter gives a comprehensive survey for translating XQuery into various query representations. The chapter relates these approaches to the way normalization and translation is implemented in Natix and discusses these two steps in detail.

Chapters 14 and 15, about XML Data Integration, discuss the challenges and techniques in XML Data Integration. Chapter 14 first presents a four step outline, illustrating the steps involved in the integration of XML data. This chapter, then, focuses on the first two of these steps: schema extraction and data/schema mapping; the next chapter focuses on the remaining steps: merging, query processing and conflict resolution.

Chapter 15 continues from the previous chapter to discuss the merging, query processing and conflict resolution steps in XML data integration. Specifically, merging integrates multiple disparate (heterogeneous and autonomous) input data sources together for further usage, while query processing is one main reason why the data need to be integrated in the first place. Besides, when supported with appropriate user feedback techniques, queries can also provide contexts in which conflicts among the input sources can be interpreted and resolved. This chapter also discusses two alternative ways XML data/schema can be integrated: conflict-eliminating (where the result is cleaned from any conflicts that the different sources might have with each other) and conflict-preserving (where the resulting XML data or XML schema captures the alternative interpretations of the data).

Section 5, XML Semantics Utilization and Advanced Application, includes how to utilize semantics to process XML update and query, as well as XML application on web service.

Chapter 16 starts from the update primitives supported by current language proposals, and deals with the data management issues that arise when documents and schema are updated and new versions created. Specifically, the chapter will provide a review of various proposals for XML document updates, their different semantics and their handling of update sequences, with a focus on the XQuery Update proposal. Approaches and specific issues concerned with schema updates are then reviewed. Document and schema versioning is considered and a review of the degree and limitations of update support in existing DBMSs is discussed.

Chapter 17 proposes a hybrid approach which integrates the two classes of exiting XML query processing approaches, i.e. the relational approach and the native approach (inverted lists), and it wants to inherit the advantages and solve the problems in the two approaches. By performing content search using relational tables before structural pattern matching, this approach not only properly solves the value constraints, but also simplifies the pattern matching process, thus improves the query processing efficiency. The chapter also proposes three optimizations based on semantic information of object. Once more object information is known in a given XML document, the approach can use such semantics to improve relational tables, and to get a better performance.

Chapter 18 describes that web applications communicate with web services through the exchange of sequences of XML messages representing requests and responses for specific operations. The available documentation for a service constitutes what is called an interface contract, which specifies the acceptable messages and sequences of messages that can be exchanged with this service. By capturing incoming and outgoing messages during an actual execution of an application and aligning them into an XML document, it is possible to determine whether a specific execution trace satisfies an interface contract. In particular, the chapter shows how sequential constraints expressed in an extension of Linear Temporal Logic with first-order quantification on data can be verified by translating them into equivalent XQuery expressions on XML trace documents.

Changqing Li, Duke University, USA
Tok Wang Ling, National University of Singapore, Singapore
Editors

Acknowledgment

We would like to express our gratitude to Professor Philip S. Yu who not only writes the Foreword for this book, but serves as a member of the Editorial Advisory Board (EAB) of this book.

We are deeply indebted to the Editorial Advisory Board (EAB) members:

Chin-Wan Chung, Korea Advanced Institute of Science and Technology (KAIST), South Korea
Torsten Grust, Universität Tübingen, Germany
H.-Arno Jacobsen, University of Toronto, Canada
Bongki Moon, University of Arizona, U.S.A.
M. Tamer Özsu, University of Waterloo, Canada
Masatoshi Yoshikawa, Kyoto University, Japan
Jeffrey Xu Yu, Chinese University of Hong Kong, Hong Kong
Philip S. Yu, University of Illinois at Chicago, U.S.A.

We want to thank all the reviewers whose valuable comments guarantee the good quality of this book.

We appreciate the contributions of all the chapter authors. Without them, this book does not exist.

Finally we would like to give our special thanks to our respective families. Thank for their constant supports and patience.

Changqing Li, Duke University, USA
Tok Wang Ling, National University of Singapore, Singapore
Editors

Section 1
XML Data Management

Chapter 1
XML Native Storage and Query Processing

Ning Zhang
Facebook, USA

M. Tamer Özsu
University of Waterloo, Canada

ABSTRACT

As XML has evolved as a data model for semi-structured data and the de facto standard for data exchange (e.g., Atom, RSS, and XBRL), XML data management has been the subject of extensive research and development in both academia and industry. Among the XML data management issues, storage and query processing are the most critical ones with respect to system performance. Different storage schemes have their own pros and cons. Some storage schemes are more amenable to fast navigation, and some schemes perform better in fragment extraction and document reconstruction. Therefore, based on their own requirements, different systems adopt different storage schemes to tradeoff one set of features over the others. In this chapter, the authors review different native storage formats and query processing techniques that have been developed in both academia and industry. Various XML indexing techniques are also presented since they can be treated as specialized storage and query processing tools.

INTRODUCTION

As XML has evolved as a data model for semi-structured data and the *de facto* standard for data exchange, it is widely adopted as the foundation of many data sharing protocols. For example, XBRL and FIXML defines the XML schemas that are used to describe business and financial information; Atom and RSS are simple yet popular XML formats for publishing Weblogs; and customized XML formats are used by more and more system log files. When the sheer volume of XML data increases, storing all these data in the file system is not a viable solution. Furthermore, users often want to query over large volumes of XML data. A customized and non-optimized query processing system would quickly reach its limits. A more scalable and sustainable solution is to load the XML data into a database system that is specifically designed for storing and updating large volumes

DOI: 10.4018/978-1-61520-727-5.ch001

of data, efficient query processing, and highly concurrent access patterns. In this chapter, we shall introduce some of the database techniques for managing XML data.

There are basically three approaches to storing XML documents in a DBMS: (1) the LOB approach that stores the original XML documents as-is in a LOB (large object) column (Krishnaprasad, Liu, Manikutty, Warner & Arora, 2005; Pal, Cseri, Seeliger, Rys, Schaller, Yu, Tomic, Baras, Berg, Churin & Kogan, 2005), (2) the extended relational approach that shreds XML documents into object-relational (OR) tables and columns (Zhang, Naughton, DeWitt, Luo & Lohman, 2001; Boncz, Grust, van Keulen, Manegold, Rittinger & Teubner, 2006), and (3) the native approach that uses a tree-structured data model, and introduces operators that are optimized for tree navigation, insertion, deletion and update (Fiebig, Helmer, Kanne, Mildenberger, Moerkotte, Schiele, & Westmann, 2002; Nicola, & Van der Linden, 2005; Zhang, Kacholia, & Özsu, 2004). Each approach has its own advantages and disadvantages. For example, the LOB approach is very similar to storing the XML documents in a file system, in that there is minimum transformation from the original format to the storage format. It is the simplest one to implement and support. It provides byte-level fidelity (e.g., it preserves extra white spaces that may be ignored by the OR and the native formats) that could be needed for some digital signature schemes. The LOB approach is also efficient for inserting or extracting the whole documents to or from the database. However it is slow in processing queries due to unavoidable XML parsing at query execution time.

In the extended relational approach, XML documents are converted to object-relational tables, which are stored in relational databases or in object repositories. This approach can be further divided into two categories based on whether or not the XML-to-relational mapping relies on XML Schema. The OR storage format,

if designed and mapped correctly, could perform very well in query processing, thanks to many years of research and development in object-relational database systems. However, insertion, fragment extraction, structural update, and document reconstruction require considerable processing in this approach. For schema-based OR storage, applications need to have a well-structured, rigid XML schema whose relational mapping is tuned by a DBA in order to take advantage of this storage model. Loosely structured schemas could lead to unmanageable number of tables and joins. Also, applications requiring schema flexibility and schema evolution are limited by those offered by relational tables and columns. The result is that applications encounter a large gap: if they cannot map well to an object-relational way of life due to tradeoffs mentioned above, they suffer a big drop in performance or capabilities.

Due to these shortcomings of the two approaches, much research has been focusing on the *native* XML storage formats. There is not, and should not be, a single native format for storing XML documents. Native XML storage techniques treat XML trees as first class citizens and develop special purpose storage schemes without relying on the existence of an underlying database system. Since it is designed specifically for XML data model, native XML storage usually provides well-balanced tradeoffs among many criteria. Some storage formats may be designed to focus on one set of criteria, while other formats may emphasize another set. For example, some storage schemes are more amenable to fast navigation, and some schemes perform better in fragment extraction and document reconstruction. Therefore, based on their own requirements, different applications adopt different storage schemes to trade off one set of features over another.

The following are examples of some of the important criteria that many real-world applications consider.

Table 1. Comparisons between LOB, OR, and native XML storages

	LOB Storage	OR Storage	Native Storage
Query	Poor	Excellent	Good/Excellent
DML	Poor/Good	Good/Excellent	Excellent
Document Retrieval	Excellent	Good/Excellent	Excellent
Schema Flexibility	Poor	Good	Excellent
Document fidelity	Excellent	Poor	Good/Excellent
Mid-tier integration	Poor	Poor	Excellent

1. **Query performance:** For many applications, query performance may be the most important criterion. Storage format, or how the tree data model is organized on disk and/or in main memory, is one of the major factors that affect query performance. Other factors include the efficiency of the query processing algorithm and whether there are indexes on the XML data. All of these will be covered in the following sections.

2. **Data manipulation performance:** This can be further measured by insertion, update, and document or fragment retrievals. Each of these may be an enabling feature for many applications.

3. **Space and communication efficiency:** XML documents are verbose and contain redundant information. A compact format benefits both the storage space and the network communication cost when they are transferred between different parties.

4. **Schema flexibility:** XML documents in data exchange often have schemas, which define common structures and validation rules among exchanged data. Many applications may have millions of documents conforming to a large number of slightly different schemas (schema chaos), or these schemas may evolve over time (schema evolution). A native storage format needs to be able to handle both schema chaos and schema evolution efficiently.

5. **Miscellaneous features:** These include partitioning, amenability to XML indexes, and seamless integration with mid-tier applications such as Java or C#.

Table 1 summarizes the comparisons LOB, OR, and the native XML storage approaches.

In the next section, we introduce different native storage formats and compare them in the context of a set of commonly encountered requirements. Some native storage formats, e.g., XMill (Liefke, L., and Suciu, D., 2000) and XGrind (Tolani, P. M., and Haritsa, J. R., 2002) concentrate on only one or a very small subset of the requirements, so we will omit them from this chapter. We then introduce different query processing techniques that have been developed for native XML systems. A large body of such work focuses on answering XPath queries efficiently. Finally, we present various XML indexing techniques for answering path queries. To a certain extent, these XML indexing techniques can be thought of as specialized storage and query processing tools.

NATIVE XML STORAGE METHODS

XML data model treats XML documents as labeled, ordered, unranked trees. Main memory data structure for trees has been studied very well. Different data structures have been proposed for efficient operations such as query, insertion, deletion, and update. However, disk-based data structure for trees had not attracted as much research until the XML data model caught on. The key difference between the main memory data structures and the disk-based data structures are that the former are based on Random Access Machine (RAM) model of computation, in which accessing two different nodes in main memory have the same cost. However, in disk-based data structures based on the paged I/O model, accessing a node in a new page is usually significantly more expensive than accessing a node in the cached page. Therefore many disk-based algorithms are designed to minimize the number of buffer cache misses according to access patterns. The solution to solve these problems is to partition a large tree into smaller trees such that:

1. Each subtree is small enough to be stored entirely into one disk page.
2. Based on some priori knowledge of access patterns, tree nodes that are accessed in consecutive order are clustered as much as possible into one partition.

The second condition is the major difference between different storage formats. For example, suppose nodes n_1 to n_{10} need to be partitioned into two clusters and each of them are free to be in either cluster. If it is known that the access pattern is $n_1, n_2, n_3, \ldots n_{10}$ in that order, then the partitions of $\{n_1, n_2, n_3, n_4, n_5\}$ and $\{n_6, n_7, n_8, n_9, n_{10}\}$ are optimal. However if the access pattern is $n_1, n_2, n_4, n_8, n_9, n_4, n_2, n_5, n_{10}, n_5, n_3, n_6, n_3,$ *and* n_7, then the partitions of $\{n_1, n_2, n_4, n_8, n_9\}$ and $\{n_3, n_5, n_6, n_7, n_{10}\}$ would be optimal. The reason is that each page (containing one partition) is accessed only once, which results in the optimal I/O cost.

It is clear from the above example that the access pattern is a key factor to consider when designing native XML storage formats. For XML applications, query access patterns are path-based pattern matching as defined in W3C XPath (Berglund, A., Boag, S., Chamberlin, D., Fernández, M. F., Kay, M., Robie, J., & Siméon, J. 2007) and

XQuery (Boag, S., Chamberlin, D., Fernández, M. F., Florescu, D., Robie, J., Siméon, J., 2007) languages. There are basically two patterns in accessing XML nodes in a tree: *breadth-first traversal* and *depth-first traversal*. The breadth-first access pattern is usually observed in the XML DOM API, e.g., through the Java getChildNodes method in the Node class. Based on this access pattern, the storage format needs to support fast access to the list of children from its parent node. The depth-first access pattern can be seen in the XML SAX API, where a pair of begin- and end-events are generated for each node visited in document order (coincident with the depth-first traversal of the XML tree). This access pattern requires the storage formats cluster tree nodes based on their document order.

Most native XML storage schemes try to optimize both access patterns, with an emphasis on one of them.

Breadth-First-Based Tree Partitioning

If a storage format favors the breadth-first access pattern, a simple clustering condition needs to be satisfied: grouping all children with their parent in the same disk page. However when a tree is large, it is hard to satisfy this simple condition. The reasons are two-fold: (1) all children should be clustered with their parent in the same page. Since the number of children is unlimited, they are not guaranteed to be stored in the same page; (2) even though all children of a node can be stashed into one page, the clustering condition implies that all its descendants need to be stored into one page as well. These two conditions are unrealistic for most large XML documents. Therefore, a partitioning algorithm based on the bread-first access pattern was proposed to group as many siblings as possible into one page, and if the page overflows, it keeps a "proxy" node (illustrated as in dotted cycles in Figure 1) that act as a linkage to the next page (Helmer, Kanne, Mildenberger, Moerkotte,

Figure 1. Breadth-first Tree Partitioning (dotted circles are proxy nodes that connect two pages)

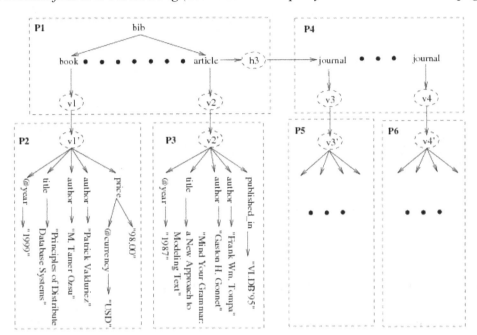

Schiele, & Westmann, 2002). Figure 1 illustrates the partitioning algorithm on a large tree where the number of children of element bib is too large to fit into one page. If the tree nodes are partitioned based on breadth-first access pattern, as many children as possible should be placed into page P1 with element bib. The proxy node h3 acts as a *horizontal link* to the next sibling of element article. Furthermore, since both child elements book and article have descendants, all their descendants will be stored into separate pages, P2 and P3, where v1 and v2 act as *vertical links* to their children. It is straightforward to see that there is at most one horizontal proxy link for each page.

Even though this storage format is optimized for breadth-first traversal, clever page caching techniques can make it optimal for depth-first traversal as well. Consider Figure 1 as an example. If each page is considered as a node and each (vertical or horizontal) proxy link as an edge, it forms a tree structure, which is called a *page tree*. In the page tree, the edges are ordered so that vertical edges are ordered in the same way

as their proxy nodes in the parent page, and the horizontal proxy link, if any, is the last child. Supposing that the elements are visited in depth-first traversal, the access pattern to pages is P1, P2, P1, P3, P4, P5, P4, and P6, which coincide with the depth-first traversal order of the page tree. Therefore, the page caching algorithm can be designed to push every visited page onto a stack during depth-first traversal, and pop it up when it is finished with the traversal (e.g., popping up P2 when P1 is visited the second time). Every page that is popped up from the stack is a candidate for page-out. In this case, depth-first traversal of the XML elements will visit each page exactly once, which is I/O optimal. The memory requirement is the size of the page times the depth of the page tree, i.e., the maximum length of the root-to-leaf path in the page tree.

This native XML storage format can also support efficient data manipulation operations. Inserting a tree node amounts to finding the page where the node should be inserted, and inserting it into the appropriate position. In case of

Figure 2. An encoded XML tree

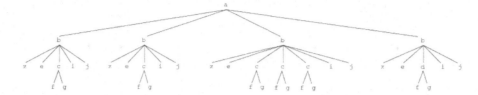

Figure 3. Balanced parentheses tree representation

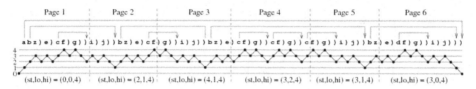

page overflow, a vertical proxy node is created that links to a new page where the new node is inserted. The only caveat of this approach is that fragment retrieval may not be optimal. For example in Figure 1, if the fragment containing the first element book is to be extracted, both P1 and P2 need to be read. In the optimal case, only one page read is necessary.

Depth-First-Based Tree Partitioning

Another approach of natively storing trees is to serialize tree nodes in document order, or depth-first order, so that depth-first traversal is optimal (Zhang, Kacholia, & Özsu, 2004). For example, suppose an encoded XML tree is depicted in Figure 2, where elements are encoded as follows:

bib → a, book → b, @year → z, author → c, title → e,

publisher → i, price → j, first → f, last → g

One way to materialize the tree is to store the nodes in pre-order and keep the tree structure by properly inserting pairs of parentheses as the form of balanced parentheses format. For example, (A(B)(C)) is a string representation of the tree that has a root A and two children B and C. The open parenthesis "(" preceding letter A indicates the beginning of a subtree rooted at A; its corresponding close parenthesis ")" indicates the end of the subtree. It is straightforward that such a string representation contains enough information to reconstruct the tree. However, it is not a succinct representation, because the open parenthesis is redundant in that each node, a character in the string, actually implies an open parenthesis. Therefore, all open parentheses can be safely removed and only closing parentheses are retained as in AB)C)). Figure 3 shows the string representations of the XML tree in Figure 2.

At the physical storage level, only the string representation in the middle is stored, the pointers above of the string and level property below the string are not. The pointers only serve to easily identify the end of a subtree to the reader, and the levels are used for efficient navigation between siblings. If the string is too long to fit in one page, it can be broken up into substrings at any point and stored in different pages as indicated in Figure 3.

This storage format is very efficient for depth-first traversal: it is only necessary to sequentially read the string from the beginning to the end, and there is no need to cache any page other than the current page. Both I/O complexity and caching size are optimal. Also practically, this storage format is more desirable than the breadth-first tree partitioning approach introduced previously. The reasons are twofold: (1) this storage format can easily take advantage of existing prefetching mechanism from the I/O component of DBMS. There is no pointer (proxy node) to follow when deciding which page to prefetch; and (2) this storage format is more CPU-cache friendly simply because nodes are ordered in depth-first order and the next node to be visited is mostly likely already loaded into the CPU cache. On the other hand, the breadth-first tree partitioning approach may see much more cache misses since the next visited node may be on the child page, and when that page is finished, the parent page is brought up again (e.g., P1, P2, P1, P3, etc. in Figure 1). . So this behavior of juggling between the parent page and children pages causes a lot of CPU cache misses.

The downside of this depth-first-based tree partitioning approach is its inefficiency in breadth-first traversal, e.g., traversing from one node to its next sibling. To solve this problem, one can store the begin and end positions of each element into an auxiliary data structure that serves as an index to find the end of a subtree. To find the next sibling of an element, what is needed is to find the end of the subtree and the next element is its next sibling. If the next character is a ')', then there is no next sibling. This method is simple and can reduce the index size by including only "large" elements in the auxiliary structure. Small elements are more likely to be within the same page so they do not save much in terms of I/O cost. This optimization is very useful during the path expression evaluation introduced in next section, where the XML tree is mostly visited in depth-first pattern and can jump to the next sibling during the traversal. However, maintaining the begin and end positions is an extra cost during inserting and deleting nodes. One insertion in the middle of a page may cause many updates of the begin and end positions of nodes after the inserted node in the page.

Another solution to trade off the navigation and maintenance costs is to keep some extra information in the page header. The most useful information for locating children, siblings and parent is the node level information, i.e., the depth of the node from the root. For example, assuming the level of the root is 1, the level information for each node is represented by a point in the 2-D space under the string representation in Figure 3 (the x-axis represents nodes and the y-axis represents level). For each page, an extra tuple (st, lo, hi) is stored, where st is the level of the last node in the previous page (st is 0 for the first page), lo and hi are the minimum and maximum levels of all nodes in that page, respectively. If all the page headers are preloaded into main memory, they can serve as a light-weight index to guess which page contains the following sibling or parent of the current node. The idea is based on the fact that if the current node U with level L has a following sibling, the page that contains this following sibling must have a character")" with level $L - 1$ (this is the closing parenthesis corresponding to U). If $L - 1$ is not in the range [lo, hi] of a page, it is clear that this page should not be loaded. This could greatly reduce the number of page I/Os for finding the following sibling of large elements. As an example, suppose the search is to find the following sibling of element b in page 3. Since the level of b is 2, the level of its corresponding end-subtree character ')' is 1. Since the [lo, hi] ranges of page 4 and 5 are [2, 4], and [1, 4] respectively, page 4 can be skipped and page 5 can be read to locate the node whose level is 1. The next character is the following sibling of b. This approach may not be as efficient as the pointer-based approach for tree navigation, but it has lower maintenance cost, since the extra cost of inserting a node may just be updating the page header in some rare cases if the minimum or maximum level statistics is changed.

QUERY PROCESSING TECHNIQUES

Path expressions in XPath or XQuery are an important focus of XML query processing. A path expression defines a tree pattern that is matched against the XML tree and specifies nodes that need to be returned as results. As an example, the path expression //book[author/last = "Stevens"] [price < 100] finds all books written by Stevens with the book price less than 100. Path expressions have three types of constraints: the tag name constraints, the structural relationship constraints, and the value constraints. They correspond to the name tests, axes, and value comparisons in the path expression, respectively. A path expression can be modeled as a tree, called a *pattern tree*, which captures all three types of constraints.

There are basically two types of path query processing techniques: query-driven and data-driven. In the query-driven navigational approach (Brantner, Helmer, Kanne, & Moerkotte, 2005), each location step in the path expression is translated into a transition from one set of XML tree nodes to another set. To be more specific, a query execution engine translates a path query into a native XML algebraic expression. Each location step (e.g., //book, book/author, or author/last) in the path expression is translated into an Unnest-Map operator that effectively replaces an input list with an output list satisfying structural relationship specified by the axis. A path expression is then translated into a chain of Unnest-Map operators. Specifically, a Unnest-Map operator defined for a child-axis takes a list of nodes and produces a list of child nodes. The breadth-first tree partitioning based storage format is most suitable for such operations, since child nodes are clustered and can be reached directly in one page or accessed through proxy links in other pages. However, it has large memory requirement since it needs to cache the intermediate results for each location step.

In the data-driven approach (Barton, Charles, Goyal, Raghavachari, Fontoura, & Josifovski, 2003; Zhang, Kacholia, & Özsu, 2004), the query is translated into an automaton and the data tree is traversed in document order according to the current state of the automaton. This approach is also referred as the streaming evaluation approach since the automaton is executed on top of the stream of input SAX events and there is no need to preprocess the XML document. This data-driven query processing approach works best with the depth-first based tree partitioning storage format. A subset of path expression is identified as a Next-of-Kin (NoK) expression when all axes are child-axis except the axis of the pattern tree root. For example, the path expression //book[author/last = "Stevens"][price < 100] is a NoK expression. A NoK expression can be evaluated by a single scan of the input stream with constant memory requirement. A general path expression containing descendant axes does not have this nice property. Algorithm 1 is the pseudocode for the NoK pattern matching.

This algorithm first finds the XML tree nodes (*snode*) that match with the root of the pattern tree (*pnode*), and invokes NoK pattern matching (*NPM*) from there. The results are put in the list *R*. The idea of the *NPM* is to maintain a set of frontier children for each pattern tree node. Whenever a pattern tree node is matched, all its children in the pattern tree are called frontier children and they are the candidates to be matched for the next incoming XML tree node in depth-first traversal. This procedure is a recursive function and traverses the XML tree in a depth-first fashion through the two function calls *First-Child* and *Following-Sibling*. Therefore, depth-first-based clustering storage formats works best with this algorithm.

STRUCTURAL XML INDEXES

There are many approaches to indexing XML documents. An XML document can be shredded into relational tables and regular B-tree indexes can

Algorithm 1. NoK pattern matching

```
NoK-Main
1.   R:= empty set;
2.   if Root-Lookup(pnode, snode) then
3.       NPM(pnode, snode, R);
4.   endif
5.   return R;


Root-Lookup (pnode, snode)
1.   if label(pnode) != label(snode) then
2.     return FALSE;
3.   endif
4.   while pnode is not the root of pattern tree do
5.       pnode:= pnode.parent;
6.       snode:= Parent(snode);
7.     Root-Lookup(pnode, snode);
8.   endwhile
9.   return TRUE;


NPM
1.   if proot is the returning node then
2.       construct or update a nlist for the candidate result;
3.       append snode to R;
4.   endif
5.   S:= all frontier children of proot;
6.   u:= First-Child(snode);
7.   repeat
8.       for each s in S that matches u with both tag name and value constraints do
9.               b:= NPM(s,u,R);
10.              if b = TRUE then
11.                      S:= S - {s};
12.                      delete s and its incident arcs from the pattern tree;
13.                       insert new frontiers caused by deleting s;
14.              endif
15.      endfor
16.  u:= Following-Sibling (u);
17. until u = NIL or S = empty set
18. if S != empty set and proot is a returning node then
19.    remove all matches to proot in R;
20.      return FALSE;
21. endif
22. return TRUE;
```

be created on their columns (Zhang, C., Naughton, J., DeWitt, D., Luo, Q., & Lohman, G., 2001; Li, Q., & Moon, B., 2001), or it can be represented as a sequence and the index evaluation algorithm is reduced to string pattern matching (Wang, H., Park, S., Fan, W., & Yu, P., 2003; Rao, P., & Moon, B., 2004). Another large body of research focuses on *structural* XML indexes, where XML tree nodes are clustered based on their *structural similarity*. To some extent, an XML index can be thought

of as a special XML storage format in that it also clusters tree nodes based on certain criteria. The differences are that XML indexes are solely created for query performance and storage formats are designed for many purposes and need to trade off between different requirements. We will focus on the structural XML indexes in this section.

Different notions of structural similarity result in different structural indexes. There are basically five notions of structural similarity: tag name,

Figure 4. An example XML tree

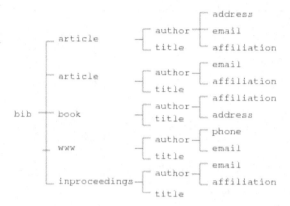

rooted path, bisimulation graph, F&B bisimulation graph, and feature vector. In the next sections, we shall introduce indexes based on these notions of structural similarity.

Tag Name Index

Under the simplest similarity notion, two nodes are similar if and only if they have the same tag name. Indexes based on this similarity notion are called tag-name indexes. The tag-name index can be easily implemented by a regular B+ tree, where the keys are the tag names and the values are the pointers to the storage that store the elements with the tag name. Elements clustered based on tag names are also used as input to many join-based path expression evaluation algorithms (Zhang, Naughton, DeWitt, Luo, & Lohman, 2001; Al-Khalifa, Jagadish, Koudas, Patel, Srivastava, & Wu, 2002; Bruno, Koudas, & Srivastava, 2002). Therefore, this evaluation strategy can be thought of as an index-based join.

Consider the XML tree in Figure 4. There are 11 distinct tag-names in the document, each of which corresponds to one key in the tag name index. Given a tag name, it is easy to find all elements with that tag name. Therefore, the tag name index is sufficiently expressive to answer path queries of length one such as //author. Since it is not suitable

for answering queries of length greater than one, it has very limited usage in practice.

Path Index

The rooted path of a node is the sequence of nodes starting from the document root to this node. If two nodes have the same rooted path, they are said to be similar in terms of their rooted path. In Figure 4, there are 22 distinct rooted paths, e.g., (bib), (bib, article), (bib, article, author), (bib, book, author), etc. Each rooted path can be assigned a distinct path ID, which serves as the key to the B+ tree. The value of the path index is the pointer to the element storage with this rooted path. For example, the two email elements under article subtrees have the same rooted path, so they can be reached by looking up in the path index with their path ID. Both DataGuide (Goldman & Widom, 1997) and 1-index (Milo & Suciu, 1999) fall into this category.

It is straightforward to see that the path index is a refinement of the tag-name index, in that all nodes under the same clusters in the path index are also under the same cluster in the tag-name index, but not vice versa. For example, the email element under the www subtree does not have the same rooted path as the two email elements under the article subtree. Because of this, the path index can answer queries involving a simple path expression having only child-axes, e.g., /bib/article/author. Even though the path index is a refinement of the tag-name index, it cannot answer the query //author since the key to the path index is the ID rather than the real path. One way to solve this is to use the reversed rooted path as the key. For example, the keys include (email, author, article, bib), (author, www, bib) etc. When the nodes are clustered based on the reversed rooted path, elements with the same tag name will be implicitly clustered as well. Therefore, this path index can also be used to answer queries such //author.

Bisimulation Graph

One of the major limitations of the above two indexes is that they cannot answer path queries with predicates. The reason is that their similarity notion is based on the current node label (tag-name index) or the label of its ancestors (rooted path). For path expressions with predicates, it is necessary to find nodes whose children or descendant match a subtree. For example, the path expression //author[address][email] finds all author elements that have both address and email as children. To be able to find all such author elements, the index needs to cluster the nodes based on their set of children. The bisimulation graph was proposed to solve this problem (Henzinger, Henzinger & Kopke, 1995).

The bisimulation graph of a node can be derived from the subtree rooted at the node. Given an XML tree, there is a unique (subject to graph isomorphism) minimum bisimulation graph that captures all structural constraints in the tree. The definition of bisimulation graph is as follows:

Definition 1 (Bisimulation Graph): Given an XML tree $T(N, A)$, where N is the set of nodes and A is set of tree edges, and a labeled graph $G(V, E)$, where V is the set of vertices and E is a set of edges, an XML tree node u in N is (forward) bisimilar to a vertex v in V (denoted as $u \sim v$) if and only

if all the following conditions hold:
1. u and v have the same label.
2. If there is an edge (u, u') in A, then there is an edge (v, v') in E such that $u' \sim v'$.
3. If there is an edge (v, v') in E, then there is an edge (u, u') in A such that $v' \sim u'$.

Graph G is a bisimulation graph of T if and only if G is the smallest graph such that every vertex in G is bisimilar to a node in T.

It is easy to see that every node in the XML tree T is bisimilar to itself. Furthermore, if there are two leaf nodes in T whose labels are the same, these two nodes can be merged together and the resulting vertex is, by definition, still bisimilar to the two nodes. It can also be proven that the bisimulation graph of a tree is a directed acyclic graph (DAG). Otherwise, if the bisimulation contains a cycle, the tree must also contain a cycle based on the definition. In fact the bisimulation graph of a DAG is a DAG.

The above properties imply that the bisimulation graph can be constructed in a bottom up fashion: merging leaf nodes with the same labels first and then keep merging upper level nodes that have the same set of children. Note that when merging non-leaf nodes, two nodes are said to have the same set of children if and only if each child can find another child in the other set such that they recursively have the same set of grandchildren. This satisfies the definition of bisimulation. For example, the bisimulation graph of the XML tree in Figure 4 is depicted in Figure 5 by merging tree nodes from bottom up.

After the bisimulation graph is constructed, each vertex in the bisimulation graph corresponds to a set of nodes in the XML tree. This actually defines an equivalent class of tree nodes: if two tree nodes are bisimilar, they should be merged in the bisimulation graph construction phase. Therefore, each equivalent class is a cluster of tree nodes (which is called *bisimulation cluster*) that

Figure 5. Bisimulation graph of the XML tree in Figure 4

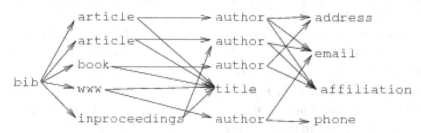

are represented by the vertex in the bisimulation graph. It is also easy to prove that for a predicated path query such as //author[address][email], if any node in the bisimulation cluster satisfies this path expression, then all nodes in that cluster do. Therefore, the bisimulation graph can be thought of as a structural index.

Since this index is a graph rather than the key-value pairs as in the tag-name and path indexes, it cannot be stored using the existing disk-based data structures such as the B+ tree. Fortunately since the bisimulation graph is usually much smaller than the XML tree, it is usually fully loaded into the main memory and then fed as an input to the tree pattern matching algorithm. The tree pattern matching algorithm is very similar to the one introduced in the previous section. However, the input event generation is different: previously the XML tree was traversed in depth-first order during which the begin and end events were generated for each element. If the input is the bisimulation graph, the DAG needs to be traversed in depth-first order, during which the begin and end events are generated when a vertex is visited the first and last time, respectively.

F&B Bisimulation Graph

As mentioned in the previous subsection, the bisimulation graph can answer predicated path queries starting with a descendant-axis with only one step in the non-predicate path. For example, it can answer queries such as //author[address][email] but not queries such as /bib/article/

author[address][email]. The reason is that the bisimulation graph clusters tree nodes only based on their subtrees, without considering their ancestors. Therefore, all author nodes that have the two children address and email will be clustered together, even though some of them do not have an ancestor element article.

To solve this problem, the F&B bisimulation graph was proposed to be the combination of the bisimulation graph and the path index (Kaushik, Bohannon, Naughton & Korth, 2002). Two nodes are F&B bisimular if and only if they have the same rooted path and they are bisimilar. Its formal definition is as follows:

Definition 2 (Backward Bisimulation Graph):
A node *u* is defined as backward bisimilar to *v* if and only if all the following conditions hold:
1. *u* and *v* have the same label.
2. *parent(u)* is backward bisimilar to *parent(v)*.

Graph *G* is a backward bisimulation graph of *T* if and only if *G* is the smallest graph such that every vertex in *G* is backward bisimilar to a node in *T*.

By this definition, it is easy to see that the path index of an XML tree is a backward bisimulation graph of the tree.

Definition 3 (F&B Bisimulation Graph):
Given an XML tree *T(N, A)* and a labeled graph *G(V, E)*, an XML tree node *u* in *N* is

Figure 6. F&B bisimulation graph of XML tree in Figure 4

F&B bisimilar to a vertex v in V (denoted as $u \approx v$) if and only if u is forward and backward bisimilar to v.

Graph G is an F&B bisimulation graph of T if and only if G is the smallest graph such that every vertex in G is F&B bisimilar to a node in T.

An F&B bisimulation graph can be constructed by clustering tree nodes that are F&B bisimilar. The construction can be extended from the construction of the bisimulation graph: if two vertices in the bisimulation graph have two different rooted paths, they will be separated into two vertices in the F&B bisimulation graph.

It is easy to see that the F&B bisimulation graph is a further refinement of both the path index and the bisimulation graph in that for any node cluster n1 under F&B bisimulation graph there is a node cluster n2 under path index or bisimulation graph such that n1 is the subset of n2. This means that the bisimulation graph can answer more path queries than the path index and the bisimulation graph. Figure 6 is an example of the F&B bisimulation graph of XML tree shown in Figure 4. Note that there are five authors in the F&B bisimulation graph, even though there are only four of them having different subtree structure (verify that the author under the second article has the same subtree structure as the author under inproceedings) as shown in Figure 4. Because of this finer granularity of clustering, the F&B bisimulation graph can answer query //article/author[email][affiliation].

It is also easy to prove that the F&B bisimulation graph is also a DAG. Therefore, given a path expression, the evaluation algorithm will do a pattern matching on the DAG in the same way as to the bisimulation graph. Since F&B bisimulation graph is a refinement of the bisimulation graph, it is usually larger than the bisimulation graph. For some complex data set, the F&B bisimulation graph could be too large to be fit into main memory. Therefore disk-based storage formats are proposed for F&B bisimulation graph.

To store the F&B bisimulation graph on disk, it is necessary to materialize it into a list of vertices, each of which keeps the pointers to its children. With carefully designed physical storage format, the F&B bisimulation graph can be used to efficiently answer a large set of queries including all queries that can be answered by all the structural indexes mentioned before. This is based on the observation that the F&B bisimulation graph is a refinement of the bisimulation graph and the path index, and both of which are also refinements of the tag-name index. The refinement relationships between these structural indexes form a lattice shown in Figure 7.

Based on this observation, when the vertices in the F&B bisimulation graph are stored, further clustering is possible so that the resulting storage format can also be treated as the path index and the tag-name index (Wang, Wang, Lu, Jiang, Lin, & Li, 2005). The clustering criteria are as follows:

Figure 7. Relationship between different structural indexes

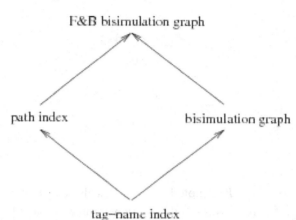

1. All XML tree nodes that are F&B bisimilar are clustered into chunks
2. All chunks having the same path ID are clustered into fragments
3. All fragments having the same tag names are clustered into tapes

These three clustering criteria have different granularity, with the chunk being the finest and the tape being the coarsest. It is easy to see that all nodes in the same type have the same tag name and all nodes with the same tag name are clusterd into one tape. Therefore, the tape has the same clustering criterion as the tag-name index, so answering queries such as //author amounts to finding the tape who is clustered based on tag name "author". Similarly the fragment has the same clustering criterion as the path index. Therefore, it can be used to answer queries that are suitable for the path indexes. Finally, the chunks are used to answer queries that can only be answered by the F&B bisimulation graph.

Feature-Based Index

As seen from the previous subsection, F&B bisimulation graph is the finest granular index and it can answer the largest set of queries. However, this also gives rise to the problem that the F&B bisimulation graph could be very large. In fact, it could grow as large as more than two million vertices for a medium sized (81 MB) complex data set (Zhang, Özsu, Ilyas & Aboulnaga, 2006). Even with the help of the disk-based clustering format introduced in the previous subsection, answering a twig query such as //author[email][address] will need to perform an expensive tree pattern matching for each vertex in the tape corresponding to tag name author. It is necessary to match against every vertex in the tape because of the need to find all author vertices whose children contains both email and address as a subset.

The feature-based index (Zhang, Özsu, Ilyas & Aboulnaga, 2006) was proposed to solve this problem by computing a list of features (or distinctive properties) of these bisimulation graphs, and use these features as filters to the tree pattern matching. To some extent, this feature-based index is similar to hash-based index in that it has pruning power to eliminate a set of inputs that are guaranteed to be non-match, and then use the more expensive matching algorithm to further check the remaining set.

The general framework of the feature-based index is as follows:

1. At the index creation phase:
   a. Compute the bisimulation graph of the XML tree.
   b. Enumerate all subgraphs of depth k (indexable units) in the data bisimulation graph, and compute their features. The reason to put a limit on the depth is that otherwise there are too many indexable units.
   c. Insert indexable units based on their distinctive features into a B+ tree.
2. At the query execution time:
   a. Compute the bisimulation graph of the query tree.
   b. If the depth of the bisimulation graph is not greater than k, then calculate the features of query bisimulation graph; otherwise, the index cannot be used.
   c. Use the query features to filter out indexed units.
   d. Perform tree pattern matching for the remaining bisimulation vertex.

The key idea of the feature-based index is to come up with the most distinctive features that have the maximum pruning power. To answer a twig query, the features need to be able to distinguish different bisimulation vertices having a certain tag name, and the capability to find subgraphs that are supergraphs of the query graph. The first is trivial since the tag name of the bisimulation graph serves the purpose. The second requirement needs some graph theory properties. In fact the following theorem lays the foundation of the feature-based indexes.

Theorem 1: Given two graphs G and H, let l_{min} and l_{max} denote the minimum and maximum eigenvalues of the matrix representation of a graph, respectively. Then the following property holds: if H is an induced subgraph of G, then $l_{min}(G) \le l_{min}(H) \le l_{max}(H) \le l_{max}(G)$.

This theorem indicates that the minimum and maximum eigenvalues of all the indexable units can be extracted as the features, and inserted, together with the root tag name, as keys into the B+ tree. Given a query bisimulation graph H, the minimum and maximum eigenvalues can be computed and searched in the B+ tree to find all graphs G such that all the following conditions hold:

1. $root\_label(G) = root\_label(H)$
2. $l_{min}(G) \le l_{min}(H)$
3. $l_{max}(H) \le l_{max}(G)$

Since the feature-based index indexes all subgraphs in the bisimulation graphs, it can answer all types of queries that a bisimulation graph can answer. Furthermore, since the features are all numbers, the feature-based index leverages the mature disk-base data structure such as B+ tree in query, creation as well as update. Another advantage of the feature-based index is that that it is very flexible to be extended to support a larger set of queries. For example, if the feature set includes the rooted path ID, then it can answer the query set covered by the F&B bisimulation graph.

CONCLUSION

In this chapter, we introduce state-of-the-art native XML storage, query processing and indexing techniques. These three techniques are closely related in that the design of the storage formats is affected by the access pattern of the XML tree nodes, which can be observed through XML query processing. The design of XML indexes is also dependent on the query processing techniques, but it focuses on how to efficiently execute a subset of queries, without considering a whole spectrum of requirements (e.g., DML, fragment retrieval etc.) that the storage formats have to.

REFERENCES

Al-Khalifa, S., Jagadish, H. V., Koudas, N., Patel, J. M., Srivastava, D., & Wu, Y. (2002). Structural joins: A primitive for efficient XML query pattern matching. In *Proceedings of the 18th International Conference on Data Engineering* (pp. 141-152). San Jose, CA: IEEE Computer Society.

Barton, C., Charles, P., Goyal, D., Raghavachari, M., Fontoura, M., & Josifovski, V. (2003). Streaming XPath processing with forward and backward axes. In *Proceedings of the 19th International Conference on Data Engineering* (pp. 455-466). Banglore, India: IEEE Computer Society.

Berglund, A., Boag, S., Chamberlin, D., Fernández, M. F., Kay, M., Robie, J., & Siméon, J. (2007, January 23). *XML Path Language (XPath) 2.0.* W3C Recommendation. Available at http://www.w3.org/TR/xpath20/

Boag, S., Chamberlin, D., Fernández, M. F., Florescu, D., Robie, J., & Siméon, J. (2007, January 23). *XQuery 1.0: An XML Query Language.* W3C Recommendation. Available at http://www.w3.org/TR/xquery/

Boncz, P. A., Grust, T., van Keulen, M., Manegold, S., Rittinger, J., & Teubner, J. (2006). MonetDB/XQuery: A fast XQuery processor powered by a relational engine. In *Proceedings of the ACM SIGMOD International Conference on Management of Data* (pp. 479-490). Chicago: ACM.

Brantner, M., Helmer, S., Kanne, C. C., & Moerkotte, G. (2005). Full-fledged algebraic XPath processing in Natix. In *Proceedings of the 21st International Conference on Data Engineering*, ICDE 2005 (pp. 705-716). Tokyo, Japan: IEEE Computer Society.

Bruno, N., Koudas, N., & Srivastava, D. (2002). Holistic twig joins: Optimal XML pattern matching. In *Proceedings of the ACM SIGMOD International Conference on Management of Data* (pp. 310-322). Madison, WI: ACM.

Fiebig, T., Helmer, S., Kanne, C. C., Mildenberger, J., Moerkotte, G., Schiele, R., & Westmann, T. (2002). Anatomy of a native XML base management system. *The VLDB Journal, 11*(4), 292–314. doi:10.1007/s00778-002-0080-y

Goldman, R., & Widom, J. (1997). DataGuides: Enabling query formulation and optimization in semistructured databases. In *Proceedings of 23rd International Conference on Very Large Data Bases* (pp. 436-445). Athens, Greece: ACM.

Henzinger, M. R., Henzinger, T. A., & Kopke, P. W. (1995). Computing simulation on finite and infinite graphs. In *Proceedings of 36th Annual Symposium on Foundations of Computer Science* (pp. 453-462). Milwaukee, Wisconsin: IEEE Computer Society.

Kaushik, R., Bohannon, P., Naughton, J. F., & Korth, H. F. (2002). Covering indexing for branching path queries. In *Proceedings of the ACM SIGMOD International Conference on Management of Data* (pp. 133-144). Madison, Wisconsin: ACM.

Krishnaprasad, M., Liu, Z. H., Manikutty, A., Warner, J. W., & Arora, V. (2005). Towards an industrial strength SQL/XML Infrastructure. In *Proceedings of the 21st International Conference on Data Engineering*, ICDE 2005 (pp. 991-1000). Tokyo, Japan: IEEE Computer Society.

Li, Q., & Moon, B. (2001). Indexing and querying XML data for regular path expressions. In *Proceedings of the 26st International Conference on Very Large Data Bases* (pp. 361–370). Rome: ACM.

Liefke, H., & Suciu, D. (2000). XMill: An efficient compressor for XML data. In *Proceedings of the ACM SIGMOD International Conference on Management of Data* (pp. 153-164). Dallas, TX: ACM.

Milo, T., & Suciu, D. (1999). Index structures for path expressions. In *Proceedings of 7th International Conference on Database Theory,* (pp. 277-295). Jerusalem, Israel: Springer.

Nicola, M., & Van der Linden, B. (2005). Native XML support in DB2 universal database. In *Proceedings of the 31st International Conference on Very Large Data Bases* (pp. 1164–1174). Trondheim, Norway: ACM.

Pal, S., Cseri, I., Seeliger, O., Rys, M., Schaller, G., Yu, W., et al. (2005). XQuery implementation in a relational database system. In *Proceedings of the 31st International Conference on Very Large Data Bases* (pp. 1175–1186). Trondheim, Norway: ACM.

Rao, P., & Moon, B. (2004). PRIX: Indexing and querying XML using Prufer sequences. In *Proceedings of the 20th International Conference on Data Engineering* (pp. 288-300). Boston: IEEE Computer Society.

Schkolnick, M. (1977). A clustering algorithm for hierarchical structures. [TODS]. *ACM Transactions on Database Systems, 2*(1), 27–44. doi:10.1145/320521.320531

Tolani, P. M., & Haritsa, J. R. (2002). XGRIND: A query-friendly XML compressor. In *Proceedings of the 18th International Conference on Data Engineering* (pp. 225-234). San Jose, CA: IEEE Computer Society.

Wang, H., Park, S., Fan, W., & Yu, P. (2003). ViST: A dynamic index method for querying XML data by tree structures. In *Proceedings of the ACM SIGMOD International Conference on Management of Data* (pp. 110-121). San Diego, California: ACM.

Wang, W., Wang, H., Lu, H., Jiang, H., Lin, X., & Li, J. (2005). Efficient processing of XML path queries using the disk-based FB index. In *Proceedings of the 31st International Conference on Very Large Data Bases* (pp. 145–156). Trondheim, Norway: ACM.

Zhang, C., Naughton, J. F., DeWitt, D. J., Luo, Q., & Lohman, G. M. (2001). On supporting containment queries in relational database management systems. In *Proceedings of the 2001 ACM SIGMOD International Conference on Management of Data* (pp. 425-436). Santa Barbara, CA: ACM.

Zhang, N., Kacholia, V., & Özsu, M. T. (2004). A succinct physical storage scheme for efficient evaluation of path queries in XML. In *Proceedings of the 20th International Conference on Data Engineering* (pp. 54-65). Boston: IEEE Computer Society.

Zhang, N., Özsu, M. T., Ilyas, I. F., & Aboulnaga, A. (2006). FIX: A feature-based indexing technique for XML documents. In *Proceedings of the 32nd International Conference on Very Large Data Bases* (pp. 259-271). Seoul, Korea: ACM.

Chapter 2
XML Data Management in Object Relational Database Systems

Zhen Hua Liu
Oracle Corporation, USA

Anguel Novoselsky
Oracle Corporation, USA

Vikas Arora
Oracle Corporation, USA

ABSTRACT

Since the advent of XML, there has been significant research into integrating XML data management with Relational DBMS and Object Relational DBMS (ORDBMS). This chapter describes the XML data management capabilities in ORDBMS, various design approaches and implementation techniques to support these capabilities, as well as the pros and cons of each design and implementation approach. Key topics such as XML storage, XML Indexing, XQuery and SQL/XML processing, are discussed in depth presenting both academic and industrial research work in these areas.

INTRODUCTION

Ever since XML has been introduced, a primary challenge associated with XML has been to persist and query XML content. As a result, there has been significant research into integrating XML data management in relational and object-relational databases. From a user point of view, it is desirable to have integrated access to both relational content and XML content in one platform and to leverage the full breadth of mature database technology to manage XML data.

There are two aspects of integrating XML data management into ORDBMS. One aspect is related to the XML storage and query processing in the database. Various techniques have been developed for storing XML in an ORDBMS including decomposed relational storage form, *aggregated storage* form, such as storing XML in a tree representation, a BLOB (Binary Large Object), or a CLOB (Character Large Object). Efficient XML query and

DOI: 10.4018/978-1-61520-727-5.ch002

update techniques for each form have been studied extensively.

A second aspect is to provide capabilities to facilitate interoperability between the Relational and XML data models. The SQL/XML standard plays a key role in this by providing users complete relational and XML duality - the capability of generating XML from relational data so that XQuery/XPath/XSLT can be used to query relational data, the capability of providing relational access over XML data so that SQL can be used to query XML data, and the capability of embedding XQuery/XSLT and SQL in each other to query and update both XML and relational data together.

In this chapter, we discuss the rationale and benefits of XML data management in ORDBMS, its capabilities of managing both XML and relational data in one platform, the industrial XML applications built by leveraging these capabilities, the design and implementation techniques to support such capabilities effectively and efficiently. We analyze different design approaches from the wealth of the literature in XML processing in the last decade. To conclude, we present the current ongoing and future work in XML data management in ORDBMS.

1 RATIONALE OF XML DATA MANAGEMENT IN ORDBMS

In this section we outline the motivation of building XML data management capabilities in ORDBMS from the perspective of user, from the perspective of data modeling and from the perspective of data engineering.

1.1 User Perspective

There is a general trend for users to increasingly prefer to manage all of their data in one platform for the benefits of easier data management, integrated query services, and sharing a common infrastructure for all types of data. This is more so

with relational databases that are widely adopted as mature platforms for managing structured data. With data extensibility mechanisms, such as user defined types, user defined functions and extensible indexes that are added into relational databases, the RDBMS has evolved into an ORDBMS with object-relational support (Stonebraker, Brown & Moore, 1999) that is capable of managing more complex data that may not fit into the relational model. Using an ORDBMS, users are able to manage various kinds of non-relational data such as object hierarchies in one platform. XML data management is a continuation of this trend with users looking for a single data management platform to avoid the overheads of partitioning and integrating data across multiple repositories. Major database vendors such as Oracle, IBM and Microsoft, in recognition of this trend have released XML capabilities in their products to support industrial strength applications that span all forms of data including relational data and XML data.

The other aspect is that XML has been used as a data exchange language to exchange data. Organizations have used XML as a portable way of exchanging data, in particular, exchanging data from and to relational systems with well-defined XML schema. This is associated with the need to generate XML from relational data at the data sending side and the need to extract relational data from XML at the data receiving side. To support this, it is critical for an ORDBMS to provide support for bridging the XML and relational data models.

1.2 Data Model Analysis Perspective

Another motivation for integrating XML data management in an ORDBMS arises from the perspective of data modeling. Although XML is based on a document centric hierarchical tree based data model, XML data in practice has been broadly classified into *document centric XML* and *data centric XML*. There also exists a wide spectrum of data between these two extremes where certain parts of the XML are more document centric and other parts are more data centric.

Reviewing the history of the evolution of data models (Stonebraker & Hellerstein, 2005), the hierarchical data model over the years came to be replaced by the relational data model. One of the key reasons is that relational model is flat without imposing a single hierarchy over the data. It is thus flexible enough to be used as a general purpose data model to model data having relationships more complex than *single hierarchical relationships* (Date, 1990). Colorful XML (Jagadish., Lakshmanan., Scannapieco, Srivastava, & Wiwatwattana, 2004) recognizes this problem and proposes an elegant multi-hierarchy XML data model to overcome the shortcomings of the single hierarchy tree model of XML.

The hierarchical data model can be leveraged as a presentation model to provide multiple hierarchical views over the relational data model. Data centric XML used for data exchange is schema based XML derived from the relational system. Consequently, data centric XML is better stored by exploiting its underlying relational structures rather than storing it directly in hierarchical tree form.

Document centric XML on the other hand has structure which is either loose or significantly varying and the data naturally fits into a *single hierarchical tree model*. As a result, an XML tree is a better physical data model for document centric XML. In this type of use case, ad-hoc XPath with text search queries are very common. Another reason why the physical model must preserve the hierarchical representation is to allow full navigational access such as parent and sibling access over XML data, particularly when XQuery is used as a general purpose programming language instead of DOM and SAX APIs to manipulate XML content.

As a result, there are multiple physical data models for different types of XML data. This has the implication that XML data management requires modeling XML as an *abstract data type* whose underlying physical storage and indexing structures can be more flexible and adaptive depending on the XML use case. (Liu & Murthy, 2009) study gives a concrete description of XML usecases and lessons learned from XML data management.

1.3 ORDBMS Engineering Perspective

The strength of an ORDBMS is that it provides a well-defined data-engineering and extensibility infrastructure to enable database implementers to define a new data type and to plug in one or more implementations of the data type along with supporting functions and index methods. This engineering infrastructure allows users to have deployment choices when selecting the proper XML storage and index for their XML use cases. Furthermore, both XQuery and SQL are based on "set at a time" declarative query language processing model. Therefore, many query transformation, optimization and execution ideas and strategies can be shared. In fact, the iterator based execution model (Graefe, 1993) adopted by SQL can be applied to XQuery processing as well. In addition, much of the database system technology infrastructure, such as, transaction system, backup and recovery system, multi-threaded kernel system, high availability management, parallel query execution infrastructure, memory management for different DBMS tasks, can be fully exploited to process XML data and query as well. It thus allows the re-use of the ORDBMS engineering infrastructure to provide the base platform to host XML data management instead of starting from scratch.

2 XML FUNCTIONALITY AND USECASE IN ORDBMS

In this section, we discuss the capabilities of XML data management in ORDBMS that provide SQL/XQuery over both XML and relational data, while leveraging the underlying database infrastructure. This section gives a description of these capabilities from a usage point of view. The underlying design and implementation techniques from academic and industrial research efforts to support these capabilities are presented and discussed in section 3.

2.1 XMLType as a Native Datatype in ORDBMS

Just as other built-in datatypes, such as VAR-CHAR, INTEGER, in SQL, XML is defined as a built-in datatype by the SQL/XML standard. XML can be used as a datatype for column of a SQL table or view, for parameters and return value of SQL functions and procedures. The XML type is based on the XQuery data model. The SQL/XML standard allows XML schemas to be managed as database objects similar to tables and views. The XML type can be constrained to a particular XML schema so that a table or column of that type are verified to conform to the XML schema. In addition, SQL/XML defines a set of SQL/XML publishing functions to generate XML data from relational data as well as XMLQuery() and XMLExists() operators to query XML with XQuery. Furthermore, the SQL/XML standard defines the XMLTable construct that can be used to define a virtual table that converts XML content into relational content.

2.2 Generating XML Data from Relational Data Using *SQL/XML generation functions*

Consider the following example. There are four relational tables: *Dept, Employee, Project, Pro-*

Table 1. Dept

Depid	DepName
1	Accounting
2	Engineering

Table 2. Employee

EmpId	EmpName	EmpSal	DepId
E1	John Smith	20000	1
E2	Allen Zhou	30000	1
E3	Fong Chu	25000	2
E4	Mary Clinton	30500	2

Table 3. Project

ProjId	ProjName
P1	ReFinance
P2	XMLQuery

Table 4. ProjAssignment

ProjId	EmpId
P1	E1
P1	E2
P2	E3
P2	E4
P1	E3
P2	E2

jAssignment. There are primary key, foreign key relationships between *Dept.Depid* and *Employee. Depid, Employee.Empid* and *ProjAssignment.Empid, ProjAssignment.ProjId* and *Project.ProjId*.

Below is the SQL/XML query Q1 used to define a view that generates the XML result R1 corresponding to the hierarchy from *Department* to *Employee* to *Project*. Q1 uses XMLAgg() with a nested sub-query to generate nested collection elements forming a hierarchical master-detail-detail relationship. A similar SQL/XML query can be written to generate XML result R2 that corresponds to the hierarchy from *Project* to *Employee* to *Department*. This reinforced the point made earlier in section 1.2 that "The *single hierarchical data model* can be leveraged as a presentation model to provide multiple hierarchical views over the relational data model". Without a single fixed hierarchy, the relational model enables user to query data starting from any entity table and then use primary key, foreign key joins for traversing the relationship chains to derive different hierarchies. Therefore, entity-relationship based relational data model serves as the best physical data model to model structured XML data.

SQL/XML GenXML Query:Q1

```
CREATE VIEW DEPT_EMP_PROJ_
VU(reportContent)
AS
SELECT XMLELEMENT("Department",
        XMLATTRIBUTES(d.depid
AS "depId"),
        (SELECT
XMLAGG(XMLELEMENT("Employee",
                XMLFOREST(e.
empname AS "empname", e.empsal
AS "empsal"),
                    (SELECT
XMLAGG(XMLELEMENT("Project",
                    XM-
LFOREST(

(SELECT projname

FROM project p

WHERE p.projid = pa.projid) AS
"projectName")))
                FROM pro-
jassignment pa
                WHERE
pa.empid = e.empid
```

```
    )))
    FROM employee e
    WHERE e.depid =
d.depid
        )
    )
FROM dept d
```

R1: Result of Q1 – Two XML Documents (department->employee->project hierarchy)

```
<Department depId="1">
    <Employee>
            <empname>John
Smith</empname>
            <empsal>20000</
empsal>
            <Project><projec
tName>ReFinance</projectName></
Project>
    </Employee>
    <Employee>
        <empname>Allen
Zhou</empname>
            <empsal>30000</emp-
sal>
        <Project><project
Name>ReFinance</projectName></
Project>

<Project><projectName>XMLQuery</
projectName></Project>
    </Employee>
</Department>
<Department depId="2">
    <Employee>
        <empname>Fong Chu</emp-
name>
        <empsal>25000</empsal>

<Project><projectName>XMLQuery</
projectName></Project>
        <Project><projectName>Re
```

```
Finance</projectName></Project>
 </Employee>
<Employee>
        <empname>Mary Clinton</
empname>
        <empsal>30500</empsal>

<Project><projectName>XMLQuery</
projectName></Project>
</Employee>
</Department>
```

Use Case: XML generation queries are widely used because XML serves as a common data exchange format. By simply defining several SQL/XML views over relational data, SQL/XML based applications can generate various XML reports, such as RSS feed, SOAP messages, XHTML web pages, without making any changes to the persistently stored relational data. A more XQuery centric way of accomplishing the same goal is discussed in section 2.6.

2.3 Querying XML Data Using XMLQuery(), XMLExists()

XQuery is the standard language to query XML. The SQL/XML standard embeds XQuery into SQL using the XMLQuery() and XMLExists() which are SQL operators taking an XQuery expression as an argument. The XMLExists() operator is typically used in a conditional check, such as the WHERE clause of SQL, to return a Boolean value that indicates if the XQuery used in XMLExists() returns an empty sequence or not. The XMLQuery() operator is typically used to extract an XML fragment or to construct new XML content. An example of a table with an XMLType column created to store XML documents is shown below.

```
CREATE TABLE DEPT_EMP_PROJ_RE-
PORT (reportId VARCHAR(20), re-
portContent XMLType)
```

The following is a SQL/XML Query Q2 that uses XMLQuery() and XMLExists(). It uses XMLExists() to qualify rows from table *DEPT_EMP_PROJ_REPORT*. For each qualified row, it uses XMLQuery() to extract and to construct new XML content from each qualified XML document.

SQL/XML Query XML Query: Q2

```
SELECT
   XMLQUERY('for $e in $x/De-
partment/Employee
                    where
$e/empsal > 2000
                     return
$e/Project/projectName' PASSING
r.reportContent AS "x"
                    RETURNING
CONTENT)
FROM DEPT_EMP_PROJ_REPORT r
WHERE XMLEXISTS('$x/Department[@
depId = 1]'

PASSING r.reportContent AS "x")
```

If two XML documents from result R1 are inserted into the table *DEPT_EMP_PROJ_REPORT*, Q2 returns the following XML document fragment shown as R2 below.

R2: Result of Q2

```
<projectName>ReFinance</project-
Name>
<projectName>XMLQuery</project-
Name>
Furthermore, the XMLQuery() and
XMLExists() operators do not
require the XML documents they
operate on to be persistently
stored. For example, the XMLQue-
ry() operator can be applied to
the XML column of a SQL/XML view
created by Q1.
```

SQL/XML Query XML Query: Q3

```
SELECT
  XMLQUERY('for $e in $x/De-
partment/Employee
                    where
$e/empsal > 2000
                      return
$e/Project/projectName' PASSING
r.reportContent AS "x"
                    RETURNING
CONTENT)
FROM DEPT_EMP_PROJ_VU r
WHERE XMLEXISTS('$x/Department[@
depId = 1]'
                    PASSING
r.reportContent AS "x")
```

Use Case: An XML schema can be registered to ORDBMS and managed as an object by ORDBMS. Users can then declare an XMLType column of a table to store XML document instances conforming to the registered XML schema. Once the XMLType column is declared to be associated with an XML schema, XQuery over the XMLType column can be optimized during query compilation time by taking advantage of the XML schema information. There can be different physical storage forms of XML. The *decomposed storage* model based on XML schema (to be discussed in section 3.1.1) can be used to shred XML data into the relational tables automatically and XQuery/XPath can be internally rewritten into equivalent SQL/XML query on the underlying storage tables by the system. This use case is common when the ORDBMS is used to load XML document instances conforming to a particular XML schema into the system so that different relational views over the XML can be used to extract data from XML into other relational applications. The *aggregated storage* model based on XML schema (to be discussed in 3.2) is used when an XML schema is either not available or is highly variant and the XML data is more document centric than data centric.

Being able to query XML independent of its physical form is the key strength of XML data management in ORDBMS. In contrast to a native XML database, this capability allows both physically stored XML and logical XML views over relational data to be queried uniformly. Also, given the variability of XML there is no one size fits all solution to store XML. Storing the XML may require *aggregated storage* (to be discussed in section 3.2) for content based document centric XML, or a decomposed relational approach (to be discussed in section 3.1) for data centric XML, or potentially combinations of these. XML is modeled as an abstract type in an ORDBMS independent of the physical storage representation that allows different physical representations to be queried uniformly without any changes in the XQuery and SQL/XML used in the applications. This *logical and physical separation of XML type abstraction* is a key strength of ORDBMS that is designed with the idea of XMLType as an *abstract datatype* (Murthy et al., 2005).

2.4 Relational Access on XML Using XMLTable Construct

Besides querying and retrieving XML fragments from XML, the SQL/XML standard also defines the XMLTable operator to bridge the gap between XML and relational content. It enables users to define a virtual table by extracting a node sequence from XML using XQuery. Each node in the sequence becomes a row which allows further projecting out columns based on XQuery expressions over the node. The typical use case of XMLTable is to traverse the XML and project out the hierarchy into a set of relational tables. Q4 shown below illustrates the XMLTable construct that yields the result shown in R4. The XMLTable construct can be chained as shown in Q4. Note that the second XMLTable construct extracts the *project* node that becomes the source for the third XMLTable construct.

Table 5. R4 – 6 rows of relational row

depid	empname	Empsal	projname
1	John Smith	20000	ReFinance
1	Allen Zhou	30000	ReFinance
1	Allen Zhou	30000	XMLQuery
2	Fong Chu	25000	XMLQuery
2	Fong Chu	25000	ReFinance
2	Mary Clinton	30500	XMLQuery

SQL/XML XMLTable Query: Q4

```
SELECT d.depId, e.empname,
e.empsal, proj.projname
FROM DEPT_EMP_PROJ_REPORT r,
     XMLTABLE('$x/Department'
PASSING r.reportContent AS "x"
            COLUMNS
                depId NUMBER
PATH '@depId'
          ) d,
     XMLTABLE('$y/Department/Em-
ployee'

PASSING r.reportContent AS "y"
            COLUMNS
                empname VAR-
CHAR2(20) PATH 'empname',
                empsal  NUMBER
PATH 'empsal',
                projx   XMLTYPE
PATH 'Project'
          ) e,
     XMLTABLE('Project' PASSING
e.projx
            COLUMNS
                projname VAR-
CHAR2(20) PATH 'projectName'
          ) proj
```

Use case: The XMLTable operator is commonly used in many application use cases where users can define a set of base relational views over XML using XMLTable constructs. These base relational views can then be used to compose other relational views or used directly in relational applications. In particular, many mature relational applications, such as OLAP and data warehouse solutions, can use the XMLTable operator to extract out relational content from XML data.

2.5 Updating XML Using XQuery Update Facility

XQUF (XQuery Update Facility 1.0) is the current proposed recommendation from W3C to update XML data. Since SQL does not provide a way to update a column value with self-mutating expression, any updates to an XML column is accomplished using the transform expression of XQUF. Q5 below shows a SQL UPDATE statement that updates the XML type column *reportContent*. It does so by executing the XMLQuery() function. XMLQuery() embeds the XQUF transform expression that makes a copy of the original XML column value, applies deletion of nodes using the 'delete node' expression to the copy, and then returns the modified XML result copy as the return value of XMLQuery(). The subsequent SQL UPDATE assignment overrides the original XML column value with the new modified XML value. That effectively updates the XML column value. This is a conceptual description of updating XML column value. Efficient mechanism can be used to update fragments of XML without actually making the logical copy. (Liu, Krishnaprasad, Warner, Angrish & Arora, 2007) studies such mechanism in depth and shows how efficient XML update can be achieved for different XML storages for a subset of XPath based XML update.

SQL/XML Update XML Statement -Q5

```
UPDATE DEPT_EMP_PROJ_REPORT r
SET r.reportContent =
XMLQUERY(
'copy $d:= .
```

```
    modify delete node $x/De-
partment/Employee/Project[projec
tName="XMLQuery"]
 return $d'
    PASSING r.reportContent As
"x" RETURNING CONTENT)
```

2.6 Standalone XQuery

Instead of accessing XML via SQL/XML standard that requires a SQL shell, there is also a concept of invoking XQuery directly. Instead of SQL, XQuery becomes the primary language to access XML data. Q6 shows such an example. An XQuery extension function sql:tab2xml() accepts a table or view name and returns the data stored in table or view in XML format: each row of the table forms an XML document with the top level element node named "ROW" and each column value of the row is tagged with the column name. Compared with Q1 of section 2.2, this way of generating XML reports from relational or XML content stored in ORDBMS is more XQuery centric and user friendly.

Q6: Top XQuery over relational data

```
for $d in sql:tab2xml('DEPT')/
ROW
return
<Department depId="{$d/DEPID}">
{
  for $e in
sql:tab2xml('EMPLOYEE')/ROW
  where $e/DEPID = $d/DEPID
  return
    <Employee>
      <empname>{$e/EMPNAME}</
empname>
      <empsal>{$e/EMPSAL}</emp-
sal>
      {
        for $p in
sql:tab2xml('PROJASSIGNMENT')/
```

```
ROW
      where $p/EMPID = $e/EM-
PID
    return
      <project>
        <projectName>{sql:ta
b2xml('PROJECT')/ROW[PROJID=$p/
PROJID]/PROJNAME}
        </projectName>
      </project>
    }
  </Employee>
}
</Department>
```

3 XML STORAGE, INDEX TECHNIQUES IN ORDBMS

In this section, we discuss various XML storage approaches and their applicable indexes that have been studied in the literature and have been implemented in the industry. For each approach, we describe how XML query processing is done and its associated advantages and disadvantages.

3.1 Decomposed Storage Using RDBMS

The general idea of this approach is to decompose or to shred XML document into relational tables. The relational table content contains enough information so that the original XML document can be reconstructed. XPath query over the original XML document is translated by the system into SQL over the relational tables. An XML document consists of structure and value. XML structure is expressed as an XML Schema or a DTD. Depending on the availability of XML structure, the shredded approach is classified into an **XML schema dependent approach** and an **XML schema independent approach**.

3.1.1 XML Schema Dependent Storage

When DTD information is available, (Shanmugasundaram et al., 1999) outlines the general principle of this approach. Each top-level element is stored in a separate table. For local elements, depending on if the local element is a *scalar* or *collection* element, the local element within a parent element is either stored inline with the table storing the parent element, or stored out of line as a separate table joined with the parent table. Scalar elements are elements that occur at most once whereas collection elements are elements that may occur more than once. The separate table holding the collection elements contains a foreign key to join with the parent table. Scalar elements are stored out of line as a separate table if referenced more than once by multiple parent elements. Consider storing XML documents in R1 of section 2.2 as an example using this approach, *department* element is stored into a *dept* table. Since both *employee* and *project* are collection elements, therefore, separate *employee* table and *project* table are created to store *employee* and *project* elements individually. Other scalar elements such as *empname*, *projname* are stored inline with their parent tables *employee* and *project*, respectively. Not surprisingly, this ends up with the same three relational tables *dept*, *employee*, *project* presented in the beginning of section 2.2. The only difference is that the project table using DTD shredding actually contains the result of joining *project* and *projAssignment* tables of section 2.2. After all, this XML schema dependent approach fundamentally does an ***entity-relationship decomposition*** of XML data that is highly structured and naturally fits into the relational model.

OR storage of XML (Murthy & Banerjee, 2003) study describes an industrial implementation of this approach based on annotations of XML schema. In addition, the OR storage approach handles other XML schema constructs that are not native to the relational model. To handle the ordering aspect of XML, the collection table is enhanced into an *ordered collection table* with an ordinal number column that keeps track of the position of each collection element. To handle non-sequence XML schema content model, such as choice of child elements under the parent element, an ***additional positional description binary column*** is added into the parent table to keep track of positions of child elements within the same parent element. Other non-relational content such as XML comments, processing instruction information, is also stored in the binary column. XPath and XQuery over OR stored XML are transformed into object relational SQL over the underlying relational storage tables using the ***XML Query Rewrite*** technique (Krishnaprasad et al. 2004; Liu, Krishnaprasad & Arora, 2005). The essence of this approach is to use XML generation functions to algebraically compose the XML from all the storage tables and to break XPath into multiple decomposition operators which are then optimized using composition and decomposition algebra. The essence of query rewrite over OR storage of XML is the same as that of optimizing XQuery and SQL/XML query over XML views defined on relational data as described in section 4.2.

Indexing OR storage XML is equivalent to creating relational B+ tree indexes, bitmap indexes over the underlying relational storage tables. In particular, a bitmap index is very useful for indexing the XML schema enumeration datatype that has limited enumerated values. The multi-column B+ tree index is very useful for multi-value search predicates.

3.1.2 XML Schema Independent Storage

When neither an XML schema or DTD is available, XML can be decomposed into one or a fixed number of universal relational tables using the *entity-attribute-value* approach that is commonly used in relational databases to represent data whose schema is not known in advance or is highly variant. An example of the entity-attribute-

Table 6. R -edge-table

Parent	Child	Ordinal	Name	Flag	Value
0	1	1	Department	Element	
1	2	1	depId	Attribute	1
1	3	2	Employee	Element	
1	4	3	Employee	Element	
3	5	1	Empname	Element	John Smith
3	6	2	Empsal	Element	20000
3	7	3	Project	Element	
7	8	1	projectName	Element	ReFinance
4	9	1	Empname	Element	Allen Zhou
4	10	2	Empsal	Element	30000
4	11	3	Project	Element	
4	13	4	Project	Element	
11	12	1	projectName	Element	ReFinance
13	14	1	projectName	Element	XMLQuery

value approach is to store E-commerce data whose schemas are constantly evolving and whose data content is sparsely populated (Agrawal,R., & Somani, A.,& Xu, 2001). An approach applying the same entity-attribute-value approach of storing XML without knowing an XML schema in advance is the edge table and node table approaches described below.

3.1.2.1 Edge Table Approach

The *Edge table* approach (Florescu & Kossmann 1999) decomposes XML as a directed graph because the XML data model is a directed tree model. Each edge of the graph is stored as a row in one edge table. The edge table content storing the first XML document in R1 of section 2.2 is shown below as R1-edge-tab. The parent and child columns indicate the parent and child relationship of the edge. The root of the XML tree has its parent column value as 0, which is the starting value. The ordinal column indicates the ordinal positions among sibling children nodes for a given parent node. The *name* column stores the tag name of the node, *flag* column indicates the type of the node and *value* column stores the value of

the node. Note for the purpose of illustrating the key point, the leaf text node is rolled up into the parent element node with the text value shown as value column of the element node. In an actual implementation, this level of detail including tracking comment nodes, processing instruction nodes, can be tracked as additional rows in the edge table (Table 6).

Construction of the original XML document can use recursive SQL query that computes transitive closure by following the parent, child column links of the edge table (Shanmugasundaram et al., 2001). Such a recursive SQL query construct is defined in SQL 1999 standard and is supported in commercial relational databases. An XPath query can be translated into a SQL query over the edge table. Each XPath step traversal is equivalent to querying the name and the flag columns of the edge table matching the node name and the node kind. The value column of the edge table is used for XPath predicate value matching. Node ordering among sibling nodes is inferred from the ordinal column at each step.

Various B+ tree indices over the parent, child, sibling columns and name, flag, value columns can be created to speed up tag name, value search and parent, child traversal required for XPath processing.

Since XML leaf node values can be of different XML schema built-in types such as number, string, date, time and interval, the value column of the edge table can be physically implemented as multiple value columns, one for each built-in type with B+ tree index created on top of it so as to facilitate efficient bottom-up value searches with different datatypes. Such a ***multi-value indexed approach*** is proposed in LORE (McHugh, Abiteboul, Goldman, Quass, & Widom, 1997).

3.1.2.2 Node Table Approach

The *Node table* approach stores each node of the XML tree as a separate row in a single node table. There are essentially two variations of this approach: **node-path** and **node-interval**. The **node-path** approach (Yoshikawa, Amagasa, Shimura, & Uemura, 2001) stores the path from the root node to each node in the tree as a separate row in a ***node-path table*** so that XPath processing can be efficiently done in a holistic manner instead of traversing each step individually as required by the edge table storage approach. The ***node-path table*** content storing the first XML document in R1 of section 2.2 is shown below as R1-node-path-tab. Each row has a path column that stores the path from the root to the current node in the row. The flag and value columns are the same as that of the edge table approach. Note that the path string stored in path column is for illustration purpose, efficient implementation of this strategy stores the binary encoding value of the path so as to provide efficient path search via B+ tree index over the path column.

However, the challenge with this approach is how to store XML document ordering relationship among nodes so that ancestor-descendant relationships, parent-child relationships and ordering among siblings can be processed efficiently during query processing. This is known as the ***structural join*** problem discussed in (Al-Khalifa

et al., 2002). The XRel approach (Yoshikawa, Amagasa, Shimura, & Uemura, 2001) stores the byte range offset of each node in the ***node-path table*** so that ancestor-descendant relationship can use range inclusion check and parent-child relationship can use minimal containing range check. The XParent approach (Jiang, Lu, Wang, & Yu, 2002) uses a similar ***node-path table*** idea but stores the ancestor-descendant relationship in a separate table with a level column so that parent-child relationship can be checked efficiently.

The **node-interval** approach, on the other hand, labels each node using its pre-order, post-order tree traversal number along with its level number within the tree. Both containment query approach (Zhang, Naughton, DeWitt, Luo, & Lohman, 2001) and accelerating XPath approach (T. Grust 2002) label each node using its pre-order, post-order traversal number and level number to keep track of node document ordering information so that an ancestor-descendant relationship is queried using range containment of pre-order and post-order numbers, while a parent-child relationship can be queried using level number. However, the path from the root node to each node is not stored in the node-interval approach.

The XML ordered relation approach (Tatarinov et al., 2002) proposes to use dewey decimal classification mechanism to label node. Each node is labeled with a string of numbers representing the path from the root to the node. Each number of the string represents the local sibling order of a given ancestor node. The indexing XML approach (Pal et al., 2004) adds the dewey column into the ***node-path table***. This is shown as the DWO (DeWey Order encoding) column of the R1-node-path table (Table 7)

One issue with node labeling is to avoid as much node re-labeling as possible in the presence of updates. The XML ordered relation approach (Tatarinov et al., 2002) studies the node re-labeling effects by comparing three node labeling mechanisms: global order, local order and dewey order and concludes that dewey order performs the

Table 7. R1-node-path-table

DWO	Path	Flag	Value
1	/Department	Element	
1.1	/Department/@depId	Attribute	1
1.3	/Department/Employee	Element	
1.3.1	/Department/Employee/empname	Element	John Smith
1.3.3	/Department/Employee/empsal	Element	20000
1.3.5	/Department/Employee/Project	Element	
1.3.5.1	/Department/Employee/Project/projectName	Element	ReFinance
1.5	/Department/Employee	Element	
1.5.1	/Department/Employee/empname	Element	Allen Zhou
1.5.3	/Department/Employee/empsal	Element	30000
1.5.5	/Department/Employee/Project	Element	
1.5.7	/Department/Employee/Project	Element	
1.5.5.1	/Department/Employee/Project/projectName	Element	ReFinance
1.5.7.1	/Department/Employee/Project/projectName	Element	XMLQuery

best on a mix of queries and updates workload. Either storing byte range offset for node ordering information or using pre-post-order labeling essentially falls into the global ordering technique and requires re-labeling large number of nodes for sub-tree inserts. Using the dewey order number, ORDPATHs approach (O'Neil 2004) suggests a 'careting' scheme to use odd numbers at the initial labeling and then to use even number between odd numbers to get another odd number. Dynamic quaternary encoding (DQE) scheme approach (Li & Ling, 2005) completely avoids the re-labeling problem when XML is updated.

Multi-value indexed approach can be applied to the value column of the node table as well. The strength of the node-path approach is that XPath processing can be done by directly querying the path column instead of traversing each path step individually as in the OR storage of XML approach or the edge table approach or the node-interval approach. In this way, XPath processing is no longer proportional to the length of steps in the path using node-path approach. However, it also leads to an increase in the cost of processing Xpath with predicates in the step since each predicate branch requires a self join on the ***node-path table***. Each self-join is a structural join using the dewey order column to determine the parent child relationship. Many such self-joins can lead to significant overhead compared with the OR storage of XML approach. Consider processing XPath *exists(/ Department[@depId = 1]/Employee[empname = "John Smith" and empsal > 20000 and empsal < 50000])*, both the SQL query for OR storage of XML approach and the node-path approach are shown below respectively.

OR_SQL for XPath Predicate Branch

```
EXISTS (SELECT 1
          FROM EMPLOYEE e,
DEPT d
          WHERE e.empname =
"John Smith" and e.empsal >
20000 and e.empsal < 50000
                    AND
e.empid = d.empid AND d.depid =
1)
```

Node-Path SQL for XPath Predicate Branch

```
EXISTS (SELECT 1
              FROM NODE_PATH_TAB
p1, NODE_PATH_TAB p2, NODE_PATH_
TAB p3,NODE_PATH_TAB p4,
                      NODE_
PATH_TAB p5, NODE_PATH_TAB p6
              WHERE p1.path = '/
Department/Employee'
              AND  p2.path =
'/Department/Employee/empname'
AND p2.value = "John Smith"
              AND p3.path =
'/Department/Employee/empsal'
AND CAST(p3.value AS INTEGER) >
20000
              AND p6.path =
'/Department/Employee/empsal'
AND CAST(p3.value AS INTEGER) <
50000
              AND IsParent(p1.
DWO, p2.DWO) AND IsParent(p1.
DWO, p3.DWO) AND IsParent(p1.
DWO, p6.DWO)
              AND p4.path = '/
Department'
              AND p5.path = '/De-
partment/@depId'
              AND p5.value = 1
              AND IsParent(p4.DWO,
p5.DWO)
              AND IsParent(p4.DWO,
p1.DWO))
```

Note the actual path match is done using binary encoding value via B+ tree index over the path column instead of path string match. However, still as shown above, there are many structural joins in the node-path SQL compared with the simple primary key foreign key joins in the OR_SQL. Furthermore, the value search is against all leaf value columns with the same type in Node-Path

approach, whereas in the OR storage approach, different value columns are created to hold specific element so that a value search reads more relevant data values than that of the *node-path table* approach. The *XMLTable Index* approach (Liu, Krishnaprasad, Chang & Arora, 2007) illustrates the performance issues with the node-path approach when XPath is used with many value based predicates and proposes the concept of the XMLTable index that leverages the strength of OR storage approach but uses it as indexing scheme for XML. This will be discussed further in section 3.2.3.2.

3.1.3 Comparison Between Schema Dependent and Independent Approach

When either an XML schema or DTD is available, the XML schema dependent shredding approach (OR storage of XML) performs better than an XML schema independent shredding approach. This is observed in both the edge table paper (Florescu & Kossmann, 1999) and ALTXML SIGMOD record (Tian, DeWitt, Chen & Zhang, 2002). The Edge table paper (Florescu & Kossmann, 1999) explains that the performance difference is due to only *relevant data* being processed in the schema dependent approach. We observe the following architectural differences between the two that contribute to better performance for the schema dependent approach:

• The Schema dependent approach does not need to do element tag matches during query run time, only value searches are needed whereas the schema independent approach needs to match both. This not only leads to better performance but also more compact storage because the element tag is part of the relational schema, which is meta-data, instead of data stored as the content of the table. Another way to understand this is that the element tag match has been pre-compiled during query compilation time into the specific tables to query on. Such a compile time data partitioning scheme is not feasible for schema independent approach.

- The value search of the schema dependent approach is restricted to more specific columns of tables instead of a single bloated value column capturing all leaf values as in the schema independent approach. Therefore, the schema dependent approach in general reads less data values than the schema independent approach.

- The structural join (Al-Khalifa et al., 2002) issue exists for both the node-interval approach and node-path approach. Efficiently implementing the structured join requires adding new physical join methods (Zhang, Naughton, DeWitt, Luo, & Lohman, 2001, Al-Khalifa et al., 2002) in an ORDBMS. However, for schema dependent approach, the structural join to determine the parent-child relationship is processed as a primary key, foreign key join that can be done very efficiently in an ORDBMS.

- Finally, the XMLTable based query as shown in section 2.4 suffers the most performance overhead using the schema independent approach compared with the schema dependent approach. This is discussed in the *XMLTable Index* paper (Liu, Krishnaprasad, Chang & Arora, 2007).

On the other hand, when an XML schema is not available or the schema has too many variations and irregularities, then the flexibility from the schema independent approach has its merits and significant strength. Indeed, the comparison between the *XML schema dependent* storage approach and *XML schema independent storage* approach is the same as comparing the *entity-relationship* model and *entity-attribute-value* model. The node-path approach has the advantage of matching the whole XPath without doing step-wise join. This is significant if the query involves lengthy path traversals. However, the node-path approach is quite costly for heavy update use cases. Furthermore, the size of the *node-path table* can be much larger relative to the original XML document size.

3.2 Aggregated Storage

One of the key performance issues for the XML *decomposed storage* approach is the cost of document reconstruction when retrieving the whole document or a large document fragment. Although this is not an issue for XMLTable based queries or for small to medium document fragment retrieval queries, it is an important argument against the use of the relational shredding approach to store XML. In this section, we look at strategies of storing XML as an aggregated unit instead of decomposing it.

3.2.1 CLOB, BLOB Approach

This strategy either stores XML text as a Character Large Object (CLOB) column or stores a certain binary encoding of the XML as Binary Large Object (BLOB) column. The advantage of this approach is that it provides the most efficient way of retrieving the XML document as a whole. The CLOB approach preserves XML text fidelity that may be important for certain usecases for example, maintaining records for auditing. However, storing XML as CLOB also means that any XML processing requires parsing and XML parsing is not cheap. Storing the SAX events of parsing XML as a BLOB can avoid the XML parsing cost and make it more efficient to process certain XPaths over the XML BLOB content efficiently. Furthermore, the XML element tag name length can be large. Encoding of the XML element tag name as integers can save both the storage space and provide fast XML tag matching. When XML is schema based, storing XML leaf data in its native binary data form instead of a text form can also save storage space and provide fast value search. Enterprise XML architecture (Murthy et al., 2005) presents this as the ***binary XML storage approach***.

However, storing SAX events of parsing XML is not enough for arbitrary XPath navigational queries that require efficient traversal from a node to its parent node or ancestor nodes as well as its sibling nodes. Such full XPath axis navigational queries are common when XQuery is used as a declarative query language over XML instead of using the XML DOM API. This motivates the need for storing DOM tree on disk as the persistent storage mechanism for XML to be discussed in the following section.

3.2.2 Tree Based Storage

The idea of XML tree storage is to have the XML DOM tree be persisted on disk. The classical organization of on-disk tree node storage consists of a set of pages, each of which stores a subset of the entire XML tree nodes. Each XML node has a unique address that can be used to retrieve the node. Each node stores node addresses of its parent node, its first child node and its preceding and following sibling nodes so that full axis DOM traversal can be done efficiently. When XPath is processed, only disk pages that contain the DOM nodes that the XPath selection needs are loaded into memory cache and it is thus more scalable than any dynamic in-memory DOM building approach. The classical RDBMS buffer pool manager, disk storage page manager, that are proven to be scalable with respect to large data sizes and high user concurrency, can be leveraged completely to support XML tree storage. Both System RX (Beyer et al., 2005) and NATIX (Kanne, Moerkotte, 2000) use the tree storage approach. Storing the parent, child, sibling link information inside each tree node, the object storage method discussed in ALTXML SIGMOD record (Tian, DeWitt, Chen & Zhang, 2002) is in principle the same as that of tree storage method.

One aspect of XML tree storage is that full axis navigation of XML tree is natively supported by the storage instead of running structural join query that is required in both the node-interval and the node-path with dewey key approaches. Certainly, the node-path approach has the advantage of using the index to search the full XPath holistically. However, the structured join issue remains when there are predicates in XPath. So the question is whether the structural join query performs better. The Node-interval XPath with RDBMS (Grust, Rittinger, & Teubner, J, 2007) appears to suggest that the node-interval approach performs better than native XML tree storage. Our thinking is that evaluating an XPath via steps, whether done via tree navigations over native tree storage or structural joins, needs to follow the same cost based join order optimization principles in relational database so that the steps that return less number of nodes are probed first. This cost based join principle is inherited fully in the Node-interval XPath with RDBMS approach (Grust, Rittinger, & Teubner, J, 2007) as the underlying RDBMS automatically applies this principle. An XML tree storage model, once equipped with such a cost based step join optimizer, should be able to show the strength of the native navigation capability in the underlying physical storage.

3.2.3 Indexing Aggregated Storage

Although aggregated XML storage provides efficient retrieval of the full XML document or large document fragments without the need of reconstruction as in the decomposed approach, ***aggregated storage*** needs to be indexed to provide fast query performance. XQuery, in particular, XPath, is about finding bits and pieces of XML satisfying certain criteria quickly and extracting them out efficiently. It turns out that both the ***node-path table*** approach and the schema dependent OR XML storage approach can be applied as indexing schemes for XML. Furthermore, the key advantage is that being an indexing scheme instead of a storage scheme, there is NO need to shred all pieces of the data. Instead only the commonly queried pieces need to be shredded for indexing. This can significantly reduce the overall size of the *node-path table* approach and number of tables needed from the OR XML storage approach.

3.2.3.1 Path and Value Index

The *node-path table* approach can be used to index aggregated XML storage. An extra locator column can be added into the *node-path table*. It stores the locator to retrieve the node in that row. For CLOB or BLOB storage, the locator can be the LOB locator that contains the offset within the LOB to reach the node along with the length of the XML fragment rooted from the node. Thus fragment retrieval given a full XPath can be done efficiently. For XML tree storage, the locator can be the address of the node so that full axis XPath navigation is possible followed by path index look up. Furthermore, since the *node-path table* is used as an index, only commonly searched paths need to be indexed. This can significantly alleviate the need of maintaining a huge *node-path table* if it is used as storage. Secondary multi-valued index can be created on the *node-path table* to support bottom up value searches from XPath predicates.

3.2.3.2 XMLTable Index

Another approach to indexing aggregated XML storage is based on using the SQL/XML XMLTable operator to define the index. Conceptually, the schema dependent XML storage (OR XML storage) model can be thought of as using the XMLTable operator to decompose XML into a set of relational tables. Each of the tables is defined by an XMLTable pattern derived from the XML schema. The row XQuery expression of

the XMLTable operator extracts out the collection elements and the column XQuery expression of the XMLTable operator extracts out the scalar elements for each collection element in the row. However, when the XMLTable operator is used as a storage mechanism, it needs to decompose every piece of data. Whereas when it is used as an indexing mechanism, it only needs to index commonly queried pieces. In fact, being an indexing mechanism, both the XQuery/XPath expressions used in the row and column expressions of the XMLTable operator can be more holistic XPaths instead of step-by-step XPaths required for storage. Such an indexing mechanism is referred to as *XMLTable Index* (Liu, Krishnaprasad, Chang, & Arora, 2007). It can be used to efficiently answer queries involving searches of multiple related property values for the same node because it avoids the structural join of the qualified nodes. Also it does not depend on the existence of an XML schema or a DTD as long as some of the commonly searched properties in user queries can be identified.

3.2.3.3 Integrated Path-Value Index

System RX (Beyer et al., 2005) indexes commonly searched paths together with the leaf values cast to specific SQL built-in datatypes so as to promote fast searches using paths and values together. It avoids the need to separately build multi-valued indexes and thus reduces the index size. However, it does not embrace the concept of *XMLTable index* where multiple leaf property values related to the same node can be pivoted into a table when they are typically searched together. This can avoid structured join among these nodes from the result of each separate probe of path-value index.

SECTION 4: XQUERY, SQL/XML PROCESSING TECHNIQUES IN ORDBMS

In this section, we discuss XQuery and SQL/XML query processing techniques in ORDBMS. We compare and contrast various approaches from research and industry to support XQuery and SQL/XML processing in ORDBMS.

4.1 XML Generation from Relational Data

A straightforward way of executing Q1 of section 2.2 is to execute the query using *iterative nested loop with immediate XML tagging* approach. For each *department* row, it runs the sub-query to find all the *employee* rows for that department which in turn runs the sub-query to find all the *project* rows for that employee. The result from each row is immediately tagged with XML element name to produce an intermediate XML result. Then all the intermediate XML results are copied from the bottom of the generation function expression tree to the top so that they are eventually copied into the output XML result buffer. The problem with this straightforward approach is that it dictates the nested loop join order of *dept, employee* and *projassignment* tables to be the same as specified in the query, and each sub-query has to be repeatedly executed per row from the outer table. The second problem is that all the intermediate XML results, which can be large, have to be repeatedly copied from the child generation function to the parent generation function.

Sorted Outer Union approach (Shanmugasundaram et al., 2000) proposes an efficient way of generating XML from relational data. The key idea is to run a pure relational query without XML tagging first to produce structured relational content in the order it needs to appear in the result XML document and then to apply XML tagging later in the second phase. A pure relational query applies the query de-correlation method and uses a left

outer join to join from *dept* to *employee* to *projassignment*. This gives the database optimizer more freedom to determine the optimal join ordering among these tables instead of relying on the join order in the query. The relational result content from the query is then sorted to ensure parent information occurs before the child information by sorting the id columns of the table based on the final XML result order.

SilkRoute (Fernandez, Morishima, & Suciu, 2001), however, proposes that generating one giant query that left outer joins all the tables and then doing sorted outer union in the end may not be always optimal. As a large query involving many table joins is more likely to increase the optimizer search space and sorting a large result set is more likely to cause an on-disk sort. So a *fully partitioned strategy* is proposed to decompose the generation query into multiple SQL queries that do not contain outer join or outer unions. Each intermediate query result is then merged and tagged to generate the final result. The optimal approach, which is in between the outer union approach and fully partitioned approach, is to generate multiple queries some of which may contain outer joins and unions.

An alternative generation mechanism is proposed in (Krishnaprasad, Liu, Manikutty, Warner, & Arora 2005) as the *top-down streaming evaluation* approach. This approach solves the problem of repeatedly copying intermediate result from the child generation function to the parent generation function by doing top-down evaluation of the generation function expression tree. A single result XML output buffer is created at the top of the generation function tree and the buffer is passed down to the descendant generation functions in a top-down, depth-first manner. Each descendant generation function writes its XML generation result to the result XML output buffer directly. This technique can also be applied to the evaluation of XQuery constructor functions which are essentially the same as the evaluation of SQL/XML XML generation functions. This can be done by creating the constructor content XML node tree by directly attaching to the final result XML tree instead of repeatedly copying intermediate content XML node trees.

4.2 Querying XML View over Relational Data

A straightforward way of executing Q3 of section 2.3 is to construct the XML result from the relational data as defined by the SQL/XML view, and then apply the XQuery to the materialized constructed XML result. However, a key observation is that the XPath traversal part of the XQuery carries the inverse operation of the XML construction. As a result, it is feasible to cancel out the XPath extraction and XML construction so that only the minimal XML fragment needs to be constructed. Such query transformations and optimizations can be accomplished by developing *composition and decomposition algebra rules* for *SQL/XML generation function* operators and the corresponding XPath traversal and extraction operators.

O2 shows the optimized query for Q3 of section 2.3 after applying the composition and decomposition approach. As shown, O2 is a relational query with SQL/XML generation functions.

(Shanmugasundaram, Kiernan, Shekita, Fan, & Funderburk, 2001) implement such techniques in the context of a middleware system outside of a database. It eliminates the need for construction of all the intermediate XML fragments and pushes down the computation to the underlying SQL query engine in the RDBMS. (Krishnaprasad et al., 2004) define the composition and decomposition algebra rules between *SQL/XML generation functions* and XPath extraction functions. It classifies these rules into normalization rules, distribution rules, cancellation rules, and nullification rules. These rules combined with relational algebra rules such as relational view merge, sub-querying un-nesting and query de-correlation, can fully optimize SQL/XML query with XQuery and SQL inside the ORDBMS kernel. This avoids the need of having two loosely integrated query engines, one for XQuery and one for SQL. This is the underlying motivation for the Native XQuery approach that provides native interoperability between the relational and XML data models (Liu, Krishnaprasad, & Arora, 2005).

O2: Optimization Result of Q6

```
SELECT XMLELEMENT("Department",
        XMLATTRIBUTES(DEPID AS
"depId"),
    (SELECT
XMLAGG(XMLELEMENT("Employee",

XMLELEMENT(NOMAPPING "empname",
                CASE WHEN
SYS_ALIAS_2.EMPNAME IS NOT NULL
                THEN
XMLELEMENT("EMPNAME",SYS_
ALIAS_1.EMPNAME)
                ELSE NULL
END),

XMLELEMENT(NOMAPPING "empsal",
                CASE WHEN
SYS_ALIAS_2.EMPSAL IS NOT NULL
                THEN
XMLELEMENT("EMPSAL",SYS_ALIAS_2.
EMPSAL)
                ELSE NULL
END),
            (SELECT
XMLAGG(XMLELEMENT("project",

XMLELEMENT("projectName",

(SELECT XMLAGG(

CASE  WHEN SYS_ALIAS_4.PROJNAME

IS NOT NULL
```

```
THEN XMLELEMENT("PROJNAME",

SYS_ALIAS_4.PROJNAME) ELSE NULL
END)

FROM PROJECT SYS_ALIAS_4

WHERE

SYS_ALIAS_4.PROJID= SYS_ALIAS_3.
PROJID))))
                        FROM PRO-
JASSIGNMENT SYS_ALIAS_3
                        WHERE
SYS_ALIAS_3.EMPID=SYS_ALIAS_2.
EMPID)))
        FROM EMPLOYEE SYS_ALIAS_2
        WHERE SYS_ALIAS_2.
DEPID=SYS_ALIAS_1.DEPID)) "RE-
SULT_PLUS_XQUERY"
FROM DEPT SYS_ALIAS_1
```

4.3 XQuery Processing

There has been a vast amount of research and industrial effort into designing and implementing XQuery processors. Almost all of the approaches use the iterator-based pipeline as the execution model where the queries are compiled into a so-called execution plan tree. During run-time, data items flow up from leaf nodes to the parent operator nodes an item at a time. The popularity of the iterator approach can easily be explained. Originally, XQuery was designed as a functional query language and pipelining is a well-established execution strategy for such languages and for relation databases as well. The alternative to pipelining is so-called sequential or eager execution strategy where programs are compiled into a sequence of virtual or hardware machine instructions. During run-time, each instruction is executed only after the previous instruction produces all of its data items. The sequential strategy is widely adopted

in processing procedural language such as Java and C.

While the iterator approach is ideal for searching and pipelining large amount of data, it is not that effective when working with sequential language constructs like user defined functions, assignments (Chamberlin, D., Engovatov, D, 2008), update expressions (Chamberlin, D., Florescu, D, 2008), try-catch expressions (Chamberlin, D., Robie, J., 2008) or when dealing with moderately sized XML data. This is because the entire execution plan tree has to be available until the last item in the sequence is computed and fetched by the client. Since the intermediate data sequence from each expression is not fully materialized but rather lazily evaluated, all the intermediate execution states for each execution plan tree have to be kept alive. Sequential execution on the other hand more efficiently handles small to moderate sizes of intermediate data but falls behind pipelining when the searched data size increases.

We discuss various XQuery processing approaches by evaluating them from several principal aspects:

- Whether the processor uses iterator lazy execution strategy or eager execution strategy or integration of both strategies;
- Which XQuery compilation and optimization strategies have been used;
- Whether the processor works with only one XML storage and indexing model or it is open to multiple storage or indexing models;
- Whether the processor is implemented within the ORDBMS by extending the underlying SQL compilation and execution infrastructures with XML constructs or implemented outside ORDBMS as a standalone engine, or implemented outside ORDBMS by translating XQuery into SQL and leveraging RDBMS as a black box.

4.3.1 Integrated XQuery/SQL/XML Processors

Since XQuery and SQL have significant conceptual overlaps and SQL/XML is the standard way of querying XML in databases, all major database vendors have adopted an ***integrated approach*** to leverage the SQL compilation and execution infrastructure to support both XQuery and SQL as a unified engine. Note that this approach is conceptually different from translation of XQuery into SQL. Native XQuery processing (Liu, Krishnaprasad, & Arora, 2005) proposes cross language optimizations between XQuery and SQL and it extends the relational algebra with XML data model and XML specific table functions and operators to cope with the semantic difference between SQL and XQuery. System RX [Beyer et al., 2005] extends its internal SQL query compiler dataflow structure: QGM (Query Graph Model) with XQuery data model and XQuery. XQuery in RDBMS (Pal et al., 2005) compiles XQuery expressions into an extended relational operator tree against a ***node-path table*** (discussed in 3.1.2.2) and then combines it with SQL query operator tree so that in the end, the underlying relational engine receives a single operator tree to optimize and execute. The merits of the integrated approach of XQuery and SQL are:

- To scale with large data sizes in a database, iterator based query execution strategy together with parallel query capabilities in databases can be fully leveraged for evaluating XQuery as well.
- Type, function and index extensibility from the ORDBMS infrastructure can be fully leveraged to model XQuery data model and XML specific expressions that are foreign to SQL. Thus database extensibility mechanism can be leveraged as an engineering mechanism to support ***XML extended relational algebra***.

- Many existing relational query transformation rewrite techniques, such as view merge (Stonebraker, 1975), sub-query un-nesting to semi-join and anti-joins (Kim, 1982), query de-correlation, can be leveraged for XQuery transformation as well.

When dealing with multi-storage and indexing model of XML, (Liu, Chandrasekar, Baby, & Chang 2008) propose the idea of separating XQuery processing steps into XML storage/index independent step (***logical rewrite***) and XML storage/index dependent step so that it can work with different XML storage and index models (***physical rewrite***). This is in principle similar to the approach of answering XML queries over heterogeneous data sources presented in the paper (Manolescu, Florescu & Kossmann, 2001). However, the key difference is that the Liu's approach does not translate XQuery into SQL. Instead, any XQuery construct foreign to SQL is modeled as an XML extension to the relational algebra in the SQL/XML engine. Other industrial XQuery in RDBMS (Pal et al., 2005) works with one node-path based XML index model. System RX (Beyer et al, 2005) works with one XML tree storage model using ***path-value index***.

As an example to show how an XQuery and SQL/XML integrated engine can optimize queries over different XML physical storage and index models, we show the optimized query for Q2 of section 2.3. O3 and O4 show the optimized query when using XML OR storage approach and XML ***aggregated storage*** with node-path as index approach respectively. For OR XML storage, the XPath in XMLEXISTS() searching @depid becomes a SQL predicate on the *dept. depid* column. The where clause *$e/empsal > 2000* of the XQuery in XMLQuery() becomes a SQL predicate on the *employee.empsal* column. Both of these can use a B+ tree index on the specific column of the specific table. For aggregated XML storage with ***node-path table*** as an Index, the XPath in XMLExists() searching @depid becomes a SQL predicate on the ***node-path table*** value column. The where clause *$e/empsal > 2000* of the XQuery in the XMLQuery() operator becomes a SQL predicate on the ***node-path table*** value column casting to integer as well. Both of these can use a B+ tree index created on the result of casting value column of the ***node-path table*** to integer. Note the OR XML storage approach does more relevant value matches than the aggregated approach with multi-type-valued index.

For returning the XML *projectName* element node in the OR storage approach, the XML result needs to be constructed using the XMLELE-MENT() function. In contrast for ***aggregated storage*** using node-path index, the ***node-path table*** has a *FRAG_LOCATOR* column (discussed in section 3.2.3.1) that can be used to directly fetch the XML fragment. Both O1 and O2 can be further optimized by the relational optimizer to un-nest the EXISTS subquery into a semi-join with the main query. For clarity, we don't show this step of optimization. However, the important point here is that in an ORDBMS, XML is an ***abstract datatype*** so that an XML Query can work with different physical XML storage and index models.

O1: Optimization Result of Q3 Using OR XML Storage

```
SELECT (SELECT XMLAGG(SELECT XM
LAGG(XMLELEMENT("projectName",
proj.projName))

FROM project proj

WHERE proj.empid = e.empid)
          FROM employee e
          WHERE e.EMPSAL >
2000
          AND e.depId IN (SELECT
depid FROM dept d WHERE d.depId
=  r.docid)
          )
FROM DEPT_EMP_PROJ_REPORT r
```

```
WHERE EXISTS (SELECT 1
          FROM DEPT d
          WHERE d.depId = 1
          AND d.docid =
r.docid)
```

O2: Optimization Result of Q3 Using Node-Path Index Over Aggregated XML Storage

```
SELECT (SELECT XMLAGG(SELECT
XMLAGG(p5.FRAG_LOCATOR)
          FROM node_path_
tab p5
          WHERE p5.path =
'/Department/Employee/Project/
projectName'
          AND
p5.docid = p3.docid
          AND
isAncestor(p3.DWO, p5.DWO))
     FROM node_path_tab p3
     WHERE p3.path = '/De-
partment/Employee'
     AND p3.docid = r.docid
     AND EXISTS(SELECT 1
          FROM node_
path_tab p4
          WHERE
          AND
p4.path = '/Department/Employee/
empsal'
          AND
IsParent(p3.DWO, P4.DWO)
          AND
CAST(p4.vaue AS INTEGER) > 2000
          AND
p3.docid = p4.docid)
     )
FROM dept_emp_proj_report r
WHERE EXISTS (SELECT 1
          FROM
node_path_tab p1, node_path_tab
p2
```

```
                            WHERE
p1.path = '/Department' AND
p2.path = '/Department/@depId'

AND CAST(p2.value AS INREGER) =
1

AND IsParent(p1.DWO, p2.DWO

AND p1.docid = p2.docid AND
r.docid = p1.docid)
```

4.3.2 Standalone Iterator-Based XQuery Processors

The BEA streaming XQuery processor (Florescu et al, 2004) is an iterator-based engine built outside a database although the XQuery transformation optimization and execution strategies it adopts are principally the same as that of the SQL engine. Being a mid-tier based XQuery engine that needs to cope with relational data sources, the BEA AquaLogic streaming eingine internally converts XQuery expressions against relational data source into efficient SQL sent to the backend relational sources (Borkar et al., 2006).

PathFinder (Grust, Rittinger, & Teubner 2008) builds an XQuery to SQL translator outside a database using the node-interval approach and leverages off-the-shelf RDBMSs to execute the translated SQL. It leverages the robust relational engine for its cost based optimizer and iterator based execution models. However, it works with only one physical XML storage model which is the node-interval approach discussed in 3.1.2.2.

Saxon (Kay, 2008) is currently (2009) a popular standalone XQuery engine. It works with XML documents stored in a file system or sent over the wire. During run-time, XML documents are converted into one of the following representations: TyneTree – a proprietary array based node storage; Linked Tree – nodes are represented as linked list; or classical DOM. The TinyTree is the most interesting one of them because it is

significantly more efficient both space-wise and processing speed-wise. Saxon doesn't scale well while working with large documents because it needs the documents to stay in-memory while processed.

Zorba (Zorba) is an open source XQuery processor, which according to its authors is suitable for embedding in wide range of application contexts including: browsers, databases, online data distribution and hosting systems. Zorba architecture resembles the BEA one but it accesses the underlying XML data via well-defined abstract interface. The processor is written in C++.

4.3.3 Hybrid XQuery Processors

As XQuery imperative extensions started to emerge (Chamberlin, D., Engovatov, D, 2008) and with XQuery 1.1 (Chamberlin, D., Robie, J., 2008) on the horizon, the limitations of an iterator-based pipeline execution strategy started to appear. Contrary to the iterator style of lazy evaluation, XVM (Novoselsky & Liu, 2008) compiles XQuery into virtual machine byte-code and executes queries using a hybrid of eager and lazy evaluation. The differences between lazy and eager strategies are illustrated bellow. Both Fig 1 and Fig 2 represent compiled forms of the following query:

```
declare variable $db external;
for $I in $db/employee
where $i/last = "Smith"
return <name> { $i/first, $i/
last } </name>
```

Figure 1 shows the compiled sequence of XVM virtual instructions and Figure 2 shows the semantically equivalent iterator based execution plan. In the pure sequential approach, the entire query is treated as an imperative programming language such as C or Java. It is compiled into byte-code, similar to the one on Figure 1 and the byte-code is executed by a virtual machine. The virtual machine uses stacks for function calls,

Figure 1. XVM byte-code

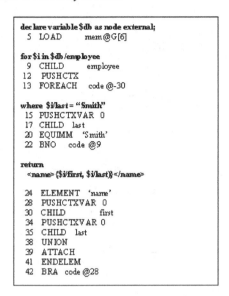

```
declare variable $db as node external;
  5  LOAD       mem@G[6]

for $i in $db/employee
  9  CHILD      employee
 12  PUSHCTX
 13  FOREACH    code @-30

where $i/last = "Smith"
 15  PUSHCTXVAR 0
 17  CHILD   last
 20  EQUIMM  'Smith'
 22  BNO     code @9

return
  <name>{$i/first, $i/last}</name>

 24  ELEMENT 'name'
 28  PUSHCTXVAR 0
 30  CHILD           first
 34  PUSHCTXVAR 0
 35  CHILD   last
 38  UNION
 39  ATTACH
 41  ENDELEM
 42  BRA  code @28
```

Figure 2. Iterator-based execution plan

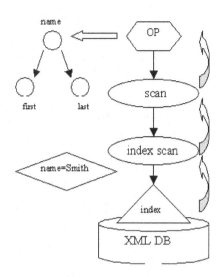

single-assigned variables, parameters and intermediate results and a heap for multi-assigned variables and some intermediate XML data. When executed, virtual instructions pop their input data items from the stack and push back the result. On the other hand when an iterator strategy is applied, the entire query is treated as a database query language and is compiled into a query plan. The query plan is executed top-down by calling the root node getNext() method and repeating the same downward with index scans at the leaf level.

As mentioned earlier both approaches have their strengths and weaknesses. This is why a well-balanced mixture of both starts to look likes a good solution, similar to one taken by creators of SQL/PSM (SQL/PSM 1999). Therefore, there is a need to develop a hybrid declarative and imperative XQuery processor so that the imperative XQuery constructs can be efficiently processed in ORDBMS. (Liu, Novoselsky, & Arora, 2008) study proposes an integrated declarative and procedural approach with XVM driving the imperative execution and with XQuery querying fragments pushed-down to the database search engine for evaluating. XQSE (Borkar 2008) proposes a similar approach. All of these approaches are in

principle the same as that of SQL/PSM but in this case the underlying data is XML. The right diagram of Figure 3 below shows how XVM byte code is integrated with an iterator based execution plan.

The query is the same as the one from Figure 1. Now the byte-code is used to execute the FLWOR return clause and the execution plan is used to drive the FLWOR search part with the help of a database index. The result of the execution of ITERATORCALL virtual instruction is an XVM iterator object. Its only difference with other XVM objects is that data items from the iterator object are retrieved lazily, one at a time.

4.3.4 XML Query Algebra

As a query language, historically, SQL was introduced after the relational algebra was proposed and studied. Relational algebra has been used as the theoretical foundation to provide rigorous reasoning and proof for SQL query transformation and optimization techniques. The development of XQuery, however, does not appear to have the XML query algebra developed first. Although there are various published works that propose

Figure 3. Integrated XVM, iterator plan

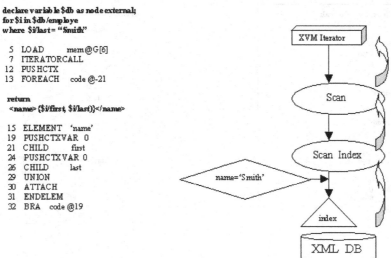

```
declare variable $db as node external;
for $i in $db/employe
where $i/last = "Smith"

    5   LOAD       mem@G[6]
    7   ITERATORCALL
   12   PUSHCTX
   13   FOREACH    code @-21

   return
   <name>{$i/first, $i/last)}</name>

   15   ELEMENT    'name'
   19   PUSHCTXVAR  0
   21   CHILD      first
   24   PUSHCTXVAR  0
   26   CHILD      last
   29   UNION
   30   ATTACH
   31   ENDELEM
   32   BRA    code @19
```

different XML query algebras to capture the semantics of XPath and XQuery, they have all been proposed after the XQuery language itself has been defined. Surveying the proposed XML query algebras show that the algebras fall into two categories: tree-based algebra and tuple-based algebra. Tree-based algebra is proposed in paper (Jagadish, Lakshmanan, Srivastava & Thompson, 2001). Tuple-based relational like algebra capturing XPath and XQuery semantics are proposed in various literatures. Complete XQuery algebra is presented in the paper (Christopher, Siméon & Fernández, 2006). XPath algebra is presented in the paper ((Brantner, Helmer, Kanne, & Moerkotte, 2005). XQuery unnesting algebra is presented in the paper (May, Helmer & Moerkotte, 2004). **XML extended relational algebra** to integrate both XQuery and SQL/XML processing is presented in the paper (Liu, Chandrasekar, Baby, & Chang 2008).

To completely integrate the XQuery and SQL languages using SQL/XML in ORDBMS, an **XML extended relational algebra** is needed which in principle is aligned with the tuple-based algebra. That is, the relational algebra can be extended with

the XQuery data model. It consists of the following key extensions from relational algebra:

- Incorporate XQuery data model (XQDM) as an ordered collection. An XQDM can be a single XQItem, which is either an atomic value with its type, or a single XML node reference. It can also be an ordered set (sequence) of such XQItems (each XQItem is implicitly associated with an ordinal position indicating the item position in the sequence).

- Incorporate operators that operate on XQDM: These operators take XQDM as inputs and return XQDM as output and are closed with respect to XQDM.

- UNNEST XQDM as a relational set: it converts an XQDM, which is a sequence of XQItems, into a set of relational tuples. There are two columns in each relational tuple. The first column *pos* is of type integer that is the ordinal position of the XQItem in the sequence, the second column *value* is an XQItem.

- NEST relational set into XQDM: it aggregates a set of relational tuples of XQItems into an XQDM. It is the opposite of the UNNEST operator. The un-nesting and nesting cancellation enables algebraic simplification of combining XQuery expressions after function inline, variable substitution and FOR clause merge etc.

- Incorporate ordered and lateral Join operator over XQDM: Joins in XQuery are ordered and have left join dependency whereas a pure relational join is unordered and has no left join dependency.

SECTION 5: SUMMARY AND FUTURE WORK

In this chapter, we have presented the XML data management capabilities in an ORDBMS environment and their associated use cases. We have also presented and discussed various work from both academic research and industry to support XML data management effectively and efficiently. In particular, we have compared various XML storage and index approaches, illustrated their advantages and disadvantages, and their proper use cases. We have compared various XQuery and SQL/XML processing strategies and their strength and weakness. In summary, we conclude with the following points and motivations for future work:

- The concept of XML is overloaded: it has a variety of characteristics and requirements depending on how XML is used and exploited. There are a wide spectrum of XML applications ranging from data centric to document centric XML. XML has been used as a data exchange language as well as a logical data storage description language. Therefore, XML storage, index and query processing techniques vary significantly depending on its usecases so that XML needs to be modeled as an abstract type in the system.

- XML has been successful particularly as a data exchange and integration mechanism. The SQL/XML standard serves as a bridge to enable data exchange among different relational stores using XML.

- The difference between XML schema dependent and schema independent decomposition of XML into the relational model is essentially the difference between the entity-relationship approach and the entity-attribute-value (name/value) approach. The tradeoff between the two is the tradeoff between query performance and data flexibility. Both of the decomposition methods can, however, be used as indexing schemes to index aggregated XML storage.

- SQL and XQuery share the same declarative set-based algebraic computation models so that many optimization and execution principles and infrastructure that have been well-researched and matured for SQL in the past 30 years can be leveraged to handle XQuery as well. Developing an *XML extended relational algebra* appears to be the right theoretical direction to follow.

- With XQuery and XQuery-P being positioned as general purpose programming languages to manipulate the XML data model, the importance of executing the language as an imperative language instead of a database query language has grown. The integration of XQuery with XSLT and XSLT processing in general has not been discussed in this chapter. In general, properly balancing XQuery and XQuery-P as both programming languages and query languages, and providing efficient implementation strategies for the two remain future research topics.

- There is also on-going work for both XQuery updating and XQuery full text search that we have not covered in this chapter.

REFERENCES

Agrawal,R., Somani, A.,& Xu, Y. (2001). Storage and querying of e-commerce data. *VLDB*, 149-158

Al-Khalifa, S., Jagadish, H. V., Patel, J. M., Wu, Y., Koudas, N., & Srivastava, D. (2002). Structural joins: A primitive for efficient XML query pattern matching. *ICDE*.

Beyer, K. S., Cochrane, R., Josifovski, V., Kleewein, J., Lapis, G., & Lohman, G. M. (2005). System RX: One part relational, one part XML. *SIGMOD Conference*, 347-358

Borkar, V. R., Carey, M. J., Engovatov, D., Lychagin, D., Westmann, T., & Wong, W. (2008). XQSE: An XQuery scripting extension for the AquaLogic data services platform. *ICDE, 2008,* 1229–1238.

Borkar, V. R., Carey, M. J., Lychagin, D., Westmann, T., Engovatov, D., & Onose, N. (2006). Query processing in the AquaLogic data services platform. *VLDB*, (pp. 1037-1048).

Brantner, M., Helmer, S., Kanne, C.-C., & Moerkotte, G. (2005). Full-fledged algebraic XPath processing in Natix. *ICDE*, (pp. 705-716).

Chamberlin, D. Florescu, D., et al. (2008). *XQuery update facility.* Retrieved from http://www.w3.org/TR/xquery-update-10/

Chamberlin, D., Carey, M. J., Florescu, D., Kossmann, D., & Robie, J. (2006). Programming with XQuery. *XIME-P.*

Chamberlin, D., Engovatov, D., Florescu, D., & Melton, J. (2008). *XQuery scripting extension 1.0.* Retrieved from http://www.w3.org/TR/xquery-sx-10/

Chamberlin, D., & Robie, J. (2008). *XQuery 1.1.* Retrieved from http://www.w3.org/TR/xquery-11/

Christopher, R., Siméon, J., & Fernández, M. (2006). *A complete and efficient algebraic compiler for XQuery.* ICDE.

Date, C. J. (1990). *An introduction to database systems,* (Vol. I, 5th Ed.). Reading, MA: Addison-Wesley.

DeHaan, D., Toman, D., Consens, M. P., & Özsu, M. T. (2003). A Comprehensive XQuery to SQL translation using dynamic interval encoding. *SIGMOD Conference*, (pp. 623-634).

Fernandez, M. F., Morishima, A., & Suciu, D. (2001). Efficient evaluation of XML middle-ware queries. *SIGMOD Conference,* (pp. 103-114).

Florescu, D., Hillery, C., Kossmann, D., Lucas, P., Riccardi, F., & Westmann, T. (2004). The BEA streaming XQuery processor. *The VLDB Journal, 13*(3), 294–315. doi:10.1007/s00778-004-0137-1

Florescu, D., & Kossmann, D. (1999). Storing and querying XML data using an RDMBS. *IEEE Data Eng. Bull., 22*(3), 27–34.

Graefe, G. (1993). Query evaluation techniques for large databases. *ACM Computing Surveys, 25*(2), 73–170. doi:10.1145/152610.152611

Grust, T. (2002). Accelerating XPath location steps. *SIGMOD Conference*, (pp.109-120.)

Grust, T., Mayr, M., Rittinger, J., Sakr, S., & Teubner, J. (2007). A SQL: 1999 code generator for the pathfinder xquery compiler. *SIGMOD Conference*, (pp. 1162-1164).

Grust, T., Rittinger, J., & Teubner, J. (2007). Why off-the-shelf RDBMSs are better at XPath than you might expect. *SIGMOD Conference*, (pp. 949-958).

Grust, T., Rittinger, J., & Teubner, J. (2008). Pathfinder: XQuery off the relational shelf. *IEEE Data Eng. Bull., 31*(4), 7–12.

Jagadish, H. V., Al-Khalifa, S., Chapman, A., Lakshmanan, L. V. S., Nierman, A., & Paparizos, S. (2002). TIMBER: A native XML database. *The VLDB Journal, 11*(4), 274–291. doi:10.1007/s00778-002-0081-x

Jagadish, H. V., Lakshmanan, L. V. S., Scannapieco, M., Srivastava, D., & Wiwatwattana, N. (2004). Colorful XML: One hierarchy isn't enough. *SIGMOD Conference,* (pp. 251-262).

Jagadish, H. V., Lakshmanan, L. V. S., Srivastava, D., & Thompson, K. (2001). TAX: A tree algebra for XML. *DBPL,* (pp. 149-164).

Jiang, H., Lu, H., Wang, W., & Yu, J. X. (2002). Path materialization revisited: An efficient storage model for XML data. *Australasian Database Conference.*

Kanne, C-C.,& Moerkotte, G. (2000). Efficient storage of XML data. *ICDE,* 198.

Kay, M. (2008). Ten reasons why Saxon XQuery is fast. *IEEE Data Eng. Bull., 31*(4), 65–74.

Kim, W. (1982, Sep 7). On optimizing an SQL-like nested query. *ACM TODS.*

Krishnaprasad,M., Liu,Z.H., Manikutty, A., Warner, J.W., & Arora, V. (2005). Towards an industrial strength SQL/XML infrastructure. *ICDE,* 991-1000.

Krishnaprasad, M., Liu, Z. H., Manikutty, A., Warner, J. W., Arora, V., & Kotsovolos, S. (2004). Query rewrite for XML in Oracle XML DB. *VLDB,* (pp. 1122-1133).

Li, C., & Ling, T. W. (2005). QED: A novel quaternary encoding to completely avoid re-labeling in XML updates. *CIKM,* (pp. 501-508).

Liu, Z. H., Chandrasekar, S., Baby, T., & Chang, H. J. (2008). Towards a physical XML independent XQuery/SQL/XML engine. *PVLDB, 1*(2), 1356–1367.

Liu, Z. H., Krishnaprasad, M., & Arora, V. (2005). Native Xquery processing in Oracle XMLDB. *SIGMOD Conference,* (pp. 828-833).

Liu, Z. H., Krishnaprasad, M., Chang, H. J., & Arora, V. (2007). *XMLTable index An efficient way of indexing and querying XML property data.* ICDE, (pp. 1194-1203).

Liu, Z. H., Krishnaprasad, M., Warner, J. W., Angrish, R., & Arora, V. (2007). Effective and efficient update of xml in RDBMS. *SIGMOD Conference,* (pp. 925-936).

Liu, Z. H., & Murthy, R. (2009). A decade of XML data management: An industrial experience report from Oracle. *ICDE,* (pp. 1351-1362).

Liu, Z. H., Novoselsky, A., & Arora, V. (2008). Towards a unified declarative and imperative XQuery processor. *IEEE Data Eng. Bull., 31*(4), 33–40.

Manolescu, I., Florescu, D., & Kossmann, D. (2001). Answering XML queries on heterogeneous data sources. In *VLDB,* (pp. 241-250).

May, N., Helmer, S., & Moerkotte, G. (2004). Nested queries and quantifiers in an ordered context. *ICDE,* (pp. 239-250).

McHugh, J., Abiteboul, S., Goldman, R., Quass, D., & Widom, J. (1997). Lore. A Database management system for semistructured data. *SIGMOD Record, 26*(3), 54–66. doi:10.1145/262762.262770

Murthy, R., & Banerjee, S. (2003). XML schemas in Oracle XML DB. *VLDB,* (pp. 1009-1018).

Murthy, R., Liu, Z. H., Krishnaprasad, M., Chandrasekar, S., Tran, A., & Sedlar, E. (2005). Towards an enterprise XML architecture. In *SIGMOD Conference* (pp. 953-957).

Novoselsky, A., & Liu, Z. H. (2008). XVM - *A hybrid sequential-query virtual machine for processing XML languages.* PLAN-X.

O'Neil, P. E., O'Neil, E. J., Pal, S., Cseri, I., Schaller, G., & Westbury, N. (2004). ORDPATHs: Insert-friendly XML node labels. In *SIGMOD Conference,* (pp. 903-908).

Pal, S., Cseri, I., Schaller, G., Seeliger, O., Giakoumakis, L., & Zolotov, V. V. (2004). Indexing XML data stored in a relational database. In *VLDB,* (pp. 1134-1145).

Pal, S., Cseri, I., Seeliger, O., Rys, M., Schaller, G., Yu, W., et al. (2005). XQuery Implementation in a relational database system. *VLDB,* (pp. 1175-1186).

Shanmugasundaram, J., Kiernan, J., Shekita, E. J., Fan, C., & Funderburk, J. E. (2001). Querying XML Views of Relational Data. *VLDB,* (pp. 261-270).

Shanmugasundaram, J., Shekita, E. J., Barr, R., Carey, M. J., Lindsay, B. G., Pirahesh, H., & Reinwald, B. (2000). Efficiently publishing relational data as XML documents. In *VLDB,* (pp. 65-76).

Shanmugasundaram, J., Shekita, E. J., Kiernan, J., Krishnamurthy, R., Viglas, S., Naughton, J. F., & Tatarinov, I. (2001). A general techniques for querying XML documents using a relational database system. *SIGMOD Record, 30*(3), 20–26. doi:10.1145/603867.603871

Shanmugasundaram, J., Tufte, K., Zhang, C., He, G., DeWitt, D. J., & Naughton, J. F. (1999). Relational databases for querying XML documents: Limitations and opportunities. In *VLDB,* (pp. 302-314).

SQL/PSM, Database Languages – SQL-Part 4: Persistent stored modules (SQL/PSM). (1999). ANSI/ISO/IEC 9075-4-1999.

SQL/XML, I.O. for Standardization (ISO). Information Technology-Database Language SQL-Part 14: XML-Related Specificaitons (SQL/XML). (n.d.).

Stonebraker, M. (1975). Implementation of integrity constraints and views by query modification. In *SIGMOD Conference,* (pp. 65-78).

Stonebraker, M., Brown, P., & Moore, D. (1999). *Object-relational DBMSs: Tracking the next great wave.* San Francisco: Morgan-Kauffman Publishers.

Stonebraker, M., & Hellerstein, J. M. (2005). *What goes around comes around. Readings in database systems,* (4th Ed.). San Francisco: Morgan Kaufmann.

Tatarinov, I., Viglas, S., Beyer, K. S., Shanmugasundaram, J., Shekita, E. J., & Zhang, C. (2002). Storing and querying ordered XML using a relational database system. In *SIGMOD Conference,* (pp. 204-215).

Tatarinov, I., Viglas, S., Beyer, K. S., Shanmugasundaram, J., Shekita, E. J., & Zhang, C. (2002). Storing and querying ordered XML using a relational database system. In *SIGMOD Conference,* (pp. 204-215).

Tian, F., DeWitt, D. J., Chen, J., & Zhang, C. (2002). The design and performance evaluation of alternative XML storage strategies. *SIGMOD Record, 31*(1), 5–10. doi:10.1145/507338.507341

Yoshikawa, M., Amagasa, T., Shimura, T., & Uemura, S. (2001). XRel: A path-based approach to storage and retrieval of XML documents using relational databases. *ACM Transactions on Internet Technology, 1*(1), 110–141. doi:10.1145/383034.383038

Zhang, C., Naughton, J. F., DeWitt, D. J., Luo, Q., & Lohman, G. M. (2001). On supporting containment queries in relational database management systems. In *SIGMOD Conference,* (pp. 425-436).

Zorba – The XQuery processor (n.d.). Retrieved from http://www.zorba-xquery.com/f

Chapter 3
XML Compression

Chin-Wan Chung
Korea Advanced Institute of Science and Technology (KAIST), Republic of Korea

Myung-Jae Park
Korea Advanced Institute of Science and Technology (KAIST), Republic of Korea

Jihyun Lee
Korea Advanced Institute of Science and Technology (KAIST), Republic of Korea

ABSTRACT

To effectively reduce the redundancy and verbosity of XML data, various studies for XML compression have been conducted. Especially, XML data management systems and applications require the support of direct query processing and update on compressed XML data, the stream based compression/decompression, and the reduction of the size of the compressed data. In order to fully support the various aspects of XML compression, existing XML compression techniques should be carefully examined and the additional requirements for XML compression techniques should be considered. In this chapter, the authors first classify existing representative XML compression techniques according to their characteristics. Second, they explain the details of XML specific compression techniques. Third, they summarize the performance of the compression techniques in terms of the compression ratio and the compression and decompression time. Lastly, they present some future research directions.

INTRODUCTION

XML (eXtensible Markup Language) (Bray et al., 2008) is a standardized markup language to represent and exchange data on the Web. Due to the proliferation of the Web, the usage of XML has tremendously increased. As a result, more data are produced as XML data and the size of XML data also increases. In order to efficiently manage such

XML data, various types of researches on issues such as XML indexing, XML query processing, and XML storage have been conducted. Moreover, to effectively manage large sized XML data, the compression on XML data was required.

Data compression is the process of encoding data with a size smaller than that of the original data using specific encoding methods. As a result, data compression provides several important advantages. First, the storage size for compressed data is reduced compared with that for original data.

DOI: 10.4018/978-1-61520-727-5.ch003

Second, the network bandwidth can be saved with the reduced data size since much more data can be transferred through the network within a given period of time. Lastly, the performance of query processing can be improved since the memory is efficiently utilized and the required number of disk I/Os is reduced.

According to those advantages of the data compression, the compression of XML data has been interested in various areas such as archiving, query processing, data dissemination and so on. Since an XML document is generally a text file, general text compression techniques such as gzip (Gailly & Adler, 2007) and bzip2 (Seward, 2008) can be employed to compress the XML document. However, an XML document is distinguished from a general plain text by the existence of the semantic structure in the XML document. Thus, various researches for XML specific compression have been conducted to effectively solve the redundancy and verbosity problems of XML data.

The XML specific compressors take advantage of the structure-awareness to improve the performance of the compression. In general, the structure of an XML document, which can be modeled as a tree composed of redundant elements and attributes, has a high regularity such that similar sub-trees repeatedly appear throughout the document. Also, data values enclosed by the same element have the same data type or are similar to each other. The regularity of data increases the compression ratio. Therefore, the XML specific techniques compress the syntactically or semantically partitioned structure and content using different encoding models to sufficiently take advantage of the local homogeneity. For the XML compression, the high compression ratio is an important goal of the XML compression. In addition, since XML data can be frequently queried and updated, the direct evaluation of queries and the direct update on compressed XML data should be possible. Since XML data are frequently exchanged in the Internet, the stream based compression/decompression should also be

considered. Until now, most studies on the XML compression have focused on the achievement of high compression ratio and the direct query evaluation on compressed XML data. In order to fully support the above aspects of XML compression, existing XML compression techniques should be carefully examined and the additional requirements for XML compression techniques should be addressed.

The objective of this chapter is to provide a better understanding on relevant theoretical frameworks and an up-to-date research trend of the XML compression. To achieve this goal, this chapter contains the following contents.

First, various existing XML compression techniques are classified according to their characteristics. The classified categories are schema-dependent compression and schema-independent compression, non-queriable compression and queriable compression, and homomorphic compression and non-homomorphic compression. The characteristics of each category are introduced in detail.

Second, representative XML specific compression techniques including the latest ones such as XMill (Liefke & Suciu, 2000), XMLPPM (Cheney, 2001), XAUST (Hariharan & Shankar, 2006), XGRIND (Tolani & Haritsa, 2002), XQzip (Ng & Cheng, 2004), XPRESS (Min et al., 2003), XBzipIndex (Ferragina et al., 2006), XCQ (Ng et al., 2006b), XQueC (Arion et al., 2007), and ISX (Wong et al., 2007) are presented. Also, the compression performance of those compression techniques is summarized in terms of compression ratio, compression time, and decompression time. Furthermore, based on their characteristics and experimental evaluation, appropriate XML compression techniques for different environments are recommended.

Lastly, several applications which adapt the XML compression techniques are introduced. Also, based on the up-to-date research trend of XML compression techniques, important future research directions required for the development of enhanced XML compression techniques are suggested.

BACKGROUND

Various types of data compression methods (known as general purpose data compression) are described first since such data compression methods are utilized to compress the structure and data values of XML data. The most widely used data compression methods are dictionary encoding, Huffman encoding (Huffman, 1952), and arithmetic encoding (Witten, 1987).

Dictionary Encoding

The dictionary encoding method assigns an integer value to each distinct word in the input data so that each word in the input data can be encoded by using a uniquely assigned integer value. For example, if 'the chapter contains the overall …' is given as an input data, '1', '2', '3', and '4' are assigned for 'the', 'chapter', 'contains', and 'overall', respectively. As a result, the given input data is compressed as '1 2 3 1 4 …'. In general, the assigned integer values by the dictionary encoding method do not keep the order information among the words in the input data. Thus, ALM, a variant of the dictionary encoding method, is devised to preserve the order information among words. In addition, there are other variants of the dictionary encoding method such as LZ77 and LZ78 to dynamically assign the dictionary values to words.

Since the basic compression unit of the dictionary encoding method is the word, the dictionary encoding method is very effective for the input data which contains a large number of repeated words. However, in the case of less repetition, the dictionary encoding method may require much more time to compress the input data since the dictionary contains a large number of words. Also,

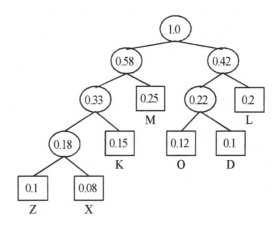

Figure 1. An example of the Huffman tree

much more space would be required to manage those words in the dictionary in the latter case.

Huffman Encoding

The Huffman encoding method is devised to assign shorter codes to more frequently appearing characters and longer codes to less frequently appearing characters. To assign a code to each character, a binary tree, called the Huffman tree, is constructed using the statistics gathered by a preliminary scan of the input data. Within this preliminary scan, the frequency of each character appearing in the input data is calculated. An example of the Huffman tree is shown in Figure 1.

The leaf nodes of the Huffman tree are associated with characters in the input data. The value in a leaf node is the frequency of the character. The left edges of the Huffman tree are labeled with 0, and the right edges are labeled with 1 so that the code assigned to each character is the sequence of labels starting from the root to the leaf node of the character. For example, if 'XML …' is given as an input data, '0001', '01', and '11' are assigned to 'X', 'M', and 'L', respectively. As a result, the given input data is compressed as '00010111 …'. Note that the codes generated by the Huffman encoding method do not keep the order information among characters. In addition, to dynamically construct the Huffman tree, an adaptive Huffman encoding method is devised. The adaptive Huffman encoding method dynamically updates the statistics of each character in the Huffman tree using the previous statistics during the compression phase.

In contrast to the dictionary encoding method, the Huffman encoding method is to compress each character in the input data. Thus, the repetition of words is not considered. However, since the Huffman encoding method utilizes the Huffman tree, the frequency of each character must be calculated and the Huffman tree must be constructed based on those frequencies before the compression. Also, the processing cost of the Huffman encoding method would be degraded due to the heavy traversal of the Huffman tree for each character in the input data. In addition, in order to process an update in the input data, the frequencies should be recalculated and the Huffman tree should be reconstructed.

Arithmetic Encoding

The arithmetic encoding method compresses an input data in the form of a sequence of characters by assigning predefined number such as the minimum value from an interval calculated by the frequencies of all the given characters. Disjoint intervals are assigned to characters based on their frequencies. Using the order of intervals for characters, the order information among characters is preserved in the compressed values. Successive characters of an input data reduce the length of the interval of the first character in accordance with the frequencies of the characters. After reducing the length of the interval by applying all the characters of the input data, the input data is transformed into a variable length bit string that represents any number within the reduced interval. Figure 2 shows an example of the arithmetic encoding method.

As described in Figure 2, the given input data 'BCB' is compressed as '0.424'. Note that the

Figure 2. An example of the arithmetic encoding method

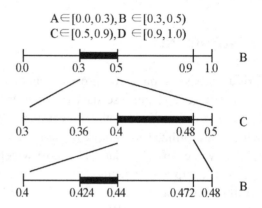

$A \in [0.0, 0.3), B \in [0.3, 0.5)$
$C \in [0.5, 0.9), D \in [0.9, 1.0)$

starting value (i.e., '0.424') of the reduced interval is chosen to represent the given input data. In addition, the adaptive arithmetic encoding method is devised. The adaptive arithmetic encoding method calculates the intervals by gathering frequencies dynamically, instead of using the predefined intervals.

Lastly, in some XML compression techniques, binary encoding and differential encoding methods are used. The binary encoding method compresses the numeric data (e.g., integer or floating) as binary. The differential encoding method (also known as delta encoding) replaces a data value with a code value that defines its relationship to a specific data value. For example, if '100 150 101 110' is given as an input data, '100 50 1 10' is generated as a compressed value in the case when '100' is chosen as the specific data value (i.e., the minimum value).

Similar to the Huffman encoding method, the repetition of words is not considered. However, since the arithmetic encoding method is based on the interval of each character, the frequencies of characters must be gathered and the intervals based on those frequencies must be calculated in advance. The processing cost of the arithmetic encoding method would be efficient since it only requires the interval computation. In addition, in the case of the update processing, similar to the Huffman encoding method, the arithmetic encoding method requires the frequency recalculation and the interval recalculation.

CLASSIFICATION OF XML COMPRESSION TECHNIQUES

XMill, XMLPPM, XGRIND, XQzip, XPRESS, XBzip/XBzipIndex, XAUST, XCQ, XQueC, and ISX are the representative XML specific compression techniques. The XML specific compression techniques can be classified into several groups according to the characteristics of them as follows:

Schema-Dependent Compression vs. Schema-Independent Compression

Schema-dependent compressors use the schema of an XML document such as the DTD to compress the document. Since the schema contains the syntax of the XML document, the compressor and the decompressor can obtain useful information such as the structure of the document, the tag names, and the type of data to increase the performance in terms of the compression ratio, and the compression/decompression time.

Additionally, many documents share a single schema. Thus, the compression of multi-documents sharing one schema together achieves better compression performance than multiple individual compressions since the common structure part represented by the DTD is compressed just once. However, the schema-dependent techniques have a critical problem that they cannot compress XML documents without the schema. XAUST and XCQ are the representative schema-dependent compressors.

Schema-independent compressors are designed to compress XML documents without the schema information. Thus, the schema-independent compressors extract the structural information (i.e., structure tree) from the XML document, and utilizes the extracted information in the compression. Thus, such schema-independent compressors require more compression time and memory usage than schema-dependent compressors. XMill, XMLPPM, XGRIND, XQzip, XPRESS, XBzip/XBzipIndex, XQueC, and ISX are the representative schema-independent compressors.

Non-Queriable Compression vs. Queriable Compression

Non-queriable compressors have been designed to maximize the compression ratio for efficient archiving. The early compression works such as XMill, and XMLPPM as well as the general text compression methods such as gzip and bzip2 belong to this category. Since these compressors do not consider the query processing over the compressed format, the full-decompression of the target document is inevitable and it significantly degrades the performance of the query processing.

Queriable compressors allow direct processing of queries on compressed data, and minimize the overhead of the decompression. XGRIND, XQzip, XCQ, XPRESS, and XQueC are the representative queriable compressors. Based on these techniques, we summarize some important factors required for an efficient query processing over the compressed data as follows:

Lazy Decompression (Compression Granule)
To minimize the overhead of the decompression during query processing, only the part required to access for the query processing should be decompressed. For this, most queriable compressors divide elements/attributes as well as data values in the XML document into multiple partitions according to contexts which are represented as incoming paths in the document, and the partitions are compressed individually. Moreover,

some techniques compress each data value in a partition individually (e.g., XQueC) or divide each data value partition into multiple blocks, and then compress the blocks separately (e.g., XCQ, ISX). Basically, the small-sized compression granule needs short decompression time and is of advantage to query processing while the compression ratio may be degraded since the regularity in the granule is low. The large-sized compression granule is opposite to that.

Query Operations

An XPath query consists of location paths and predicates. For processing an XPath query, the evaluation of the location path requires a traversal of the structure in the XML data. In order to directly and efficiently find the nodes matching to the location paths in the compressed format, an appropriate compression technique for the structure is required. Such compression technique should preserve the structural relationships among elements/attributes in the original document as well as encode the structure in a compact format. For instance, XPRESS encodes the structure of an XML document using the reverse arithmetic encoding and XBzip/XBzipIndex transforms an XML document by the XBW transform scheme.

In addition, various types of predicates (e.g., prefix string matching, equality check, range comparison) can appear in an XPath query. According to the compression techniques, different types of predicates can be treated. For example, the Huffman encoding method supports equality check and prefix matching predicates but cannot process range compression predicates since it cannot preserve the order of values. In order to support the direct evaluation of rich query predicates on the compressed format, an appropriate compression technique should be selected according to the type of data values and the query predicates on the data values. A schema like DTD and a query workload can be useful sources to provide the type information of data values and frequent query predicates. For example, XQueC

exploits the query workload to choose an effective compression technique.

Selective Access

For efficient query processing, the parts relevant to a query should be directly accessed. For this, many queriable compressors use a kind of path index. Also, some techniques construct the summary or signature on the compressed block in order to avoid access and decompression for irrelevant blocks for queries. For example, XQueC and XCQ construct a kind of a structural summary like a path index to efficiently access the nodes matching to an XPath query, and XCQ, XBzipIndex, and ISX construct signatures or indexes on data values for fast evaluation of query predicates.

The queriable compressors provide an efficient query processing on the compressed XML document. However, they have the following disadvantages due to the support of the direct query processing: First, since the partitioning of XML document decreases the regularity of the content in the compressed granule, the compression ratio of the queriable compressors is lower than that of the non-queriable compressors in general. Second, employing appropriate compression techniques according to the type of the compressed content and constructing the index require more compression time than the non-queriable comporesors.

Homomorphic Compression vs. Non-Homomorphic Compression

Homomorphic compressors (i.e., XPRESS, XGRIND) preserve the structure of the original XML document in the compressed format. In other words, the structural relationships among all components (i.e., element, attribute, data values) as well as their positions in the compressed data are the same as those of the original data. Thus, existing XML tools like parsers and validation tools as well as query processing techniques can handle the compressed data. However, the homomorphic compressors only support the top-down strategy for query evaluation.

Non-homomorphic compressors (e.g., XMill, XMLPPM, XCQ, XQueC) partition the original data syntactically or semantically and then compress the partitions individually using general compression techniques like gzip and bzip2. Thus, in general, it can achieve a higher compression ratio compared with the homomorphic compressors. Moreover, in contrast to the homomorphic compression which only supports the top-down strategy for query evaluation, non-homomorphic compression allows the bottom-up strategy as well as the top-down strategy. However, the information of links among separated parts should be managed in order to reconstruct the original document. Also, since the structure of compressed data is different from that of the original one, the existing XML tools cannot be directly utilized. Figure 3 shows an example of homomorphism.

Lastly, Table 1 provides the classification of XML compression techniques in order to provide better understanding of the differences and similarity among the existing XML compression techniques.

REPRESENTATIVE XML SPECIFIC COMPRESSION TECHNIQUES

XMill

XMill Compresses XML Data Based on the Following Three Principles

First, XMill separates the structure from data values. For the structure part, start tags are compressed by the dictionary encoding method, while all end tags are replaced by the special token '/'. Then, those compressed structure of XML data are maintained in a special container, called 'Structure Container'.

Second, XMill groups semantically related data values into containers. In other words, the data

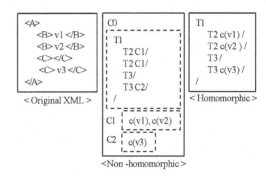

Figure 3. An example of homomorphism

values are partitioned by the common incoming path from the root to the value. Each container is separately compressed. For example, all data values of 'author' form one container and all 'nationality' data values form another container. When compressing XML data, data values are replaced by their container number. To find the container for the data values, the path processor is used. For each XML data value, the path processor checks the incoming path of the data value against each container's path, and determines a proper container for that data value. If there is no proper container, the path processor creates a new container for that value. Note that a user can also control this mapping by providing a series of container expressions in the command line.

Last, XMill can apply different encoding methods to compress different containers. Some containers may contain text based data values, while other containers can contain numbers. In such a case, XMill uses different compressors to compress those containers. For example, the 'delta' compressor can be applied for integers, and the 'dictionary' compressor can be used for enumerations. However, in order to apply specialized compressors, a user should specify compressors for certain containers in the command line. Otherwise, XMill applies the default 'text' compressor to containers. The default 'text' compressor simply copies its input to the container without

Table 1. The classification of XML compression techniques

	Schema-dependent	Queriable (Language;Predicates)	Homomorphic	Updatable	Streaming
XMill					Stream-compression
XMLPPM					Stream-decompression
XQzip		V (XPath)			
XGRIND		V (XPath; prefix, =)	V		Stream-decompression
XPRESS		V (XPath; prefix, =, <)	V	V	Stream-decompression
XQueC		V (XQuery; prefix, =, <)			
XAUST	V				Stream-compression
XCQ	V	V (XPath; aggregation predicates)			
XBzip					
XBzipIndex		V (XPath; prefix, =)			
ISX		V (XPath)		V	

any compression. Figure 3 <Non-homomorphic> provides an example of XML data compressed by XMill.

Once the structure and data values of XML data are compressed and maintained in the corresponding containers, containers are kept in a main memory window of 8MB. When the main memory window is full, all containers are gzipped, stored on disk, and the compression resumes.

XMLPPM

XMLPPM (XML Prediction by Partial Matching) is based on a streaming XML compression technique. In order to compress XML data, XMLPPM utilizes an Encoded SAX (ESAX) for parsing and Multiplexed Hierarchical PPM (MHM) model for compressing. MHM is composed of four different PPM models; 'Syms' for the element and attribute names, 'Elts' for the elements, 'Atts' for the attributes, and 'Chars' for the strings. In general, PPM is considered as the theoretically optimal method. For each symbol, the PPM model estimates a probability range for the symbol within the context and this probability range is used to compress the symbol using the arithmetic encoding method.

In XMLPPM, XML data is processed as a sequence of SAX events and each token in the event sequence is compressed by the corresponding PPM model. For example, if a start element token for 'A' element is given, 'A' is first compressed by the 'Syms' model. In simplicity, a byte value 01 can be generated to the start element of 'A' if 'A' appears for the first time. Otherwise, the previously assigned value is used to compress the element. Then, the byte value 01 for the start element of 'A' is given to the 'Elts' model, which indicates that 'A' is the element currently being processed. In the case a data value 'V1' for 'A' is given, the data value is compressed by the 'Chars' model.

Figure 4. An example of DTD and DFA for the element B

```
<!ELEMENT A ( B* ) >
<!ELEMENT B ( C | ( D , E ) ) >
<!ELEMENT C ( #PCDATA ) >
<!ELEMENT D ( F, G ) >
<!ELEMENT E ( #PCDATA ) >
```
DTD

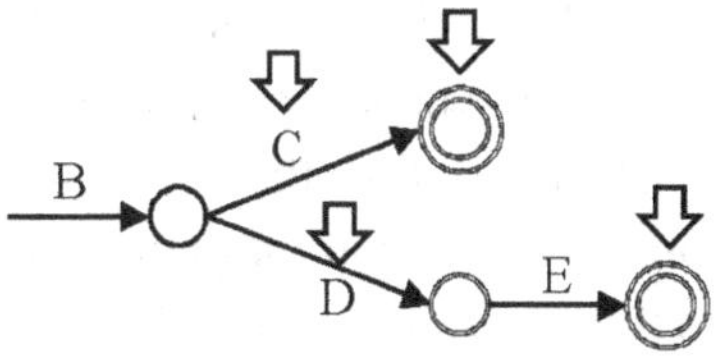

DFA for element B (encoding point = ⬇)

Lastly, all end tags are replaced by the special character 'FF'.

XAUST

XAUST (XML Compression with AUtomata and STack) is a schema-aware compression method. Since DTD specifies the syntax of an XML document, both the compressor and the decompressor can predict the next element to be compressed or decompressed from the DTD. By sharing the DTD between the compressor and the decompressor, it is sufficient for the compressor to encode only the part which cannot be inferred from the DTD for reconstructing the original document.

XAUST compresses XML data by the adaptive arithmetic algorithm. At the leaf element with PCDATA and the element having multiple-choice child elements, the arithmetic algorithm encodes the PCDATA and the next element, respectively. Each element definition can be transformed into a deterministic finite automaton (DFA). Thus, XAUST maintains a DFA per element to predict an element to appear after the element during the compression or decompression. In order to encode PCDATAs and multiple-choice child elements, the DFA states corresponding to the leaf element and the multiple-choice elements are associated to statistics table for arithmetic encoding. Figure 4 shows an example of DTD and the DFA for element B defined in the DTD. In addition, XAUST uses a stack to maintain the context from root to the current element when traversing the structure of the XML document.

XGRIND

XGRIND supports the direct evaluation of queries on compressed XML data. In order to do so, XGRIND retains the structure of the original XML data in the compressed XML data, known as the homomorphic compression.

XGRIND compresses XML data by using different compression methods for structure, enumerated-type attribute values, and data values. For the structure compression, XGRIND compresses each start tag as a 'T' followed by a uniquely assigned element ID. All end tags are replaced by the special character '/'s. An attribute name is similarly compressed by an 'A' followed by a uniquely assigned attribute ID. For the enumerated-type attribute value compression, XGRIND can use the DTD if exists. If an attribute is defined as the enumerated-type, XGRIND compresses attribute values of that attribute using the dictionary encoding method. Lastly, XGRIND compresses other types of data values by using the Huffman encoding method. As described in Background, two passes have to be made over the XML document since the statistics required to construct the Huffman tree must be collected before the actual compression. Note that XGRIND constructs a separate Huffman tree for each element and non-enumerated attribute.

Since XGRIND compresses at the granularity of individual data values, the direct evaluation of queries on compressed XML data is possible. To evaluate a path expression, whenever an element is visited by the query processor, the identifier sequence which represents the incoming path from the root element to the currently visited element is found, and the query processor checks whether this identifier sequence satisfies the path expression. In XGRIND, exact-match and prefix-match queries are directly executed on the compressed XML data. However, range or partial-match queries require the partial decompression of only those element/attribute values that appear in the query predicates since the Huffman encoding and dictionary encoding methods do not preserve any order information among data items.

XQzip

XQzip is another XML compression technique which supports the direct evaluation of queries on compressed XML data. In contrast to XGRIND and XPRESS, XQzip separates the structure from data values. Thus, XQzip is a non-homomorphic compression.

To remove the duplicate structures in XML data and improve the query performance, an index structure called the Structure Index Tree (SIT) is used to maintain the structural information of XML data. To avoid full decompression when evaluating, XQzip separates data values into a sequence of blocks which is decompressed individually. Those blocks can be efficiently accessed from the hashtable where the element/attribute names are stored, and the sequence of blocks is compressed by the built-in library, zlib. In addition, XQzip manages a buffer pool for the decompressed blocks of compressed XML data in order to reduce the decompression overhead during the query evaluation.

For the query processing, the query executor uses the SIT index to evaluate queries. To process data values, the query executor checks with the buffer manager which applies the LRU rules to manage the buffer pool for the decompressed data blocks. If the data values are already in the buffer pool, the query executor retrieves them without decompression. Otherwise, the query executor checks with the hashtable to retrieve the data values.

XPRESS

XPRESS also supports the direct evaluation of queries on compressed XML data by maintaining the homomorphic compression. XPRESS uses a novel encoding method, called the reverse arithmetic encoding method, which encodes path expressions as intervals. XPRESS also uses a simple mechanism to automatically infer the type of data values of each XML element. The inferred type information is used to apply proper compression methods to various kinds of data values of XML elements so that the overhead of partial decompression is minimized when processing queries on compressed XML data. Moreover, the extended version of XPRESS (Min et al., 2006) provides the direct update on compressed XML data, which does not require the complete decompression of compressed XML data.

The reverse arithmetic encoding method of XPRESS first partitions the entire interval $[0.0, 1.0)$ into subintervals, one for each distinct element name. The subinterval is calculated based on the frequency of the element name. Suppose that the frequencies of elements $\{a,b,c,d,e,f\}$ are $\{0.1, 0.1, 0.1, 0.3, 0.3, 0.1\}$. Then, the entire interval $[0.0, 1.0)$ is partitioned as $a \in [0.0, 0.1)$, $b \in [0.1, 0.2)$, $c \in [0.2, 0.3)$, $d \in [0.3, 0.6)$, $e \in [0.6, 0.9)$, and $f \in [0.9, 0.1)$. Then, the reverse arithmetic encoding method encodes the simple path of an element as the corresponding interval by reducing the interval of the element according to the intervals of tags appearing in the simple path of the element. For example, for the element 'd' with the simple path '/a/d', the interval $[0.3, 0.33)$ is generated while the interval $[0.69, 0.6999)$ is generated

Figure 5. An example of XBW transform

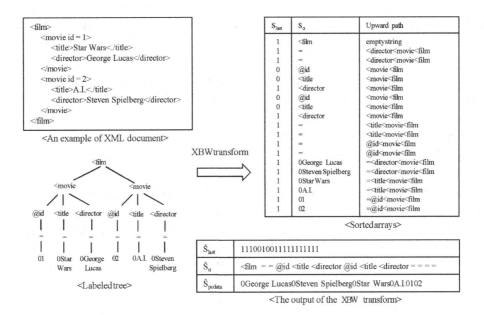

<An example of XML document>

<Labeled tree>

<Sorted arrays>

<The output of the XBW transform>

for the element 'e' with the simple path '/a/d/e'. XPRESS compresses the start tag of the element by the minimum value of the interval generated by the reverse arithmetic encoding method.

In XPRESS, data values are compressed by applying proper compression methods, chosen by automatically inferred types. For example, XPRESS uses the u8 encoder for data values of an element where max-min $< 2^7$, the dictionary encoder for enumeration typed data, and the Huffman encoder for textual data.

To directly evaluate queries on compressed XML data, the query processor of XPRESS first partitions a long label path expression into short label path expressions. Then, a partitioned short label path expression is transformed into a sequence of intervals. Finally, the query processor checks compressed values of elements in compressed XML data whether their compressed values are in an interval of the sequence or not. For the exact matching query, the query processor compares the data values of the elements which satisfy the label path expression without any decompres-

sion. For the range query, the range condition for numeric typed elements is checked without any decompression. However, in the case of the textual typed data values, a partial decompression is required.

XBzip/XBzipIndex

XBzip and XBzipIndex are compressors based on the XBW transform for XML data. The XBW transform represents XML data tree in two arrays, $S_\alpha[1,t]$ and $\hat{S}_{last}[1,t]$ where t is the number of nodes: $S_\alpha[i]$ is the label of the ith node and $\hat{S}_{last}[i]$ is set to 1 if the ith node is the rightmost child of its parent. These arrays are sorted in the lexicographical order of the upward path from its parent to root. $S_\alpha[0,n]$ ($=\hat{S}_\alpha$) contains the labels of internal nodes and $S_\alpha[n+1,t]$ ($=\hat{S}_{pcdata}$) contains the labels of the leaf nodes (i.e., PCDATA) where n is the number of internal nodes. The XBW transform supports an efficient navigation and search on the XML tree. Figure 5 shows an example of the XBW transform.

In the sorted S_α, nodes with the same prefix of upward paths are consecutive in the sorted S_α. Thus, it can compress data enclosed in a certain path together. As this property is likely to increase the regularity in a compressed unit, XBW transform is of great advantage to increasing the compression ratio.

XBzip is a compressor designed to compress as compactly as possible. $\hat{S}_{last}$ and $\hat{S}_\alpha$ are merged into a single array. Then, the merged array and $\hat{S}_{pcdata}$ are compressed separately using PPMDI which a variant of PPM. XBzipIndex is designed to support navigation and search on the compressed data. The three arrays are compressed separately. First, both $\hat{S}_\alpha$ and $\hat{S}_{last}$ are partitioned into variable-length or fixed length blocks, and the compression using gzip is performed to each block. Second, $\hat{S}_{pcdata}$ is partitioned into buckets according to the upward paths. Then, the content of each bucket is treated as strings, and FM-index is constructed on each bucket, which is the state-of-art string index to support efficient substring search.

XCQ

XCQ (XML Compression and Querying system) is a schema-aware compression and querying system designed to support the direct query processing on compressed XML data.

XCQ extracts the structure stream and the data streams from the SAX event stream according to the DTD. The structure stream contains the necessary information which is required to reconstruct the tree structure of the XML document, but cannot be inferred from analyzing DTD. The data values in the document are partitioned into data streams using the path-based grouping. The structure stream and each data stream are separately compressed by gzip or bzip2.

Each data stream is divided again into fix-sized blocks and the data blocks are individually compressed. In order to facilitate retrieval of only the data block relevant to a query, Block Statistics Signature (BSS) index is constructed to data

blocks with numeric data values. Since the BSS index contains the summary of the data values (i.e., min, max, sum, count) in the data block, the query processor can efficiently find the target data blocks including data values relevant to a query without the decompression of the data blocks. Especially, the BBS index is useful for the queries containing aggregation predicates.

XQueC

XQueC (XQuery Processor and Compressor) is an XML data management system which is designed to support an efficient XML query processing with a wide set of queries on the compressed XML data. XQueC divides an XML document into a structure tree and the data values of the document, and compresses them separately. First, nodes (i.e., element or attribute) in the structure tree are partitioned according to distinct incoming paths in the tree. Also, in order to preserve the structural relationships among the nodes, the structural identifier is assigned to each node by using a traditional labeling scheme. Eventually, the structure tree is encoded as a set of ID sequences each of which is a sequence of identifiers of nodes included in a path-based partition. Second, the data values are also partitioned into containers according to distinct incoming paths. Each record in a container consists of the individually compressed data value and the identifier of its parent node. Additionally, in order to support the selective access to the data values, XQueC maintains the structure summary for each XML document. The structural summary is a tree which is composed of only distinct paths in the document, and each leaf node of the tree corresponds to a container according to its incoming path.

XQueC supports a wide set of XQuery queries including various predicates (i.e., $=$, $<$, prefix) on the compressed data. For efficient processing of the rich query predicates on compressed data values, XQueC chooses different compression algorithms for containers (i.e., data values) according to the applicable predicates. For example, the Huffman encoding as a prefix- and equality-preserving compressor can be selected to support prefix selection and equality predicates (selection or joins) in the compressed data while ALM as an order-preserving compressor can be used to support inequality predicates.

For an efficient query processing, XQueC chooses suitable compression granules (i.e., a set of containers compressed together) and compression algorithms according to the query workload based cost model.

ISX

ISX (Integrated Succinct XML system) is an XML data management system to maintain an XML data in a more compact structure and to support an efficient navigation and update on the structure. The storage layer of ISX system consists of three layers: topology layer, internal node layer, and leaf node layer. First, the topology layer stores the tree structure of an XML document using the balanced parentheses encoding, and the encoding is physically represented in a bit array (i.e., 0 indicates an open tag and 1 indicates an end tag). The balanced parentheses encoding supports an efficient node navigation. Second, the internal node layer maintains the labels of elements and attributes, and the signature of text data facilitates an efficient text query processing. Lastly, the leaf node layer stores the text data and the text data is compressed by a general compression technique like gzip.

For an efficient node navigation, in the topology layer, two auxiliary tiers are added on the top of the base tier including the entire topology information. Each tier is partitioned into fixed sized blocks, and each entry of an upper tier holds the summary information of a single block in the lower tier. By using these auxiliary tiers, the linear scan of the base tier can be avoided and the performance of primitive navigation operations is improved.

ISX considers direct insertions and deletions on the compressed data. For an efficient handling of the update operations, ISX leaves some empty space in each block of the topology layer. The empty spaces are eventually filled up by newly inserted data. In order to manage the empty space equally among the blocks for the frequent insertions and deletions, ISX observes the state of the empty spaces of the blocks by keeping the block density in the virtual balanced binary tier and decides the right time to redistribute the empty space among the blocks and the blocks to be involved in the redistribution.

Applications of Compression Techniques

XML Data Management System

Many XML compression techniques have been designed to support compact archiving as well as direct query processing in the compressed data. Those techniques can be adapted to the XML data management systems. BLAS (Chen et al., 2004), for example, is a representative XML data management system adapting the reverse arithmetic encoding method of XPRESS to the labeling scheme for an efficient XPath query processing.

Also, native XML repositories store XML fragments in a cache for an efficient query processing. In order to improve the memory utilization and the effectiveness of the cache, the compact representation of XML fragments and the direct query processing on the cached fragment are necessary. Since an XML fragment can also be regarded as an XML document, the existing compression methods can be applied to this domain.

Internet Applications Exchanging XML Data

Many Internet applications using the XML data requires an efficient transmission of XML documents or XML fragments as well as a compact representation of them to reduce archiving cost. Therefore, the compression technique is useful to improve the performance of the XML data dissemination over the Internet.

The XML publish and subscribe system is a representative application which demands an efficient XML data dissemination. For example, He et al. (2006) suggests an efficient framework for multi-query processing over the compressed XML data in the publish and subscribe environment. The framework uses XPRESS to compress the disseminated XML documents/fragments.

In publish and subscribe systems as well as stream processing systems, a large number of queries are registered, and they should be resident in the memory. Thus, a compact representation and an efficient handling of them are very important issues in the above applications. Since an XML query (e.g., XPath) can be represented in a tree structure like the structure of XML data, the compression techniques can be applied to the compression for a set of XML queries. For instance, XTREAM (Min et al, 2007) uses the reverse arithmetic encoding to represent the query structure, and it facilitates efficient multi-query processing over the XML data stream. In addition, Li et al. (2008) proposes the subscription covering mechanism which summarizes the subscriptions registered to routers in order to compactly manage those registered subscriptions. To more effectively represent the summarized subscriptions, XML compression techniques can be applied.

Recently, many Web applications have migrated to the mobile Web environment. However, since the mobile devices have the limitations on computational capacity, storage spaces, network bandwidth, and so on, the widespread deployment of the mobile applications is restricted. Thus, the compression technique is a promising solution to overcome the limitations simultaneously. For instance, EXEM (Natchetoi et al., 2007), first, minimizes the size of an XML document transmitted from the server to a mobile client by pruning the part irrelevant to the mobile application. Then, it compresses the remaining part based on the dictionary encoding.

EVALUATION OF COMPRESSION TECHNIQUES

According to the experimental evaluation results from the literatures mentioned in this chapter and some survey papers (Ng et al., 2006a; Gupta, A., & Agarwal, S., 2008), we summarize the comparative analysis of XML compression techniques as follows:

Compression Ratio

The compression ratio is the ratio between the compressed data and the original data. The compression ratio is defined as follows:

Compression ratio = (1 − Size of compressed XML data / Size of original XML data)*100%

XML specific compression techniques increase the regularity of data in a compression unit by separating the structure and the data values syntactically and semantically. Among these, the non-queriable XML specific compression techniques like XMill, XMLPPM and XBzip achieve better compression ratios than general compression techniques like gzip.

On the other hand, queriable XML specific compression techniques split the data into finer granules in order to reduce or minimize the decompression overhead during the query processing. As the compression unit gets smaller, the redundancy of the data in the unit also decreases. Thus, the compression ratio of queriable compression techniques such as XGRIND and XPRESS is worse than that of non-queriable compression techniques.

Also, the statistics based encoding method like PPM has better performance than non-statistics based compression method like gzip. Therefore, the non-queriable compression technique like XMLPPM achieves better compression ratio than XMill.

Ng et al. (2006a) conduct experiments to observe the compression ratio of the existing XML compressors such as XMLPPM, XMill, Gzip, and XGrind which are publically released. According to the experimental results, non-queriable compression techniques such as Gzip, XMill, and XMLPPM provide better compression ratios than queriable compression techniques. In most cases, XMLPPM provides the best compression performance. This experimental results support the above analysis result on the compression ratio of the XML compressors.

Compression Time

The compression time is the total time taken to compress XML data and then to write the compressed data to disk. The compression includes the following phases: pre-processing, encoding, and writing to disk.

The XML specific compression techniques require the pre-processing phase in contrast to the general text compression techniques. The pre-processing phase can contain the separation of data and the collection of the information required to compress the data. Thus, in general, the compression time of the general text compression techniques is shorter than that of the XML specific compression technique. For example, XMill divides the data into multiple containers, and then compress the data while gzip can start compressing without any pre-processing. Thus, XMill needs more time than gzip.

To improve the compression ratio or to support direct query processing on the compressed data, many XML specific compression techniques use various statistics based encoding methods. Note that the statistics based encoding methods such as Huffman encoding, and arithmetic encoding needs the statistics of the data, and the compression techniques employing the statistic encoding methods require two scan of the data to collect the statistics. Even if an adaptive encoding method is used in the compression, the overhead caused by maintaining (updating) the statists is inevitable. Thus, the compression times of XMLPPM, XGRIND, and XPRESS are much slower than those of XMill and XCQ using gzip and bzip2.

The encoding time is dependent on the encoding method, and the time to write compressed data to the disk is determined by the size of the compressed data.

Decompression Time

The decompression time is the total time taken to decompress a compressed XML document and then reconstruct the original document. Similar to the compression cost, the decompression cost is mainly determined by the encoding method used in the compression technique. In the case of using the Huffman encoding method, compressed values can be decompressed by the massive traversal of the same Huffman tree used for the compression. Thus, it takes much time to decompress. The decompression overhead for PPM is also due to the complexity of the encoding method.

In addition, XML specific compressors divide the XML document into multiple partitions in order to increase the compression ratio. Thus, they require to merge the separated parts in the compressed format to recover their original positions in the original document. Thus, it takes longer time for the XML specific compressors like XMill and XCQ to decompress the data than the general compressors like gzip.

Ng et al. (2006a) also provide experimental results on the compression and decompression times of the existing XML compressors. Similar to the case of the compression ratio, the above analysis result on the compression and decompression times of the XML compressors is validated.

DISCUSSION

In general, the compression ratio of the queriable compressors is worse than that of the non-queriable compressors since they are designed to support an efficient query processing in the compressed format. Therefore, for an efficient archiving or the network transmission of XML data, the non-queriable compressors are suitable. Especially, XMLPPM achieves the best compression ratio in general.

The queriable compressors basically support simple and partial matching path expressions with partial decompression. Their differences in the query processing can be found in what kinds of value based predicates are supported without decompression, and they are summarized in Table 1. XQueC can handle a wide set of XQuery queries in the compressed format. Also, it provides a configuration mechanism to select a suitable compression granule and a suitable compression algorithm for an efficient query processing as well as a compact compression. Thus, XQueC is the most powerful queriable compressor with a good compression ratio. On the other hand, XCQ can efficiently process the aggregation queries since it maintains the summary information about the compressed data block. For dynamic XML data, XPRESS is the most useful compressor since it can update without decompression and it supports an efficient query processing and compression ratio.

FUTURE RESEARCH DIRECTIONS

Even though existing XML compression techniques provide several important achievements, there are still issues to be addressed in order to fully support the aspects of XML compression.

First, most existing XML compression techniques have not considered the direct update on the compressed XML data. However, as the update on XML data is frequent, updatable XML compression techniques which directly support insertions and deletions on compressed XML data without the decompression or with the minimal decompression are required. In order to support the direct update on compressed XML data, XML compression techniques should be queriable and minimize the portion to be affected (e.g., partial decompression and adjustment after the update) by insertions or deletions. Currently, only XPRESS and ISX provide direct update techniques for compressed XML data.

Second, as various Internet applications exchange XML data in real time, XML compression techniques should also support streaming XML data. XML compression techniques applicable to streaming XML data can effectively reduce the size of XML data being transmitted. As a result, the memory usage for managing streaming XML data can be minimized and the compression time for compressing streaming XML data can be reduced. Such XML compression techniques should compress XML data through a single-pass reading of streaming XML data. The early decompression for streaming XML data can effectively reduce the network latency since the decompression can be started even if the entire XML data has not been arrived yet. In order to support the early decompression, all the information required for the decompression should be located in the header of compressed XML data and the size of the header should be small enough to fit into the available memory.

Third, in order for XML compression techniques to be fully utilized in various applications, XML compression techniques should be extended to support much larger subset of XML queries such as full axes supported by either XPath or XQuery, aggregates, complex queries containing joins or nested predicates. Moreover, the direct evaluation of queries on compressed XML data should be more optimized in order to improve the query processing performance. To reflect the real world environment, XML compression techniques should be able to compress much large sized XML data since 1GB of XML data is not unusual.

Last, since XML is the standardized representation format, various languages such as RDF/XML (Beckett, 2004) and OWL (McGuinness & Harmelen, 2004) are expressed in the XML syntax. Note that ontologies in the Semantic Web, the next generation Web, are described by using such languages. As a result, XML compression techniques should be properly applied to other data formats. In such a case, the advantages of using XML compression techniques can be delivered to various ontology related systems and applications.

CONCLUSION

In this chapter, through comprehensive studying and analyzing existing XML compression techniques, we suggested the following four categories of XML compression techniques:

- General compression vs. XML specific compression
- Schema-dependent compression vs. Schema-independent compression
- Non-queriable compression vs. Queriable compression
- Homomorphic compression vs. Non-homomorphic compression

For each category, we explained its characteristics, strength, and weakness. Also, based on the evaluation results from the literatures of the XML compression, we summarized the performance of the compression techniques as follows: first, since the compression ratio is determined by the redundancy of the compression unit, non-queriable XML specific compression techniques provide the best compression ratio, followed by the general text compression techniques and the queriable compression techniques. Second, since the compression time is heavily affected by the pre-processing time, the compression techniques using statistics based encoding methods to support a high compression ratio and direct query evaluations in the compressed data require longer compression time than others. Finally, the decompression time is dependent on the encoding methods as well as the needs of recovering the original positions of separated parts in the compressed format.

Moreover, we addressed the future research directions as follows: the direct update on compressed data, the compression/decompression on stream data, the improvement of the direct query processing performance with the support of complex queries including various predicates, the scalability of the compressed data, and the effective deployment of the XML compression technique to various related applications.

We expect that this chapter will provide better understanding on the background, the up-to-date research trend, and the future direction of the research on the XML compression, and aid the utilization of the existing compression techniques and the development of appropriate new compression techniques.

ACKNOWLEDGMENT

This research was supported in part by Basic Science Research Program through the National Research Foundation of Korea(NRF) funded by the Ministry of Education, Science and Technology (grant number 2009-0081365), and in part by the Ministry of Knowledge Economy, Korea, under the Information Technology Research Center support program supervised by the Institute of Information Technology Advancement (grant number IITA-2009-C1090-0902-0031).

REFERENCES

Antoshenkov, G. (1997). Dictionary-based order-preserving string compression. *The VLDB Journal, 6*(1), 26–39. doi:10.1007/s007780050031

Arion, A., Bonifati, A., Manolescu, I., & Pugliese, A. (2007). XQueC: A query-conscious compressed XML database. *ACM Transactions on Internet Technology, 7*(2), 1–35. doi:10.1145/1239971.1239974

Beckett, D., & McBride, B. (2004). *RDF/XML Syntax Specification (Revised) W3C Recommendation*. Retrieved February 10, 2004, from http://www.w3.org/TR/rdf-syntax-grammar

Bray, T., Paoli, J., Sperberg-McQueen, C. M., Maler, E., & Yergeau, F. (2008). *Extensible Markup Language (XML) 1.0 (Fifth Edition) W3C Recommendation*. Retrieved November 26, 2008, from http://www.w3c.org/TR/2008/REC-xml-20081126/

Chen, Y., Davidson, S. B., & Zheng, Y. (2004). BLAS: An efficient XPath processing system. *ACM SIGMOD International Conference on Management of Data* (pp. 47-58). New York: ACM.

Cheney, J. (2001). Compressing XML with multiplexed hierarchical PPM models. *Data Compression Conference* (pp. 163-172). Washington, DC: IEEE.

Ferragina, P. Luccio, & F., Muthukrishna, S. (2006). Compressing and searching XML data via two zips. *International World Wide Web Conference* (pp. 751-760). New York: ACM.

Gailly, J., & Adler, M. (2007). *gzip (GNU zip) compression utility*. Retrieved from http://www.gnu.org/software/gzip

Gupta, A., & Agarwal, S. (2008). A review on XML compressors and future trends. *International Journal of Computer Sciences and Engineering Systems, 2*(4), 227–234.

Hariharan, S., & Shankar, P. (2006). Evaluating the role of context in syntax directed compression of XML documents. *Data Compression Conference* (pp. 453). Washington, DC: IEEE.

He, J., Ng, W., Wang, X., & Zhou, A. (2006). An efficient co-operative framework for multi-query processing over compressed XML data. *International Conference on Database Systems for Advanced Applications*, (LNCS Vol. 3882, pp. 218-258).

Huffman, D. A. (1952). A method for the construction of minimum redundancy codes. *The Institute of Radio Engineers, 9*(40), 1098–1101.

Liefke, H., & Suciu, D. (2000). XMill: An efficient compressor for XML data. *ACM SIGMOD International Conference on Management of Data* (pp. 153-164). New York: ACM.

McGuinness, D. L., & Harmelen, F. V. (2004). OWL Web Ontology Language Overview WC3 Recommendation. Retrieved February 10, 2004, from http://www.w3.org/TR/owl-features

Min, J., Park, M., & Chung, C. W. (2003). XPRESS: A queriable compression for XML data. *ACM SIGMOD International Conference on Management of Data* (pp. 122-133). New York: ACM.

Min, J., Park, M., & Chung, C. W. (2006). A compressor for effective archiving, retrieval, and update of XML documents. *ACM Transactions on Internet Technology, 6*(3), 223–258. doi:10.1145/1151087.1151088

Min, J., Park, M., & Chung, C. W. (2007). XTREAM: An efficient multi-query evaluation on streaming XML data. *Information Sciences, 177*(17), 3519–3538. doi:10.1016/j.ins.2007.03.009

Natchetoi, Y., Wu, H., & Dagtas, S. (2007). EXEM: Efficient XML data exchange management for mobile applications. *Information Systems Frontiers, 9*(4), 439–448. doi:10.1007/s10796-007-9045-4

Ng, W., & Cheng, J. (2004). XQzip: Querying compressed XML using structural indexing. *International Conference on Extending Database Technology* (pp. 219-236). New York: ACM.

Ng, W., Lam, W., & Cheng, J. (2006a). Comparative Analysis of XML Compression Technologies. *World Wide Web: Internet and Web Information Systems, 9*, 5–33.

Ng, W., Lam, W., Wood, P. T., & Levene, M. (2006b). XCQ: A queriable XML compression system. *Knowledge and Information Systems, 10*(4), 421–452. doi:10.1007/s10115-006-0012-z

Salomon, D. (1998). *Data compression, The complete reference*. New York: Springer-Verlag, Inc.

Seward, J. (2008). *bzip2 and libbzip2, version 1.0.5 A program and library for data compression*. Retrieved from http://bzip.org/1.0.5/bzip2-manual-1.0.5.html

Tolani, P., & Haritsa, J. (2002). XGRIND: A Query-friendly XML compressor. *International Conference on Data Engineering* (pp. 225-234). Washington, DC: IEEE.

Witten, I. H., Neal, R. M., & Cleary, J. G. (1987). Arithmetic coding for data compression. *ACM Communication, 30*(6), 520–540. doi:10.1145/214762.214771

Wong, R. K., & Lam, F. Shui, & W. M. (2007). Querying and maintaining a compact XML storage. *International World Wide Web Conference,* (pp. 1073-1082). New York: ACM.

Ziv, J., & Lempel, A. (1977). An universal algorithm for sequential data compression. *IEEE Transactions on Information Theory, 30*(6), 520–540.

Ziv, J., & Lempel, A. (1978). Compression of Individual Sequences via Variable-rate Coding. *IEEE Transactions on Information Theory, IT-24*(5), 530–536. doi:10.1109/TIT.1978.1055934

Chapter 4
XML Benchmark

Ke Geng
University of Auckland, New Zealand

Gillian Dobbie
University of Auckland, New Zealand

ABSTRACT

Benchmarks are widely used in database-related research, helping users choose suitable database management systems and helping researchers evaluate their new methods. Recently benchmarks for XML have been designed to support the development of XML tools and systems. In this chapter, XML benchmarks are categorized into four groups: application benchmark, micro benchmark, XML generator and real dataset. Characteristics of each benchmark are discussed and compared. Finally, the future direction of XML benchmarks are discussed.

INTRODUCTION

A benchmark is a standard that enables users to evaluate the performance of a system. A benchmark also helps researchers decide what to evaluate and how to evaluate their system (Gray,1993). DBMS (database management system) benchmarking is used by researchers and industry practitioners to evaluate products to determine their strengths and weaknesses. In particular, industry practitioners use benchmarks to determine which database system best meets their needs while researchers use benchmarks to evaluate the results of their research. A

benchmark usually consists of a dataset and a set of queries. The dataset may be provided or the user may generate it the meet their own requirements. Users can also choose which queries to execute to fulfill their evaluation. Serious work on benchmarks has been carried out in DBMS-related areas for many years, for the different flavours of database systems, e.g. hierarchical, relational, object-oriented, etc.

XML (eXtensible Markup Language) has attracted attention because of its flexibility and powerful semi-structured data management capability. XML is designed to store, transport and display semi-structured data. Research into XML databases, including both native XML databases and XML-enabled databases, has been carried out and

DOI: 10.4018/978-1-61520-727-5.ch004

XML databases have been widely implemented. Traditional DBMS benchmarks, such as the Wisconsin benchmark (Gray,1993) and the TPC series benchmarks (Gray,1993), cannot satisfy the demand of XML DBMSs' implementation and development. In particular, traditional benchmarks cannot satisfy the evaluation of some characteristics, such as hierarchy structure, which exists in XML but is not found in traditional databases. Benchmarks for XML are needed to support the development of XML products and to evaluate the performance of XML-related systems.

Current XML benchmarks can be classified into two main groups: application benchmarks and micro benchmarks. Application benchmarks are designed to evaluate the overall performance of an XMLDB (XML database system). With application benchmarks, users can evaluate and compare XML database systems to identify the main characteristics of the XML database system, such as: whether a system supports data-centric document operations or whether a system has effective methods for dealing with text. These benchmarks are useful for choosing which XML engine/database system meets the users' specific demands.

Micro benchmarks evaluate single operations on XML database systems. Usually, these benchmarks provide single or multiple datasets that imitate possible characteristics, including both structure and value characteristics, which can be found in real data. Individual operations can be executed against the provided datasets and the system's performance can be recorded and evaluated. These benchmarks are important for finding more specific information in XML-research, in areas such as query processing and optimization.

Sometimes, the existing XML benchmarks do not satisfy the demands of users, and so the users build XML documents with particular characteristics for their own research. Several XML generators have been developed to undertake experiments or evaluations that need specific characteristics in their datasets. An XML generator allows users to set and control characteristics, such as selectivity of elements for experimentation.

Real dataset is another option for evaluating XML-related research. Some organizations publish their data in XML format and these XML documents can be used for proving or demonstrating new methods/algorithms.

In this chapter, application benchmarks, micro benchmarks and XML document generators are introduced. Characteristics for different benchmarks are discussed and compared. This comparison will help users choose which benchmark best fits their needs. We will also introduce three popular real datasets and discuss the future work of XML benchmarks.

APPLICATION BENCHMARK

An application benchmark evaluates the overall performance of a DBMS or query engine. For example, a user may need a database that handles large documents where the data is seldom updated, such as an electronic dictionary. While other people may want a database to store a large number of small XML documents where the data is updated frequently, such as e-commercial transactions. In this situation, application benchmarks may help users to understand the characteristics of the XML databases they evaluate and choose a database system that is suitable for their specific needs. We use the following features to compare application benchmarks:

Document-centric & Data-centric: XML documents can be classified into two groups: document-centric documents and data-centric documents. It is possible that an XML DBMS will perform better on either document-centric documents or data-centric documents, or equally well on both. Similarly some benchmarks concentrate more on one type of document than the other. In order to explore the performance of the XML DBMS and choose the suitable XML DBMS for specific demands, users need a benchmark that evaluates how well a DBMS handles different kinds of XML documents.

Single-document & Multiple-document: Because XML is flexible, that is a document can be composed in many different ways. People can use one document to record everything or build many documents to record different parts or aspect of the whole thing. Handling both single- and multiple-documents has their own difficulties. For example, when information is stored in one document, the size of the document may be very big. Manipulating the large document will influence the performance of the whole XML database system. On the other hand, storing information across a number of documents adds the difficulty of joining the documents. Some benchmarks evaluate whether a system is optimized for dealing with single- or multiple-document.

Big document & small document: In XML databases, some documents can be very big, such as dictionaries. On the other hand, some documents may be very small, such as transaction data. To choose the right database system for their application, users need to know whether their XML database is better for handling big documents or small documents. Benchmarks can evaluate the DBMS's capability of handling documents of various sizes if this is of interest to users.

Single-user & Multiple-user: XML databases have been widely utilized in website construction. In some situations, single-user models can satisfy the demands of users. However, there are times when evaluation in single-user situations does not satisfy the user's demands and a multiple-user model is necessary for DBMS performance evaluation. So this feature is important for some systems in benchmark evaluation.

Basic operations of DBMS: These operations include selection, updating, aggregation, sorting and join. Evaluation of each of these operations can be provided by the benchmark, allowing users to evaluate the performance of the DBMS and find

out the strengths and weaknesses of individual operations of the XML DBMS under test.

Special features of XML: Namespace and schema. Namespace is used to solve element name conflicts. Various namespaces may be found in XML documents. The manipulation of namespaces in the DBMS should not be ignored in the benchmarks. Schemas are used to describe the structure of XML. Although XML is touted as schemaless, many database systems use the schema if it is available. Schema validation and update can influence the DBMS performance, especially when XML Schema-based optimization methods are included. So these special features, though they are sometimes ignored in evaluation are important in XML DBMS and consequently for investigation in XML benchmarks.

In this section, five application benchmarks, XBench, XMark, XMach-1, XOO7 and TPoX, will be introduced. Also, the features of the benchmarks will be compared and discussed.

XBench

XBench (Yao, Özsu and Khandelwal, 2004) differs from other XML application benchmarks in that it contains sets of XML documents that capture various XML application characteristics, and the user can choose which dataset best suits their purpose.

Dataset

The datasets of XBench are classified along two dimensions: application characteristics, which classify the XML documents in the datasets as data-centric documents (DC) and text-centric documents (or document-centric document) (TC), and document characteristics, which classify the XML documents in the datasets into single document (SD) and multiple documents (MD) (Yao, Özsu and Khandelwal, 2002). So there are four kinds of datasets, which are shown in Table 1.

Table 1. XBench dataset classification and examples(Yao, Özsu and Khandelwal, 2002)

	Single document	**Multiple document**
Text-centric document	Online dictionary	News corpus, Digital libraries
Data-centric document	E-commerce catalogs	Transactional data

In order to scale the dataset, XBench Benchmark defines datasets in four classes, which are small (10 MB), normal (100MB), large (1GB) and huge (10GB). The default size is normal (100MB).

Text-Centric Documents

The content of the dataset for text centric single documents is composed from two dictionaries: GUN version of the Collaborative International Dictionary of English (GCIDE) and the Oxford English Dictionary (OED). The multiple documents' content is composed from a collection of XML documents that make up the Reuters news corpus along with a part of Springer-Verlag digital library. The data from the OED and the Springer library is converted from SGML to XML.

The data generation can be carried out in three steps:

1. Analyzing the XML documents, which are introduced above, and recording the following parameters:
    -   **Element types:** This parameter records all the elements that appear in the XML document.
    -   **Tree structure of element types:** This parameter records the relationships between elements.
    -   **Distribution of children to elements:** For each element type, if there are children elements nested in it, the possible distribution of occurrences of all the children elements will be recorded with this parameter.
    -   **Distribution of element values to types:** For each element type, if they

have values, the value distribution will be recorded.
    -   **Attribute names:** This parameter records all attribute names that appear in the XML document.
    -   **Distribution of attribute values to names:** Similar as the distribution of element values, this parameter records the value distribution for each attribute.
    -   **Distribution of attributes to elements:** This parameter records the attributes of each element type.
2. Generalizing the characteristics for the XML document. In this step, the maximum and minimum value of each parameter should be defined.
3. Generating the XML documents for the benchmark.

Data-Centric Documents

The content of data-centric single document dataset is built based on the TPC-W benchmark. Four tables, which include **ITEM, AUTHOR, ADDRESS** and **COUNTRY**, are inherited from the TPC-W benchmark and two new tables, **AUTHOR_2** and **PUBLISHER**, are included for the XML benchmark. The six tables are joined and mapped to an XML document, which is called "*catalog.xml*". A flat translation method is implemented to translate tables into XML documents.

The data-centric multiple document datasets consist of transactional data. Eight basic tables are chosen from the TPC-W benchmark (Gray, 1993) database and transformed to XML documents. In particular, the ORDERS, ORDER LINE, and

Table 2. Queries in XBench (Yao, Özsu and Khandelwal, 2004)

Group	ID	Functionalities
Exact match	Q1 (DC/SD)	Top level exact match
	Q2 (TC/MD)	Deep level exact match
Function application	Q3 (TC/SD)	Function application
Order access	Q4 (TC/MD)	Relative ordered access
	Q5 (DC/MD)	Absolute ordered access
Quantification	Q6 (TC/MD)	Existential quantifier
	Q7 (DC/SD)	Universal quantifier
Path expression	Q8 (TC/SD)	Regular path expressions (unknown element name)
	Q9 (DC/MD)	Regular path expressions (unknown subpaths)
Sorting	Q10 (DC/MD)	Sorting by string types
	Q11 (TC/SD)	Sorting by non string types
Document construction	Q12 (DC/SD)	Document structure preserving
	Q13 (TC/MD)	Document structure transforming
Irregular data	Q14 (DC/SD)	Missing elements
	Q15 (TC/MD)	Empty values
Retrieval of individual documents	Q16 (DC/MD)	Retrieve individual documents
Text search	Q17 (TC/SD)	Uni-gram search
	Q18 (TC/MD)	N-gram search
References and joins	Q19 (DC/MD)	References and joins
Datatype casting	Q20 (DC/SD)	Datatype casting

CC XACT tables are broken into fragments and a set of XML documents are built based on the fragments.

Data Generation

XBench uses ToXgene (Barbosa, Mendelzon, Keenleyside and Lyons, 2002), which is a template-based synthetic generator, to generate XML documents. The details of ToXgene can be found in the "XML generator" section.

Queries

A set of queries is designed to cover the full XQuery (Boag et al., 2007) functionality. The queries cover twelve aspects and the queries' classifications and functions are listed in Table 2.

The queries are composed in XQuery. Both the queries and their explanation can be found at the XBench website (Yao, 2003).

XMach-1

The XMach-1 (XML Data Management benchmark, Version 1) benchmark was the first XML database benchmark, which was developed at the University of Leipzig in 2000 (Böhme and Rahm 2001). The benchmark includes a database of XML documents and a series of operations, which investigate the performance of the operations against the XML DBMSs.

The benchmark imitates a multi-user and multi-layer XML data management system and it can also be applied in single-user mode. The

Figure 1. Structure of XMach-1(Böhme and Rahm 2001)

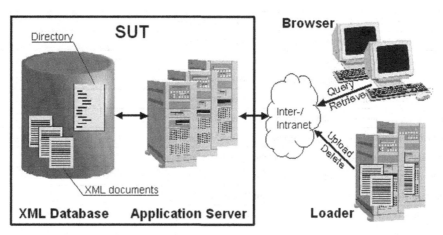

benchmark includes four parts: the XML database, Application server, Browser and Loader.

System Structure

Users' operations (queries or updates) are input through the Browser and all operations will be sent to the Application server, which runs a web server, middle ware and contacts the XML database. The Loader simulates loading XML documents from different data sources from the Internet.

Dataset

All XML documents in the benchmark are stored in the XML database and the information about the documents (metadata) is stored in a data-centric directory. The directory is stored in the XML database too and the document information it stores includes document URL, name, insert and update time. The XML documents contain both document-centric documents and data-centric documents. The XML documents are synthetically generated and the documents vary in structure and size, from 2-100KB. The generation procedure can be controlled by a set of parameters, such as number of sections per document, number of paragraphs per section, etc. The text contents in

the XML documents is generated from the 10000 most frequent English words with a distribution corresponding to natural language text.

The database can be scaled to different system configurations by changing the initial number of managed document. There are four possible initial numbers of XML documents: 10.000, 100.000, 1.000.000 and 10.000.000. The initial numbers will be increased using the insertion operation.

Queries

Eight queries and three update operations are provided to evaluate the performance of the DBMS. The queries cover features such as complete reconstruction of complex documents, full text retrieval, navigational queries, queries using sorting and grouping operators, etc. The update operations include insert, delete and update text content. The queries, which are composed in XQuery, can be downloaded from XMach-1 website (Database Group Leipzig, n.d.).

XMark

XMark (Schmidt et al. 2002) is the popular benchmark developed in CWI (Centrum Wiskunde & Informatica) Amsterdam. This benchmark consists

Table 3. Queries in XMach-1(Böhme and Rahm 2001)

ID	Functionalities
Q1	Return a complete document (complex hierarchy with ordering preserved)
Q2	Text retrieval query. The phrase is chosen from the phrase list. Join needed to get URL for qualifying documents
Q3	Simulates navigating a document tree using sequential operators
Q4	Restructuring operation simulating creation of a table of contents
Q5	Browse directory structure. Operation on structured unordered data
Q6	Find chapters of a given author. This tests efficiency of index implementation
Q7	Get important documents. Needs some kind of group by and count operation
Q8	Needs count, sort, join and existential operations and accesses metadata
U1	The loader generates a document and URL and sends them to the HTTP server
U2	A robot requests deletion, e.g. because the corresponding original document no longer exists on the web
U3	Update directory entry

of one XML document and twenty queries that evaluate essential aspects of XQuery.

Dataset

The XMark benchmark employs an XML document which imitates an online auction website. The root element called "site" has six subtrees and each subtree has information for the website.

- **Regions:** Which record items from different regions. Each item is assigned a unique identifier. The item elements have sub-elements including description, reserve, name, etc.
- **People:** Which saves information about people who register on the website. Subelements include homepage, credit card details, name, profile and income.
- **Open_auction:** Which are auctions in progress. Subelements include bidder, initial, itemref, annotation and description.
- **Closed_auction:** Which records the auctions that have been finished. The subelements include price, itemref, annotation and description.

- **Categories:** Consist of a name and a description, which are used to implement a classification scheme of items.
- **A category graph:** Connects the categories into a network.

The structure is given in Figure 2.

Consider two of the elements, annotation and description. These elements work as document-centric elements and are embedded into subtrees to which they semantically belong. Both length of the strings and the internal structure of sub-elements vary greatly to simulate the natural language.

The subtrees are connected with references and the reference map is given in figure 3. For more detail about the reference definition, please refer to (Schmidt et al. 2002).

A data generator is designed for data generation. Users can control the generation procedure by specifying the possible size. A generator is provided for four operating systems, Win32, Linux, Solaris and IRIX. Also a ready-made document, with size 100 MB, can be downloaded from the XMark website (Schmidt, 2003).

Figure 2. Element relationships between most of the queried elements (Schmidt et al. 2001)

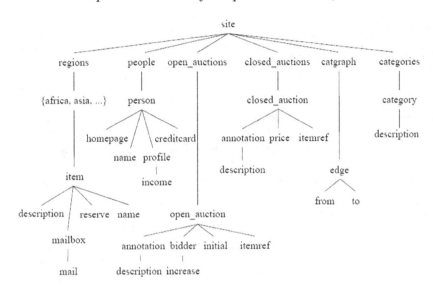

Figure 3. References between elements (Schmidt et al. 2001)

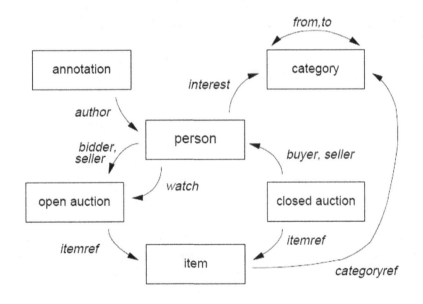

Queries

XMark has twenty queries, which are written in XQuery. The queries cover fourteen aspects of XQuery. The test aspects and functionalities are listed in Table 4.

XOO7

XOO7 is the XML benchmark developed at the National University of Singapore. The XOO7 benchmark is based on OO7 (Carey, DeWitt and Naughton, 1993), which is a comprehensive benchmark for Object-Oriented Database system.

Table 4. Queries in XMark (Schmidt et al. 2002)

Group	Functionalities	Description
Group 1	Exact match	This query is used to test the capability of string match with a specific XPath expression.
Group2	Ordered access	These queries evaluate the capability for managing the essential order of XML documents and demonstrate how efficiently queries with order constraints are executed. Three queries are designed for this test.
Goup3	Casting	This query tests the DBMS' capability for handling different datatypes.
Group4	Regular path expressions	XPath expressions are fundamental element for XML query languages. These queries evaluate the capability of the query engine to optimize path expressions. Two queries are designed for this investigation
Group5	Chasing references	References define relationships between elements. These queries investigate how well the query engine handles references. There are two queries in this group.
Group6	Construction of complex results	XQuery provides the capability for users to compose results in a specific structure. This query tests the DBMS's result construction.
Group7	Joins on values	This query investigates the DBMS's capability to handle intermediate results. Two queries are designed for this evaluation and the two queries differ in the size of the result set and provide various optimization opportunities.
Group8	Reconstruction	This query tests the ability of DBMS's to reconstruct portions of the original XML documents. The complementary action is to reconstruct the original document from its broken-down representation.
Group9	Full text	This query tests the capability of full-text searching.
Group10	Path traversals:	These queries are designed to quantify the costs of specified long path traversals without wild cards. Two queries are included in this group.
Group11	Missing elements	This query is designed to test the special capability of semi-structured data or XML.
Group12	Function application	This query puts the application of user defined functions (UDF) to the proof.
Group13	Sorting	This query is designed to test the sorting ability of DBMS's.
Group14	Aggregation	This query is designed not only to test the simple aggregation but also semi-structured data handling: some elements included in the query may have missing values.

Dataset

XOO7 (Bressan et al. 2001) can be considered an XML version of OO7. The structure (DTD) is transformed from OO7. New elements and queries are added to the benchmark to test characteristics specific to XML databases.

The structure of the XOO7 dataset is both complex and comprehensive. It involves recursive elements, attributes, text data, numerical data, document-centric data etc. Because XML does not support ISA relationships, the inheritance of attributes and relationships has been preprocessed before data transformation.

An element named "Module" is defined as the root of the XML document. Three attributes are included in "Module": MyID, type and buildDate. There are two elements nested in each Module

element: Manual and ComplexAssembly. Manual contains big text data and the big text data is useful for evaluating document-centric operations. Each Manual has three attributes: MyID, with value integer, title, with value string, and textLen, with value integer. The different datatypes of attribute values is useful for evaluating the performance of different datatype handling. ComplexAssembly is a recursive element. The recursive structure is an important characteristic in XML and the design of this element evaluates the handling of recursive structures. There are two sub-elements in ComplexAssembly: ComplexAssembly and BaseAssembly. Each BaseAssembly has one or multiple CompositePart elements. Each CompositePart has one Document element and several Connection elements. Element para is a new element that is created under element Document to present the document-centric characteristics of XML. Text-related evaluation can be carried out with both element para and Manual. The DTD is shown in Figure 4.

Queries

In order to evaluate features specific to XML, extra queries are designed especially to evaluate the functionality of XQuery. Queries in XOO7 can be classified into three groups:

- **Group 1 traditional database queries:** Test the performance on tradition database operations.
- **Group 2 navigation queries:** Test the capability of navigation with XPath expressions.
- **Group 3 document queries:** Evaluate the performance on text-related operations.

Each query is simple and evaluates a few functionalities. With all three groups of queries, most functionalities of XQuery can be tested. The queries are listed in Table 5. All queries are composed in Kweelt (Sahuguet, 2001) and the queries are available at the XOO7 website (Li, n.d.).

TPoX

TPoX, which stands for "Transaction processing over XML", is the XML benchmark from IBM (Nicola, Kogan and Schiefer, 2007). This benchmark simulates a financial multi-user system and evaluates different aspects of XML databases, including searching, updating, aggregating, etc.

Dataset

The dataset of TPox is built based on the FIXML Schema 4.4, which is an industry-standard XML schema for trade-related messages and developed from FIX (Financial Information eXchange). The structure of the dataset is shown in Figure 5.

Each customer may have one or more accounts and each customer is described in one XML document, CustAcc, which includes personal information. For every account, multiple orders will be executed. Each order buys or sells shares of one security. Orders are represented using the FIXML 4.4 schema. A holding is a number of shares of a security, which may be stock, bonds or funds.

In TPox, there are a total of 20833 security documents and the sizes of security documents range from 3KB to 10KB. Because stock and fund descriptions have large text values of different sizes, the evaluation of text-related operations can be executed. CustAcc documents are between 4KB and 20 KB while Orders are from 1KB to 2KB. The database can be scaled from extra small to extra large by increasing the number of Order and CustAcc documents.

The XML documents are not isolated. In fact, the three kinds of documents are connected by the information inside. For example, the order documents and security documents are connected with the value of attribute "symbol" and order documents and CustAcc documents are connected with the value of attribute "account_id". The data is generated with the generator ToXgene. All TPoX documents contain namespaces.

Queries

There are a total of 17 queries included in TPoX. All queries are composed in XQuery and each query includes one or more fundamental operations, which include insert, delete, update and query. All queries are listed in Table 6.

Discussion

XMach-1, XMark, XBench, XOO7 and TPoX are all designed to evaluate the performance of XML query engines or XML Database systems. Each of the benchmarks chooses comprehensive datasets to imitate characteristics of real XML datasets

Figure 4. DTD of XOO7 (Bressan, Lee, Li, Lacroix, and Nambiar, 2001)

```
<!DOCTYPE Module>
<!ELEMENT Module        (Manual, ComplexAssembly)>
<!ATTLIST Module        MyID            NMTOKEN #REQUIRED
                        type            CDATA           #REQUIRED
                        buildDate       NMTOKEN         #REQUIRED>
<!ELEMENT Manual        (#PCDATA)>
<!ATTLIST Manual        MyID            NMTOKEN         #REQUIRED
                        title           CDATA           #REQUIRED
                        textLen         NMTOKEN         #REQUIRED>
<!ELEMENT ComplexAssembly (ComplexAssembly+ | BaseAssembly+)>
<!ATTLIST ComplexAssembly
                        MyID            NMTOKEN         #REQUIRED
                        type            CDATA           #REQUIRED
                        buildDate       NMTOKEN         #REQUIRED>
<!ELEMENT BaseAssembly (CompositePart+)>
<!ATTLIST BaseAssembly
                        MyID            NMTOKEN         #REQUIRED
                        type            CDATA           #REQUIRED
                        buildDate       NMTOKEN         #REQUIRED>
<!ELEMENT CompositePart (Document, Connection+)>
<!ATTLIST CompositePart
                        MyID            NMTOKEN         #REQUIRED
                        type            CDATA           #REQUIRED
                        buildDate       NMTOKEN         #REQUIRED>
<!ELEMENT Document      (#PCDATA | para)+>
<!ATTLIST Document      MyID            NMTOKEN         #REQUIRED
                        title           CDATA           #REQUIRED>
<!ELEMENT para          (#PCDATA)>
<!ELEMENT Connection (AtomicPart, AtomicPart)>
<!ATTLIST Connection
                        type            CDATA           #REQUIRED
                        length NMTOKEN          #REQUIRED>
<!ELEMENT AtomicPart EMPTY>
<!ATTLIST AtomicPart
                        MyID            NMTOKEN         #REQUIRED
                        type            CDATA           #REQUIRED
                        buildDate       NMTOKEN         #REQUIRED
                        x               NMTOKEN         #REQUIRED
                        y               NMTOKEN         #REQUIRED
                        docId           NMTOKEN         #REQUIRED>
```

Table 5. Queries in XOO7 (Chaudhri, A. B., Rashid, A., & Zicari, R.,2003)

Group	ID	Functionalities
Group 1	Q1	Simple selection. Number comparison is evaluated.
	Q2	String comparison and element ordering are evaluated in this query.
	Q3	Range query. Users can change the selectivity.
	Q4	Tests join operation.
	Q5	Text data handling. Contains-like functions are evaluated.
	Q6	New structure reconstruction test.
	Q7	Test count aggregate function.
	Q8	Test sorting and use of environment information.
Group2	Q9	Querying a single level of the XML document without child nodes included.
	Q10	Compare attributes in parent nodes and child nodes. It tests the hierarchy relationship in XML data.
	Q11	Selection from multiple XML documents. It performs string and number comparison as well.
	Q12	Users may have various choices to store the same data, so they always require switching the parent nodes with the child nodes.
	Q13	Test regular path expression handling.
	Q14	Robustness in the presence of negation.
	Q15	Avg function and groupby-like functions are evaluated in this query.
	Q16	Part-of information of an element is evaluated in this query. Tests data transformation.
Group3	Q17	Test element order preservation. It is a document query.
	Q18	Similar as Q17. This is to check if some optimization is done.

Figure 5. TPoX documents structure (Nicola, Kogan and Schiefer, 2007)

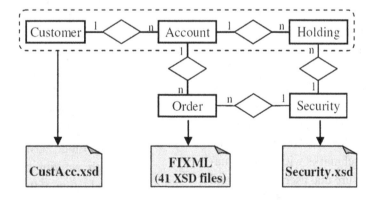

and carefully designed queries to investigate the execution of basic operation.

In Table 7, the features of each application benchmark are listed. This table breaks the features of each application benchmark into three groups:

1. The first six rows, Dataset type, Evaluation destination, Number of users, Number of documents, Documents, Total operations, are the fundamental aspects of each XML application benchmark.

Table 6. Descriptions of transactions (Nicola, Kogan and Schiefer, 2007)

ID	Functionalities
I1	Insert
I2	Insert & schema validation
D1	Delete & Exact match
D2	Delete & Exact match
U1	Subtree delete & Exact match
U2	Subtree insert & Exact match & element construction & schema validation
U3	Value update
U4	Value update & schema validation
U5	Value update & subtree insert/replace & join
U6	Value update & subtree delete/replace & join
Q1	Exact match
Q2	Exact match & document retrieve
Q3	Exact match & element construct
Q4	XPath expression processing & element construct
Q5	Exact match & element construct
Q6	Exact match & element construct
Q7	Exact match & join & aggregation

2. The basic operations of DBMSs, which are provided by each application benchmark, are listed in the rows: navigation, selection, update, aggregation, join and sorting.

3. The last six rows are XML-specific operations.

   ○ Because results of XQuery can be composed to a specific format, element construction evaluates the capability of XML DBMSs to construct results. Benchmarks with this evaluation will ensure that users have a good understanding on the DBMSs' capability of result organization and construction. Also, element construction is an important function of XQuery. So evaluation on this function is inevitable for XML benchmarks.

   ○ Sometimes the XML documents are not equipped with XML Schema and there is no information about the datatype of element values. How the element values are handled will greatly influence query execution with regard to both accuracy and efficiency. To test the capability of the execution of basic operations, the evaluation of the treatment of information-less values is necessary in a benchmark.

   ○ Schema validation is necessary for some XML applications. So Schema validation is needed when these kind of applications are implemented.

   ○ One of the XQuery requirements is operations on XML Schema. Because this requirement has not been met in DBMSs, there is no XML application benchmark that supports this kind of evaluation.

   ○ Namespace should not be ignored because it is an important and effective method to avoid element name conflicts. Whether namespace can be quickly recognized and handled will influence the performance of basic operations when there are namespaces involved. To this end, namespace awareness should be considered when an XML DBMS is evaluated.

   ○ Text-related operations are operations such as full-text search, matching. These operations are very important for text-centric document operations and other basic DBMS operations, such as join based on values. The evaluation of the performance of text-related operations is important for an XML benchmark, especially when users are interested in the DBMS for document-centric documents.

From the table, it can be seen that XMach-1 and TPoX are designed to imitate the multiple-user environment while the other three Benchmarks

Table 7. Features of XML application benchmarks

	XMach-1	XMark	XBench	XOO7	TPoX
Aspects of Benchmarks					
Dataset type	Document-centric && data-centric	Data- centric	Document-centric && data-centric	Data-centric	Data-centric
Evaluation destination	XML DBMS	XML query engine	XML DBMS	XML query engine	XML DBMS
Number of users	Multiple	Single	Single	Single	Multiple
Number of document	Multiple	Single	Single/ Multiple	Single	Multiple
Document Size	2-100KB	10MB-10GB	10MB-10GB	4MB-1GB	2-25KB
Total operations	8 queries and 3 updates	20 queries	20 queries	23 queries	7 queries and 10 updates
Standard Database Operations					
Navigation	√	√	√	√	√
Selection	√	√	√	√	√
Update	√				√
Aggregation		√	√	√	√
Join	√	√	√	√	√
Sorting	√	√	√	√	√
XML Specific Operations					
Element construction	√	√	√	√	√
Casting	√	√	√	√	√
Schema validation					√
Schema evolution					
Namespace awareness					√
Text-related operation	√	√	√	√	√

are single-user benchmarks. XBench imitates four possible situations: TC /SD, TC/MD, DC/SD and DC/MD (TC = text-centric document; DC = data-centric document; SD = single document; MD = multiple documents). And there are different groups of queries designed for the four situations. XMark chooses an XML document which simulates the auction website. The queries almost cover all aspects of query execution. But there is no updating operation involved. XOO7 is based on the dataset from OO7, the object-oriented database benchmark, with additional elements to simulate the characteristics of XML. More que-

ries are included to investigate the performance of XML query execution. TPoX, which is the most recent benchmark, is developed based on a standard Schema and this benchmark pays more attention to updating operations than other benchmarks. Each application benchmark has its own characteristics and may be suitable for different evaluations. Armed with the information above, users can choose the most suitable application benchmark to test their specific requirements are fulfilled when evaluating XML database systems and XQuery engines.

Table 8. Attributes in Basetype (Runapongsa et al. 2002)

Attribute name	Value
aUnique1	A unique integer (element ID) generated by traversing the tree in a breath-first manner.
aUnique2	A random integer
aLevel	An integer used to store the level number
aFour	An integer set to aUnique mod 4
aSixteen	An integer set to aUnique1 + aUnique2 mod 16
aSistyFour	An integer set to aUnique2 mod 64.
aSrting	An approximately 32 byte string

MICRO BENCHMARK

Introduction

In this section, we will introduce micro benchmarks for XML. The difference between micro benchmark and the application benchmarks introduced in the previous section is that micro benchmarks are designed to evaluate the performance of basic query operations, such as selection and join, while the application benchmarks are designed to evaluate the performance of the XML database systems and they are not suitable for evaluating the performance of individual operations. Sometimes, application benchmarks may be used to evaluate the performance of basic query operations, but the results do not reflect the performance accurately. This is because:

- First, the aims are different. Application benchmarks evaluate the overall performance of a DBMS while micro benchmarks evaluate the performance of individual operations.
- Second, the datasets are different. Datasets of micro benchmarks are designed to imitate all possible characteristics, including both structure characteristics and value characteristics, which can be found in the real world data. Datasets of application benchmarks are generated to imitate one or several kinds of real world data. So

the dataset of application can not cover as many characteristics as micro benchmark dataset.

- Third, the queries are different. Queries for application benchmarks usually include more operation while queries for micro benchmarks concentrate on individual operations.

To date four micro benchmarks have been developed for XML, Michigan, MemBeR, XSelMark and a duplicated detection benchmark. Because the last two benchmarks are not general purpose, we will only discuss Michigan and MemBeR in detail.

Michigan Benchmark

Michigan benchmark (Runapongsa et al. 2002) was the first micro benchmark for XML, and is inspired by Wisconsin Benchmark (Gray, 1993), a micro benchmark for relational database. Michigan benchmark consists of one XML document and 56 queries.

Data Set

The dataset of the Michigan Benchmark is built based on an element called "BaseType". The "BaseType" element has seven attributes, which are listed in Table 8. All attributes are necessary for the queries to explore the performance of query executions with different structural characteristics.

Each "BaseType" element has two kinds of subelements: BaseType element and OccasionalType element. The repetition of "BaseType" is decided by the fanout of the parent element. The occurrence of "OccasionalType" element is determined by the value of attribute "aSixtyFour" of the parent element. An OccasionalType element will appear if the parent element's aSixtyFour attribute has value "0". The content of each BaseType element is a long string that is approximately 512 bytes in length.

The depth of the Michigan benchmark dataset is 16 and the fanout of each level is between 2 to 13.

Queries

The queries of the Michigan benchmark are classified into 6 groups, which are:

- Returned structure (QR1-QR4)
- Simple selection (QS1-QS35)
- Value-based join (QJ1-QJ2)
- Point-based join (QJ3-QJ4)
- Aggregation queries (QA1-QA6)
- Update (QU1-QU7)

Some queries are provided with high selectivity and low selectivity for users to explore the performance of the XML database system operations.

MemBeR

MemBeR (Afanasiev, Manolescu and Michiels, 2005) is another kind of micro benchmark, which is a group of data sets with carefully designed query groups for each data set. Users of MemBer have different choices of data sets and queries:

- Download existing data sets and queries

- Generate their own data sets with the generator provided by MemBeR and design their own queries for specific purposes

Another important characteristic of MemBeR is that MemBeR is an open repository. Users can share their experimental datasets and queries with other XML-researchers by submitting their own data sets and queries to MemBeR. Users are also encouraged to submit their experimental results to MemBeR. So MemBeR users can compare their experimental results with the results from the MemBeR website to highlight the strengths and weakness of their methods.

MemBeR Generator

MemBeR provides a synthetic XML generator, which can generate arbitrarily sized XML documents. Users can control the generator by specifying several statistical properties of an XML document. There are three modes provided ("*MemBeR XML Generator*", n.d.):

Depth Based Mode
This kind of generator is designed to generate XML documents by specifying the fanout and the size of the destination XML document. The depth of the XML document will be calculated automatically from the size and the fanout. Subtrees will be inserted randomly at the leaf level to achieve the desired size.

Fanout Based Mode
With this kind of generator, users can generate XML documents by specifying the depth and the size of the target XML document. The generator will calculate the fanout of the XML document.

Advanced Mode
This mode provides a sophisticated method to control the generating procedure, where users have to specify each tag that occurs in the tree,

Table 7. Queries in Michigan Benchmark (Runapongsa et al. 2003)

ID	Functionalities
QR1	Return only the elements in question, not including any sub-elements.
QR2	Return the elements and all their immediate children
QR3	Return the entire sub-tree rooted at the elements
QR4	Return the elements and their selected descendants
QS1-QS2	Selection based on the value of a string attribute & low selectivity
QS3-QS4	Selection based on the value of a integer attribute & low selectivity
QS5	Selection based on range values
QS6	Selection with sorting
QS7	Multiple-attribute selection
QS8	Selection based on element name
QS9-QS10	Selection of child node with different parent node fanout
QS11-QS12	Selection based on the value of element content & low selectivity
QS13-QS14	Selection based on the element content with different string distance & low selectivity
QS15-QS17	Order-sensitive parent-child structure selection
QS18-20	Parent-child structure selection
QS21-QS23	Ancestor-descendant structure selection
QS24-QS27	Ancestor nesting in ancestor-descendant selection
QS28-QS30	Parent-child Complex Pattern Selection
QS31- QS34	Ancestor-descendant complex pattern selection
QS35	Negated selection
QJ1-QJ2	Value-based join
QJ3-QJ4	Pointer-based join
QA1	Value aggregation
QA2	Value aggregation with groupby
QA3	Value aggregation with selection
QA4	Structural aggregate
QA5	Structural aggregate selection
QA6	Structural exploration
QU1	Point insert
QU2	Point delete
QU3	Bulk insert
QU4	Bulk delete
QU5	Bulk load
QU6	Bulk reconstruction
QU7	Reconstruction

at which level it should appear and the frequency of appearances at the specified level.

Data Sets and Queries

MemBeR provides 34 queries, which are executed against four XML documents. We list the queries, functionalities, and destination documents in table 10. All queries and data sets can be found at the MemBeR website.

Features List

Both Michigan benchmark and MemBeR are very effective tools for users to evaluate the performance of basic operations against their database system. In this section, the features of the two benchmarks are listed.

Both of the two micro benchmarks provide data generators to the users, and dedicated designed queries help users to master the characteristics of the database system and highlight the strength and weakness of their system. The queries of Michigan benchmark almost cover all basic operations of database system. MemBeR continues to be developed and users can compare their experimental result with others.

XSelMark

Although the Michigan benchmark and MemBeR provide queries to evaluate the performance of basic operations against XML documents, they do not always satisfy the demands of research in specific areas. Estimating the sizes of query results and intermediate results is important in any effective query optimization process. An example of selectivity estimation implementation is in Lore (McHugh and Widom, 1999) from Stanford University. In this system, query execution is optimized by choosing sub-query execution order. The decision of sub-query execution order is based on each sub-query selectivity estimation.

In fact, selectivity estimation is a crucial part of effective query optimization.

Selectivity estimation in the XML domain is more complex than that of relational database system because (Sakr, 2008):

- Not all XML documents follow their XML schema and some XML documents do not have a schema
- Both value and structure are involved in XML queries
- The high expressiveness of XML query languages
- Randomly distributed elements and attributes
- Complex relationships between elements

XSelMark (Sakr, 2008) is the micro benchmark that is designed to assess and evaluate the different selectivity estimation approaches of XML queries. XSelMark satisfies the demands of selectivity estimation- related research in the following areas (Sakr, 2008):

- **It supports both value and structural queries.** In XML implementations, structure qualification is always involved in the XML queries. A selection operation based on structure will influence the XML query execution greatly. So both value and structural queries should be evaluated.
- **It is strongly capable.** XML queries are very complex. Traditional operations of DBMS, which include search, join, aggregation, etc., should be executed on both value and structure. Also, special structure operations, such as XPath expression navigation, are important parts of XML queries. So a selectivity estimation approach should have the capability to treat different possible situations.
- **It is composable.** Because XML query languages enable users to compose XML

Table 10. MemBeR queries and data sets (Afanasiev, L., Manolescu, I., & Michiels, P., n.d.)

Query name	Functionalities	Data set
CHILD-ATTRIB	Navigation (XPath)	exponential2.xml
CHILD-EXISTENTIAL-ATTRIB	Navigation (XPath)	exponential2.xml
CHILD-FIRST-ATTRIB	Navigation (XPath)	exponential2.xml
CHILD-LAST-ATTRIB	Navigation (XPath)	exponential2.xml
CHILD	Navigation (XPath)	exponential2.xml
DESCENDANT	Navigation (XPath)	exponential2.xml
EXISTENTIAL-ATTRIB	Existential branch, then attribute step (XPath)	exponential2.xml
FLWR-COPY-CHILD-POSITION	Navigation (XQuery)	flat2.xml
FLWR-COPY-DESCENDANT-NAME	Navigation (XQuery)	flat2.xml
FLWR-COPY-LEVEL-ATTRIB	Navigation (XQuery)	flat2.xml
FLWR-COPY-LEVEL	Navigation (XQuery)	flat2.xml
FLWR-NESTED-RETURN-LEAF	Navigation (XQuery)	flat2.xml
FLWR-RETURN-CHILD-POSITION	Navigation (XQuery)	flat2.xml
aggr_where:	Aggregate	Generated by **Toxgene and reldata.tsl**
universal_quantifier	Universal quantification	Generated by **Toxgene and reldata.tsl**
exist_gencom	Existential quantifier and general comparison.	Generated by **Toxgene and xmp.tsl**
implicit_unary_grouping	Aggregate and general comparison	Generated by **Toxgene and xmp.tsl**
multi_level_exist	Existential quantification	Generated by **Toxgene and reldata.tsl**
multi_level_exist2	Existential quantification	?
simple_aggr	Aggregate	Generated by **Toxgene and reldata.tsl**
exist_gencom2	General comparison	Generated by **Toxgene and xmp.tsl**
implicit_grouping_gencom_both	Aggregate function and general comparison	Generated by **Toxgene and xmp.tsl**
implicit_grouping_gencom_inner	Aggregate function and general comparison	Generated by **Toxgene and xmp.tsl**
implicit_grouping_gencom_outer	Aggregate function and general comparison	Generated by **Toxgene and xmp.tsl**
implicit_grouping_neq	Aggregate function and non-equality comparison.	Generated by **Toxgene and reldata.tsl**
theta_exist:	Existential quantification	Generated by **Toxgene and reldata.tsl**
theta_forall	Universal quantification	Generated by **Toxgene and reldata.tsl**
exist_gencom3	Node comparison	Generated by **Toxgene and xmp.tsl**
forall_gencom	Universal quantification	Generated by **Toxgene and xmp.tsl**
Implicit-unary-grouping	Aggregate function	Generated by **Toxgene and xmp.tsl**

queries with sub-expressions. So the selectivity estimation approach should estimate both sub-expressions and the final results.

- **It is practical.** Selectivity estimation is an important procedure for optimization methods, which consider the selectivity. So

the estimation procedure should be finished quickly and provide accurate results.

- **It is accurate.** Because the selectivity estimation results will influence the XML query optimization execution, accurate results are an required for selectivity estimation.

Table 11. Fundamental features

Features	Michigan	MemBeR
Open	√	√
Continues to grow		√
Data generator	√	√
Data set provided	√	√
Queries provided	√	√
Experimental results comparison		√
XPath support	√	√
XQuery support	√	√

- **It is independent.** The selectivity estimation approach should not work only on specific query engines or XML query optimization methods.

Data Set and Queries

XSelMark uses the XML document "auction.xml", which is the data set of XMark, as its data set and 25 queries are designed against the XML document. The queries are composed in XPath and XQuery. The queries are classified into groups and each group represents a kind of basic operation.

Duplication Detection Benchmark

Duplication detection benchmark (Weis, Naumann and Brosy, 2006) is another specific micro benchmark that is designed to evaluate the methods and algorithms for duplicate detection. Duplicate detection is an important technique that has a close relationship with data warehousing, data mining or data integration. The duplication detection benchmark is developed to support the research of duplication detection. This benchmark is designed in XML because XML is more flexible than relational database, but relational database researcher can use the benchmark by mapping the data to flat relational data.

The benchmark differs from other benchmarks in the following ways:

- There are no queries in the benchmark. This is because this benchmark is used to evaluate the methods or algorithms, rather than to evaluate a database system.
- A website is designed for the benchmark implementation. Users can finish their method evaluation and compare the results with other methods through the website.

Dataset

The data of the benchmark is based on five fundamental data sets, which can be classified into two groups: synthetic generated data and real-world data. The synthetic generated data can be generated by the XMach-1 generator, XMark generator and Customer Relationship Managements. The two sources of real-world data are a digital library, which is similar to DBLP, and a movie database, which is similar to the Internet Movie Database (IMDB).

The Dirty XML Generator was developed for the benchmark, which inserts duplicated data into the fundamental data sets. All the dirty data is appended to the end of the XML documents. Currently the Dirty XML Generator can generate dirty data in three ways:

1. Exact duplicate elements, which copies elements from the original document and assigns an identifier to the copied elements.
2. Contradictory text, which inserts, deletes, swaps or replaces a specified number of characters in the text.
3. Missing data, which deletes text or elements.

Website

A website is built for users to evaluate their method of duplication detection. An advantage of using the benchmark through a website is that all the developed methods or algorithms can be executed under the same conditions. So the comparison of

Table 12. Evaluation functionalities

Functionalities	Michigan	MemBeR
Specify nagivation		√
Selection*	√	√
Update⁺	√	
Aggregation^	√	√
Join #	√	√
Sorting	√	
Element construction	√	√
Different selectivity	√	√
Different fanout	√	
dataTypes operation	√	√
Reference		
Collections		√
Schema availability		
Namespace awareness		
Text and element boundaries	√	
Universal and existential quantifiers		√
Hierarchy and sequence	√	√
Combination	√	√
Composition of operation	√	√
Null Values	√	√
Structural preservation	√	√
Identity preservation	√	√
Operations on literal data	√	√
Operations on names	√	√
Closure	√	

* Selection includes element name selection, element content selection and element structure selection.

⁺ Update includes insert, delete, restructure.

^ Aggregation includes value aggregation and structure aggregation.

Join includes value-based join, simple structure join and complex structure join.

the experimental results can help users to highlight the strengths and weakness of their methods. Currently users can submit their algorithm using one of two options: executable code or Java packages. After running the submitted algorithm on duplication detection, the results will be generated and the results can be downloaded and compared with the results of other algorithm. A comparator is provided to compare experimental results and the comparison results will be generated automatically. The submitted algorithms can be evaluated in two ways: effectiveness, which includes precision, recall and f-measure, and efficiency, which concentrates on the number of comparisons and the observed runtime.

Table 13. Queries in XSelMark (Sakr, 2008)

Group	Query	Functionality
Path Expressions	Q1	Path expression with non-recursive axes
	Q2	Path expression with recursive axes
	Q3	Path expression with wild cards
	Q4	Path expression with ordered-based axes
	Q5	Branching XPath Expressions
Twig Expressions	Q6	Simple twig expression
	Q7	Twig expression with element construction
Predicates	Q8	Positional Predicates
	Q9	Equality Predicates
	Q10	Range Predicates
	Q11	Conjunctive/Disjunctive Predicates
	Q12	Predicates with merged nodes from different paths
	Q13	Predicates with merged nodes from different paths and hybrid natures
	Q14	String Predicates
Value Based Join	Q15	Value comparison where the values of each operand are constructed by path expression
	Q16	Value comparison where the values of one operand are constructed by path expression and the values of the other operand are constructed by path expression manipulated with arithmetic expression
	Q17	Values Join
Data value Based Join	Q18	Arithmetic Operations on Statistical Summaries 1
	Q19	Arithmetic Operations on Statistical Summaries 2
	Q20	Arithmetic Operations on Statistical Summaries 3
Nested Expression	Q21	Let – Aggregates
	Q22	Predicates with values constructed by aggregate function
Data Dependent	Q23	Sub-String Matching
	Q24	Distinct Values
	Q25	Document Order

Discussion

In this section, four micro benchmarks are introduced. Both Michigan benchmark and MemBeR provide data set generators. The queries of the two benchmarks can help users to evaluate performance of individual operation execution and highlight the weakness of the XML database system. Both Michigan benchmark and MemBeR are micro benchmarks for general purposes evaluation. XSelMark and Duplication detected benchmark are designed for specific research. XSelmark is designed for selectivity estimation, which concentrates on the selectivity of both final results and intermediate results. Duplication detected benchmark will help for duplication detection research with a multiple function website, which can evaluate the user methods and compare the results of different methods automatically.

XML DOCUMENT GENERATOR

In this section, we introduce four XML document generators. An XML document generator is necessary when the existing dataset, including both XML benchmark and real XML documents, cannot satisfy the specific demands of the research. Subsequently researchers need a tool to build their own dataset with specific characteristics. The generators introduced in this section are Synthetic XML generator, ToXgene, XML generator for XSQO research and IBM XML generator.

Synthetic XML Generator

This generator was developed at the University of Wisconsin, Madison (Aboulnaga, Naughton and Zhang, 2001). With this generator, users can generate complex XML data to simulate real data for their experiments. By setting input parameters, the generated XML data set can be built with specific characteristics, which enable users to evaluate the performance of proposed techniques with different XML data.

Path Tree

The generation of a path tree is the first step of the XML data generation. A path tree is the tree structure that describes the structure of the XML data. The root node of the path tree will be the root node of the generated XML document. Every node of the path tree represents a kind of element with the same element name that can be reached from the root node with the same XPath expression. A number is always assigned for each node, which provides the frequency of this kind of node. The path tree is generated in a depth first manner. Users can control the generator procedure by specifying the depth of the XML document, and the minimum and maximum fanout for each level.

Figure 6. Examples of path tree (Aboulnaga, Naughton and Zhang, 2001)

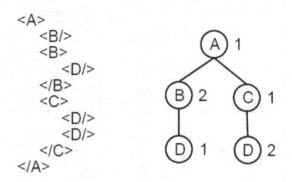

```
<A>
    <B/>
    <B>
        <D/>
    </B>
    <C>
        <D/>
        <D/>
    </C>
</A>
```

Tag Names

The second step of the XML data generation is to assign tag names (element names) to the path tree. This procedure is achieved in breadth first order.

The tag names can be assigned in two ways:

- In some situations, each tree node may be assigned a unique name.
- In some situations, there will be repeated tag names in the path tree.

Assigning the same tag name to different nodes will benefit users in the following areas (Aboulnaga, Naughton and Zhang, 2001):

- There will be recursion in the XML data, such as an element has the same tag name as one of its ancestors.
- Same name elements may be reached from the root element with different XPath expressions.
- Same name elements may increase the Markov memory of the paths in the path tree.

The tag names can be assigned in two kinds of recursion methods: direct recursion, which means some elements share the same names with their parent nodes, and indirect recursion, which means some elements share the same names with their ancestors.

Frequency Distribution

The frequency distribution assigned to path tree nodes specifies the total number of XML elements to generate for every node. The generator will specify the frequency distribution of the path tree nodes in breadth first order. Currently the generator supports ascending order, descending order and random order.

Element Values

The values of Elements in the generated XML data are strings that consist of one or more text words. The text words follow a Zipfian frequency distribution. The words generations are controlled by specifying the number of XML documents to generate, the number of words to generate and the number of distinct words to generate.

ToXgene

ToXgene (Barbosa, Mendelzon, Keenleyside and Lyons, 2002) is a template-based XML document generator, which was developed for the ToX (the Toronto XML Server) project in University of Toronto. The generator is designed to provide comprehensive methods for users to generate XML documents for their research.

TSL

The ToXgene template is specified using a language called TSL (Template Specification Language), which is a subset of XML Schema with newly defined annotations.

Features

Element Specification

The two important annotations for element specification are type and gene. Type defines the content of elements in XML documents, which includes SimpleType and ComplexType. The SimpleType is used to define base type, such as string, integer, etc., ComplexType defines the complex content of elements, which may include subelements, CDATA content, or both of them. With these two annotations, a structure can be defined. Gene consists of a name (element name/attribute name) and a type. When a gene consists of an element name and a type, an element structure is defined. When a gene consists of an attribute name and a type, the structure of an attribute is specified.

Distribution Control

Another feature of elements that can be specified is their probability distributions. Currently ToXgene supports uniform, normal, exponential, log-normal distributions and arbitrary discrete distributions. In order to insure the consistency of the templates, maximum and minimum value of distribution should be specified.

Content Sharing

ToXgene supports different elements with the same content. The elements, which have the same content, may be located in different parts of one document or located in different documents. This feature enables the generator to generate correlated documents, which will provide evaluations for operations, such as "join".

Integrity Constraints

The content sharing is implemented by generating the shared content before generating the documents. The generating content is stored in a specified list, tox-list. The ToXgene enable users

Figure 7. The structure of ToXgene API (Barbosa, Mendelzon, Keenleyside and Lyons, 2002)

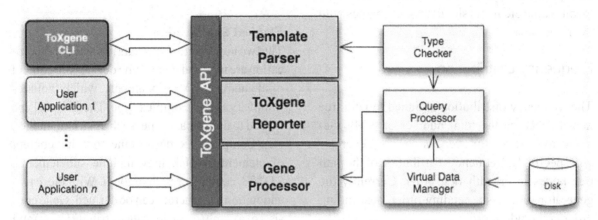

to specify integrity constraints over the content of a list to ensure the consistency of the generated documents.

Existing Data Reuse

ToXgene supports the existing data reuse. Sometimes users need some special data, such as DNA sequences, in their XML documents. ToXgene enables users to load the existing data into the toxlist. This allows users to reuse their own content generator or mix the real data together with the synthetic data to simulate real XML documents.

Extensibility

ToXgene provides interfaces for users to combine their own applications with ToXgene to build XML documents for the experiences with specific requirements.

Structure

The API of ToXgene consists of three main modules: template parser, ToXgene reporter and Gene processor.

1. The Template parser transforms the input templates into the format which will be recognized by the generation engine.

2. ToXgene reporter provides the interface between the generator and human being.
3. Gene processor generates and stores the documents.

The structure of ToXgene API is shown in figure 7.

IBM XML Generator

An XML generator was developed in IBM (*IBM XML generator*, n.d.). This generator is a template-based generator. The structure of the generated XML documents can be specified in a DTD. However, the generator does not provide users with much control over the generation procedure. For example, the users can specify the maximum level of the destination document but the exact number of levels cannot be specified. Currently the IBM XML Generator has become part of Visual Age for Java.

XML Generator for XSQO Research

This generator was developed to support research into XSQO (XML Semantic Query Optimization). XSQO optimizes XML query execution based on information, such as classification of attributes, abstracted from the XML document. In order to evaluate the performance of the methods developed for XSQO, XML documents with built-in classification are needed. With this generator, users can build data sets with different classifications for specific conditions (Geng and Dobbie, 2006).

Features

- **Scalable:** The generator can modify documents of different sizes.
- **Multi-operation:** different operations, including insertion, deletion and value modification, are provided for users to modify the documents with specific requirements.
- **XPath compatible:** XPath expression is an essential part for XML-related query languages. This generator can execute all operations specified as XPath expressions.
- **Multi-purpose:** Content and structure are the two important parts of XML documents. This generator can modify both to satisfy the demands of the experiments.
- **Distribute changes uniformly:** When one or more lists of elements are involved in the modification, the destination elements are chosen by a uniform distribution calculator.
- **Selectivity control:** Queries with different selectivity are useful to evaluate the optimization method performance and find out the suitable situation for optimization method execution. This generator enables users to specify different proportions to evaluate their optimization methods.
- **Schema independent:** Because not all XML documents are equipped with XML Schema or DTD, operations on XML should not rely on the information from the structure description documents. The generator can operate on all XML documents, including both XML documents with Schema and XML documents without Schema.

Functionality

Insert Single Elements
This function inserts same name elements to specific positions.

Set Element Values
This function will modify the values of the specified elements in the XML documents.

Remove Element
This function removes the specified elements from the XML documents.

Insert Multiple Elements
This function enables users to insert at most three elements together with a specified structure. For example, if three elements, a, b and c are inserted into the element E, which exists in the XML document, the possible structures are shown in Figure 8.

Discussion

In this section, four XML document generators are introduced. IBM XML generator, Synthetic XML generator and ToXgene are template-based generators. Users of IBM XML generator can specify the structure and other parameters, but the IBM generator parameters are not very fine grained. Synthetic XML generator enables users to define the levels and minimum and maximum children nodes of each level. ToXgene provides more control for the generating procedure. XML Generator for XSQO (XML semantic query optimization) is developed for the research of XSQO, and can both generate an XML document and modify existing XML documents.

REAL DATA SET

Some people are not satisfied with experiments that are carried out based on synthetic data set.

Figure 8. Possible structures for multiple element insertion (Geng and Dobbie, 2006)

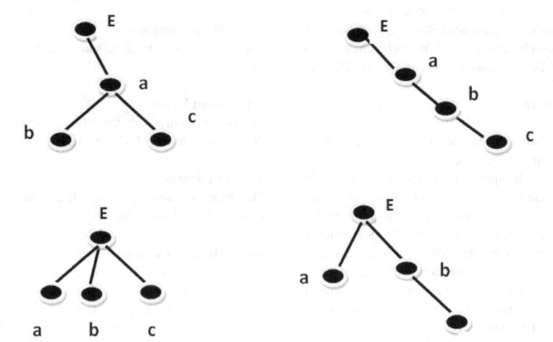

So they will choose real data sets to evaluate and demonstrate the performance of their systems. The popular real datasets are: DBLP, SIGMOD and NASA.

- **DBLP:** The DBLP website is a popular tool for computer science researchers to trace the work of colleagues and to retrieve bibliographic details (Ley, 2009).In June 2009, the DBLP computer science bibliography had already recorded more than 1.2 million bibliographic records (Ley, 2009). Recently, more and more researchers have begun to use the data from DBLP in another way: using the DBLP data set to evaluate their systems and algorithms. The XML document, which contains the records from DBLP on-line website can be downloaded from http://dlp.uni-trier.de/xml/. More information about DBLP can be found in http://dblp.uni-trier.de.

- **SIGMOD:** The ACM SIGMOD on-line website is a digital library for the database systems research community (*"the ACM SIGMOD Anthology"*, n.d.) The SIGMOD data set is an XML version of portion of ACM SIGMOD website, which records information from ACM SIGMOD in XML format (*"the ACM SIGMOD Anthology"*, n.d.). All the data of SIGMOD.xml is abstracted from DBLP website because the original ACM SIGMOD website is organized in HTML and the DBLP website contains a large number of SIGMOD issues (*"the ACM SIGMOD Anthology"*, n.d.). More information about the SIGMOD dataset can be found in http://www.dia. uniroma3.it/Araneus/Sigmod/.

- **NASA:** The NASA dataset stores the published astronomical data from Astronomical Data Center (ADC at GSFC/NASA). The ADC supports a series of research projects to store raw observational or experimental data that was published in the scientific journals in machine understandable formats (Cover, 2000). The research also provides a greater understanding of ongoing research and aids in the planning of new missions, observations, or experiments. (Shaya et. al., 2000). More information about NASA.xml can be found at NASA website.

Real data sets are widely used because it is believed that experimental results based on real data set are more realistic and therefore more practical. But there is a big obstacle in the use of real data sets, in that the characteristics of real data set are hard to characterise. One reason for this is that real datasets are updated regularly. This makes it difficult not only to test particular characteristics in an experiment but also to compare results over an extended period of time. For example: the size of DBLP.xml was only 127M in 2001 while the size has become 609M in 2009. More real datasets can be found at (XML Data Repository, n.d.)

FUTURE WORK

We have listed the existing XML benchmarks in this chapter. All the benchmarks are designed for systems that are based on XML 1.0. To date XML 2.0 is still under development and no official standard or description has been published. With XML 2.0, we will need to see futher extensions to the benchmarks. However even when we concentrate on XML 1.0, we can see that of two XML characteristics need to be enhanced in XML benchmarks: XML schema-related research and namespace (including QName) technology.

XML Schema (Fallside & Walmsley, 2004) is the document structure description language that is designed specifically for XML. Compared with DTD, XML Schema provides more description methods. For example, users may specify the data type for an XML element with XML Schema while in DTD users can only specify two data types for the values of elements/attributes: CDATA and PCDATA. Users can do more validation of their XML documents with XML Schema, which may reduce work on data maintenance. Another important characteristic of XML Schema is that XML Schema has the same grammar as XML. XML Schema will be accepted by more users with the use of XML becoming more popular. Currently the existing XML benchmarks do not provide enough evaluation for XML Schema-related technology (only TPoX supports Schema validation). So there will be a need for XML benchmarks that can provide more evaluation for XML Schema related technology.

XML namespaces provide a simple and effective method for qualifying element and attribute names used in XML documents by associating them with namespaces identified by URI references (**Bray,** Hollander, Layman, & Tobin, 20006). With XML namespaces, both human beings and XML application systems can effectively identify elements/attributes with the same name from different documents, reduce collisions and simplify the procedure of elements recognition. Most existing XML Benchmarks do not provide evaluation of namespace (and QName) awareness. With the increasing use of XML and the development of the Internet, abstracting information from multiple sources needs the support of namespaces. So namespace (including QName) awareness should be given more attention by XML benchmark developers.

CONCLUSION

In this chapter, we introduced the benchmarks for XML. There are five application benchmarks. XBench consists of a set of XML documents, including both data-centric documents and document-centric documents. XMach-1 is designed based on a web application. XOO7 is based on OO7, which is an Object-Oriented database benchmark, with new elements and queries added. XMark imitates an auction website. TPoX is built based on a financial application scenario. XBench, XMach-1 and TPoX provide multiple XML documents. There is only one XML document in XMark and XOO7. XMach-1 and TPoX support multiple-user models while the other three benchmarks are designed as single-user models. As the latest application benchmark, TPoX provides more queries that evaluate update operations than the other application benchmarks.

Four micro benchmarks have been introduced in the chapter. Michigan benchmark and MemBeR are two micro benchmarks developed for general purpose use. Michigan provides a carefully designed dataset, which imitates most characteristics that can be found in real XML documents, and a series of queries to explore different aspects of XML query execution. MemBeR is an open repository. Users can download existing datasets and queries from MemBeR. Also users can submit their own dataset, queries and experimental results to the repository. XSelMark is the micro benchmark for selectivity-related research. Duplication detection benchmark is developed for the duplicate detection related research.

IBM XML generator, Synthetic complex-structure XML generator and ToXgene are all template-based XML document generators. IBM XML generator has become a part of Visual Age for Java. Synthetic complex-structure XML generator generates XML documents based on a path tree, which describes the structure of the destination XML document. Users can also define parameters, such as levels and fanout. ToXgene is designed to generate large and complex XML datasets. XML generator for XSQO (XML semantic query optimization) research is developed to support the research of XSQO. This generator can not only build XML documents but also modify existing XML documents.

NASA, DBLP and SIGMOD are three popular real datasets, which are often used in XML related experiments. Because the datasets change regularly, the characteristics and statistics are hard to master. We have provided the website for each data set and users can find the latest information easily from there.

The future work of XML benchmark is discussed at the end of the chapter. We believe that XML Schema and XML Namespace are two areas that need more attention. Because the XML 2.0 description is not published yet, our discussion is still limited to XML 1.0.

REFERENCE

Aboulnaga, A., Naughton, J. F., & Zhang, C. (2001). *Generating Synthetic Complex-structured XML Data*. Paper presented at the Fourth International Workshop on the Web and Database (WebDB), Santa Barbara, USA.

Afanasiev, L., Manolescu, I., & Michiels, P. (2005). *MemBeR: A Micro-benchmark Repository for XQuery*. Paper presented at Third International XML Database Symposium (XSym), Trondheim, Norway. Afanasiev, L., Manolescu, I., & Michiels, P. (n.d.). *MemBeR: XQuery Micro-Benchmark Repository*. Retrieved April 1, 2009, from http://lips.science.uva.nl/Resources/MemBeR/index.html

Barbosa, D., Mendelzon, A. O., Keenleyside, J., & Lyons, K. (2002). *Toxgene: An extensible template-based data generator for XML*. Paper presented at the Fifth International Workshop on the Web and Database, Madison, WI.

Boag, S., Chamberlin, D., Fernández, M. F., Florescu, D., Robie, J., & Siméon, J. (2007). *XQuery 1.0: An XML Query Language*. Retrieved March 25, 2006. from http://www.w3.org/TR/xquery/

Böhme, T., & Rahm, E. (2001). *XMach-1: a benchmark for XML data management*. Paper presented in the German Database Conference BTW2001, Berlin, Germany.

Bray, T., Hollander, D., Layman, A., & Tobin, R. (2006). *Namespaces in XML 1.0* (2nd Ed.). Retrieved April 24, 2009, from http://www.w3.org/TR/REC-xml-names/

Bressan, S., Dobbie, G., Lacroix, Z., Lee, M. L., Li, Y. G., Nambiar, U., & Wadhwa, B. (2001). *XOO7: Applying OO7 Benchmark to XML Query Processing Tools.* Paper presented at the 10th ACM International Conference on Information and Knowledge Management (CIKM), Atlanta, GA.

Bressan. S., Lee, M. L., Li, Y. G., Lacroix, Z. & Nambiar, U.(2001). *The XOO7 XML management system benchmark.* Retrieved March 12, 2009, from http://www.comp.nus.edu.sg/~ebh/XOO7/download/XOO7_TechReport.pdf

Carey, M. J., DeWitt, D. J., & Naughton, J. F. (2003). The OO7 Benchmark. *SIGMOD Record, 22*(2), 12–21. doi:10.1145/170036.170041

Chaudhri, A. B., Rashid, A., & Zicari, R. (2003). *XML Data management: Native XML and XML-enabled database systems.* Reading, MA: Addison-Wesley publisher.

Cover, R. (2000). *NASA Goddard Astronomical Data Center (ADC) 'Scientific Dataset' XML.* Retrieved June 17, 2009, from http://xml.coverpages.org/nasa-adc.html

Data Repository, X. M. L. (n.d.). Retrieved June 17, 2009, from http://www.cs.washington.edu/research/xml datasets/www/repository.html

Database Group Leipzig. (n.d.). *XMach-1: A benchmark for XML Data Management.* Retrieved Febrary 20, 2009, from http://dbs.uni.leipzig.de/en/projeket/XML/XmlBenchmarking.html

Fallside, D. C., & Walmsley, P. (2004). *XMLSchema Part 0: Primer Second Edition.* Retrieved March 14, 2009. From http://www.w3.org/TR/xmlschema-0/

Geng, K., & Dobbie, G. (2006). *An XML document generator for semantic query optimization experimentation.* Paper presented at the 8th International Conference on Information Integration and Web-based Application & Services, Yogyakarta, Indonesia.

Gray, J. (1993). *The Benchmark Handbook (2nd ed.).* San Francisco, USA: Morgan Kaufmann Publishers, Inc.

IBM XML Generator. (n.d.). Retrieved from http://www.alphaworks.ibm.com/tech/xmlgenerator

Ley, M. (2009). *DBLP—Some lessons learned.* Paper presented at the VLDB' 09, Lyon, France.

Li, Y. G. (n.d.). *The XOO7 benchmark.* Retrieved Febrary 28, 2009, from http://www.comp.nus.edu.sg/~ebh/XOO7.html

Manolescu, I., Miachon, C., & Michiels, P. (2006). *Towards micro-benchmarking XQuery.* Paper presented at the first International Workshop on Performance and Evaluation of Data Management Systems (EXPDB), Chicago, IL.

McHugh, J., & Widom, J. (1999). *Query optimization for XML.* Paper presented in the 25th International Conference on Very Large Data Bases, Edinburgh, Scotland.

MemBeR XML Generator. (n.d.). Retrieved April 3, 2009, from http://ilps.science.uva.nl/Resources/MemBeR/member-generator.html

Nicola, M., Kogan, I., & Schiefer, B. (2007). *An XML transaction processing benchmark.* Paper presented at SIGMOD'07, Beijing, China.

Runapongsa, K., Patel, J. M., Jagadish, H. V., Chen, Y., & Al-Khalifa, S. (2002). *The Michigan benchmark: towards XML query performance diagnostics.* Retrieved from http://www.eecs.umich.edu/db/mbench

Runapongsa, K., Patel, J. M., Jagadish, H. V., Chen, Y., & Al-Khalifa, S. (2003). *The Michigan benchmark: towards XML query performance diagnostics*. Paper presented at the 29th VLDB Conference, Berlin, Germany.

Sahuguet, A. (2001). *Kweelt: More than just "yet another framework to query XML!* Paper presented at ACM SIGMOD, Santa Barbara, CA.

Sakr, S. (2008). *XSelMark: A micro-benchmark for selectivity estimation approaches of XML queries*. Paper presented at the 19th International Conference on Database and Expert Systems Applications (DEXA 2008), Turin, Italy.

Schmidt, A. (2003). *XMark-An XML Benchmark project*. Retrieved Febrary 25, 2009, from http://monetdb.cwi.nl/xml/

Schmidt, A., Waas, F., Kersten, M., Carey, M. J., Manolescu, I., & Busse, R. (2002). *XMark: A benchmark for XML data management*. Paper presented at the 28th Very Large Data Base (VLDB), Hong Kong, China.

Schmidt, A., Waas, F., Kersten, M., Florescu, D., Manolescu, I., & Carey, M. J. & Busse, R. (2001). *The XML Benchmark Project*. (Tech. rep. INS-R0103). Amsterdam, The Netherlands, CWI.

Shaya, E., Gass, J., Blackwell, J., Thomas, B., Holmes, B., Cheung, C., et al. (2000). *XML at the ADC: Steps to a Next Generation Data Repository*. Retrieved June 17, 2009, from http://www.adass.org/adass/proceedings/adass99/O9-05/

The, A. C. M. *SIGMOD Anthology*. (n.d.). Retrieved June 17, 2009, from http://www.sigmod.org/sigmod/anthology/index.htm

Weis, M., Naumann, F., & Brosy, F. (2006). *A duplicate detection benchmark for XML (and relational) data*. Paper presented at the SIGMOD workshop on Information Quality for Information Systems (IQIS), Chicago, IL.

Yao, B. B. (2003). *XBench- A family of benchmarks for XML DBMSs*. Retrieved February 15, 2009, from http://se.uwaterloo.ca/~ddbms/projects/xbench/

Yao, B. B., Özsu, M. T., & Keenleyside, J. (2002). *XBench—A family of benchmarks for XML DBMSs*. Paper presented at Efficiency and Effectiveness of XML Tools and Techniques and Data Integration over the Web, (EEXTT), Hong Kong, China.

Yao, B. B., Özsu, M. T., & Khandelwal, N. (2004). *XBench benchmark and performance testing of XML DBMSs*. Paper presented at the 20th International Conference on Data Engineering, Boston, MA.

Section 2
XML Index and Query

Chapter 5
Index Structures for XML Databases

Samir Mohammad
Queen's University, Canada

Patrick Martin
Queen's University, Canada

ABSTRACT

Extensible Markup Language (XML), which provides a flexible way to define semistructured data, is a de facto standard for information exchange in the World Wide Web. The trend towards storing data in its XML format has meant a rapid growth in XML databases and the need to query them. Indexing plays a key role in improving the execution of a query. In this chapter the authors give a brief history of the creation and the development of the XML data model. They discuss the three main categories of indexes proposed in the literature to handle the XML semistructured data model and provide an evaluation of indexing schemes within these categories. Finally, they discuss limitations and open problems related to the major existing indexing schemes.

INTRODUCTION

XML is becoming the dominant method of exchanging data over the Internet. It was endorsed as a W3C recommendation in 1998 (Bary, Paoli, & Sperberg-McQueen, 1998). Its roots go back to SGML (Standard Generalized Markup Language) (Bary et al., 1998). XML poses a nested hierarchical nature. An example XML document is illustrated in Figure 1. It is based on DBLP (The DBLP Computer Science Bibliography, 2009), a popular computer

science bibliography dataset. The data-tree shape in Figure 2 represents the data in the XML document of Figure 1.

The growth in the use of XML for data exchange has led to the introduction of native XML databases to store and manage the data directly in its XML representation. Since the repetition of XML data is irregular due to missing and/or repeated arbitrary elements, its storage structure can be scattered over many different locations on the disk, which decreases the performance of XML queries (Chung, Min, & Shim, 2002). Furthermore, the flexibility of specifications of the XML queries (e.g. use of

DOI: 10.4018/978-1-61520-727-5.ch005

Figure 1. DBLP like XML document

```
<Bib>
    <book>
        <author>Tim</author>
    </book>
    <paper> </paper>
    <paper>
        <author>Sarah</author>
    </paper>
    <paper @reviewer="Ahmad">
        <author>Wang</author>
    </paper>
</Bib>
```

wild cards) adds to the challenge of indexing methods (Wang, Park, Fan, & Yu, 2003; Zou, Liu, & Chu, 2004).

The best way to judge the strength of an indexing technique is to compare it with other techniques using common criteria that are applicable for all of them and can act as a benchmark. The main contributions in this chapter are:

• A set of common criteria to summarize the characteristics of the most popular indexing techniques used for XML databases.

• Classify novel classification of graph indexes that is based on the presence/degree of determinism and the bisimilarity direction(s) of indexing, which control the size of an index and its query answering power, respectively.

In the remainder of this chapter we discuss a number of approaches to XML indexing. We first give an overview of XML data models and the XPath query language. We next explain the three types of indexing techniques used for XML data, namely, Node index scheme, Graph index scheme, and Sequence index scheme; and compare approaches of each type. We divide the comparison criteria into four basic groups:

• **Retrieval power:** Which includes the precision and completeness of the result, and the type of queries supported.

• **Processing complexity:** Which involves the need to compute the relationship between elements (such as the parent/child and the ancestor/descendent relationships), the need for structural joins to answer a

Figure 2. Edge-labeled data-tree

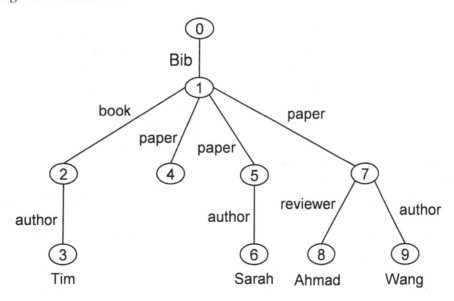

query, and the need for additional refine-ment steps to fine-tune answers.

- **Scalability** of the index and its *adaptabil-ity* to queries with different path lengths.
- **Update cost:** Which is measured by the number of nodes that are touched during update.

BACKGROUND

XML documents can be represented as directed graphs. For example, the directed graph in Figure 2 represents the XML document in Figure 1. The "mapping" of an XML document to a graph may result in an acyclic graph (e.g. Figure 2), which is tree shaped, or in a cyclic graph (if ID/IDREF tokens are used). While some indexes support all graph data (cyclic and acyclic graphs), others only support tree-shaped data. In this section, we review two common models for semistructured documents and the XPath query language, which is used in this chapter to express queries.

Data Models

Gou and Chirkova (2007) identify four basic data models to represent the hierarchical structure of XML documents: edge-labeled tree data model, node-labeled tree shaped data model, directed acyclic graph (DAG) data model, and directed graph with cycles data model. In this chapter we only review the first two data models.

Edge-Labeled Tree Data Model

Figure 2 is an example of an edge-labeled model for the XML document in Figure 1. Each edge represents an element or an attribute in the XML document. For example, "author" is an element, and "@reviewer" is an attribute. The leaf nodes represent the values of the elements or attributes. For example, "Ahmad" and "Wang" are values for the "@reviewer" attribute and "author" ele-

ment, respectively. The element in the fifth line in Figure 1 is an example of an empty element. Note that in a tree structure an element cannot have more than one parent.

Node-Labeled Tree Data Model

Figure 3 is an example of a node-labeled data-tree for the XML document in Figure 1. As in the edge-labeled model, it contains three main components: elements, attributes, and values. The main difference is that a node in the node-labeled tree represents an element as opposed to an edge in the edge-labeled model. The hierarchal and nesting structure of both models is self-evident in the trees that they represent.

X-Path

Many APIs (Application Program Interfaces) have been proposed to access XML data, such as the standard Document Object Model (DOM) (Goldman, McHugh, & Widom, 1999) and Simple API for XML (SAX) (Megginson & Brownell, 2004). However, neither one of these APIs provides enough capabilities to manipulate and query XML data. Motivated by this fact, query languages such as XPath (XML Path Language) (Clark & DeRose, 1999) and XQuery (Vakali, Catania, & Maddalena, 2005) were proposed. XPath supports thirteen types of relationships or axes including child ("/"), descendant ("//"), parent, ancestor, ancestor-or-self, descendant-or-self, following, following-sibling, preceding, preceding-sibling, attribute, self, and namespace. In this chapter we concentrate on the child "/" and descendent "//" axes.

An XML query may be either a simple single-path query with or without a predicate, or a complex twig query with or without a predicate. A complex twig query with a predicate specifies patterns of selection on multiple elements related to one another by a tree structure. For example, "q1" below is a simple path query.

Figure 3. Node-labeled data-tree

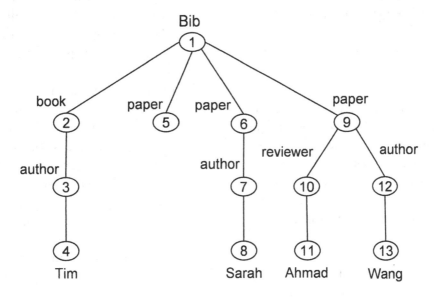

```
q1: /Bib/paper/author
```

If we run this query against the XML document in Figure 3, it returns the results "Sarah" and "Wang," which are the values of the "author" elements under the "paper" elements under the "Bib" element. Query "q2" is an example of a complex twig query. It asks for the author of a paper that has a reviewer "Ahmad," and the query returns the author "Wang."

```
q2: //paper[/reviewer="Ahmad"]/
author
```

STRUCTURAL INDEXING SCHEMES FOR XML DATA

Generally, structural indexes can be grouped into three categories:

- *Node indexes* (Li & Moon, 2001; Zhang, Naughton, Dewitt, Luo, & Lohman, 2001)

depend on labeling schemes including interval labeling (Dietz, 1982) and prefix labeling (Tatarinov, Viglas, Beyer, Shanmugasundaram, Shekita, & Zhang, 2002; Online Computer Library Centre, 2008; Lu, Ling, Chan, & Chen, 2005).

- *Graph indexes* include indexes that cover either path queries only (Chung et al., 2002; Cooper, Sample, Franklin, Hjaltason, & Shadmon, 2001; Goldman & Widom, 1997) or both path and twig queries (Kaushik, Bohannon, Naughton, & Korth, 2002). We divide graph indexes in this chapter into three types depending on their deterministic property and bisimilarity direction(s) (see *Graph Indexing Schemes* section).

- *Sequence indexes* (Rao & Moon, 2004; Wang et al., 2003) interpret a query as a structured series of sequences and search for a match in the structured encoded sequence of an XML document.

Criteria for Evaluation of Structural Indexing Schemes

We evaluate the indexing schemes according to the following set of criteria:

- **Precision:** When a query is evaluated, the results returned may be complete and precise, or they may require further processing. Obviously, the first option is more efficient if the measurements of time taken to produce the initial answer for the two options are approximately equal. A structural index is precise iff the returned answer does not contain any incorrect answers.

- **Recall:** This is the probability that all relevant documents are retrieved by the query. If the recall achieved is 100%, we say that the result is complete.

- **Processing complexity:** This criterion covers different kinds of complexity depending on the type of indexing scheme that is used. It covers the primary processing procedure as well as additional join processing.

- **(A) Scalability:** Large indexes may involve many I/O accesses. These accesses increase the processing time of a query. Some indexes expand linearly with the size of the source data, while others increase exponentially with the size of the data. The second type imposes restrictions on the data growth.

- **(B) Adaptability:** Graphical indexes partition the data into equivalence classes based on their determinism and bisimilarity (backward bisimilarity, or forward and backward bisimilarity). Two nodes are backward bisimilar if they share the same incoming paths and forward bisimialr if they share the same outgoing paths. The bisimilarity can be specified by a factor "k". Two nodes are backward k-bisimilar if they share the same incoming paths of a

length = "k." Setting the value of "k" to a small value results in a small index, while a large value of "k" results in a large index. The length of the path in queries varies depending on the users' needs. If a graph index is used regularly to evaluate short-path queries, then a small k-value index is sufficient. In contrast, long-path queries need a large k-value index. Based on these observations, and depending on the queries, it would be useful if the size of the index could be adjusted by a given parameter "k" that represents the length of bisimilarity according to the users' need.

- **Type of queries supported:** The two types of XML queries are path queries and twig queries.

- **Update cost of insertion of a node or a subtree:** The nodes in a given tree index have to be maintained in a certain organization in order to reflect ancestor/descendent, parent/child, and sibling relationships. When a new node is inserted into the tree, these relationships have to be preserved. Consequently, the index has to reflect its position with regard to these relationships, which adds more complexity, especially if there are no gaps in the numbering scheme that is used to label nodes. We study two types of updates: (1) the insertion of a node, which represents a small incremental change for an edge addition (for all indexing schemes); (2) the insertion of a subtree, which represents the addition of a new file (for some indexing schemes).

Node Indexing Schemes

Node indexes hold values that reflect the nodes' positions within the structure of an XML tree. They can be used to find a given node's parent, child, sibling, ancestor, and descendent nodes. These numbers can be used to solve simple path and twig path queries. Paths are solved through many steps. At each step, a structural join is performed between two nodes starting from one end of the path and finishing at the other end (Al-Khalifa, Jagadish, Koudas, Patel, Srivastava, & Wu, 2002; Li & Moon, 2001; Zhang et al., 2001).

Two of the most widely used labeling schemes are interval and prefix labeling. In the following, we take the (Beg, End) labeling scheme as an example of the interval labeling and the Dewey scheme as an example of the prefix labeling.

Criteria for Evaluation of Node Indexes

In addition to the general evaluation criteria listed above, we refine the processing complexity criterion into the following specific criteria.

Processing complexity:
- **Relationship computation:** To confirm a relationship between two given nodes, certain operations have to be performed. These operations depend on the type of the relationship. They also depend on the type of the labeling scheme that is used.
- **Relationships supported:** Basically there are three types of relationships:
  - *Ancestor/descendent relationship*: This relationship is needed to solve queries with the "//" axis.
  - *Parent/child relationship*: It is useful to solve queries with the "/" axis.
  - *Sibling relationship*: In some cases, a group of sibling nodes form an answer for a twig query.
- **Ability to infer parent/ancestor and child/descendent nodes:** There are two approaches for solving queries, especially the ones with predicates, that is, top-down and bottom-up. A bottom-up approach is useful

when the parent/ancestor nodes of a matched leaf node, for a given query, can be inferred from the matched leaf node. Also, identifying child/descendent nodes is helpful when the top-down approach is used to solve a query.
- **Data type used in indexing scheme:** Comparing different data types involves different algorithms with different operations. As an illustration, comparing two numbers usually requires less time than that of comparing two sequences of strings.

Interval Labeling Scheme

The (Beg,End) labeling schemes is an examples of interval labeling scheme. Zhang et al. (2001) introduce it to index the elements in a document. It assigns a pair of numbers to each node in an XML document according to its sequential traversal order. Since the value of an element is a leaf node, the "Beg" number of this value is equal to the "End" number. Figure 4 is an example of (Beg,End) labeling scheme for the XML document in Figure 1. The beginning and the ending numbers imply the positions of the opening tag (<..>) and the closing tag (</..>), respectively, in an XML document.

This labeling scheme enables us to find the ancestor-descendant relationship as indicated in "property 1" below. A "Level" is added to the (Beg,End) label to form a node-triplet identification label (Beg,End,Level) for each node in the tree, where "Level" represents the depth of an element in the tree (Zhang et al., 2001). This triplet identification label is used to infer the parent-child relationship as indicated in "property 2."

- *Property 1* (Ancestor-descendant relationship): In a given data-tree, node "x" is an ancestor of node "y" iff x.Beg < y.Beg < x.End.

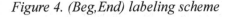

Figure 4. (Beg,End) labeling scheme

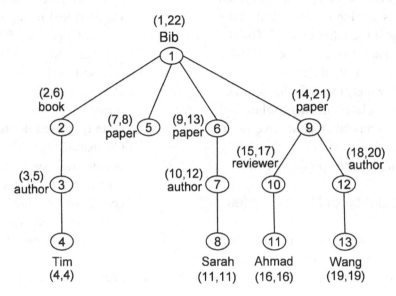

For example, in Figure 4, node (1,22) is an ancestor of the node (3,5).

*   *Property 2* (Parent-child relationship): In a given data-tree, node "x" is a parent of node "y" iff x.Beg < y.Beg < x.End and y.Level = x.Level + 1.

For example, in Figure 4, node (1,22,1) is a parent to the node (2,6,2).

The (Beg,End) scheme can be used to solve a twig query by using structural joins. The relations that are supported by the node approach are the parent/child ("/") and the ancestor/descendent ("//") relationships. The (Beg,End) labeling scheme is used to infer the relationship between two nodes at a time. It requires only a single comparison to infer any of these two relations. However, the number of joins required to evaluate an XML query using a node index is equal to the number of nodes in the query minus one, which is high for large twig queries.

The (Beg,End) labeling scheme can be used to solve both path queries and twig queries. For a given query, the relationship between any two nodes within a path in the query is investigated separately because this indexing scheme's granularity is defined at the level of each node and hence the answer for a given query will be precise and complete.

Since the nodes' index numbers are chosen sequentially, or randomly in an increasing order, and the tree is not necessarily balanced, there is no way to locate the siblings of a given node, using only the knowledge of its index numbers. Furthermore, the exact ancestor and descendent index numbers of a node can-not be inferred. It is possible to know the range within which the parent/ancestor or the child/descendent nodes are located, but the exact number of these nodes can-not be determined.

Unlike a prefix labeling scheme, which we explain in the next section, the interval labeling scheme is best used for immutable encoding. Some "durable" schemes, for example Li and

Figure 5. Dewey labeling scheme

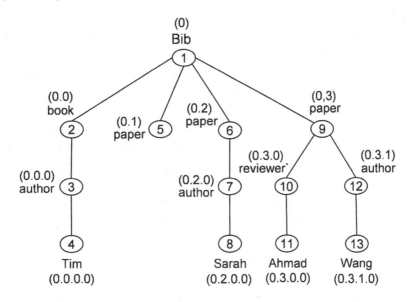

Moon (2001), suggest leaving gaps between the interval values for new nodes to be inserted. After filling these gaps, renumbering or other solutions are required. Cohen, Kaplan, and Milo (2002) proved that immutable (persistent) labeling, which preserves the order of an XML tree, requires O(n) bits per label where "n" is the size of the tree. The complexity is measured in the size of the interval labels because this size determines the total size of the index. It is desirable to keep the used number of bits small enough so that the index can fit in memory. Silberstein, He, Yi, and Yang (2005) designed dynamic labeling structures for interval indexes that allow relabeling by using only O(log n) bits per label.

Interval labeling schemes require modest storage space. Regardless of the depth of the data-tree, each node is represented by only two numbers, and we can determine the relationship between any two nodes in constant time by using a comparison operation between the index numbers. Nevertheless, updating the labeling scheme of these types of indexes is costly. When a new

node is inserted into the tree, then all the nodes in the tree, except the left sibling subtrees of the inserted node, have to be updated.

Prefix Labeling Scheme

Dewey labeling, which is an example of a prefix labeling scheme, is another coding scheme that was originally made for general knowledge classification (Online Computer Library Centre, 2008). Tatarinov et al. (2002) first used it for XML tree-shaped data. Figure 5 is an example of the Dewey labeling scheme for the XML document in Figure 1. Each node label represents the node location within a path by including its ancestors' coding as a prefix (vertical coordinate), and it also includes the node number within its siblings of the same parent (horizontal coordinate). The level is implicitly included by counting the number of segments that are separated by a delimiter (dot in our example in Figure 5) in the Dewey label.

To decide if a parent/child or an ancestor/descendent relationship exists, we perform a prefix matching operation on the index string. In a given data-tree, node "x" is an ancestor of node "y" if the label of node "x" is a substring of the label of node "y." For example, node (0.3) is an ancestor of node (0.3.1.0). Unlike the (Beg,End) labeling scheme, the Dewey labeling scheme does not require any additional information in order to evaluate the parent/child relationship. For example, it is easy to see that node (0.3) is the parent of node (0.3.1).

The sibling relationship can be computed in the same way without the need for any additional information (e.g. level number or parent ID). The Dewey label provides direct support for the sibling relationship. In a given tree, node "x" and node "y" are siblings if nodes "x" and "y" have the same number of fragments in their labels (call it "n") and x.prefix = y.prefix (where the prefix length equal to "n" minus one). For example, node (0.3.0) and node (0.3.1) are siblings.

Dewey labels are much easier to update than (Beg,End) labels. When a new node is inserted, only the nodes in the subtree rooted at the following sibling need to be updated (Tatarinov et al., 2002). However, its storage size increases with the depth of the tree. Furthermore, as the depth increases, it becomes more costly to infer the parent/child or the ancestor/descendent relationship between any two arbitrary nodes because the string prefix matching becomes longer.

Fisher, Lam, Shui, and Wong (2006) propose a dynamic labeling approach that can be applied to Dewey labels with identifiers of size O(log n) when there is type information in the form of a DTD or Schema, where "n" is the size of the database. Similar to all labeling schemes, immutable Dewey labeling requires O(n) bits per label (Cohen et al., 2002).

It is easy to infer the exact ancestor or descendent of a given node in Dewey labeling scheme indexes. For example, in Figure 5 the ancestors of the node (0.3.1) are the nodes that start with (0.3) or (0) prefix, and the descendents are the nodes that start with the (0.3.1) prefix such as node (0.3.1.0). Since the complete path is recorded

within a node index, Dewey labeling scheme indexes return a precise and a complete answer for both path queries and twig queries. Path and twig queries need join operations in order to be solved, specifically the number of nodes in the query minus one operations are required.

Summary of Node Indexes

Table 1 contains a summary of the two types of labeling schemes; for further discussion see (Mohammad & Martin, 2009). The precision of an index scheme is either precise (does not return any false answers) or imprecise (may contain some false answers along with the correct answers). If the recall achieved is 100% then the result is complete, otherwise it is incomplete. Relationship computation is constant if we can determine the relationship between any two arbitrary nodes in constant time, regardless of the depth of the data-tree. The relationships supported are ancestor/descendent, parent/child, and sibling relationships. The data type is either a number or a string. The types of queries supported by these node indexing schemes are path and twig queries. The evaluation of these queries may require join operations. The maintenance cost of the indexes depends on the number of elements and whether or not the index is mutable or immutable.

Both types are equivalent with respect to precision, completeness (recall), and maintainability. However, they differ with respect to the other characteristics. The (Beg,End) labeling scheme requires constant time to compute a relationship between any two arbitrary nodes for two reasons. First, it uses numerical values to index the nodes. Second, the size of the label that is used to index each node is fixed regardless of the level (depth) at which each node is located. On the other hand, in Dewey labeling schemes, the time that is required to compute the relationship between any two arbitrary nodes is directly proportional to the depth of the nodes for two reasons. First, Dewey labeling schemes use strings to represent labels instead of integers. Second, the labels' size

Table 1. Comparison of interval labeling scheme and prefix labeling scheme

No.	Criteria		Interval Labeling (Beg,End)	Prefix Labeling (Dewey)
1	Precision		Precise	Precise
2	Recall		Complete	Complete
3	Computation Complexity	Relationship Computation	Constant	Directly proportional to depth increase
		Relationship supported	- Ancestor/Descendent - Child/Parent (if "Level" is available)	All
		Can infer exact ancestor & descendent nodes	No	Yes
		Data type	Numerical	String
4	Size/Scalability for increasing depth		Linear	Exponential
5	Type of queries Supported efficiently		None	None
6	Maintenance cost	Mutable	O (log n)	O (log n)
		Immutable	O (n)	O (n)

increases as the depth increases. Unlike (Beg,End) labels, each Dewey label contains the root path (the path from the root to the designated node) information. Therefore, with Dewey labels, we can infer any node's parent/child or ancestor/ descendent from the label of the node. Finally, prefix labels are often easier to update than interval labels, although, the cost of maintaining prefix labels can be the same as the cost of maintaining interval labels in the worst case.

Graph Indexing Schemes

A graph index (a.k.a. summary index) is a structural path summary that can be used to improve query efficiency, especially for single path queries. It is also capable of solving twig queries but with an additional cost of multiple join operations.

Graph indexes consider paths, during query evaluation, as a whole path instead of dealing with each node in the path separately. A subsequent step is needed to join simple paths together in order to solve a twig query. In contrast to node indexes, the number of joins is reduced during

query processing and consequently query performance is improved.

Graph indexes have been categorized according to many criteria. For example, Gou and Chirkova (2007) group them into two classes, path indexes, which are able to cover simple path queries (such as DataGuides and 1-index), and twig indexes, which are able to cover twig queries (such as F&B-index). Graph indexes can also be categorized according to their path exactness (Polyzotis & Garofalakis, 2002). Some schemes are exact such as strong DataGuide, Index Fabric, 1-index, and F&B-index; while others are approximate such as approximate DataGuide, A(k)-index, D(k)-index, and (F+B)^k-index.

Our classification considers the important properties of an index:

- **Path determinism:** If the index tree is a Deterministic Finite Automata, then the paths of the tree are considered to be deterministic paths. This feature assures that every distinct path in an index graph is represented only once. Otherwise, multiple identical paths may exist in the index, which may add to the complexity of query evaluation. Deterministic indexes guarantee uniqueness of paths, and non-deterministic indexes guarantee the uniqueness of elements. Deterministic indexes are therefore suitable for simple path queries, where the complete path is known.

- **Bisimilarity:** There are two types of bisimilarity, namely, forward and backward bisimilarity. The direction of bisimilarity significantly affects the size of an index and the answering power of an index to a given query. Non-deterministic graph indexes with only backward bisimilarity tend to have lower accuracy (which is corrected by some post-processing steps) but their sizes are minimal. In contrast, graph indexes with forward and backward bisimilarity have higher accuracy and cover twig queries, but their sizes are larger than those of backward bisimilar indexes.

Based on path determinism and bisimilarity, we classify graph indexes as follows:

- **Deterministic graph indexes:** This includes DataGuides (Goldman & Widom,1997), approximate DataGuide (Goldman & Widom, 1999), and Index Fabrics (Cooper et al., 2001).
- **Non-deterministic graph indexes with backward bisimilarity:** This includes 1-index (Milo & Suciu, 1999), A(k)-index (Kaushik, Shenoy, Bohannon, & Gudes, 2002), and D(k)-index (Chen, Lim, & Ong, 2003).
- **Non-deterministic graph indexes with forward and backward bisimilarity:***This includes* F&B-index (Gou & Chirkova, 2007; Abiteboul, Buneman, & Suciu, 2002) and (F+B)^k-index (Kaushik, Bohannon, Naughton, & Korth, 2002).

We elaborate the development of graph index schemes according to these three classes and analyze the schemes using the general criteria given earlier.

Deterministic Graph Indexes

In deterministic graph indexes, each unique path in a data graph is listed once in the summary graph, and every path in a summary graph has at least one matching path in the data graph. Two indexing schemes of this type are strong DataGuides and Index Fabrics.

Strong DataGuide

Goldman and Widom (1997) present one of the early structure summaries called a strong DataGuide. In this scheme, the nodes in the source data are partitioned based on their root path. The graph index of an XML data-graph is a strong DataGuide if it fulfills two conditions:

- Every distinct root path in the source data appears only once in the graph index.
- All the paths in the graph index have at least one matching root path in the original source data. In other words, there are no invalid paths in the graph index.

Figure 7 contains an XML data tree and its associated graph indexes. To simplify the comparison between different schemes in Figure 7, we assume an edge-labeled graph structure, use numbers inside the nodes to represent the node IDs, and use letters to represent the elements (tag types) of the source XML data. The letters (B,P,A, and R) in Figure 7(B) stand for book, paper, author, and reviewer in Figure 7(A), respectively. Figure 7(A) is a modified version of the XML data-tree in Figure 2. Unlike node indexes, graph indexes are capable of supporting DAG data such as in Figure 7(A).

The graph index in Figure 7(B) is a strong DataGuide for the data in Figure 7(A). Note that

Figure 7. XML data-tree and its corresponding graph indexes

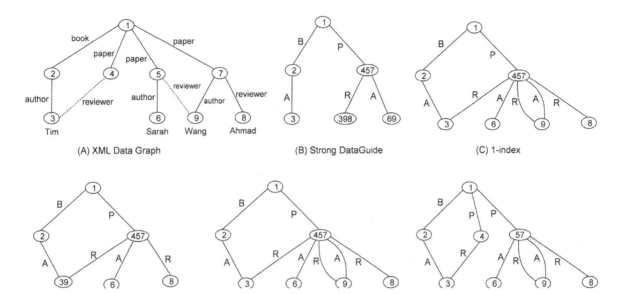

(A) XML Data Graph   (B) Strong DataGuide   (C) 1-index

node number "3" occurs in both the "/B/A" and "/P/R" paths. Node number "9" occurs in both the "/P/R" and "/P/A" paths. One may argue that being deterministic is an advantage of the strong DataGuide structure index. Nevertheless, a node's repetition is directly proportional to the existence of multiple parent nodes and cycles in the source data. In the worst case, the structural index size may exceed the original size of the data and hence it may lose its essential characteristic of a *summary*. In the case of DAG data, the size may be exponential in the size of the original data. Tree-shaped XML data, on the other hand, requires storage space, in the worst case, equal to the size of the data itself.

Strong DataGuides are capable of giving a complete and precise result for simple parent/child path queries (Kaushik, Bohannon, Naughton, & Korth, 2002) such as "/B/A" in our example, which returns the node {3}. They are also complete and precise for ancestor/descendent path queries. For instance, the query "//R," in our example, returns the nodes {3,8,9}.

Strong DataGuides are complete for twig queries but not precise (Kaushik, Bohannon, Naughton, & Korth, 2002). For example, evaluating query "/P[/A]/R," which returns an "R" node that has a "P" parent node and an "A" sibling node, over the strong DataGuide index in Figure 7(B) returns index nodes {3,8,9}. This answer is complete because the returned set includes the correct answer {8,9}, but it is not precise as node {3} does not belong to the correct answer.

The complexity of maintaining strong DataGuides depends on the structural effect of the updates. Updating strong DataGuides could be as simple as inserting a new leaf into tree-structured data, which requires only one target set to be recomputed and one new object to be added to the strong DataGuide. In the worst case, updating a tree with a subgraph of structured data that has loops and sharing may incur recomputation of a large portion of the strong DataGuide. An edge insertion update requires touching a number of nodes and edges that is equal to $O(n + m)$ in the worst case, where "n" is the number of nodes (objects) and "m" is the number of edges of a strong DataGuide.

Figure 8. Index Fabric of the data-tree in Figure 2

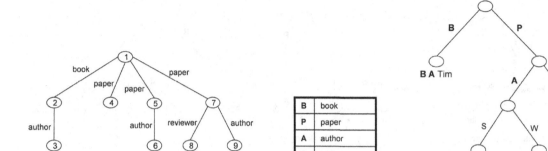

B	book
P	paper
A	author
R	reviewer

Index Fabric

Index Fabric is proposed by Cooper et al. (2001) as a solution for very large indexes that may not fit in memory. Index Fabric utilizes its paging capabilities to solve the size problem. It uses prefix-encoding to represent paths as strings. These strings are classified and sorted by a special index called the Index Fabric. The index structure is designed specifically for complete path queries that start from the document root node. Other paths such as descendent path queries "//" require a post-processing stage and expensive index look-ups. The notion of *refined paths* (template paths) is proposed by the authors to solve this problem. However, the refined paths are not dynamic and need to be determined prior to index creation and loading time.

The Index Fabric indexes both paths and values in a tree. As an example, each edge of the data-tree in Figure 8(A) (which is the same as the XML data-tree in Figure 2) is given a designator as illustrated in Figure 8 (B). The edge labels along with the content of the data-tree are combined at the leaf nodes to form a path index for each value in the tree. Note that compression is used to minimize the size of the tree as follows. In Figure 8(C), since "book" edges are followed by an "author" edge,

the bold capital "B" designates the path "/B/A" (book and author), instead of "/B" alone.

A major contribution of the Index Fabric is its layered-based paging strategy to index large data. This feature makes it possible to handle very large indexes. The index structure is stored on disk and divided into multiple blocks of approximately equal size, each of which holds a small sub-Trie. The Tries of the lower levels are referenced by higher level Tries in the Index Fabric, and so forth until we reach the root Trie, which can fit in one block. The number of the Index Fabric levels is based on the size of the original data.

Index Fabric is conceptually similar to strong DataGuide (Wang et al., 2003; Chung et al., 2002). It is deterministic and its size may grow exponentially in the size of the original data for the DAG data, and linearly for the tree-shaped data. Furthermore, it is complete and precise for path queries, and complete for twig queries but not precise. DAG data can be indexed by an Index Fabric, but Index Fabric is more efficient for tree-shaped data.

The Index Fabric is a balanced structure tree like a B-tree. Updating an Index Fabric may include a deletion of one record and an insertion of another. The insertion may cause one block per level of the tree to split in the worst case.

Non-Deterministic Graph Indexes with Backward Bisimilarity

The 1-index, the A(k)-index, and the D(k)-index are based on backward bisimilarity partitioning. While the 1-index backward bisimilarity length is equal to the length of the longest path in the data-graph, the A(k)-index and the D(k)-index backward bisimilarity lengths are set by a value "k." The "k" value in the A(k)-index is set manually, and the "k" value in the D(k)-index is set automatically. In this section we only review the 1-index and the A(k)-index.

(1-index)

Milo and Suciu (1999) propose 1-index as an attempt to reduce the size of a structural summary to less than that of a strong DataGuide by relaxing the determinism constraint. Figure 7(C) is an example of 1-index for the data in Figure 7(A). The 1-index partitions the data nodes of a document into equivalence classes based on their backward bisimilarity from the root node to the indexed node. Both strong DataGuide and 1-index are identical in the case of simple XML data-trees. In the case of DAG data, however, a 1-index may contain similar root paths, but represents each node in the source data-graph only once, and hence it is possible for a node to be reachable by multiple paths (see nodes "3" and "9" in Figure 7(C) for example). Based on this fact, we can say that the 1-index scheme is non-deterministic in nature. In the worst case, the size of 1-index will never exceed the size of the original data regardless of whether the data source is a basic tree or a graph. Nevertheless, 1-index structural summaries are often too large, and are considered inefficient when the original source data is large and irregular (Chen, et al., 2003).

It is easy to see from Figure 7(C) that 1-index is complete and precise for evaluating path queries such as "/B/A" and "//R", and is complete but not precise for evaluating twig queries like "/P[/A]/R". In General, 1-index is always complete, but not necessarily precise (Kaushik, Shenoy, et al., 2002).

Kaushik, Bohannon, Naughton, and Shenoy (2002) review two kinds of updates for the 1-index, namely, the addition of a subgraph, and the addition of an edge. Let the data-graph before the addition of the new file be G, the 1-index be IG, H is a new subgraph, and the 1-index for H be IH. Let the number of nodes in IG, H, and IH be nIG, nH, and nIH, respectively, and the number of edges be mIG, mH, and mIH, respectively. The time taken by the subgraph addition is $O(mHlog(nH) + (mIH + mIG)log(nIH + nIG))$. Note that this is independent of the size of G, but dependent on the size of IG, which is usually smaller than the size of the data-graph.

The complexity of edge addition is measured by the number of nodes and edges touched in the data-graph during propagation, which can be $O(n + m)$ in the worst case scenario, where m is the number of edges in G (Kaushik, Bohannon, Naughton, & Shenoy, 2002).

A(k)-Index

The dominant disadvantage of strong DataGuide and 1-index is the size of their indexes when the source data is large and irregular. A(k)-index is proposed by Kaushik, Shenoy, et al. (2002), mainly to overcome the size problem. Similar to 1-index, A(k)-index (Figure 7 (D & E)) is based on backward bisimilarity and is non-deterministic. A(k)-index uses a mechanism to minimize the size of the graph indexes by specifying a factor "k" that is used to decide the length of the backward bisimilarity of the indexed nodes.

The size of an A(k)-index is generally smaller than that of a strong DataGuide and a 1-index. Similar to the 1-index scheme, A(k)-index grows linearly in the size of the source data regardless of the shape of the data. A smaller value of "k" results in a smaller index. A(k)-index gains the advantage of having a smaller size at the expense of precision since the index does not necessarily reflect the complete path from the root node.

Since the A(k)-index is based on equivalence-class partitioning of nodes in a data-graph, it is usually complete but not necessarily precise (Kaushik, Shenoy, et al., 2002). Let us take an A(1)-index for the data in Figure 7(A), which is illustrated in Figure 7(D), as an example. For path queries such as "//R", A(1)- index is complete and precise as it will return the node set {3,8,9}. Although, it is complete for the path queries such as "/B/A", as it will return {3,9}, which is a superset of the correct answer {3}, it is not precise as the answer set contains the wrong answer "9." It is only precise for path queries with a length that is less than or equal to the length set by the "*k*" value. For example, an A(2)-index, as illustrated in Figure 7(E), is complete and precise for both "/B/A" and "//R" queries. Note that Figure 7(E) is identical to the 1-index in Figure 7(C). Actually, a 1-index is a special case of A(k)-index where "*k*" value is equal to the depth of a data-tree (the longest path in a tree). A(k)-index is complete but not precise for twig queries like "/P[/A]/R".

The subgraph addition algorithm for the 1-index extends to the A(k)-index. Unfortunately, the edge insertion algorithm does not extend and hence the edge insertion for the A(k)-index remains an open problem (Kaushik, Bohannon, Naughton, & Shenoy, 2002).

Non-Deterministic Graph Indexes with (Forward & Backward) Bisimilarity

We review two types of indexing schemes under this class of graph indexes: the F&B-index and the (F+B)^k-index. They are non-deterministic like the above type of graph indexes (1-index and A(k)-index), but they differ with respect to size and query answering power as they are larger and they cover twig queries as well as path queries.

F&B-index

The F&B-index was introduced by Abiteboul et al. (2002). It is based on the incoming and the outgoing (forward and backward) bisimilarity of all nodes in the source data-graph. It is therefore considered to be a twig structural index scheme.

To demonstrate the benefits of this indexing scheme, consider the twig query "/P[/A]/R". Evaluating this query over strong DataGuide (Figure 7(B)), 1-index (Figure 7(C)), or A(2)-index (Figure 7(E)), returns a set of "R" nodes {3,8,9}. We see that "R" node "3" does not contribute to the correct answer, yet it is returned in the initial steps by all the indexes. Eventually, it is eliminated from the final answer after performing some additional join steps. In contrast, as illustrated in Figure 7(F), the F&B-index detects this mismatch early and is able to exclude "R" node "3", therefore avoiding the additional joins and improving efficiency. F&B-index therefore is complete and precise for twig queries as well as for path queries.

The F&B-index is non-deterministic. The size of the index grows linearly in the size of the source data document, and in the worst case does not exceed the original data size for both data shapes (tree and graph). Kaushik, Bohannon, Naughton, and Korth (2002) proved that F&B-index is the smallest index covering all branches of a given XML graph. However, the size of an F&B-index is often too large to fit in memory. To update the F&B-index when a subgraph or an edge is added to the data-graph, approaches similar to those used for updating the 1-Index by Kaushik, Bohannon, Naughton, and Shenoy (2002) can be adopted.

Kaushik, Bohannon, Naughton, and Korth (2002) propose (F+B)^k-index, which is a modified version of the F&B-index. They manage the size of the F&B-index by specifying the value of "*k*" (Gou & Chirkova, 2007). A low value of "*k*" results in an index that can cover limited classes of branching path queries, but the index size is often small. A high value of "*k*," on the other hand, can cover a wide range of classes of branching path queries at the expense of the size since the size of the index is often large. With regard to the rest of the comparison criteria, both F&B-index and (F+B)^k-index have the same features. The idea of (F+B)^k-index as an extension to F&B-

Figure 9. Comparison between the three categories of graph indexing approaches

Criteria		Deterministic	Non-deterministic Backward Bisimilar	Non-deterministic Forward & Backward Bisimilar
Criteria		Strong DataGuide, Index Fabric	1-index, A(k)-index	F&B-index, (F+B)^k-index
1-Precision	Path	Precise	Precise	Precise
1-Precision	Twig	Not Precise	Not Precise	Precise
2-Recall	Path	Complete	Complete	Complete
2-Recall	Twig	Complete	Complete	Complete
3- Complexity (joins required)	Path	No	No	No
3- Complexity (joins required)	Twig	Yes	Yes	No
4-Size (initial, worst)	Tree	Same	Same	Same
4-Size (initial, worst)	Graph	Exponential	Same	Same
4-Size (scalability, growing)		Linearly (for tree data), Exponentially (for cyclic data)	Linearly	Linearly
5- Query supported efficiently		Path	Path	Path (Twig by F&B-index)
6- Maintain ability (Edge insertion)		O (n + m)	O (n + m)	O (n + m)
Notes			- Path queries are precise for $k \geq$ path length for A(k)-index - Edge addition to A(k)-index is not available (open for research)	- Precision and the need for joins depend on "k" value for (F+B)^k-index

index is analogous to A(k)-index as an extension to 1-index.

Summary of Graph Indexes

Figure 9 contains a summary of the graph indexing schemes; for further discussion see (Mohammad & Martin, 2009). The initial size (when it is first created) of a graph index for both tree-shaped and graph-shaped data could be either the same as the size of the data or exponential in the size of the data, in the worst case. The scalability (growing size) could be either linear or exponential in the size of data. The type of queries that are supported efficiently could be path, twig, or both.

Non-deterministic forward and backward bisimilar indexes are the only type of graph indexes that are capable of supporting twig queries if the index is exact (i.e. F&B-index). Note that the size of a deterministic index grows linearly in the original size of the source data if the shape of the source data is tree, and it grows exponentially if the shape of the source data is graph.

Before moving into the third type of structural indexes, it is worth mentioning here that graph indexes can facilitate use of statistics and other features that can aid query processing and optimization. For example, it can hold sample values for each node or statistics about the extended data such as fan-in and fan-out of each node.

Sequence Indexing Schemes

Sequence indexes (Wang et al., 2003; Rao & Moon, 2004) transform XML documents and queries into structure-encoded sequences. Answering a query requires sequence string matching between the encoded sequences of the data and the query.

Figure 10. Data trees and a query

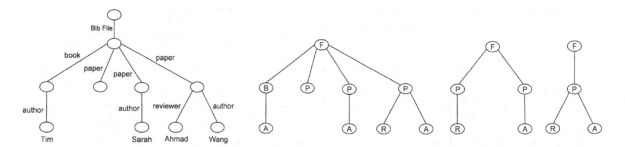

This eliminates the need for joins to evaluate twig queries. We must be careful, however, when using matching to answer a query since the sequence may not necessarily reflect a structural tree match. Sequence indexes combine the structure and the values of XML data into an integrated index structure. They are used to efficiently evaluate path queries and twig queries with keyword components without any extra join operations.

Specific Comparison Criteria of Sequence Indexes

In addition to the general comparison criteria listed above, we include the following specific comparison criteria for this type of index:

- **Computational complexity, indexing direction.** The shape of an XML graph is similar to a triangle. At the top there is only one root element and at the bottom there may be many leaf nodes, which are usually value nodes. A top-down search for a value in a data-tree starts from the root element then goes down the tree according to a given query path specification. In contrast, a bottom-up approach starts the search from the values at the leaf nodes. Since the selectivity of leaf nodes is higher than that of nodes in the top and the middle of the tree, bottom-up search results in fewer paths in the tree being examined. Therefore, the

indexing direction has an effect on the efficiency of a query evaluation.

- **Refinement step.** Sequence schemes suffer from two anomalies, namely, false positives and false negatives. Refinement steps are added to the evaluation process of a query to overcome these problems. On the one hand, the fact that these anomalies exist in the encoded sequence is an issue by itself. On the other hand, the way that these anomalies are dealt with is another issue. With regard to this criterion, we are only concerned with how efficiently these problems are resolved.

Based on the importance of tree mapping direction, we divide sequence indexes into two types, namely, top-down sequence indexing schemes and bottom-up sequence indexing schemes. ViST and PRIX are examples of top-down and bottom-up indexes, respectively.

ViST (Top-Down Sequence Indexes)

The ViST (Virtual Suffix Tree) index structure is proposed by Wang et al. (2003). Before we illustrate an example of ViST, please note that the data-tree in Figure 10 (B) is an encoded form of the data-tree in Figure 10 (A) by substituting the edge labels Bib File, book, author, paper, and reviewer with the letters F, B, A, P, and R, respectively. Furthermore, Figure 10 (A) is the same as the example edge-labeled data-tree in Figure 2. As an example of ViST, consider the data-tree in Figure 10 (B) and the query tree in Figure 10 (D). Both trees are transformed into structure-encoded sequences as illustrated below. Note that each pair in the sequence consists of the nodes' tag and the root path of the node's parent.

Data Tree 2 (D2): <u>(F,0)</u> (B,F) (A,FB) (P,F) (P,F) (A,FP) <u>(P,F)(R,FP)(A,FP)</u>

Query (Q): <u>(F,0)(P,F)(R,FP)(A,FP)</u>

The underlined subsequences of "D2" match the query sequence of "Q," so we return the matched subsequence in the data-tree as an answer to the query.

We should be aware of any existing false-positives in the solution. For example, consider the data-tree 3 in Figure 10 (C), the sequence of this tree is illustrated below.

Data Tree 3 (D3): <u>(F,0)(P,F)(R,FP)</u> (P,F) <u>(A,FP)</u>

To evaluate the above query "Q" over the "D3" data, we notice that the underlined sequence forms an answer for the query. It is not a correct answer, however, because the "R" and the "A" nodes do not have the same parent "P" node. This is an example of a false-positive answer.

In addition to false-positives, the sequence schemes also have the problem of false-negatives, which is caused by the isomorphic tree problem. It occurs when a branch node has multiple identical child nodes. For example, the two tree combinations which are illustrated in Figure 11, have the following structural sequences.

Data Tree 1: (F,0) (P,F) (A,FP) (P,F) (R,FP)
Data Tree 2: (F,0) (P,F) (R,FP) (P,F) (A,FP)

If we run any one of these two trees as a query over the other tree, we will not find a match as can

Figure 11. Example of false-negative

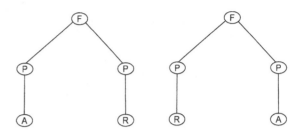

be seen from the translated sequences. However, logically both trees have the same structure and same number and types of elements. To solve this problem in ViST, which occurs when there are similar tag siblings in a query, we have to rewrite the given query into all possible combinations of sequence order. After that, we solve each query separately, and then union the result of all queries. In the worst case, permutations of the query sequence are exponential in the number of the similar siblings.

ViST is based on top-down traversal tree. As a result, for deep and large XML documents, the size of the index becomes a problem as it does not scale well with an increase in data size because the top elements have to be included within the sequence of the newly inserted elements. As the paths in XML data get longer, the sequence length will increase and hence the size of the index will increase exponentially in the size of data.

The false-positives problem is resolved by disassembling the query tree at the branch into multiple trees, and using join operations to combine their result. This solution is definitely expensive, since it involves additional join operations. ViST is based on B+-tree (Wang et al., 2003), which is physically implemented as two levels of B+-trees (Gou & Chirkova, 2007). If we assume that the fan-out of the used B+-tree is equal to "b," then $O(b \log_b n)$ nodes are touched during a sequence index update at each level.

115

Figure 12. An example of Prufer sequence

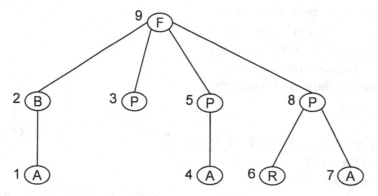

PRIX (Bottom-Up Sequence Indexes)

ViST's top-down transformation approach weakens the query processing because it results in a large number of nodes (paths) being examined during subsequence matching for commonly occurring non-contiguous tag names. Motivated by this fact, Rao and Moon (2004) propose another approach that implements bottom-up transformation instead. This approach is called PRIX (Prufer sequences for Indexing XML). It is based on Prufer Sequences as indicated by the name. The bottom-up transformation of XML data-trees in PRIX plays a crucial role in reducing the query processing time.

Basically, the top-level elements of an XML tree are shared with lower-level elements by being their parent or ancestor nodes. Thus, if we index a tree starting from the top, the chances are high of having a large number of elements that share the same starting tags in a given query path. In contrast, indexing a tree starting from the bottom and moving upward to the top of the tree reduces the chance of having a large number of shared elements for a given query path as the selectivity is higher at the bottom. A bottom-up index is more efficient than a top-down index and PRIX therefore is more efficient than ViST (Rao & Moon,2004).

PRIX is based on Prufer sequences. To illustrate how a Prufer sequence is used to denote a

tree, we use the data-tree in Figure 12, which is the same as the data-tree in Figure 10 (B). The letters inside the node circles represent the tag types (labels) and the numbers shown beside the nodes represent the post-order numbering of the tree. To encode the tree in Figure 12 with a Prufer sequence, we repeatedly delete the leaf node that has the smallest number and append the label of its parent to the sequence.

As we can see in Figure 12, the smallest post-order number is "1" so we delete it and add "2" to the sequence, so it becomes {2}. We delete the node numbered "2" and add its parent "9" to the sequence to become {2,9}, and so forth. At the end of this process, we have the sequence {2,9,9,5,9,8,8,9}, which represents the following tag sequence {B,F,F,P,F,P,P,F}.

In PRIX the string/character data in the XML document tree are extended by adding dummy child nodes before the transformation process so it can be indexed using the Prufer sequence. Similarly, query twigs are also extended before transforming them into sequences. Indexing extended-Prufer sequences is useful for processing twig queries with values. Since queries with value nodes usually have high selectivity, they are processed more efficiently than those without values.

The size of a PRIX grows linearly in the total length of the sequences stored in it because an increase in the path length will result in a se-

Figure 13. Comparison between Top-down (ViST) and Bottom-up (PRIX) sequencing schemes

No	Criteria		Top-down (ViST)	Bottom-up (PRIX)
1	Precision		False-positives (imprecise)	False-positives (imprecise)
2	Recall		False-negatives (incomplete)	False-negatives (incomplete)
3	Computation Complexity	Refinement step	Expensive Joins	Complicated four-phase process
		Indexing direction	Top-down	Bottom-up
4	Scaling/Size		Exponential	Linear
5	Type of queries supported efficiently		Path & Twig	Path & Twig
6	Maintainability		$O(b\log_b n)$	$O(b\log_b n)$

quence addition which is equal to the amount of the increase. In the PRIX approach, the length of a Prufer sequence, as we noticed from the above example, is linear in the number of nodes in the tree. Hence, the index size is linear in the total number of tree nodes regardless of the depth of the tree.

PRIX uses a complex four-phase refinement process to deal with false-positives and false-negatives. Basically, PRIX overcomes the false-positives problem by using document by document post-processing which is time consuming process. PRIX is based on the B+tree, and it is built in a way similar to ViST (Rao & Moon, 2004). It is mainly implemented as two levels of B+-trees. If we assume that the fan-out of the used B+-tree is equal to "b," then $O(b \log_b n)$ nodes are touched during a sequence index update at each level.

Summary of Sequence Indexes

Figure 13 includes a summary of the sequence indexing schemes. Both path and twig queries are supported efficiently by sequence indexes .

Structural Indexes Critique

In this subsection we compare the three categories of structural indexes, namely, node index schemes, graph index schemes, and sequence index schemes.

Criteria for Comparison among Structural Indexing Schemes

In addition to the general criteria listed previously we use the following specific criteria to compare the above three types of structural indexing schemes:

- *(A) Computational complexity: Does it require structural joins?* Structural joins are considered for path queries and twig queries. In general, to achieve high performance for a query execution, we need to minimize the number of joins. *(B) Computational complexity: Granularity of usage to evaluate a query.* The granularity of an XML index depends on the type of the indexing scheme. For example, the granularity could be at the node level, the path level, or the twig level (for twig queries). As the granularity of the index that is used to evaluate a query increases, the execution time becomes shorter.

- *Data supported.* The types of data supported by the XML indexing schemes are mainly tree-shaped data and graph-shaped data. The main difference between them is that the graph-shaped data can be represented by an XML document with the ID/ IDREF attribute tokens. The tree-shaped data can be considered as a subclass of the graph-shaped data where a node cannot have more than one parent. The indexing schemes that are capable of supporting the graph-shaped data are more powerful than the ones that support only the tree-shaped data.

- *Ability to facilitate the use of statistics and other features.* The ability to facilitate the use of statistics, such as the fan-in and the fan-out of nodes, helps to provide query optimization with the capability to choose the most efficient evaluation plan for a given query.

- *Values integrated into the index structure.* If the values of the elements and attributes are indexed separately from the structure, and a query with some predicates needs to be evaluated over that data, then joins between the structural index and the value indexes are necessary and hence increases the complexity of the XML query evaluation process. In contrast, integrating values into the structural index saves some additional joins and narrows down the matching procedure during the evaluation process, since the selectivity of the values are always higher than that of the elements in a structural index.

Comparison Among Structural Indexes

Generally, sequence indexes may initially produce a wrong answer to a query then correct it at a later stage in the evaluation process. The deterministic graph indexes and non-deterministic graph indexes with backward bisimilarity may produce some wrong initial answers. The non-deterministic graph indexes that are based on forward and backward bisimilarity, on the contrary, are more accurate and often return only the correct answers. Finally, since the node indexes are used for binary joins, they do not produce any initial wrong answers.

Without some extra post-processing steps, false-negatives may occur when we use the sequence indexing scheme to evaluate a query. On the other hand, node and graph indexes always return a complete answer because the order of the nodes is not encoded within the structure of the index.

The number of structural joins that are required to evaluate a path or a twig query varies among the different schemes. It has a significant impact on the query processing time. Node indexes are the least efficient with respect to structural joins since they require joins for both path and twig queries. Graph indexes support path queries without the need for structural joins but structural joins are required (for all graph indexes except F&B-index) at the branching node to evaluate twig queries. Finally, sequence indexes are the best because the structure is encoded within the sequence so they do not require any structural joins for path or twig queries.

There are three levels of granularity used to evaluate a twig query: the pair-wise, path, and twig levels. For illustration, in order to evaluate a twig query using a node index, we break the query into nodes, then join nodes a pair at a time until all nodes are joined together for the complete twig paths to solve the query. On the other hand,

Figure 14. Summary of comparison among the 3 categories of structural indexing schemes

Criteria		Node Indexes	Graph Indexes	Sequence Indexes
1- Precision (wrong initial answer, false positive)		No	Yes/No	Yes
2- Recall (missing initially correct answer, false negative)		No	No	Yes
3- Computation complexity (structural join required)	Path	Yes	No	No
	Twig	Yes	Yes / No	No
3- Computation complexity (granularity of usage to evaluate a query)		Nodes Pair-wised Evaluation	Path Evaluation	Twig Evaluation
4- Size / Scalability		Linear-Exponential	Linear-Exponential	Linear-Exponential
5- Type of queries supported <u>efficiently</u>		None	Path (Twig by exact (F&B) indexes)	Path & Twig
6- Maintainability for adding an edge		$O(n)$ immutable $O(\log n)$ mutable	$O(n + m)$	$O(b\log_b n)$
7- Data supported		Tree	Graph	Tree
8- Can facilitate the use of statistics		No	Yes	No
9- Hold value		No	Yes/No	Yes

to evaluate a twig query using all graph indexes except F&B-index, we break the query into several paths and solve each path separately, then join the results of all paths to form the answer to the query. Finally, to evaluate a twig query by using a sequence index, we process the twig query as a whole.

Node indexes can only support tree-shape data because of the containment rule that is used to specify the relationship between two nodes in a data-tree. In order for node "*a*" to be an ancestor of node "*b*", *a*'s interval code has to contain *b*'s interval code, and not vice versa, which may be caused by a graph-shaped data. In contrast, graph indexes support the graph-shaped data well. Like node indexes, sequences indexes only support tree-shaped data.

Some indexes provide valuable utilities for the query optimization. For example, strong DataGuides (Goldman & Widom, 1997) are used in Lore (McHugh, Abiteboul, Goldman, Quass, & Widom, 1997) to facilitate annotation of sample values and statistical data. The annotated information is associated with the DataGuide objects (nodes). This information assists in estimating the cost of

the evaluation plans for a given query. The node and the sequence indexes do not facilitate these kinds of supporting information.

There are some attempts to integrate values into graph indexes (Cooper et al., 2001), although, the majority of graph indexes do not carry any values within the structural summary. Node indexes cannot contain values, and values have to be indexed separately. The only indexing schemes that are designed to efficiently integrate values into the structural index are the sequence indexing schemes. We summarize our comparison of the three categories of structural indexing schemes in Figure 14.

Future Research Directions

The main challenge in indexing XML data is the irregularity of data and structure. Value-based queries can be evaluated by using traditional indexing schemes, such as B+-trees or inverted lists. However, efficient support for the structural part is a challenging task. The semistructured nature of XML data and the flexibility of the query languages pose another distinctive concern for deriving or selecting proper indexing methods. Designing representations for efficient storage of semistructured data is also a difficult task.

Making the existing numbering index schemes dynamic so that they adapt gracefully to deletion and insertion of new nodes is not an easy task. Node indexes require the highest number of joins among the three indexing schemes to solve an XML query. In order to reduce this shortcoming, it is useful to explore a method to optimally use node indexes together with graph indexes to solve XML queries. Each type of index plays a different role. A graph index is used for path selection, whereas a node index is used for path joining (Gou & Chirkova, 2007).

Node indexes are implemented by two dominant labeling schemes: the prefix (e.g. Dewey) and the interval (e.g., (Beg, End)) labeling schemes. Each one of these schemes has its own advantages and disadvantages. The size of the interval indexes grows constantly regardless of the data-tree depth, while it grows exponentially in the prefix indexes. Processing time of interval indexes is shorter than that of prefix indexes. The information for a data-tree path is included within the prefix labels, while it is not included within the interval labels and require extra processing step to be computed. Prefix indexes are relatively easy to update while interval indexes are harder. A possible research area would be to investigate integrating these two types of node indexing schemes into one scheme that retains all the desired characteristics in an index. The integrated scheme may have, but should not be limited to, the following characteristics: a reasonable size; based on numbers (not string); a path can be calculated within a relatively small cost; and easy to be updated.

Choosing an appropriate index definition that covers a given query workload is an open problem for $(F+B)^k$-index. Also, efficient index building and updating algorithms are needed for non-deterministic forward and backward bisimilar indexes. Efficient integration of graph indexes with value indexes is another interesting area. This will minimize the I/O accesses by eliminating the need to access two different indexes to solve an XML query with a predicate. Identifying a suitable set of statistics for given graph-based data that can be efficiently computed and stored without having a fixed graph index is an open problem (McHugh & Widom, 1999).

Sequence indexes support solving a twig query only in a certain order. If the query order does not match the index order it will return an incorrect answer. To run a query against a sequence index all possible orders of the query nodes have to be tested in order to get an accurate result. The node and graph indexes do not have this problem. Another limitation of sequence indexes is that they may require a large number of accesses to the index, consequently, it might result in expensive random I/O accesses (Gou & Chirkova, 2007). Finally, the overhead of the false-positives problem is a major drawback of sequence indexes.

CONCLUSION

Indexing is key factor in improving the performance of XML queries (Zou et al., 2004). Indexes are used during most of the optimization stages. Indexing the XML data has to reflect the structure in order to be able to support the path queries as well as the twig queries.

Our classification of XML graph indexes is novel. It is based on their deterministic property in addition to forward and backward bisimilarity, which determines the possible size and accuracy of an index. Deterministic indexes may grow exponentially in the worst case, while non-deterministic indexes grow linearly. Forward and backward bisimilar indexes are more accurate than backward bisimilar indexes. Deterministic indexes guarantee uniqueness of paths, and are suitable for simple path queries. They evaluate a simple path query by traversing one path only. In contrast, non-deterministic graph indexes may traverse more than one index path to solve a simple path query.

Our classification of XML sequence indexes is also novel. It is based on the mapping direction of data-trees, because the mapping direction is the main factor that drastically affects the size of sequence indexes. We use common criteria to analyze the characteristics of the most common types of XML structural indexes.

Our analysis of structural indexes is based on the following key issues: retrieval power, which covers the precision and the completeness of an index; processing complexity, which demonstrates how efficient an index can be used to answer a query; scalability of the index and its adaptability to queries with different path lengths; and finally update cost of the index.

We observe that no single indexing scheme is capable of satisfying all users' needs; deciding which index scheme to use depends on the users' preferences. There is a trade-off between the size of the structural index and its precision. For example, graph indexes with only backward bisimilarity tend to have lower accuracy (which is corrected by some post-processing steps) but their sizes are minimal. In contrast, graph indexes with forward and backward bisimilarity tend to have high accuracy but at the expense of the size. Node and sequence indexes can be used only for tree-shaped data, while graph indexes can be used for both tree-shaped and graph-shaped data. Graph indexes can be used to efficiently facilitate additional information such as some statistical information, which can be used during a query optimization process. Some indexes cover twig and path queries, while others cover only path queries.

Finally, the ultimate goal of researchers is to create an indexing scheme that will occupy minimal storage without compromising the precision, if possible, or at least improve the trade-off in favor of precision (i.e. have a small increase in the size to achieve higher precision).

ACKNOWLEDGMENT

This work was supported by the Natural Science and Engineering Research Council of Canada (NSERC).

REFERENCES

Abiteboul, S., Buneman, P., & Suciu, D. (2002). *Data on the Web: From Relations to Semistructured Data and XML.* San Francisco, CA: Morgan Kaufmann Publishers.

Al-Khalifa, S., Jagadish, H. V., Koudas, N., Patel, J. M., Srivastava, D., & Wu, Y. (2002, February 26-March 1). Structural Joins: A Primitive for Efficient XML Query Pattern Matching. In R. Agrawal, K. Dittrich, & A.H.H. Ngu (Eds.), *Proceedings of the 18th International Conference on Data Engineering,* San Jose, CA, USA (pp.141-154). Los Alamitos, CA: IEEE Computer Society.

Bary, T., Paoli, J., & Sperberg-McQueen, C. M. (Eds.). (1998, February 10). *Extensible Markup language (XML) 1.0.* Retrieved January 22, 2009, from http://www.w3.org/TR/1998/REC-xml-19980210.html

Chen, Q., Lim, A., & Ong, K. (2003, June 9-12). D(k)-Index: An adaptive Structural summary for graph-structured data. In *Proceedings of the ACM SIGMOD International Conference on Management of Data*, San Diego, CA (pp.134-144). New York: ACM Press.

Chung, C., Min, J., & Shim, K. (2002, June 3-6). APEX: An Adaptive Path Index for XML data. In *Proceedings of the ACM SIGMOD International Conference on Management of Data*, Madison, WI, (pp.121-132). New York: ACM Press.

Clark, J., & DeRose, S. (Eds.). (1999, November 16). *XML Path Language (XPath) Version 1.0.* Retrieved January 22, 2009, from http://www.w3.org/TR/xpath

Cohen, E., Kaplan, H., & Milo, T. (2002, June 3-5). Labeling Dynamic XML Trees. In *Proceedings of the 21ˢᵗ ACM SIGMOD-SIGACT-SIGART symposium on Principles of Database Systems,* Madison, WI, (pp. 271-281). New York: ACM Press.

Cooper, B., Sample, N., Franklin, M., Hjaltason, G., & Shadmon, M. (2001, September 11-14). A Fast Index for Semistructured Data. In P.M.G. Apers, P. Atzeni, S. Ceri, S. Paraboschi, K. Ramamohanarao, & R.T. Snodgrass (Eds.), *Proceedings of 27th International Conference on Very Large Data Bases VLDB,* Roma, Italy (pp.341-350). San Francisco, CA: Morgan Kaufmann Publishers Inc.

Dietz, P. (1982, May 5-7). Maintaining order in a linked list. In *Proceedings of the fourteenth annual ACM symposium on Theory of Computing,* San Francisco, California, USA (pp.122 –127). New York: ACM Press.

Fisher, D. K., Lam, F., Shui, W. M., & Wong, R. K. (2006, January 16-19). Dynamic Labeling Schemes for Ordered XML Based on Type Information. In G. Dobbie, & J. Bailey (Eds.), *Proceedings of the 17ᵗʰ Australasian Database Conference,* Hobart, Australia (Vol. 49, pp. 59-68). Darlinghurst, Australia: Australian computer Society, Inc.

Goldman, R., McHugh, J., & Widom, J. (1999, June 3-4). From semistructured data to XML: Migrating the Lore data model and query language. In S. Cluet, & T. Milo (Eds.), *Proceedings of the 2nd International Workshop on the Web and Databases, ACM SIGMOD Workshop,* Philadelphia, PA (pp. 25-30).

Goldman, R., & Widom, J. (1997, August 25-29). DataGuides: Enabling query formulation and optimization in semistructured databases. In M. Jarke, M.J. Carey, K.R. Dittrich, F.H. Lochovsky, P. Loucopoulos, & M.A. Jeusfeld (Eds.), *Proceedings of 23rd International Conference on Very Large Data Bases, VLDB'97,* Athens, Greece, (pp.436-445). San Francisco, CA: Morgan Kaufmann Publishers Inc.

Goldman, R., & Widom, J. (1999, January 13). Approximate Data Guide. In *Proceedings of the Workshop on Query Processing for Semistructured Data and Non-Standard Data Formats,* Jerusalem, Israel.

Gou, G., & Chirkova, R. (2007, October). Efficiently Querying Large XML Data Repositories: A Survey. *Transactions on Knowledge and Data Engineering, 19*(10), 1381–1403. doi:10.1109/TKDE.2007.1060

Kaushik, R., Bohannon, P., Naughton, J., & Korth, H. (2002, June 3-6). Covering indexes for branching path queries. In *Proceedings of the ACM SIGMOD International Conference on Management of Data,* Madison, WI, (pp.133-144). New York: ACM Press.

Kaushik, R., Bohannon, P., Naughton, J., & Shenoy, P. (2002, August 20-23). Updates for Structure Indexes. In P.A. Bernstein, Y.E. Ioannidis, R. Ramakrishnan, & D. Papadias (Eds.), *Proceedings of 28th International Conference on Very Large Data Bases,* Hong Kong, China (pp.239-250). San Francisco, CA: Morgan Kaufmann.

Kaushik, R., Shenoy, P., Bohannon, P., & Gudes, E. (2002, 26 February - 1 March). Exploiting local similarity for indexing paths in graph-structured data. In A.D. Williams, & S. Kawada (Eds.), *Proceedings of 18th International Conference on Data Engineering,* San Jose, California, USA (pp. 129-140). Los Alamitos, CA: IEEE Computer Society.

Li, Q., & Moon, B. (2001, September 11-14). Indexing and querying XML data for regular path expressions. In P.M.G. Apers, P. Atzeni, S. Ceri, S. Paraboschi, K. Ramamohanarao, & R.T. Snodgrass (Eds.), *Proceedings of 27th International Conference on Very Large Data Bases,* Roma, Italy (pp.361-370). San Francisco, CA: Morgan Kaufmann.

Lu, J., Ling, T., Chan, C., & Chen, T. (2005, August 30-September 2). From region encoding to extended Dewey: On efficient processing of XML twig pattern matching. In K. Bohm, C.S. Jensen, L.M. Haas, M.L. Kersten, P. Larson, & B.C. Chin (Eds.), *Proceedings of the 31st International Conference on Very Large Data Bases, VLDB,* Trondheim, Norway (pp. 193-204). New York: ACM Press.

McHugh, J., Abiteboul, S., Goldman, R., Quass, D., & Widom, J. (1997, September). Lore: A database management system for semistructured data. *SIGMOD Record, 26*(3), 54–66. doi:10.1145/262762.262770

McHugh, J., & Widom, J. (1999, September 7-10). Query Optimization for XML. In M.P. Atkinson, M.E. Orlowska, P. Valduriez, S.B. Zdonik, & M.L. Brodie (Eds.), *Proceedings of 25th International Conference on Very Large Data Bases, VLDB '99,* Edinburgh, Scotland, UK (pp.315-326). San Francisco, CA: Morgan Kaufmann Publishers Inc.

Megginson, D., & Brownell, D. (2004, April 27). *Simple API for XML (SAX).* Retrieved January 22, 2009, from http://www.saxproject.org/

Milo, T., & Suciu, D. (1999, January 10-12). Index Structures for Path Expressions. In C. Beeri, & P. Buneman (Eds.), *Database Theory –ICDT'99, Proceedings of 7th International Conference on Database Theory,* Jerusalem, Israel (LNCS 1540, pp.277-295). Berlin, Germany: Springer.

Mohammad, S., & Martin, P. (2009). *XML Structural Indexes* (Technical Report No. 2009-560). Kinston, Ontario, Canada: Queen's University.

Online Computer Library Center. (2008). *Dewey decimal classification.* Retrieved January 13, 2009, from http://www.oclc.org/dewey/versions/ddc22print/intro.pdf

Polyzotis, N., Garofalakis, M., & Ioannidis, Y. (2004, June 13-18). Approximate XML Query Answers. In G. Welkum, A.C. Konig, & S. Dessloch (Eds.), *Proceedings of the ACM SIGMOD International Conference on Management of Data,* Paris, France (pp.263-274). New York: ACM Press.

Rao, P., & Moon, B. (2004, March 30-April 2). PRIX: Indexing and querying XML using Prufer sequences. In *Proceedings of the 20th International Conference on Data Engineering, ICDE 2004,* Boston, MA (pp.288-300). Washington, DC: IEEE Computer Society.

Silberstein, A., He, H., Yi, K., & Yang, J. (2005, April 5-8). BOXes: Efficient Maintenance of Order-Based Labeling for Dynamic XML Data. In *Proceeding of the 21st International Conference on Data Engineering, ICDE 2005,* Tokyo, Japan (pp.285-296). Washington, DC: IEEE Computer Society.

Tatarinov, I., Viglas, S., Beyer, K., Shanmugasundaram, J., Shekita, E., & Zhang, C. (2002, June 3-6). Storing and Querying Ordered XML Using a relational Database System. In *Proceedings of the ACM SIGMOD International Conference on Management of Data,* Madison, Wisconsin, USA (pp.204-215). New York: ACM Press.

The DBLP Computer Science Bibliography. (2009, January). *DBLP XML records* [Data file]. Retrieved January 22, 2009, from http://www.informatik.uni-trier.de/~ley/db/

Vakali, A., Catania, B., & Maddalena, A. (2005, March-April). XML Data Stores: Emerging Practices. *Internet Computing, IEEE, 9*(2), 62–69. doi:10.1109/MIC.2005.48

Wang, H., Park, S., Fan, W., & Yu, P. (2003, June 9-12). ViST: A Dynamic Index Method for Querying XML Data by Tree Structures. In *Proceedings of the ACM SIGMOD International Conference on Management of Data,* San Diego, CA (pp.110-121). New York: ACM Press.

Zhang, C., Naughton, R., Dewitt, D., Luo, Q., & Lohman, G. (2001, May 21-24). On Supporting containment Queries in Relational Database Management Systems. In T. Sellis (Ed.), *Proceedings of ACM SIGMOD International Conference on Management of Data*, Santa Barbara, CA (pp.425-436). New York: ACM Press.

Zou, Q., Liu, S., & Chu, W. (2004, November 12-13). Ctree: A Compact Tree for Indexing XML Data. In A.H.F. Laender, D. Lee, & M. Ronthaler (Eds.), *Proceedings of the 6th annual ACM international workshop on Web Information and Data Management, WIDM 2004,* Washington, DC, (pp.39-46). New York: ACM Press.

Chapter 6
Labeling XML Documents

Jiaheng Lu
School of Information and DEKE, MOE, Renmin University of China, China

Liang Xu
School of Computing, National University of Singapore, Singapore

Tok Wang Ling
School of Computing, National University of Singapore, Singapore

Changqing Li
Duke University, USA

ABSTRACT

XML labeling schemes play an important role in XML query processing. Containment and Prefix labeling schemes are two of the most popular labeling schemes. In order to perform efficient XML query processing, this chapter shows how to extend the traditional prefix labeling scheme to speedup query processing. In addition, for XML documents that are updated frequently, many labeling schemes require relabeling which can be very expensive. A lot of research interest has been generated on designing dynamic XML labeling schemes. Making labeling schemes dynamic turns out to be a challenging problem and many of the approaches proposed only partially avoid relabeling. This chapter describes some recently emerged dynamic labeling schemes that can completely avoid relabeling, making efficient update processing in XML database management systems possible.

INTRODUCTION

XML has become a de facto standard for data exchange and representation on the World Wide Web and elsewhere. To facilitate query processing over XML data that conforms to an ordered tree-structured data model, two main techniques have been proposed including structural index and labeling approach. Compared with the traditional

methods that performs hierarchical traversal of the XML tree, the labeling approach benefits from smaller storage size and efficient establishment of various relationships such as Ancestor-Descendant (AD) and Parent-Child (PC). As a result, we consider labeling as the preferred approach for XML query processing.

We classify existing labeling schemes into two main bodies: **static labeling schemes** and **dynamic labeling schemes** which are designed for static and

DOI: 10.4018/978-1-61520-727-5.ch006

dynamic XML data respectively. **Containment labeling scheme** (Li&Moon, 2001; Zhang, 2001) and Prefix labeling scheme (Abiteboul, 2006; Tatarinov, 2002) are two of the most popular static labeling schemes. Many variants of them also have emerged that serve different purposes. For example, **extended Dewey labeling scheme** (Lu&Ling, 2005) is prefix-based and designed to further enhance the performance of twig pattern matching queries. The significance of extended dewey is that it provides not only structural information, but also the information about the names of the corresponding nodes. Twig pattern matching can benefit from extended dewey labels because only the leaf node labels need to be scanned, significantly reducing I/O cost during query processing. However, the static XML labeling schemes can suffer from high cost of re-labeling when the XML tree structure is subjected to change. To efficiently process updates for dynamic XML documents, a lot of works have been done on designing dynamic XML labeling schemes.

In this chapter, we present a survey on the existing labeling schemes. We begin with the introduction of static labeling schemes, describing how they support XML queries. Next we introduce dynamic XML labeling schemes which are developed to facilitate XML query processing as well as efficient updating. Finally we introduce the encoding schemes (Li&Ling, 2005; Li&Ling 2006; Xu&Ling, 2007) which can be applied to static labeling schemes to generate dynamic XML labels.

STATIC XML LABELING SCHEMES

In order to perform XML query processing efficiently, one way is to develop a labeling scheme to capture the structural information of XML documents to facilitate query processing without traversing the original XML documents.

The existing labeling scheme use a tree-traversal order (e.g. extended preorder [Li&Moon, 2001]) or textual positions of start and end tags (e.g. containment [Bruno, Koudas, & Srivastava 2005]) or path expressions (e.g. Dewey ID [Tatarinov et al. 2002]) or prime numbers (e.g. [Wu&Lee, 2004]). By applying these labeling schemes, one can determine the relationship (e.g. ancestor-descendent and parent-child) between two elements in XML documents from their labels alone. We introduce the labeling schemes for static documents as follows.

Containment Labeling Schemes

In the containment labeling scheme (or called region encoding) [Bruno et al. 2005, Shanmugasundaram 2001], each label includes 3-tuple (*start, end, level*). Based on the strictly nested property of labels, we can use them to evaluate the PC and AD relationships between element pairs in a data tree. Formally, element u is an ancestor of another element v if and only if

```
u.start < v.start and v.end >
u.end
```

That is, the region of v is contained by that of u. To check the PC relationship, we additionally test whether element u is exactly one level above element v in the data tree (i.e., $u.level = v.level-1$). For example, Figure 1 shows an example XML tree with containment labels.

Dewey ID Labeling Schemes

In the Dewey ID labeling scheme [Tatarinov et al. 2002, Lu&Ling 2004] (or called prefix scheme), each element is presented by a vector:

1. The root is labeled by a empty string ε; and

2. For a non-root element u, label(u)= label(s).x, where u is the x-th child of s.

Figure 1. Example of the containment labeling scheme

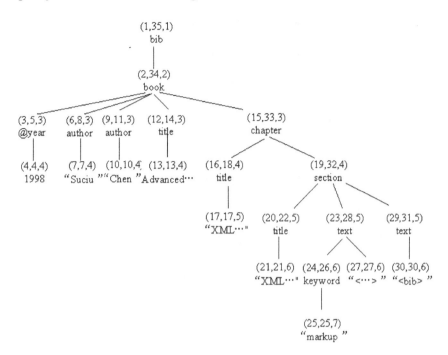

For example, Figure 2 shows an XML document tree with Dewey ID labels. Dewey ID supports efficient evaluation of structural relationships between elements. That is, element u is an ancestor of element v if and only if

```
label(u) is a prefix of label(v)
```

In order to check the PC relationship, we additionally test whether the number of integers separated by a delimiter (e.g. dot in our example in Figure 2) in the label of element *u* is one less than that of element *v*.

Extended Dewey Labeling Scheme

We now present a powerful labeling scheme, called extended Dewey ID (for short, extended Dewey). The unique feature of this scheme is that, from the label of an element alone, we can derive the names of all elements in the path from the root to this element. For example, Figure 3 shows an XML document with extended Dewey labels. Given

the label "0.5.1.1" of element text alone, we can derive that the path from the root to text is "/bib/book/chapter/section/text". An immediate benefit of this feature is that, to evaluate a twig pattern, we only need to access the labels of elements that satisfy the leaf node predicates in the query. Further, this feature enables us to easily match a path pattern by string matching. Take element "0.5.1.1" as an example again. Since we see that its path is "/bib/book/chapter/section/text", it is quite straightforward to determine whether this path matches a path query (e.g. "//section/text"). As a result, the extended Dewey labeling scheme provides us an extraordinary chance to develop a new efficient algorithm to match a twig pattern.

In order to extending Dewey ID labeling scheme to incorporate the element-name information. A straightforward way is to use some bits to present the element-name sequence with number presentation, followed by the original Dewey label. The advantage of this approach is simple and easy to implement. However, this method faces the problem of the large label size. In the

Figure 2. Example of the Dewey ID labeling scheme

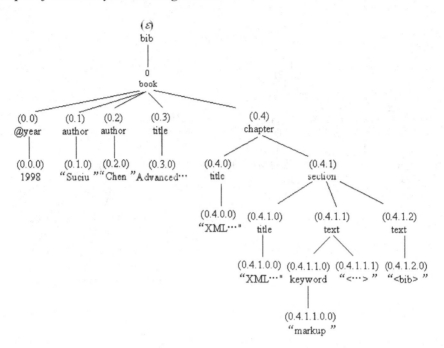

Figure 3. Example of the extended Dewey labeling scheme

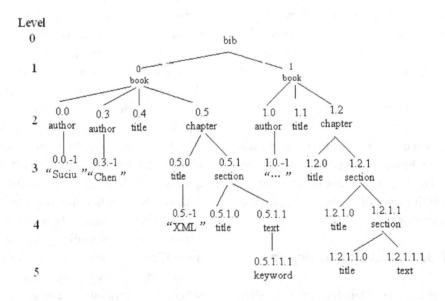

following, a more concise scheme is shown to solve this problem. In particular, we first encode the names of elements along a path into a single Dewey label. Then we present a **Finite State**

Figure 4. DTD for XML document in Figure 3

```
<!ELEMENT bib (book*)>
<!ELEMENT book ( author+, title, chapter* ) >
<!ELEMENT author (#PCDATA)>
<!ELEMENT title (#PCDATA)>
<!ELEMENT chapter (title, section*)>
<!ELEMENT section (title, (text | section)*)>
<!ELEMENT text (#PCDATA | bold | keyword | emph) *>
<!ELEMENT bold (#PCDATA | bold | keyword | emph )*>
<!ELEMENT keyword (#PCDATA | bold | keyword | emph )*>
<!ELEMENT emph (#PCDATA | bold | keyword | emph) *>
```

Transducer (FST) to decode element names from this label. For simplicity, we focus the discussion on a single document. The labeling scheme can be easily extended to multiple documents by introducing document ID information.

Extended Dewey

The intuition of extended dewey is to use modulo function to create a mapping from an integer to an element name, such that given a sequence of integers, we can convert it into the sequence of element names.

In the extended Dewey, we need to know a little additional schema information, which we call a child names clue. In particular, given any tag t in a document, the child names clue is all (distinct) names of children of t. This clue is easily derived from DTD, XML schema or other schema constraint. For example, consider the DTD in Figure 6.4; the tag of all children of bib is only book and the tags of all children of book are author, title and chapter. Note that even in the case when DTD and XML schema are unavailable, our method is still effective, but we need to scan the document once to get the necessary child names clue before labeling the XML document.

Let us use $CT(t) = \{t_0, t_1, \cdots, t_{n-1}\}$ to denote the child names clue of tag t. Suppose there is an ordering for tags in $CT(t)$, where the particular ordering is not important. For example, in Figure 4, $CT(book) = \{author, title, chapter\}$. Using child

names clues, we can easily create a mapping from an integer to an element name. Suppose $CT(t) = \{t_0, t_1, , t_{n-1}\}$, for any element e_i with name t_i, we assign an integer x_i to e_i such that $x_i \mod n = i$. Thus, according to the value of x_i, it is easy to derive its element name. In the following, we extend this intuition and describe the construction of extended Dewey labels.

The extended Dewey label of each element can be efficiently generated by a depth-first traversal of the XML tree. Each extended Dewey label is presented as a vector of integers. We use label(u) to denote the extended Dewey label of element u. For each u, label(u) is defined as label(s).x, where s is the parent of u. The computation method of integer x in extended Dewey is a little more involved than that in the original Dewey. In particular, for any element u with parent s in an XML tree,

1. If u is a text value, then $x = -1$;
2. Otherwise, assume that the element name of u is the k-th tag in CT(ts) (k=0,1,...,n-1), where ts denotes the tag of element s.

   2.1 If u is the first child of s, then $x = k$;

   2.2 Otherwise assume that the last component of the label of the left sibling of u is y (at this point, the left sibling of u has been labeled), then

$$x = \begin{cases} \left| \dfrac{y}{n} \right| \times n + k \\ \dfrac{y}{n} \times n + k \end{cases}$$

Example 1.*Figure 3shows an XML document tree that conforms to the DTD inFigure 4. For instance, the labels of four nodes "author, author, title, chapter" under book("0") are computed as follows. Firstly, "author" is labeled as "0.0", as this "author" is the first child of "book". Secondly, the "author" is labeled as "0.3".This is because 3 is the minimal number which is greater than 0, and 3mod3 = 0. Thirdly, the "title" is "0.4". Finally, the "chapter" is 0.5. This is because 5 is the minimal number which is greater than 4, and 5 mod 3 =2. We also show how to get the label "0.5" for "chapter" according to our formula. k = 2 (for "chapter" is the third tag in its child names clue, starting from 0), y = 4 (for the last component of "0.4" is 4), and n=3, so y mod 3 = 1 < k. Then $x = \left| 4/3 \right| * 3 + 2$ = 5. So "chapter" is assigned the label "0.5". We show the space complexity of extended Dewey using the following theorem.*

Theorem 1:*The extended Dewey does not alter the asymptotic space complexity of the original Dewey labeling scheme.*

Proof: According to the formula in (2.2), it is not hard to prove that given any element s, the gap between the last components of the labels for every two neighboring elements under s is no more than $|CT(t_s)|$. Hence, with the binary representation of integers, the length of each component i of extended Dewey label is at most $\log_2 |CT(t_{s_i})|$ more than that of the original Dewey. Therefore, the length difference between an extended Dewey label with m components and an original one is at most $\sum_{i=1}^{m} \log_2 |CT(t_{s_i})|$. Since m and $|CT(t_{s_i})|$ are small, it is reasonable to consider this difference is a small constant. As a result, the extended Dewey does not alter asymptotic space complexity of the original Dewey.

Finite State Transducer (FST)

Given the extended Dewey label of any element, we can use a finite state transducer (FST) to convert this label into the sequence of element names which reveals the whole path from the root to this element. We begin this section by presenting a function F(t, x) which will be used to define FST.

Figure 5. A sample FST for DTD in Figure 4

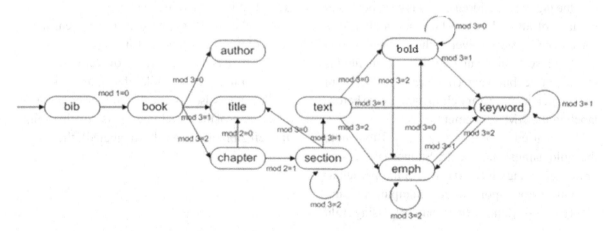

Definition 1: Let Z denotes the non-negative integer set and Σ denotes the alphabet of all distinct tags in an XML document T. Given an tag t in T, suppose CT(t) = $\{t_0, t_1, \ldots, t_{n-1}\}$, a function F(t, x): $\Sigma \times Z \to \Sigma$ can be defined by F(t, x) $= t_k$, where k= x mod n.

Definition 2: (Finite State Transducer) Given child names clues and an extended Dewey label, we can use a deterministic finite state transducer (FST) to translate the label into a sequence of element names. FST is a 5-tuple (I, S, i, δ, o),where (i) the input set $I = Z \cup \{-1\}$;(ii) the set of states $S = \sum \cup \{PCDATA\}$,where PCDATA is a state to denote text value of an element;(iii) the initial state i is the tag of the root in the document; (iv) the state transition function δ is defined as follows. For $\forall t \in \varepsilon$, if x=-1, $\delta(t, x) = PCDATA$, otherwise $\delta(t, x) = F(t, x)$. No other transition is accepted. (v) the output value o is the current state name.

Example 2.*Figure 5shows the FST for DTD inFig 4. For clarity, we do not explicitly show the state for PCDATA here. An input -1 from any state will transit to the terminating state PCDATA. This FST can convert any extended Dewey label to an element path. For instance, given an extended Dewey label "0.5.1.1", using the above FST, we derive that its path is "bib/book/chapter/section/text".*

As a final remark, it is worth noting three points:(i) the memory size of the above FST is quadratic to the number of distinct tags in XML documents, as the number of transition in FST is quadratic in the worst case; and (ii) we allow recursive element names in a document path, which is demonstrated as a loop in FST; and (iii) the time complexity of FST is linear in the length of an extended Dewey label, but independent of the complexity of schema definition.

Properties of Extended Dewey

In this section, we summarize the following five properties of extended Dewey labeling scheme.

1. **[Ancestor Name Awareness]** Given any extended Dewey label of an element, we can know all its ancestors' names (including the element itself).
2. **[Ancestor Label Awareness]** Given any extended Dewey label of an element, we can know all its ancestors' label.
3. **[Prefix relationship]** Two elements have ancestor -descendant relationships if and only if their extended Dewey labels have a prefix relationship.
4. **[Tight Prefix relationship]** Two elements a and b have parent-child relation-ships if and only iftheir extended Dewey labels label (a), label (b) have a tight prefix relationship. That is: (i) label (a) is a prefix of label (b); and (ii) label (b).length-label (a).length=1.
5. **[Order relationship]** Element a follows (or precedes) element b if and only if label (a) is greater (or smaller) than label (b) with lexicographical order.

The containment labeling scheme also can be used for determining ancestor- descendant, parent-child and order relationships between two elements. But it cannot see the ancestors of an element and therefore has not Properties 1 and 2.The original Dewey labeling scheme has Properties 2 to 5, but not Property 1. The first property is unique for extended Dewey. Note that Property 1 and 2 are of paramount importance among five properties for XML twig query processing, since they provide us an extraordinary chance to efficiently process XML path (and twig) queries. For example, given a path query "a/b/c/d", according to the **Ancestor Name and Label Awareness**, we only need to read the labels of "d" to answer this query, which will significantly reduce I/O cost compared to previous algorithms based on

Figure 6. An example of ORDPATH labeling

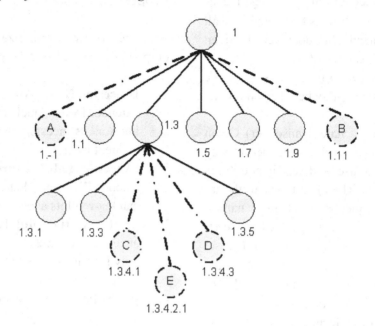

the containment labeling scheme, because those algorithms need to read labels for all four nodes a, b, c, d to answer the path query. One may use extended Dewey labels to design a novel and efficient holistic twig join algorithm, which efficiently utilizes the above five properties (See [Lu, et al. 2005] for details).

DYAMIC XML LABELING SCHEMES

We classify dynamic labeling schemes into three categories: region-based, prefix-based and prime labeling scheme. Lastly we introduce several encoding schemes which can be applied to containment and dewey ID labeling schemes to generate dynamic XML labels.

Region-Based Dynamic Labeling Schemes

A simple approach to make containment labeling scheme more flexible is to leave some gaps at initial labeling (Li&Moon, 2001). This approach

can have poor updating performance if nodes are continuously inserted into the smallest gap, since re-labeling is necessary when the gap is consumed. In addition, gaps make labels less compact and therefore less efficient to process.

Using floating-point numbers (Amagasa, 2003) instead of integers only adds limited dynamism to region-based labeling scheme. A floating-point number typically consist of three fields: the sign bit, the exponent and the significand (mantissa). The fact that the significand field is represented by fixed number of bits implies that floating-point numbers only have finite accuracy, i.e. there are finite numbers of floating-point numbers between any two floating-point numbers. In this sense, using floating-point number is equivalent to leaving gaps and therefore suffers from the same weaknesses.

Prefix-Based Dynamic Labeling Schemes

Compared with region-based labeling scheme, prefix-based labeling scheme is inherently more robust for insertions. For example, dewey ID labeling scheme (Tatarnov, 2002) can easily accommodate insertions below a leaf node or after the last child of a node. However, re-labeling is still unavoidable for insertions between two consecutive siblings.

ORDPATH Labeling Scheme

ORDPATH (O'Neil, 2004) solves the re-labeling problem by dynamically extending the number of components based on a special 'careting in' technique. We illustrate the processing of ORDPATH labels with the following example.

Example 3.*An example of ORDPATH labeling is shown in Figure 6. The circles with solid lines represent nodes from the initial labeling. It can be seen that the initial labeling of ORDPATH is similar to dewey ID except that only odd numbers are used. The circles with dotted lines represent the new nodes that are inserted into the XML tree. The order in which they are inserted follows from the alphabetical order of their associated letters. Node A is inserted before the root's first child with label 1.1. The new label is generated by adding -2 to the last component of 1.1, which gives 1.-1. Similarly, by adding 2 to the last component of 1.9, we can get the new label 1.11 for node B. To insert node C between 1.3.3 and 1.3.5, we use 4 which falls between 3 and 5 as the `caret'. The new label is 1.3.4.1 which is the concatenation of the parent label and the caret, followed by a 1. The new label for D can be generated in the same way as a rightmost insertion: by adding 2 to the last component of C, the label of D is 1.3.4.3. Inserting E between C and D requires another caret 2, which is between 1 and 3, to be used and the new label is 1.3.4.2.1.*

Given two ORDAPTH labels A: $a_1.a_2...a_m$ and B: $b_1.b_2...b_n$, A is an ancestor of B if and only if m<n and $a_1.a_2...a_m$ is a prefix of $b_1.b_2...b_n$. Document order can be deduced by comparing A and B based on lexicographical order. To determine parent and sibling relationships from ORDPATH

labels are more complicated because every level of an ORDPATH label is possibly represented by a variable number of even numbers followed by an odd number.

Although ORDPATH labeling scheme allows dynamic insertions without re-labeling, it comes with considerable costs even when no update actually happens: a) The initial ORDPATH labels are less compact than Dewey ID labels because even numbers are not used; and b) The 'careting technique' significantly complicates the processing of ORDPATH labels. For example, to infer the level information from an ORDPATH label requires checking the parities of all of its components. These costs, in terms of storage and query processing, are especially un-desirable for documents that are seldom updated.

DDE Labeling Scheme

Compared with ORDPATH, Dynamic DEwey (DDE) labeling scheme (Xu&Ling, 2009) has the advantage of being tailored for static XML documents, while being able to avoid re-labeling when updates take place. The initial labeling of DDE is the same as dewey ID. However, determining the various relationships based on DDE labels is different from dewey ID.

- **AD relationship:** Given two DDE labels A: $a_1.a_2...a_m$ and B: $b_1.b_2...b_n$, A is an ancestor of B if and only if m<n and $a_1/b_1 = a_2/b_2 = ... = a_m/b_m$.
  - **PC relationship** can be established if, in addition to AD relationship, the level difference of the two labels is one.
- **Sibling relationship:** Given two DDE labels A: $a_1.a_2...a_m$ and B: $b_1.b_2...b_n$, A is an ancestor of B if and only if m=n and $a_1/b_1 = a_2/b_2 = ... = a_{m-1}/b_{m-1}$.
  - **Document order:** Given two DDE labels A: $a_1.a_2...a_m$ and B: $b_1.b_2...b_n$, A precedes B in document order if

and only if one of the following conditions holds:

1. $m < n$ and $a_1/b_1 = a_2/b_2 = \ldots = a_m/b_m.$
2. There exits $k \leq min(m, n)$ (min is a function which takes in two numbers and returns the smaller number as output), such that $a_1/b_1 = a_2/b_2 = \ldots = a_{k-1}/b_{k-1}$ and $a_k \times b_1 < b_k \times a_1.$

It can be seen that the properties of DDE labels are the same as those of dewey ID labels if we have $a_1 = b_1 > 0$. That is, the initial labels of DDE can be treated exactly like dewey ID labels if no update takes place. Given that the initial DDE labels are the same as and can be treated in the same way as dewey ID labels, we consider DDE labels tailored for static XML documents.

To facilitate updates, we introduce an addition operation on DDE labels:

Definition 3: (DDE label addition) Given two DDE labels A: $a_1.a_2 \ldots a_m$ and B: $b_1.b_2 \ldots b_m$, addition of A and B (denoted as A+B) is defined as:

A+B= $(a_1+b_1).(a_2+b_2) \ldots .(a_m+b_m).$

We illustrate how DDE handles updates with an example.

Example 4. *Consider the example of DDE labeling in Figure 7, the circles with solid lines represent nodes from the initial labeling which is the same as dewey ID labeling scheme. Node A is inserted before node 1.1 which is the first child of the root. The new label is generated by adding -1 to the last component of 1.1, which gives 1.0. Likewise, by adding 1 to the last component of 1.5, we can get the new label 1.6 for node B. To insert node C between 1.2.2 and 1.2.3, we add the two labels and the new label is 2.4.5 (1.2.2+1.2.3). Similarly, the labels for D and E are 3.6.8 (2.4.5+1.2.3) and 5.10.13 (2.4.5+3.6.8). respectively.*

When a new node is inserted between two sibling nodes with labels A and B, we assign label A+B to the new node. We refer the readers to Xu&Ling (2009) for the complete description of DDE labeling scheme as well as the proof of correctness of its algorithms.

Prime Labeling Scheme

In prime labeling scheme (Wu&Lee, 2004), every node is assigned a unique prime number (self-label). The label of a node is the product self-labels of the nodes along the path from the root to that node, or equivalently, the product of its self-label and its parent's label. Given that all self-labels are unique prime numbers, the factorization of a label can be used to uniquely identify a path in the XML tree (this property resembles prefix labeling scheme in some respects). Based on the path information contained in the prefix labels, establishing AD and PC relationships can be easily achieved. Determining document order, however, requires a Simultaneous Congruence (SC) value which is used to derive the one-to-one mappings from a self-label to its global order. In practice, to avoid the SC value from becoming too large, usually a list of SC values is used where each SC value maintains the global ordering of a subset of the nodes. While updates in prime labeling scheme require no re-labeling of existing nodes, the SC values need to be re-computed every time a node is inserted or deleted.

Prime labeling scheme suffers from the following drawbacks:

a. **Label size:** Each prime number can only be used once. Thus, the self-label of a new node is always larger than self-labels of existing nodes. This implies that, as the number of nodes increases, the rate at which prime label size increases becomes faster. In addition, prime labels are computed based on multiplications and therefore have large label size;

Figure 7. An example of DDE labeling

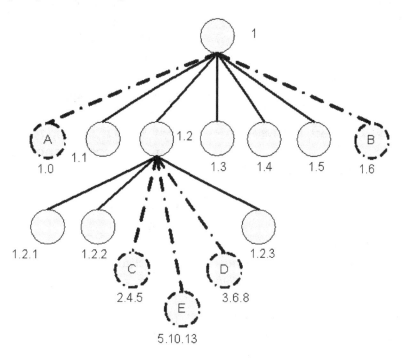

b. **Computational cost:** Prime labeling schemes involves many costly computations such as: (1) a single insertion demands determining the next un-used prime number as well as the re-computation of multiple SC values and (2) determining AD and PC relationships requires modulus operations of possibly large numbers.

The Encoding Schemes

Recently several encoding schemes (Li&Ling, 2005; Li&Ling 2006; Xu&Ling, 2007) have been proposed as a new approach to produce dynamic labels. These encoding schemes can be applied to containment or dewey labeling schemes and transform their labels into dynamic formats.

Dynamic Formats

Compact Dynamic Binary String (CDBS) (Li&Ling 2006) encoding scheme transforms the original labels into CDBS codes which are binary strings that end with '1's.

Definition 4: (Binary string) Given the set a binary numbers A= {0, 1} where each number can be stored with 1 bit, a binary string is a sequence of elements in A.

CDBS codes are compared based on lexicographical order. From Algorithm 1, given any two CDBS codes C_l and C_r such that C_l is lexicographically less than C_r (denote as $C_l <_{lex} C_r$), we can always find another CDBS code C_m, such that $C_l <_{lex} C_m <_{lex} C_r$.

<u>Algorithm 1: InsertCDBSCode(Cl, Cr)</u>

```
    Data: C_l and C_r which are
two CDBS codes such that C_l <_lex-
C_r.
    Result: Another CDBS code C_m
which satisfies C_l <_lex C_m <_lex C_r.
1   if(length(C_l)≥length(C_r))
then
2      C_m = C_l ⊙'1'  //⊙ means con-
catenation
3   elseC_m = C_r with the last '1'
changed to '01'
4   returnC_m
```

Example 5. *Let C_l and C_r be '001' and '01' such that '001' $<_{lex}$ '01', we can find C_m by concatenating C_l with '1' and the result is '0011' (Algorithm 1, line 2). It can be seen that '001' $<_{lex}$ '0011' $<_{lex}$ '01'. Let C_l and C_r be '01' and '011' such that '01' $<_{lex}$ '011', we can deduce that C_m = '011' with the last '1' changed to '01' ='0101' (Algorithm 1, line 3). As a result, we have '01' $<_{lex}$ '0101' $<_{lex}$ '011'.*

Although CDBS encoding can produce compact and dynamic labels, overflow problem can happen to the physical representation of binary strings. There are two formats to store binary strings: (1) attach a length field to each binary string. The lengths fields should have the same length; or (2) store all binary strings with the same length. If a binary string is shorter than the fixed length, attach '0's to its front . For both formats, there is a limit on the maximum length that can be represented. Overflow happens when the length of some binary string exceeds that limit.

Quaternary Encoding for Dynamic XML data (QED) (Li&Ling 2006) is similar to CDBS encoding scheme in many aspects, but solves the overflow problem. QED encoding scheme transforms the original labels into QED codes which are quaternary strings that end with '2' or '3'.

Definition 5: (Quaternary string) Given the set a binary numbers A= {1, 2, 3} where each number can be stored with 2 bits, a quaternary string is a sequence of elements in A. Note that 0 is reserved as the delimiter for quaternary strings.

Algorithm 2: InsertQEDCode(Cl, Cr)

```
    Data: C_l and C_r which are
two QED codes such that C_l <_lex C_r.
    Result: Another QED code C_m
which satisfies C_l <_lex C_m <_lex C_r.
1   if(length(C_l)<length(C_r))
then
2      C_m = (C_r with the last sym-
bol changed to '1') ⊙ '2'  //⊙
means concatenation
3   else if
(length(C_l)>length(C_r))
4   if the last symbol of C_l is
'2'
5          then C_m = C_r with the
last '2' changed to '3'
6   else //the last symbol of C_l
is '3'
7      C_m = C_l ⊙ '2'
8   else //length(C_l)=length(C_r)
9   C_m = C_l ⊙ '2'
10  returnC_m
```

Algorithm 2 illustrates how a QED code can be inserted between two QED codes in lexicographical order. Given any two QED codes, it follows from Algorithm 2 that we can always find another QED code which falls between them in lexicographical order.

Example 6. *Let C_l and C_r be '22' and '223' such that '22' $<_{lex}$ '223' and length('22')<length('223'), Algorithm 2 will output '2212' ('223' with the last symbol changed to '1' ⊙ '2', line 2). Let C_l and C_r be '22' and '23' such that '22' $<_{lex}$ '23' and length('22')=length('23'), we can deduce that C_m ='222' which it the concatenation of C_l with '2'.*

Vector encoding scheme (Xu&Bao, 2007) transforms labels into vector codes.

Definition 6: (Vector code) A vector code is a pair of positive decimal numbers which represents a vector in the first quadrant of the two dimensional space. We denote a vector code as (x, y).

Vector codes are ordered based on Gradient.

Definition 7: (Gradient) Given a vector code V (x, y), the Gradient of V (denote as $G(V)$) is defined as y/x.

Suppose $V_1(x_1, y_1)$ and $V_2(x_2, y_2)$ are two vector codes, V_1 precedes V_2 in vector order (denote as $V_1 <_v V_2$) if and only if $G(V_1) < G(V_2)$, or equivalently, $y_1x_2 < x_1y_2$. Additions of the two vector codes, $V1+V2$ is defined as $(x_1 + x_2, y_1 + y_2)$. An important property of the addition operation as follows,

Theorem 2: Given two vector codes $V_1(x_1, y_1)$ and $V_2(x_2, y_2)$ such that $V_1 <_v V_2$, we have $V_1 <_v (V_1 + V_2) <_v V_2$.

Proof: $V_1 <_v V_2$ implies that $y_1x_2 < x_1y_2$. We have $y_1 \times (x_1 + x_2) = y_1x_1 + y_1x_2 < y_1x_1 + x_1y_2 = (y_1 + y_2) x_1$. As a result, $V_1 <_v (V_1 + V_2)$. Proving $(V_1 + V_2) <_v V_2$ is similar so we ignore it here.

Based on Theorem 2, we can insert $V_1 + V_2$ between V_1 and V_2 in vector order. Vector codes therefore allow dynamic insertions without relabeling.

Encoding Algorithm

What lies at the core of all the encoding schemes is how to transform a range of integers into the corresponding dynamic codes. The transformation process should guarantee the following two properties:

- Order preserving: for any two start or end values i and j in the range such that i<j, their corresponding codes C_i and C_j should satisfy $C_i < C_j$.
- Optimal size: the label size after transformation should be as small as possible.

Next we introduce the encoding algorithms of the three encoding schemes that satisfy the above two properties. First we illustrate how CDBS encoding scheme performs encoding with an example. Suppose we want to encode a range from 1 to 18. Their corresponding CDBS codes which are shown in the second column of Table 1 can be derived from the following steps:

1. Extend the range by adding a 0 before 1 and a 19 after 18. Assign empty strings to positions 0 and 19.
2. Apply Algorithm 1 with the two empty strings that correspond to 0 and 19 as input (note that we treat empty strings as CDBS codes in this case). Assign the output CDBS code '1' to the middle position 10 (round $(0+19)/2$) of range $[0, 19]$.
3. Use the middle position to divide range $[0, 19]$ into two sub-ranges $[0, 10]$ and $[10, 19]$. Repeat step 1 for each of the sub-ranges, i.e. apply Algorithm 1 with the CDBS codes of the two end positions as input. Assign the output CDBS code to the middle position of the current range.

Step 3 is recursively applied until all positions in the original range $[0, 19]$ are encoded.

To encode a range from 1 to 18 by QED encoding scheme, the results are shown in Table 1 column 3. The encoding process of QED encoding scheme is derived from the following steps:

1. Extend the range by adding a 0 before 1 and a 19 after 18. Assign empty strings to both 0 and 19.

Table 1. The encoding table for CDBS, QED and Vector encoding

Decimal Number	CDBS code	QED code	Vector code	Gradient (accurate to 0.01)
1	00001	112	(5,1)	0.2
2	0001	12	(4,1)	0.25
3	001	122	(3,1)	0.33
4	0011	13	(5,2)	0.4
5	01	132	(2,1)	0.5
6	01001	2	(7,4)	0.57
7	0101	212	(5,3)	0.6
8	011	22	(3,2)	0.67
9	0111	222	(4,3)	0.75
10	1	223	(1,1)	1
11	10001	23	(4,5)	1.25
12	1001	232	(3,4)	1.33
13	101	3	(2,3)	1.5
14	1011	312	(3,5)	1.67
15	11	32	(1,2)	2
16	1101	322	(2,5)	2.5
17	111	33	(1,3)	3
18	1111	332	(1,4)	4

2.   Calculate the $(1/3)^{th}$ and $(2/3)^{th}$ positions of range [0, 19]
   a. $(1/3)^{th}$ position = round(0+(19-0)/3)=6 and
   b. $(2/3)^{th}$ position = round(0+(19-0)×2/3)=13.

Next we apply Algorithm 2 with the QED codes of positions 0 and 19 as input (Note that we treat empty strings as QED codes) and assign the output QED code to position 6 ($(1/3)^{th}$ position). Similarly, we can apply Algorithm 2 again with the QED codes of positions 6 and 19 as input and assign the output QED code to position 13 ($(2/3)^{th}$ position).

A straightforward optimization of the above encoding process is to modify Algorithm 2 so that it outputs two QED codes for the $(1/3)^{th}$ and $(1/2)^{th}$ positions at one time.

3.   Use the $(1/3)^{th}$ and $(2/3)^{th}$ positions to divide the range [0, 19] into three sub-ranges [0, 6], [6, 13] and [13, 19]. Then we repeat step 2 for each of the sub-ranges.

This process continues until all positions in the original range [0, 19] are encoded.

The result of vector encoding for the range from 1 to 18 is shown in Table 1 column 4. Vector encoding performs the following steps:

1.   Extend the range by adding a 0 before 1 and a 19 after 18. Assign Vector code (1, 0) to position 0 and (0, 1) to position 19.

2.   Add the vector codes of positions 1 and 19 and assign the sum (1, 1) (= (1, 0) + (0, 1)) to the middle position 10 (round(0+19)/2).

3.   Use the middle position 10 to divide the range [0, 19] into two sub-ranges [0, 10] and [10, 19]. Repeat step 2 for each of the sub-ranges.

Figure 8.Applying QED encoding scheme to containment labeling scheme

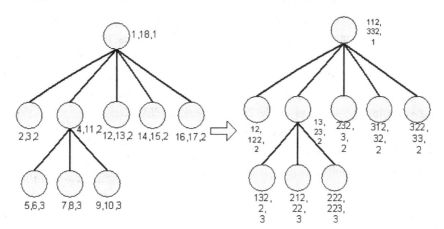

Table 2. Comparison of different labeling schemes (initial labels)

	Update	Space Complexity	Time Complexity to get level	Time Complexity to compare AD/PC	Time Complexity to compare Sibling	Special property
Containment	Static	O(nlog(n))	O(1)	O(log(n))	N/A	
Dewey	Static	O(n²)	O(1)	O(n)	O(n)	
Extended Dewey	Static	O(n²)	O(1)	O(n)	O(n)	Ancestor-type-aware
ORDPATH	Dynamic	O(n²)	O(n)	O(n)	O(n)	
DDE	Dynamic	O(n²)	O(1)	O(n)	O(n)	

The encoding process stops when all position in [0, 19] are encoded.

Application of Encoding Schemes

To illustrate the application of encoding schemes, we use the application of QED to containment labeling scheme as an example.

The *start* and *end* values of the containment labels shown in Figure 8 ranges from 1 to 18. We have shown how to derive the mapping from the range 18 to QED codes and the results are shown in Table 1 column 3. Based on the encoding table, the containment labels can be transformed to QED codes with *level* fields unchanged. We refer to the resulting labels as QED-Containment labels. Given the dynamic property of QED codes, QED

Containment labels allow dynamic insertions without relabeling.

CONCLUSION

In this chapter, we have presented existing works on XML labeling schemes which we classify mainly into static and dynamic labeling schemes. Static labeling schemes facilitate efficient determination of various relationships of the nodes in an XML tree which is essential for XML query processing. We introduce three types of static labeling schemes: containment, dewey ID and extended dewey schemes. Extended dewey scheme extends the original dewey labels by adding the element name information to speedup query processing.

Dynamic labeling schemes, while inheriting the basic properties of static labeling schemes, should also accommodate dynamic updates with low costs. We introduce three types of dynamic labeling schemes: region-based, prefix-based and prime labeling scheme. The comparison of selected labeling schemes is shown in Table 2. In addition, we have introduced the encoding schemes, which can be applied to static labeling schemes to generate dynamic labels.

REFERENCES

Abiteboul, S., Alstrup, S., Kaplan, H., Milo, T., & Rauhe, T. (2006). Compact Labeling Scheme for Ancestor Queries. *SIAM Journal on Computing, 35*(6), 1295–1309. doi:10.1137/S0097539703437211

Amagasa, T., Yoshikawa, M., & Uemura, S. (2003). QRS: a robust numbering scheme for XML documents. In *Proceedings of the 19th International Conference on Data Engineering* (5-8 March 2003), (pp. 705 – 707).

Bruno, N., Koudas, N., & Srivastava, D. (2002). Holistic twig joins: optimal XML pattern matching. In *Proceedings of the 2002 ACM SIGMOD international Conference on Management of Data,* Madison, Wisconsin, June 03 - 06, 2002 (pp. 310-321). New York: ACM.

Cohen, E., Kaplan, H., & Milo, T. (2002). Labeling dynamic XML trees. In *Proceedings of the Twenty-First ACM SIGMOD-SIGACT-SIGART Symposium on Principles of Database Systems,* Madison, Wisconsin, June 03 - 05, (pp. 271-281). New York: ACM.

Li, C., & Ling, T. W. (2005). QED: a novel quaternary encoding to completely avoid re-labeling in XML updates. In *Proceedings of the 14th ACM international Conference on information and Knowledge Management,* Bremen, Germany, October 31 - November 05, (pp. 501-508). New York: ACM.

Li, C., Ling, T. W., & Hu, M. (2006). Efficient Processing of Updates in Dynamic XML Data. In *Proceedings of the 22nd international Conference on Data Engineering,* April 03 - 07, ICDE (pp. 13). Washington, DC: IEEE Computer Society.

Li, Q., & Moon, B. (2001). Indexing and Querying XML Data for Regular Path Expressions. In P. M. Apers, P. Atzeni, S. Ceri, S. Paraboschi, K. Ramamohanarao, and R. T. Snodgrass, (Eds.), *Proceedings of the 27th international Conference on Very Large Data Bases,* September 11 - 14, Very Large Data Bases, (pp. 361-370). San Francisco, CA: Morgan Kaufmann Publishers.

Lu, J., Chen, T., & Ling, T. W. (2004). Efficient processing of XML twig patterns with parent child edges: a look-ahead approach. In *Proceedings of 2004 International Conference on Information and Knowledge Management (CIKM),* Washington, DC, November 8-13, (pp. 533–542).

Lu, J., & Ling, T. W. (2004). Labeling and querying dynamic XML trees, In *Proceedings of the Sixth Asia Pacific Web Conference,* Hangzhou, China, April 14-17, APWeb, (pp. 180–189).

Lu, J., Ling, T. W., Chan, C., & Chen, T. (2005). From region encoding to extended dewey: on efficient processing of XML twig pattern matching. In *Proceedings of the 31st international Conference on Very Large Data Bases,* Trondheim, Norway, August 30 - September 02, Very Large Data Bases, VLDB Endowment, (pp. 193-204).

O'Neil, P., O'Neil, E., Pal, S., Cseri, I., Schaller, G., & Westbury, N. (2004). ORDPATHs: insert-friendly XML node labels. In *Proceedings of the 2004 ACM SIGMOD international Conference on Management of Data*, Paris, France, June 13 - 18, *SIGMOD '04* (pp. 903-908). New York: ACM.

Shanmugasundaram, J., Shekita, E. J., Kiernan, J., Krishnamurthy, R., Viglas, S., Naughton, J. F., & Tatarinov, I. (2001). A general techniques for querying XML documents using a relational database system. *SIGMOD Record, 30*(3), 20–26. doi:10.1145/603867.603871

Silberstein, A., & He, H. nd Yi, K. & Yang J. (2005). Boxes: Efficient maintenance of order-based labeling for dynamic XML data, In *Proceedings of the 21st International Conference on Data Engineering,* 5-8 April, Tokyo, Japan, (pp. 285–296).

Tatarinov, I., Viglas, S. D., Beyer, K., Shanmugasundaram, J., Shekita, E., & Zhang, C. (2002). Storing and querying ordered XML using a relational database system. In *Proceedings of the 2002 ACM SIGMOD international Conference on Management of Data,* Madison, WI, June 03 - 06, *SIGMOD '02* (pp. 204-215). New York: ACM.

Wu, X., Lee, M. L., & Hsu, W. (2004). A Prime Number Labeling Scheme for Dynamic Ordered XML Trees. In *Proceedings of the 20th international Conference on Data Engineering,* March 30 - April 02, *ICDE* (pp. 66). Washington, DC: IEEE Computer Society.

Xu, L., Bao, Z., & Ling, T. W. (2007). A Dynamic Labeling Scheme Using Vectors. In R. Wagner, N. Revell, & G. Pernul, (Eds.), *Proceedings of the 18th international Conference on Database and Expert Systems Applications,* Regensburg, Germany, September 03 - 07, (LNCS Vol. 4653, pp. 130-140). Berlin: Springer-Verlag.

Xu, L., Ling, T. W., Wu, H., & Bao, Z. (2009). DDE: From Dewey to a Fully Dynamic XML Labeling. To appear in *Proceedings of the 2009 ACM SIGMOD international Conference on Management of Data* Providence, Rhode Island, United States, June 29 – July 2, 2009.

Zhang, C., Naughton, J., DeWitt, D., Luo, Q., & Lohman, G. (2001). On supporting containment queries in relational database management systems. In T. Sellis, (Ed.), *Proceedings of the 2001 ACM SIGMOD international Conference on Management of Data,* Santa Barbara, CA, May 21 - 24, *SIGMOD '01* (pp. 425-436). New York: ACM.

ADDITIONAL READING

Alstrup, S., Bille, P., & Rauhe, T. (2003, January 12-13). Labeling Schemes for Small Distances in Trees. In Proceedings of the 14th Annual ACM-SIAM Symposium on Discrete Mathematics, Baltimore, Maryland, USA (pp. 689-698). Society for Industrial and Applied Mathematics.

Chen, Y., Mihaila, G. A., Bordawekar, R., & Padmanabhan, S. (2004, March 14-18). L-Tree: a Dynamic Labeling Structure for Ordered XML Data. In W. Lindner, M. Mesiti, C. Turker, Y. Tzizikas, & A. Vakali (Eds.). Current Trends in Database Technology - EDBT 2004 Workshops, Herakleion, Greece (LNCS 3268, pp. 209-218). Germany, Berlin: Springer.

Duong, M., & Zhang, Y. (2005, January 31 – February 3). LSDX: A New Labeling Scheme for Dynamically Updating XML Data. In H.E. Williams, & G. Dobbie (Eds.), Database Technologies 2005, Proceedings of 16th Australasian Database Conference, Newcastle, Australia (Vol.39, pp. 185-193). Melbourne, Australia: Victoria University.

Fisher, D. K., Lam, F., Shui, W. M., & Wong, R. K. (2006, January 16-19). Dynamic Labeling Schemes for Ordered XML Based on Type Information. In G. Dobbie, & J. Bailey (Eds.), Proceedings of the 17th Australasian Database Conference, Hobart, Australia (Vol. 49, pp. 59-68). Darlinghurst, Australia: Australian computer Society, Inc.

Harder, T., Haustein, M., Mathis, C., & Wagner, M. (2007, January). Node labeling schemes for dynamic XML documents reconsidered. *Data & Knowledge Engineering*, *60*(1), 126–149. doi:10.1016/j.datak.2005.11.008

Kaplan, H., Milo, T., & Shabo, R. (2002, January 6-8). A comparison of labeling schemes for ancestor queries. In Proceedings of the 13th annual ACM-SIAM Symposium on Discrete Algorithms, San Francisco, CA, USA (pp. 954-963). Philadelphia, PA, USA: Society for Industrial and Applied Mathematics.

Li, C., & Ling, T. W. 2005. QED: a novel quaternary encoding to completely avoid re-labeling in XML updates. In *Proceedings of the 14th ACM international Conference on information and Knowledge Management* (Bremen, Germany, October 31 - November 05, 2005). CIKM '05. ACM, New York, NY, 501-508.

Li, C., Ling, T. W., & Hu, M. 2006. Efficient Processing of Updates in Dynamic XML Data. In *Proceedings of the 22nd international Conference on Data Engineering* (April 03 - 07, 2006). ICDE. IEEE Computer Society, Washington, DC, 13.

Li, C., Ling, T. W., and Hu, M. 2008. Efficient updates in dynamic XML data: from binary string to quaternary string. *The VLDB Journal* 17, 3 (May. 2008), 573-601.

Lu, J., Ling, T. W., Chan, C., & Chen, T. 2005. From region encoding to extended dewey: on efficient processing of XML twig pattern matching. In *Proceedings of the 31st international Conference on Very Large Data Bases* (Trondheim, Norway, August 30 - September 02, 2005). Very Large Data Bases. VLDB Endowment, 193-204.

O'Neil, P., O'Neil, E., Pal, S., Cseri, I., Schaller, G., & Westbury, N. 2004. ORDPATHs: insert-friendly XML node labels. In *Proceedings of the 2004 ACM SIGMOD international Conference on Management of Data* (Paris, France, June 13 - 18, 2004). SIGMOD '04. ACM, New York, NY, 903-908.

Tatarinov, I., Viglas, S. D., Beyer, K., Shanmugasundaram, J., Shekita, E., & Zhang, C. 2002. Storing and querying ordered XML using a relational database system. In *Proceedings of the 2002 ACM SIGMOD international Conference on Management of Data* (Madison, Wisconsin, June 03 - 06, 2002). SIGMOD '02. ACM, New York, NY, 204-215.

Wu, X., Lee, M. L., & Hsu, W. 2004. A Prime Number Labeling Scheme for Dynamic Ordered XML Trees. In *Proceedings of the 20th international Conference on Data Engineering* (March 30 - April 02, 2004). ICDE. IEEE Computer Society, Washington, DC, 66.

Xu, L., Bao, Z., & Ling, T. W. 2007. A Dynamic Labeling Scheme Using Vectors. In *Proceedings of the 18th international Conference on Database and Expert Systems Applications* (Regensburg, Germany, September 03 - 07, 2007). R. Wagner, N. Revell, and G. Pernul, Eds. Lecture Notes In Computer Science, vol. 4653. Springer-Verlag, Berlin, Heidelberg, 130-140.

Xu, L., Ling, T. W., Wu, H., & Bao, Z. DDE: From Dewey to a Fully Dynamic XML Labeling. To appear in *Proceedings of the 2009 ACM SIGMOD international Conference on Management of Data* (Providence, Rhode Island, United States, June 29 – July 2, 2009).

Zhang, C., Naughton, J., DeWitt, D., Luo, Q., & Lohman, G. 2001. On supporting containment queries in relational database management systems. In *Proceedings of the 2001 ACM SIGMOD international Conference on Management of Data* (Santa Barbara, California, United States, May 21 - 24, 2001). T. Sellis, Ed. SIGMOD '01. ACM, New York, NY, 425-436.

Chapter 7
Keyword Search on XML Data

Ziyang Liu
Arizona State University, USA

Yi Chen
Arizona State University, USA

INTRODUCTION

Information search is an indispensable component of our lives. Due to the vast collections of XML data on the web and in enterprises, providing users with easy access to XML is highly desirable. The classical way of accessing XML data is through issuing structured queries, such as XPath/XQuery. However, in many applications it is inconvenient or impossible for users to learn these query languages. Besides, the requirement that the user needs to comprehend data schemas may well be overwhelming and infeasible, as the schemas are likely complex, fast-evolving, or unavailable. A natural question to ask is whether we can empower users to effectively access XML data simply using keyword queries.

Ideally the result of a keyword search on XML will automatically assemble relevant pieces of data

that are in different locations but are inter-connected and collectively relevant to the query. There are several advantages of such an approach. First, it can relieve casual users from the steep learning curve of studying structured query languages and data schemas when accessing structured data. Second, it allows users to easily access heterogeneous databases. For instance, for websites with back-ends storing XML data, this approach provides a more flexible search method than the existing solution that uses a fixed set of pre-built template queries. Furthermore, this approach helps to reveal interesting or unexpected relationships among entities. Making XML data searchable will substantially increase the information volume that a user can access, have potential to provide search results with better quality compared with keyword search on textual documents, and thus increase the usability of XML and make significant impact to people's lives.

DOI: 10.4018/978-1-61520-727-5.ch007

The objective of this chapter is to provide an overview of the state-of-the-art in supporting keyword search on XML data, outline the problem space in this area, introduce representative techniques that address different aspects of the problem, and discuss further challenges and promising directions for future work. The problem spectrum that will be covered in this chapter ranges from identifying relevant keyword matches and an axiomatic framework to evaluate different strategies, identifying other relevant data nodes, ranking, indexes and materialized views, to result snippet generation.

1.1 QUERY MODEL AND QUERY RESULT

1.1.1 Keyword Query

A keyword search, as the name indicates, is a query which consists of a set of keywords. A keyword may be required (it must appear in each result) or optional. Each keyword may match elements, attributes names and/or values in the XML document. Some search engines, such as XSEarch (Cohen, Jamou, Kanza, & Sagiv, 2003), has a slightly structured query format: each query term is one of the three formats: l:k, l: or:k, where l and k are keywords, l must match name nodes (element names and/or attribute names) and k must match value nodes.

1.1.2 Query Result

A result of a keyword search on textual documents is usually a whole document. On the other hand, due to the structure of XML, each result is not an entire XML document, but a fragment of it. When the user does not separate the keywords into required keywords and optional keywords, a system may opt to use AND semantics or OR semantics. As the names suggest, AND semantics requires a query result to have all keywords in the query, while OR semantics only requires a result to have some of the keywords.

XML search engines generate results as subtrees / subgraphs of the XML document. A query result should contain both relevant keyword matches (i.e., the XML nodes that match the keywords) and other relevant nodes that are deemed relevant. The details of how query results are constructed will be discussed later in this chapter.

In this chapter, "query" and "search" are used interchangeably.

1.2 WHAT ARE THE PROBLEMS INVOLVED?

Due to the structure of XML data, processing keyword search on XML requires fundamentally different techniques than on textual documents. In fact, the structure of XML data provides us with better opportunities than textual documents to generate meaningful results, as long as they can be properly exploited. We summarize processing XML keyword search as the following problems, including generating query results (including finding relevant matches and relevant non-matches), improving efficiency, ranking and generating result snippets.

1. **Identifying relevant keyword matches.** Each keyword can have multiple matches in the XML document. Not all of them are relevant to the query. Consider query *"Greg, position"*, on the XML data in Figure 1. By issuing this query, the user would like to find the *position* of the player named *Greg*. In Figure 1, there are multiple *"position"* nodes, but only the one labeled (20) is relevant to the query.

2. **Identifying relevant non-matches.** Merely returning relevant matches to users as query results is undesirable. A user who issues a keyword search is usually interested in some information other than the keyword

matches. Consider Q_1: "*Greg, position*" and Q_2: "*Greg, forward*" on the XML data in Figure 1. The queries look similar but the intentions of the user are completely different. For Q_1, the user is likely seeking the "*position*" information of *Greg*. On the other hand, by issuing Q_2, very likely the user is interested in the general information of the player whose name is "*Greg*" and who is a "*forward*" in the team. Therefore, in addition to the relevant matches, we should also return other information of this player, such as nationality and former teams.

3. **Generating results efficiently.** Indexes and materialized views are widely used in answering structured queries (SQL/XPath/XQuery, etc.) and have achieved big success in speeding up the query processing. Indexes support various common operations on the data efficiently. A materialized view is a query whose results are computed and physically stored, which can answer a new query without accessing the source data. Indexes and materialized views can also potentially be used in XML keyword search to achieve improvement in efficiency.

4. **Ranking.** Since keyword searches are inherently ambiguous and it is impossible for users to clearly specify their intentions in keyword queries, search engines will inevitably generate irrelevant results. As a result, a proper ranking of the results is highly desirable.

5. **Result snippets.** Result snippets are widely used in web search engines as a complement of ranking schemes to help users find the relevant results. Since keyword searches are ambiguous, it is impossible for any ranking scheme to perfectly gauge the result relevance, which may even be different for different users. A concise snippet for each query result helps the user quickly evaluate the result and find the relevant ones to click.

1.3 IDENTIFYING RELEVANT KEYWORD MATCHES

Keyword searches are inherently ambiguous: there can be many interpretations for a single query. As a result, existing search engines adopt best effort approaches to infer the "best" possible results from the data. A notable characteristics of keyword search on XML is that, although there can be multiple matches to a keyword, not all of them are relevant to the query. Therefore, various approaches have been proposed to identify relevant keyword matches based on the XML data structure.

1.3.1 XML Trees

Generally in XML trees, keyword matches are connected by a set of LCA (*Lowest Common Ancestor*) nodes, which depict node relationships. As an example, consider query "*Greg, nationality*". As we can see from Figure 1, *Greg* (17) and *nationality* (18) are connected by their LCA, *player* (15), i.e., they belong to the same player. On the other hand, *Greg* (17) and *nationality* (29) are connected by LCA *players* (14), indicating that they belong to different players. In this section, we introduce existing strategies for identifying relevant matches on XML trees, all of which are based on pruning LCA nodes that likely connect irrelevant match nodes, such as LCA *players* (14).

1.3.1.1 Identification Strategies

When there is no ID/IDREF in an XML document, it can be modeled as a tree. There are two types of query result definition on XML trees, which lead to different types of strategies in identifying relevant matches: multi-match semantics and single-match semantics. In multi-match semantics, each result may contain multiple matches to a keyword, while in single-match semantics, each result contains exactly one match to each keyword. A set of nodes in the XML data consist-

Figure 1.

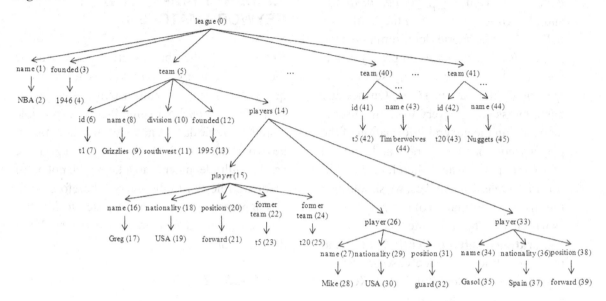

ing of one match to each keyword is referred as a *pattern match*. In single-match semantics, the keyword matches in selected pattern matches are considered as relevant.

Single-match semantics include XSEarch (Cohen et al. 2003) and MLCA (Li & Jagadish, 2004). Multi-match semantics include SLCA (Xu &Papakonstantinou, 2005) and MaxMatch (Liu & Chen, 2008). They are all refinements of LCA, i.e., each of them is a subset of the LCA of all pattern matches.

XSEarch (Cohen et al. 2003). Each result of XSEarch is a pattern match for either semantics. As introduced in Section 1.1.1, XSEarch uses slightly more expressive search terms than keywords. However, it is not much different from considering each term as a keyword, except that there are restrictions on the position of the matches, such as only internal nodes may match term *l:*.

The interconnection relationship defined in XSEarch is used to identify the qualified pattern matches.

Definition 1.1: Two nodes u, v in an XML tree are *interconnected* if and only if there are no two nodes in the paths from $LCA(u, v)$ to u and

v that have the same label, or the only two nodes that have the same label are u and v.

For example, nodes *name* (27) and *nationality* (36) in Figure 1 are not interconnected due to nodes *player* (26) and *player* (33), which have the same label. Intuitively, they are attributes of two different players. On the other hand, *name* (27) and *nationality* (29), which belong to the same player, are interconnected.

As we can see, the interconnection relationship is a way to specify whether the relationship between two nodes is meaningful.

There are two different XSEarch semantics, namely *all-pair semantics* and *star semantics*. In the all-pair semantics of XSEarch, each result contains a pattern match, such that any two of them are interconnected. In the star-semantics, each result contains a pattern match, such that there exists a "star node" in the pattern match and every other node is interconnected with the star node. For example, for query ":*Grizzlies, :forward, nationality*:" on the XML tree in Figure 2, there are two qualified pattern matches in all-pair semantics: {*name* (8), *position* (20), *nationality* (18)} and {*name* (8), *position* (38), *nationality* (36)}.

Figure 2.

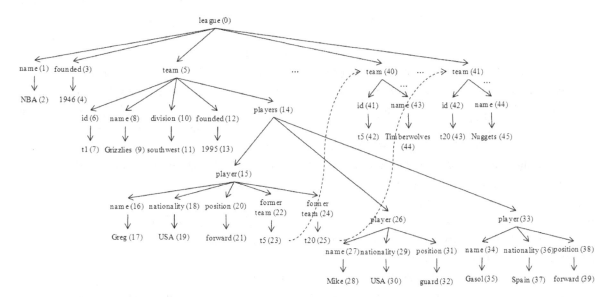

In star semantics, pattern matches such as {*name* (8), *position* (29), *nationality* (18)} are also valid, with the star node being *name* (8).

Meaningful Lowest Common Ancestor (MLCA) (Li & Jagadish, 2004). The concept of MLCA is proposed with schema-free XQuery which allows users to mix keyword search and structured query when it is beneficial to do so. Each result under MLCA semantics is a pattern match, in which every two nodes are *meaningfully related* as defined below.

Definition 1.2: Two nodes *u, v* in the XML data that match keywords k_1, k_2 are *meaningfully related* if there does not exist nodes *u', v'* matching keywords k_1, k_2, such that *LCA(u, v)* is an ancestor of *LCA(u', v')*. Intuitively, if we can find nodes *u'* and *v'* with a lower LCA, then *u'* and v' depict a more specific relationship that *u* and *v* do not have, and thus *u* and *v* are considered as not meaningfully related. Consider *name* (27) and *nationality* (36), whose LCA is node *players* (14). They are not meaningfully related as the LCA of *name* (27) and *nationality* (29) is a descendant of *players* (14). Indeed,

name (27) and *nationality* (36) belong to different players and their relationship is not meaningful.

In MLCA semantics, a result consists of a qualified pattern match. A pattern match is qualified if every pair of nodes in the pattern match are meaningfully related. As we can see, in XSEarch all-pair semantics and MLCA semantics, a result is a pattern match in which every two nodes satisfy certain conditions. The difference is that XSEarch requires every two nodes to be interconnected, while MLCA requires every two nodes to be meaningfully related. We leave the comparison of these two approaches in terms of pros and cons to the reader.

Smallest Lowest Common Ancestor (SLCA) (Xu & Papakonstantinou, 2005). This is a commonly used keyword search semantics on XML. The SLCA node of a keyword search on XML is defined as follows. The keyword matches in the subtree rooted at an SLCA node are considered as relevant.

Definition 1.3: An XML node *u* is an SLCA of a keyword search if (1) there is at least one match to each keyword in the subtree rooted at *u*, and (2) there is no descendant of *u* that satisfies (1).

As an example, the SLCA nodes of query *"forward nationality"* on the data in Figure 1 are nodes *player* (15) and *player* (33). Note that node *players* (14) satisfies condition (1), but not (2).

MaxMatch (Liu & Chen, 2008). MaxMatch is based on the observation that although SLCA semantics is able to identify and discard some irrelevant matches, there can be still many irrelevant matches in the subtree of an SLCA. MaxMatch further prunes the matches by disqualifying nodes with "stronger" siblings, i.e., a node *u* is pruned if it has a sibling *v*, such that the set of keywords appearing in *u*'s subtree is a proper subset of those appearing in *v*'s subtree. Intuitively, *u* contains strictly less information than *v*, thus it is likely that u does not satisfy the semantics of the query.

Consider keyword query *"Grizzlies, Gasol, position"* on Figure 1 as an example. There is one SLCA node which is *team* (5), and therefore all *position* nodes in the figure are considered as relevant by SLCA semantics. On the other hand, MaxMatch prunes the subtree rooted at nodes *player* (15) and *player* (26) as they only contain keyword *"position"*, while their sibling, *player* (33), contains keywords *"position"* and *"Gasol"*. As a result, MaxMatch prunes the subtree rooted at *player* (15) and *player* (26).

Formally, let *dMatch*(*u*) be the set of keywords contained in the subtree rooted at node *u*. MaxMatch defines "contributor" whose subtree is potentially relevant to the query.

Definition 1.5: For an XML tree *D* and a query *Q*, a node *u* in *D* is a contributor to *Q* if (i) *u* has an ancestor-or-self *u'* which is an SLCA node, and (ii) *u* does not have a sibling *v*, such that *dMatch*(*v*) is a proper superset of *dMatch*(*u*).

In the above example, *player* (15) and *player* (26) are not contributors, as *dMatch*(*player*(15)) and *dMatch*(*player*(26)) are proper subsets of *dMatch*(*player*(33)).

A match *m* is considered relevant by MaxMatch if (i) *m* has an ancestor-or-self *n*, which is an SLCA node, and (ii) every node on the path from *n* to *m* is a contributor to the query.

As we can see, the set of relevant matches identified by MaxMatch is a subset of that identified by SLCA.

1.3.1.2 Desirable Properties for Evaluation

Due to the ambiguity of XML keyword search, evaluating different approaches using ground truth obtained from user study can be prohibitively expensive and inconvenient. A result, an axiomatic framework is proposed by Liu and Chen (2008) which includes four properties to evaluate a strategy for identifying relevant matches. Evaluating different approaches using axiomatic frameworks has been successfully adopted in many areas including mathematical economics (Osborne & Rubinstein, 1994), clustering (Kleinberg, 2002), discrete location theory (Hansen & Roberts, 1996) and collaborative filtering (Pennock, Horvitz & Giles, 2000).

The four properties used for evaluating strategies for identifying relevant matches are data/query monotonicity and data/query consistency. These properties assume that each result is a rooted subtree; the roots of two results are not the same and do not have ancestor-descendant relationship. Besides, AND semantics is adopted.

Monotonicity describes the desirable change to the number of query results with respect to data updates and query updates.

Definition 1.6 (Data Monotonicity): If we add a new node to the data, then the data content becomes richer, therefore the number of query results should be (non-strictly) monotonically increasing. Analogous to keyword search on text documents, adding a word to a document that is not originally a query result may qualify the document as a new query result.

We now use examples to illustrate these properties. In the following examples, let D_1 be the XML tree in Figure 1 without the subtree rooted at position (38), and D_2 be the entire XML tree.

Example 1.1 Adding a new data node may increase the number of query results. Consider query "*forward, name*" on D_1, which searches for the name of a forward. Ideally, there should be one query result, rooted at *player* (15) with the matches in its subtree: *name* (16) and *forward* (21), and the paths connecting them. Now consider an insertion of a *position* node (38) and its value *forward* (39) to D_1, which results in XML tree D_2. Now, we should have one more query result: a tree rooted at *player* (33), the matches in its subtree: *name* (34) and *forward* (39), and the paths connecting them.

The number of query results may also stay the same after a data insertion. Consider query "*Grizzlies, Greg, Gasol, position*", searching for the positions of *Greg* and *Gasol* in *Grizzlies*, on D_1 and D_2, respectively. For each document there should be a single query result tree, rooted at *team*, as this subtree contains at least one relevant match to each keyword. Though the set of relevant matches in the subtree rooted at the *team* node are different for D_1 and D_2, the number of query result is one for both XML documents.

Definition 1.7 (Query Monotonicity): If we add a keyword to the query, then the query becomes more restrictive, therefore the number of query results should be (non-strictly) monotonically decreasing. Analogous to keyword search on text documents, adding a keyword to the query can disqualify a document that is originally a query result to be a result of the new query.

Example 1.2 Adding a new keyword may decrease the number of query results. For query "*forward, name*" on Figure 1, there should be two results rooted at *player* (15) and *player* (33), respectively. Now suppose we add one more keyword "*USA*" to this query, which searches for the *name* related to *forward* and *USA*. The query result rooted at node *player* (15) is still a relevant query result. However, the one rooted at *player* (33) becomes invalid, as it does not contain any match to *USA* in its subtree.

The number of query results may also stay the same after insertion of a new query; the example of this case is left for the reader to work out.

To explain the other two properties, we define a delta result tree in XML keyword search as the subtree that newly becomes part of the set of query results upon an insertion to the data or query. Note that a delta result tree could be a query result itself, or could be part of a query result.

Definition 1.8: Let R be a set of query results of processing query Q on data D, and R' be the set of updated query results after an insertion to Q or D. A subtree rooted at a node n in a query result tree $r' \in R'$ is a delta result tree if $desc - or - self(n, r') \cap R = \phi$; and $desc - or - self(parent(n, r'), r') \cap R \neq \phi$, where *parent*($n$, r') and *desc-or-self*(n, r') denotes the parent, and the set of descendant-or-self nodes of node n in a tree r', respectively. The set of all delta result trees is denoted as $\delta(R, R')$.

Definition 1.9 (Data Consistency): After a data insertion, each additional subtree that becomes (part of) a query result (i.e., delta result tree) should contain the newly inserted node. Analogous to keyword search on text documents, after we add a new word to the data, if there is a document that becomes a new query result, then this document must contain the newly inserted word.

Again, In the following example, let D_1 be the XML tree in Figure 1 without the subtree rooted at *position* (38), and D_2 be the entire XML tree.

Example 1.3 Consider query *"forward, name"* on D_1, which searches for the *name* of a *forward*. There is one query result, consisting of *player* (15) and the matches in its subtree. Now consider D_2 obtained after an insertion of a *position* (38) node along with its value *forward* to D_1. This insertion qualifies a new query result of this query, consisting of *player* (33) and the matches in its subtree. This new query result is a delta result tree, as it is the biggest subtree that is in the new result but not the original one. It is valid with respect to data consistency since the delta result tree contains the newly inserted match node *forward* (39).

As another example, consider query *"Gasol, position"* on D_1 and D_2, searching for the position of Gasol. Although the newly inserted node *position* (38) is a match of Q_1, the query result should not change. Intuitively, this match refers to the *position* of a player other than *Gasol*, and therefore is irrelevant. In this case, there does not exist a delta result tree, and data consistency holds trivially.

Definition 1.10 (Query Consistency): If we add a new keyword to the query, then each additional subtree that becomes (part of) a query result should contain at least one match to this keyword.

Example 1.4 Consider again query *"forward, name"* on the XML data in Figure 1. We have two query results: *player* (15) and the matches in its subtree; *player* (33) and the matches in its subtrees. If we add one more keyword *USA*, which results in query "forward, name, *USA*", then *player* (33) should no longer be a query result (which satisfies query monotonicity). On the other hand, the query result related to *player* (15) should add the subtree rooted at *nationality* (18), which is a delta result tree. This is valid with respect to query consistency

since this subtree contains a node (19) matching the new keyword *USA*.

As reported by Liu and Chen (2008), these properties are non-redundant (it is possible to satisfy some properties but fail the others) and satisfiable. MaxMatch (Liu & Chen, 2008), a strategy for identifying relevant keyword matches, is proven to satisfy all these properties.

1.3.2 XML Graphs

On XML graphs, the lowest common ancestor concept is no longer applicable. As a result, existing approaches define a query result as a minimal subtree/subgraph of the XML graph that contains all or part of the query keywords (Golenberg, Kimelfeld and Sagiv 2008; Kimelfeld & Sagiv 2006; He, Wang, Yang & Yu, 2007; Hristidis & Balmin 2003; Li, Ooi, Feng, Wang & Zhou, 2008; Kacholia, Pandit, Chakrabarti, Sudarshan, Desai & Karambelkar, 2005). A minimal subtree/subgraph indicates that no nodes can be removed from the subtree/subgraph such that it is still connected and contains all keywords. Note that a minimal subtree is not necessarily a group Steiner tree, which is the minimum over all minimal subtrees.

As an example, consider the XML graph shown in Figure 3 and query *"Greg, USA, Nuggets"*. A minimal subtree consists of *Greg* (17), *USA* (19), and *Nuggets* (45) and their connectioning paths, including the reference edge from *t20* (25) to *team* (41). Another minimal subtree consists of *Greg* (17), *USA* (30), *Nuggets* (45) and their connections.

Li et al. (2008) adopts OR semantics while others use AND semantics.

For minimal subtrees/subgraphs on XML graphs, all keyword matches are relevant, except that when AND semantics is adopted and a result is defined as rooted subtree, in which case the keyword matches that do not compose a rooted subtree with the matches to other keywords are irrelevant. As a result, the number of valid results can be huge. For example, if there are k keywords

Figure 3.

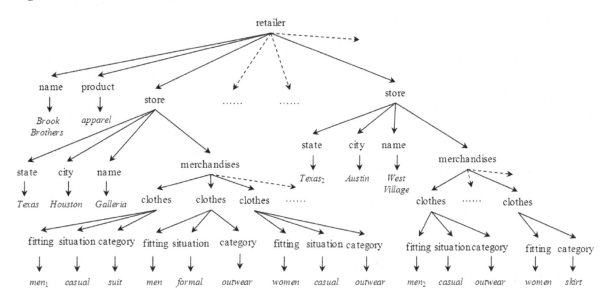

and each having n matches in the XML graph, then potentially the total number of query results can be k^n. Therefore, effective and efficient ranking is highly important to ensure that the most relevant results can be found by the user. The discussion of their ranking functions and algorithms can be found in Section 1.6.

1.4 IDENTIFYING OTHER RELEVANT DATA NODES

In most cases it is not sufficient for a result to have only relevant matches and their connections. Other XML nodes that do not match keywords may also be relevant.

Example 1.5 Consider query Q_1: "Greg, forward" and Q_2: "Greg, position" on the XML data in Figure 1. By issuing Q_1, the user is likely interested in information about the player whose name is *Greg* and who is a *forward*. In contrast, Q_2 indicates that the user is likely interested in a particular piece of information: the *position* of *Greg*. Note that if we only consider explicit relevant nodes, then these two queries have similar results. However, they have different semantics

and their results should be different. This can be addressed by considering relevant nodes other than keyword matches. The relevant nodes for Q_1, intuitively, should be those in the subtree rooted at *player* (15), while the relevant node for Q_2 is node *forward* (21).

To infer relevant data nodes besides keyword matches, we can get some hint by analyzing keyword categories. From these two queries, we can see that an input keyword can specify a predicate that restricts the search (analogous to "where" clause in XQuery), such as *Greg* and *forward* in Q_1. Or, a keyword may specify a desired return node (analogous to "return" clause in XQuery and "select" clause in SQL), such as position in Q_2. The subtree rooted at a return node, albeit not necessarily on the paths connecting relevant keyword matches, are usually interesting to the user. For Q_2, for instance, the return node is *position* (20), therefore, its child node *forward* is an implicit return node. However, return nodes are not always specified in the query, such as Q_1 in which both keywords specify predicates. In this case, intuitively the user is interested in the general information about the entities related to the search, which is *player* (15) for Q_1.

An immediate question is how to infer return nodes for a keyword query. Since a keyword can specify a predicate or a return node, the first step is to categorize keywords into predicates and return nodes.

XSeek (Liu & Chen, 2007) proposes the following inference of keyword category:

- A keyword specifies a return node if it matches internal nodes and has no descendant matches. Otherwise it is a predicate.
- A keyword specifies a predicate otherwise.

In Q_1, both keywords match leaf nodes, thus they both specify predicates. In Q_2, keyword *position* matches internal node (20) with no keyword matching its descendant, *forward* (21). Therefore, it specifies a return node. Intuitively, if an internal node is queried but none of its descendants is, then the user is likely interested in the subtree rooted at the node.

If return nodes are specified in the keywords, then the nodes in the subtree rooted at each match to the return node are considered relevant nodes. Otherwise, XSeek infers implicit return nodes by categorizing data nodes:

- An XML node is an entity if it is a *-node in the DTD, i.e., it can have multiple siblings of the same name, such as *team* and *player*.
- An XML node is an attribute name if it has only one leaf child, and an attribute value if it is a leaf.
- An XML node is a connection node otherwise.

When there is no return node specified in the query, which is the case of Q_1, XSeek considers the entities in the paths connecting keyword matches as return nodes. For example, for Q_1, the return node is *player* (15). The subtree of the implicit return nodes are considered as relevant nodes.

Although it is intuitive that return nodes are the information of user's interest, the inference of return nodes by XSeek may not always be accurate. For example, if a person has multiple addresses or phone numbers, then address and phone number will be considered as entities, while they actually are not. Besides, the quality of XSeek depends largely on the quality of identifying relevant matches. An incorrect or undesirable relevant match may change XSeek's categorization of keywords into return nodes or predicates.

Prior to XSeek, some other works (Hristidis, Papakonstantinou & Balmin, 2003; Koutrika, Simitsis & Ioannidis, 2006) can also identify relevant non-matches, but requires user elicitation or specification from system administrators. Specifically, Hristidis et al. (2003) requires a system administrator to split the schema graph into target schema segments (TSS) for each result, and Koutrika et al. (2006) requires users or a system administrator to specify a weight for each edge in the schema graph, and then a user needs to specify a degree constraint and a cardinality constraint in order to determine the return information.

1.5 GENERATING QUERY RESULTS EFFICIENTLY

To improve the efficiency of generating query results, indexes and materialized views are widely adopted for structured query processing. Similarly, they can potentially be helpful for processing XML keyword searches as well.

1.5.1 Indexes

Common indexes used for XML keyword search include inverted indexes and B-tree indexes. Each entry of an inverted index consists of a keyword and IDs of the nodes that match the keyword. Inverted indexes are used to find the nodes containing the query keywords. B-tree indexes contain information of each node, clustered by node IDs.

It is used for efficient access to the children, parent and siblings of a node.

The ID of a node usually uses the Dewey labeling scheme (Tatarinov, Viglas, Beyer, Shanmugasundaram, Shekita & Zhang, 2002). A Dewey label records the relative position of a node among its siblings, and then concatenate these positions using dot '.' starting from the root to compose the Dewey ID for the node. For example, node with Dewey ID 0.2.3 is the 4-th child of its parent node 0.2. Dewey ID can be used to detect the order, sibling and ancestor information of a node.

- The start tag of a node u appears before that of node v in an XML document if and only if *Dewey(u)* is smaller than *Dewey(v)* by comparing each component in order.
- A node *u* is an ancestor of node *v* if and only if *Dewey(u)* is a prefix of *Dewey(v)*.
- A node *u* is a sibling of node *v* if and only if *Dewey(u)* differs from *Dewey(v)* only in the last component.

1.5.2 Materialized Views

Materialized views have been proved successful for performance optimization in evaluating structured queries on XML and databases. They have also been widely used in web applications. Caching query results as materialized views at the application tier can decrease the workload of the servers. Exploiting materialized views at client side can further decrease the number of network accesses.

A framework has been recently proposed by Liu and Chen (2008b) that use materialized views for efficient evaluation of keyword queries on XML. This approach adopts a relatively widely used semantics, SLCA, to define query results. As different approaches further return different subtrees of each SLCA node as results, materialized views in Liu and Chen (2008b) are used only for computing SLCA nodes.

It is shown by Liu and Chen (2008b) that given a query Q, a subquery Q' of Q (i.e., the queries with a subset of keywords in Q) can be used for computing the SLCA of Q. In other words, it is possible to compute the SLCA of Q from the SLCA of Q'. However, if a query has some keywords that are not in Q, then it is unhelpful. Given a query Q, the goal is to find a set of views, such that their union is as close to Q as possible, and that the cost of computing the SLCA of Q using the materialized views is minimized. This problem is proved to be NP-hard, and a greedy algorithm similar as the one for the set cover problem is proposed.

There are still plenty of open questions on this topic, e.g., whether it is possible to answer keyword queries using views for other XML search semantics (XSEarch, MLCA, etc.); whether it is possible to efficiently maintain the views; what is the best strategy to choose a set of views to materialize; how to use materialized views to compute top-k results, and so on.

1.6 RANKING

Due to the ambiguity of keyword searches, various ranking strategies have been proposed and studied for keyword search on XML. As discussed in Section 1.3.2, ranking is especially critical for XML graphs, on which a query usually have a very large number of results and most of them are in fact irrelevant. The score of a query result is mainly evaluated from the following two types of ranking factors.

Ranking Factor for Individual Nodes. This type of ranking factors include variants of TFIDF (term frequency and inverse document frequency) (Cohen et al., 2003, Bao, Ling, Chen & Lu, 2009), PageRank (Guo et al., 2003; Li et al., 2008), and other factors (He et al., 2007). A ranking factor for individual nodes calculates scores for individual nodes with respect to the query, which can be aggregated to compute a score of the result.

As an example of individual scores, consider XSEarch (Cohen et al., 2003). It defines the weight of a node with respect to a keyword, denoted by $w(k, n_l)$, in the following way similar as the TFIDF measurement in information retrieval.

$$w(k, n_l) = tf(k, n_l) \times idf(k)$$

$$tf(k, n_l) = \frac{occ(k, n_l)}{\max\{occ(k', n_l) \mid k' \subset words(n_l)\}}$$

$$idf(k) = \log(1 + \frac{|N|}{|\{n' \in N \mid k \in words(n')\}|})$$

where $occ(k,n)$ denotes the number of times keyword k occurs in node n, $words(n)$ is the set of words that is contained in node n, and N is the set of all nodes in the XML document.

Score of the entire result. The score of the entire result can be obtained by aggregation of individual node scores. For example, to aggregate the individual scores into the score of the result, XSEarch interprets the result and the query as vectors, and computes the vector similarity. Besides, the score of a result can also be measured from the result tree structure, such as result tree size and keyword proximity. Intuitively, a compact result tree indicates a closer relationship between keywords in the tree, and therefore is favored in the ranking. The compactness of a result subtree is defined in a variety of ways (Cohen et al., 2003; Guo et al., 2003; He et al., 2007; Li et al., 2008; Barg & Wong, 2001; Hristidis et al., 2003; Hristidis, Koudas, Papakonstantinou & Srivastava, 2006).

As an example, XRank (Guo, Shao, Botev & Shanmugasundaram, 2003) computes a rank for the root of a result denoted as v_1, which is treated as the rank of the result. The rank of a node v_1 with respect to keyword k is calculated as:

$$r(v_1, k_i) = ElemRank(v_t) \times decay^{t-1}$$

where *ElemRank* measures the objective importance of an XML node, which is conceptually similar as Google's PageRank. v_t is a descendant of v_1 whose depth is t-1 bigger than that of v_1, which directly contains keyword k_i. decay is a parameter from 0 to 1. Intuitively, the farther away v_1 is from v_t, the lower rank it gets.

Then, the overall ranking of the result root v_1 with respect to a query $Q = (k_1, k_2, ..., k_n)$ is defined as:

$$R(v_1, Q) = \left(\sum_{1 \le i \le n} r(v_1, k_i) \right) \times p(v_1, k_1, k_2, ..., k_n)$$

where $r(v_1, k_i)$ is an aggregation of the scores of matches to k_i. If k_i has m matches and their ranks are $r_1, r_2, ..., r_m$, respectively, then

$$r(v_1, k_i) = f(r_1, r_2, ..., r_m)$$

where f is an aggregation function.

As another example, in XSEarch and Hristidis et al. (2003), a ranking factor is the size of the result tree, which penalizes large results. EASE (Li et al., 2008) uses a more sophisticated way to measure result compactness, in which the structural similarity between two nodes n_i and n_j is defined as:

$$Sim(n_i, n_j) = \sum_{n_i \leftrightarrow n_j} \frac{1}{(|n_i \leftrightarrow n_j| + 1)^2}$$

where $n_i \leftrightarrow n_j$ is any path between ni and nj, and $|n_i \leftrightarrow n_j|$ is its length.

Function *Sim* is used to measure the structural relevancy of two keywords k_i and k_j:

$$Sim(< k_i, k_j > \mid R) = \frac{1}{|C_{k_i} \cup C_{k_j}|} \sum_{n_i \in C_{k_i}, n_j \in C_{k_j}} Sim(n_i, n_j)$$

Figure 4.

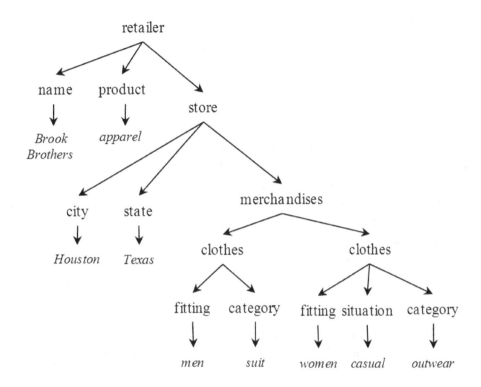

where R is the result; C_{ki} is the set of nodes that match keyword ki.

Finally, one of the scores of a result is the total structural relevancy of all pairs of keywords:

$$Score_{DB}(R) = \sum_{1 \le i \le j \le m} Sim(< k_i, k_j >| R)$$

where m is the number of keywords.

Other approaches may use different ranking functions, but they all fall into the above two categories.

Since the efficiency of processing keyword search is very important to the user, it is often desirable to generate ranked results incrementally, so that the top-k results will be shown to the user without generating all results and sorting them. Unfortunately, we are currently yet to see an approach that achieves this goal. This is an important open question in XML keyword search.

1.7 RESULT SNIPPETS

Although ranking schemes are studied in XML keyword search, it is impossible to design a ranking scheme that always perfectly gauges query result relevance with respect to users' intentions. Indeed, even for the same query, different users may be interested in different results and thus desire different rankings. To compensate the inaccuracy of ranking functions, result snippets are used by almost every text search engine. The principle of result snippets is orthogonal to that of ranking functions: let users quickly judge the relevance of query results by providing a brief quotable passage of each query result, so that users can choose and explore relevant ones among many results.

The problem of generating informative and concise result snippets in XML keyword search has been studied by Huang, Liu and Chen (2008). It attempts to generate snippets with four properties:

Figure 5.

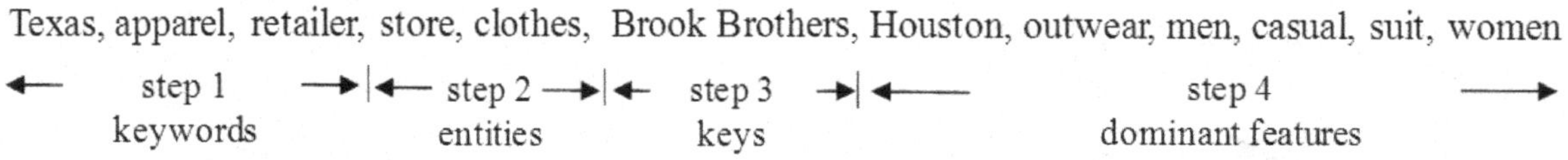

Texas, apparel, retailer, store, clothes, Brook Brothers, Houston, outwear, men, casual, suit, women

◄———— step 1 ————►|◄—— step 2 ——►|◄— step 3 —►|◄————   step 4   ————►
        keywords   entities   keys   dominant features

self-contained, distinguishable, representative and small. A snippet information list is constructed for each result, which contains the information of the result to be shown in its snippets in order to be self-contained, distinguishable, and representative. Then, the instances of the items in the snippet information list are carefully chosen from the result, such that the maximum number of items are included in the snippet subject to a limit of snippet size. As an example, consider the result of query "*Texas, apparel, retailer*" in Figure 4.

First of all, the snippet of a query result should show the query keywords. Therefore, the keywords of the query are added to the snippet information list, shown as step 1 in Figure 5. Next, we illustrate the four goals for generating snippets.

Self-contained. A result snippet should be *self-contained* so that the users can understand it. In text search, result snippets usually consist of one or more "windows" on the document containing the complete phrases/sentences where the keyword matches appear, which are self-contained and can be easily read. In contrast, in XML documents, each entity is a semantic unit. We include the names of the entities involved in the query result as context information, even though names of such entities may not necessarily appear between two keyword matches in the XML document, as shown in step 2 in Figure 5.

Distinguishable. Different result snippets should be *distinguishable* so that the users can differentiate the results from their snippets with little effort. To achieve this in text document search, result snippets often include the document titles. In XML keyword search, intuitively, the key of a result can be used for distinguishing results. A

query result may contain several entities, whose keys can potentially serve as the key of a result. The question is which entities' keys should be considered as the key of the query result. The entities in a query result are classified into two categories.

- Return entities, which are what the users are looking for when issuing the query;
- Supporting entities, which are used to describe the return entities in a query result.

An entity in a query result is a return entity if its name matches a query keyword or its attribute name matches a keyword, such as entity *retailer*. If there is no such entity, then the highest entity in the result is considered as the return entity. The key of the return entity is added to the snippet information list in step 3 in Figure 5.

Representative. a snippet should effectively summarize the query result. To this end, we should identify important features in a result. A feature is defined as an entity-attribute-value triplet, and the type of a feature is the entity-attribute pair. For example, *clothes:fitting:men* in Figure 4 is a feature, whose type is *clothes:fitting*. A feature is considered as dominant if it has a large number of occurrences compared with similar features, such as *store:city:Houston* and *store:fitting:men*.

To effectively summarize the result, only those features that are dominant in the result should be included in the snippet. Intuitively, a feature is considered dominant if it has a large number of occurrences compared with features of the same type. For example, if most clothes in Figure 4 are for men, then feature *clothes:fitting:men* is a dominant feature. Based on this observation, the dominance score of a feature f, denoted by $DS(f)$, is defined as the ratio between the number of occurrences of the feature and the average number of occurrences of all features of the same type:

$$DS(f) = \frac{N(e,a,v)}{\dfrac{N(e,a)}{D(e,a)}}$$

where $N(x)$ denotes the number of occurrences of x in the result; $D(e, a)$ denotes the number of distinct features of type (e, a).

Features with a dominance score greater than or equal to 1 are added to the snippet information list in the order of their dominance score, e.g., in the result in Figure 4, there are 4 dominant features, which are added to the information list as shown in the last step of Figure 5.

Small. A result snippet should be small so that the users can quickly browse several snippets. As a result, snippets should have an upper bound of size (in terms of number of nodes), which can be specified by users.

After the snippet information list of a result is constructed, the items in the list are added to the snippet in the order they appear in the list, until the size upper bound is reached. Since each item may have multiple instances in the result, the choice of instances will impact the number of items that can be included. For example, if we want to choose one instance for *Houston* and one for *men*, then choosing men_1 results in a smaller tree than men_2, which means more space is saved to include other items.

It is shown by Huang et al. (2008) that, given a size limit, including the maximum number of items in the snippet information list is NP-hard. A greedy algorithm is given in the paper, which outputs the snippet shown in Figure 1.5 for the result in Figure 4.

1.8 CONCLUSION AND FUTURE RESEARCH DIRECTIONS

This chapter describes the importance and various challenges for supporting XML keyword search. Then it presents and compares representative state-of-the-art techniques from multiple aspects, including identifying relevant keyword matches and an axiomatic framework to evaluate different strategies, identifying other relevant data nodes, ranking schemes, indexes and materialized views, and result snippet generation. These studies enable casual users to easily access XML data without the need to learn XPath/XQuery and data schemas, and yet to obtain high-quality results. In this section we discuss some important issues in XML keyword search that have not yet been well studied and demand further investigation.

Ranking and top-k query processing. Due to the inherent ambiguity of keyword searches, ranking is highly important for any keyword search engine. A ranking scheme considers both ranking factors for individual nodes, such as variants of TF, IDF, PageRank, and ranking factors for the entire result, such as the aggregation of individual node scores, keyword proximity and result size (Bao et al. 2009, Cohen et al. 2003, He et al. 2007, Li et al. 2008).

However, none of the existing approaches on XML keyword search supports top-k query processing. They need to generate all the results, compute a score for each result and finally sort them. This can be potentially very inefficient when the number of results is large. It is highly desirable but challenging to develop efficient top-k algorithms for XML keyword search.

Utilization of user relevance feedbacks. In information retrieval, user relevance feedbacks have been widely exploited for deducing users' interests and have achieved big success in improving search quality. Existing work on utilizing feedbacks for XML search focuses on finding the structural relationships among keywords using explicit feedbacks (Schenkel and Theobald, 2006). How to use relevance feedbacks, especially implicit feedbacks, in different aspects of XML keyword search is largely an open question. With the structure of XML data, there are plenty of opportunities of utilizing user relevance feedbacks to improve search quality, from relevant node inference in result generation to ranking and snippet generation in result presentation in a keyword search engine.

Evaluation of XML keyword search systems. Since there are many approaches of generating and presenting results for XML keyword search, a framework to evaluate them is critical for users to understand the trade-offs of existing systems. The quality of an XML keyword search system is often gauged empirically with respect to the ground truth over a large and comprehensive set of test data and queries. INEX (http://inex. is.informatik.uni-duisburg.de/) is an initiative for developing empirical benchmark for evaluating XML search. Two important factors are proposed to measure result relevance: exhaustivity, measuring how well a node satisfies user's information need; and specificity, measuring how well a node focuses on the user's information need (Amer-Yahia & Lalmas, 2006). A cost-effective alternative to an empirical benchmark is to evaluate XML keyword search systems based on a set of axioms that capture broad intuitions, such as Liu and Chen (2008) which evaluates strategies for identifying relevant keyword matches using axioms (as reviewed in Section 3.1). We believe it is essential for the community to actively contribute to comprehensive frameworks for XML keyword search evaluation.

REFERENCES

Amer-Yahia, S., & Lalmas, M. (2006). XML Search: Languages, INEX and Scoring. *SIGMOD Record*, *35*(4). doi:10.1145/1228268.1228271

Bao, Z., Ling, T. W., Chen, B., & Lu, J. (2009). Effective XML Keyword Search with Relevance Oriented Ranking. In *Proceedings of ICDE*.

Barg, M., & Wong, R. K. (2001). Structural proximity searching for large collections of semistructured data. In *Proceedings of CIKM*. 175-182.

Cohen, S., Mamou, J., Kanza, Y., & Sagiv, Y. (2003). XSEarch: A semantic Search Engine for XML. In *VLDB*.

Guo, L., Shao, F., Botev, C., & Shanmugasundaram, J. (2003). XRANK: Ranked Keyword Search over XML Documents. In *Proceedings of SIGMOD*, (pp. 16-27).

Hansen, P., & Roberts, F. S. (1996). An Impossibility Result in Axiomatic Location Theory. In *Mathematics of Operations Research*.

He, H., Wang, H., Yang, J., & Yu, P. S. (2007). BLINKS: Ranked Keyword Searches on Graphs. In *Proceedings of SIGMOD*.

Hristidis, V., Koudas, N., Papakonstantinou, Y., & Srivastava, D. (2006). Keyword Proximity Search in XML Trees. *IEEE Transactions on Knowledge and Data Engineering*, *18*(4). doi:10.1109/TKDE.2006.1599390

Hristidis, V., Papakonstantinou, Y., & Balmin, A. (2003). Keyword Proximity Search on XML Graphs. In *ICDE*.

Huang, Yu., Liu, Z., & Chen, Y. (2008). Query Biased Snippet Generation in XML Search. In *SIGMOD*.

Kleinberg, J. (2002). An Impossibility Theorem for Clustering. In *NIPS*.

Koutrika, G., Simitsis, A., & Ioannidis, Y. E. (2006). Pr'ecis: The Essence of a Query Answer. In *ICDE*.

Li, G., Ooi, B. C., Feng, J., Wang, J., & Zhou, L. (2008). EASE: an Effective 3-in-1 Keyword Search Method for Unstructured, Semi-structured and Structured data. In *SIGMOD*.

Li, Y., Yu, C., & Jagadish, H. V. (2004). Schema-Free XQuery. In *VLDB*.

Liu, Z., & Chen, Y. (2007). Identifying meaningful return information for xml keyword search. In *SIGMOD*.

Liu, Z., & Chen, Y. (2008). Reasoning and Identifying Relevant Matches for XML Keyword Search. In *VLDB*.

Liu, Z., & Chen, Y. (2008b). Answering Keyword Queries on XML Using Materialized Views. In *ICDE*.

Osborne, M. J., & Rubinstein, A. (1994). *A Course in Game Theory*. Cambridge, MA: MIT Press.

Pennock, D. M., Horvitz, E., & Giles, C. L. 2000. An Impossibility Theorem for Clustering. In *AAAI*.

Schenkl, R., & Theobald, M. (2006). Structural Feedback for Keyword-Based XML Retrieval. In *ECIR*.

Tatarinov, I., Viglas, S., Beyer, K. S., Shanmugasundaram, J., Shekita, E. J., & Zhang, C. (2002). Storing and Querying Ordered XML Using a Relational Database System. In *SIGMOD*.

Xu, Y., & Papakonstantinou, Y. (2005). Efficient Keyword Search for Smallest LCAs in XML Databases. In *Proceedings of SIGMOD*.f

Chapter 8
A Framework for Cost-Based Query Optimization in Native XML Database Management Systems

Andreas M. Weiner
University of Kaiserslautern, Germany

Theo Härder
University of Kaiserslautern, Germany

ABSTRACT

Since the very beginning of query processing in database systems, cost-based query optimization has been the essential strategy for effectively answering complex queries on large documents. XML documents can be efficiently stored and processed using native XML database management systems. Even though such systems can choose from a huge repertoire of join operators (e. g., Structural Joins and Holistic Twig Joins) and various index access operators to efficiently evaluate queries on XML documents, the development of full-fledged XML query optimizers is still in its infancy. Especially the evaluation of complex XQuery expressions using these operators is not well understood and needs further research. The extensible, rule-based, and cost-based XML query optimization framework proposed in this chapter, serves as a testbed for exploring how and whether well-known concepts from relational query optimization (e. g., join reordering) can be reused and which new techniques can make a significant contribution to speed-up query execution. Using the best practices and an appropriate cost model that will be developed using this framework, it can be turned into a robust cost-based XML query optimizer in the future.

INTRODUCTION

In the last few years, XML became the de-facto standard for exchanging structured and semi-structured data in business as well as in research. The database research community took this development into account by proposing—among others—native *XML database management systems* (XDBMSs) for efficient and transactional processing of XML documents.

DOI: 10.4018/978-1-61520-727-5.ch008

As in the relational world, the quality of query optimizers plays an important role for the acceptance of database systems by a wide range of users, especially in business scenarios where longer-than-necessary running queries can cause high costs. One of the main tasks in query evaluation is plan generation, where physical operators are arranged in such a way, that the given optimization goal (e. g., maximum throughput) is satisfied while the semantics of the query is still preserved.

In recent years, several join operators for the evaluation of structural relationships like *child* or *descendant* have been proposed. All of them belong to one of the major classes of XML join operators: *Structural Joins (SJs)* (Al-Khalifa et al., 2002) and *Holistic Twig Joins (HTJs)* (Bruno, Koudas, & Srivastava, 2002). Being binary join operators, SJ operators decompose tree-structured query patterns, which are also called twig query patterns, into binary relationships and evaluate each of them separately, before they merge intermediate results to get the final query result. On the other hand, HTJ operators are able to evaluate twigs holistically. A precondition for the efficient evaluation of SJ and HTJ operators is a node labeling scheme (O'Neil et al., 2004; Härder, Haustein, Mathis, & Wagner, 2007) that assigns to each node in an XML document a unique identifier that (1) allows to decide, without accessing the document, for two given nodes whether they are structurally related to each other and (2) that does not require re-labeling even after modifications to the document.

Besides SJ and HTJ operators, several approaches for indexing XML documents were proposed. These approaches can be classified into a hierarchy of access methods w. r. t. their availability in a native XDBMS. *Primary access paths (PAPs)* provide input for navigational primitives as well as for SJ and HTJ operators. The most important representative of this class is a *document index* that indexes a document using the unique node labels as keys. *Secondary access paths[1]* (SAPs) provide more efficient access to specific element nodes using *element indexes* (Bruno et al., 2002). They are absolutely necessary for efficient evaluation of structural predicates by SJ or HTJ operators. *Tertiary access paths (TAPs)* like *path indexes* (Milo & Suciu, 1999) employ structural summaries such as *DataGuides* (Goldman & Widom, 1997) for providing efficient access to nodes satisfying structural relationships like *child* or *descendant*. *Content indexes* (McHugh & Widom, 1999) support efficient access to text nodes or attribute-value nodes. Finally, *hybrid indexes* (Wang, Park, Fan, & Yu, 2003), which are also called *content-and-structure (CAS) indexes*, are a promising approach for indexing content and structure at a time. Compared to PAPs, which are available per default in a native XDBMS, SAPs and TAPs have to be manually created by the database administrator. Furthermore, TAPs like path indexes or CAS indexes can replace complete trees of SJ and HTJ operators and become—if available—first-class citizens for query evaluation. As maintenance and updates of TAPs can cause substantial overhead, they will only be created by the database administrator in rare cases, e.g., for frequently queried subtrees.

Motivation

If we have a look at the status quo of native XML query evaluation, several unsolved problems arise. In the presence of a rich variety of physical operators, most of all empirical evaluations were performed using self-generated or slightly modified well-known documents with simple queries. By doing so, the superiority of a particular operator was shown and probable weaknesses were suppressed. Today, it is unknown how these operators really behave in realistic native XDBMS scenarios. For example, real-world XQuery expressions are provided by the XMark benchmark queries (Schmidt et al., 2002) or by the TPoX benchmark queries (Nicola, Kogan, & Schiefer, 2007) that are more complex than simple path expressions or the twig patterns used for the evaluation of HTJ algorithms. There is—to the best of our knowledge—no query evaluation framework that can employ SJ, HTJ, and various indexes in combination or exclusively for query evaluation. Cost-based query optimization using these operators is not possible yet, because there is little knowledge on the characteristics of SJ and HTJ operators in real-world scenarios as well as on the effectiveness of logical query rewrites like SJ reordering, and, as a consequence, no cost model for driving the query optimization process is available.

To overcome these deficits, we need a framework, which serves at the beginning as a testbed, allowing to enumerate different query execution plans (QEPs) for a given XQuery expression and its corresponding logical algebra representation using a rich physical algebra and execute them all under the same conditions provided by a full-fledged native XDBMS infrastructure. Based on the best practices and the resulting cost model developed using the testbed, the framework must be easily extensible to a complete and efficient cost-based query optimizer.

Contribution

In this chapter, we first discuss the differences between relational and XML query optimization and show which new challenges are raised by querying semi-structured data. We define several requirements for cost-based XML query optimizers and show why present approaches do not fully meet them. Based on these findings, we describe a modular and extensible plan enumeration framework for XML queries that takes different access methods and join operators into account and can be further extended to a full-fledged cost-based query optimizer usign an appropriate cost model.

In general, there are two major tasks for query optimization: (1) choosing the cheapest access

method for feeding joins and (2) selecting the optimal evaluation strategy for join trees. To solve these problems, a query optimizer explores the search space of semantically equivalent query plans and assigns costs to them that permit to wipe out expensive plans. To tackle the first problem, we develop an initial cost model describing the IO and CPU costs of PAPs and SAPs in a system-independent way. For relational query optimization, a query optimizer can use *join associativity* (reordering of join operators) and *join commutativity* (exchange of join partners) for query rewrite to generate different join trees. We present *join fusion* (Weiner, Mathis, & Härder, 2008; Weiner & Härder, 2009) as an additional rewrite for joins evaluating structural predicates (SJs and HTJs) that allows fusing two adjacent join operators to an n-way join operator. Using these rewrites, the framework is ready for joint evaluation of XML queries using SJ and HTJ operators.

Based on the framework developed before, we (1) show how an initial instance of it can be used within the *XML Transaction Coordinator* (XTC) (Haustein & Härder, 2007)—our prototype of a native XDBMS—to perform plan generation. We explore the QEPs of different XPath and XQuery expressions w. r. t. the impact of join reordering and join fusion on their overall query execution performance.

BACKGROUND

In this section, we point out the challenges raised by query optimization in native XML database management systems. Afterwards, we discuss important contributions related to our plan generation framework, which emerged within the last 30 years of research on cost-based query optimization in relational DBMSs. Finally, we show which concepts have been introduced so far to support XML query optimization.

Challenges of Native XML Query Optimization

Even though we have seen many years of research on cost-based query optimization in relational database systems—which itself is a complex task—cost-based optimization for XML query languages like XPath or XQuery is different. It is much more than simple value-based join reordering and thus raises additional challenges:

In the world of XML, schema evolution will occur much more often than in the relational world. This adds an additional degree of fuzziness to element-cardinality estimation.

In the relational world, value-based cardinality estimation works fine, because of the simplicity of the data model with its homogeneous rows. As XML explicitly supports heterogeneity, two documents complying with a given schema do not necessarily share the same structure, e. g., an element e can occur in document d_1 several times, but never in document d_2. XML is based on a hierarchical data model where structural relationships, e. g., *child* and *descendant*—in addition to classic value-based relationships—play an important role especially during query evaluation. As a consequence, an XML query optimizer has to deal with value-based joins as well as with structural joins and has to arrange them in an at least near-optimal way.

Nowadays, structural relationships are evaluated using physical SJ and HTJ operators. Both classes of operators must provide their results in document order and sometimes need to perform duplicate elimination that adds additional complexity to these operators. Compared to classic value-based join operators like nested-loops join or sort-merge join, estimating the CPU costs of SJ or HTJ operators is hard and needs much more effort and empirical analysis. For example, HTJ operators have to maintain several stacks and some of them can skip input nodes by "jumping" to more promising nodes in the input stream (Fontoura, Josifovski, Shekita, & Yang, 2005).

The search space of a cost-based XML query optimizer is increased tremendously in two dimensions: (1) Besides classical value-based joins, we have to additionally deal with structural joins as well as with equivalent twig joins, and (2) the confusing variety of different index access operators further expands the search space, because they are not only providing input streams for join operators, e. g., by using element indexes, but can also completely replace them like hybrid content-and-structure (CAS) indexes. Consequently, CAS indexes are competing with SJ and HTJ operators for a first-class citizenship.

Related Work

In this section, we give a brief literature review of related works. A more detailed historical reflection on query optimization in relational database systems can be found in important survey articles (Jarke & Koch, 1984; Graefe, 1993; Chaudhuri, 1998).

Important Concepts of Relational Cost-based Query Optimization

Selinger et al. (1979) introduced the first cost-based query optimizer, which was part of *System R*—the prototype of the first relational database system. The optimizer was capable of optimizing simple and linear SPJ (select, project, and join) queries. The authors provide a simple cost model based on weighted IO and CPU costs and use statistics concerning the number of data pages consumed by relations to bind the cost model's variables to concrete values. Their dynamic programming algorithm works in a bottom-up style where optimal operator fittings for access paths are selected first. Afterwards, an optimal join order is determined based on a local optimality assumption. To early prune the search space, not all possible enumerations are considered. Instead, they only consider so-called *interesting join orders,* i.e., orders that do not require additional introductions of Cartesian products.

Graefe & DeWitt (1987) introduced the *EXODUS Optimizer Generator*. This system is independent of any data model and allows specifying algebraic transformations as rules. These rules serve as input for an optimizer generator—together with a concrete data model—that generates a tailor-made query optimizer.

The *Starburst* project (Haas, Freytag, Lohman, & Pirahesh, 1989; Pirahesh, Hellerstein, & Hasan, 1992) contributed valuable concepts to the emerging research field of query optimization. Amongst others, they presented the so-called *Query Graph Model (QGM)*—an extended relational algebra with a strong emphasis on structural relationships between language constructs. Furthermore, they introduce the concepts of rule-based query optimizers, which can be easily modified by adding new rules for query transformation and query translation. Consequently, this approach improves the extensibility of such systems very much.

The *Volcano* project (Graefe & McKenna, 1993) as well as the *Cascades* project (Graefe, 1995) are descendants of the EXODUS project (Graefe & DeWitt, 1987). The authors make a distinction between transformation rules that serve for algebra-to-algebra transformations and implementation rules describing the mapping from logical algebra expressions to operator trees. Compared to the query optimization approach of System R (Selinger et al., 1979), they use a top-down query optimization algorithm.

Software Engineering Approaches to Query Optimization

Lanzelotte & Valduriez (1991) described an extensible framework for query optimization that models the search space independent of a particular search strategy. Thus, their search-space model can be used for enumerative and probabilistic search strategies. Using this technique, developers can build highly-extensible plan enumeration frameworks.

OPT++ (Kabra & DeWitt, 1999) is an object-oriented method for extensible query optimization. By combining an extensible search component with an extensible logical and physical algebra representation, they extend the work of Lanzelotte & Valduriez (1991).

First Steps Towards Cost-Based XML Query Optimization

Because the research directions of cost-based XML query optimization and XML cost modeling are just emerging, there are only few related publications. The classic work of McHugh & Widom (1999) addressing the optimization of XML queries focuses only on optimizing path expressions using navigational access primitives and lacks support for SJ and HTJ operators.

Wu, Patel, & Jagadish (2003) proposed five novel dynamic programming algorithms for structural join reordering. Their approach is orthogonal to our work, i.e., it can be employed to choose the best join order in SJ-only scenarios. Compared to our work, they use only a very simple cost model for driving the join reordering process and do not consider the combination of SJ and HTJ operators as well as different index access operators.

Zhang et al. (2005) introduced several statistical learning techniques for XML cost modeling. In contrast to our work, which will follow a static cost modeling approach, they demonstrate how to model the cost of a navigational access operator. Unfortunately, they do not cover SJ and HTJ operators.

Balmin et al. (2006) sketched the development of a hybrid cost-based optimizer for SQL and XQuery being part of DB2® XML. Compared to our approach, they evaluate every path expression using an HTJ operator and cannot decide on a fine-granular level whether to use SJ operators or not. By omitting SJs as alternative, they remove all room for binary join-order optimization. As indicated by Weiner & Härder (2009), HTJ operators are inferior to SJ operators in high-selectivity scenarios.

THE QUERY EVALUATION PROCESS

Query processing in native XDBMSs can be described as a process consisting of three consecutive stages: analysis, optimization, and code generation.

During the *analysis* stage, a query is parsed and checked for syntactic and semantic correctness. Afterwards, normalization removes "syntactic sugar" by mapping the query to a common normal form expression (XQuery Core Language). Next, static type checking serves for inferring static typing information. Thereafter, a simplification of the query is performed by wiping out redundant or unnecessary query parts. Finally, the query is mapped to a logical algebra expression (*Query Graph*).

The second stage of the query evaluation process, which is our focus in this chapter, is called *optimization*. Within this stage, cost-based query transformation and query translation are performed. Query transformation manipulates a query graph by applying query rewrite in such a way, that a semantically equivalent but more efficient query graph is found. For this task, optimization must be performed in two orthogonal dimensions at the same time: (1) finding an optimal arrangement of operators and (2) selecting the cheapest access paths and the best plan-operator fittings. After a plan is found, which is optimal in both dimensions, it is mapped onto a physical algebra expression (QEP) during the translation step.

Finally, the *code generation* stage serves for the execution of the QEP, either by direct interpretation or by translating it first to an executable module. It is furthermore responsible for providing the final query result.

Example 1. XMark benchmark query Q6

```
let $auction:= doc("auction.xml") re-
turn  for $b in $auction//site/regions
return  count($b//item)
```

MOTIVATING EXAMPLE

To illustrate different aspects of query optimization, we use the XMark benchmark query Q6 (Schmidt et al., 2002), which returns the total number of items listed on all continents, as a running example throughout the rest of this chapter. (see Example 1)

A FRAMEWORK FOR COST-BASED NATIVE XML QUERY OPTIMIZATION

In this section, we describe our framework for cost-based query optimization in native XML database systems. First, we define several design goals that must be met to provide a next-generation XML query optimizer. Second, we detail the architecture of our flexible query optimization framework.

Design Goals

We designed the optimization framework having several requirements in mind: (1) *Extensibility*: An optimization framework can only be useful, if it can be easily extended by adding new operator types or search strategies. (2) *Rules rule everything*: A query optimizer has several tasks to perform. Besides selecting appropriate physical operators, it explores the search space by applying several algebraic rewrites like join reordering. Performing such operations can be described by transformations that transform a state in the search space into another semantically equivalent state. When the most promising state is found, it has to be translated onto a physical QEP. Both, translations and transformations, should be described by rules that can be easily added to the framework. (3) *Graph-structured plan support*: Because sharing of results of (sub-)expressions is a common task while evaluating XQuery expressions (e. g., by the multiple occurrence of reference $i in the example), the plan generator must support the generation of linear join graphs as well as complex graph-structured query plans. (4) *Join support*: Because XML queries can refer to structural as well as to value-based predicates, the framework must support these classes of operators. (5) *Independence of search strategies*: The query optimization framework should not be tailored to any specific search strategy. Though, it must support the rapid implementation of new search strategies. Furthermore, exchanging search strategies—even at runtime of the DBMS—must be supported.

Preliminaries

We do not explicitly promote this framework as a stable cost-based query optimizer, even though such a system can be built using it. Because XML query processing is still in its infancy, little is known what really pays off in XML query optimization. Therefore, this framework primarily serves as a testbed for (1) exploring how and whether well-known concepts from relational query optimization can be reused in the context of XML query optimization and (2) which new optimization strategies are necessary to further improve XML query processing.

To compare different but equivalent physical operators (e. g., join or index operators) in the first place, and query optimization strategies in the second place, we need a common system environment that allows for the execution of different QEPs under equal and fair conditions. Consequently, we rely on a prototype of a native XML database management system with full transactional support and record-oriented storage structures.

XQuery Fragment Considered

Due to the lack of space, we do not discuss the sophisticated process of translating an XQuery or XPath expression into a logical algebra expression (Mathis, 2009). We assume that a query, which serves as input for our framework, is already translated into a logical XML algebra expression. For our system and without loss of generality, we use the *XML Query Graph Model* (XQGM) (Mathis, Weiner, & Härder, 2008) as logical XML algebra. The XQGM is a tailor-made version of the original *Query Graph Model* (Pirahesh, Hellerstein, & Hasan, 1992) that works on nested tuples. For example, Figure 3 shows the XQGM instance of XMark query Q6 (Example 1). Here, inputs are provided by sequence-access operators and structural relationships are evaluated using logical SJs. All operators are connected to tuple variables, which are illustrated as circles, and have a for-loops semantics.

Using the XQGM, we can express all core XQuery features such as FLWOR expressions, path expressions, comparison and positional predicates, quantifications, and node-construction expressions. Currently, we do not support type-related expressions, module and function declarations, and if-then-else expressions. The following XQuery grammar excerpt (Boag et al., 2007) shows the language constructs, we explicitly support:

```
[29] EnclosedExpr ::= "{"Expr"}"
[31] Expr ::= ExprSingle (","Ex-
prSingle)*
[32] ExprSingle ::= FLWORExpr |
QuantifiedExpr | OrExpr
[33] FLWORExpr ::= (ForClause |
LetClause)+ WhereClause? Order-
ByClause? "return" ExprSingle
[34] ForClause ::= "for" "$"
VarName PositionalVar? "in" Ex-
prSingle ("," "$" VarName Posi-
tionalVar? "in" ExprSingle)*
```

```
[35] PositionalVar ::= "at" "$"
VarName
[36] LetClause ::= "let" "$"
VarName ":=" ExprSingle ("," "$"
VarName ":=" ExprSingle)*
[37]  WhereClause ::= "where"
ExprSingle
[38] OrderByClause ::= ("order"
"by") OrderSpecList
[39] OrderSpecList ::= OrderSpec
("," OrderSpec)*
[40] OrderSpec ::= ExprSingle
OrderModifier
[41] OrderModifier ::= ("ascend-
ing" | "descending")?
[42] QuantifiedExpr ::= ("some"
| "every") "$" VarName "in" Ex-
prSingle ("," "$" VarName "in"
ExprSingle)* "satisfies" ExprS-
ingle
[46] OrExpr ::= AndExpr ("or"
AndExpr)*
[47] AndExpr ::= ComparisonExpr
```

```
("and" ComparisonExpr)*
[48] ComparisonExpr ::= Range-
Expr ((ValueComp | GeneralComp |
NodeComp) RangeExpr)?
[49] RangeExpr ::= AdditiveExpr
("to" AdditiveExpr)?
[50] AdditiveExpr ::= Multipli-
cativeExpr (("+" | "-") Multi-
plicativeExpr)*
[51] MultiplicativeExpr ::=
UnionExpr (("*" | "div" | "idiv"
| "mod") UnionExpr)*
[52] UnionExpr ::= IntersectEx-
ceptExpr (("union" | "|") Inter-
sectExceptExpr)*
[53] IntersectExceptExpr ::=
UnaryExpr (("intersect" | "ex-
cept") UnaryExpr)*
[58] UnaryExpr ::= ("-" | "+")*
PathExpr
[60] GeneralComp ::= "=" | "!="
| "<" | "<=" | ">" | ">="
[61] ValueComp ::= "eq" | "ne" |
```

Figure 1. Architecture of the query optimization framework

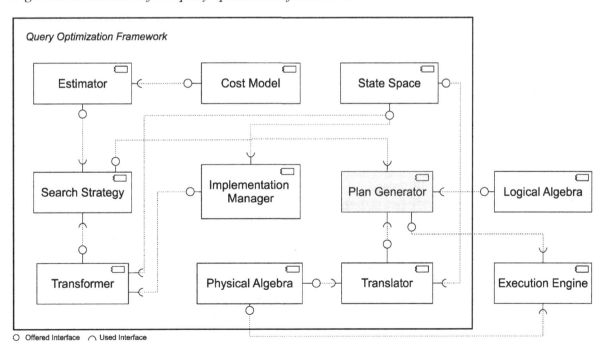

"lt" | "le" | "gt" | "ge"

[62] NodeComp ::= "is" | "<<" | ">>"

[68] PathExpr ::= ("/" RelativePathExpr?) | ("//" RelativePathExpr) | RelativePathExpr

[69] RelativePathExpr ::= StepExpr (("/" | "//") StepExpr)*

[70] StepExpr ::= FilterExpr | AxisStep

[71] AxisStep ::= (ReverseStep | ForwardStep) PredicateList

[72] ForwardStep ::= (ForwardAxis NodeTest) | AbbrevForwardStep

[73] ForwardAxis ::= ("child" "::") | ("descendant" "::") | ("attribute" "::") | ("self" "::") | ("descendant-or-self" "::") | ("following-sibling" "::") | ("following" "::")

[74] AbbrevForwardStep ::= "@"? NodeTest

[75] ReverseStep ::= (ReverseAxis NodeTest) | AbbrevReverseStep

[76] ReverseAxis ::= ("parent" "::") | ("ancestor" "::") | ("preceding-sibling" "::") | ("preceding" "::") | ("ancestor-or-self" "::")

[77] AbbrevReverseStep ::= ".."

[78] NodeTest ::= KindTest | NameTest

[79] NameTest ::= QName | Wildcard

[80] Wildcard ::= "*" | (NCName ":" "*") | ("*" ":" NCName)

[81] FilterExpr ::= PrimaryExpr PredicateList

[82] PredicateList ::= Predicate*

[83] Predicate ::= "[" Expr "]"

[84] PrimaryExpr ::= Literal | VarRef | ParenthesizedExpr | ContextItemExpr | FunctionCall | Constructor

[85] Literal ::= NumericLiteral | StringLiteral

[86] NumericLiteral ::= IntegerLiteral | DecimalLiteral | DoubleLiteral

[87] VarRef ::= "$" VarName

[88] VarName ::= QName

[89] ParenthesizedExpr ::= "(" Expr? ")"

[90] ContextItemExpr ::= "."

[93] FunctionCall ::= QName "(" (ExprSingle ("," ExprSingle)*)? ")"

[94] Constructor ::= DirectConstructor | ComputedConstructor

[95] DirectConstructor ::= DirElemConstructor

[96] DirElemConstructor ::= "<" QName DirAttributeList ("/>" | (">" DirElemContent* "</" QName S? ">"))

[97] DirAttributeList ::= (S (QName S? "=" S? DirAttributeValue)?)*

[98] DirAttributeValue ::= ('"' (EscapeQuot | QuotAttrValueContent)* '"') | ("'" (EscapeApos | AposAttrValueContent)* "'")

[99] QuotAttrValueContent ::= QuotAttrContentChar | CommonContent

[100] AposAttrValueContent ::= AposAttrContentChar | CommonContent

[101] DirElemContent ::= DirectConstructor | CommonContent | ElementContentChar

[102] CommonContent ::= PredefinedEntityRef | CharRef | "{{" | "}}" | EnclosedExpr

[109] ComputedConstructor ::= CompDocConstructor | CompElemConstructor | CompAttrConstruc-

```
tor | CompTextConstructor
[110] CompDocConstructor ::=
"document" "{"Expr"}"
[111] CompElemConstructor ::=
"element" (QName | ("{"Expr"}"))
"{"ContentExpr?"}"
[112] ContentExpr ::= Expr
[113] CompAttrConstruc-
tor ::= "attribute" (QName |
("{"Expr"}")) "{"Expr?"}"
[114] CompTextConstructor ::=
"text" "{" Expr "}"
[123] KindTest ::= DocumentTest
| ElementTest | AttributeTest |
TextTest | AnyKindTest
[124] AnyKindTest ::= "node" "("
")"
[125] DocumentTest ::= "docu-
ment-node" "(" ElementTest ")"
[126] TextTest ::= "text" "("
")"
[129] AttributeTest ::= "at-
tribute" "(" (AttribNameOrWild-
card)? ")"
[130] AttribNameOrWildcard ::=
AttributeName | "*"
[133] ElementTest ::= "element"
"(" (ElementNameOrWildcard)? ")"
[134] ElementNameOrWildcard ::=
ElementName | "*"
[137] AttributeName ::= QName
[138] ElementName ::= QName
```

The Architecture of the Query Optimization Framework

Figure 1 shows the different components of the query optimization framework. The *Plan Generator* component offers an interface that allows for configuring the query optimization framework according to the needs of the database developers. It is the entry point where a concrete instance of the query optimization framework is established. Therefore, a *Search Strategy* is selected that drives

the process of search-space exploration. Using the *Transformer* component, for a given logical algebra expression, all semantically equivalent expressions are generated. The *Implementation Manager* component provides metadata on the characteristics of physical operators, e. g., whether an operator requires sorted inputs or not. Furthermore, this component knows everything about physical alternatives for logical operators. Because the search space can become very large during query optimization, not all alternatives may be considered for consecutive optimization steps. Hence, the *Estimator* component estimates the costs of each alternative and prunes expensive ones. The cost estimation is based on a system-dependent model provided by the *Cost Model* component.

The Plan Generator

The Plan Generator component receives a logical algebra expression as input and returns the best physical alternative according to the cost estimation provided by the cost model. Because the framework is very modular, it would be possible to choose for every query optimized by this framework a different search strategy.

The State Space

Solutions to a combinatorial optimization problem can be described as states in a solution space of semantically equivalent states. The main task of query optimization is to find this solution based on an initial state by manipulating it in such a way that the optimal or at least a near-optimal state is reached while the optimization goal (e. g., maximum throughput) is satisfied.

At the beginning of query optimization, for every logical algebra operator in a query graph, a corresponding state graph is generated. It contains all *static properties* of a query plan, e. g., structural predicates, projection specifications, or orderings that have to be preserved and which

Figure 2. Hierarchy of search strategies

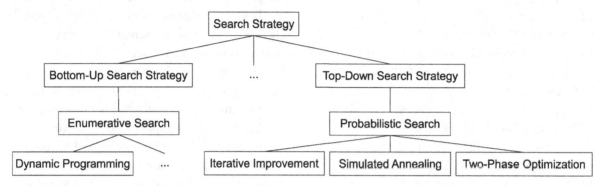

are not changed during the query optimization process. Furthermore, each state contains *dynamic properties*, e. g., required sorting on inputs, assigned cost-estimation values, and the currently assigned physical implementation. In contrast to static properties, dynamic properties can change during every state transition.

The Search Strategy

Since the beginning of relational cost-based optimization, many search strategies have been proposed. Today, we are not sure whether the local-optimality assumption made in the context of classical relational query optimization still holds for XML databases. Moreover, it is not clear which search strategy is the default choice for an XML query optimization framework. Thus, our framework supports different algorithms for exploring the search space of semantically equivalent query plans, which can be classified into bottom-up search strategies and top-down search strategies (Figure 2).

Bottom-up search strategies perform a full-enumerative exploration of the search space and are guaranteed to find the cheapest solution. Because a full-enumeration is hardly applicable due to the exponential growth of the search space, dynamic programming algorithms iteratively construct a search tree formed by all possible alternatives for a (sub)-tree and prune expensive

plans. For constructing this search tree, they start at the leaf nodes of a query plan and enumerate all possible input operations. For a consecutive operator (e. g., a join operator), they create all possible combinations. This process continues until the root of the query plan is reached. This strategy was used by the seminal System R query optimizer (Selinger et al. 1979). Our dynamic programming algorithm follows this classical principle. Compared to the System R optimizer, which was only capable of creating left-deep join trees, our algorithm also supports the generation of bushy and right-deep plans (Graefe, 1993).

The *top-down search strategies* currently provided by our framework can perform a probabilistic search. Consequently, there is no guarantee that they find the best possible solution. Nevertheless, they allow for the optimization of very large join trees, because the space complexity of bottom-up strategies is bound by $n!$, where n is the number of input operators involved. The prominent top-down search strategies currently supported by our framework are: Iterative Improvement, Simulated Annealing, and Two-Phase Optimization (Ioannidis & Kang, 1990). *Iterative Improvement* performs down-hill moves in the search space and can get trapped in local cost minima. On the other hand, the *Simulated Annealing* algorithm can perform down-hill and up-hill moves and consequently increases the probability to find the optimal solution. Finally, Two-Phase optimization is the combination of the former two approaches. In the first phase, a plan with locally minimal cost is determined using Iterative Improvement. This plan serves as input for the second phase, where the plan is further optimized using Simulated Annealing.

The Transformer Component

The Transformer component creates for a given query plan semantically equivalent query plans by performing state transitions using query rewrite. Every rewrite is specified as a *transformation rule* that contains a condition part and an action part. If the condition is satisfied, the action is applied to the state graph. Using this rule-based approach, the implementation of new rewrite rules is straightforward. In the relational world, join commutativity and join associativity are the most important rewrite rules. Both rules can be applied for structural as well as value-based join rewriting. Join commutativity simply replaces the left with the right join partner and vice versa. Join associativity allows exchanging the order in which two adjacent join operators are evaluated. For structural joins, we add an additional rewrite rule, which we call *join fusion* (Weiner, Mathis, & Härder, 2008). It permits to fuse two adjacent structural join operators, which only evaluate the *child* or the *descendant* axis, by a single twig join operator that evaluates both predicates holistically.

For example, if we reconsider the query of Example 1 and use join associativity and join fusion as transformation rules, then Figure 4 shows possible QEPs for this query. Figure 4 a) shows a left-deep plan for this query that is gained by directly mapping the XQGM expression of Figure 3 to a QEP. In Figure 4 b), a possible QEP resulting from join reordering is illustrated. If we apply the join fusion rule once to the logical algebra expression, we get the QEP depicted in Figure 4 c).

Figure 3. XQGM Instance for query Q6

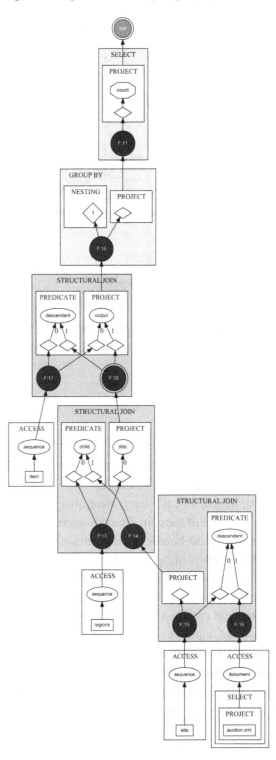

Figure 4. Semantically equivalent query execution plans

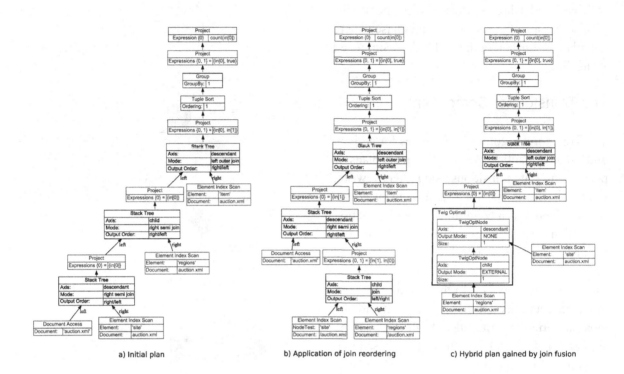

a) Initial plan   b) Application of join reordering   c) Hybrid plan gained by join fusion

The Implementation Manager

Creating semantically equivalent query plans is only one side of the coin. The orthogonal dimension, where cost-based optimization is performed, is the selection of optimal input operators for a query plan and the best implementation for inner-graph operators. For that reason, the Transformer component creates all possible and valid combinations of input operators for every equivalent query plan. Which input operators are available in the database system is described by the *Implementation Manager* component that manages the metadata describing all physical algebra operators. For example, this component knows where path or content indexes can be exploited and which physical alternatives are available for a logical SJ operator.

The Cost Model and the Cost Estimator

The cost model is a system-dependent set of formulae describing the costs of every physical algebra operator in the XDBMS. In combination with statistics provided by the system catalog as well as with the cardinality estimates provided by the system's cardinality estimation framework (Aguiar Moraes Filho & Härder, 2008) the cost model allows to assign costs to every possible query plan.

Because of the exponential growth of alternatives, not every semantically equivalent query plan provided by the Transformer component can be considered for subsequent optimization steps. Therefore, expensive query plans are wiped out early. The cost estimator assigns to each query plan a cost that is estimated using the cost model.

Only the cheapest plan is considered in the future; the remaining *n-1* query plans are pruned.

The Translator Component

After finding the optimal query plan for a given query, this plan is mapped to a QEP. The translator component performs rule-based logical-to-physical operator mappings. Each translation of a logical operator to one or more physical operators is described by so-called translation rules. A *translation rule* has a condition part (a structural pattern) and an action part. Every condition must not be in conflict with other conditions to overcome the problem of several rules matching at the same time. During translation, a query plan is traversed in left-most depth-first order. If a rule matches, the affected sub-tree is translated according to the action part. For example, Figure 4 shows possible QEPs for the query of Example 1.

The Physical Algebra

Currently, our framework encompasses approximately 50 physical algebra operators. These operators belong to the following equivalence classes:

Access operators, for which our framework supports two different kinds, exist with a number of variations. First, the Document Access operator provides the virtual document root of an XML document that serves as the initial evaluation context. Second, we can employ different kinds of operators that give access to document nodes via navigational primitives or index accesses. The so-called Document Index operator is a primary access path and provides navigational access to the document. We additionally provide a kind of inverted-list mechanism that is called Element Index. This secondary access path offers efficient access to element nodes. As tertiary access paths, we provide different kinds of path, content, and content-and-structure indexes.

Navigational operators evaluate structural predicates like the attribute axis using a nested-loops join.

Structural Join operators can be considered as a kind of stack-based merge-join operators that work on two sequences of element-node streams and provide all nodes fulfilling the structural predicate sorted by the left or right input stream. Whenever possible, these operators are semi-join operators.

Holistic Twig Join operators are stack-based n-way join operators. Because they are managing a global state, rather than Structural Join operators, they reduce the amount of intermediate results not being part of the final query result and outperform Structural Join operators in some situations (Weiner & Härder, 2009). Some Holistic Twig Join operators can perform jumps on the input streams to minimize IO costs.

Besides evaluating structural joins, XML query languages like XPath or XQuery also require *Value-Based Join operators*. Therefore, our framework supports the three types of value-based join operators well-known from the relational world: nested-loops join, sort-merge join, and hash-join for equality predicates.

Filter operators allow for the evaluation of aggregate functions like count or for the evaluation of value-based predicates like equality of text values.

Because XML relies on an ordered data model, a *Sort operator* allows sorting a tuple sequence if this property cannot be preserved by the physical operator that produced it. For example, during structural-join reordering, additional sorting can become necessary.

Group-By operators are used for the evaluation of positional predicates and *Set operators* serve for the evaluation of set operations (union, intersection, and difference) on ordered tuple sequences. *Unnest operators* allow for unnesting tuple sequences for example after the evaluation of positional predicates.

In more complex XQuery expressions, variables bound by let expressions are reused several times. For example, if we consider the XMark Benchmark query Q5 (Schmidt et al., 2002), the variable $i is referred to in three cases. Therefore, we employ a so-called *Split operator* that allows to calculate the path expression $auction/site/open_auctions/closed_auction only once, instead of three times, and provides input for the referring sub-trees. The so-called *Merge operator* serves as a counterpart to the Split operator and finally merges the different tuple sequences according to a predicate check.

AN INSTANCE OF THE QUERY OPTIMIZATION FRAMEWORK

In this section, we describe the instance of our query optimization framework that is used throughout the experimental evaluation. The query optimizer performs a bottom-up search and can dispose of PAPs and SAPs for getting the required XML node sequences.

Access Paths

In general, the costs for accessing all instances of element node E can be calculated using the following formula, where the weighting factor w pays attention to CPU-bound or IO-bound hardware settings.

$$Cost_{access}\left(E\right) = IOcost + w * CPUcost$$

Structural Join and Holistic Twig Join operators can only work efficiently on inputs provided by element-node streams. These streams must be sorted in document order and need to be labeled using a node labeling scheme. In this case, we assume DeweyIDs (O'Neil et al., 2004; Härder, Haustein, Mathis, & Wagner, 2007) as node labeling scheme.

Per default, the so-called *document index* (Haustein & Härder, 2007) serves as our primary access path. Figure 6 a) shows a sample document index for the XML tree illustrated in Figure 5. The tree contains the DeweyIDs assigned to each node in the document as keys in ascending order. Each key refers to the data page that contains the corresponding record.

For accessing all E element nodes, we first have to access the left-most data page by descending the index, resulting in h_d page accesses. Next, all data pages have to be scanned to find all E nodes. Let P_d be the number of data pages allocated by document d and $Card_d(E)$ be the total number of occurrences of E elements, then we

Figure 5. Sample XML document (Adapted from Haustein & Härder, 2007)

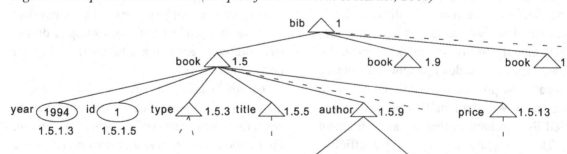

Figure 6. Access structures (Adapted from Haustein & Härder, 2007)

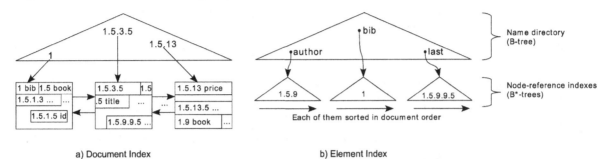

a) Document Index   b) Element Index

model the costs for accessing all element nodes E as (Weiner & Härder, 2009):

$$Cost_{access_{dix}}\left(E\right) = h_d + \left(P_d - 1\right) + w * Card_d(E)$$

It is obvious that document index accesses can only be efficient in high-selectivity scenarios. Therefore, we can make use of a secondary access structure, which is called *element index* (Figure 6 b; Haustein & Härder, 2007). It consists of a name directory where the element names serve as keys and point to node-reference indexes implemented as B*-trees. Each node-reference index contains the DeweyIDs of the corresponding element node instances in ascending document order. Using this structure, efficient access to element nodes can be assured. Accessing all E element nodes requires us first to find the corresponding key in the name directory causing h_{nd} page fetches in the worst case. Next, we have to reach the left-most data page holding the corresponding record by descending the node-reference index (h_{nr} page fetches), and, finally, we must scan all data pages containing E element nodes that raises $\left(P_e - 1\right)$ additional page fetches. This results in the following cost formula (Weiner & Härder, 2009):

$$Cost_{access_{eix}}\left(E\right) = h_{nd} + h_{nr} + \left(P_e - 1\right) + w * Card_d(E)$$

Join Operators

In this plan generation setup, two different join operators can be used during query evaluation. The *StackTree* operator (Al-Khalifa et al., 2002) is a binary SJ operator that is able to evaluate parent/child and ancestor/descendant predicates. The *TwigOptimal* operator (Fontoura, et al., 2005) is a HTJ operator and operates on *n* input streams. Compared to the classic HTJ operator of Bruno, Koudas, & Srivastava (2002), this operator can skip input stream nodes that are guaranteed to be not part of the query result.

In this setup, the plan enumerator uses join associativity and join fusion to generate all possible query evaluation plans using a full-enumeration of the search space.

To estimate the costs of StackTree or TwigOptimal, we apply the following formulae, respectively (Weiner & Härder, 2009):

$$Cost_{ST}\left(E_1, E_2\right) = \left(Cost_{access}\left(E_1\right) + Cost_{access}\left(E_2\right)\right) * f_{ST}$$

$$Cost_{TO}\left(E_1, E_2\right) = \left(Cost_{access}\left(E_1\right) + Cost_{access}\left(E_2\right)\right) * f_{TO}$$

The factors f_{ST} and f_{TO} are correcting weights that return the *relative performance gain* (RPG) for both operators depending on the selectivity of the currently evaluated location.

Figure 7. XPathMark results

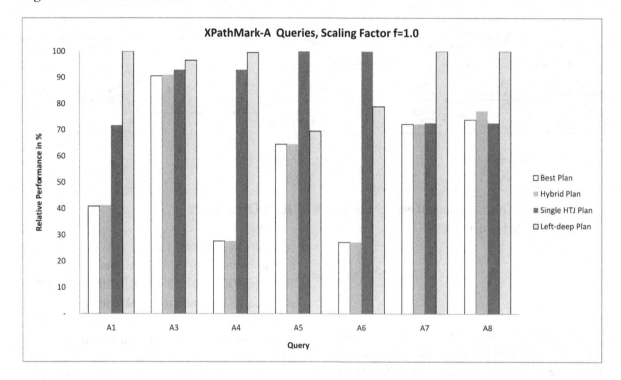

EMPIRICAL EVALUATION

In this section, we show how we can use our query optimization framework to generate and compare different QEPs for XPath and XQuery expressions.

Figure 7 and Figure 8 show the experimental results for the XPathMark-A queries and the XMark benchmark queries, respectively. For all queries, we generated and executed all possible QEPs. For every query, we normalized the presented experimental results to the overall slowest QEP, i.e., the slowest plan has always a relative performance of 100%. The fastest plan for each query is referred to as b*est plan. Hybrid plans* are the fastest combinations of SJ and HTJ operators, which are generated by allowing the plan generator to perform join fusion and structural-join reordering. A s*ingle HTJ plan* is a QEP that evaluates the complete query holistically using a single TwigOptimal (Fontoura, et al., 2005) operator. Finally, a l*eft-deep plan* evaluates path expressions

using cascades of StackTree (Al-Khalifa, et al., 2002) operators, which are not reordered.

Experimental Setup

All experiments were done using an Intel Pentium IV computer (two 3.20 GHz CPUs, 1 GB of main memory, 80 GB of external memory) running Linux with Kernel version 2.16.13. Our native XDBMS server—implemented using Java version 1.6.0 06—was configured with a page size of 4 KB and a buffer size of 250 4KB frames. The experimental results on a 100MB XMark document (scaling factor f=1.0) reflect the average of 5 runs of each query on a cold database buffer.

XPathMark Queries

The XPathMark queries (Franceschet, 2005) are a set of simple to complex XPath queries. Figure 7 shows the experimental results for the

Figure 8. XMark benchmark results

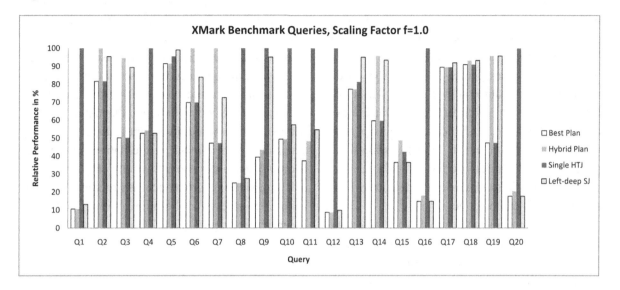

XPathMark-A query set[2] using a linear scale on the y axis.

For these queries, hybrid plans were the best or at least near-optimal choices. Single HTJ plans are faster in 5 out of 7 cases than left-deep plans. Nevertheless, for linear (or almost linear) path expressions such as A1 and A4, they performed worse. We also observed this behavior for similar queries on different documents. This indicates that HTJ operators alone do not serve as a silver bullet for the evaluation of simple XPath expressions in real-world scenarios. They are only fast if some path predicates are involved and, thus, start forming a twig query pattern. For query A3, even a left-deep query execution plan is a good choice, because the difference between the best and worst plan is negligibly small.

XMark Benchmark Queries

Figure 8 illustrates the experimental results for the XMark benchmark queries (Schmidt et al., 2002). For these queries, we did not evaluate all possible QEPs that were generated using our framework. For example, even if we only consider an element index as access path for query Q20, our framework

generated 10,367 different QEPs. Therefore, for every query, we generated all possible QEPs, but evaluated only a sample of 5 randomly chosen QEPs to get the bounds for best plans and worst plans depicted in Figure 8.

Even though some of these queries are very complex and evaluating them requires a lot of different operators, hybrid plan generation does a good job in reducing the query execution time to up to 1/10 of the worst plan's query execution time. Moreover, hybrid plans were in 14 out of 20 cases (70%) optimal or near-optimal choices. In 9 out of 20 cases (45%), single HTJ plans were the worst QEPs. By considering TAPs in the future, we believe that an even more noticeable speed-up can be expected.

FUTURE RESEARCH DIRECTIONS

Cost-based query optimization in native XDBMs is a new and emerging research field. In relational query optimization, plenty of best practices were developed, which nowadays provide default settings for cost-based query optimizers. Such rules-of-thumb are completely missing in the context of native XML query optimization. Therefore, it will be of utmost importance to establish such general cornerstones, which must be condensed into an appropriate cost model.

In the XML world, index-usage advisory needs a closer look, because there is a huge variety of indexing approaches with different power. For example, sophisticated CAS indexes can completely evaluate large fragments of XQuery expressions and become substitutes for conventional join trees. Today, it is neither known nor modeled in which situations this can be done.

Green Computing will become very important in the next few years. Developing cost models that allow for minimizing energy consumption and—to a certain degree—maximizing throughput will become a challenging task. This is especially true, when new hardware technologies, such as flash disks, with completely different access patterns must be considered.

CONCLUSION

In this work, we introduced a cost-based XML query optimization framework for a large fragment of the XQuery language. It uses XTC (Haustein & Härder, 2007)—our prototype of a transactional native XDBMS—as an efficient infrastructure, providing equal and fair conditions for evaluation. This system offers a testbed for exploring which concepts and techniques of relational query optimization can be reused in the context of native XDBMSs. Based on these findings, the first cost-based XQuery optimizer for a native XDBMS can be established.

Even though we are just starting to develop a cost-based XQuery optimizer, our experimental evaluation revealed that hybrid plans, i.e., QEPs using SJ and HTJ operators in combinations for the evaluation of path expressions, can reduce the query execution time tremendously, without requiring sophisticated but costly tertiary index structures. Hybrid plans outperform other plans

by up to two orders of magnitude. If the plan generator explores different join orders, our experiments showed that left-deep join trees are the worst choice in almost all cases. Compared to hybrid plans, even the best join orders are in most situations not competitive to them. As a consequence, we recommend that a plan generator of a cost-based query optimizer should only consider hybrid plans as alternatives and should omit query plans consisting only of SJ operators. By considering tertiary access structures like path or CAS indexes in the future, we believe that a further acceleration of XQuery evaluation can be noticed.

ACKNOWLEDGMENT

We thank the anonymous reviewers for their valuable hints to improve the readability of this work.

REFERENCES

Aguiar Moraes Filho, J., & Härder, T. (2008, September 10–12). EXsum—An XML summarization framework. In *Proceedings of the 12th International Database Engineering and Applications Symposium, Coimbra, Portugal, 2008,* (pp. 139–148). New York: ACM Press.

Al-Khalifa, S., Jagadish, H. V., Patel, J. M., Wu, Y., Koudas, N., & Srivastava, D. (2002, February 26–March 1). Structural joins: A primitive for efficient XML query pattern matching. In *Proceedings of the 18th International Conference on Data Engineering,* San Jose, CA. (pp. 141–154). Washington, DC: IEEE Computer Society.

Balmin, A., Eliaz, T., Hornibrook, J., Lim, L., Lohman, G. M., & Simmen, D. E. (2006). Cost-based optimization in DB2 XML. *IBM Systems Journal, 45*(2), 299–320.

Boag, S., Chamberlin, D., Fernández, M. F., Florescu, D., Robie, J., & Siméon, J. (2007). XQuery 1.0—W3C Recommendation January 23, 2007, Retrieved April 1, 2009 from http://www.w3.org/TR/2007/REC-xquery-20070123/

Bruno, N., Koudas, N., & Srivastava, D. (2002, June 3-6). Holistic twig joins: Optimal XML pattern matching. In *Proceedings of the 2002 ACM SIGMOD International Conference on Management of Data, Madison, Wisconsin* (pp. 310–321). New York: ACM Press.

Chaudhuri, S. (1998, June 1-4). An Overview of Query Optimization in Relational Systems. In *Proceedings of the Seventeenth ACM SIGACT-SIGMOD-SIGART Symposium on Principles of Database Systems, Seattle, Washington* (pp. 34–43). New York: ACM Press.

Fontoura, M., Josifovski, V., Shekita, E., & Yang, B. (2005, October 31-November 5). Optimizing Cursor Movement in Holistic Twig Joins. In *Proceedings of the 14th ACM International Conference on Information and Knowledge Management, Bremen, Germany* (pp. 784–791). New York: ACM Press.

Franceschet, M. (2005, August 28-29). XPath-Mark: An XPath Benchmark for XMark Generated Data. In S. Bressan, S. Ceri, E. Hunt, Z. G. Ives, Z. Bellahsene, M. Rys, & R. Unland (Eds.), *Database and XML Technologies, Third International XML Database Symposium, XSym, Trondheim, Norway* (LNCS Vol. 3671, pp. 129-143). Berlin: Springer.

Goldman, R., & Widom, J. (1997, August 25-29). DataGuides: Enabling Query Formulation and Optimization in Semistructured Databases. In N. Jarke, M. J. Carey, K. R. Dittrich, F. H. Lochovsky, P. Loucopoulos, & M. A. Jeusfeld (Eds.), *Proceedings of the 23rd International Conference on Very Large Data Bases, Athens, Greece* (pp. 436-445). San Francisco: Morgan Kaufmann Publishers.

Graefe, G. (1993, June). Query evaluation techniques for large databases. *ACM Computing Surveys, 25*(2), 73–169. doi:10.1145/152610.152611

Graefe, G. (1995). The Cascades framework for query optimization. *A Quarterly Bulletin of the Computer Society of the IEEE Technical Committee on Data Engineering, 18*(3), 19–29.

Graefe, G., & DeWitt, D. J. (1987, May 27–29). The EXODUS optimizer generator. In U. Dayal (Ed.), *Proceedings of the 1987 ACM SIGMOD International Conference on Management of Data, San Francisco, California* (pp. 160-172). New York: ACM Press.

Graefe, G., & McKenna, W. J. (1993, April 19-23). The volcano optimizer generator: Extensibility and efficient search. In *Proceedings of the Ninth International Conference on Data Engineering, Vienna, Austria* (pp. 209–218). Washington, DC: IEEE Computer Society.

Haas, L. M., Freytag, J. C., Lohman, G. M., & Pirahesh, H. (1989, June). Extensible query processing in Starburst. *SIGMOD Record, 18*(2), 377–388. doi:10.1145/66926.66962

Härder, T., Haustein, M., Mathis, C., & Wagner, M. (2007). Node labeling schemes for dynamic XML documents reconsidered. *Data & Knowledge Engineering, 60*, 126–149. doi:10.1016/j.datak.2005.11.008

Haustein, M., & Härder, T. (2007). An efficient infrastructure of native transactional XML processing. *Data & Knowledge Engineering, 61*, 500–523. doi:10.1016/j.datak.2006.06.015

Ioannidis, Y. E., & Kang, Y. (1990, May 23–26). Randomized algorithms for optimizing large join queries. In *Proceedings of the 1990 ACM SIGMOD International Conference on Management of Data, Atlantic City, NJ*, (pp. 312–321). New York: ACM Press.

Jarke, M., & Koch, J. (1984, June). Query optimization in database systems. *ACM Computing Surveys, 16*(2), 111–152. doi:10.1145/356924.356928

Kabra, N., & DeWitt, D. (1999, April). OPT++: An object-oriented implementation for extensible database query optimization. *The VLDB Journal, 8*(1), 55–78. doi:10.1007/s007780050074

Lanzelotte, R. S., & Valduriez, P. (1991, September 3–6). Extending the Search Strategy in a Query Optimizer. In G. M. Lohman, A. Sernadas, & R. Camps (Eds.), *Proceedings of the 17th International Conference on Very Large Data Bases, Barcelona, Spain* (pp. 363–373). San Francisco: Morgan Kaufmann Publishers.

Mathis, C. (2009). *Storing, indexing, and querying XML documents in native XML database management systems*. Doctoral Dissertation, Dept. of Computer Science, University of Kaiserslautern, Germany.

Mathis, C., Weiner, A. M., Härder, T., & Hoppen, C. R. F. (2008). XTCcmp: XQuery compilation on XTC. In . *Proceedings of the VLDB Endowment, 1*(2), 1400–1403.

McHugh, J., & Widom, J. (1999, September 7-10). Query Optimization for XML. In M. P. Atkinson, M. E. Orlowska, P. Valduriez, S. B. Zdonik, & M. L. Brodie (Eds.), *Proceedings of the 25th International Conference on Very Large Data Bases*, Edinburgh, Scotland, UK (pp. 315–326). San Francisco: Morgan Kaufmann Publishers.

Milo, T., & Suciu, D. (1999, January 10–12). Index Structures for Path Expressions. In C. Beeri & P. Buneman (Eds.), *Proceedings of the 7th International Conference on Database Theory, Jerusalem, Israel* (LNCS Vol. 1540, pp. 277–295). Berlin: Springer.

Nicola, M., Kogan, I., & Schiefer, B. (2007, June 11–14). An XML Transaction Processing Benchmark. In *Proceedings of the 2007 ACM SIGMOD International Conference on Management of Data, Beijing, China* (pp. 937–948). New York: ACM Press.

O'Neil, P., O'Neil, E., Pal, S., Cseri, I., Schaller, G., & Westbury, N. (2004, June 13–18). ORDPATHs: Insert-Friendly XML Node Labels. In *Proceedings of the 2004 ACM SIGMOD International Conference on Management of Data, Paris, France* (pp. 903–908). New York: ACM Press.

Paparizos, S., Wu, Y., Lakshmanan, L. V., & Jagadish, H. V. (2004, June 13–18). Tree Logical Classes for Efficient Evaluation of XQuery. In *Proceedings of the 2004 ACM SIGMOD International Conference on Management of Data, Paris, France* (pp. 71–82). New York: ACM Press.

Pirahesh, H., Hellerstein, J. M., & Hasan, W. (1992, June 2–5). Extensible/Rule Based Query Rewrite Optimization in Starburst. In M. Stonebraker (Ed.), *Proceedings of the 1992 ACM SIGMOD International Conference on Management of Data, Sun Diego, California* (pp. 39–48). New York: ACM Press.

Schmidt, A., Waas, F., Kersten, M., Carey, M. J., Manolescu, I., & Busse, R. (2002, August 20–23). XMark: A Benchmark for XML Data Management. In *Proceedings of the 28th International Conference on Very Large Data Bases, Hong Kong, China* (pp. 974–985). San Francisco: Morgan Kaufmann Publishers.

Selinger, P. G., Astrahan, M. M., Chamberlin, D. D., Lorie, R. A., & Price, T. G. (1979). Access Path Selection in a Relational Database Management System. In *Proceedings of the 1979 ACM SIGMOD International Conference on Management of Data, Boston, Massachusetts,* (pp. 23–34). New York: ACM Press.

Wang, H., Park, S., Fan, W., & Yu, P. S. (2003, June 9–12). ViST: A Dynamic Index Method for Querying XML Data by Tree Structures. In *Proceedings of the 2003 ACM SIGMOD International Conference on Management of Data, San Diego, California* (pp. 110–121). New York: ACM Press.

Weiner, A. M., & Härder, T. (2009, September 7–10). Using Structural Joins and Holistic Twig Joins for Native XML Query Optimization. In *Proceedings of the 13th East European Conference on Advances in Databases and Information Systems, Riga, Latvia.* Berlin: Springer.

Weiner, A. M., Mathis, C., & Härder, T. (2008, March 25). Rules for Query Rewrite in Native XML Databases. In *Proceedings of the 2008 EDBT Workshop on Database Technologies for Handling XML Information on the Web, Nantes, France,* (pp. 21–26). New York: ACM Press.

Wu, Y., Patel, J. M., & Jagadish, H. V. (2003, March 5–8). Structural Join Order Selection for XML Query Optimization. In U. Dayal, K. Ramamritham, & T. M. Vijayaraman (Eds.), *Proceedings of the 19th International Conference on Data Engineering, Bangalore, India* (pp. 443–454). Washington, DC: IEEE Computer Society.

Zhang, N., Haas, P. J., Josifovski, V., Lohman, G. M., & Zhang, C. (2005, August 30–September 2). Statistical Learning Techniques for Costing XML Queries. In K. Boehm, C. S. Jensen, L. M. Haas, M. L. Kersten, P. Larson, & B. C. Ooi (Eds.), *Proceedings of the 31st International Conference on Very Large Data Bases, Trondheim, Norway* (pp. 289–300). New York: ACM Press.

ADDITIONAL READING

Barta, A., Consens, M., & Mendelzon, A. (2004, June 17–18). XML query optimization using path indexes. In I. Manolescu, & Y. Papakonstantinou (Eds.), *Proceedings of the First International Workshop on XQuery Implementation, Experience, and Perspectives, in cooperation with ACM SIGMOD, Paris, France* (pp.43-48). New York: ACM Press.

Buneman, P., Davidson, S., Hillebrand, G., & Suciu, D. (1996, June 4-6). A Query Language and Optimization Techniques for Unstructured Data. In J. Widom (Ed.), *Proceedings of the ACM SIGMOD International Conference on Management of Data, Montreal, Quebec, Canada* (pp. 505–516). New York: ACM Press.

Che, D., Aberer, K., & Ozsu, M. T. (2006). Query optimization in XML structured-document databases. *The VLDB Journal, 15*(3), 263–289. doi:10.1007/s00778-005-0172-6

Chien, S., Vagena, Z., Zhang, D., Tsotras, V., & Zaniolo, C. (200, August 20–23). Efficient structural joins on indexed XML documents. In *Proceedings of 28th International Conference on Very Large Data Bases, Hong Kong, China* (pp. 263–274). San Francisco: Morgan Kaufmann Publishers.

Gardarin, G., Gruser, J., & Tang, Z. (1996, September 3–6). Cost-Based Selection of Path Expression Processing Algorithms in Object-Oriented Databases. T.M. Vijayaraman, A.P. Buchmann, C. Mohan, and N.L. Sarda (Eds.), *Proceedings of the 22nd International Conference on Very Large Data Base, Bombay, India* (pp. 390–401). San Francisco: Morgan Kaufmann Publishers.

Li, H., Lee, M. L., Hsu, W., & Chen, C. (2004, September). An evaluation of XML indexes for structural join. *SIGMOD Record, 33*(3), 28–33. doi:10.1145/1031570.1031576

ENDNOTES

[1]   Note, we also consider path indexes supporting only paths like *//a* as representatives of this class.

[2]   Note, we do not display results for query A2, because a hybrid version does not make sense for a two-step query.t

Section 3
XML Stream Processing, Publish/Subscribe, and P2P

Chapter 9
XML Stream Processing:
Stack–Based Algorithms

Junichi Tatemura
NEC Laboratories America, USA

ABSTRACT

This chapter reviews recent advances on stream XML query evaluation algorithms with stack-based encoding of intermediary data. Originally proposed for disk-resident XML, the stack-based architecture has been extended for streaming algorithms for both single and multiple query processing, ranging from XPath filtering to more complex XQuery. The key benefit of the stack-based architecture is its succinct encoding of partial query results, which can cause exponential enumeration if encoded naively. In addition, the chapter discusses opportunities to integrate benefits demonstrated in the reviewed work. For single-query processing, a sketch is given for an integrated algorithm, StreamTwig²Stack, that achieves all the benefits of existing algorithms in terms of functionality, time complexity, and buffer memory optimality.

INTRODUCTION

XML has become an essential format in data exchange application domains, where an application processes data in XML documents sent from other systems. In order to ensure interoperability, XML data is usually sent as text data, which needs parsing before being consumed by the application. Various XML stream processing technologies have been developed to enable query processing over streaming XML documents for such scenarios.

XML stream processing is to evaluate queries only by a single scan over an XML document. It requires different technologies from querying over disk-resident XML data where an XML can be converted into proprietary data structure with indexing. Moreover, in this streaming environment, we should avoid materializing the entire document as a tree in the main memory. A system often needs to evaluate a query in a low memory-profile environment. In

DOI: 10.4018/978-1-61520-727-5.ch009

some cases, XML processing is embedded in an application as a utility component. In other cases, a system must achieve high throughput to process a large amount of documents and/or queries.

XML stream processing has been extensively studied in recent years. Motivated by a variety of applications, these studies address various issues under different assumptions and problem statements.

Earlier work typically targets information filtering applications, where a query is a pattern matching expression that returns a Boolean value. Received an XML document, the system should identify a small fraction of matching queries from a large set of registered queries. Many filtering algorithms naturally employ an automaton-based approach, where the query results are modeled as acceptance states of automaton.

As XML became pervasive in data exchange, various application needs emerged beyond filtering. Many applications use queries to express more complex patterns that extract structured data from an XML document. In such a scenario, structural pattern matching in XML queries can generate a large amount of intermediary data, which has been recognized as a challenging research issue.

In this chapter, we give a review mainly on recent advance on stream XML query evaluation algorithms that efficiently manage intermediary data in a special data structure based on multiple stacks. Originally, this succinct encoding of intermediary data was proposed for processing disk-resident XML data (Bruno, Koudas, & Srivastava, 2002). However, the proposed algorithms, PathStack and TwigStack, have inspired various streaming algorithms, which have been demonstrated to be efficient for various applications.

We categorize algorithms into two types and review them separately: single-query processing and multi-query processing. At the end of each review, we discuss approaches to integrate benefits of the reviewed algorithms. For single-query processing, we also give a sketch of an integrated algorithm, StreamTwig²Stack, that achieves all the benefits of existing algorithms (functionality, time complexity, and buffer memory optimality).

BACKGROUND

Queries

XPath and XQuery

In the context of stream processing, most research focuses on *Univariate XPath*, a subset of standard XPath 1.0, with the following major limitations: (1) it only supports forward axes (child, descendant, and attribute axes); (2) it does not allow a predicate that compares values of multiple nodes (e.g., A[B > C] is not allowed). Some work also supports backward axes (parent and ancestor axes) in addition. Also, it is known that an XPath query with a backward axis can be rewritten into one only with forward axes (Olteanu, Meuss, Furche, & Bry, 2002).

In order to specify various fragments of XPath within Univariate XPath, the literature often uses a notation P^S, where S is a subset of features $\{/,//,*,[]\}$ that are supported by a query. For instance, $P^{\{/,//\}}$ is XPath that supports child and descendant axes, and $P^{\{/,//,*,[]\}}$ supports predicates and a wildcard in addition.

XQuery is a further complex query language. Most research work on streaming XQuery processing focuses on how to support FOR, LET, WHERE, and RETURN clauses.

Twig Query

With a research focus on structural pattern matching, many studies do not directly discuss XPath/XQuery but model a query as a tree pattern, called a *twig query*. A node (query node) of the twig corresponds to a node test, and an edge between two nodes represents their structural relationship (i.e., axes). The query result is an ordered or unordered list of tuples, each of which is a combination of data nodes that matches the twig pattern. For brevity, we use a non-standard way to describe a twig query that looks similar to XPath, e.g. //A[//B]/C. Unlike XPath, it returns all the combinations of data nodes {A, B, C}.

We also introduce a non-return node, which semantically means that the node is projected out from the result tuples and de-duplication is applied. In this way, an XPath query can be seen as a twig query that has only one return node.

Generalized Tree Pattern

Whereas a twig query captures an important core of XML query processing, it is not powerful enough to efficiently describe FOR-LET-WHERE-RETURN clauses of XQuery. Chen et al. proposed a structure, called generalized tree pattern (GTP), that can represent such clauses, a significant fragment of XQuery (Chen, Jagadish, Lakshmanan, & Paparizos, 2003). A tree structure in GTP features an optional axis and a grouped return node, which enable efficient representation of LET and RETURN clauses. Note that whereas XPath patterns in FOR and WHERE clauses are mandatory to match, patterns in LET and WHERE clauses are optional. Also the matching results in LET and WHERE is associated with matching nodes in the FOR clause as a group.

Data

The system accesses the document as an event stream of the following types: (1) startDocument(), (2) endDocument(), (3) startElement(n), (4) endElement(n), and (5) text(t), where n is tag information of a data node and t is text data. The standard SAX API is available for parsing a document to generate this event stream.

The characteristics of XML documents that have impact to query processing performance include the following: (1) document size |D|, which is the number of elements (nodes) in the document tree; (2) document depth d; (3) document recursion. A document is said to be *recursive* if it contains multiple elements of the same tag that have ancestor-descendant relationship (i.e., they are in the same path from the document root).

In this chapter, we use a capital letter for a tag name (e.g., A) and a lower case letter with subscripts (e.g., a1, a2) for individual nodes whose tag names are the corresponding capital letter. A document is illustrated as a tree whose nodes are elements in this notation.

Technical Challenges

In this section, we highlight technical challenges in evaluating queries over streaming XML data, which have motivated the extensive studies we review in this chapter.

Exponential Enumeration

A path expression, such as //A//B//C is a combination of structural relations ("//"). Whereas it may be naturally implemented as an automaton to check only if it matches, the output of matching nodes may cause enumerating an exponential number of partial results during evaluation. This problem is especially challenging when a document is recursive. Note that, even when the final result is not very large, its partial matches can be much larger. Thus, enumeration of the final result must be done carefully.

Execution of a twig query is more complicated. A straightforward approach is to decompose it into linear path queries and join their results. For instance, a twig //A//B[//C]//D can be decomposed into //A//B//C and //A//B//D. The results of these path queries are joined based on the node identity of B. This process is possibly expensive and inefficient since each path query may result in an exponential number of path matches and many of them may not be part of the final results.

Buffering Data

The complexity of a query has large impact to the required memory for streaming evaluation.

If a linear path query $P^{\{/,//,*\}}$ is required to return only a Boolean value (i.e., filtering) or a matching node at the leaf query node, the system only has to keep the current state of a finite machine. However, if a query has a predicate, the system has to remember that all the leaves in a query twig are satisfied in the current context. Bar-Yossef et al. formalized this issue of maintaining twig match as the *query frontier size*, which is derived from fan-out of query nodes, and proved that it gives a lower bound for a large fragment of XPath (Bar-Yossef, Fontoura, & Josifovski, 2004).

When it needs to output result nodes, instead of a Boolean value, the system needs to buffer potential result nodes for $P^{\{/,//,*,[]\}}$ since the predicates of the query might become satisfied after the system observe the result candidates. In the worst case, the buffer size might be $O(|D|)$, which cannot be avoided by any streaming algorithm. To formalize this buffering problem, Bar-Yossef et al. gives a lower bound, formalized as the concurrency of the document with respect to the query (Bar-Yossef, Fontoura, & Josifovski, 2005).

Sharing

In order to execute multiple queries (query workload) in a scalable manner, a multi-query processing system should consolidate redundant computation and memory among individual query evaluation. Many techniques have been proposed to leverage various commonalities among query expressions, such as prefix, suffix, and substring. Typically, queries $P^{\{/,//,*,[]\}}$ are first decomposed into linear paths $P^{\{/,//,*\}}$, and their query nodes in the common prefixes (or suffixes) are shared among these queries. Whereas decomposition increases sharing opportunities among multiple queries, it loses optimization opportunities for a single query. Efficient algorithm for a single twig may no longer applicable after decomposition.

Preliminaries: Technology background

Related Approaches

Automaton-Based Filtering Algorithms

XFilter is one of the earliest works to address path query evaluation over streaming XML data for information filtering applications (Altinel & Franklin, 2000). It builds a separate finite state machine for each path query and offers no sharing. YFilter extended this work to represent a path query as a nondeterministic finite automaton (NFA), which is easy to combine based on the prefix commonality (Diao, Altinel, Franklin, Zhang, & Fischer, 2003).

An NFA-based algorithm has to manage the number of active runtime states. In order to address this issue, the XMLTK system translates NFA-based query workload into DFA which enables higher throughput (Green, Gupta, Miklau, Onizuka, & Suciu, 2004). The problem of a naïve approach to use DFA is that the number of states can be exponentially larger than the original NFA. The XMLTK thus generates DFA states only when they are required.

XPush (Gupta & Suciu, 2003) directly handles XPath with predicates and shares common predicates among the workload. It introduces a single deterministic pushdown automaton, called XPush machine, that evaluates XPath in a bottom-up manner.

Automaton-Based Query Algorithms

In order to support query processing that returns data nodes, the automaton-based approach is extended as transducers that manipulate intermediary data driven by state transition. XSQ is an automaton-based system for single XPath query processing (Peng & Chawathe, 2003). It uses a hierarchy of non-deterministic push down automata associated with buffers. The time complexity is however exponential with respect to the query size. XSM (Ludäscher, Mukhopadhyay, & Papakonstantinou, 2002) and SPEX (Olteanu, 2007) both employ a network of transducers for single query processing.

Most automaton-based approaches target either filtering or single query processing. A notable exception is that YFilter is extended to support multi-query processing for message brokering applications (Diao & Franklin, 2003).

Non-Automaton-Based Filtering Algorithms
For filtering applications, various approaches that are not based on automaton have been proposed, too. MatchMaker proposed an index structure for matching multiple tree patterns, which requires two passes of the XML document (Lakshmanan & Parthasarathy, 2002). FiST represents a twig query as a sequence and solves twig filtering as a sequence matching problem (Kwon, Rao, Moon, & Lee, 2005). However, it is limited to handle ordered twig queries. XTrie is an XPath filtering algorithm that leverages the commonality of substrings among path expressions (Chan, Felber, Garofalakis, & Rastogi, 2002). An XPath is decomposed into sequences of node tests separated only by child axes, e.g. A/B/C, which are indexed in a trie.

Single-Stack Architecture
In fact, many existing systems use stack-based data structure. However, unlike PathStack, they typically employ a single stack to maintain the current matching context. In this chapter, we call it *single-stack architecture* and distinguish it from multi-stack encoding of query results, which is our focus of review. TurboXPath (Josifovski, Fontoura, & Barta, 2005) is a streaming twig query processor. Its data structure WA (Work Array) takes single-stack architecture to perform state transition in a manner similar to the transitions of the NFA. XAOS is XPath query processing algorithm that

supports both backward and forward axes (Barton, Charles, Goyal, Raghavachari, Fontoura, & Josifovski, 2003). Its matching structure is also regarded as single-stack architecture. In fact, YFilter also employs single-stack architecture to manage active states of the NFA.

Holistic Twig Join

In this section, we describe holistic twig join, an approach proposed by Bruno et al. to address the issue of large intermediary data, and the algorithms PathStack and TwigStack that implement this holistic approach (Bruno, Koudas, & Srivastava, 2002).

Structural Join
First, we review a join-based XML processing, called *structural join*. In the storage, an XML document is physically shredded into individual nodes, and a query A // B is implemented as a join over two sets of nodes.

Zhang et al. proposed a structural join algorithm based on region encoding (Zhang, Naughton, Dewitt, & and Lohman, 2001), which is a widely used scheme to represent the structural relationship among nodes in a tree. Region encoding associates each node with a triple of integer values (left, right, level). Here, level is the depth of the node in the document tree. The values of left and right are assigned as follows: assign a sequential number to each tag (both start and end tags are put together) in the document order. The left and right values of a node are the sequential numbers of start and end tags, respectively. With this encoding, we can identify structural relationship between two nodes a and b as follows:

- Node a is an ancestor of node b (i.e., a // b) if and only if a.left < b.left < a.right.
- Node a is the parent of node b (i.e., a / b) if and only if a // b and a.level + 1 = b.level.

Figure 1. PathStack example

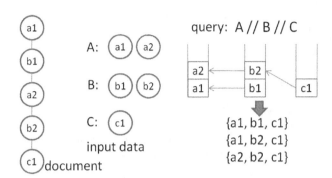

Based on the range encoding, Zhang et al. proposed the MPMGJN algorithm, which is a specialized merge join algorithm for structural relation. Al-Khalifa et al. proposed an improved algorithm, called Stack-Tree, which utilizes a single stack to operate a binary structural join (Al-Khalifa, Jagadish, Koudas, Patel, Srivastava, & Wu, 2002).

The structural join algorithms described above decompose a twig or path query into a tree of multiple binary joins, which might generate a large amount of intermediary results.

PathStack/TwigStack

Bruno et al. proposed a holistic approach that manages all the input lists of nodes together in order to minimize intermediary join results in the main memory. The PathStack algorithm is introduced for a linear path query and extended as TwigStack for a general twig query.

To preserve intermediary results, the authors introduced a succinct encoding scheme based on multiple stacks, each of which is associated with an individual query node. A stack is maintained such that a node is descendant of the all the nodes below in the same stack. When a data node is pushed into a stack, it is associated with a pointer to the closest ancestor node in the parent stack (i.e., the stack top). The stack-structure and pointers

together maintain ancestor-descendant relation in a way we can easily traverse.

Figure 1 illustrates a running example of PathStack for a query A//B//C. The algorithm maintains cursors for the three input lists. Each list is sorted by the left value in increasing order, and the algorithm processes the node with the minimum left value among the top of the cursors (i.e., it traverses the document tree in preorder). The current node (e.g., c1) is put into the corresponding stack if and only if it satisfies the structural relationship with the stack top of the parent query node (e.g., b2).

Once it reaches the leaf query node, the result is enumerated through traversal of pointers. If the structural relationship is ancestor-descendant (e.g., B//C), the traversal also goes to lower nodes in the stack. In this way, a possibly exponential number of pattern matches are succinctly encoded with the stacks, and unnecessary enumeration of partial results is avoided.

The algorithm must maintain the stack to keep ancestor-descendant relationship. This is achieved by popping a node out if its right value is smaller than the left value of the current node to be pushed.

A straightforward extension to a twig query is to apply linear-path decomposition, which may generate many unnecessary path results. The au-

Figure 2. The getNext operation of TwigStack

```
getNext of TwigStack
    getNext(q) {
1       if (q.leaf) return q;
2       for (c in q.children) {
3          n = getNext(c);
4          if(n != c) return n;
5       }
6       cmin = minarg(c in q.children) { c.next().left };
7       cmax = maxarg(c  in q.children) { c.next().left };
8       while(q.next().right < cmax.next().left)  q.advance(); // advances q's cursor
9       return (q.next().left < cmin.next().left)? q : cmin;
    }
```

thors proposed the TwigStack algorithm, which employs careful selection of data nodes from the cursors with assuring that a node is a part of the twig query result.

The TwigStack algorithm consists of the main procedure that constructs stacks and getNext function that returns the next data node to be processed (Figure 2). The main procedure constructs the stacks in a top-down manner from the root query node. A data node is put if and only if there exists a matching data node in the parent stack. The getNext operation returns a query node q that has the following property: the current node at q's cursor (given by q.next()) and the current nodes of the descendants' cursors satisfy a subtwig query whose root is q. Together with the top-down construction of the main procedure, it assures that a node to put into q.stack is a part of the final result. The main procedure process merge join over path results as a post-processing.

Benefits of Stack-Based Architecture

As demonstrated for the disk-resident data, the key benefit of the stack-based architecture is its succinct encoding of intermediary data that enables efficient holistic processing of twig queries. As we will review later, this benefit is applicable to the streaming environment. Key challenge is that TwigStack is not directly applicable to the streaming environment since getNext looks up multiple node lists and such look-ahead access is not available. In addition, we do not know the right value of a data node when its start tag is observed.

Whereas its benefit is apparent for twig queries, the stack-based architecture is also effective even for a simpler XPath query, for which maintenance of states for predicates can cause exponential cost. For a single XPath query processing, stack-based algorithms, LQ/EQ, achieve time compexity $O(|Q||D|)$, which is independent of the document recursion.

Another benefit of the stack-based architecture, especially against the automaton-based approach, is its flexibility of data processing due to decoupling of a stack construction process and a result enumeration process. AFilter exploits such flexibility to avoid eager state management of automaton-based algorithms for multi-query processing.

On the other hand, the stack-based architecture is not really meaningful if the workload does not involve document recursion, which causes explosion of the intermediary data. Such a case is often seen when relational data is published as XML data.

STACK-BASED SINGLE-QUERY PROCESSING

Baseline Framework

We first introduce a common framework of a single query processing to present the algorithms in a uniform manner.

An algorithm has to implement a query node data structure q and two procedures startBlock(q,n,level) and endBlock(q,level). A query processor, configured with a specific algorithm, evaluates a single query as follows: upon an event startElement(n) or endElement(n), the processer looks up query nodes that match with n. For each matched query node, it calls the corresponding procedure. The processor also maintains the level of the current node.

As a baseline algorithm, PathStack can be naturally adapted to this framework. Recall that PathStack consumes data nodes in preorder traversal, which is the same order startBlock is called. A query node q has a stack (q.stack) and a pointer to the parent query node (q.parent). Given a node n and its level, the algorithm checks a node at the stack top of q.parent (q.parent.stack.top()). When the axis (q.axis) is parent-child, the document level must be compared as follows: q.parent.stack.top(). level + 1 = level. In order to pop out nodes from stack, we do not need range encoding. Instead, we can pop a node out when its end tag is observed (i.e., endBlock is called).

We review two algorithms for XPath query and two algorithms for twig query processing. Here, XPath query $P^{\{/,//,*,[]\}}$ is seen as a special case of a twig query. We introduce the following terms. A query node q is a *predicate node* if the sub-twig rooted at q does not contain return nodes. Such a sub-twig is called a *predicate twig*, which corresponds to a predicate in XPath expression. Other non-return nodes are called *axis nodes*. A *predicate path* with respect to a predicate node q is a path

to q from the closest axis node. The *axis path* is the path from the root to the return node.

TwigM

Given an XPath query represented as a twig, we immediately have the following observations:

- When PathStack reaches a leaf predicate node, its predicate path becomes true.
- When PathStack reaches a return node, the matching data node is a candidate result.

Then a problem is how to combine the above information without possibly expensive merge join.

Chen et al. proposed the algorithm called TwigM for this problem (Chen, Davidson, & Zheng, 2006). It propagates matching condition of predicate paths and result candidates through data nodes in the stacks. By the end of traversal, the result has been aggregated at the root node. The pseudo code is given in Figure 3.

In TwigM's stack (q.stack), a stack element s for node n maintains the following information.

- *Branch match* s.flags: an array of Boolean values that specify if n has descendant data nodes that satisfy predicate twigs that are branched from q.
- *Candidates* s.list: a list of candidate data nodes that are descendant of n.

If s.flags is evaluated to be true, the data nodes in s.list are the result of the sub-query whose root is q when it is applied to the sub-document whose root is n. The algorithm constructs this information recursively from leaves to the root (i.e., postorder) whereas it constructs stacks in a top-down manner (i.e., preorder). The propagation is performed in endBlock, depending on the axis type: child (lines 6-7) or descendant (line 9).

Figure 3. TwigM algorithm

```
TwigM
        startBlock(q,n,level) {
   1      if (q.parent.stack.isEmpty()) return;
   2      if (q.axis == D || q.parent.stack.top().level + 1 == level) {
   3        s = q.newElement(level);
   4        if (q.type == R) s.list.add(n);  // q is return node
   5        q.stack.push(s);
   6      }
        }
        endBlock(q,level) {
   1      if (q.stack.isEmpty()) return;
   2      s = q.stack.top();
   3      if (s.level == level && q.eval(s.flags)) { // sub-twig q(s) is satisfied
   4        if (q.root) { output(s.list);  return;}
   5        if (q.axis == C) { // child axis
   6          sp = q.parent.stack.top();
   7          if (sp.level + 1 == level) propagate(q,s,sp);
   8        } else { // descendant axis
   9          for (sp in q.parent.stack) propagate(q,s,sp);
  10        }
  11      }
        }
        propagate(q,s,sp) {
   1      sp.flags[q.pos] = true;  // q.pos is the position of q in the children of q.parent
   2      sp.list.append(s.list);
        }
```

The time complexity of TwigM is polynomial $O((|Q| + dB)|Q||D|)$.

LQ/EQ

It is known that XPath $P^{\{/,//,*,[]\}}$ can be evaluated in $O(|Q||D|)$ time in the non-streaming environment (Gottlob, Koch, & Pichler, 2005). However, TwigM is still more expensive. The major cost is its propagation procedure. Especially, it has to scan all the data nodes in a stack.

Gou et al. proposed two algorithms LQ and EQ that evaluate $P^{\{/,//,*,[]\}}$ in $O(|Q||D|)$ time in the streaming environment (Gou & Chirkova, 2007).

LQ

LQ employs stack-based structure and bottom-up propagation scheme similar to TwigM. Unlike TwigM, however, its propagation procedure only accesses the top of stacks for each node visit: for each data node popped out from q.stack, the algorithm propagates information to the following (a constant number of) destinations:

- **Propagation 1:** The new stack top of q.
- **Propagation 2:** The stack top of q.parent.
- **Propagation 3:** The stack top of the *host* node of q.

Propagation 2 is similar to TwigM except that it only propagates information to the stack top. LQ eventually propagates the information to the rest of data nodes in the stack after they appear at the top, which is achieved by Propagation 1 and 3 for branch match and candidates, respectively. Propagation 1 propagates a value in the branch match only if it branches with descendant axs. The candidate list is not propagated in the same way since it causes duplication of candidate lists. Propagation 3 is introduced to avoid this.

The key idea in Propagation 3 is a notion of *host* node defined as follows. First, notice that candidates are propagated only though the axis path. We segment this axis path by splitting at descendant axes ("//"). For instance, an axis path //A/B//C/D is partitioned into two segments: A/B and C/D. We call the axis node at the tail of a segment the *segment host*. In this example, B is the host of A and B, and C and D have no host. A query node q is extended to have a pointer (q.host) to its host.

Figure 4 gives a running example //A[//D]/B[//E]//C. Here we focus the segment A/B and stacks A and B. Figure 4 (c) shows the state of stacks A,B after the algorithm observes the end tag of e1. The data node b2 has a candidate c1 and its branch match (for E) is true. When the algorithm observes the end tag of b2, b2 is popped out from the stack. Propagation1 sets b1's branch match for E to be true, and Propagation 2 moves the candidate c1 to the top of the parent stack (i.e., a2). The result of this propagation is seen in Figure 4 (d). Then, a2 is popped out from the stack, and its branch match is evaluated to be false. Propagation 3 moves the candidate c1 from a2 to the stack top of its host, i.e., b1 (Figure 4 (e)). The branch match of b1 will become all true after visiting d1, and the branch match and c1 will be propagated to a1 when b1 is popped out. Finally, c1 will be returned as a result when a1 is popped out.

EQ

Another limitation of TwigM, as well as LQ, is its laziness of result output. It is desirable to output results as early as possible in order to minimize memory consumption for candidate buffering. EQ realizes this by extending LQ to evaluate and propagate partial results in an eager manner.

The eager evaluation is done with two procedures: bottom-up evaluate (BUE) and top-down propagate (TDP). BUE is triggered when the traversal reaches a leaf predicate node. It propagates the change along the predicate path. If it reaches an axis node and the predicate twig becomes true, TDP propagates this information down along the axis.

Notice that this information propagation must be done at data level (a tree of matched data nodes) instead of query level (a tree of query nodes). Two pointers are added to the data node in a stack: (1) s.parent: a pointer to s's closest ancestor in q.parent; (2) s.child: a pointer to s's closest descendant in the axis node that is a child of q (s.child is added only if q is an axis node).

Each data node has two additional flags: s.self (the sub-query is true at s) and s.up (predicate twigs are true for all the descendant axis nodes).

When the algorithm reaches a return node s, if both s.self and s.up bits are true, the algorithm can immediately output the node as a part of the result. Otherwise, the candidate is propagated in a similar way to LQ. The propagated list associated with a data node will be output during TDP when the up and self bits of the node become true.

When there is a descendant axis, BUE has to visit lower nodes in the stack. However, the traversal of the stack is carefully designed to avoid redundant paths from the current predicate node to the axis nodes. Data nodes no longer contribute to further propagation are eagerly removed from the stacks during BUE/TDP procedures.

The authors showed that EQ also has time complexity $O(|Q||D|)$. Although it eagerly traverses stacks, such costs are amortized when the end tags are processed in the future.

Twig²Stack

Twig²Stack is a holistic twig join algorithm that avoids merge join post-processing of Twig-Stack based on postorder traversal (Chen S., Li, Tatemura, Hsiung, Agrawal, & Candan, 2006). Although it is not proposed as a streaming al-

Figure 4. LQ example

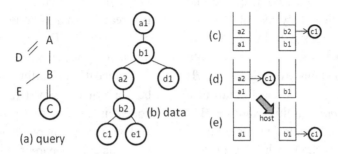

(a) query

(b) data

gorithm, the authors suggest applicability to the streaming environment since it does not employ look-ahead data access. In this chapter, we discuss the Twig^{2}Stack algorithm in the context of stream processing.

Twig^{2}Stack can efficiently evaluate not only a twig query but also a GTP query by employing hierarchical stack encoding. It constructs the stacks at the time cost O(|Q||D|) and evaluates a GTP query at the time cost O(|D||Q| + |R|), where |R| is the number of sub-twig results.

Hierarchical Stack Encoding

In order to avoid possibly expensive merge join, the authors proposed a stack-based data structure, called a hierarchical stack encoding scheme, to compactly represent twig results. Figure 5 illustrates a running example of hierarchical stacks constructed for a query and data in the figure.

Each query node q is associated with a *hierarchical stack* HS[q] that consists of an ordered sequence of *stack trees*. A stack tree is an ordered tree whose nodes are stack of data nodes. A stack tree efficiently encodes ancestor-descendant relationship between two data nodes that matched with q. It has the following properties:

- A node in a stack is an ancestor of all nodes below in the same stack and is also an ancestor for all nodes in the descendant stacks

in the stack tree.
- If two stacks have no ancestor-descendant relationship in a stack tree, no data node in one stack has ancestor-descendant relationship with any data nodes in the other stack.

For instance, in HS[A] in Figure 5, a2 is ancestor of both a3 and a4, whereas a3 and a4 have no such relationship.

A hierarchical stack can be constructed through postorder document traversal. Construction involves merging stack trees. For instance, consider constructing HS[A] in the example. When the algorithm tries to put a2, there are two stack trees (for a3 and a4) that are descendant of a2. In order to put a2, the algorithm merges them into one whose root is an empty stack that has the original stack trees as its children.

Twig^{2}Stack

Twig^{2}Stack runs similar process to PathStack in a bottom-up manner. A data node s is pushed only when there exists a result of sub-twig query whose root is s. It associates s with pointers to the closest descendant in the child query nodes. Note that this process may require merge of stack trees in a child query node. For instance, when a2 is put to HS[A], there are two stack trees in HS[B] that are descendant of a2. Thus they are

Figure 5. Hierarchical stack encoding

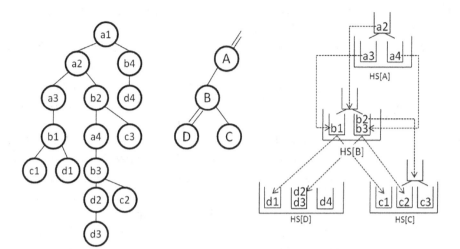

merged into a single stack tree, and a2 points to the bottom of its empty root stack.

In Figure 6, the procedure endBlock implements this construction. Given a matching data node to a query node q, the algorithm checks existence of sub query results and merges stack trees of child hierarchical stacks when needed (lines 5-8). If there exists a sub-query result, the data node is pushed to HS[q] (lines 9-12).

Twig^{2}Stack enumerates the results in a top-down manner and visits data nodes that are in the final results. The authors give detailed enumeration algorithms for GTP queries. Here we only note that grouping node is automatically achieved in the hierarchical stack encoding, and expensive grouping operation is avoided.

Optimization for Memory Cost

One issue of the basic Twig^{2}Stack algorithm is the memory requirement: (1) data nodes must be buffered to evaluate in postorder. The buffer size is the depth of the document; (2) whereas Twig-Stack ensures that a node put into the stacks are guaranteed to be part of final stacks, Twig^{2}Stack may contain data nodes that are not the part of the final result.

Figure 6. Twig^{2}Stack adapted for streaming

Twig2Stack	
	startBlock(q, n, level) {
1	PathStack.startBlock(q,n,level);
	}
	endBlock(q,level) {
1	n = PathStack.endBlock(q,level);
2	if(n == null) return;
3	s = newElement(n,level);
4	satisfied = true;
5	for (c in q.children) {
6	satisfied = c.hs.merge(s, c.axis);
7	if (!satisfied) break;
8	}
9	if(satisfied) {
10	q.hs.merge.(s,"");
11	q.hs.push(s);
12	}
13	if(q.topBranch && q.ps.isEmpty())
14	enumareteResults(q);
	}

The authors proposed an improvement through *early result enumeration*, which is also applicable to the streaming environment. It takes a hybrid approach with top-down (preorder) and bottom-up (postorder) methods with PathStack and the hierarchical stack, respectively.

A stream version of the Twig^{2}Stack in Figure 6 implements early result enumeration. When the algorithm observes a start tag (the procedure startBlock), a node n is put into a PathStack (q.ps) of the corresponding query node q. When the algorithm observes the end tag of n, it is popped out from q.ps and put into the hierarchical stack q.hs.

This approach enables us to enumerate the query results earlier and all the data in the hierarchical stacks can be cleaned up. Assume that q is the *top branch* node in a query. Whenever the data in q.ps is all popped out (line 13), we can start enumerating the query results and then clean up all the hierarchical stacks (line 14).

Notice the difference in trigger condition between the early enumeration and EQ. Unlike XPath, it does not help to reduce memory to output a twig match as soon as it is found, because the nodes in the twig match may be a part of another twig match found in the future. Line 13 makes sure that there will no such future mathes.

There is another performance optimization related to the memory, proposed by Qin et al (Qin, Yu, & Ding, 2007). Their algorithm Twig-List is basically a list-based implementation of the Twig^{2}Stack algorithm. Compared to naïve implementation of hierarchical stacks, a list-based implementation avoids random access of the memory and is easy to extend to an external algorithm. A close look at the Twig^{2}Stack algorithm reveals that a hierarchical stack, i.e., an ordered sequence of ordered trees of stacks, is constructed in the document order and can be implemented as a single list to which a new data node is appended. A pointer to the stack top can be implemented as a range in the list. They reported that even the external algorithm, which maintains all lists on disk, outperformed a naïve Twig^{2}Stack implementation.

StreamTX

StreamTX is another approach to extend Twig-Stack to the streaming environment (Han, Jiang, Ho, & Li, 2008). The key issue of TwigStack

for streaming data is look-ahead data access in getNext operation. Recall that getNext is the key component to guarantee the memory optimality of the stacks, i.e., a node in the stacks is guaranteed to be part of the final results. Twig^{2}Stack is ready for stream processing since it does not look ahead, but, at the same time, it abandons this optimality.

The key idea of StreamTX is intelligent buffering of the incoming document event stream in order to emulate multi-cursor data scan of getNext.

A simple buffering can be done as follows: The document is progressively parsed as much as the getNext operation advances cursors. When it advances a cursor, there can be other data nodes preceding the target node for the cursor. They are buffered in queues until they are consumed by other cursors. This approach, however, can buffer a large number of data nodes wasting the memory. The problem is that each cursor aggressively searches for its next node without considering other cursors. Instead of advancing the cursor, we may find data nodes in the buffer for other cursors that are ready to process.

The algorithm StreamTX coordinates the cursors with *blocking*. A cursor whose buffer does not have a data node is said to be *blocked*. The algorithm tries to continue the matching with non-blocked cursors as much as possible. Figure 7 shows the getNext operation with blocking. The key differences are lines 9-12.

The new getNext algorithm consumes data in a best-effort manner and achieves the optimality for the stack size. However, it does not guarantee the optimality of the buffers. There can be a data node in the buffer we can guarantee that it is *not* part of the result. The authors proposed two pruning techniques to minimize the size of the buffers:

- **Query-path pruning:** When a start tag is observed, all the ancestors of the node have been observed. We put a new node to the buffer only if it satisfies a query path (i.e., the path from the root to the corresponding

Figure 7. The getNext operation of StreamTX

getNext of StreamTX	
	getNext(q) {
1	if (q.leaf) return q;
2	for (c in q.children) {
3	n = getNext(c);
4	if(n != c && !n.blocked) return n;
5	}
6	cmin = minarg(c in q.children) { c.next().left };
7	cmax = maxarg(c in q.children) { c.next().left };
8	while(q.next().right < cmax.next().left) q.advance();
9	if(q.blocked) return cmin.blocked? q : cmin;
10	if(cmin.blocked) return cmin;
11	if(cmax.blocked) return q.next().left < cmin.next().left ? cmax : cmin;
12	return q.next().left < cmin.next().left ? q : cmin;
	}

query node). This check is similar to PathStack and can be done at $O(1)$ cost.

- **Existential-match pruning:** When an end tag is observed, all the descendants of the node have been observed. We purge the node from the buffer if it does not satisfy a sub-twig result with its ancestor nodes. This check is similar to postorder traversal of Twig^{2}Stack and can be done at $O(1)$ cost.

Discussion: A Unified Approach

In this section, we discuss a possibility to achieve an efficient streaming GTP processing algorithm with the buffer optimality and illustrate a sketch of an algorithm, StreamTwig^{2}Stack, that takes a unified approach of the ideas reviewed above.

Buffer Optimality for a Stream Twig Query Processing

First we discuss limitations of the two stream twig query processing algorithms Twig^{2}Stack and StreamTX.

Twig^{2}Stack, when it is combined with PathStack, guarantees that a data node is put into the stack if and only if it satisfies both a query path

and a sub-twig query. Although it is better than the basic Twig^{2}Stack, it does not achieve the optimality of TwigStack. Consider, for instance, a twig query A[//E]//B[//C]//D. A data node b is put into the stack of B if it is part of the results of A//B[//C]//D. But it does not check existence of a data node for E that is part of the final result together with b. In the streaming environment, we cannot always guarantee that at the time the algorithm observes the end tag of a node. This means that, in the streaming environment, even postorder traversal cannot achieve the optimality in the same sense with TwigStack.

Let us revisit StreamTX's proposal to handle this problem. It manages buffers (queues) between TwigStack and a parser, which is optimal in a sense that: A buffered data in a queue is (1) put into stacks as soon as it turns out to be in part of the final result, and (2) purged from a queue as soon as it turns out *not* to be in the final result.

Here, notice a subtle difference in the concept of optimality between the streaming environment and the disk-based environment. In the streaming environment, the entire data must be scanned and put into the memory. It does not make fundamental difference in the impact of memory cost whether a node is kept in a queue or a stack, both of which reside in the main memory.

Thus, we can take the following approach to achieve the same buffer optimality of StreamTX:

1. A data node is put into a stack if the information already observed *cannot* guarantee that it can be discarded without missing the final results.
2. It is purged from the stack as soon as it turns out *not* to be in the final result.

In addition, we notice that the following optimization must be achieved to minimize the buffer space for result data, which was out of the scope of StreamTX:

3. It is purged from the stack, after result enumeration, as soon as it will no longer be part of the future results.

StreamTX does not focus on the performance of the main part of TwigStack in the streaming environment. The original TwigStack executes merge-join over path matches at the end of the entire process, meaning that the partial solutions are preserved in the memory. Eager processing over partial solutions is desired in order to achieve the optimal buffering cost *as a whole*.

Twig^{2}Stack already achieve the third property by early result enumeration, as well as the first property by PathStack. The second property of the memory optimality is achieved by introducing eager purging to the management of the hierarchical stacks, which is illustrated in Figure 8.

If a query node q has multiple children (i.e., q.branch is true) and the current node is not a part of the sub-twig result with respect to q. It is possible that the hierarchical stack contains nodes that can be discarded. Procedures purgeAll and purgeC identify and purge such nodes by invoking the purge procedure introduced to the hierarchical stack.

Although this purge algorithm traverses multiple hierarchical stacks for each endBlock call,

it only accesses each stack tree at most once (i.e., when it is purged), and the number of stack tree is not larger than the number of data nodes matched with the query nodes. Similar to EQ, this cost is amortized by the end of traversal. Thus, this additional procedure does not change the $O(|Q||D|)$ cost of stack construction. During enumeration, Twig^{2}Stack only accesses nodes that are part of the final result. Thus the cost of enumeration is not affected at all.

Moreover, the access pattern of this purge process is uniform, and the list-based implementation of the hierarchical stack (TwigList) is still applicable. When it is combined with an external algorithm, the purge process can be selectively applicable to the latest page (i.e., the page that contains the list tail) in the main memory, avoiding unnecessary disk I/O to save the main memory.

Optimization for a Twig with Predicate Nodes

In the above discussion, we assumed that the all query nodes are return node. However, there is a chance to further reduce the buffer space when a twig query has non-return nodes. Note that the EQ algorithm achieves this for a special case where a query has only one return node.

We generalize the notion of axis nodes in the discussion of a twig for XPath. Unlike XPath, non-predicate nodes does not conform a linear path (axis). We call the structure of non-predicate nodes an *axis twig*. When an axis node has multiple non-predicate children, we say that it is an *axis branch*. We also call the top-most one the *top axis branch* of a query.

First, the authors of Twig^{2}Stack already proposed optimized construction of the hierarchical stack of a predicate node (which they call an existence-checking query node). (1) For a predicate node with the ancestor-descendant axis, any descendant stacks or non-top elements in a root stack of a stack tree can be safely removed. (2) For one with the parent-child axis, a child node

Figure 8. StreamTwig²Stack: Optimization for buffer memory

```
StreamTwig2Stack
    endBlock(q, level) {
        ...
        If(!satisfied && q.branch) {
            If(q.ps.isEmpty()) for (c in q.children) purgeAll(c,s);
            else for (c in q.children) if(c.axis == C) purgeC(c,s);
        }
        ...
    }
    purgeAll(q, s) {
1       purged = q.hs.purge(s); // purge stack-trees that are descendant of  s
2       if(purged) for(c in q.children)  purgeAll(c, s);
    }
    purgeC(q,s) {
1       if(q.ps.isEmpty()) {
2           purgeAll(q,s);
3       } else {
4           purged = q.hs.purge(s);
5           if(purged)
6               for(c in q.children)
7                   if(c.axis == C) purgeC(c,s);
8       }
    }
```

can be discarded after visiting its parent. (3) We need not create any pointers to a data node of a predicate node.

In addition to their proposal, the eager purge can also be optimized for a predicate node: (4) if PathStack of the parent query node is empty, a child query node can be cleared.

The above optimization schemes, however, do not achieve the optimality in terms of early result enumeration. Consider an extreme case, when it evaluates an XPath query.

The optimal early result enumeration is achieved by combining the Twig²Stack algorithm with the EQ algorithm. Given a twig query Q, it can be partitioned into two queries: (1) Q_{down}: a sub-twig query whose root is the top axis branch of Q. (2) Q_{up}: the rest of Q, i.e., a path from the root to the top axis branch, as well as predicate twigs branched from the path. The basic idea is to handle Q_{down} with Twig²Stack and Q_{up} with EQ.

The outline of the integrated algorithm, StreamTwig²Stack, is as follows:

- In the startBlock procedure, if the query node q belongs Q_{up}, process based on the EQ algorithm. The TDP procedure propagates down the up bit only up to the top axis branch.

- In the endBlock procedure, if the query node q is the top branch node and q.ps (which is enhanced by the EQ algorithm) is empty, do the following:
  - If the self and up bits are both true, enumerate the result and clear the hierarchical stack.
  - Otherwise, append the enumerated results to the candidate list of the parent node, which will be managed by the EQ algorithm, and clear the hierarchical stacks.

Detailed interaction between Twig²Stack and EQ is straightforward and omitted for brevity.

STACK-BASED MULTI-QUERY PROCESSING

IndexFilter

IndexFilter (Bruno, Gravano, Koudas, & Srivastava, 2003) is the first attempt to apply stack-based encoding of PathStack to multi-query processing. It shares the prefix commonality of the path query workload. A prefix tree is constructed, and a stack is allocated to each query node in the tree. As an extension of PathStack/TwigStack, each query node is also associated with a cursor to scan the data node with a particular tag name. Thus, IndexFilter is not directly applicable to the streaming XML data. Instead, it first preprocesses the streaming data to generate disk-resident index data with the region encoding.

The key idea is an efficient scheduling of cursor advancement to avoid processing large portions of the input document that are guaranteed not to be part of any match. Experiments showed that IndexFilter can outperform YFilter when the document is very large, meaning that it sometimes pays off to preprocess the input document to build an index.

However, as the number of queries increases, the advantage of indexing is canceled. This implies the limited efficiency of sharing query execution in IndexFilter.

AFilter

Both IndexFilter and YFilter need to manipulate a possibly large number of states for each node arrival. Most of these active states will be wasted without contributing to the final results. It is desirable to avoid such unnecessarily eager result/state enumerations and trigger an enumeration process in a lazy manner with more stringent conditions.

AFilter (Candan, Hsiung, P., Chen, Tatemura, & Agrawal, 2006) proposes an alternative way to share stacks across multiple queries to achieve lazy enumeration. It also leverages both prefix and suffix commonalities across queries.

The number of stacks is bounded by the number of distinct tag names $|\sum|$, and the cost of stack construction is independent of the number of queries: The time complexity is $O(|D||\sum|)$; The number of stack elements is bounded by $2d + 1$, and the number of pointers is bounded by $2d|\sum|$, where d is the depth of a document.

Figure 9 shows an example with a set of path queries. A suffix tree, called SFLabel-tree, is constructed based on suffix commonality. Each branch is associated with a suffix label (s_i), and each leaf corresponds to an individual query. Each suffix label corresponds to a cluster of steps (i.e. pairs of an axis and node) that appear in the query workload. For instance suffix label s1 corresponds to query steps (Q1,0), (Q2,3), and (Q3,2), where (Q,i) denotes the i-th step of query Q.

AFilter's stack structure, called StackBranch, has only one stack for each tag name. In this example, they are A, B, C, and root. If there exists wildcards ("*") in the query workload, StackBranch has a single stack for "*". When the algorithm pushes a node to a stack, it only guarantees existence of single query step results for the node (whereas PathStack/IndexFilter guarantees existence of query path results). When the leaf step of a query is checked, the algorithm needs result enumeration to confirm if all the steps from the root have been matched.

Figure 9 (c) shows a data structure called AxisView that serves as a blueprint to construct the stacks upon node arrival. Its nodes correspond to distinct tag names (i.e. stacks). An edge (N_i, N_j) exists if and only if there exists a query that contains step, N_j/N_i or $N_j//N_i$. An edge is annotated with a set of corresponding suffix labels. A suffix label that includes a leaf step is annotated with "!", meaning that it triggers enumeration.

Figure 10 illustrates a running example. A document tree is traversed in preorder, and the example shows the states when b1, b2, and c1 are observed, respectively. When a node is pushed,

Figure 9. AFilter: AxisView and SFLabel-tree

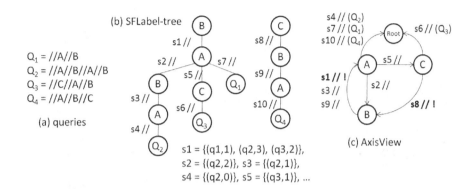

it is associated with pointers to the top of stacks based on the edges of AxisView. When b2, for instance, is pushed, suffix label s1 triggers enumeration, resulting in outputs for Q1 and Q2. Note that traversal for Q1 and Q2 is done in a clustered manner by following the SFLabel-tree.

Notice that, during enumeration, it traverses the same paths to the root many times. AFilter introduces prefix caching to share the effort of traversal both within a single query and across multiple queries. A prefix tree, called PRLabel-tree, is introduced to enable multiple queries share caching results. Similar to the suffix tree, each branch is associated with a prefix label. The cache maintains mapping from a pair of a pointer in a stack and a prefix label to the traversed result.

However, there is one non-trivial issue to apply this caching scheme: traversal is clustered as suffix labels whereas the cache is shared as prefix labels. There may be many-to-many relationship between suffix and prefix labels. In order to benefit from prefix caching, suffix-based clustering may need *unfolding*. The authors propose two strategies, early and late unfolding, and report that late unfolding outperformed in experiments.

GFilter

GFilter (Chen S., Li, Tatemura, Hsiung, Agrawal, & Candan, 2008) is a stack-based multi-query processing algorithm that employs postorder traversal. GFilter shares the following common properties with AFilter: (1) it shares common suffixes, and (2) it benefits from the heuristics that the leaf selectivity is often more stringent.

However, it differs in the following features that benefit from postorder traversal:

- The postorder traversal naturally enables the processing of the common document prefixes. Unlike AFilter, a path in the document is visited only once without help of caching.
- The bottom-up path matching enables succinct encoding of the matching results into tree structure, called TOP (Tree-of-Path) encoding, that achieves more efficient join processing for twig query results, and enumeration for more powerful GTP queries.

Figure 11 illustrates an example of shared bottom-up path matching conducted by GFilter. First, similar to other algorithm, twig (or GTP) queries are decomposed into linear path queries. Note that, in the bottom-up matching scheme, the common prefix of linear paths in a twig needs to be evaluated only once by one of the paths. The paths in the query workload are integrated together into a shared suffix query plan. Each node, called a suffix query node, is associated with an identity

Figure 10. AFilter: Runntine example

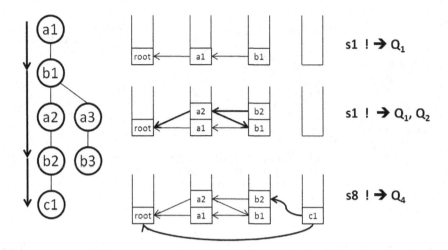

s_i. A node that corresponds to a root of original twigs is annotated with "+".

Assume that we visit b2 in the document tree in Figure 11, which means that we have visited all the descendants. The matching process of b2 (i.e., s2, s5, s6) is done based on prior matches on the descendants (i.e., s1 at descendants and s4 at children). To maintain the active states at each step, the algorithm introduces two tables, PC table and AD table.

In addition, we also need to maintain matching data nodes that are part of the final results. GFilter introduces a data structure, TOP encoding, which is theoretically equivalent to the hierarchical stack but is seamlessly integrated into the path matching algorithm.

Figure 12 shows how matching results are encoded within PC/AD tables. Each matching suffix query node in the tables is associated with a set of matching data node ids. For instance, in the AD table of b3, s1 is associated with $\{c1, c2\}$. This s1 is propagated from b3 to b2. Instead of copying the list of ids, the table maintains a pointer to it, denoted by $b3^{//}$. Here $n^{//}$ associated with s_i is a pointer to the s_i entry at the AD table of n, and $n^{+//}$ is a short form of $\{n, n^{//}\}$. For instance, given $s2\{b1^{+//}\}$ in a1's AD table, we can enumerate the matching data nodes $\{b1, b2, b3\}$ through traversal of the pointers.

For each path query, the matching results are given as a sequence of TOP encodings (SOT: Sequence of Trees). The authors propose a multi-way merge join algorithm over SOTs that efficiently generates a GTP query result. Since the data nodes in SOT are duplicate-free, we can avoid redundant join probes of full-path matches. Note that there can be an exponential number of full-path matches in the worst case. The total join cost for the entire query workload is bounded by $O(|Q||D|)$, where $|Q|$ is the number of suffix query nodes and $|D|$ is the document size. Moreover, being equivalent to the hierarchical stack, the TOP encoding enables efficient enumeration for GTP queries.

Discussion

The stack-based encoding (and the TOP encoding as its variants) has been demonstrated as effective not only for single-query processing but also multi-query processing. In addition to provide succinctness of intermediary data, it offers flexibility in query processing by separating node matching process and result enumeration. Both AFilter and GFilter leverage this flexibil-

Figure 11. GFilter: bottom-up suffix query matching

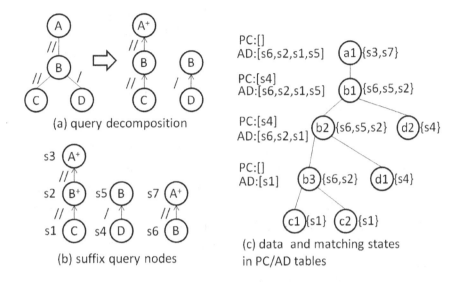

(a) query decomposition

(b) suffix query nodes

(c) data and matching states in PC/AD tables

ity to avoid unnecessary computation in eager, automaton-based approaches.

Both GFilter and AFilter have their own benefits. It is reported that, in experiments on linear path queries, AFilter outperforms GFilter when the query workload is highly selective, and GFilter outperforms otherwise. It is desirable to integrate the two benefits.

GFilter's query state activation is less stringent than AFilter's trigger-based enumeration. In the original GFilter algorithm, a simple stack is employed to preserve all the ancestor nodes of the current node. We can replace this stack with AFilter's StackBranch and apply the trigger condition to the leaf query nodes.

This combined approach reduces both computation and memory by avoiding unnecessary construction of TOP data. However, unlike PathStack for a single path query, it does not guarantee that nodes in the TOPs are part of the final path results, since StackBranch does not guarantee existence of query path results.

This observation opens a new issue on trade-off between computation and memory, which is analogous to garbage collection. We can trig-

ger query path existence check (i.e., traversal of pointers in StackBranch) at the cost of extra computation, only when the available memory becomes scarce.

Another possible issue is a case when matching results are too large to fit the available main memory. YFilter and AFilter enumerate full-path results when they reach a leaf query node, and these full-path results can be spilled into external memory if needed. On the other hand, postorder traversal requires GFilter to hold enumeration later. Similar to the above trade-off, an adaptive strategy may spill a partial TOP result earlier without waiting for end tags. Note that SOTs in this case are no longer duplicate-free, sacrificing the merge join performance. Adaptation of the data structure suitable for this external algorithm is also an open issue.

FUTURE RESEARCH DIRECTIONS

The algorithms we have reviewed do not assume availability of schema information. It is a future research direction to incorporate semantic query

Figure 12. GFilter: TOP encoding

a1: PC:[]
    AD:[s6{b1$^{+//}$}, s2{b1$^{+//}$},
        s1{b3$^{//}$}, s5{b1$^{+//}$}]

b2: PC:[s4{d1}]
    AD:[s6{b3}, s2{b3},
        s1{b3$^{//}$}]

b1: PC:[s4{d2}]
    AD:[s6{b2$^{+//}$}, s2{b2$^{+//}$},
        s1{b3$^{//}$}, s5{b2}]

b3: PC:[]
    AD:[s1{c1,c2}]

optimization (Su, Rundensteiner, & Mani, 2005) to the stack-based framework.

It is also an important research direction to develop efficient streaming algorithms for larger classes of pattern matching beyond twigs and GTPs. For instance, stack-based algorithms for DAG (Chen, Gupta, & Kurul, 2005) and partial path query (path with partial order) (Wu, Souldatos, Theodoratos, Dalamagas, & Sellis, 2008) have been proposed for non-streaming environments. Another class of XML queries is keyword query over XML data, which has been extensively studied in the context of information retrieval.

Finally, beyond XML, the stack-based data encoding might be introduced to other types of streaming queries and data, such as event stream processing and regular expression, when they extract large amount of matching data.

CONCLUSION

In this chapter, we have reviewed stack-based algorithms to evaluate queries over streaming XML data. Originally proposed for disk-resident data, the stack-based encoding of intermediary data has been successfully applied to various query workloads in the streaming environment, from XPath to more complex GTP queries, and from a single-query processing to multi-query processing. In the discussions, we have presented opportunities to integrate benefits that demonstrated in the reviewed work. For single-query processing, we illustrated a sketch of an integrated algorithm, StreamTwig²Stack, which has the same time

complexity with Twig2Stack and has optimized buffer memory performance. For a multi-query processing, we identified an open issue of trade-off between memory and computation in an integrated approach.

REFERENCES

Al-Khalifa, S., Jagadish, H. V., Koudas, N., Patel, J. M., Srivastava, D., & Wu, Y. (2002). Structural joins: a primitive for efficient xml query pattern matching. In *Proceedings of 18th International Conference on Data Engineering*, (pp. 141-152).

Altinel, M., & Franklin, M. J. (2000). Efficient filtering of xml documents for selective dissemination of information. *VLDB '00: Proceedings of the 26th International Conference on Very Large Data Bases*, (pp. 53-64), San Francisco, CA.

Bar-Yossef, Z., Fontoura, M., & Josifovski, V. (2004). On the memory requirements of xpath evaluation over xml streams. In *PODS '04: Proceedings of the twenty-third ACM SIGMOD-SIGACT-SIGART symposium on Principles of database systems* (pp. 177-188). New York: ACM Press.

Bar-Yossef, Z., Fontoura, M., & Josifovski, V. (2005). Buffering in query evaluation over xml streams. In *PODS '05: Proceedings of the twenty-fourth ACM SIGMOD-SIGACT-SIGART symposium on Principles of database systems* (pp. 216-227). New York: ACM.

Barton, C., Charles, P., Goyal, D., Raghavachari, M., Fontoura, M., & Josifovski, V. (2003). Streaming XPath processing with forward and backward axes. In *Proceedings. 19th International Conference on Data Engineering,* (pp. 455-466).

Bruno, N., Gravano, L., Koudas, N., & Srivastava, D. (2003). Navigation- vs. index-based XML multi-query processing. In *Proceedings. 19th International Conference on Data Engineering, 2003,* (pp. 139-150).

Bruno, N., Koudas, N., & Srivastava, D. (2002). Holistic twig joins: optimal xml pattern matching. In *SIGMOD '02: Proceedings of the 2002 ACM SIGMOD international conference on Management of data* (pp. 310-321). New York: ACM Press.

Candan, S. K., & Hsiung, P. W., Chen, S., Tatemura, J., & Agrawal, D. (2006). AFilter: adaptable XML filtering with prefix-caching suffix-clustering. In *VLDB '06: Proceedings of the 32nd international conference on Very large data bases* (pp. 559-570). VLDB Endowment.

Chan, C.-Y., Felber, P., Garofalakis, M., & Rastogi, R. (2002). Efficient filtering of XML documents with XPath expressions. In *Proceedings. 18th International Conference on Data Engineering,* (pp. 235-244).

Chen, L., Gupta, A., & Kurul, E. M. (2005). Stack-based algorithms for pattern matching on DAGs. In *VLDB '05: Proceedings of the 31st international conference on Very large data bases,* (pp. 493-504).

Chen, S., Li, H. G., Tatemura, J., Hsiung, W. P., Agrawal, D., & Candan, S. K. (2006). Twig2Stack: bottom-up processing of generalized-tree-pattern queries over XML documents. In *VLDB '06: Proceedings of the 32nd international conference on Very large data bases* (pp. 283-294). VLDB Endowment.

Chen, S., Li, H.-G., Tatemura, J., Hsiung, W.-P., Agrawal, D., & Candan, S. K. (2008). Scalable filtering of multiple generalized-tree-pattern queries over xml streams. *IEEE Transactions on Knowledge and Data Engineering, 20*(12), 1627–1640. doi:10.1109/TKDE.2008.83

Chen, Y., Davidson, S. B., & Zheng, Y. (2006). An Efficient XPath Query Processor for XML Streams. In *ICDE '06: Proceedings of the 22nd International Conference on Data Engineering.* Washington, DC: IEEE Computer Society.

Chen, Z., Jagadish, H. V., Lakshmanan, L. V., & Paparizos, S. (2003). From tree patterns to generalized tree patterns: on efficient evaluation of XQuery. In *VLDB '2003: Proceedings of the 29th international conference on Very large data bases* (pp. 237-248). VLDB Endowment.

Diao, Y., Altinel, M., Franklin, M. J., Zhang, H., & Fischer, P. (2003). Path sharing and predicate evaluation for high-performance XML filtering. *ACM Transactions on Database Systems, 28*(4), 467–516. doi:10.1145/958942.958947

Diao, Y., & Franklin, M. (2003). Query processing for high-volume XML message brokering. In *VLDB '2003: Proceedings of the 29th international conference on Very large data bases* (pp. 261-272). VLDB Endowment.

Gottlob, G., Koch, C., & Pichler, R. (2005). Efficient algorithms for processing XPath queries. *ACM Transactions on Database Systems, 30*(2), 444–491. doi:10.1145/1071610.1071614

Gou, G., & Chirkova, R. (2007). Efficient algorithms for evaluating xpath over streams. In *SIGMOD '07: Proceedings of the 2007 ACM SIGMOD international conference on Management of data* (pp. 269-280). New York: ACM Press.

Green, T. J., Gupta, A., Miklau, G., Onizuka, M., & Suciu, D. (2004). Processing xml streams with deterministic automata and stream indexes. *ACM Transactions on Database Systems, 29*(4), 752–788. doi:10.1145/1042046.1042051

Gupta, A. K., & Suciu, D. (2003). Stream processing of xpath queries with predicates. In *SIGMOD '03: Proceedings of the 2003 ACM SIGMOD international conference on Management of data* (pp. 419-430). New York: ACM Press.

Han, W. S., Jiang, H., Ho, H., & Li, Q. (2008). StreamTX: extracting tuples from streaming XML data. *Proc. VLDB Endow., 1*(1), 289-300.

Josifovski, V., Fontoura, M., & Barta, A. (2005). Querying XML streams. *The VLDB Journal, 14*(2), 197–210. doi:10.1007/s00778-004-0123-7

Kwon, J., Rao, P., Moon, B., & Lee, S. (2005). FiST: scalable xml document filtering by sequencing twig patterns. In *VLDB '05: Proceedings of the 31st international conference on Very large data bases* (pp. 217-228). VLDB Endowment.

Lakshmanan, L. V., & Parthasarathy, S. (2002). On Efficient Matching of Streaming XML Documents and Queries. In *EDBT '02: Proceedings of the 8th International Conference on Extending Database Technology*, (pp. 142-160).

Ludäscher, B., Mukhopadhyay, P., & Papakonstantinou, Y. (2002). A transducer-based xml query processor. In *Proceedings of the 28th international conference on Very Large Data Bases VLDB 2002* (pp. 227-238). VLDB Endowment.

Olteanu, D. (2007). SPEX: Streamed and Progressive Evaluation of XPath. *IEEE Transactions on Knowledge and Data Engineering, 19*(7), 934–949. doi:10.1109/TKDE.2007.1063

Olteanu, D., Meuss, H., Furche, T., & Bry, F. (2002). XPath: Looking Forward. *XML-Based Data Management and Multimedia Engineering — EDBT 2002 Workshops*, (pp. 892-896).

Peng, F., & Chawathe, S. S. (2003). Xpath queries on streaming data. *SIGMOD '03: Proceedings of the 2003 ACM SIGMOD international conference on Management of data* (pp. 431-442). New York: ACM Press.

Qin, L., Yu, J., & Ding, B. (2007). TwigList: Make Twig Pattern Matching Fast. *DASFAA 2007*, (LNCS Vol. 4443, pp. 850-862). Berlin: Springer.

Su, H., Rundensteiner, E. A., & Mani, M. (2005). Semantic query optimization for XQuery over XML streams. In *VLDB '05: Proceedings of the 31st international conference on Very large data bases*, (pp. 277-288).

Wu, X., Souldatos, S., Theodoratos, D., Dalamagas, T., & Sellis, T. (2008). Efficient evaluation of generalized path pattern queries on XML data. In *WWW '08: Proceeding of the 17th international conference on World Wide Web* (pp. 835-844). New York: ACM.

Zhang, C., Naughton, J., Dewitt, D. L., & Lohman, G. (2001). On supporting containment queries in relational database management systems. In *SIGMOD '01: Proceedings of the 2001 ACM SIGMOD international conference on Management of data* (pp. 425-436). New York: ACM.

Chapter 10
Content–Based Publish/ Subscribe for XML Data

Yuan Ni
IBM China Research Laboratory, China

Chee-Yong Chan
National University of Singapore, Singapore

ABSTRACT

Content-based publish/subscribe system is an effective means to deliver relevant data to interested data consumers. As the emergence of XML, it quickly becomes the de facto for data exchange on the Internet. Therefore, to use XML format in the content-based publish/subscribe system attracts increasing interests. This chapter firstly introduces the content-based publish/subscribe system for XML data; followed by the discussion of issues in this system and introduction of solutions to these issues. Finally, this chapter points out some possible research directions for the content-based publish/subscribe system for XML data.

INTRODUCTION

The Internet has considerably increased the scale of distributed information systems, where information is published on the Internet anywhere at any time by anybody. To avoid overwhelming users with such huge amount of information, the publish/subscribe systems have emerged, where users subscribe a set of queries to the system to express the kinds of information they are interested in and the system will automatically deliver newly published information to proper users. With the emergence of XML, it quickly becomes the standard for data exchange

on the Internet. There is a new trend to publish the data contents in XML format and to provide users with a more expressive subscription language such as XPath to address both the content and structure of the data, which makes the publish/subscribe system for XML data becomes increasingly important.

The publish/subscribe system could be divided into two categories: (1) topic-based publish/subscribe system which has been implemented by many industrial solutions, such as VITRIA (Skeen, 1999), TIB/Rendezvous (TIBCO, 1999), JEDI (Cugola, et al., 2001). Publishers associate some keywords with each message to indicate the topic the message belongs to; subscribers express their interests using keywords. Then all messages belonging to a

DOI: 10.4018/978-1-61520-727-5.ch010

topic will be delivered to the users who subscribe to this topic. (2) content-based publish/subscribe system which improves the expressiveness by allowing the subscribers to use some subscription language to address the content of the information in which they are interested. In topic-based publish/subscribe, the information is delivered towards a group of users; while in content-based publish/subscribe, the information is delivered towards each individual user. The content-based system guarantees the users to receive accurate information they are interested in, which makes it more attractive than the topic-based system. A variety of content-based publish/subscribe systems are implemented by academy or industry, such as Gryphon (Banavar et al. 1999), Siena (Carzaniga et al., 2000), Elvin (Segall et al., 2000) and ONYX.(Diao et al, 2004). Compared with topic-based publish/subscribe, content-based publish/subscribe provides a fine grain way to address the content of the documents. Thus this chapter focuses on the content-based publish/subscribe system for XML data.

This chapter firstly gives an introduction about the content-based publish/subscribe system for XML data and three components, i.e. publisher, subscriber and XML routing network, in such system. The content-based publish/subscribe system for XML data has two important issues, i.e. the efficiency of the system and the functionalities of the system. Therefore, secondly this chapter categories and introduces the existing approaches that are proposed to improve the above two aspects of the XML publish/subscribe system. Finally, this chapter will point out some possible future work in the content-based publish/subscribe system for XML data domain.

BACKGROUND

In the content-based publish/subscribe system for XML data, the information is published as XML documents and the subscriptions are expressed using some XML query language such as XPath (1999) or XQuery (2006). Figure 1 illustrates the architecture for the content-based publish/subscribe system. There are three components in the system:

- **Publishers.** The left part in Figure 1 shows the data publishers, which are also called the data producers for the system. They generate the information and encode it as XML documents, and send these documents to the system. Published XML documents could come from various resources, such as newspapers, databases, libraries, mobile sensors, etc. Various publishers generate the XML documents independently, thus XML documents for the same domain by different publishers may conform to different schemas.

- **Subscribers.** The right part in Figure 1 gives the subscribers which are also called the data consumers, who receive the information from the data publishers. The subscribers register their interests to the system by subscribing their profiles to the system. In the system for XML data, their profiles are rewritten using some XML query language such as XPath (1999) or XQuery (2006). The subscribers would receive all and exactly the information that matches their subscriptions. When the subscribers do not want the information anymore, they need to unsubscribe their queries.

- **XML routing network**. The central part in Figure 1 illustrates the XML routing network, which contains a set of XML routers that are inter-connected. Each XML router receives the subscriptions from end-users or other XML routers; and receives the XML documents from the publishers or other XML routers. A routing table is stored at each router to store the set of queries subscribed to the router, and the routing table also maintains the information about the

Figure 1. The architecture of content-based publish/subscribe system for XML data

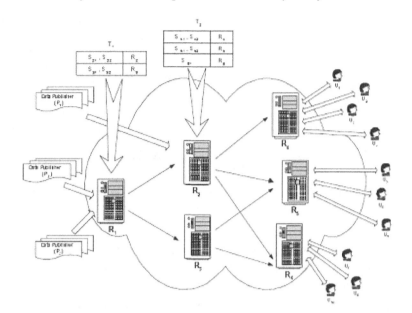

destination of a document if the document matches some query in the table. For each incoming document, the router parses the XML document to match all the queries. If a router R_i determines that document d matches a query q which is subscribed from router R_j, then R_i will forward d to R_j. Here R_i is considered as the upstream router of R_j and R_j is considered as the downstream router of R_i.

There exists a batch of approaches proposed to efficiently match the set of XPath expressions (Altinel & Franklin, 2000; Chan, 2002; Diao, 2003; Gong, 2005; Shuang Hou & H.-Arno Jacobsen, 2006; Kwon, 2005; Green, 2003; Gupta, 2003; Selcuk, 2006; Skeen, 1999). In traditional query processing, the XML documents are stored statically in the database and some kinds of indexes for the documents may be provided. The indexes are exploited or the documents are navigated to process each query. While in content-based publish/subscribe, a large number of subscriptions are relatively static on the routers and these

subscriptions are indexed for efficient evaluation. The XML documents continuously arrive at the routers as streams from publishers or other routers, and these documents are parsed to match the set of subscriptions on the routers. Figure 2 shows a schematic diagram of the key components in a typical content-based router. The incoming XML data is first parsed by an event-based XML document parser. The parsed events are used to drive the matching engine which relies on some efficient index on the subscriptions to quickly detect matching subscriptions in its routing table; data is then forwarded to neighboring routers and local subscribers with matching subscriptions.

The SAX API (2000) is used to parse the XML document on-the-fly in the router. The SAX API brings two advantages: (1) the query processing is started immediately once the XML document arrives. There is no need to wait for the receiving of the complete document, which improves the response time considerably; (2) it only incurs small memory overhead in SAX API, which makes the router be able to handle large XML documents. SAX provides a mechanism for reading data in-

Figure 2. Content-based routing of XML data

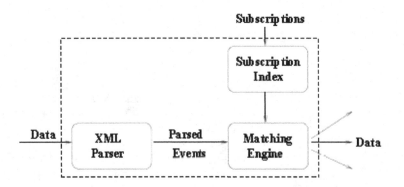

crementally from an XML document. The XML stream is accessed unidirectionally such that the previously accessed data can not be re-read unless re-parsing the document.

The SAX parser is implemented using an event-driven model in which the developer provides the callback methods with respect to events which are invoked by the parser as it serially traverses the document. There exist several SAX API implementations, such as Apache Xerces (2007) and Libxml (2000). Figure 3(b) illustrates the sequence of events by the SAX parser for the document in

Figure 3(a). There are three main kinds of events reported by the SAX API:

- **Start_document/end_document:** The start_document event reports the beginning of an XML document, and the end_document event reports the end of the document.
- **Start_element/end_element:** The start_element event indicates the start tag of an element, it carries the information for the name of the element, the attributes

Figure 3. (a) An Example XML Document (b) An Example of SAX Parsed Sequence

```
<?xml version = "1.0"? >
<Courses>
    <Course Code = "CS3230">
        <Title> Database Management < /Title>
        <Instructor>
            <Name> Jim < /Name>
            <Email> jim@comp.nus.edu.sg < /Email>
        < /Instructor>
        <Time> Wed, 16:00 - 18:00 < /Time>
        <Location> LT33 < /Location>
    < /Course>
< /Courses>
```

a

start_document	
start_element	Courses
start_element	Course Code = "CS3230"
start_element	Title
characters	Database Management
end_element	Title
start_element	Instructor
...	
end_element	Instructor
start_element	Time
characters	Wed, 16:00 - 18:00
end_element	Time
...	
end_element	Course
end_element	Courses
end_document	

b

associated with the element and their values. And the end_element event indicates the end of the element, which corresponds to the previously nearest start_element event.

- **Characters:** The characters event contains the text information between two XML tags.

CONTENT-BASED PUBLISH/ SUBSCRIBE SYSTEM FOR XML DATA

As aforementioned, there are two important issues to consider in content-based publish/subscribe system for XML data, i.e. the matching efficiency for XPath queries and the functionalities supported by this system.:

Matching Efficiency for XPath Queries in the System

Content-based publish/subscribe system is to provide the data consumers with the newest published information. Some information is only useful for a small period. For example, in the stock market, the stock quote is changing frequently, users are only interested in the most up-to-date stock quote; also in monitoring systems, users should be alerted about abnormal events immediately so that they can response in time. Therefore, the efficiency of the publish/subscribe system is critical. To publish XML data and to use XPath queries as the subscriptions improves the expressiveness of the publish/subscribe system. However, matching XPath queries with XML documents incurs larger processing cost than matching simple predicates with attribute-value pairs as in the traditional publish/subscribe system. Therefore, an efficient algorithm to match the XPath queries with XML documents is indispensable.

Functionality of the System

Besides the efficiency issue of the system, the functionalities provided by the system are also important aspects to consider. Three kinds of functions would be useful for the content-based publish/subscribe system for XML data:

- **To handle the fragmented XML data.** The popularity of the mobile devices, such as mobile phones, laptops and personal digital assistants, and the advance of the wireless networks has fostered the increasing use of mobile devices in current distributed systems. Some work have addressed the publish/subscribe in a mobile environment (Cugola, 2000; Huang, 2004). To employ the resource-constrained mobile devices for accessing and monitoring data requires a memory-efficient technique to process queries on *fragmented* data. Furthermore, the data collected by sensor devices is often in fragments such that the querying should be performed on the fragmented data. For example, in a military battlefield, many mobile sensors are equipped to report the fragment of information for their monitored locations. The information from various sensors forms the complete information for the battlefield.

- **To handle heterogeneous XML data.** In content-based publish/subscribe system, data publishers and data consumers are *loosely-coupled*, *anonymous*, and do not necessarily agree on the same schema. Data consumers may have no knowledge about the schemas from data publishers, and various data publishers generate and publish their data independently. Therefore, publications from different publishers may conform to heterogeneous schemas although they satisfy the same kinds of users' interests. Thus, although the users' subscriptions do not exactly match the publications, the publications do satisfy the users' interests. There is indeed a requirement for the system to handle such heterogeneous data, while the supporting of the heterogeneous data should not be at the cost of the dissemination efficiency.

- **To support stateful subscriptions.** The traditional content-based publish/subscribe system only allows the subscriptions to address an individual event, which is called *stateless subscriptions*. However, some users may be interested in the trends of a sequence of events happened in a period of time. For example, in the stock ticker system, some user may have the request for a stock whose price consistently increases in an hour. Such kind of request is represented using the *stateful subscriptions* and the approaches are required to handle the *stateful subscriptions*.

IMPROVING THE MATCHING EFFICIENCY OF THE SYSTEM

Many approaches have been proposed to improve the efficiency of the content-based publish/subscribe system for XML data. Based on how the optimization is applied, these approaches could be classified into two categories:

- **Local optimization:** The approaches in this category focus on improving the efficiency at each individual router.
- **Global optimization:** The approaches in this category leverage the collaboration among routers to optimization the matching efficiency.

Local Optimization

The approaches in local optimization could be classified into three categories based on the mechanism to optimize the matching:

- **Approaches to share the processing.** Each router stores a large number of XPath expressions, thus there is a high probability that the common parts exist in XPath queries. Shared the processing of these common parts could improve the matching efficiency. YFilter (Diao, 2003), YFilter* (Zhang, 2004) and LazyDFA (Green, 2003) share the processing of common prefixes; XTrie (Chan, 2002) share the processing of common substrings; AFilter (Selcuk, 2006) shares the processing of both common prefixes and su±xes; and XPush machine (Gupta, 2003) shares the processing of common predicates.
- **Approaches to reduce the number of processed queries.** The matching time increases as the number of processed XPath queries grows. This kind of approaches intends to reduce the number of processed queries during the parsing of the document. The approach to use precomputed views (Gupta, 2002; Gupta, 2003) and the tree pattern aggregation approach (Chan, 2002) belong to this category.
- **Approaches to reduce the matching complexity.** To match the path expressions especially the tree pattern queries incurs larger cost. Some approaches are proposed to convert the tree pattern matching to some simple matchings. The BloomFilter (Gong, 2005) uses the Bloom to hash the path expression and converts the matching of tree patterns to be the matching of corresponding bits. FiST (Kwon, 2005) converts both the XPath queries and XML document to be sequence, such that the matchings can be detected using string matching.

In the following, we introduce these approaches in detail.

Figure 4. Created NFA in YFilter for the example queries

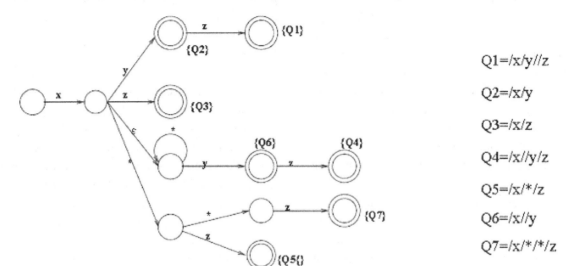

Q1=/x/y//z

Q2=/x/y

Q3=/x/z

Q4=/x//y/z

Q5=/x/*/z

Q6=/x//y

Q7=/x/*/*/z

Approaches to Share Processing

YFilter (Diao, 2003) converts the collection of XPath expressions on a router to a single *nondeterministic finite state automata* (NFA). The common prefixes in different XPath expressions are combined into one path in NFA such that the processing of these common prefixes are shared, thus the filtering efficiency can be improved. Figure 4 shows the NFA in YFilter for the set of XPath expressions in the right part of this figure. A circle stands for a state in NFA and two concentric circles stand for a final state, which is associated with the identities of the queries it accepts. The symbol "*" matches any element in the document. The "//" axis in XPath expressions is converted to an ε transition followed by a "*" loop in the NFA. This figure clearly illustrates the shared processing for the common prefix /x in all queries. The state transitions of the NFA in YFilter are driven by the events generated by the SAX parser. When the final state is reached, the queries associated with the final state are found to be matched.

YFilter* (Zhang, 2004) is proposed to further enhance the performance of YFilter on the pro-cessing of tree pattern queries. The NFA in YFilter can only handle the matching of single path expressions. To process the tree pattern queries, YFilter conducts an expensive post-processing to join the matching of single paths which are decomposed from the tree pattern queries. Then a large number of temporary matching results for the single paths have to be maintained in the memory, and may be discarded finally in the join procedure. YFilter* is to optimize the processing by either detecting a matching tree pattern query or discarding an unnecessary partial matching as early as possible. YFilter* additionally maintains the information for *branch point nodes* of the tree pattern queries. The checking of whether the tree pattern queries are matched is performed during the evaluation of single paths using NFA. If some tree pattern query is determined to be matched, the processing of the single paths decomposed from it can be short-circuited in the following processing. The maintained *branch point nodes* can also help to determine that a matched single path cannot generate the matching of the tree pattern query such that the matching of the single path can be discarded immediately.

The *Deterministic Finite Automata* (DFA) (Green, 2003) is also used to process the large number of XPath expressions on the routers. The DFA is built in two steps: the collection of XPath expressions is converted into *Nondeterministic Finite Automata* (NFA) at first and then the NFA is converted into a DFA. The DFA approach has two variants: *eager* DFA and *lazy* DFA. The *eager* DFA method completely computes all the states before the query evaluation; while the *lazy* DFA computes the states on demand during the query evaluation. It shows that the wildcard (i.e. "*") and the descendant axis (i.e. "*") incur the significant exponential growth in the number of states, which makes the *eager* DFA prohibitive in practice. However, for the *lazy* DFA, it is theoretically proved that an upper bound of the number of states exists depending on the character of the XML data, thus the number of states in *lazy* DFA is manageable.

The above approaches only exploit the common parts in the prefixes. The XPath expressions, however, can contain the common parts in other places. For example, the two XPath queries /a/*/b/c and /e/*/b/c have the common parts /b/c which is not the prefix, and such common parts will not be shared using the above approaches. The approach XTrie (Chan, 2002) can share the processing of common substrings in the XPath queries. XTrie achieves the shared processing for common substrings by decomposing the XPath expressions into substrings. It requires that each pair of consecutive elements in substrings must be separated by a parent-child ("/") operator, and each substring has the maximal length. A substring-table (ST) is used to store these substrings. Each row in ST corresponds to one substring from some XPath expression. Physically, the substrings from the same XPath expression are clustered together and are ordered by the simple decomposition of the expression. Logically, the same substring from different XPath expressions are chained together using a linked list to facilitate the following match-

ing process. Each substring (denoted as s_i) in ST has five attributes:

- **ParentRow:** Specifies the row number of the substring in ST corresponding to the parent substring of s_i (If s_i is the root substring, ParentRow = 0).
- **RelLevel:** Is the relative level of s_i with its parent substring. Let x denote the distance in document level between the last element in s_i and the last element in s_i's parent substring, if there are "//" between s_i and its parent substring, then the RelLevel of s_i is $[x, \infty)$; otherwise *RelLevel* = $[x,x]$.
- **Rank:** The substring s_i having rank k means that s_i is the kth child of its parent substring.
- **NumChild:** Indicates the total number of children of s_i.
- **Next:** Is an integer indicates the row number of the substring s_j such that s_j is the first substring behind s_i satisfying the requirement that s_j is the same with s_i. *Next* is used to logically group the substrings with same labels. Actually, a linked list is formed, and the head of the linked list is substring with the smallest row number in ST.

The above five attributes are used to check the matching of substring and further the matching of XPath expressions with the XML document. The set of decomposed substrings is indexed by a *trie* structure T. For the substrings with the same label, only the substring with the smallest row number is indexed in the *trie* T, and other substrings can be looked up using the *Next* attribute in ST. The *trie* T is a rooted tree. Each edge of T is associated with an element name, and each node N of T is labelled with a string formed by concatenating the edge labels along the path from the root node of T, which is denoted as label(N). Each node N in T is also associated a value, denoted as $\alpha(N)$, which is determined as follows: if label(N) corresponds to a decomposed substring, then $\alpha(N)$ is

Figure 5. The example for XTrie

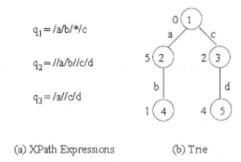

$q_1 = /a/b/*/c$

$q_2 = //a/b//c/d$

$q_3 = /a//c/d$

(a) XPath Expressions (b) Trie

	ParentRow	RelLevel	Rank	NumChild	Next
1	0	[2,2]	1	1	3
2	1	[2, ∞)	1	0	0
3	0	[2,2]	1	1	0
4	3	[2, ∞)	1	0	6
5	0	[1,1]	1	1	0
6	5	[2, ∞)	1	0	0

(c) ST

the row number of this substring in ST; otherwise $\alpha(N) = 0$. The *trie* T is used to check whether the substring parsed from the XML document has some matchings in XPath expressions.

XTrie method needs to construct another table called substring-table (ST). When a start-element event *e* is encountered, the algorithm searches in the *trie* T. If there is an edge label *e* from the current node to a node N, the search continues on node N. For each node N visited, if $\alpha(N) <= 0$, a matching algorithm will be invoked to check the matching of all substrings in the linked list pointed by the substring at row$\alpha(N)$ in ST. The matching algorithm uses the attributes in the ST table to check if the constraints are satisfied and return the XPath expressions that matched. On the other hand, if there is no edge out the current node labeled *e*, the search in the *trie* T will backtrack to the node that is the longest suffix of the current node to check for other potential matchings.

Let us use the following example to illustrate the XTrie method. Considering the collection of XPath expressions in Figure 5(a), the Trie structure and ST table for them are shown in Figure 5(b) and (c) respectively. The numbers at the left of nodes in the Trie structure point to the first rows of the substrings with the same labels in ST. Given a data path /a/b/c/d in some document, when the start element of a is reported, the Trie moves the current node from node 1 to node 2. Then the number 5 is used to find the substring,

i.e. a, in row 5 of the ST. Comparing the element a in the document with the information in ST, the method detects substring a is matched. When the start element of b is reported, the node in the Trie further moves to node 4, which corresponds to row 1, i.e. substring /a/b, in ST. The Next attribute of row 1 is used to find the substring /a/b in row 3. The processor detects that both two substrings are matched. Similarly, when the substrings c in row 2 and c/d in row 4 and 6 are matched. The matchings of substrings are propagated from the child substring to its parent substring, and the RelLevel is used to check the level requirement. Finally, the processor detects are q_2 and q_3 are matched.

AFilter (Selcuk, 2006) leverages the shared processing in both common prefixes and suffixes. An *AxisView* is created to capture the information of all nodes and all axes in the collection of XPath expressions. Specifically, the *AxisView* (denoted A_{view}) is a directed graph such that: (1) for an element name e_i in some XPath expression, there exists a unique node with name e_i in A_{view}; (2) if there exists an axis e_i/e_j or $e_i//e_j$ in some XPath expression, then A_{view} has an edge from node n_i to n_j; (3) if the XPath expression with identity k has the axis e_i/e_j (resp. $e_i//e_j$) at the rth step, then the edge from n_i to n_j is annotated with an assertion $(q_k, r) |$ (resp. $(q_k, r) \|$). Each node in A_{view} is associated with a stack. During the parsing of the XML document, these stacks maintain the currently active data nodes. The data nodes in stacks have the pointers to the data nodes in other stacks to maintain the ancestor/descendant and parent/child relationships for them. When the data node that matches a leaf node in some XPath expression is encountered, a backward checking procedure is triggered to determine whether the XPath expression is matched.

A *trie* structure is used to index the XPath expressions based on the commonalities in their prefixes. The backward checking procedure would cache the matching results for some expressions. Thus, next time when the same checking from the same pointer needs to be validated, the results in the cached can be returned immediately. Similarly, a *trie* structure is also used to cluster the XPath expressions based on their overlapping suffixes. The matchings of XPath expressions are triggered by the matchings of some leaf nodes. To cluster the common suffixes can reduce the number of assertions to consider. It shows that by combining the shared processing on both common prefixes andsuffixes, AFilter achieves better performance than YFilter.

Besides the common parts in the *axis navigation*, the XPath expressions are also likely to have some common parts in predicates. For example considering the two XPath queries /b/a[@c = 2] and /e//a[@c = 2], the fact that the predicate [@c = 2] is common in both queries can be exploited to speed up the filtering further. The XPush machine approach (Gupta, 2003) can eliminate the redundant processing caused by such common predicates. *XPush machine* uses the *deterministic pushdown automata* to index the queries. Besides the element names, *XPush machine* also converts the predicates to be the states of the automata. The XPush Machine uses a modified pushdown automata in which the states in XPush Machine have two components: a top-down state and a bottom-up state. The top-down phrase builds the stack for the automata, and the bottom-up phrase is the matching of the automata with the document. The bottom-up state in the top of the stack stands for the total subquery that has been evaluated to

be true so far. The states transition is driven by the events reported from the SAX parser. When an XML document is exhausted, the current state will return a set of XPath expression identities that are matched with the document.

To construct an XPush machine for a collection of XPath expressions, firstly each of the XPath expression needs to be converted to an *Alternating Finite Automaton* (AFA). The construction of AFA is like the construction of NFA in YFilter, and it only needs to add an AND, OR, or NOT label to a state after constructing the NFA. The construction of the bottom-up XPush machine follows the construction of AFA. Each bottom-up state in XPush Machine stands for one common part (including both the navigation part and the predicate part) in every AFA. Therefore, the XPush machine can eliminate the redundant work in both structural navigation part and predicate part.

When queries have multiple predicates, the query evaluation time may be dominated by the predicate evaluation. To eliminate redundant processing in predicate evaluation further improves the matching efficiency. In this case, XPush Machine is more efficient. However since XPush machine incorporates the predicate information in the states of automata, it may need more states than other approaches, especially when the number of predicates in the XPath expression is large. The construction of XPush Machine may also take more time.

Discussion. The above approaches make use of some index structures on the set of XPath queries to improve the matching efficiency. The following table gives a summarization and comparison of these approaches. It compares the approaches based on the four features: (1) query type indicates what kind of XPath queries are supported. The tree pattern query is the query with branches; the ordered query means that the query tree is treated as an ordered tree for matching and the unordered query means that the query tree is treated as an unordered tree for matching; (2) index structure indicates the kind of index that is created on the

Table 1. A comparison for approached to share the processing

	Query Type	Index Structure	Shared Part
YFilter	Tree pattern & unordered	NFA	prefix
YFilter*	Tree pattern & unordered	NFA	Prefix
LazyDFA	Path query & unordered	DFA	prefix
XTrie	Tree pattern & both ordered and unordered	Trie structure & ST table	common substring
AFilter	Tree pattern & unordered	AxisView & trie structure	both prefix and suffix
XPush Machine	Tree pattern & unordered	AFA	value predicate

XPath queries; (3) shared part indicates the part of XPath expressions whose processing are shared for optimization.

Approaches to Reduce the Number of Queries

The matching time increases as the number of processed XPath queries grows. This kind of approaches intends to reduce the number of processed queries during the parsing of documents.

The methods in (Gupta, 2002; Gupta, 2003) use the attached additional information (i.e. *pre-computed-view*) with the published documents to detect matching subscriptions before evaluations. This approach assumes that publishers have some knowledge about the queries issued by subscribers such that the publishers can pre-compute some information to benefit the matching on each router. Such information is attached with the document as the *header* to be forwarded together. Specifically, the views include a set of XPath expressions and their matching results. When a router receives an XML document with the header, it first tries to answer the XPath expressions using the header. For the XPath expressions that match the header, their evaluation can be skipped during the parsing of documents. Furthermore if all XPath expressions are matched, the parsing of the XML document can be skipped.

The methods in (Chan, 2002) use query aggregations to reduce the number of subscriptions.

One disadvantage of these approaches is that the aggregation may cause the irrelevant information to be forwarded to some users. The problem of subscription aggregation is defined as follows. Given a set of tree pattern subscriptions S and a space constraint k on the total size of aggregated subscriptions, the aggregation computes a set of subscriptions S' which satisfies the following conditions:

- All the documents that are matched with S are also matched with S'.
- The number of nodes in S' is not greater than the constraints k.
- The error of the matching results between the two sets is minimized.

To solve the above subscription aggregation, an algorithm to compute the aggregation of two XPath expressions is required, which is addressed in (Gupta, 2002; Gupta, 2003). Given two tree patterns p and q, the algorithm iteratively traverses the subtree of p and q. "*" is the aggregation of the nodes at the same level with different name, and "//" is the aggregation for the root nodes of the common sub-pattern at different level of p and q. Then the aggregation of a set of XPath expressions S to another set of XPath expressions S' can be handled. The approach in (Gupta, 2002; Gupta, 2003) iteratively selects the pair of XPath expressions to aggregate such that the aggregation maximizes the gain in space while minimizes the loss in selectivity.

The method in (Li, 2009) exploits the containment relationship among XPath queries to reduce the number of processed queries. This method adapts the use of advertisements to optimize the XML data dissemination. Advertisements are specifications of information that the publisher publishes in the future. Advertisements are used to avoid broadcasting subscriptions in the network so that subscriptions are only routed to the publishers who advertise what the subscribers are interested in. In (Li, 2009), the DTD is used to generate advertisements about the information a data producer is going to publish. This method also proposes a subscription tree structure to capture the covering relations among XPath queries and speed up the covering detection. Finally, the method exploits the merging possibility among XPath queries to further reduce the number of XPath queries.

Approaches to Reduce the Matching Complexity

To match the path expressions especially the tree pattern queries incurs larger cost. Some approaches are proposed to convert the tree pattern matching to some simple matchings.

The BloomFilter (Gong, 2005) approach uses the Bloom filter (Bloom, 1970) to convert the tree pattern matching to the matchings of bit-vectors, which can be performed more efficient. A Bloom filter is a bit-vector of length m used to efficiently test whether an element y is a member of a set S = $\{x_1, x_2, ..., x_n\}$. The BloomFilter approach uses one Bloom filter to store all queries for each user. Given a set of users U = $\{u_1, u_2, ..., u_n\}$, their corresponding Bloom filters are denoted as B = $\{b_1, b_2, ..., b_n\}$. During the parsing of the XML document, let n denote the currently parsed element, then all possible paths (including the paths with wildcard "*" and axis "//") are enumerated. For a certain path p enumerated, if there exists

a Bloom filter b_i such that $p \in b_i$, then the document is considered to be matched u_i's interest and will be forwarded to u_i. The efficient matching of bit-vectors leads to the better performance of the BloomFilter approach. However, as the depth of the XML document increases, the number of enumerated paths increases exponentially which may diminish the improvement by the BloomFilter and the BloomFilter may cause the false positive such that some irrelevant information may be disseminated to the users.

FiST (Kwon, 2005) converts the tree pattern matching to be the sequence matching. The XML documents and XPath expressions are encoded using the Prüfer sequences. The matching of an XPath expression with an XML document can be determined by the matching of Prüfer sequence of the query with the Prüfer sequence of the XML document. The set of XPath expressions on each router will be converted to a collection of sequences, and these sequences are organized using a dynamic hash based index. The matching is conducted in two phrases. Firstly, a progressive subsequence matching procedure is used to obtain a set of XPath expressions whose Prüfer sequences match some Prüfer sequences generated during the parsing of the XML document. This phase identifies a superset of XPath expressions that potentially match the incoming XML document. The second phase is conducted to refine the results to eliminate the *false positive* matchings. By converting the tree pattern matching to a holistic sequence matching, FiST avoids the joint operations for tree pattern queries in other approaches, which makes FiST better for the XPath expressions with more branch nodes.

The SemCast (Papaemmanouil & Cetintemel 2005) approach makes use of the multiple channels in the interior dissemination network such that the time-consuming content-based filtering at the interior routers is eliminated. In the SemCast, a number of multicast channels are created for disseminating information. Each channel consists of several routers which form a dissemination tree.

The channel is represented by some predicates expressions to specify the content. Data sources publish the information to one or more channels in terms of the overlapping between the content of the data source and the content of the channel. Data consumers subscribe to one or more channels whose content collectively cover their interests. There are five kinds of routers in Sem-Cast system:

- **Coordinator:** Is responsible for creating and managing channels. It communicates with both the source routers and gateway routers to inform them about the content of the existing channels.
- **Source routers:** Receive the information from the publishers. By comparing the content of the information with the content of channels from the coordinator, the source routers determine the set of dissemination trees for forwarding the information.
- **Rendezvous routers:** Take charge of the dissemination trees and serve as the roots of the dissemination trees.
- **Internal routers:** Forwards the information by identifying the identity of the channels that correspond to this information.
- **Gateway routers:** Take charge of forwarding the information to the end users.

The SemCast improves the filtering efficiency by eliminating the content-based matching at internal routers. However, SemCast may incur a large number of channels to be maintained.

Global Optimization

One limitation of the local optimizations is that they only consider the opportunity to improve the performance on each individual router. However, in the content based XML data publish/subscribe system, the same document D is being repeatedly processed against related sets of subscriptions on the upstream and downstream routers. This opens up a new opportunity to improve the filtering efficiency by exploring the collaboration among various routers. Given a set of routers in the system, suppose R_i is passing the data to R_j, we say that R_i is the upstream router of R_j and R_j is the downstream router of R_i. The piggyback optimization (Chan & Ni, 2007) leverages the collaboration among routers where the upstream router R_i is allowed to pass along some hint information (which is referred to as annotations) to its downstream router R_j when it forwards D to R_j. Such hint information is generated based on the matching of document D with the set of subscriptions on R_i. On receiving the document D with annotations, the downstream router R_j tries to exploit the hint information to optimize its own processing of D. There are two key ways that a downstream router R_j can optimize its processing and matching of D by exploiting additional hint information from its upstream router R_i:

- The hint could enable R_j to quickly determine that D is to be forwarded to a downstream router R_k without requiring R_j to parse and process D.
- The hint could enable R_j to quickly detect that a portion S'_j of the subscriptions in R_j's routing table are guaranteed not to match D, and R_j can therefore speed up its matching of D against the smaller set ($S_j - S'_j$) instead of S_j.

Four types of useful annotations are proposed which is summarized as follows:

- Positive subscription annotation specifies a data pattern in *D* that matches some subscription in T_i. Such an annotation can benefit R_j if the specified data pattern also matches some subscription s_y in T_j that aggregates to s_x. When this happens, R_j can very quickly detect that *D* matches s_y without having to actually process *D*. R_j can then immediately forward *D* to the relevant downstream router.

- Positive data annotation is to specify some useful property about the data D that can potentially be exploited by a downstream router R_j to skip the matching of some of its subscriptions in T_j thereby reducing R_j's processing overhead.

- Negative subscription annotation for a downstream router R_j (w.r.t. D) is a list of the identities of all the non-matching subscriptions in S_j (detonated as $S_j^-(D)$). This information can be exploited by R_j to skip the matching of all the aggregating subscriptions that were aggregated to $S_j^-(D)$.

- Negative data annotation specifies the absence of certain data patterns in D to skip the matching of all subscriptions in R_j that contain such patterns.

Evaluation of the Approaches to Improve the Matching Efficiency

The proposed approaches are evaluated by measuring the filtering time on processing a large number of XPath queries. The XPath queries are generated by a generator provided in (Diao, 2003). The number of steps in XPath queries, the probability of "//" and the probability of "*"; the number of nested paths in the XPath queries could be controlled to generate the XPath queries.

In the local optimization, the goal is to improve the matching efficiency at each individual router. The metric used to evaluate the performance is the query processing time on each router which is defined as follows:

Query processing time = Filtering time – Document parsing time;

Filtering time = Wall clock time from the start of document parsing to the end of output

In the global optimization, it is to leverage the collaboration among routers to improve the

filtering efficiency. The metric used to evaluate the performance is the response time which is defined as follows.

Response time = Wall clock time taken to disseminate a published document from its source to the relevant users.

It should be pointed out that the global optimization approach is orthogonal to the local optimization approaches. Therefore the local optimization and global optimization could be combined to achieve the best performance. Besides the filtering efficiency, these approaches also demonstrate the scalability by increasing the number of queries and increasing the complexity of the queries.

EXTENDING THE FUNCTIONALITIES OF THE SYSTEM

The Approach to Handle the Fragmented XML Data

As aforementioned, more and more data may be collected and published in terms of fragments, thus there is indeed a need to provide the functionality to support the XML data that is published in fragments. An approach (Chan & Ni, 2006) is proposed to match the XPath-based subscriptions *directly* on fragmented XML documents without reconstructing the original documents. The proposed approach of processing Boolean XPath queries on fragmented XML data consists of three main steps.

The first step identifies *what* relevant subqueries to evaluate on each fragment; the second step decides on the *order* in which the fragments are evaluated; and the third step deals with *how* each fragment is evaluated. Figure 6 gives an overview of our approach. The following describes each of the above steps.

Figure 6. Overview of processing XML fragments

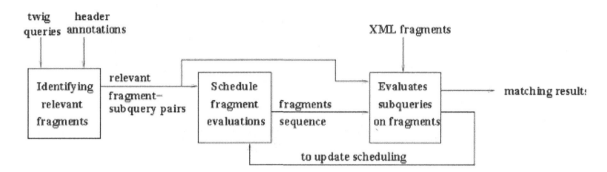

- **Identify relevant fragments.** Since the data nodes are partitioned among several fragments, finding a matching of an input query q in a fragmented XML document generally requires finding the matchings of different query nodes of q in the various fragments. Thus, the first step is to make use of the collection of fragment header information to identify a set of "relevant"' matchings to determine for each fragment. The goal is to minimize both the number of relevant matchings as well as the number of fragments to be evaluated.

- **Schedule fragment evaluations.** The second step is to determine an order in which to process the fragments based on the relevant fragment-subquery pairs obtained in the first step. The goal is to "short-circuit" the query evaluation as early or as much as possible: in the case that there is a matching of the input query, the schedule should identify the matching data nodes early; otherwise, the schedule should avoid processing

- **Evaluate subqueries on fragments.** This step deals with how to efficiently optimize and process the set of relevant subqueries associated with each fragment. The evaluation results on one fragment may affect the scheduling for the remaining fragments. Therefore we may update the scheduling

during the evaluations. A key challenge is how to efficiently maintain the intermediate set of matching nodes to facilitate the detection of a matching if it exists.

The Approach to Handle the Heterogeneous XML Data

In content-based publish/subscribe system for XML data, the data publishers are autonomous and independent, thus they generally do not use the same schemas even when their published data are related and belong to the same domain. Therefore, we need an approach to handle the heterogeneous XML data in content-based publish/ subscribe system. In traditional query processing, the query rewritten approach is leveraged to handle the heterogeneous data. However, different with the traditional scenario where the data amount is large and the number of queries is small, in publish/subscribe system, the number of queries is large while the data amount is small. Therefore, a new mechanism is required to handle heterogeneous data in the publish/subscribe system. A data rewriting based framework is proposed (Ni & Chan, 2008) to solve this problem.

There are three main approaches to perform the data rewriting. These approaches can be classified based on where the rewriting is done. The data rewriting step is introduced in three possible locations as illustrated in Figure 7: (a)

Figure 7. Data rewriting approaches

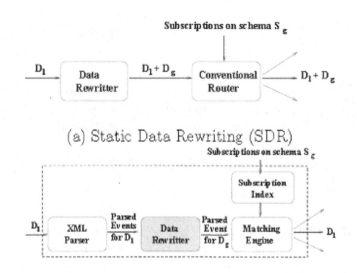

(a) Static Data Rewriting (SDR)

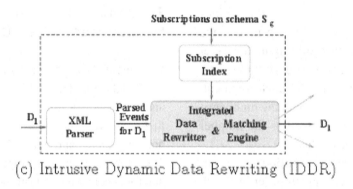

(b) Non-Intrusive Dynamic Data Rewriting (NDDR)

(c) Intrusive Dynamic Data Rewriting (IDDR)

outside of the router, (b) between the parser and matching engine components of the router, and (c) within the matching engine component. These three architectural options have different implementation-performance tradeoffs. In terms of implementation complexity, the last method is an *intrusive* approach in that it requires making substantial changes to some software component: in this case, the data rewriting step needs to be integrated into the matching engine. In contrast, the first two approaches are *non-intrusive* and have a lower implementation effort. The different methods can also be classified into *static* or

dynamic approaches depending on whether the data is rewritten only once before being forwarded to the routers (e.g., the first approach) or rewritten dynamically by each router (e.g., last two approaches).

Static Data Rewriting (SDR). In the *static data rewriting* (SDR) approach (illustrated in Figure 7(a)), each published data D_1 (based on some publisher's local schema S_1) is rewritten to D_g (based on the integrated global schema S_g) statically (but only once) by either the publisher itself or the mediator agent (MA). The advantage of employing the MA to rewrite the data is that the publishers are shielded from the details of the schema mappings and rewriting processing; however, this requires each publisher to first forward D_l to the MA for the rewriting before the MA forwards the transformed data to the routers for dissemination. Once D_l has been rewritten to D_g, both D_l and D_g are forwarded together to the network of routers. Here, D_g serves as metadata to enable the forwarding of the payload data D_l. Since the subscriptions stored in each router are based on the global schema S_g, D_g is used for matching against the subscriptions to detect matching subscriptions and decide to which router(s) the data needs to forwarded next. For forwarding to the local subscribers at a router, only the actual data D_l needs to be forwarded. One advantage of SDR is that it is a non-intrusive approach that can be easily implemented. However, the tradeoff is that the amount of data that is being forwarded is roughly doubled compared to the conventional approach.

Dynamic Data Rewriting (DDR). To avoid the transmission overhead of SDR, an alternative strategy is for each router to forward only D_l but the tradeoff is that each router now needs to rewrite the data D_l *dynamically*. This approach is referred to as *dynamic data rewriting* (DDR) approach. Note that DDR does not materialize D_g. Instead, the data rewriting is conducted during the parsing of documents for query evaluation. Specifically, the XML parser still parses D_l, while the evaluation of queries is equivalent to match these queries against D_g. Two dynamic data rewriting approaches are proposed based on the location to perform data rewriting.

- **NDDR.** The first option is to perform the rewrite outside of the matching engine by installing a new software component, called the *data rewriter*, between the document parser and matching engine as shown in Figure 7(b). The data rewriter essentially rewrites D_l to D_g by intercepting the sequence of events E_l that is generated by the

event-based XML parser (as it parses the input document D_l) and generating a modified sequence of events E_g to the matching engine such that E_g is equivalent to the sequence of events generated by parsing D_g. We refer to this approach as *non-intrusive dynamic data rewriting* (NDDR) approach since it does not require making any changes to the existing XML parser and matching engine components.

- **IDDR.** The second option is to rewrite the data within the matching engine itself as shown in Figure 6(c); we refer to this approach as *intrusive dynamic data rewriting* (IDDR) approach. The challenge of IDDR is how to match queries against the parsed events that are encountered out of document order.

The Approach to Handle the Stateful Subscriptions

PADRES (Li & Jacobsen, 2005) is a system to support the stateful subscriptions, in which the *composite subscriptions* are proposed to address a sequence of events. The *composite subscriptions* are formed by linking the traditional subscriptions using some logical or temporal operators. Each *composite subscription* is matched by a set of events that satisfy its correlation requirements. The PADRES supports four kinds of composition operators on subscriptions, i.e. *parallelization*, *alternation*, *sequence* and *repetition*. The *parallelization* operator is to address the set of events that occur together; the *alternation* operator on two subscriptions s_1 and s_2 is matched if an event matches either s_1 or s_2; the *sequence* operator is to address a set of events that occur in a sequence, and the attribute *time-span* can be used to specify the time interval between two events; and the *repetition* operator matches the events that occur in aperiodically or periodically. The PADRES proposed a mechanism to decompose the composite subscriptions and allocate the parts of subscriptions in the distributed environment. A rule-based matching engine is extended to support the matching of composite subscriptions.

The Cayuga (Demers, 2006) system also allows users to express subscriptions that span a set of events. Four kinds of binary operators, addressing on subscriptions s_1 and s_2, are proposed to support the stateful subscriptions. The first operator is *union*, which is similar with *alternation* operator in PADRES. The second operator is called conditional sequence, which requires that s_1 and s_2 are the sequence of two consecutive and non-overlapping events, and s_2 satisfies the condition with s_1. The third operator is *iteration* operator, which is the repeated application of the conditional sequence operator. The *iteration* iteratively applies the *conditional sequence* operator on a sequence of events. This operator enables the powerful parameterized subscriptions. The last operator is *aggregate*, which occurs over a sequence of events. For example, to compute the summarization or average for some attribute over a sequence of events needs the *aggregate* operator.

FUTURE RESEARCH DIRECTIONS

This section discusses some possible future directions in content-based publish/subscribe system for XML data.

QoS Constraints in the Content-Based Dissemination. Many existing publish/subscribe systems are based on the best effort principle. Subscribers are only allowed to issue their interests for the kind of XML document, but there are no parameters addressing the quality of the dissemination service provided to them. However, in some cases the Quality-of-Service of the filtering of XML documents should be considered. For example real-time trading systems need to guarantee the deadline for the arrival of current prices, and air-traffic control systems require up-to-date data on aircraft position and status. Although the quality-of-service considered in

publish/subscribe systems may reduce the whole systems' throughput, the requirement of users about the quality-of-service should be guaranteed. To consider QoS problem in publish/subscribe systems, we need to provide more parameters for users to specify, such as the deadline to receive some information and the priority of some queries. The publish/subscribe system should be modified to adopt some strategy to match the incoming documents against subscriptions such that all users' requirements are best satisfied.

Hybrid Content-Based Publish/Subscribe. The existing content-based dissemination systems either handle pure XML data or process pure attribute-value pairs. However, both XML data and attribute-value based data are published on the Internet, and there may be even other formats of data. A hybrid content-based publish/subscribe system can provide users with a uniform interface to subscribe their queries, while the routers in the system take charge of matching the queries with various formats of published information. For such kind of publish/subscribe systems, we need to consider what type of query interface is proper for users and how to index the queries such that the processing on different data formats can be optimized.

CONCLUSION

The information explosion nowadays makes the *push-based* communication model more suitable for large scale distributed information system. The features of XML make it become the *de facto* standard for information exchange on the Internet. The above two reasons lead to the importance of content-based publish/subscribe of XML data in the large-scale distributed information systems. In this chapter, we introduced the content-based publish/subscribe system for XML data and introduced the approaches to improve the efficiency and effectiveness of the system. Finally, this chapter also presented some possible future directions in content-based publish/subscribe system for XML data.

REFERENCES

W3C (1999). *XML Path Language (XPath) 1.0.* Retrieved from http://www.w3.org/TR/xpath

W3C (2006). *XQuery 1.0.* Retrieved from http://www.w3.org/TR/xquery

Altinel, M., & Franklin, M. (2000). Efficient filtering of XML documents for selective dissemination of information. In *Proceedings of the 26th International Conference on Very Large Data Bases*, 53-64.

Apache Xerces. (2007). Retrieved from http://xml.apache.org/xerces-c/

Banavar, G., Chandra, T., Mukherjee, B., & Nagarajarao, J. (1999). An efficient multicast protocol for content-based publish-subscribe systems. In *Proceedings of the 19ᵗʰ International Conference of Distributed Computing Systems*, (pp. 262-271).

Bloom, B. H. (1970). Space/time trade-offs in hash coding with allowable errors. *Communications of the ACM, 13*(7), 422–426. doi:10.1145/362686.362692

Carzaniga, A., Roseblum, D. S., & Wolf, A. L. (2000). Archieving scalability and expressiveness in an internet-scale event notification services. In *Proceedings of the 19ᵗʰ ACM Symposium on Principles of Distributed Computing*, (pp. 219-227).

Chan, C.-Y., Fan, W. F., Felber, P., Garofalakis, M., & Rastogi, R. (2002). Tree pattern aggregation for scalable XML data dissemination. In *Proceedings of the 28th International Conference on Very Large Data Bases (VLDB)*, (pp. 826-837).

Chan, C.-Y., Felber, P., Garofalakis, M., & Rastogi, R. (2002). Efficient filtering of XML documents with XPath Expressions. *The International Journal on Very Large Data Bases, 11*(4), 354–379. doi:10.1007/s00778-002-0077-6

Chan, C.-Y., & Ni, Y. (2006). Content-based dissemination of fragmented XML data. In *Proceedings of the 26th International Conference on Distributed Computing Systems (ICDCS)*, (pp. 44-53).

Chan, C.-Y., & Ni, Y. (2007). Efficient XML data dissemination with piggybacking. In *Proceedings of the ACM International Conference on Management of Data (SIGMOD)*.

Cugola, G., Nitto, E. D., & Picco, G. P. (2000). Content-based dispatching in a mobile environment. In *Proceedings of the Workshop su Sistemi Distribuiti: Algoritmi, Architetture e Linguaggi*.

Cugola, G., Nittom, E. D., & Fuggeta, A. (2001). The JEDI event-based infrastructure and its application to the development of the OPSS WFMS. *IEEE Transactions on Software Engineering, 27*(9), 827–850. doi:10.1109/32.950318

Demers, A., Gehrke, J., Hong, M. S., Riedewald, M., & White, W. (2006). Towards expressive publish/subscribe systems. In *Proceedings of the 10th International Conference on Extending Database Technology (EDBT)*, (pp. 627-644).

Diao, Y., Altinel, M., Franklin, M., Zhang, H., & Fischer, P. (2003). Path sharing and predicate evaluation for high-performance XML filtering. *ACM Transactions on Database Systems, 28*(4), 467–516. doi:10.1145/958942.958947

Diao, Y., Rizvi, S., & Franklin, M. (2004). Towards an Internet-scale XML dissemination service. In *Proceedings of the 30ᵗʰ International Conference on Very Large Data Base,* (pp. 612-623).

Gnome Libxml2. (2000). Retrieved from http://xmlsoft.org/

Gong, X. Q., Qian, W. N., Yan, Y., & Zhou, A. Y. (2005). Bloom filter-based XML packets filtering for millions of path queries. In *Proceedings of the 21st International Conference on Data Engineering,* (pp. 890-901).

Green, T. J., Miklau, G., Onizuka, M., & Suciu, D. (2003). Processing XML streams with deterministic automata. In *Proceedings of the 9th International Conference on Database Theory,* (pp. 752-788).

Gupta, A., Halevy, A., & Suicu, D. (2002). View selection for XML stream processing. In *Proceedings of the 5th International Workshop on the Web & Database,* (pp. 83-88).

Gupta, A., & Suciu, D. (2003). Streaming processing of XPath queries with predicates. In *Proceedings of the ACM International Conference on Management of Data,* (pp. 419-430).

Gupta, A., Suicu, D., & Halevy, A. (2003). The view selection problem for XML content based routing. In *Proceedings of the 22nd International Conference on Principles of Database System,* (pp. 68-77).

Hou, S., & Arno Jacobsen, H. (2006). Predicate-based filtering of XPath expressions. In *Proceedings of the 22nd International Conference on Data Engineering (ICDE),* (pp. 53-62).

Huang, Y. Q. & Molina, H. G. (2004). Publish/subscribe in a mobile environment. *Wireless Networks. Special Issue: Pervasive computing and communications, 10*(6), 643-652.

Kwon, J., Rao, P., Moon, B., & Lee, S. (2005). FiST: scalable XML document filtering by sequencing twig patterns. In *Proceedings of the 31st International Conference on Very Large Data Bases,* (pp. 217-228).

Li, G. L., Hou, S., & Jacobsen, H. A. (2009). Routing of XML and XPath queries in data dissemination network. In *Proceedings of the 29th International Conference of Distributed Computing Systems,* (pp. 627-638).

Li, G. L., & Jacobsen, H.-A. (2005). Composite subscriptions in content-based publish/subscribe systems. In *Proceedings of ACM/IFIP/USENIX International Middleware Conference,* (pp. 249-269).

Ni, Y., & Chan, C.-Y. (2008). Dissemination of heterogeneous XML data (Poster Paper). In *Proceedings of the 17th International World Wide Web Conference,* (pp. 1059-1060).

Papaemmanouil, O., & Cetintemel, U. (2005). SemCast: semantic multicast for content-based data dissemination. In *Proceedings of the 21st International Conference on Data Engineering,* (pp. 242-253).

SAX. (2000). Retrieved from http://www.sax-project.org/

Segall, B., Aronld, D., Boot, J., Henderson, M., & Phelps, T. (2000). Content-based routing with Elvin4. In *Proceedings of the Australian UNIX and Open Systems User group Conference.*

Selcuk Candan, K., Hsiung, W.-P., Chen, S., Tatemura, J., & Agrawal, D. (2006). AFilter: adaptive XML filtering with prefix-caching and suffix-clustering. In *Proceedings of the 32nd International Conference on Very Large Data Bases,* (pp. 559-570).

Skeen, D. (1998). *Publish-subscribe architecture: publish-subscribe overview.* Retrieved from http://www.vitria.com

TIBCO. (1999). *TIB/Rendezvous.* Retrieved from http://www.tibco.com

Zhang, X., Yang, L. H., Lee, M. L., & Hsu, W. (2004). Scaling SDI systems via query clustering and aggregation. In *Proceedings of the 9th International Conference on Database Systems for Advanced Applications,* (pp. 21-23).

Chapter 11
Content–Based XML Data Dissemination

Guoli Li
University of Toronto, Canada

Shuang Hou
University of Toronto, Canada

Hans-Arno Jacobsen
University of Toronto, Canada

ABSTRACT

XML-based data dissemination networks are rapidly gaining momentum. In these networks XML content is routed from data producers to data consumers throughout an overlay network of content-based routers. Routing decisions are based on XPath expressions (XPEs) stored at each router. To enable efficient routing, while keeping the routing state small, we introduce advertisement-based routing algorithms for XML content, present a novel data structure for managing XPEs, especially apt for the hierarchical nature of XPEs and XML, and develop several optimizations for reducing the number of XPEs required to manage the routing state. The experimental evaluation shows that our algorithms and optimizations reduce the routing table size by up to 90%, improve the routing time by roughly 85%, and reduce overall network traffic by about 35%. Experiments running on PlanetLab show the scalability of our approach.

INTRODUCTION

Over the past decade, XML has rapidly evolved as the standard for data representation and exchange. XML marked-up message traffic in intranets and on the Internet ranges from insurance claims, health-care requests, corporate memos, online ads to news items and entertainment information. The standardization of the mark-up language, the wide range of related standards, and the wide-spread adoption of this technology are further amplifying the network externalities created by this technology.

XML-based data dissemination networks are starting to become a reality. In a dissemination network, data messages, marked-up in XML, are routed based on filter expressions stored at intermediate nodes that indicate where the XML message is to be routed to. These routing nodes are often referred to as *content-based routers* or *brokers*, as they route messages to interested recipients by

DOI: 10.4018/978-1-61520-727-5.ch011

Figure 1. Distributed dissemination network

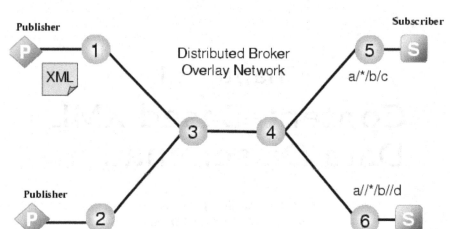

inspecting the message content. Filter expressions, often expressed as XPath expressions (XPEs), are submitted by data consumers who express interest in receiving certain kinds of documents. This architecture is depicted in Figure 1. For instance, a globally operating insurance company with many branch offices distributed world-wide is linked by an overlay network of content-based routers that comprise the XML dissemination network. An insurance claim, an insurance bid, or a request for proposal can be submitted anywhere into the overlay network (e.g., by a third party insurance broker or an online client) and be routed toward a currently online, specific expert employee, speaking the same language as the requester. Note, the latter constraints are expressed as XPE filter expressions against which the XML document is evaluated in transit. This design fully decouples information requesters and information providers, avoids a single point of control and a single point of failure, and increases scalability due to decentralization and distribution.

The fundamental concepts underlying the content-based dissemination of XML messages are the algorithms and data structures for matching and routing of XML documents against XPEs, the definition of advertisements that efficiently summarize the kind of XML documents that data producers will publish, the interpretation and the development of algorithms for intersecting advertisements with subscriptions, and the definition of covering and merging of XPEs.

This chapter addresses the XML/XPath routing problem. More specifically, this chapter focuses on the problem of efficiently routing an XML document emitted from a data producer at one point in the network to a set of data consumers located anywhere throughout the network. Prior to receiving XML documents, consumers must have expressed interest in receiving XML documents by registering XPEs with the network. This problem statement is akin to the well-known publish/subscribe matching problem. However, the main difference here is that in the case of data dissemination networks, there exists no one single centralized publish/subscribe system, but a network of content-based routers (i.e., a network or federation of publish/subscribe systems.) In the dissemination network, XML documents are routed based on their content and not based on IP address information, which is, due to the completely decoupled design, not available – all routing decisions are exclusively based on content information. Figure 2 provides an overview of the dissemination network this chapter assumes. In the overlay network depicted in Figure 2 each

Figure 2. Content-based routing

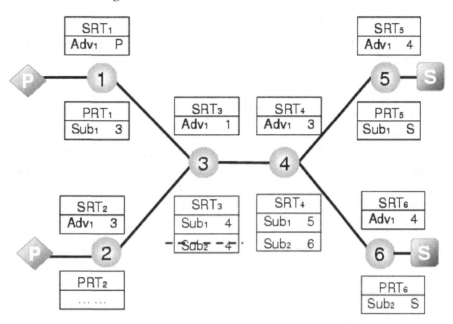

content-based router, referred to as broker, only knows its neighbors (i.e., in terms of IP network address information.) However, none of the clients – neither data producers nor data consumers – know about each other or about the network topology, except the router they connect to. This design eases system management while offering flexibility to the application design.

In the context of XML-based data dissemination, one of the main challenges is the ability to efficiently deliver relevant XML documents to a large and dynamically changing group of consumers. Not only data sinks (consumers) can change dynamically, but also data sources (producers) can change dynamically. Existing producers and consumers can go away and reappear, and new ones can appear at any time. Furthermore, the challenges are to evaluate high rates of XML messages against large numbers of possibly overlapping XPEs to decide where to send an XML message to. Moreover, XPEs can dynamically change, which has to be reflected in the whole dissemination network. A further challenge is that XPEs may operate over XML

document structure, XML tag attributes, and XML document content. XPath expressions can define very complex expressions.

Centralized XML filtering (Altinel & Franklin, 2000; Chan et al., 2002b; Diao et al., 2003; Hou & Jacobsen, 2006) and distributed query-based XML retrieval approaches (Chan et al., 2002a; Koloniari & Pitoura, 2004; Koudas et al., 2004) have found wide-spread interest, but do not address the distributed, content-based routing problem articulated above and addressed in this chapter. ONYX is a query-based XML retrieval approach for XML data dissemination in distributed environments (Diao et al., 2004). It is closely related to our approach, but complementary in objectives. ONYX aims at reducing the XML message size. ONYX achieves this through only disseminating parts of an XML message selected by subscriber queries. Several techniques are presented and evaluated to achieve this objective. In the context of our work, subscriber queries are meant to select messages that match the query, however, the subscriber requires the full message and not just parts of it. It is therefore difficult to quantitatively compare both approaches. Content-based routing in distributed publish/subscribe architectures (Carzaniga et al., 2004; Cugola et al., 2001; Li & Jacobsen, 2005; Mühl, 2001), has been studied for non-XML-based data. Their operational model assumes sets of attribute-value pairs joined by Boolean operators. It is not at all obvious how to extend these approaches for semi-structured data, especially due to the hierarchical data model of XML.

Our own prior research on content-based routing and matching develops architectures, algorithms and protocols for content-based routing of non-XML based data (Cheung & Jacobsen, 2006; Fidler et al., 2005; Li et al., 2005; Li & Jacobsen, 2005; Liu & Jacobsen, 2002; Liu & Jacobsen, 2004; Liu et al., 2009). It is a non-trivial problem, as we argue in this chapter, to extend these approaches to the hierarchical structure of XML. Our prior work on developing efficient matching algorithms for XML addresses part of the problem (Hou & Jacobsen, 2006), and another work on efficient routing protocols addresses the important problem of efficiently computing routing decisions, inducing advertisements from XML DTDs, and determining covering and merging relations (Li et al., 2008a; Li et al., 2008b). This chapter is an extended version of our prior work (Li et al., 2008a). This chapter combined with our earlier work on XML matching (Hou & Jacobsen, 2006) and routing (Li et al., 2008a) comprises all components required to build an efficient content-based router for an XML data dissemination network. The research presented in this chapter complements our PADRES content-based publish/subscribe system effort (Fidler et al., 2005; Jacobsen, 2006; Li et al., 2007b). PADRES has to date not investigated the routing of XML content against XPEs. PADRES is based on a proprietary subscription language and publication data model. Subscriptions are conjunctions of predicates, which define filter constraints over attribute value pairs. Publications are sets of attribute value pairs. Unique to PADRES are its capabilities

to subscribe to past events (i.e., query the event space for historic data) (Li et al., 2007a; Li et al., 2008c), to correlate past and future events, and to detect composite events by correlating individual atomic and composite events. PADRES achieves this flexibility through a powerful subscription language based on composite subscription expressions that form the basis of its SQL-like subscription language. A composite subscription defines the subscriber's interest in composite events. PADRES proposes novel algorithms for the routing of composite subscriptions and the detection of composite events based on data source intensity and past matching statistics. PADRES also proposes routing protocols that exploit cyclic overlay topologies to handle failures, react to congestion and peak loads, and to generally offer a robust publish/subscribe service. In PADRES, robustness is achieved by supporting alternate message routing paths (Li et al., 2008b), load balancing techniques to distribute load (Cheung & Jacobsen, 2008), and fault resilience techniques to react to broker failures (Sherafat Kazemzadeh & Jacobsen, 2007; Sherafat Kazemzadeh & Jacobsen, 2008). PADRES also studies client mobility (Muthusamy & Jacobsen, 2005; Muthusamy & Jacobsen, 2007; Petrovic et al., 2005), service selection (Chau et al., 2008; Hu et al., 2008; Muthusamy et al., 2007; Muthusamy & Jacobsen, 2008) and resource and service discovery (Yan et al., 2009). All these concepts complement the work presented in this chapter. However, PADRES does not support the routing of XML messages against XPEs, which is the missing link to briding and combining the work presented in this chapter with PADRES.

In this chapter, we develop algorithms for dissemination of XML data throughout a network of content-based routers towards data consumers who have specified their interests through XPEs. Our contributions are: first, we adapt the use of advertisements to optimize data dissemination. While this idea is common in the publish/subscribe literature (Carzaniga et al., 2004; Cugola et al., 2001; Mühl, 2001), it is not clear how to extend the concepts to the data model of XML. We demonstrate how to use the XML Document Type Definition (DTD) to generate advertisements about the information a data producer is going to publish. We distinguish between a non-recursive and a recursive case depending on the DTD defining the data emitting source. We then develop advertisement-based routing algorithms for both cases. Second, we propose a novel data structure to maintain XPEs by identifying the covering relations among them. We present covering algorithms for XPEs to reduce the routing table size stored at each router and speed up routing computation in the routers. Third, we present an optimization of merging similar XPEs to further reduce routing computation. Finally, we perform a detailed experimental evaluation of our approach on an overlay network comprised of 127 XML routers deployed over a cluster with 20 nodes and deployed on PlanetLab. Our experimental results demonstrate the effectiveness of the approach by reducing the routing table size by up to 90% and improving the routing time by roughly 85%.

BACKGROUND

Content-Based Routing

Content-based publish/subscribe systems provide a flexible and extensible environment for information exchange (Carzaniga et al., 2004; Cugola et al., 2001; Fidler et al., 2005; Jacobsen, 2006; Mühl, 2001). Publishers and subscribers are clients to the publish/subscribe system, are loosely coupled in space and time, and have no knowledge of each other. Messages in content-based publish/subscribe systems are routed based on their content rather than the IP address of their destinations. In order to handle a large amount of dynamic information and reduce the network traffic many optimization techniques, such as advertisements

(Carzaniga et al., 2004), covering technique and merging technique (Carzaniga et al., 2004; Cugola et al., 2001; Mühl, 2001) have proven to offer significant benefits for non-XML based publish/subscribe systems. While conceptually, these ideas apply to XML-based data as well, it is not obvious how to apply these concepts to XML due to the structural complexity of XML data. These are the challenges addressed by this chapter.

In advertisement-based publish/subscribe systems, advertisements are specifications of information that the publisher publishes in the future. Advertisements are flooded in the publish/subscribe overlay. The common assumption is that the number of advertisements is much smaller than the number of subscriptions and publications. Advertisements are used to avoid broadcasting subscriptions in the network, so that subscriptions are only routed to the publishers who advertise what the subscribers are interested in. Subscriptions define filters to select publications of interest. Matching publications are delivered to subscribers along the paths built by subscriptions. Figure 2 shows a scenario for advertisement-based content-based routing. The subscription routing table (SRT) consisting of <advertisement, last-hop>-tuples stores advertisements in order to route subscriptions. Publications trace back along the path setup by subscriptions to interested subscribers. The publication routing table (PRT) maintains the path information. For example, in Figure 2, advertisement adv_1 is broadcast in the network, and is stored on each broker of the network with a different last hop. Consequently, subscriptions that match adv_1 are routed according to these last hops (e.g., sub_1 is routed along the link 5−4−3−1). Note that the subscription sub_1 is not forwarded to Brokers 2 and 6, respectively, since adv_1 indicates that matching publications are from Broker 1. Therefore, publication pub_1 is routed along the reverse path 1−3−4−5 to the subscriber. In the rest of this chapter, we use the notations $P(s)$ and $P(a)$ to refer to the set of publications that match subscription *s* and advertisement *a*, respectively.

Covering and Merging

The goal of covering-based routing is to remove redundant subscriptions from the network in order to obtain a compact routing table and reduce the network traffic (Carzaniga et al., 2004; Li et al., 2005; Mühl, 2001). In Figure 2, if subscription sub_1 covers subscription sub_2 at Broker 4, sub_2 is not forwarded to Broker 3. That is, we can safely remove sub_2 at Broker 3 obtaining a compacter routing table while maintaining the same information delivery behavior. All publications matching sub_2 must also match sub_1. A formal definition of the covering relation is as follows: A subscription sub_1 covers sub_2, if and only if, $P(sub_1) \supseteq P(sub_2)$, denoted as $sub_1 \sqsupseteq sub_2$. The covering relation defines a partial order on the set of all subscriptions with respect to $\sqsupseteq$. Since advertisements have the same format as subscriptions, the covering relations among advertisements can be defined in the same manner.

If two subscriptions are not in a covering relation, but their publication sets intersect each other, the two subscriptions can be merged to a more general subscription, which covers the original subscriptions. Suppose subscription sub_m is a merger of sub_1 and sub_2, then we have $P(sub_m) \supseteq P(sub_1) \cup P(sub_2)$. There are two kinds of mergers. If the publication set of the merger is exactly equal to the union of the publication set of the original subscriptions, the merger is a *perfect merger*; otherwise, if $P(sub_m) \supset P(sub_1) \cup P(sub_2)$, it is an *imperfect merger*. After merging, only the merger is forwarded into the network. The merging technique (Li et al., 2005; Mühl, 2001) is used for further minimizing the routing table size, since the merger may introduce new covering relations among subscriptions. Covering and merging are complementary routing optimizations.

RELATED WORK

A large body of work has focused on developing publish/subscribe-style matching algorithms for evaluating an XML message against a set of XPEs (Altinel & Franklin, 2000; Bruno et al., 2003; Chan et al., 2002b; Diao et al., 2003; Hou & Jacobsen, 2006). However, all these approaches exclusively address centralized matching architectures, not the distributed, content-based XML dissemination networks we address in this work. While matching is an integral step in a content-based router, other routing operations studied in this chapter are equally important in distributed data dissemination architecture. Thus, our work complements matching algorithms for the design of a content-based XML router.

Recent research has focused on XML data dissemination (Altinel & Franklin, 2000; Diao et al., 2003; Diao et al., 2004; Fenner et al., 2005; Koloniari & Pitoura, 2004; Koudas et al., 2004; Snoeren et al., 2001). Among the earlier work on XML dissemination, XFilter (Altinel & Franklin, 2000) is probably among the first approaches. It defines a finite state machine (FSM) for each XPath query, then it proposes an index over these FSMs. These FSMs are executed concurrently for each XML document. When a matching state is reached, the XML document is delivered to the subscriber who issued the query. YFilter (Diao et al., 2003) improved the matching performance by proposing one unique FSM for all queries, which allowed common query paths to be processed only once. The matching performance is improved by sharing common query paths. Other FSM-baed approaches use different techniques for building the FSMs for queries, as well as different type of FSMs. For instance, Deterministic Finite Automaton (DFA) have been built in Green *et al.* from XPath queries (Green et al., 2004). The authors construct a DFA lazily. A lazy DFA is one whose states and transitions are computed from the corresponding NFA at runtime, not at compile time.

The number of states in the lazy DFA is small, which guarantees the efficient matching of XML documents.

Holistic information is first used in the matching process by FiST (Kwon et al., 2005), which performs a different, bottom-up approach based on ordered twig patterns using Prüfer sequences. FiST organizes the sequences into a dynamic hash-based index for efficient filtering. Another FSM-based approach BUFF also uses a bottom-up approach (Moro et al., 2007), but it avoids translating documents and queries to Prüfer sequences, but employs a novel pruning technique based on lower and upper bound estimations to reduce the query space.

Another methodology is to aggregate the queries using some index technique. XTrie supports efficient filtering of streaming XML documents based on XPath expressions (Chan et al., 2002b). The authors proposed a novel index structure, termed XTrie, for large-scale filtering with complex XPath expressions, not limited to simple, single-path specifications. It supports both ordered and unordered matching of XML documents. XTrie is space-efficient since the space cost of XTrie is dominated by the number of substrings in each tree pattern.

There are some related research in peer-to-peer networks. Koloniari *el al.* present a decentralized approach for XML dissemination in a peer-to-peer network (Koloniari & Pitoura, 2004). However, in their approach queries are severely restricted in that no wildcards are allowed. Koudas *et al.* propose a flexible routing protocol for XML routers to enable scalable XPath query and update processing in a data-sharing peer-to-peer network (Koudas et al., 2004). Both approaches are solutions to the *location problem*. The location problem states that given a dynamic collection of XML database servers and an XPath query, find the databases that contain data relevant to the query. Our approach evaluates an XML document against a set of XPath queries, and decides where to route the XML document.

Instead of matching XML documents against individual queries, generating a compact set of XPath queries from a given set of XPEs could improve the matching performance as well. This problem is similar to the covering and merging problem discussed in this chapter. Query containment and aggregation address how a compact set could be generated theoretically and practically (Chan et al., 2002a; Dong et al., 2003; Miklau & Suciu, 2004). In Miklau *et al.* it is shown that for a simple fragment of XPath that contains descendant axis (//), wildcards(*), and qualifiers([...]), but without either tag variables or disjunctions (Miklau & Suciu, 2004), query containment is coNP-complete. If any of the above constructs is dropped, (Amer-Yahia et al., 2002) shows that the query containment problem can be reduced to PTIME. Dong *et al.* (Dong et al., 2003) further studies the nested XML queries and shows for queries with fixed nesting depth, the containment problem is coNP-complete.

One of the challenges brought by the query containment and aggregation problem is to guarantee the equivalence between the compact set and the original set. That is, the aggregate query set does not introduce or control false positives (i.e., takes XML documents not originally matched) or false negatives (i.e., misses XML documents originally matched.) The efficient tree-pattern aggregation algorithm proposed in Chan *et al.* makes effective use of document-distribution statistics in order to compute a precise set of aggregate tree patterns within the allocated space budget (Chan et al., 2002a). However they try to minimize the loss in precision due to the aggregation, not to avoid it. While we try to eliminate the false positives and false negatives in the covering approach and quantify the imprecision in the merging approach. These are non-trivial extensions to their work. Furthermore, the tree aggregation approach does not address the generation of advertisements from DTDs, which is central to our approach. Chand *et.al.* discuss a scalable protocol for XML-based data dissemination (Chand & Felber, 2003). They explore subscription aggregation to provide efficient message routing and use a tree structure to maintain the covering relation among subscriptions. They maintain part of the covering relation in their substitution tree. We use extend the tree structure with *super pointers* to cache a complete covering relationship, which is used for covering-based routing.

Advertisement-based techniques for optimizing content-based routing have been developed in the area of distributed publish/subscribe (Carzaniga et al., 2004; Cugola et al., 2001; Mühl, 2001). It has been demonstrated that the network traffic and routing table size can be reduced by using different routing strategies, including advertising, covering and merging techniques. However, the main differences between these approaches and our approach lie in the subscription language and publication data format. Our approach is based on the hierarchical, tree-based XPath and XML model; while the traditional content-based routing approaches operate with attribute-value pairs and predicate constraints over these pairs. The advertising carried out by XML and XPath data sources is different and more complex than predicate-based languages, for the hierarchical and recursive structure of the model needs to be taken into account. A DTD of an XML document does not have an equivalent in traditional publish/ subscribe approaches. Galanis *et al.* explore XML data dissemination based on a distributed hash table (DHT) (Galanis et al., 2003), which is a decentralized distributed system that provides a lookup service similar to a hash table: (key, value) pairs are stored in the DHT, and any participating node can efficiently retrieve the value associated with a given key. The authors use data summaries to ensure that queries are only sent to relevant servers. These data summaries could be taken as a form of advertisements. The data summary is generated from an XML document, so the expressiveness of the data summary is part of the DTD. Our contribution is to generate a complete advertisement set once from a DTD for all related XML documents.

ONYX (Diao et al., 2004) and XTreeNet (Fenner et al., 2005) are systems similar in conception to the one we describe in this chapter. However, their objectives are quite different making a comparison difficult. ONYX (Diao et al., 2004) describes an architecture to deploy XML-based services on an Internet-scale. The approach is based on performing incremental message transformations to reduce message size instead of sending and receiving the entire XML message, published by a data source. ONYX only delivers the parts of the message actually selected by the data sinks' subscribing queries. For many applications, this approach is not feasible, as the entire message published by a source needs to be delivered in its entirety to all subscribing data sinks, which is the message delivery semantic realized by our system and algorithms. To further reduce message size and processing cost, ONYX investigates various representations for XML messages. While a binary message representation will certainly speed up XML message processing, we have found in prior work that XML processing, such as parsing, is not the dominating cost for an XML router (Hou & Jacobsen, 2006) and optimizations of that component are therefore of questionable utility in this context. ONYX uses an NFA-based operator network for representing routing tables. This approach supports the sharing of common prefixes among queries. Our approach goes beyond this by identifying all covering relations among queries processed when constructing the routing tables, so that all covered queries are eliminated completely from the routing computation. Moreover, our work introduces merging and advertising for XML data not addressed in the earlier approach. Our unique contribution is to enable these techniques for the XML data model, which is fundamentally different from the data models underlying non-XML-based content routing approaches, such as (Carzaniga et al., 2004; Cugola et al., 2001; Li et al., 2005; Mühl, 2001). XTreeNet (Fenner et al., 2005) elegantly unifies the publish/subscribe and the query/response model in an XML-aware overlay network. XTreeNet proposes a dissemination protocol to avoid repeatedly matching XML data against queries at intermediate routers. This is an orthogonal optimization that our approach can also employ by attaching the path of overlay hops to the XML query when the subscription tree is constructed in the network. XML messages only match against the queries at the first router, and are forwarded along the subscription paths to the subscribers.

To the best of our knowledge, our work is the first to address the problem of advertisement for XML data dissemination. However, the advertisement-based routing has been widely studied in the area of content-based publish/subscribe system (Carzaniga et al., 2004; Cugola et al., 2001; Mühl, 2001). They reduce the network traffic and routing table size by using different routing strategies, including advertisement, covering and merging techniques. In contrast to the format of advertisement, conjunction of attribute-value pairs, in the context of content-based publish/subscribe system, our chapter focuses on a more complex format (as the advertisement in our work is defined as recursive and non-recursive with respect to different DTDs), which includes both data contents and structure. The query aggregation scheme given in (Chan et al., 2002a) addresses the problem as part of our work, and they do not address the advertisement-based optimization and support powerful language like recursive advertisement format.

ADVERTISEMENT-BASED ROUTING

Upon receiving a subscription, a broker matches the subscription against its advertisements. If there is an advertisement whose publication set intersects that of the subscription, it means there is a *match* between the subscription and the advertise-

ment. The broker then routes the subscription to the broker where the advertisement came from.

XML-Based Advertisements

In the context of XML/XPath routing, advertisements are generated by exploiting DTD information. The purpose of a DTD is to define the legal building blocks of an XML document. The main building blocks of XML documents are elements surrounded by tags, e.g., *<root>...</root>*, where *root* is the element name in the document. All elements appearing in the XML document must be defined in the corresponding DTD, which determines the structure of elements and their sequence in the document. In this chapter, our discussion focuses on the main building block – elements. Our approach could be easily extended to element attributes and content Hou & Jacobsen (2006), which we omit due to space limitations.

In this chapter, we use the common interpretation of an XML document as a tree of nodes and consider each path from the root node to a leaf node. Thus, we decompose each XML document into a set of XML paths and each path is represented as $e=/t_1/t_2/.../t_n$, where t_i is the XML element name. These paths are extracted from the document before the publisher submits the document to the network. Thus, a publication routed in our system is actually an XML path annotated with a *pathId* and *docId*. This is transparent to publishers and subscribers who handle entire XML documents. Publishers submit entire XML documents, commonly referred to as publications, and subscribers submit XPath expressions (XPEs), commonly referred to as subscriptions. We use the terms XPE and subscription interchangeably in the rest of this chapter.

We use an absolute XPath expression without //-operators as the format of advertisements in the context of XML/XPath data routing. Note that this is not a restriction of our subscription language. Advertisements are a system internal mechanism, which is not exposed to the application or to the user. An advertisement is described as $a=/t_1/t_2/.../t_{n-1}/t_n$, where t_i can be either an element name or a wildcard, and a has the same length as the publication it advertises. In our approach, advertisements are derived from the DTD, since the DTD allows deriving all possible paths from the root to the leaves appearing in related XML documents.

We call an advertisement a *non-recursive* advertisement if it is extracted from a non-recursive DTD. The above advertisement a is an example of non-recursive advertisement. A DTD is recursive if it contains elements that are defined in terms of the elements themselves. The popular NITF DTD, often used for experimentation, is recursive. We call an advertisement a *recursive* advertisement if it is extracted from a recursive DTD. An advertisement may have multiple recursive parts that appear in sequence or are embedded in each other. We classify recursive advertisements into three categories as described below.

Simple-recursive advertisements: A simple-recursive advertisement has only one recursive pattern. The advertisement is described as $a=/t_1/t_2/...t_{i-1}(/t_i/.../t_i^+/.../t_n)$, where the + operator declares that elements $/t_i/.../t_j/$ must occur one or more times in the advertisement. Note that this is not part of XPath syntax. Advertisements are only used within the system, so the extended XPath syntax has no effect on clients and applications. In the proposed algorithms, we use $a=a_1(a_2)^+a_3$ to simplify the expression, where a_k $(1 \leq k \leq 3)$ is a non-recursive advertisement.

Series-recursive advertisements: A series-recursive advertisement includes more than one recursive pattern in sequence. For example, an advertisement containing two recursive patterns in sequence can be described as $a=/t_1/t_2/...t_{i-1}(/t_i/.../t_j)^+/t_{j+1}.../t_{l-1}(/t_i/.../t_o)^+/.../t_n$, or as simplified expression with non-recursive advertisements, denoted as $a=a_1(a_2)^+a_3(a_4)^+a_5$.

Embedded-recursive advertisements: An embedded-recursive advertisement recursively embeds patterns in other patterns. A possible

case is $a=/t_1/t_2/.../t_{i-1}(t_i/.../t_{l-1}(/t_i/.../t_o)^+/.../t_j)^+/.../t_n$, or $a=a_1(a_2(a_3)^+a_4)^+a_5$. The embedded-recursive advertisement can be more complex.

More types of recursive advertisements can be easily defined based on the above three types of advertisements. We discuss the matching algorithms for non-recursive and recursive advertisements in the following sections, respectively.

Non-Recursive Advertisement

In this section, we discuss the algorithms for subscription and non-recursive advertisement matching in the context of XML/XPath. An advertisement a matches a subscription s if the publication sets $P(a)$ and $P(s)$ intersect, that is, $P(a) \cap P(s) \neq \varnothing$. Figure 3(a) shows all possible relations between the two sets. To forward subscriptions, we need to identify the first two intersecting cases in Figure 3 (a). In this chapter, we focus on the subscriptions including parent-child operator (/), wildcard operator (*), and ancestor-descendant operator (//). For other operators appearing in the subscription, such as attribute filters, our approach can be easily extended to support them through value comparison. We discuss the matching algorithm for the following three subscription cases.

Absolute simple XPEs: A simple XPE only contains parent-child and wildcard operators. We describe the matching algorithm for absolute XPEs (without //-operator) and advertisements (AbsExprAndAdv) in Figure 4. For example, $s=/st_1/st_2/...st_k$ and $a=/at_1/at_2/.../at_n$, where st_i is the i-th element of s and at_j is the j-th element of a. We use this notation in all algorithms in this chapter. First, the algorithm does not have to be applied, if the given XPE is longer than the advertisement. This observation is exploited because the advertisement has the same length as its publications, and thus, publications in $P(a)$ do not match all the elements in the longer XPE. Next, the algorithm compares each pair of elements or wildcards in the advertisement and the subscription, according to the matching rules

Figure 3. Advertisement and Subscription Relations

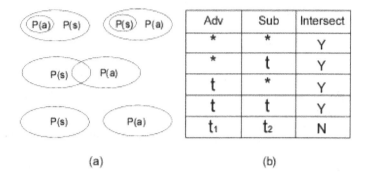

(a)   (b)

Figure 4. AbsExpr. and Adv. Matching

Input: advertisement *a*, and subscription *s*
Output: 1 if $P(a) \cap P(s) \neq \varnothing$, 0 if $P(a) \cap P(s) = \varnothing$

1: **If** $|s|>|a|$ **then return** 0
2: **For** $i=1:|s|$ **do**
3: **If** matching rules are not satisfied for at_i and st_i **then return** 0
4: **Return** 1

---

shown in Figure 3(b). It returns 0, if some pair does not intersect; otherwise it returns 1. For example, given $a=/b/*/*/c/c/d$ and $s=/*/c/*/b/c$, the algorithm returns 0, since the matching rules fail to satisfy for $i=4$. As shown in Figure 3(b), the fifth row indicates that the advertisement includes an element *c* and the subscription includes an element *b* at the same position that do not intersect. That is publications matching the advertisement cannot match the subscription.

Relative simple XPEs: These expressions are similar to absolute simple XPEs except for the first operator, which cannot be a "/". That is the XPE is relative. The matching could start at any position of the advertisement because the subscription is relative. A naive matching algorithm for this case is repeatedly calling AbsExprAndAdv. In iteration *i*, the algorithm takes the subscription as an absolute one and starts the matching from the *i*-th position of the advertisement. We skip the details of the naive algorithm as it is straightforward.

The complexity of the naive algorithm is $O(n*k)$ where *n* is the length of the advertisement and *k* is the length of the subscription. We propose an optimized version of the matching algorithm for relative simple XPEs.

The matching algorithm for relative simple XPEs and advertisements (RelExprAndAdv) is a string matching problem (Knuth et al., 1977). We try to find the XPE, *s*, inside the advertisement, *a*, by starting at the first element of *a* that matches st_1 and continue (i.e., comparing to st_2 and so on) until we either complete the match or find a mismatch. In the latter case, we must go back to the place where we started. The difference between the traditional string matching problem and ours is that the wildcard "*" can match any element in our matching rules, as shown in Figure 3(b). To improve this algorithm, the KMP algorithm (Knuth et al., 1977) is applied to reduce the number of comparisons to $O(n)$. As shown in Figure 5, KMP computes a *next* table, recording all repeat-

Figure 5. Next Table for Subscription

Input: e subscription s
Output:*next* table for s (an array of size $|s|$)

1: *next*(1) = -1, *next*(2) = 0
2: **For** i=3:$|s|$ **do**
3: j = *next* (i−1)+1
4: **While** matching rules are not satisfied for st_{i-1} and st_j, and j>0 **do** j = *next* (j)+1
5: *next*(i) = j
6: **Return***next*

Figure 6. Optimized Matching

Input: advertisement a, and subscription s
Output:*matchPos* if $P(a) \cap P(s) \neq \varnothing$, 0 if $P(a) \cap P(s) = \varnothing$

1: **If** $|s|$>$|a|$ **then return** 0
2: j = 1, I = 1, *matchPos* = 0
3: **While***matchPos* = 0 and $i \leq |a|$ **do**
4: **If** matching rules are satisfied for at_i and st_j **then**j++, i++
5: **Else** j = *next* (j)+1, **if**j=0 **then** j = 1,i++
6: **If**j=k+1 **then***matchPos* = i - k
7: **Return***matchPos*

---

ing patterns of s, to avoid backtracking. Figure 6 performs the matching by taking advantage of the *next* table.

Descendant operators in XPEs: Descendant operators indicate that more than one element should appear in the matching advertisement. The matching algorithm for XPEs with descendant operators and advertisements (DesExprAndAdv) is based on the above XPE matching algorithms (i.e., AbsExprAndAdv and RelExprAndAdv). We split the XPE in maximal length sub-XPEs that do not contain any descendant operators, and match each sub-XPE against the advertisement with sequence comparison. As shown in Figure 7, lines 1-2 guarantee that the advertisement is

longer than the subscription. Next, we match s_1 against the advertisement according to the different types of s (lines 3-4), and, recompute the next available matching position in the advertisement (lines 5-6). k_i is the length of s_i. In the rest of this chapter, we use the same notation in other algorithms. The algorithm repeats this process until the end of the subscription is reached (lines 7-10), or returns 0 immediately if it finds the rest of the advertisement is shorter (lines 11-12). For instance, given a=/a/*/e/*/d/*/c/b and s=*/a//d/*/c//b, the algorithm matches all sub-XPEs in s against a in order. It returns 1 because it finds each sub-XPE */a, d/*/c and b matches different parts in a (e.g., a/*, */d/* and b).

Figure 7. DesExpr. and Adv. Matching

Input: advertisement a, and subscription $s=s_1//\ldots//s_p$
(s_1 is absolute or relative, and s_i, $2 \leq i \leq p$, is relative)
Output: 1 if $P(a) \cap P(s) \neq \varnothing$, 0 if $P(a) \cap P(s) = \varnothing$

01: **For** $i=1:p$ **do**
02: **If** $\left|s_1\right| + \ldots + \left|s_i\right| > |a|$ **then return** 0
03: **If** s is absolute **then** $temp = \text{AbsAdv}(a, /s_1)$
04: **Else** $temp = \text{RelAdv}(a, s_1)$
05: **If** $temp = 0$ **then return** 0
06: **Else** $j = k_l + temp$, $temp = 0$
07: **For** $i=2:p$ **do**
08: $temp = \text{RelAdv}(/t_j/\ldots/t_n, s_i)$
09: **If** $temp = 0$ **then return** 0
10: **Else** $j = j + k_i - 1 + temp$
11: **For** $l=i+1:p$ **do**
12: **If** $\left|s_{i+1}\right| + \ldots + \left|s_i\right| > n - j + 1$ **then return** 0
13: **Return** 1

Recursive Advertisement

We focus on the matching of absolute XPEs and recursive advertisements. The matching of other types of XPEs and recursive advertisements can be implemented based on this algorithm. In Figure 8, the matching algorithm for absolute XPEs and simple recursive advertisements (AbsExprAndSimRecAdv) calls AbsExprAndAdv if the subscription is not longer than the recursive pattern (Line 1). If the subscription is longer, the algorithm estimates the maximum number that the recursive pattern would be repeated in the advertisement according to the length of both subscription and advertisement (Lines 4-6). Next, the algorithm tries all possible advertisements according to the maximum number of repeated recursive patterns (Lines 7-12). For example, given $a=/a/*/c(/e/d)^+/*/c/e$ and $s=/*/a/c/*/d/e/d/*$, first, the algorithm compares $/a/*/c/e/d$ in a with $/*/a/c/*/d$ in s, and computes $q=0$ and $p=1$ in Lines 4-6. Second, it supposes that the recursive

pattern is repeated only once, compares $*/c/e$ in a with $e/d/*$ in s (Line 8) and fails to match. Next, it repeats the recursive part e/d twice, and continues the comparison (Line 11). Finally, it returns 1 (Line 9) if it finds a matches s with double recursive patterns in a. The complexity of the algorithm is $O(n^2)$, since it actually matches the subscription against each possible advertisement without recursive pattern. From a practical point of view, it is reasonable to limit the maximum nesting depth of items in a document, which would reduce the complexity of processing DTDs.

The matching algorithm for absolute XPE and series-recursive advertisements (AbsExprAndSerRecAdv), where $a=a_1(a_2)^+a_3(a_4)^+a_5$, is implemented by calling the algorithm from Figure 8 recursively as shown in Figure 9. The matching determines how many times the first recursive pattern could be repeated, and calls the algorithm from Figure 8 repeatedly to try all possible advertisement formats. The matching of XPE and embedded recursive advertisements

Figure 8. AbsExpr. & Simple RecAdv.

Input: advertisement $a=a_1(a_2)^+a_3$, and subscription s
(a_k, $1{\leq}k{\leq}3$, is an advertisement)
Output: 1 if $P(a) \cap P(s){\neq}\varnothing$, 0 if $P(a) \cap P(s)=\varnothing$

01: **If** $|s| \leq |a_1a_2|$ **then return** AbsAdv(a_1a_2, s)
02: **Else**$temp$ = AbsAdv(a_1a_2, $/st_1 / \ldots / st_{|a_1a_2|}$)
03: **If**$temp$ = 0 **then return** 0
04: **If** $|s| \leq |a_1a_2a_3|$ **then**$q = 0$
05: **Else**$q = Int((|s| - |a_1a_2a_3|)/|a_2|) + 1$
06: $p = Int((|s| - |a_1a_2|)/|a_2|) + 1$
07: **For**$c{=}q$:p**do**

08: $temp$ = AbsAdv(a_3, $/st_{c^*|a_2|+|a_1a_2|+1} / \ldots / st_{|s|}$)
09: **If**$temp$ =1 **then return** 1
10: **If**$c{=}p$**then**$temp$ = AbsAdv(a_2, $/st_{c^*|a_2|+|a_1a_2|+1} / \ldots / st_{|s|}$)

11: **Else**$temp$ = AbsAdv(a_2, $/st_{c^*|a_2|+|a_1a_2|+1} / \ldots / st_{(c+1)^*|a_2|+|a_1a_2|}$)
12: **If**$temp$ =0 **then return** 0
13: **Return** 1

(AbsExprAnd- EmbRecAdv) is similar to AbsExprAndSerRecAdv. Figure 10 describes that, first, it determines how many times the outer recursive pattern could be repeated, and calls AbsExprAndSerRecAdv (not restricted to two recursive patterns) repeatedly.

COVERING AND MERGING

In this section, first, we describe a novel data structure called *subscription tree* for maintaining subscriptions. The data structure captures the covering relations among subscriptions and speeds up the covering detection. Second, we present the covering algorithms for absolute simple XPEs, relative simple XPEs, and XPEs with descendant operators. Last, we explore the merging technique, and discuss the merging rules in the context of XPEs.

Subscription Tree

In covering-based routing, if an arriving subscription is covered by an existing subscription in the routing table, the new subscription is not forwarded to the next-hop broker. On the other hand, if the arriving subscription covers existing subscriptions, before it is forwarded, the broker needs to unsubscribe all the subscriptions that are covered by the new subscription. Therefore, the subscription traffic in the network is reduced by removing the redundant subscriptions and the routing table in the next-hop broker is compacted.

At each broker, subscriptions are maintained in a tree data structure. The idea is to store the subscriptions according to the covering relations among them. A subscription at a node in the tree covers all subscriptions in its subtree. Since a covering relation defines a partial order among subscriptions, a tree data structure cannot capture all the covering relations. A subscription node can

Figure 9. AbsExpr. & Series RecAdv. Matching

Input: advertisement $a=a_1(a_2)^+a_3(a_4)^+a_5$, and subscription s
Output: 1 if $P(a) \cap P(s) \neq \varnothing$, 0 if $P(a) \cap P(s) = \varnothing$

1: **If** $|s| \leq |a_1a_2|$ **then return** AbsAdv(a_1a_2, s)
2: **Else** $p = Int((|s| - |a_1a_2|) / |a_2|) + 1$
3: *temp* = 0
4: **For** c=0: p **do**
5: **If** *temp* = 1 **then return** 1
6: **Else** *temp* = SimRecAdv($a_1(a_2)^{c+1}a_3(a_4)^+a_5$, s)
7: **Return** *temp*

Figure 10. AbsExpr.& Embedded RecAdv.

Input: advertisement $a=a_1(a_2(a_3)^+a_4)^+a_5$, and subscription s
Output: 1 if $P(a) \cap P(s) \neq \varnothing$, 0 if $P(a) \cap P(s) = \varnothing$

1: **If** $|s| \leq |a_1a_2a_3a_4|$ **then return** SimRecAdv($a_1a_2(a_3)^+a_4$, s)
2: **Else** $p = Int((|s| - |a_1a_2a_3a_4|) / |a_2a_3a_4|) + 1$
3: *temp* = 0
4: **For** c=0: p **do**
5: **If** *temp* = 1 **then return** 1
6: **Else** *temp* = SerRecAdv($a_1(a_2(a_3)^+a_4)^{c+1}a_5$, s)
7: **Return** *temp*

---

have only one parent in the tree, but it may be covered by several subscriptions. We allow each node having a set of *super pointers*, which indicate the covering relations with nodes outside its subtree, as shown in Fig 11. *Super pointers* are shortcuts to subscriptions that the node covers. The tree and the super pointers form a directed acyclic graph (DAG) capturing the covering relations among subscriptions. With super pointers, a node covers its subtree, the nodes with subtrees pointed to by its super pointers, and the nodes with subtrees pointed to by its offsprings' super pointers.

The tree is maintained as follows. When a new subscription arrives, a breadth first search traverses the tree in order to find a place to insert the subscription. At a given node the following three cases are distinguished.

Case 1: If the new subscription has no covering relation with the node, the node's siblings are searched. If neither sibling has a covering relation with the new subscription, the subscription is inserted as new sibling, After insertion, super pointers maintained by the parent node are updated. If there is a super pointer of the parent pointing to a subscription that is also covered by the new subscription, then the super pointer is moved from the parent node to the new node.

Case 2: If the new subscription covers the current node, the new subscription is inserted between the current node and its parent. As a

Figure 11. Subscription Tree

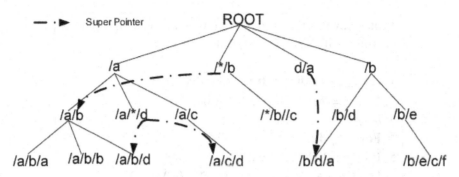

result, the new subscription becomes the parent of the current node, the old parent becomes the new subscription's parent. The old parent's super pointers are updated and moved to the new node, if there is a covering relation between the inserted subscription and a subscription pointed to by the super pointer.

Case 3: If the new subscription is covered by the current node, its children are searched until the new subscription is inserted. If the current node is a leaf node, the new node is inserted as the current node's child.

Existing super pointers are maintained while inserting. The new subscription may cause new covering relations and new super pointers to be added. Every time a new subscription arrives, we add new super pointers into existing nodes that cover the new subscription while searching the tree. However, this becomes expensive when the subscription tree grows larger. The reason we maintain the updated super pointers is for covering-based routing. When a subscription arrives, if it is not covered by existing subscriptions but it covers a set of subscriptions, we need to unsubscribe the subscriptions it covers and only forward the new subscription to neighbors. In this case, we need the super pointers to tell us what subscriptions should be unsubscribed. That means the updating of super pointers can be postponed to that point. The search space is reduced by super pointers. Note that we only need to unsubscribe subscriptions

in the higher level of the tree since nodes in the subtrees are covered and unsubscribed already.

In the worst case, it takes $O(n)$ to identify the covering relations and insert a subscription to the subscription tree. For example, a subscription is covered by all subscriptions which are organized in one path. If the subscription tree created from a subscription workload is balanced, the best case run time is $O(log(n))$, which is the height of the tree.

Optimizations for the subscription searching and insertion can be performed based on the following two properties of the subscription tree.

Property of an Absolute XPE node: For all the absolute simple XPEs which have no wildcard and //-operators, the children's path length is always longer than their parent's path length. The parent is the prefix of its children.

Based on this property, we can perform depth-first search for an XPE to find a start node which has the same length as itself and start breadth-first search at that level. If an absolute XPE has a wildcard or //-operator in the middle of the expression, it is one or more levels higher than other simple XPEs of the same length in the subscription tree. Based on this property we can stop the search earlier.

Property of a Relative XPE node: A relative XPE is a child node of either the root node or another relative node. It will never be inserted in a subtree rooted by an absolute XPE. This property reduces the search space in the subscription tree.

Figure 12. Absolute Simple XPEs Covering

Input: two subscriptions s_1 and s_2
Output: 1 if s_1 covers s_2, 0 if s_1 does not cover s_2

1: **If** $|s_2| < |s_1|$ **then return** 0
2: **For** $i = 1 : |s_1|$ **do**
3: **If** covering rules are not satisfied for $s_1 t_i$ and $s_2 t_i$ **then return** 0
4: **Return** 1

Covering Algorithm

The key problem is how to determine the relationship between two given subscriptions. The covering relation between subscriptions is the containment problem in the context of XPEs. It has been proven that containment of simple path expressions can be tested in PTIME (Milo & Suciu, 1999). It is studied as a part of the problem that checking/finding a prefix replacement for a simple query is in PTIME. In this section, we detect covering relations of XPEs containing wildcard, /- and //-operator in PTIME, and present covering rules and algorithms for determining covering relations between single path XPEs. We say Sub_1 containing an element t_i covers Sub_2 containing an element m_i at the corresponding position, if t_i is a wildcard no matter what m_i is, or $t_i = m_i$, where none of t_i and m_i is a wildcard.

Absolute simple XPEs: The covering relation between two absolute XPEs (without //-operator) is the simplest case. We describe the covering algorithm for two absolute XPEs (AbsSimCov) (e.g., s_1 and s_2) in Figure 12. An important observation is that s_1 must be shorter than s_2 if s_1 covers s_2. This is exploited because a shorter XPE s has less constraints on items in an XML document, and refers to a bigger matching set $P(s)$. Next, the algorithm compares each pair of $s_1 t_i$ and $s_2 t_i$ in s_1 and s_2, respectively, according to the covering rules.

Relative simple XPEs: Figure 13 shows the covering algorithm for relative simple XPEs

(RelSimCov), e.g., s_1 is relative, and s_2 is absolute or relative, calls AbsSimCov repeatedly to determine if s_1 contains subscription s_2 or not. An absolute XPE s_1 cannot cover a relative XPE s_2, as the absolute XPE definitely refers to a smaller matching set $P(s_1)$ than $P(s_2)$.

It is important to note that the covering algorithm RelSimCov is also a string matching problem, as we pointed out in the RelExprAndAdv algorithm. The covering algorithm uses covering rules that are different from subscription and advertisement matching rules used in RelExprAndAdv, however, a similar optimization can be applied to reduce the complexity of the covering algorithm from $O(k*n)$ to $O(k)$.

Descendant operators in XPEs: Figure 14 describes the covering algorithm for XPEs with descendant operators (DesCov), where both s_1 and s_2 can be relative or absolute. It splits the XPE into sub-XPEs without //-operator, and matches each sub-XPE in s_1 against sub-XPEs in s_2 with sequence comparisons. First, it guarantees that s_2 is longer than s_1. Next, it matches the first sub-XPE in s_1 against s_2 according to different types of s_1 and s_2. The algorithm moves to the next sub-XPE in s_1 if it finds a match, and moves to the next sub-XPE in s_2 if it does not find a match. For example, given $s_1 = /*/a//*/c$ and $s_2 = /a/a/*//c/e/c/d$, first, the algorithm compares the sub-XPE $/*/a$ in s_1 with the sub-XPE $/a/a/*$ in s_2. Second, it moves to the next sub-XPE $*/c$ in s_1 and compares it with $*$ in s_2. Next, it compares $*/c$ in s_1 with the next sub-XPE $c/e/c/d$ in s_2, and finally, it returns *true* since the end of s_1 is reached and a match is found. Generally speaking, a sub-XPE in s_1 could not match a part of s_2 that includes a //-operator. For instance, given $s_1=/*/a//*/c$ and $s_2=/a/a/*//c/b/d$, the sub-XPE $*/c$ in s_1 does not cover $*//c$ in s_2 since $*/c$ refers to a smaller matching set. However, there is a special case that the sub-XPE s_{1i} in s_1 could cover a part of s_2 that includes a //-operator if s_{1i} ended with a wildcard and the matched part in s_2 ended with $//t$, where t can be either a wildcard or an element. For example, given $s_1=/a/*//*/d$ and $s_2=/a//b/c/d$, first, the algorithm compares $/a/*$ in s_1 with $/a//b$ in s_2, where *flag*=1 is used to record the current sub-XPE in s_1 matches a part of s_2 with //-operator. Second, it moves to the next sub-XPE $*/d$ in s_1 and compares it with c/d in s_2. Finally, it returns *true* since a match is found.

It is important to note that the covering detection between non-recursive advertisements is the same with the covering detection for subscriptions, since the non-recursive advertisement has the same format with an absolute simple subscription.

Merging

If there is no covering relation among a set of subscriptions, subscriptions can be merged into a new subscription to create a more concise routing table. In this section, we exploit the merging rules for XPEs.

In the subscription tree, child nodes of the same parent have a better chance to be merged. As shown in Fig 15, node $/a/b/a$, $/a/b/b$ and $/a/b/d$ can be merged and they are represented by a new node $/a/b/*$ which is a union of the original XPEs. There was a super pointer pointing to node $/a/b/d$ before merging. This pointer should be removed because there is no covering relation between the pointer owner and the merger. If two nodes are merged, their subtrees become siblings of the merger. For example in Fig 15, after $/b/d$ and $/b/e$ are merged to $/b/*$, their children are the new node's children. The super pointer at $/b/d/a$ is not

changed. To perform the merging in the subscription tree, we define several merging rules.

The subscriptions can be merged if they have only one difference (e.g., different elements). For instance, two subscriptions $s_1=a/*/c/d$ and $s_2=a/*/c/e$ can be merged into $s=a/*/c/*$. Note that if they differ in one operator, they should be in a covering relation to each other. The general form of this rule is:

- $s_1=o_1t_1... o_i t_1 o_{i+1} \mathbf{m} o_{i+2} t_{i+1} ... o_{n+1} t_n$
- $s_2=o_1t_1... o_i t_1 o_{i+1} \mathbf{k} o_{i+2} t_{i+1} ... o_{n+1} t_n$

are merged to

- $s=o_1t_1... o_i t_1 o_{i+1} * o_{i+2} t_{i+1} ... o_{n+1} t_n$

where m and k are different elements, o_i is either a /-operator or a //-operator, and t_i is a wildcard or an element. The number of merging candidates in this rule is not limited to 2.

Another rule is to merge subscriptions with two differences (e.g., different operators or different elements). For example, two subscriptions $s_1=/a/c/*/*$ and $s_2=/a//c/*/c$ that do not cover each other can be merged to $s=/a//c/*/*$. That is, different operators are merged to //-operator, and different elements are merged to *. We represent the general form of this rule as:

- $s_1=o_1t_1... o_i t_1 o_{i+1} m ... o_{j+1} t_j / t_{j+1} ... o_{n+2} t_n$
- $s_2=o_1t_1... o_i t_1 o_{i+1} k ... o_{j+1} t_j // t_{j+1} ... o_{n+2} t_n$

are merged to

- $s=o_1t_1... o_i t_1 o_{i+1} * ... o_{j+1} t_j // t_{j+1} ... o_{n+2} t_n$

where m, k and t_i is a wildcard or an element, and o_i is a /-operator or a //-operator.

A more general rule is to replace the different parts in two subscriptions with the //-operator. We generalize this rule to:

- $s_1=o_1t_1... o_i t_1 XPE_1 o_{i+1} t_{i+1} ... o_n t_n$

Figure 13. Relative Simple XPEs Covering

Input: two subscriptions s_1 and s_2 (s_1 is relative, s_2 is absolute or relative)
Output: *matchPos* if s_1 covers s_2, 0 if s_1 does not cover s_2

1: **If** $|s_2| < |s_1|$ **then return** 0
2: **For** $i = 1 : |s_2| - |s_1| + 1$ **do**
3: **If** $\text{AbsCov}(/s_1, /s_2 t_i / \ldots / s_2 t_{|s_2|}) = 1$ **then return** *matchPos*$=i$
4: **Return** 0

Figure 14. Descendant XPEs Covering

Input: two subscriptions $s_1 = s_{11} // \ldots // s_{1q}$, and $s_2 = s_{21} // \ldots // s_{2p}$
(both s_1 and s_2 can be relative or absolute subscription)
Output: 1 if s_1 covers s_2, 0 if s_1 does not cover s_2

01: **If** $|s_1| > |s_2|$ **then return** 0
02: **If** both s_1 and s_2 are absolute **then** *temp* = AbsCov(s_{11}, s_{21}), *flag* = 0
03: **If** *temp* = 0, and $|s_{11}| = |s_{21}|$, and s_{11} ends with *, and $p \geq 2$ **then** *temp* =
   AbsCov($s_{11} t_1 / \ldots / s_{11} t_{|s_{11}|-1}, s_{21}$), *flag* = 1
04: **If** *temp* = 0 **then return** 0
05: **Else if** s_1 is relative **then** *temp* = RelCov(s_{11}, s_{21}), *flag* = 0
06: **If** *temp* = 0, and $|s_{21}| \overset{3}{} |s_{11}|$, and s_{11} ends with *, and $p \geq 2$ **then** *temp* =
   RelCov($s_{11} t_1 / \ldots / s_{11} t_{|s_{11}|-1}, s_{21} t_{|s_{21}|-|s_{11}|+2} / \ldots / s_{21} t_{|s_{21}|}$), *flag* $\neg$ 1
07: **Else return** 0
08: $i = 1, j = 1, temp_m = 0, temp_1 = 0$
09: **While** $i \leq q$ and $j \leq p$ **do**
10: **If** *temp* = 0 **then** $j = j + 1, temp_m = 0$
11: **If** $j \neq p+1$ **then** *temp* = RelCov($s_{1i}, s_{2j} t_{1+temp_1} / \ldots / s_{2j} t_{|s_{2j}|}$), *flag* = 0
12: **If** *temp* = 0, and $|s_{2j}| \overset{3}{} |s_{1i}| + temp_1$, and s_{1i} ends with *, and $p \geq j$ **then** *temp* =
   RelCov($s_{1i} t_1 / \ldots / s_{1i} t_{|s_{1i}|-1}, s_{2j} t_{|s_{2j}|-|s_{1i}|+2} / \ldots / s_{2j} t_{|s_{2j}|}$), *flag* = 1
13: $temp_1 = 0$
14: **Else return** 0
15: **Else** $temp_m = temp + temp_m + |s_{1i}| - 1, i++$
16: **If** $i \neq q+1$ and *flag*=0 **then** *temp* = RelCov($s_{1i}, s_{2j} t_{1+temp_m} / \ldots / s_{2j} t_{|s_{2j}|}$), *flag* = 0
17: **If** *temp* = 0, and $|s_{2j}| \overset{3}{} |s_{1i}| + temp_m$, and s_{1i} ends with *, and $p \geq j$ **then** *temp* =
   RelCov($s_{1i} t_1 / \ldots / s_{1i} t_{|s_{1i}|-1}, s_{2j} t_{|s_{2j}|-|s_i|+2} / \ldots / s_{2j} t_{|s_{2j}|}$), *flag* = 1
18: **Else if** $i \neq q+1$ and *flag*=1 **then** *temp* = 0, $temp_1 = 1$
19: **Else return** 1

Figure 15. Subscription Tree

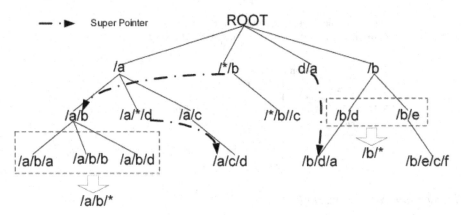

- $s_2 = o_1 t_1 \ldots o_i t_i XPE_2 o_{i+1} t_{i+1} \ldots o_n t_n$

are merged to

- $s = o_1 t_1 \ldots o_i t_i // t_{i+1} \ldots o_n t_n$

where XPE_1 and XPE_2 are different XPath expressions, t_i is a wildcard or an element, and o_i is a /-operator or a //-operator. This rule is applied if most parts in two subscriptions are equal, otherwise, more false positives will be introduced.

We periodically apply the above merging rules on the subscription tree to aggregate nodes that could be merged. We can compute an *imperfect merging degree* if each broker in the network knows the DTD relative to the XML data producer. An imperfect merger was first introduced in (Li et al., 2005). The imperfect degree of a new merger s, derived from $s_1, s_2, \ldots, s_n$, is:

$$D_{imperfect} = \frac{|P(s) - \cup_{i=1}^{n} P(S_i)|}{|P(s)|}$$

It measures the imperfectness of an individual new merger. If the publications are distributed uniformly, the bigger the imperfect degree, the more false positive are introduced by the new merger. For example, two subscriptions $s_1 = /a/*/c/d$ and $s_2 = /a/*/c/e$ can be merged into $s = /a/*/c/*$. If the

corresponding DTD indicates that the elements a, b, c, d, e are allowed at the fourth position, 60% false positive will be introduced at position 4. We need to consider the distribution of other elements in the subscription, e.g., the probability of each element appearing at other positions, to compute the total number of false positive introduced. Based on the DTD information, if $D_{imperfect}$ is 0, the merger is a perfect merger, and no false positives are introduced in this case. The false positives are not delivered to subscribers. They only occur in the network introduced due to imperfect merging. Clients are not exposed to false positives.

EVALUATION

In this section, we experimentally evaluate the performance of our routing and covering algorithms. All algorithms are implemented in C++. We perform all experiments on a local cluster of 20 nodes and on PlanetLab. Each node in the cluster has an Intel Xeon 2.4GHz processor with 2GB RAM. For generating the XPE workload, we use the XPath generator released by Diao *et al.* (Diao et al., 2003). Queries are distinct, and we set the maximum length of an XPE to 10. We use the IBM XML Generator (Diaz & Lovell, 2003) to create the XML document workload. We use default parameters in this generator except that we

Figure 16. RTS

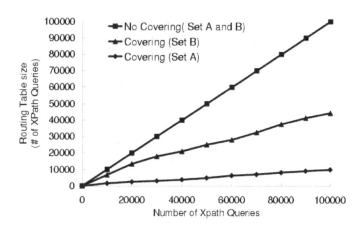

set the maximum number of levels of the resulting XML documents to 10, which is consistent with the maximum length of XPEs. We use two different DTDs: the NITF (News Industry Text Format) DTD (NITF, 2005) and the PSD (Protein Sequence Database) DTD (PSD, 2005). The performance metrics we measure include routing table size, XPE processing time and publication routing time in a single broker. We compare the network traffic (i.e., number of messages) and notification delay (i.e., the time between issuing a publication and receiving a notification) in two broker topologies with 7 brokers and 127 brokers, respectively. We also deployed our system on PlanetLab (PlanetLab, 2006) and measured the notification delay to validate the scalability of our approach.

Routing Table Size (RTS): Our algorithms exploit the covering relations among XPEs. We generate two data sets for NITF which include 100,000 XPEs each. We vary the probability of "*" occurring at a location step (W) and the probability of "//" occurring at a location step (DO) to generate two data sets A and B with different covering rates 90% and 50%, respectively. The covering rate indicates the similarity of subscriptions, that is, how many subscriptions are redundant and can be removed from the subscription set to create a compact routing table. For each data set, we

evaluate the effect of the covering optimization on routing table size. The routing table size is the number of XPEs in the table. As shown in Figure 16, for Set A, the routing table size is reduced dramatically by covering. The subscriptions in Set A have a higher degree of overlap. The results suggest that the covering algorithm performs better on data sets with higher degree of overlap. That is, the covering technique achieves more benefit when subscribers have similar interests.

Merging can further reduce the routing table size by merging some XPEs according to our merging rules. When $D_{imperfect}$ is 0, the merger is a perfect merger. Figure 1.17 shows that applying perfect merging reduces the routing table size to 87%. When $D_{imperfect}$ increases, more XPEs can be merged. For instance, the routing table is compacted to 67% with $D_{imperfect}$ equal to 0.1.

XPE Processing Time: We measure the XPE processing time of the covering algorithm. In covering-based routing, we first check the covering relationship when an XPE arrives at a broker. If the XPE is covered by existing XPEs, it will not be forwarded. Otherwise, we match the XPE against all advertisements and determine where to route it to. Without a covering algorithm, every XPE needs to be matched against all advertisements in order to be forwarded. We issue 5000 XPEs, and Figure 18 shows the processing time per XPE. Each data

Figure 17. RTS

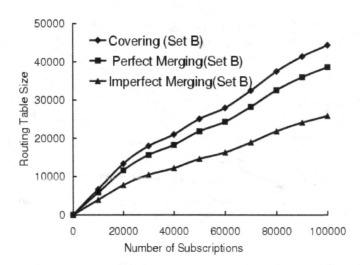

point in Figure 18 is the average processing time for 500 XPEs. Although detecting covering relations takes extra time, the experiment shows that the XPE processing time is less in covering-based routing, which avoids matching the covered XPEs against advertisements. For example, among the 5000 PSD XPEs, 90% of the XPEs are covered. The more XPEs are covered, the greater the improvement we achieve. Covering-based routing improves the XPE processing time of NITF XPEs by up to 49.2%, which is more than for the PSD XPEs. The reason is because the number of advertisements generated from the NITF DTD is 35 times larger than that of the PSD DTD. As a result, we benefit more from avoiding advertisement matching, especially when the broker has a large number of advertisements.

Publication Routing Time: In this experiment, we evaluate the covering-based routing time of each message using data sets *A* and *B*. Note that the performance of non-covering-based routing in the original system has been evaluated against YFilter (Diao et al., 2003) in our previous work (Hou & Jacobsen, 2006). For some scenarios (i.e., the XPE workload with a high percentage of matched expressions, and with many wildcards and descendant operators), our system outperformed YFilter. For a contrasting workload with a very

low matching percentage, YFilter outperformed us. We generate 500 XML documents and extract 23,098 publications from these documents. Table 1 shows the routing time of the publications against 100,000 XPEs. The measurements are obtained by averaging the time taken to route all publications. Both Set *A* and Set *B* exhibit benefits, derived from subscription covering. After applying the covering algorithm, the routing time for Set *A* and Set *B* are reduced by 84.6% and 47.5%, respectively. The merging technique generates a more compact routing table, with which we can further improve the publication routing time.

Network Traffic: The network traffic can be influenced by the broker topology, the distribution of subscribers and publishers, and the routing strategy. In this experiment, we investigate the impact of advertisement-based routing and covering techniques on network traffic, given a tree-like broker topology. The broker overlay network is a tree in which each broker is connected to 2 subordinate brokers. We build two overlays for the experiment. One has three levels, which consists of 7 brokers. The other broker overlay has seven levels with 64 leaf brokers, and 127 brokers in total. Each leaf broker is connected with a subscriber. We extend the size of the broker network

Figure 18. XPE Process Time

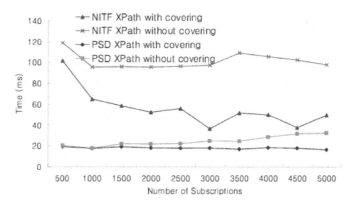

Table 1. Publication Routing Performance

Method	Set A (ms)	Set B (ms)
No Covering	13.96	14.23
Covering	2.15	7.47
Perfect Merging	1.87	6.88
Imperfect Merging	1.27	6.38

to show the scalability of our approach. Publishers randomly connect to the broker overlay.

In this experiment, we compare routing strategies with different optimization techniques, including the routing with neither advertisement nor covering technique (no-Adv-no-Cov), the routing with covering only (no-Adv-with-Cov), the routing with advertisement only (with-Adv-no-Cov), the routing with both advertisement and covering techniques (with-Adv-with-Cov), the routing with advertisement, covering and perfect merging (with-Adv-with-CovPM), and the routing with advertisement, covering and imperfect merging (with-Adv-with-CovIPM). We generate 1,000 distinct XPEs for each subscriber using the PSD DTD, and 50 XML documents for the publishers. 4,182 publications are extracted from these documents. Table 2 and Table 3 show the total number of messages in the two broker overlays generated by one publisher. These messages, including advertisements, publications

and subscriptions, are received by all brokers in the network under different routing strategies. As can be seen, the two advertisement-based routing methods significantly reduce the network traffic, because in this case a subscription is not flooded, and it is only forwarded to brokers that are on a path from the subscriber to potential publishers. The introduction of advertisements reduces the network traffic to 68.5% and 75.6% for non-covering-based and covering-based routing strategies, respectively. Moreover, applying both advertisement-based routing and covering-based routing techniques can reduce the overall network traffic to 66.2% and 49.9% in the two topologies. The experiment suggests that using advertisements to avoid subscription flooding and removing redundant queries by exploring covering and merging relations among subscriptions can reduce network traffic, save system resources and reduce the publication routing delay. Note that since imperfect merging may introduce false positives, the network traffic due to imperfect merging increases by 1.38% and by 1.04% in the two overlays, respectively. Overall, we achieve more benefit in a larger broker network. The scalability of the system is improved.

False Positives from Imperfect Merging: If the system allows a larger error tolerance, more subscriptions can be merged. An imperfect merger may match more publications than

Table 2. 7 Broker Network

Method	Network Traffic	Delay (ms)
no–Adv–no–Cov	58,138	29.02
no–Adv–with–Cov	50,931	7.50
with–Adv–no–Cov	39,849	28.9
with–Adv–with–Cov	38,492	7.45
with–Adv–with–CovPM	25,789	5.15
with–Adv–with–CovIPM	26,146	3.92

Table 3. 127 Broker Network

Method	Network Traffic	Delay (ms)
no–Adv–no–Cov	654,871	97.82
no–Adv–with–Cov	572,890	20.74
with–Adv–no–Cov	398,810	98.09
with–Adv–with–Cov	326,796	20.89
ith–Adv–with–CovPM	254,900	16.78
with–Adv–with–CovIPM	257,567	12.24

Figure 19. False Positives

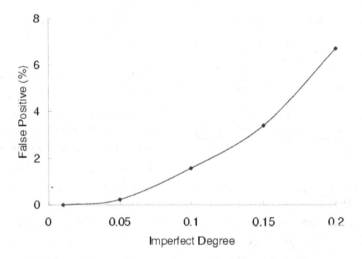

expected. Therefore, a larger $D_{imperfect}$ means that the system allows more false positives. We show the relation between $D_{imperfect}$ and false positives in Figure 1.19. The larger $D_{imperfect}$ is, the greater the number of matched publications, among which some are false positives introduced by imperfect mergers. If the system tolerates up to 2% of false positives, a $D_{imperfect}$ with value less than 0.1 can satisfy the requirement. False positives only occur in the network and are not delivered to clients. Thus, they induce overhead but do not violate the subscription semantic expected by clients.

Notification Delay on PlanetLab: In this experiment, we measure the notification delay on PlanetLab and demonstrate the scalability of our system. Due to the performance variation

on PlanetLab nodes, which in our experiment is up to 15% per data point, we average the results from four experimental runs, as shown in Figure 20 and Figure 21. We setup a broker network with the maximum end-to-end distance equal to 7 hops. We measure the notification delay from publishers to subscribers for different number of broker hops and different XML document sizes. The experiment shows that the notification delay in covering-based routing is reduced by up to 74% compared with the routing without covering for both NITF and PSD documents. Moreover, the notification delay is linear in the number of hops. In covering-based routing, it increases less with the number of hops than in the content-based routing without covering. The reason is that the routing

Figure 20. PSD XML

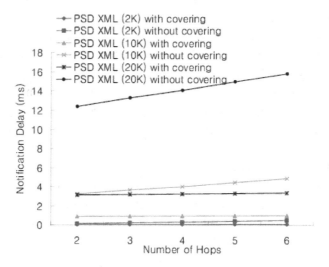

Figure 21. NITF XML

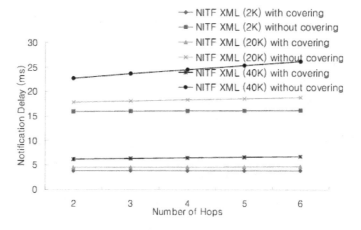

table size along the routing path has been reduced by the covering technique, as a result, the XML document matching time at each hop decreases, for instance, the routing table size is reduced to 6% for PSD XPEs. The result also indicates that the larger the document the longer the notification delay. A larger document saves more matching time with a condensed routing table. Therefore, the larger the document, the greater the improvement in routing delay we can achieve from the covering technique.

CONCLUSION

In this chapter, we studied the problem of efficiently routing XML data through a data dissemination network comprised of an overlay network of content-based routers. In the dissemination network, publishers' DTD files are transformed into advertisements expressed using XPath-like expressions. An advertisement creates a spanning tree rooted at the publisher. Subscribers specify XPath filters which are forwarded along the reverse paths of this tree for *intersecting* advertisements. XML documents from publishers are forwarded along these routing paths to subscribers with *matching* XPEs. By defining and exploiting covering and merging relations for XPEs, a compact routing table results. Our techniques improve the routing time at each broker by up to 85% in the most favorable cases. Our experiments demonstrate that the scalability of the system is improved by applying advertisement-based routing, covering, and merging techniques for routing XML documents in a data dissemination network.

There are several directions for future work that will contribute to the more wide-spread adoption of XML dissemination networks. While the text-based nature of XML has clear advantages, it comes at a cost, which may counteract its continued proliferation in many application domains. For example, in many finance applications, processing speeds are critically important. This opens up several venues for future work. A binary XML representation standard may help reduce processing, if the matching and routing algorithms can adequately take advantage of this representation without repeated pre-processing. Also, a compressed representation combined with matching and routing that can operate on the compressed data could help reduce processing. In addition, hardware-software co-designs that allocate compute-intensive loops to hardware blocks can help speed up processing. The adaptation of existing algorithms and the development of new algorithms in this operation context constitute important avenues for future work. Questions that are simple to answer in software, such as how to support dynamic subscription expression updates, become much more challenging under the constraints imposed by hardware-based solutions. Moreover, the future development of applications that exploit the content-based publish/subscribe model described in this chapter will help to understand how to best use the model described in this chapter.

ACKNOWLEDGMENT

This research project was sponsored by CA, Inc., Sun Microsystems, the Ontario Centers of Excellence, the Canada Foundation for Innovation, the Ontario Innovation Trust, the Ontario Early Researcher Award, and the Natural Sciences and Engineering Research Council of Canada. The completion of the research described in this chapter was also made possible in part thanks to the support through Bell Canada's Bell University Laboratories R&D program, the IBM's Center for Advanced Studies and various IBM Faculty Awards.

REFERENCES

Altinel, M., & Franklin, M. J. (2000). Efficient filtering of XML documents for selective dissemination of information. In *Proceedings of the 26th International Conference on Very Large Data Bases (VLDB'00)*, (pp. 53–64), San Francisco, CA.

Amer-Yahia, S., Cho, S., Lakshmanan, L. V. S., & Srivastava, D. (2002). Tree pattern query minimization. *The VLDB Journal*, *11*(4), 315–331. doi:10.1007/s00778-002-0076-7

Bruno, N., Gravano, L., & Doudas, N. (2003). Navigation-vs. index-based XML multi-query processing. In *Proceedings of the 19nd International Conference on Data Engineering (ICDE'03)*, (pp. 139–150), Washington, DC.

Carzaniga, A., Rutherford, M. J., & Wolf, A. L. (2004). A routing scheme for content-based networking. In *Proceedings of IEEE Conference on Computer Communications (INFOCOM'04)*, Hong Kong, China.

Chan, C.-Y., Fan, W., Felber, P., Garofalakis, M., & Rastogi, R. (2002a). Tree pattern aggregation for scalable XML data dissemination. In *Proceedings of the 28th international conference on Very Large Data Bases (VLDB'02)*, (pp. 826–837), Hong Kong, China.

Chan, C.-Y., Felber, P., Garofalakis, M., & Rastogi, R. (2002b). Efficient filtering of xml documents with xpath expressions. *The VLDB Journal, 11*(4), 354–379. doi:10.1007/s00778-002-0077-6

Chand, R., & Felber, P. (2003). A scalable protocol for contentbased routing in overlay networks. In *Technical Report RR-03-074, Institut EURECOM, Feb.*

Chau, T., Muthusamy, V., Jacobsen, H. A., Litani, E., Chan, A., & Coulthard, P. (2008). Automating SLA modeling. In *Proceedings of the 2008 conference of the Centre for Advanced Studies on Collaborative Research*, Richmond Hill, Ontario, Canada.

Cheung, A., & Jacobsen, H.-A. (2008). Efficient Load Distribution in Publish/Subscribe. Technical report, Middleware Systems Research Group, University of Toronto.

Cheung, A. K., & Jacobsen, H.-A. (2006). Dynamic load balancing in distributed content-based publish/subscribe. In *Proceedings of the ACM/IFIP/USENIX 2006 International Conference on Middleware (Middleware'06)*, (pp. 141–161), New York.

Cugola, G., Nitto, E. D., & Fuggetta, A. (2001). The JEDI event-based infrastructure and its application to the development of the OPSS WFMS. *IEEE Transactions on Software Engineering, 27*(9), 827–850. doi:10.1109/32.950318

Diao, Y., Altinel, M., & Franklin, M. J. (2003). Path sharing and predicate evaluation for high-performance XML filtering. *ACM Transactions on Database Systems, 28*(4), 467–516. doi:10.1145/958942.958947

Diao, Y., Rizvi, S., & Franklin, M. J. (2004). Towards an internet-scale XML dissemination service. In *Proceedings of the Thirtieth international conference on Very large data bases (VLDB'04)*, (pp. 612–623), Toronto, Canada.

Diaz, A. L., & Lovell, D. (2003). *XML generator*. Retrieved from http://www.alphaworks.ibm.com/tech/xmlgenerator

Dong, X., Halevy, A., & Tatarinov, I. (2003). *Containment of nested XML queries*. Tech. Rep. UW-CSE-03-12-05, University of Washington.

Fenner, W., Rabinovich, M., Ramakrishnan, K. K., Srivastava, D., & Zhang, Y. (2005). XTreeNet: Scalable overlay networks for XML content dissemination and querying (synopsis). In *Proceedings of the 10th International Workshop on Web Content Catching and Distribution*, French Riviera, France.

Fidler, E., Jacobsen, H.-A., Li, G., & Mankovski, S. (2005). The PADRES distributed publish/subscribe system. In *International Conference on Feature Interactions in Telecommunications and Software Systems (ICFI'05)*, (pp. 12–30), Leicester, UK.

Galanis, L., Wang, Y., Jeffery, S. R., & DeWitt, D. J. (2003). Locating data sources in large distributed systems. In *Proceedings of the 29th international conference on Very Large Data Bases (VLDB'03)*, (pp. 874–885), Berlin, Germany.

Green, T. J., Gupta, A., Miklau, G., Onizuka, M., & Suciu, D. (2004). Processing XML streams with deterministic automata and stream indexes. *ACM Transactions on Database Systems, 29*(4), 752–788. doi:10.1145/1042046.1042051

Hou, S., & Jacobsen, H.-A. (2006). Predicate-based filtering of XPath expressions. In *Proceedings of the 22nd International Conference on Data Engineering (ICDE'06)*, (p. 53), Washington, DC.

Hu, S., Muthusamy, V., Li, G., & Jacobsen, H.-A. (2008). Distributed Automatic Service Composition in Large-Scale Systems. In *Proceedings of the second international conference on Distributed event-based systems* (pp 233-244), ACM: New York.

Jacobsen, H.-A. (2006). *The PADRES content-based publish/subscribe system web site*. Retrieved http://padres.msrg.toronto.edu/Padres/

Knuth, D. E., Morris, J. H., & Pratt, V. R. (1977). Fast pattern matching in strings. *SIAM Journal on Computing, 6*(2), 323–350. doi:10.1137/0206024

Koloniari, G., & Pitoura, E. (2004). Content-based routing of path queries in peer-to-peer systems. In *Proceedings of the 7th International Conference on Extending Database Technology (EDBT'04)*, (pp. 29–47).

Koudas, N., Rabinovich, M., Srivastava, D., & Yu, T. (2004). Routing xml queries. In *Proceedings of the 20th International Conference on Data Engineering (ICDE'04)*, (p. 844), Washington, DC.

Kwon, J., Rao, P., Moon, B., & Lee, S. (2005). Fist: Scalable xml document filtering by sequencing twig patterns. In *Proceedings of the 31rd international conference on Very large data bases (VLDB'05)*, (pp. 217–228), Trondheim, Norway.

Li, G., Cheung, A., Hou, S., Hu, S., Muthusamy, V., Sherafat, R., et al. (2007a). Historic data access in publish/subscribe. In *Proceedings of the 2007 inaugural international conference on Distributed event-based systems* (pp 80-84), Toronto, Ontario, Canada.

Li, G., Hou, S., & Jacobsen, H.-A. (2005). A unified approach to routing, covering and merging in publish/subscribe systems based on modified binary decision diagrams. In *Proceedings of the 25th International Conference on Distributed Computing Systems (ICDCS'05)*, (pp. 447–457), Columbus, OH.

Li, G., Hou, S., & Jacobsen, H.-A. (2008a). Routing of XML and XPath queries in data dissemination networks. In *Proceedings of The 28th International Conference on Distributed Computing Systems (ICDCS'08)*, (pp. 627–638), Washington, DC.

Li, G., & Jacobsen, H.-A. (2005). Composite subscriptions in content-based publish/subscribe systems. In *ACM/IFIP/USENIX, 6th International Middleware Conference (Middleware'05)*, (pp. 249–269), Grenoble, France.

Li, G., Muthusamy, V. & Jacobsen, H-A. (2007b). *NIÑOS: A Distributed Service Oriented Architecture for Business Process Execution*. The Journal of ACM Transactions on Computational Logics, 4(1), Article 2, Jan 2010.

Li, G., Muthusamy, V., & Jacobsen, H.-A. (2008b). Adpative content-based routing in general overlay topologies. In *Proceedings of the 9th ACM/IFIP/USENIX International Middleware Conference* (pp 249-269). Berlin: Springer.

Li, G., Muthusamy, V., & Jacobsen, H.-A. (2008c). Subscribing to the past in content-based publish/subscribe. Technical report, Middleware Systems Research Group, University of Toronto.

Liu, H., & Jacobsen, H.-A. (2002). A-ToPSS: A Publish/Subscribe System Supporting Approximate Matching. In *Proceedings of 28th International Conference on Very Large Data Bases* (pp 1107-1110), Hong Kong, China.

Liu, H., & Jacobsen, H.-A. (2004). Modeling uncertainties in publish/subscribe systems. In *Proceedings of the 20th International conference on Data Engineering* (pp 510-522), Boston.

Liu, H., Muthusamy, V., & Jacobsen, H.-A. (2009). Predictive Publish/Subscribe Matching. Technical report, Middleware Systems Research Group, University of Toronto.

Miklau, G., & Suciu, D. (2004). Containment and equivalence for a fragment of XPath. *Journal of the ACM, 51*(1), 2–45. doi:10.1145/962446.962448

Milo, T., & Suciu, D. (1999). Index structures for path expressions. In *Proceedings of the 7th International Conference on Database Theory (ICDT'99)*, (pp. 277–295), London, UK.

Moro, M. M., Bakalov, P., & Tsotras, V. J. (2007). Early profile pruning on xml-aware publish-subscribe systems. In *Proceedings of the 33rd international conference on Very large data bases (VLDB'07)*, (pp. 866–877), Vienna, Austria.

Mühl, G. (2001). Generic constraints for content-based publish/subscribe systems. In *Proceedings of the 6th International Conference on Cooperative Information Systems (CoopIS'01)*, (LNCS vol. 2172, pp. 211–225), Trento, Italy.

Muthusamy, V., & Jacobsen, H.-A. (2005). Small-scale Peer-to-peer Publish/Subscribe. In *Proceedings of the MobiQuitous Conference* (pp 109-119). New York: ACM.

Muthusamy, V., & Jacobsen, H.-A. (2007). Infrastructure-less Content-Based Pub. Technical report, Middleware Systems Research Group, University of Toronto.

Muthusamy, V., & Jacobsen, H.-A. (2008). SLA-driven distributed application development. In *Proceedings of the 3rd Workshop on Middleare for Service Oriented Computing* (pp. 31-36), Leuven, Belgium.

Muthusamy, V., Jacobsen, H.-A., Coulthard, P., Chan, A., Waterhouse, J., & Litani, E. (2007). SLA-Driven Business Process Management in SOA. In *Proceedings of the 2007 conference of the center for advanced studies on Collaborative research* (pp 264-267), Richmond Hill, Ontario, Canada.

NITF. (2005). NITF DTD. Retrieved from http://www.nitf.org/IPTC/NITF/3.3/documentation/nitf.html

Petrovic, M., Muthusamy, V., & Jacobsen, H.-A. (2005). Content-based routing in mobile ad hoc networks. In *Proceedings of the Second Annual International Conference on Mobile and Ubiquitous Systems: Networking and Services* (pp 45-55), San Diego, CA.

PlanetLab. (2006). *PlanetLab*. Retrieved from https://www.planet-lab.org/

PSD. (2005). *PSD DTD*. Retrieved from http://matra.sourceforge.net/dtdtree/bio/psdml_dtdtree.php

Sherafat Kazemzadeh, R., & Jacobsen, H.-A. (2007). δ-Fault-Tolerant Publish/Subscribe systems. Technical report, Middleware Systems Research Group, University of Toronto.

Sherafat Kazemzadeh, R., & Jacobsen, H.-A. (2008). Highly Available Distributed Publish/Subscribe Systems. Technical report, Middleware Systems Research Group, University of Toronto.

Snoeren, A. C., Conley, K., & Gifford, D. K. (2001). Mesh-based content routing using XML. *ACM SIGOPS Operating Systems Review, 35*(5), 160–173. doi:10.1145/502059.502050

Yan, W., Hu, S., Muthusamy, V., Jacobsen, H.-A., & Zha, L. (2009). Efficient event-based resource discovery. In *Proceedings of the 2009 inaugural international conference on Distributed event-based systems*, Nashville, TN.

Chapter 12
XP2P:
A Framework for Fragmenting and Managing XML Data over Structured Peer-to-Peer Networks

Angela Bonifati
ICAR-CNR and University of Basilicata, Italy

Alfredo Cuzzocrea
ICAR-CNR and University of Calabria, Italy

ABSTRACT

This chapter presents XP2P (XPath for P2P), a framework for fragmenting and managing XML data over structured peer-to-peer networks. XP2P is characterized by an innovative mechanism for fragmenting XML documents based on meaningful XPath queries, and novel fingerprinting techniques for indexing and looking-up distributed fragments based on Chord's DHT. Efficient algorithms for querying distributed fragments over peer-to-peer networks are also presented and experimentally assessed against both synthetic and real XML data sets. A comprehensive analysis of future research directions on XML data management over peer-to-peer networks completes the contribution of the chapter.

INTRODUCTION

XML is a data format available in the Internet and, with increasing popularity, in P2P networks. Here, the nature of XML data, which are intrinsically *semi-structured*, naturally couples with the topology and structure of P2P networks, which are usually wide and loosely connected. Numerous are the scenarios in which XML and P2P ties together such as *Knowledge P2P Management Systems and Advanced P2P Information Retrieval Systems*, to mention a few examples.

However, there are still many challenges to investigate in order to realize a full-fledged *P2P XML Data Management System*, among which query performance and support for complex XML queries are the most relevant ones. A solution to these issues could be considering new data models and storage schemes for XML data over P2P networks, along with highly-efficient algorithms for retrieving useful knowledge from large XML repositories across the network.

Inspired by these considerations, in this chapter we address the problem of storing and retrieving XML data in a DHT-based P2P network. DHTs are

DOI: 10.4018/978-1-61520-727-5.ch012

widely known because of their accuracy, logarithmic efficiency and greater scalability, as discussed by (Aberer et al., 2003). In light of this, DHTs are starting to be considered as the foundational indexes for data management applications on top of P2P networks. However, the kinds of queries so far allowed in such DHT-based architectures are mainly lookup queries, i.e. queries that return singleton items.

First, we focus on identifying the pieces of data which are of interest to a peer. Indeed, *for either space or relevance reasons*, a peer is not interested to store an XML document as a whole, but to store a subpart of it, namely a *fragment*. Space constraints are relevant for any distributed system, and become crucial for DHT-based systems, which heavily rely on load balancing. Relevance metrics should be attentively considered in a network of peers sharing a large XML document. As an example, consider a P2P data repository sharing the DB research data (may be DBLP or other DB research data, such as that employed in the *Piazza* system (Halevy et al., 2003)). It is conceivable that a DB lab peer working on "streaming" only stores locally the XML data of other DB labs working on the same topic, while still wishing to fetch data on other topics/labs whenever needed. Another example is XML biological data, such as *SwissProt* and *Protein Sequence Data Base* (PSDB), which is of interest to several biological peer databases. None of the peers is willing to locally store such large XML documents, but only to hold part of them, depending on their current interest. For instance, SwissProt contains the description of proteins and genes, their features and the papers in which they were first studied. A peer would be interested to store the genes and their citations locally, while others would be interested to store their characteristics and still keeping links to their citations. A similar behaviour would occur with the PSDB, which has a full description of each protein.

Secondly, we study how the querying mechanism is affected by the presence and availability of XML fragments. Lookup queries in the most traditional sense cannot be adopted in such a case, and need to be properly re-defined. We have devised a system, called *XP2P* (*XPath for P2P*), first presented in (Bonifati et al., 2004), to *share XML documents in a P2P environment such that the sharing is kept transparent to queries*. More precisely, we focus on *efficiently storing and retrieving XML data within an arbitrarily large DHT-based P2P network*. To this purpose, we have designed a fragmentation and replication model for global XML documents, which allows them to remain re-buildable and queryable. The whole path leading to a given tag needs to be used to identify XML data, as indeed the only tag names are not sufficient. Thus, we enable a *path-based identification mechanism* for XML fragments, which couples well with the DHT of structured P2P networks. We do not assume a global mediated schema, which would not be conceivable in a P2P setting, but instead build a decentralized catalog that relies on a few *path expressions*. Similarly to XP2P, (Galanis et al., 2003) proposes to use the tag names to build the DHT keys and guarantee efficient lookup of XML data. However, their approach is found on maintaining a global catalog of data, which is feasible for small communities of peers but unfeasible for large scalable networks.

XP2P OVERVIEW

XP2P is an extension of *Chord* (Stoica et al., 2001) that uses Rabin's fingerprints (Broder, 1993; Rabin, 1981) instead of hash keys (Stoica et al., 2001). The former ones have a remarkable software efficiency, a well-understood probability of collisions (also verified in our system) and nice algebraic properties. We refer the reader to the fourth Section for details.

One of the most relevant goals in our work has been that of handling non-conventional XML queries. In XP2P, we are able to address full *XPath 1.0* (XPath, 2006) queries on the XML data obtained from the fragmentation. Our approach is similar in spirit to *IrisNet* (Gibbons et al., 2003), which solves XPath queries in hierarchical P2P networks. As opposed to IrisNet, which is effective for queries matching the hierarchical paths, XP2P achieves efficiency for arbitrary queries, and particularly for *descendant queries*. Only recently, more complex database-style queries are being taken into account, in order to enrich DHT-based systems with extra functionalities. In this direction, (Gupta et al., 2003) consider each peer holding partitions on relational tables and extend the DHT for addressing approximate range queries by means of *Locality Sensitive Hashing* (LSH). (Crainiceanu et al., 2004) proposes to augment the DHT with a B^+-tree for answering exact range queries on tuples, thus forming the so-called *P-Trees*.

Once the XML fragments have been obtained and stored in XP2P, a key problem is to efficiently locate the data of interest. Recent works, such as that by (Koloniari & Pitoura, 2004), and that by (Galanis et al., 2003), have devised mechanisms to quickly find with high probability the peers of interest to address a specific lookup of XML data. They build on the replication on each peer of more or less sophisticated data summaries/catalog information (data summaries and histograms by (Galanis et al., 2003)), bloom-filters by (Gong et al., 2005) and multi-level bloom-filters by (Koloniari & Pitoura, 2004) to guide the lookup towards the most relevant peers. However, these solutions may not be scalable for a large number of peers and for arbitrarily deep XML documents to be shared. Moreover, since these data summaries describe the local data as well as the data of the peer neighbors, it is difficult to maintain them up-to-date w.r.t. the changes in the network.

In XP2P, we use an exact query answering approach as opposed to probabilistic approaches already studied for XML data and mentioned above. We inspect the actual data, neither the data summaries nor the probabilistic schemes of (Galanis et al., 2003; Gong et al., 2005; Koloniari

& Pitoura, 2004). Indeed, the set of path expressions that serve to store the fragments are the same paths used for query evaluation and for biasing the search towards the relevant peers. Particularly, an arbitrary XPath query is decomposed into segments, these segments being evaluated one at a time in a top-down fashion. We present suitable algorithms to address the evaluation of three kinds of query segments: *exact-match, partial-match and descendant queries*. The final result is built by gathering the partial results from previous segments in top-down order.

There are several motivations behind this work. File-sharing systems, customarily known as such, are being considered the new architectures for data integration, as discussed by (Kementsietsidis et al., 2003) but are not limited to playing that role, as recognized by (Gribble et al., 2001). We believe that XP2P is widely applicable in all those cases when there is no mediation between the peer schemas and a common knowledge of the global schema is unforeseeable. An example would be that of organizations that, for *privacy* reasons, tend to keep, within each peer, only partial information of external peers XML data and still want to query that data when a complete schema knowledge is lacking. As highlighted by recent important research, such a complete schema knowledge may be impossible to achieve even in a centralized scenario, thus leading to schema-free XML querying, first proposed by (Li et al., 2004).

BACKGROUND

In recent years, there has been a strong interest in P2P data sharing systems, such as (Gnutella, 2006; KaZaA, 2006, Tsoumakos & Roussopoulos, 2003). A P2P network is a collection of heterogeneous sites sharing any kind of data and using a common intercommunication protocol that doesn't need a central coordination. Every host in this kind of network is a peer, i.e. a machine running a software with the same functionality of any other node. Each peer can join, leave and publish data on the network over time introducing high unpredictability. Evolution of research defined a dichotomy on P2P networks topology: unstructured and structured networks. *Gnutella* (Gnutella, 2006) and *Kazaa* (KaZaA, 2006) are examples of unstructured networks where queries are broadcasted to every known peer. This kind of lookup procedure can find any related document on the network but it is very costly in term of bandwidth, as studied by (Tsoumakos & Roussopoulos, 2003). To mitigate the inefficiency of broadcasting queries as in Gnutella, the concept of *super-peer* has been introduced: it is a peer that contains information on all or part of its neighbors and it is used to drive a query towards the most promising subset of peers. Very recently, structured P2P networks are gaining popularity among the database people for their efficiency due to a strictly controlled topology that allows to bound the query lookup time. This kind of networks is based on the definition of a DHT that uniquely maps data to peer identifiers and that allows to see the entire network as a distributed dictionary by means of **put** and get operations. Successful structured networks are using the notion of a d-dimensional virtual space where every peer "owns" a portion of this space. Lookup operations on the pair $\langle key, value \rangle$ are processed via (i) hashing the key on the virtual space and (ii) inquiring the peer that owns the portion of the space to which the hashed key is mapped.

Thus, *Content-Addressable Network* (CAN) (Ratnasamv et al, 2001) uses a virtual d-dimensional Cartesian space while Chord (Stoica et al., 2001) uses a linear space of identifiers that forms a ring. These techniques allow us to bound the lookup time to $O(log\ N)$ where N is the number of participating peers in the network. Structured P2P networks are becoming very popular in the database community for their scalability and efficiency. Among the works presented these last years, we cite *PierSearch* by (Loo et al., 2004),

Irisnet by (Gibbons et al., 2003), the LSH-based system for relational data by (Gupta et al., 2003), P-Trees by (Crainiceanu et al., 2004), which are discussed next.

PierSearch (Loo et al., 2004) presents a hybrid approach between Gnutella (Gnutella, 2006) and *PierDB* (Huebsch et al., 2003), first proposed by (Huebsch et al., 2003), which is a general purpose relational database targeted at a P2P architecture of millions of nodes. It addresses distributed querying, and settles several features of relational DBMS in an Internet scale. IrisNet (Gibbons et al., 2003) has similar goals to Pier, with the difference that it works with hierarchical data (XML) on hierarchical overlay networks (DNS). It is best used when the hierarchy changes infrequently and the queries exactly match the hierarchy. IrisNet is close in principle to XP2P, inasmuch as it uses XPath as query language. However, the evaluation of queries follow the guidelines of DNS directories, using the *Least Common Ancestor* (LCA) to seek the result. To our knowledge, XP2P is the first framework to devise ad-hoc path queries algorithms for DHT-based overlay networks.

In the LSH-based technique proposed by (Gupta et al., 2003), the shared data are horizontal partitions of relational tables and approximate range queries are supported. A locality preserving hash function is used to map query ranges on the network: this significantly improves the query response time because similar ranges are very likely hashed to the same peer. Relational range queries in P2P networks are also addressed by (Crainiceanu et al., 2004) using P-Trees such that every peer contains a subset of the tree and some routing information. However, P-Trees are not highly scalable even for relational data since every peer can hold at most one tuple. In XP2P, we focus on the general case when a peer can hold one or more XML fragments at a time. Moreover, the replicated index consists of few path expressions and is in general smaller than an arbitrary P-Tree.

Previous work by (Bremer & Gertz, 2003) deals with the problem of building XML distributed repositories, where each site holds local indexes and global information (up to 47% of the original data overall). This is not feasible in a P2P, because, the latter being very dynamic, the approach adopted in (Bremer & Gertz, 2003) would lead to replicate global information on every peer and to maintain this information up-to-date each time there is a variation in the network. In an highly dynamic P2P context, one is mainly interested to lookups, i.e. to know that a peer holds a fragment, to retrieve it and to possibly cope with network changes without global disruption. Past works utilized catalogs and data summaries (i.e., multi-level bloom filters (Koloniari & Pitoura, 2004), distributed path summaries, B^+-trees and histograms (Galanis et al., 2003)) that partially or entirely describe the local/global data. These approaches are probabilistic, and are proved to work in small communities of data providers, but not in large and dynamic P2P networks.

Our target is conceivably P2P networks with an high turnover of nodes. Such networks maintain as less as possible global information at every peer to avoid global refreshments of all the network. A graceful solution is that of using a light *distributed* index structure that allows the peer to know about a few (but sufficient in practice) other peers.

XML distributed query evaluation is addressed by (Suciu, 2002) that presents theoretical results valid for communities of peers, not for arbitrary P2P networks. Thus, the problem is still unsolved for large dynamic P2P networks, except for very recent papers on this topic (Galanis et al., 2003; Koloniari & Pitoura, 2004; Sartiani et al., 2004; Crainiceanu et al., 2007; Abiteboul et al., 2008).

(Galanis et al., 2003) extends Chord for XML data by using tag names as hash keys. However, this approach introduces overhead when a large number of sites has the same tag. The authors say that their framework is extensible for supporting paths instead of tag names but they do not discuss the extensions needed to handle linked XML fragments. Similarly to (Galanis et al., 2003), *XPeer* (Sartiani et al., 2004) is a system for sharing XML data, which uses full tree-guides to perform query evaluation. Differently from (Galanis et al., 2003), however, XPeer is not DHT-based and assumes the presence of super-peers. (Koloniari & Pitoura, 2004) proposes to use a probabilistic approach, in which the data of a peer neighborhood is summarized by means of multi-level bloom-filters. Thus, the probability of false positives is examined within hierarchical P2P networks. Both approaches (Galanis et al., 2003; Koloniari & Pitoura, 2004) lack scalability for a large number of peers. In particular, multi-level bloom-filters are only applicable for XML data having limited depth, whereas XP2P does not have such limitation.

While (Crainiceanu et al., 2007) handles range queries, *KadoP* (Abiteboul et al., 2008) is able to efficiently evaluate the descendant axes by means of local postings of query terms. They also handle predicates on textual content of nodes, if words have been added to the posting lists. The final aim is that of alleviating the burden of large sets of posting, and providing a scalable algorithm to evaluate queries. For the time being, XP2P does not support range queries. However, the system can be easily be extended in this direction. Moreover, since simple paths are encoded in the DHT, the search complexity is still $O(log\ N)$ in XP2P, where for KadoP simple paths needs to be split into as many terms as the number of steps and the obtained terms need to be matched to posting lists. By contrary, the evaluation of descendant axes is more efficient in KadoP.

The use of fingerprinting resembles the use of message digests in cryptography (*RSA* and *AES* (Menezes et al., 1996)). Fingerprints allow us to guarantee that the peers who answer the query are trustworthy (details in the fourth Section).

Data integration and exchange for P2P networks are addressed by (Kementsietsidis et al., 2003), and by (Tatarinov & Halevy, 2004). In

(Kementsietsidis et al., 2003), mapping tables on peers represent the aliases of the same item in the network. Then, a lookup search on a peer is conducted by looking at its mapping table to find the name aliases on other peers. (Tatarinov & Halevy, 2004) proposes a framework for data integration based on a global mediated schema: every query is first translated w.r.t. this global schema and then forwarded to the peers whose local schema can be mapped to the global schema. In XP2P, we do not deal with data heterogeneity, but the extension of P2P for data integration is an interesting future direction.

Similarly to XP2P, PeerDB (Ooi et al., 2003) also does not assume schema knowledge. Metadata are provided by the user for query matching and rewriting. No user intervention is required in the work of (Kantere et al., 2004), which relies on finding bandwidth-efficient paths to route queries within unstructured networks. However, the addressed queries are primarily relational.

XP2P FRAGMENTATION AND REPLICATION MODEL

We assume that the network is holding a set of XML fragments conforming to a given data model. These fragments stem from one or more global documents. A first question which naturally comes to our mind is: how are these fragments obtained from the global document? While several strategies for effectively and efficiently driving the fragmentation process that generates final fragments have been proposed recently, such as latest approaches based on *Data Mining* algorithms for supporting distribution and replication tasks over very large XML documents in *Data Warehousing* architectures (e.g., see (Cuzzocrea et al., 2009)), in our research we essentially focus on two possible fragmentation strategies that are suitable to the context of large and dynamic P2P networks, namely the *user-centered fragmentation strategy* and *query-centered fragmentation strategy*,

respectively. In particular, the query-centered fragmentation strategy can be alternatively realized by both a user again that edits queries, or, more realistically, an external application interacting with our P2P XML fragmentation framework (e.g., in the context of *Web-Service-* or *Grid-Service-based systems*). A peer entering the network declares its interest in sub-documents and can get them by asking a partitioning of the original document (user-centered fragmentation strategy) or, alternatively, by querying them directly (query-centered fragmentation strategy). In the former case, the whole document is shredded into fragments and the entering peer chooses the fragments it is interested in. In this Section, we will show how this fragmentation is done. The latter case happens when the entering peer queries the global document in order to identify one or more fragments. The query result amounts to a forest of XML fragments, which are then expressed in terms of their identifying path expressions. We will present in this Section the language subset of XPath 1.0, in which these path expressions are encoded.

The latter case also makes sense with virtual documents (Abiteboul et al., 2003b; Abiteboul et al., 2004) that, besides actual data, may also include method calls. Our identifying path expressions may be considered as special kinds of method calls without the extra overhead due to calls. We aimed at keeping the path expressions as more lightweight as possible to be used in large P2P scenarios.

Fragmenting XML Data

An XML fragment is a valid subdocument of the original document, identified by the unique path leading from the root of the document to the root of the fragment. We express the unique path that characterizes a fragment as a path expression and call *fragment identifier* the unique path expression that identifies a fragment. We ensure the validity of the obtained fragment by adding the necessary

Figure 1. An example of linked fragments with their related path expressions

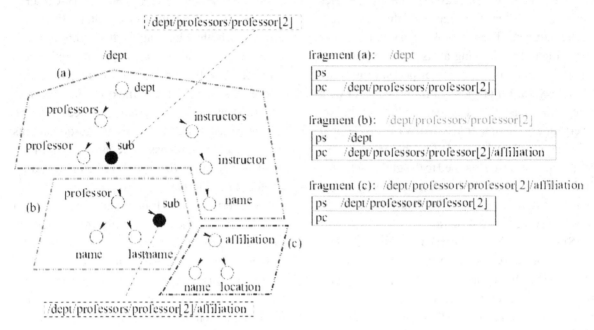

header elements, which makes it well-formed, and correctly parsed as XML. We now discuss the language subset we use for identifying XML fragments. In principle, we could use all XPath 1.0, thus including arbitrary selection filters, wildcards etc. and giving the whole expressiveness of a query language. However, we thought that such language would be too arbitrary to yield semantically meaningful path expressions. In other words, we expect a fragment identifier to also give an intuition of the kind of data stored locally on the peer and elsewhere outside. Indeed, we restrict the language to path expressions $/s_1/s_2/.../s_n$ which only uses the *child* axis and optional positional filters $[i]$, $[j]$, ..., $[k]$ on steps $s_1, s_2, ..., s_n$, respectively[1]. Positional filters $[i]$, $[j]$, ..., $[k]$ indicate the positions of elements/attributes in *document order*. This simple language allows us to derive useful information on the network data. For instance, a fragment identified by the path expression $/s_1/s_2/s_3[1]$ carries out different information: (*i*) that the local data is rooted in element s_3, which is the first in document order; (*ii*) that

in some other external peer there may exist nodes $s_3[i]$, with $i \geq 1$, which are sibling of the current fragment; (*iii*) that the elements s_1 and s_2 may also exist in the network, either as roots or internal nodes of fragments. This only partially would be given by more general paths, e.g. with wildcards, such as $s_1//*/s_3$. Notice that these path expressions carry out an intrinsic semantics, which is given by their own definition. These path expressions may give hints on what data is present in a peer to any external application. Thus, in Figure 1, a query which starts from fragment (b), is able to guess the content of fragment (a) by only looking at the super-fragment path expression.

A fragment may also keep links to other fragments, possibly distributed on an external peer. This is important to be able to reconstruct the whole document or part of it on a peer wishing to do so. These external fragments are stored as outgoing links from the bottom of the fragment, thus pointing to children fragments and/or as an outgoing link from the root of the fragment, thus pointing to a (unique) super-fragment.

Given an XML fragment, we can define the set of *related path expressions* of that fragment as follows:

- *super-fragment* path expression p_s: it is the path expression of the parent-fragment of the current fragment, which is stored apart from the fragment itself;
- *child-fragment* (or sub-fragment) path expressions p_c: they are the path expressions of the child-fragments of the current fragment, which are stored as PCDATA within sub tags in the fragment.

Notice that the parent-fragment in the previous definition *may not* correspond to the parent axis. Indeed, the super-fragment of the current fragment may be rooted in a different node that the parent axis of the current fragment, e.g. in any ancestor node. More formally, we give the following definition:

Definition 1 (XML Fragment).*Let t be an unranked labeled tree representing the global XML document and r_t be the root of this tree. A valid fragment f of t is a well-formed sub-tree of t, uniquely identified by the path expression f_i leading from r_t to r_f, r_f being the root of f. Moreover, a valid fragment includes: /r_t/.../$r_f$being the fragment identifier f_p, stored apart of f; a super-fragment path expression p_s, whose path expression is either equal to /r_t/... or a prefix of it, stored apart of f; the child path expressions p_c, whose paths have the prefix /r_t/.../r_f in common with the fragment identifier f_p, stored within sub tags in f.*

The path expressions included in a fragment, according to the previous definition, are named as related path expressions. Unfolding these path expressions leads to identify linked fragments. Obviously, while a fragment can have several p_c, it can only have one p_s. Note that all the related sub-fragments of a given fragment appear in document order in the latter. This fragmentation model, which is reminiscent of vertical partitioning of relational data (Ozsu & Valduriez, 1999)

(vertically partitioned attributes belonging to the same table), is customized for XML data.

Example 1. An example of local fragment is the following, identified for instance by the unique path expression /dept/professors/professor[2], and also depicted in Figure 1 (b):

```
<professor>
<name> Till </name>
<lastname> Tyler </lastname>
<sub> /dept/professors/professor[2]/affilia-
tion </sub>
</professor>
```

The super-fragment of the current fragment is /dept/, which in such a case does not coincide with the fragment rooted in the parent axis (/dept/professors/). Its sub-fragment is identified by the path expression enclosed within the sub tags, which has the prefix in common with the fragment identifier.

An example of linked XML fragments are illustrated in Figure 1, where fragment (a) is the root fragment (its identifying path expression is exactly the root) and has one p_c path expression to fragment (b), whose p_s is the path expression of fragment (a). Finally, fragment (b) points to fragment (c), which has no child path expression. Note that fragments (a), (b) and (c) taken separately (i.e., without looking at the related path expressions) are found to be affiliated by simply matching their identifiers prefixes. This mechanism will be further elaborated in the sixth Section, when discussing the query processing mechanism.

In XP2P, any XML fragment comes equipped with its identifier, plus (possibly) a set of p_c path expressions and a p_s path expression. These fragments are stored on the peer with their actual content and with its related p_c and p_s path expressions. Figure 1 (right) illustrates the set of *light* path expressions stored along each fragment, for fragments (a), (b) and (c), respectively. The overhead introduced by these extra path expressions is minimal and at most comparable to global indexes (actual numbers from our experiments appear in the seventh Section). In more detail, maintaining links among fragments has a *linear* cost in the number of fragments generated by the fragmentation process. On the other hand, both ps and pc path expressions are critical components of our XPath query engine (see the sixth Section), which is largely based on the capability of flooding the target P2P network throughout (linked) fragments stored in peers.

Finally, what is further needed to store the fragment content is a node scheme. More precisely, we assign to each node within the global XML tree a positional identifier. These identifiers, introduced in the *Timber* system (Srivastava et al., 2002), are of the form $\langle docId, startPos: endPos, levelNum \rangle$, where *docId* is the identifier of the document, *startPos* and *endPos* represent the numbers given by counting words between the starting and ending tags of the element, and *levelNum* is the level of the element in the XML hierarchy. Since this scheme only works for elements, and not for attributes, we made a simple extension assigning attributes identifiers as follows.

Remark We do not assume that a fragment must be linked to other fragments for being indexed in the network. Indeed, it may happen that the fragment does not own any related path expression and/or its identifier does not refer to a super-fragment identifier. In such a case, the fragment can still exist in the network, and thus queried by means of its identifier. Note that if the same path expression comes from two distinct documents, it simply suffices to prefix it with the name of the originating document.

Replicating and Updating XML Data

We underlined the importance of storing few extra bytes for the path expressions, as to guarantee that there is little overhead during query processing. We also said that, compared to the use of global indexes, our approach ensures that a distributed catalog aids the biasing of queries towards the right peers.

Thus, we adopt the choice of replicating on each peer the schema of the global document (if any), to help the user in formulating the queries. This is compatible with what we said on the assumption of a global schema, as indeed we do not expect that the schema versions present on each peer are synchronized or are needed to bias the search. In XP2P, we only advocate schemas in order to aid query formulation. Conversely, when no schema is present, queries may be formulated by looking up the local data and the related path. Also, they can bear from the *churn* mechanism, which is used in overlay networks, when a query "lives" just because of propagation from other peers.

Another important issue we want to discuss concerns the handling of updates in XP2P. Our path identification mechanism would allow restricted kinds of updates in XP2P, i.e. updates that won't entirely disrupt the related paths within fragments. Updates are feasible in XP2P whenever they are local to a fragment. It should be noted that the latter application scenario is quite common in modern P2P networks. As an example, consider a B2B e-commerce P2P application such that product (XML) database is fragmented across peers of the underlying P2P network, and each fragment peer database is handled by outsourcing to a third-part application (e.g., for privacy preservation issues). In the described application scenario, updates are clearly feasible in local fragments only. In such a way, if those updates do not affect the fragment root r_f, the fragment leaves sub and all elements but the set of related path expressions, they only affect local fragments and do not need to be propagated to the external fragments. Updates to the fragment root r_f instead implies that the path expression identifying the fragment and the related ones must be changed accordingly. The same happens for the elements used in the set of related path expressions, which once changed require to propagate the changes in the corresponding steps of the path expressions. For instance, inserting a new element age in fragment (b) under professor in Figure 1 does not induce further changes in the rest of the network, whereas replacing or deleting professors in fragment (a) implies to change all the paths that contain it, along with the actual change of the local element. Obviously, more complicated updates, such as insertion/deletion of complex fragments would imply to make more changes on the path expressions. Notice that this is different from what happens with global catalogs in P2P networks, used for instance in (Galanis et al., 2003). Indeed, since the global catalog is replicated on every peer, even a small modification of local data on a peer needs to be propagated to all the network. By contrary, a distributed index, such as that given by our lightweight path expressions, is already transparent to a restricted class of updates, as explained above.

PATH-BASED LIGHTWEIGHT DISTRIBUTED INDEXES

Fingerprinting Path Expressions

Path identifiers can be converted into unique keys in a straightforward manner. In the previous Section, we said that each path identifier is distinct from any other path identifier of the document. Moreover, each light path expression actually represents a string which can be transformed into a unique numeric key[2]. Our further assumption is to allocate such keys in structured P2P networks, such as Chord, CAN, Pastry etc. and to permit their subsequent efficient search. As opposed to unstructured networks, which rely on flooding to propagate a request, structured P2P networks ensure that each node identifier is reachable by means of a distributed index, the DHT. Thus, our light path expressions being transformed into numeric keys, represent a lightweight decentralized catalog. We recall that each path expression despite being a key in the DHT, still keeps its intrinsic semantics. Indeed, each key derived by a path lets seamlessly identify the content of external fragments. Precisely, the child-fragments let identify

the children elements of the fragments assigned to external peers, while the super-fragment path expression and the path identifier itself are aware of the elements positioned up in the XML hierarchy. These are useful information, which can be fruitfully exploited in the content search.

Along with the path identifier, we store on each peer the fragment content itself. Each peer thus keeps its own XML repository, which is partial w.r.t. the global document and might be still complete at will, by unfolding the related paths stored within the peer.

We recall that there is no necessity to store the global schema of the document on each peer, which would not be feasible in a dynamic P2P environment. The only use one can make of a global schema in XP2P is to pose queries against the data.

We have chosen Chord (Stoica et al., 2001) as a basis for building XP2P. The Chord network is organized as a ring, in which each node is aware of only $O(\log N)$ other nodes for efficient routing. Thus, the Chord protocol constituting a distributed routing table guarantees high scalability to large and dynamic network sizes, as opposed to other protocols in which each node is mapped to any other node.

In Chord, a key is associated to a data item and a ⟨*key, value*⟩ pair is mapped onto a node. Thus, the keys range exactly correspond to the nodes range. Moreover, this structure must be highly adaptive to the changes of the network, i.e. it must ensure that the entire network does not disrupt when a peer is unreachable. Indeed, the Chord network adapts efficiently when the network status is continuously changing, i.e. several nodes join and leave the network. With high probability, any node leaving or joining a *N-nodes* Chord network will use $O(\log^2 N)$ messages to re-establish the routing tables. The Chord routing table is left unchanged in XP2P, but extended to accommodate paths instead of document identifiers. As a result, the XP2P system is exactly as dynamic as the original Chord system.

Figure 2. XP2P extension of the Chord ring

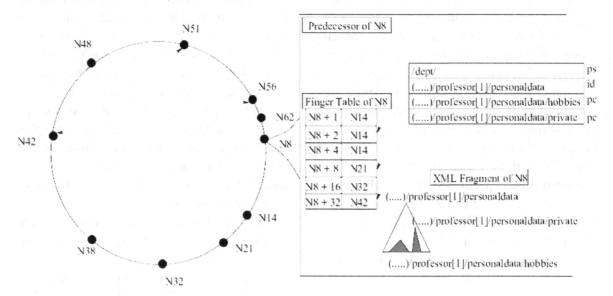

In original Chord, each node (e.g., N_8 in Figure 2) stores both the hashed keys of the successors at logarithmic distance (the so-called *Finger Table* (FT)) and of the node predecessor. XP2P keeps these hash keys to ensure logarithmic lookup and further extends the Chord ring (see Figure 2) by storing on a node the following information: the local content of a fragment(s), and its related path expressions, i.e. the list of their child-fragments and their super-fragment path expressions. These can be hashed directly in the Chord hash space and may exploit the Chord FT and the node predecessor in order to be resolved in the DHT.

Suppose we are looking for the fragment /dept/ professors/professor[1]/personaldata/ in the Chord ring in Figure 2, i.e. fragment (b) of Figure 1. We can hash it directly in the Chord hash space. The same happens with child-fragments /dept/professors/professor[1]/personaldata/hobbies and /dept/ professors/professor[1]/personaldata/private and with the super-fragment /dept. They can be accessed by means of Chord lookup mechanism, which uses the FT and the node predecessor. However, in order to embed path expressions in Chord, we need to further modify the ring, i.e. to *equip each node with the additional capability* of *"hashing" path expressions*. Moreover, for better manageability, we have chosen to store the path expressions in a different format, other than hash keys. We describe our approach in the fourth Section.

According to the data model presented in the fourth Section, the fragments may be linked one to another and their identifiers, i.e. the linear path expressions identifying them, are distinct one w.r.t. the others. However, in order to guarantee reliability, XP2P admits fragments replica in a *controlled manner*. Each fragment having an identifier path expression is stored on the peer uniquely accessible through that identifier and *may be replicated* on all its successor nodes.

Thus, for instance, in Figure 2, the fragment identified by /dept/professors/professor[1]/ personaldata belongs to the peer N8 and can be redundantly replicated on each successor peer in the FT. This is done in the spirit of *DHASH* (Brunskill, 2001), which first added a storage layer to Chord. The level of redundancy can be varied and can successfully cope with the situations in which node failures occur. In this chapter, we adopt a simple well-known solution for replication. More complex solutions may be devised, and further issues, e.g. the consistency of the obtained replicas, may raise, which are beyond the scope of the chapter.

Related path expressions are distinct path expressions sharing a prefix between each others. We preferred shorter fingerprints (Rabin, 1981; Broder, 1993; Broder et al., 2003) to SHA-1 hash functions used in Chord. Fingerprints exhibit a remarkable software efficiency, a well-understood probability of collisions and nice algebraic properties. They are basically bit tokens having the same length overall (at most 8-9 bytes against 20 bytes obtained with SHA-1 used in Chord). Path fingerprinting in XP2P closely resembles URL fingerprinting, first proposed by (Broder et al., 2003)[3]. However, since path expressions carry over an intrinsic semantics, their fingerprints turn to be more meaningful than URL fingerprints. Thus, besides reducing the occupancy of the original strings for URL caching as done in (Broder et al., 2003), fingerprinting in our case brings two main advantages. First, it has a nice *concatenation* property, which leads to quickly computing path expressions for fragments lookups. Such a property, discussed in detail below, only pertains to fingerprints and not to hash keys, thus motivating the encoding of path expressions as fingerprints rather than as hash keys. Secondly, we foresee the use of fingerprints to address the authenticity problems in P2P networks, as discussed next.

The fingerprinting function is similar to hash functions as it can be seamlessly applied when the items to be fingerprinted differ in at least one bit (Rabin, 1981; Broder, 1993), which is always true for distinct path expressions. Thus, even collections of instances of the same documents can be reduced to distinct fingerprints by differentiating them with namespaces. In the remainder, for the sake of clarity, we will ignore this technicality.

Computing Path Fingerprints

Let $A = \langle a_1 a_2 \dots a_m \rangle$ be a binary string. We assume that $a_1 = 1$, otherwise a prefix bit can be used. We associate to the string A a polynomial $A(t)$ of degree $m - 1$ with coefficients in the algebraic field Z_2, $A(t) = a_1 \times t^{m-1} + a_2 \times t^{m-2} + \dots + a_m$. Let $P(t)$ be an irreducible polynomial of degree k over Z_2. Given $P(t)$, the fingerprint of A is the following: $f(A) = A(t) \bmod P(t)$. The irreducible polynomial can be easily found following the method proposed by Rabin (Rabin, 1981) and an interesting example can be found in Knuth's book (Knuth, 1973). The method lets pick uniformly at random a polynomial of degree k and compute the probability that $A(t)$ divides it. The latter being the probability that two strings have the same fingerprint, must be kept sufficiently small

Path identifiers happen to have prefixes in common and naturally lend themselves to fast re-computation with fingerprints. Indeed, we can exploit the fingerprinting concatenation property (Rabin, 1981): the fingerprinting of the concatenation of two strings can be computed via the equality: $f(concat(A,B)) = f(concat(f(A),B))$. Consider for instance the following path expression: /dept/professors/professor/private, and suppose we are given the fingerprint of /dept/professors/professor, i.e. f(/dept/professors/professor), then f(concat(/dept/professors/professor/private)) = f(concat(f(/dept/professors/professor),/private)). The same holds for steps and filters of a path expression, which are concatenated one after the other (e.g., /professor[1] as concatenation of /professor and [1]). The above property is extremely useful when updates are performed locally on the fragments roots. Indeed, instead of re-computing the fingerprint of the modified fragment from scratch, the fingerprint of the parent is concatenated to the new root tag.

Moreover, the other advantage of fingerprinting is that it only suffices to store on each peer the irreducible polynomial to compute fingerprints. The polynomial has a fixed degree equal to $N_f + 2 \times D_{max} + Q$, where 2^{N_f} is the number of fragments in the network, $2^{D_{max}}$ being the length of the longest path expression in the network and 2^Q

being a threshold due to the probability of collision between two arbitrary distinct tokens, as shown by (Broder, 1993). In our setting, we use a degree of 64, which leads to an acceptable probability of 2^{-10}, and allows us to exploit a maximum length for path expressions of 50 steps (averaged on a length of 10 symbols per step) and a maximum number of fragments equal to 2^{30}, which is quite huge. Observe that this polynomial is a quite small structure to be *replicated on each participating peer* if compared to replicated structures used in other approaches (e.g., multi-level Bloom filters, restricted to documents with 50 distinct elements and 3-steps paths, in (Koloniari & Pitoura, 2004) and a combination of P-Indexes, A-Indexes and T-Indexes, measuring from 22% up to 47% of the whole document, in (Bremer & Gertz, 2003)). Moreover, such a polynomial can accommodate changes of the network until the maximum number of fragments, 2^{30} and until the maximum depth of a document (i.e., 50)[4].

XPATH QUERIES IN XP2P

P2P networks naturally lend themselves to enable queries on their shared data. In XP2P, we can handle both complete and incomplete queries. By complete queries, we mean the queries whose answers are computed by exhaustively searching the entire network. However, an exhaustive search is unlikely in a large network, as peers may not be alive or available and they may be simply too numerous to look for. By incomplete queries, we mean the queries which are evaluated until a specified *Time-To-Live* (TTL), as in many popular P2P networks (Gnutella, 2006; KaZaA, 2006). We consider in XP2P query processing the *semantics of incomplete answers* according to which the search stops after a given TTL or a certain number of hops.

This Section is devoted to explain (*i*) which queries we deal with and how they are formulated in XP2P, (*ii*) the content-based search of XPath

exact-match queries, (*iii*) the content-based search of XPath partial-match queries and, finally, to illustrate (*iv*) the algorithm employed for XPath descendant queries.

Handling XML Content

We must distinguish between fragment lookups, belonging to our previous work [10], and content-based XPath queries we discuss in this chapter. Indeed, elements or paths lookups as intended in (Bonifati et al., 2004) are XML elements lookups which do not assume reconstruction of the sub-fragments. In other words, a query such as //name on a fragment such as that of Example 1 would return the element name as stored with the identifier scheme, and a vector of element names in case multiple names are found.

Here, we implement content-based XPath queries, which also reconstruct the result under the form of well-formed XML. More precisely, reconstruction happens according to the algorithm in the Timber system (Srivastava et al., 2002), which reconstructs structural relationships of encoded nodes very easily. Indeed, descendant relationships between two nodes n_1 with ID $\langle D_1, S_1 : E_1, L_1 \rangle$ and n_2 with ID $\langle D_2, S_2 : E_2, L_2 \rangle$ are established iff $D_1 = D_2$, $S_1 < S_2$ and $E_1 < E_2$. Similarly, child relationships between n_1 and n_2 hold iff $D_1 = D_2$, $S_2 < S_1$, $E_2 < E_1$ and $L_1 + 1 = L_2$.

The supported queries in XP2P are those expressed in XPath 1.0. More precisely, the entire XPath 1.0 language can be used to formulate the queries. Indeed, the query evaluation mechanism ensures that the part of the query which contains only '//', '/', and positional filters can be matched against the DHT, whereas the rest of the query is evaluated on the peers local data.

We address three kinds of queries in XP2P, *exact-match*, *partial-match* and *descendant*, which lead to define separate algorithms for each kind. An arbitrary query is solved by separating the original query into *query segments* of the kinds above. The results of each segment is then joined with the results of the other segments by means of the structural relationships above.

Exact-Match XPath Queries

Once the path expressions have been fingerprinted, we need to understand how to use them for queries. A straightforward use is to query the full paths as present in the DHT. These queries are feasible if expressed in the language we have used for related path expressions, i.e. the ones that can be encoded in the DHT. More precisely, given an XPath query (or a query fragment) having only '/' and positional filters, this query is fingerprinted with the corresponding polynomial present on each peer and it is matched directly with the paths encoded in the DHT. In case a match is not found within the specified timeout, an empty result is returned.

For instance, consider the case in which the fragment of Figure 2 located on peer N_8 is looked up. N_8 is reached through the DHT, and its fragment is returned. Depending on the timeout, the two sub-fragments rooted in sub tags may or not be retrieved.

To represent the query pattern, we use the formalism introduced by (Amer-Yahia et al., 2001). Answering a tree pattern t_p of length n in $\{/, []\}$ is done by fingerprinting it in the Chord ring directly. However, this search will be successful only when there is an *exact-match* between the tree pattern and an existing fragment. We call a *miss* the lack of a fragment on the network, after an exact-match fails. A miss can be due to the absence of a fragment on the network for two reasons: (*i*) the fragment was never placed on the peers; (*ii*) the fragment is temporarily not accessible because the corresponding peer left. When a miss happens for a tree pattern, the search is biased towards finding at least a *partial-match*, which is discussed next.

Partial-Match XPath Queries

When an exact-match query outputs an empty result representing a miss, a partial-match can be attempted. Thus, the tree pattern representing the original query is *pruned* by a step at time (by step we mean a compound step, composed of a step name plus a positional filter) as shown in Figure 3. More precisely, we start looking exhaustively at the $n - 1$ prefix path expressions corresponding to t_p in a bottom-up order. As soon as one of these prefixes is hashed on a peer p_i, we can stop the bottom-up evaluation at p_i. Henceforth, we start analyzing the local content of p_i and its sub-fragment list in a top-down fashion and further on, until a result is found or the time-out expires. The evaluation of a tree pattern varying in $\{/, []\}$ is thus done in a composite bottom-up/top-down fashion. This *hybrid* evaluation allows to bi-directionally navigate the network since it may happen that a miss happens while doing bottom-up evaluation (for example, for a temporary node failure) and that the miss can be recovered when doing top-down (due to new node joins in the network).

As an example of evaluation on the data of Figure 1, consider Figure 3, which shows a tree pattern issued on a network constituted of peers p_1, p_2 and p_3. The peer S starts the evaluation at step (1), when a lookup is performed on path expression /professor/personaldata[1]/private[2]/pictures. The fragment does not belong to the network, thus its prefix /professor/personaldata[1]/private[2] is looked up (2) but not found, and so on, /professor/personaldata[1] (3) is searched, but not found since the peer p_3 is temporarily down, until /professor (4), which is instead correctly found on peer p_1. Thus, we can start the top-down evaluation from /professor (4), look in its sub-fragments and check again /professor/personaldata[1] (5), which is now up and can correctly answer our query ((6) and (7) are evaluated locally on peer p_3). Results are

Figure 3. An example of lookup for a path expression in {/, []}

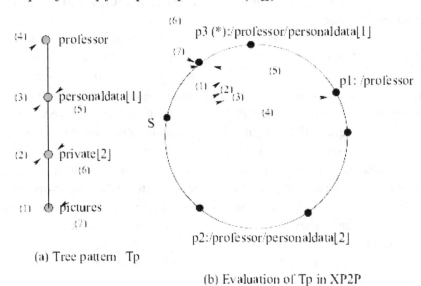

(a) Tree pattern Tp

(b) Evaluation of Tp in XP2P

shipped back on peer *S* and reconstruction of results is done on peer *S* that originated the query.

As a final remark, we give the complexity of the search algorithm for the evaluation of the addressed queries. We only include the complexity of lookups on the DHT, and we disregard the cost of inspecting the local fragments, which is proportional to the data size. The same considerations hold for the other complexity result given in the remainder. While the complexity of the search algorithm for the exact-match queries follows the Chord lookup complexity ($O(log N)$), the complexity of the search algorithm for the partial-match queries is $O(N_s \times log N)$, where N_s is the number of steps of the path expression and N the number of peers in the network.

Descendant XPath Queries

Evaluation of the descendant-axis is noticeable as it cannot be done by fingerprinting the tree pattern (or its prefixes) directly. In addition, no global schema is available in XP2P to guide the evaluation of the descendant axis towards some particular peers. One naive solution is an exhaustive search over the entire ring that starts at an arbitrary peer. However, this solution, although complete, would lead to many useless accesses. We have devised a better solution, which searches the space of the peers (and thus of the fragments located on those) by selecting *peer by peer* the most promising direction. The algorithm relies on two key observations: (*i*) the evaluation of a tree pattern containing a '//' may take place bottom-up or top-down w.r.t. the parse tree, but top-down is preferred, as demonstrated by (Gottlob et al., 2002); (*ii*) a fragment can always exploit information about the sub-fragments, since it stores their fingerprints.

We first discuss observation (*i*). To enable the evaluation of the descendant axis in XP2P, we follow the result of (Gottlob et al., 2002), which proved that top-down and bottom-up have both polynomial time complexity in a centralized setting, but top-down yields less intermediate results than bottom-up. In XP2P, evaluation of a step with '//' proceeds as much as possible *top-down*. We optimistically start evaluation of '//' from a given peer. This peer may contain the root fragment or is picked at random otherwise.

Hierarchical containment of XML data in XP2P can be further exploited with local evaluation of descendant queries. As an example, consider the query //professor running on the document instance depicted in Figure 1. Suppose the query has been originating on the peer having fragment (a). In a top-down evaluation, the elements which are relevant to the query, i.e. the elements with tag professor, are either local to the peer (e.g., the lhs element professor) or the last step of child path expressions (e.g., /dept/professors/professor[2]). We generalize this result in the following Proposition.

Proposition 1. Let q be a descendant query $//s_i$ to be evaluated on a peer P_j. In a top-down evaluation, elements s_i relevant to query q are either local on peer P_j or the last steps of child path expressions of P_j.

We now describe the evaluation of a tree pattern of the kind $/s_1/.../s_i//s_j/.../s_{j+k}$, as handling multiple descendant-axes is done via a composition of the former. Given an arbitrary peer, we can explore the local information and the related path expressions to find the answer to the above tree pattern. At an arbitrary peer p_j, we can have four cases, i.e. either find (1) local s_j elements, i.e. contained in the fragment; (2) intermediate steps s_j of the related path expressions; (3) last steps s_j of the related path expressions or (4) not find them at all as steps in the related path expressions. In case (1) the elements are local and can be retrieved. Case (2) is not meaningful (as stated by Proposition 1) when evaluation is proceeding top-down, since it means that s_j elements which appear as intermediate steps were encountered in the past and are already included in the query result. Cases (3) and (4) are the most significant ones as they provide new directions to explore: let us call first path expressions (3) *promising* path expressions LP_{Pi}, and the remaining ones (4) OT_{Pi}.

These considerations lead to the optimistic step-wise decomposition algorithm in Figure 4 for a tree pattern containing a descendant-axis. In its first step, the algorithm performs a local search on the current peer, and proceeds by following the promising directions indicated by sub-fragments

having as root the searched element. All the other remaining sub-fragments are probed afterwards. Let N_f the total number of fragments in the network, the complexity of the search algorithm for the descendant axis query evaluation is bounded by $O(N_f \times \log N)$, where N is the number of peers in the network (N corresponds to L_p in the algorithm in Figure 4).

Finally, observe that once the context node / $s_1/..../s_i$ (i.e., the node on which evaluation of a path expression starts) has been found, retrieval of s_j can proceed in parallel on all the paths in LP_{Pi} (OT_{Pi}, respectively). This leads to a quite flexible distributed query processing, which has been validated by our experiments. Similarly to what happens with the former kinds of queries, the peer who originated the descendant query will receive the results of parallel executions as soon as these are yielded.

The Composite Query Evaluation Algorithm

When an arbitrary XPath query (in the syntax of XPath 1.0) is issued other than exact-match, partial-match and descendant queries, then a *path decomposition* into *path segments* occurs. Given an arbitrary XPath query, this is split into as many segments as the number of descendant axes and of the remaining / sub-paths. To give an example, a query like /dept/*//name is decomposed into / dept and //name. The evaluation then proceeds in top-down order from /dept to its * sub-elements, which provide the context for //name. Stitching together the various results is done according to structural relationships, whereas the reconstruction of results is done on the last step of the path expression. Particularly, the name elements are reconstructed with their internal content, being the PCDATA in such a case.

When no structural relationship occurs (which is normally the case of updates to the local data, not mirrored outside), for instance for de-correlated fragments as discussed in the fourth Section,

Figure 4. Optimistic step-wise decomposition algorithm for descendant axis

	Algorithm **Optimistic Step-wise Query Decomposition of Descendant Axis**
	Input: a tree pattern t_p containing '$//$',
	a list of peers L_P, each peer p_i with a list of paths L_{p_i}
	Output: query decomposition over L_P
1	start at peer p_i containing the root fragment
2	or, alternatively, at a random peer p_i
3	while L_P is not empty
4	within L_{p_i}, seek "promising" path expressions w.r.t. t_p
5	let these "promising" path expressions be LP_{p_i}
6	let the remaining ones be OT_{p_i}
7	while LP_{p_i} is not empty
8	find the peer owning a path p_j in LP_{p_i}
9	evaluate the path p_j in LP_{p_i}, $L_P = L_P + p_j$
10	while OT_{p_i} is not empty
11	find the peer owning a path p_k in OT_{p_i}
12	evaluate the path p_k in OT_{p_i}, $L_P = L_P + p_k$
13	$L_P = L_P - p_i$

we rely on prefix-matching to reconstruct the results. Thus, for instance, if the fragment (b) looses its link to fragment (c), we do a simple pattern-matching to figure out whether two paths are related or not.

EXPERIMENTAL ASSESSMENT

The Experimental Framework

XP2P is implemented in Java, C++ and Tcl/Tk. The core layer consists of the open-source Chord simulator (Stoica et al., 2001), which has been extended to support path expressions identifiers instead of original document IDs. The original Chord methods *find* and *insert*, respectively targeted to search/add new document IDs within the Chord ring, have been customized to support the search/insertion of XML fragments. As storage back-end for XML data, we have chosen *BerkeleyDB* (BDB) (Berkeley DB, 2006)[8], which is an embedded database library. Indeed, the fragments content and the related path expressions

properly fingerprinted are physically stored in BDB B^+-trees. When reconstruction occurs, a BDB cursor is opened over these trees to retrieve the desired fragments data. The fragmentation model has been entirely implemented in Java. This is detached from the main body of the simulator as fragmentation may take place earlier enough than the actual network start-up. The output of the fragmentation is an enumeration of possible paths, which correspond to the fragments that are stored as actual peers data. Finally, a suitable user interface has been added to the simulator, by allowing a generic user to perform the simulation. In particular, the GUI allows the user to track the peers life, their evolution from joining the network and querying it till their leave. Figure 5 shows how XP2P GUI looks like. To avoid clutter, we only represent a few peers on the ring. It can be noted that a windows pops up on each peer showing the finger table and the fragments stored within it. Each of these fragments can be visualized as both plain XML and tree-shaped data within cascading windows.

Figure 5. Network status window in XP2P. To avoid clutter, we report only few peers in the ring

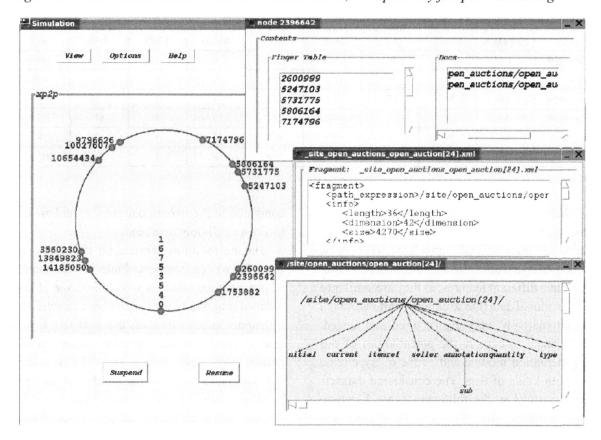

Experimental Setup

The experiments we conducted to validate the XP2P prototype aim at both proving the efficiency of the related path expressions in answering queries and their little overhead in affecting the fragments size.

In particular, we conducted all the experiments according to the following *guidelines*: (*i*) an entire XML dataset is shredded into a number of random fragments, by using the fragmentation module; more precisely, given an XML document *D* as input, our fragmentation module generates as output a set of *random* fragments extracted from *D*, using a Uniform distribution defined on the domain of all the unique path expressions in *D*; (*ii*) these fragments and their path expressions are materialized into BDB, in order for them to

be used later for querying; (*iii*) the three kinds of queries analyzed in the sixth Section are then experimentally probed to show the performance of our system. As regards the proper fragment generation process, other distributions could have been used, such as the *Zipf* or the *Gaussian* distribution. However, Uniform distribution is the one that better models typical fragment generation processes one can find in real-life P2P settings. As regards the metrics of our experimental analysis, we yield two kinds of plots, one showing the *number of hops* versus the *number of peers*, and the other showing the *percentage of query completed* versus a specified *simulation time*. The experiments ran on a *AMD Athlon XP 2600+* machine, equipped with a 2.14 GHz CPU and 1GB RAM, and running SuSe Linux 9.1.

Table 1. Datasets/fragments in the experiments and relative size of related paths

Name	Size (MB)	#Frag	MinFS (KB)	MaxFS (KB)	AvgFS (KB)	MaxD	MinD	PEsO (KB)	#PEs
xmark100	111	1000	56	860	255	9	1	59	2094
dblp	127	200	288	3.9	521	1	1	4.3	400
swissprot	109	200	252	4.1	1.48	4	1	9.35	599
xmark30	33	1000	56	816	217	9	1	81	2305
treebank	82	200	96	3.2	479	7	1	12	540
nasa	23	1000	236	6.1	1.98	6	1	56	2153

We have used synthetic XMark documents (Schmidt et al., 2002) and some real XML datasets (University of Washington XML Repository, 2006). As a first observation, note that these datasets have different features, as they are similar to flat relational data (the so called 'shallow' XML) or, alternatively, very unstructured and nested. We wanted to explore the potentialities of our fragmentation module and of the query engine for both kinds of data. The considered datasets are described in the following Table 1, where their complete size is shown, the number and sizes of fragments (*#Frag*) generated within our experiments. Moreover, as an important information, depicting the 'shallowness' of a dataset, we report the minimum and maximum path length (*MaxD* and *MinD*). To measure the relatively small impact of paths on the overall size of fragments, we summed up the occupancy of all the related path expressions in KB (*PEsO*, standing for path expressions overhead), while we indicate the total number of paths present in the network (thus including path identifiers, p_c and p_s path expressions) with *#PEs*.

First, we attempted to vary the maximum size of the fragments, *Maximum Fragment Size* (*MaxFS*), as to accommodate relatively big fragments, but not to raise too much the *Average Fragment Size* (*AvgFS*), which has been kept small in order to guarantee a non-trivial distribution of the document. Secondly, the *PEsO* size is negligible if compared to the overall dataset size and always incurs a negligible overhead.

The most shallow datasets, i.e. *dblp* and *swissprot*, have been fragmented into 200 fragments, whose path expressions size is inferior of one order of magnitude w.r.t. the other datasets. The fragments in such datasets are also less linked than in others, as the maximum depth (*MaxD*) is relatively small. By opposite, XMark is very structured and deep and the number of path expressions (*#PEs*) is significantly higher than for shallow datasets. Indeed, the occupancy of path expressions (i.e., their size in KB) reflects this number, and, in particular, only makes a slight difference for *xmark100* and *xmark30*. Indeed, the fragmentation leads to slightly more linked fragments for *xmark30* than for *xmark100* (2305 against 2094), provided the same number of fragments in both cases (1000).

Experimental Results

In our experiments, we have explored the performance of the three kinds of queries analyzed in the sixth Section: (*i*) exact-match queries containing /, corresponding to any arbitrary set of related paths present in the network; (*ii*) partial-match queries containing /, and referring paths that are prefixes of related paths present in the network; (*iii*) queries of the kind $/s_1/..../s_i//s_j/.../s_{j+k}$, employing algorithm of Figure 4.

The query set for experiment (*i*) has been chosen by randomly picking path expressions of fragments present in the DHT. Conversely, the query set for experiment (*ii*) has been chosen by constructing synthetic path expressions that do not belong to the DHT and may have in common a prefix with a path expression present in the DHT. For example, in Figure 1, a synthetic path expression is /dept/instructors. The query set for experiment (*iii*) has been chosen by randomly building queries of the kind $/s_1/..../s_i//s_j/.../s_{j+k}$, where the first segment $/s_1/..../s_i$ corresponds to an exact-match query. This is done to make the experiment non-trivial, i.e. to certainly enable descendant queries evaluation.

Figure 6 shows the number of hops required to gather the query results, while varying the number of peers present in the network. The number of queries present in each query set for the various datasets is shown as a descriptive information on top of each plot and is always equal to the number of fragments. We have chosen a number of peers scaling w.r.t. the number of fragments for each dataset and decided the interval of peers accordingly. For instance, for those datasets having 200 fragments, we have chosen a network ranging 10-100 peers to vary the number of fragments owned by the peers. Moreover, we have set up a common timeout of 500*ms* for all these experiments.

These experiments aim at showing that XP2P keeps the same efficiency of Chord DHT, when working on XML fragments identified by unique paths. The number of hops is important in DHT-based networks to guarantee that the querying mechanism does not lead to flooding.

The plots in Figure 6 clearly show an interesting trend. First, the number of hops for the three kinds of queries smoothly scales with the number of peers. Secondly, even if the relative gap depends on the employed dataset, it can be noted that the number of hops for descendant queries only slightly overcome the number of hops for exact-

match queries. The reason why the two curves are close enough is due to the fact that descendant queries do start from an exact fragment and attempt to find exact solutions, whenever they do not fail otherwise. Conversely, partial-match queries exhibit an higher number of hops w.r.t. descendant queries, as the algorithm for partial-match leads to jump over external peers several times when pruning the path expression. Nevertheless, these queries are the most significant ones for our datasets as they show that even in the *worst case*, i.e. when numerous hops occur, the number of hops is always bound to one order of magnitude at most (i.e., inferior to 12 for all datasets).

Figure 7 shows the second kind of experiment that measures the percentage of average queries completed while varying the simulation time (i.e., since the simulator started running). For each dataset, we set the number of peers as the maximum number shown on *x* axis of the corresponding plot of Figure 6. We have separately plotted results for the big datasets from the small ones, as to describe two different scenarios. In Figure 7 (left), we plot the big datasets, i.e. *dblp, swissprot, xmark100, treebank*. The percentage of average queries completed is as much higher as the number of hops in the previous experiment is lower. In particular, *dblp* and *swissprot*, exhibiting an higher number of hops for descendant queries in Figure 6 w.r.t. *xmark100* and *treebank*, are completing a lower number of descendant queries in the current experiment. A similar behavior is observed for small datasets (Figure 7 right). These also show an early cut-off point, as they quickly reach a 100% completion at around 3000*ms*, whereas the large datasets reach a 100% completion in between 3500*ms* and 4500*ms*. This yet negligible difference is imputable to the fact that the network needs a 'warm-up' time in both cases, i.e. for small and large datasets and that this time is going to have a similar impact on query completion for both datasets.

Figure 6. No. of hops versus no. of peers, measured for the three kinds of queries on dblp, swissprot, xmark100, xmark30, treebank and nasa

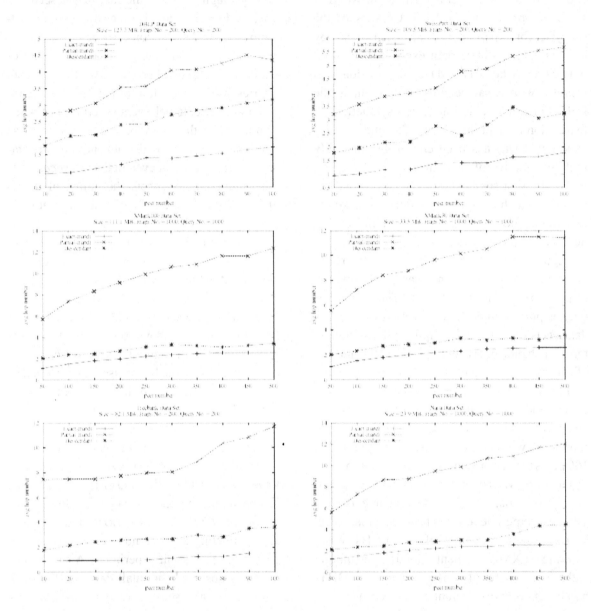

FUTURE RESEARCH DIRECTIONS

XP2P query model offers several possible extensions, mainly focused on enriching the set of covered XPath queries. In fact, lookup queries supported in XP2P can be exploited as baseline operations for evaluating more complex XPath queries such as range queries, structural joins, aggregate queries and so forth. These queries are useful not only for native P2P XML databases, but also for more challenging scenarios such as XML data integration on P2P networks, and XML processing over uncertain P2P data.

Figure 7. % of average queries completed versus simulation time, measured for descendant queries on dblp, swissprot, xmark100, treebank (left) and nasa, xmark30 datasets (right)

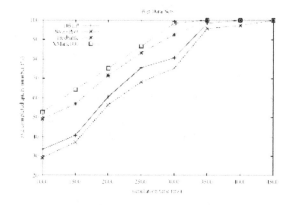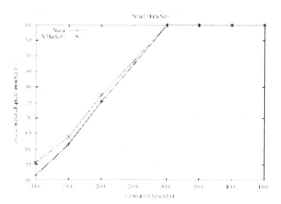

Similarly to systems based on bloom-filters (Koloniari & Pitoura, 2004; Gong et al., 2005; Abiteboul et al., 2008), XP2P is prone to support a wide range of novel P2P queries and operators. However, contrary to those systems, lightweight path expressions in XP2P are able to scale better on large and highly-dynamic P2P networks, yet introducing low computational overheads during query evaluation. The latter feature is indeed crucial for novel applications over P2P networks (e.g., sensor network data management).

Another possible extension of XP2P is represented by efficiently exploiting query caching solutions (e.g., (Mandhani & Suciu, 2005)) in order to improve XML fragment and replica management. This would lead to more efficiency during query evaluation, while also contribute to enlarge the range of applicability of XP2P in novel application scenarios such as P2P Data Warehousing and OLAP (e.g., (Espil & Vaisman, 2007)).

CONCLUSION

We have presented XP2P, a P2P framework for answering XPath queries. XP2P uses XPath to identify XML fragments in a P2P network and only needs to store a few related path expressions and a polynomial on each participating peer. Our system has been implemented on top of Chord (Stoica et al., 2001). We have conducted an extensive experimental study targeted to prove the lightweight indexing mechanism provided by related path expressions. Such a highly decentralized catalog allows us to answer queries in still reasonable time and offers scalability w.r.t. the number of peers and fragments in the network. Our prototype, previously enabled for paths lookups (Bonifati et al., 2004) is now enhanced with a suitable reconstruction module, which lets perform content-based queries. Future work will be devoted to investigate ad-hoc evaluation mechanisms of more expressive XQuery queries and full-text queries (XQuery 1.0 and XPath 2.0 Full Text, 2006), which are also interesting for XML data (Amer-Yahia et al., 2004). In particular, full-text queries represent a broad extension of IR-style queries that are made suitable for XML data.

REFERENCES

Aberer, K., Cudre-Mauroux, P., Datta, A., Despotovic, Z., Hauswirth, M., Punceva, M., & Schmidt, R. (2003). P-Grid: A Self-Organizing Structured P2P System. *SIGMOD Record*, *32*(3), 29–33. doi:10.1145/945721.945729

Abiteboul, S., Alexe, B., Benjelloun, O., Cautis, B., Fundulaki, I., Milo, T., & Sahuguet, A. (2004). An Electronic Patient Record "On Steroids": Distributed, Peer-to-Peer, Secure and Privacy-Conscious (demo). In *Proceedings of VLDB* (pp. 1273–1276).

Abiteboul, S., Baumgarten, J., Bonifati, A., & Cobena, G. Cremarenco, Dragan, C.F., Manolescu, I., Milo, T., & Preda, N. (2003). Managing Distributed Workspaces with Active XML (demo). In *Proceedings of VLDB* (pp. 1061–1064).

Abiteboul, S., Bonifati, A., Cobena, G., Manolescu, I., & Milo, T. (2003). Dynamic XML Documents with Distribution and Replication. In *Proceedings of ACM SIGMOD* (pp. 527–538).

Abiteboul, S., Manolescu, I., Polyzotis, N., Preda, N., & Sun, C. (2008). XML Processing in DHT Networks. In *Proceedings of IEEE ICDE* (pp. 606–615).

Amer-Yahia, S., Cho, S., Lakshmanan, L. V. S., & Srivastava, D. (2001). Minimization of Tree Pattern Queries. In *Proceedings of ACM SIGMOD* (pp. 497–508).

Amer-Yahia, S., Laksmanan, L. V. S., & Pandit, S. (2004). FlexPath: Flexible Structure and Full-Text Querying for XML. In *Proceedings of ACM SIGMOD* (pp. 83–94).

Berkeley DB Data Store. (2006). Retrieved from http://www.sleepycat.com/products/data.shtml

Bernstein, P. A., Giunchiglia, F., Kementsietsidis, A., Mylopoulos, J., Serafini, L., & Zaihrayeu, I. (2002). Data Management for Peer-to-Peer Computing: a Vision. In *Proceedings of ACM WebDB* (pp. 89–94).

Bonifati, A., Cuzzocrea, A., Matrangolo, U., & Jain, M. (2004). XPath Lookup Queries in P2P Networks. In *Proceedings of ACM WIDM* (pp. 48–55).

Bremer, J.-M., & Gertz, M. (2003). On Distributing XML Repositories. In *Proceedings of ACM WebDB,* (pp. 73–78).

Broder, A. Z. (1993). *Some Applications of Rabin's Fingerprinting Method.* Berlin: Springer-Verlag.

Broder, A. Z., Najork, M., & Wiener, J. L. (2003). Efficient URL Caching for World Wide Web Crawling. In *Proceedings of ACM WWW* (pp. 679–689).

Brunskill, E. (2001). Building Peer-to-Peer Systems with Chord, a Distributed Lookup Service. In *Proceedings of IEEE HotOS,* (pp. 81–86).

Crainiceanu, A., Linga, P., Gehrke, J., & Shanmugasundaram, J. (2004). Querying Peer-to-Peer Networks using P-Trees. In *Proceedings of ACM WebDB,* (pp. 25–30).

Crainiceanu, A., Linga, P., Machanavajjhala, A., Gehrke, J., & Shanmugasundaram, J. (2007). P-Ring: An Efficient and Robust P2P Range Index Structure. In *Proceedings of ACM SIGMOD,* (pp. 223–234).

Cuzzocrea, A., Darmont, J., & Mahboubi, H. (2009). (to appear). Fragmenting Very Large XML Data Warehouses via K-Means Clustering Algorithm. *Journal of Business Intelligence and Data Mining, 4*(3).

Espil, M. M., & Vaisman, A. A. (2007). Aggregate Queries in Peer-To-Peer OLAP. In *Proceedings of ACM DOLAP* (pp. 102–111).

Galanis, L., Wang, Y., Jeffery, S. R., & DeWitt, D. J. (2003). Locating Data Sources in Large Distributed Systems. In *Proceedings of VLDB* (pp. 874–885).

Gibbons, P. B., Karp, B., Ke, Y., Nath, S., & Seshan, S. (2003). IrisNet: an Architecture for a World-Wide Sensor Web. *IEEE Pervasive Computing / IEEE Computer Society [and] IEEE Communications Society*, *2*(4), 22–33. doi:10.1109/MPRV.2003.1251166

Gnutella Homepage. (2006). Retrieved from http://www.gnutella.com/

Gong, X., Yan, Y., Qian, W., & Zhou, A. (2005). Bloom Filter-based XML Packets Filtering for Millions of Path Queries. In *Proceedings of IEEE ICDE* (pp. 890–901).

Gottlob, G., Koch, C., & Pichler, R. (2002). Efficient Algorithms for Processing XPath Queries. In *Proceedings of VLDB*, (pp. 95–106).

Gribble, S. D., Halevy, A. Y., Ives, Z. G., Rodrig, M., & Suciu, D. (2001). What can Database do for Peer-to-Peer? In *Proceedings of ACM WebDB*, (pp. 31–36).

Gupta, A., Agrawal, D., & El Abbadi, A. (2003). Approximate Range Selection Queries in Peer-to-Peer Systems. In *Proceedings of CIDR*. Retrieved from http://www-db.cs.wisc.edu/cidr/cidr2003/program/p13.pdf

Halevy, A. Y., Ives, Z. G., Suciu, D., & Tatarinov, I. (2003). Schema Mediation in Peer Data Management Systems. In *Proceedings of IEEE ICDE* (pp. 505–516).

Huebsch, R., Hellerstein, J. M., Lanham, N., Loo, B. T., Shenker, S., & Stoica, I. (2003). Querying the Internet with Pier. In *Proceedings of VLDB*, (pp. 321–332).

Kantere, V., Tsoumakos, D., & Roussopoulos, N. (2004). Querying Structured Data in an Unstructured P2P System. In *Proceedings of ACM WIDM*, (pp. 64–71).

Kementsietsidis, A., Arenas, M., & Miller, R. J. (2003). Mapping Data in Peer-to-Peer Systems: Semantics and Algorithmic Issues. In *Proceedings of ACM SIGMOD*, (pp. 325–336).

Knuth, D. E. (1973). *The Art of Computer Programming III: Sorting and Searching*, (2nd Ed.). Reading, MA: Addison-Wesley.

Koloniari, G., & Pitoura, E. (2004). Content-based Routing of Path Queries in Peer-to-Peer Systems. In *Proceedings of EDBT* (pp. 29–47).

Li, Y., Yu, C., & Jagadish, H. V. (2004). Schema-free XQuery. In *Proceedings of VLDB* (pp. 72–83).

Loo, B. T., Huebsch, R., Hellerstein, J. M., Stoica, I., & Shenker, S. (2004). Enhancing P2P File-Sharing with an Internet-Scale Query Processor. In *Proceedings of VLDB* (pp. 432–443).

Mandhani, B., & Suciu, D. (2005). Query Caching and View Selection for XML Databases. In *Proceedings of VLDB* (pp. 469–480).

Menezes, A. J., van Oorschot, P. C., & Vanstone, S. A. (1996). *Handbook of Applied Cryptography*. Boca Raton, FL: CRC Press.

Ooi, B. C., Tan, K. L., Zhou, A. Y., Goh, C. H., Li, Y. G., Liau, C. Y., et al. (2003). PeerDB: Peering into Personal Databases. In *Proceedings of ACM SIGMOD*, (pp. 659–659).

Ozsu, M. T., & Valduriez, P. (1999). *Principles of Distributed Database Systems*. Upper Saddle River, NJ: Prentice-Hall.

Pang, X., Catania, B., & Tan, K. (2003). Securing your Data in Agent-based P2P Systems. In *Proceedings of IEEE DASFAA* (pp. 55–62).

Rabin, M. O. (1981). *Fingerprinting by Random Polynomials*. CRCT TR-15-81, Harvard University, Cambridge, MA.

Ratnasamy, S., Francis, P., Handley, M., Karp, R., & Shenker, S. (2001). A Scalable Content-Addressable Network. In *Proceedings of ACM SIGCOMM* (pp. 161–172).

Sartiani, C., Manghi, P., Ghelli, G., & Conforti, G. (2004). XPeer: A Self-Organizing XML P2P Database System. In . *Proceedings of P, 2PDB,* 456–465.

Schmidt, A., Waas, F., Kersten, M., Carey, M., Manolescu, I., & Busse, R. (2002). XMark: A Benchmark for XML Data Management. In *Proceedings of VLDB,* (pp. 974–985).

Srivastava, D., Al-Khalifa, S., Jagadish, H. V., Koudas, N., Patel, J. M., & Wu, Y. (2002). Structural Joins: A Primitive for Efficient XML Query Pattern Matching. In *Proceedings of IEEE ICDE,* (pp. 141–152).

Stoica, I., Morris, R., Karger, D., Kaashoek, M. F., & Balakrishnan, H. (2001). Chord: A scalable Peer-to-Peer Lookup Service for Internet Applications. In *Proceedings of ACM SIGCOMM,* (pp. 149–160).

Suciu, D. (2002). Distributed Query Evaluation on Semistructured Data. *ACM Transactions on Database Systems, 27*(1), 1–62. doi:10.1145/507234.507235

Tatarinov, I., & Halevy, A. Y. (2004). Efficient Query Reformulation in Peer-Data Management Systems. In *Proceedings of ACM SIGMOD,* (pp. 539–550).

TheKaZaA Homepage. (2006). Retrieved from http://www.kazaa.com

Tsoumakos, D., & Roussopoulos, N. (2003). A Comparison of Peer-to-Peer Search Methods. In *Proceedings of ACM WebDB,* (pp. 61–66).

University of Washington XML Repository. (2006). Retrieved from http://www.cs.washington.edu/research/xmldatasets/

XML Path Language. (2006). Retrieved from http://www.w3.org/TR/xpath

XQuery 1.0 and XPath 2.0 Full-Text. (2006). Retrieved from http://www.w3.org/TR/2005/WD-xquery-full-text-20050404/

KEY TERMS AND DEFINITIONS

Chord: It is the reference open-source implementation for DHT networks, featuring the logarithmic scalable search of resources among peers. It has been defined by Ian Stoica and other people at Berkeley.

DHT: Distributed Hash Table – it is an hash table having the property of distribution over a networked setting. In a broader sense, a DHT identifies a class of P2P networks, which are also known as structured P2P networks. A key in the DHT identifies the resource of a node, and it can be set-up/retrieved by means of put/get methods.

Fingerprinting: It is a technique that computes fingerprints, i.e. unique signatures, by means of means of random polynomials. Fingerprints exhibit a remarkable software efficiency, a well-understood probability of collisions and nice algebraic properties.

Path Expression: A path expression over an XML document is a sequence of steps, each of which is a element or attribute name in the XML document (or a wildcard) and has an axis that indicates the direction of navigation (the main axes are child, descendant, following and preceding).

Peer-to-Peer (P2P) Network: it is a network environment composed by hosts and services where each node acts in the role of server exposing a set of services as well as in the role of client invoking a set of services.

Routing: It is the process to redirect a request or a query on a peer through the network. In DHTs, routing is done by using the routing tables, which store the neighbor peers at a logarithmic distance.

Tree Pattern: It is an abstraction used to represent the tree behind a query expressed in XPath. Indeed, since XPath is a language for querying XML, its expressions can be modeled as a tree, with nodes for each step in the path expression and edges between the nodes, representing the axes of XPath.

XML: eXtensible Markup Language – it is a markup and data exchange language that is the standard language for the Web of the future, defined and approved by the W3C, the World Wide Web consortium.

XPath: XML Path – it is a navigational language for XML, which lets identify the paths that lead from the root of an XML document to the leaves. This language is one of the standards defined by the W3C, the World Wide Web consortium.

ENDNOTES

[1]   Obviously, the only positional filter admitted on the root s_j is [1], which is omitted for conciseness.

[2]   We assume that the same path belonging to different documents is distinguishable by means of different document names, whenever present, and/or by different namespaces, whenever the document names are the same.

[3]   Linked URLs are reminiscent of path expressions sharing the same prefix.

[4]   These are quite acceptable bounds since the degree of the polynomial needs to be adjusted, only if the bounds abundantly overcome of (*at least* one order of magnitude, e.g. from 2^{30} to 2^{31}).

Section 4
XML Query Translation and Data Integration

Chapter 13
Normalization and Translation of XQuery

Norman May
SAP Research, CEC Karlsruhe Vincenz-Prießnitz-Str. 1 Germany

Guido Moerkotte
Database Research Group, University of Mannheim, Germany

ABSTRACT

Early approaches to XQuery processing proposed proprietary techniques to optimize and evaluate XQuery statements. In this chapter, the authors argue for an algebraic optimization and evaluation technique for XQuery as it allows us to benefit from experience gained with relational databases. An algebraic XQuery processing method requires a translation into an algebra representation. While many publications already exist on algebraic optimizations and evaluation techniques for XQuery, an assessment of translation techniques is required. Consequently, they give a comprehensive survey for translating XQuery into various query representations. The authors relate these approaches to the way normalization and translation is implemented in Natix and discuss these two steps in detail. In their experience, their translation method is a good basis for further optimizations and query evaluation.

INTRODUCTION

As XQuery is used in an increasing number of applications, the execution time of these queries becomes more important for the acceptance of this query language. Especially for queries where potentially large amounts of XML are processed, strategies to reduce the query processing time need to be applied. The first XQuery processors often implemented a number of heuristics for this pur-

pose. As XQuery becomes more popular, specific storage and index structures as well as specialized execution strategies were implemented.

Recently algebraic optimization techniques, as they are standard in relational databases, were used to build XQuery processors where optimizations are stated as algebraic equivalences, e.g. (Naughton et al., 2001; Jagadish et al., 2002; Fiebig et al., 2002; May et al., 2006; Ozcan et al., 2005; Nicola & van der Linden, 2005; Florescu et al., 2004; Boncz et al., 2006; Liu et al., 2005; Pal et al., 2005). This development is motivated by the ability (1) to apply

DOI: 10.4018/978-1-61520-727-5.ch013

optimizations known from relational databases and adopt them for XML processing, (2) to prove the correctness of query optimizations based on a formally defined query representation. Relational query optimizers today approach query optimization in a sequence of six steps:

1. **Scan and Parse the query statement** to analyze the lexical structure of the query.

2. **Normalization of the query, translation into an internal representation, type checking, and semantic analysis**: This phase checks the semantic correctness of the query. At the same time, additional information is attached to the parse tree, e.g. type information, references to schema information, or references to available statistics. As the parse tree is not the most convenient representation of the query to apply optimizations, it is translated into an internal query representation – usually an algebraic or calculus representation. The translation step may require some normalization to be applied before. The XQuery specification gives some rules for typing XQuery expressions (Draper et al., 2007), but more precise results can sometimes be obtained. In this chapter, we will focus on this optimization phase, in particular the normalization and translation step.

3. **First heuristic optimization phase**: In this phase the query optimizer applies heuristic optimizations. Some of these optimizations are hard to implement in a cost-based optimizer, e.g. predicate-move-around. Other optimizations applied in this phase prepare the query so that the search space of the cost-based optimizer is increased, e.g. query unnesting (May et al., 2004), (May et al., 2006) or view merging, and thus, often drastically improve the overall quality of the resulting query execution plan.

4. **Cost-based optimization phase**: Based on cardinality estimates and a cost-model for possible implementations of a query, the cost-based optimizer generates equivalent plan alternatives, called query execution plan (QEP). These alternatives differ in the order of the involved operators or their implementations. Among all alternatives examined in this phase, the most efficient one is chosen. Several metrics are used as efficiency criteria, e.g. resource consumption or expected query execution time.

5. **Second heuristic optimization phase**: This phase applies heuristic optimizations that are not considered in the previous phase, e.g. merging adjacent operators.

6. **Code generation**: This phase transforms the QEP into an executable form.

In this chapter, we first discuss how an XQuery query can be translated into an internal representation that is close the well-known QGM-model used in IBM Starburst/DB2 (Haas et al., 1989). As several other query optimizers use a similar query representation, it is desirable to reuse their infrastructure to implement a query optimizer for XQuery. As (Grust et al., 2004) have pointed out, some care is required when a relational database is used to evaluate XQuery. Others discussed algebraic optimizations for XQuery based on native XML database management systems, e.g. (May et al., 2006; May, 2007; Re et al., 2006).

After surveying existing approaches to algebraic XQuery optimization and translation approaches, we introduce an algebra to represent XQuery statements that serve as input to algebraic optimizations. This algebra is defined over sequences of tuples as it is required to preserve the semantics of XQuery. Hence, it is not possible to directly apply algebraic optimizations known for SQL and relational databases to XQuery.

Then, we define the fragment of XQuery that is supported by our translation approach. This fragment covers a large fraction of the XQuery 1.0 language. After that, we introduce a number of normalization rules that prepare the XQuery statement for the translation step. We use rewrite rules that formally state the normalization rewrite. Such a formal notation is desirable because we can prove of correctness of these rewrites. In the core part of this chapter, we introduce the translation function that maps a normalized XQuery expression into the algebra as it is used in the Natix native XML database system. This algebraic expression can later be rewritten by cost-based algebraic optimizations.

We conclude this chapter with a summary of the main contributions of this chapter. Furthermore, we outline how the resulting algebraic expressions can be mapped to a calculus representation, and we discuss some open issues related to the translation and normalization of XQuery queries.

APPROACHES TO XQUERY NORMALIZATION AND TRANSLATION

In this section, we survey approaches to represent XQuery queries for the purposes of query optimization. There are a number of specifically tailored representations, e.g. (Kay, 2008). In contrast to these approaches formalisms based on algebras or calculus representations are advantageous for two reasons. First, these optimizations can be better expressed and implemented based on this internal query representation. Second, as a prerequisite for leveraging these optimization techniques, the XQuery statement needs to be translated into the desired internal representation. Early approaches to XML query processing focused on XPath which is a proper sublanguage of XQuery. Hence, we discuss approaches to XPath translation before we extend our scope to the XQuery language.

Query Representations for XQuery Optimization

XQuery optimizations typically transform a representation of the original XQuery statement into an equivalent form that supposedly is more efficient to evaluate. In this section we structure this variety of representations that were proposed as a logical algebra or calculus for XQuery or XPath.

Extensions to Relational Algebras. Extensions to relational algebras leverage the power and experiences of optimizing OQL and SQL by extending the logical algebras used for these languages. Relational algebras are based on sets (Maier, 1983). For SQL, this algebra was extended to support bag semantics (Dayal et al., 1982; Albert, 1991) or OQL (Cluet & Moerkotte, 1993; Steenhagen et al., 1994). Because the XQuery data model is based on sequences of items, algebras for XQuery need to handle both duplicates and order. Algebras proposed for order- and duplicate-aware data models (Slivinskas et al., 2002; Lerner & Shasha, 2003) and specifically for XQuery include (Beeri & Tzaban, 1999; Frasincar et al., 2002; May et al., 2004; Grust & Teubner, 2004).

Tree Algebras. An alternative approach represents queries as pattern trees (Jagadish et al., 2002). XPath expressions are translated into a pattern tree. Computing the result of an XPath expression corresponds to finding all embeddings of the tree pattern in the XML tree instance. The use of tree algebras is motivated by the fact that one can formally reason about trees (Suciu, 2001). A particularly interesting result is that query containment is *coNP* complete once either two features //, [], * are combined with the child axis (Miklau & Suciu, 2002). For more restricted cases query containment is in *P*. As query containment is an important test for applicability of views to answer a query, these results affect our translation procedure discussed later in this chapter. On the other hand, tree algebras seem to lack the expressiveness needed to represent any query formulated in XQuery. Most tree algebras are restricted to a subset of axis steps and have difficulty in expressing advanced XQuery constructs such as node construction or type-based constructs (Hosoya & Pierce, 2000).

Calculus Representations. The third camp translates the XQuery query into a representation close to the query language level. This includes representations as query graph (Haas et al., 1989), (Jarke & Koch, 1984) or in comprehension calculus (Fegaras & Maier, 1995). Both the query graph model (Shanmugasundaram et al., 2001), (Ozcan et al., 2005) and the comprehension calculus (Fegaras et al., 2002) required extensions to support XQuery. Calculus representations do not define a strict execution strategy for an XQuery statement. As a consequence, optimizations such as unnesting rewrites are easier to implement because pattern matching needs to consider fewer cases. On the other hand, another translation step into a query execution plan (QEP) is needed.

Other Approaches. In the literature on XQuery optimization the distinction between logical and physical algebra is often blurred (Brantner et al., 2005; Re et al., 2006). The reason is that heuristics are used to directly derive an efficient QEP from the query. We prefer to clearly separate logical and physical algebra, as it is done e.g. in (Jagadish et al., 2002; Florescu et al., 2004; Liu et al., 2005; Boncz et al., 2006) where the logical algebra is not concerned with specific implementations of operators. These implementations are defined by the physical algebra. Overall, this separation shall lead to a cleaner architecture of the XQuery processor.

Normalization and Translation of XQuery

To enable a query statement to be optimized using algebraic optimizations, it needs to be translated into an algebra expression. Most systems prepare this translation with a normalization step. In this section, we give a historic account on these steps and relate them to the normalization and translation of XQuery.

Classic Techniques for Normalization and Translation of SQL. There are two main approaches to optimize a query. In the first one, the query is transformed into an internal representation that can be interpreted by the query evaluation system (Astrahan & Chamberlin, 1975; Wong & Youssefi, 1976). In this approach, called *interpretation*, there are only limited possibilities for optimizations.

Thus, the *translation* of a query into an internal representation is now the dominant technique in query processing. Relational algebra and relational calculus equivalences became prime targets for the translation of query languages because one can formally prove the equivalence of two expressions. It is then the task of query optimization to find equivalent expressions that can be evaluated more efficiently.

(Ceri & Gottlob, 1985) translate a SQL query into an algebraic expression in two steps: The first step transforms the SQL syntax into a restricted one establishing a normalized syntax. This simplifies the translation, the second step, in which the restricted SQL syntax is translated into the algebra. The authors argue that the resulting algebraic expression can be optimized and, thus, efficiency of the resulting algebraic expression is not an issue. Moreover, it is shown that their translation establishes a normal form because syntactically different queries are translated into the same algebraic expression.

Calculus representations are another representation into which SQL is translated (Negri et al., 1991; von Bültzingsloewen, 1987; Fegaras & Maier, 1995). (Fegaras & Maier, 1995) and (von Bültzingsloewen, 1987) use a normal form established during their translation as the basis for further optimizations. Optimizing nested queries either containing quantifiers or aggregate functions are the prime subjects of research here (Jarke & Koch, 1984; Bry, 1989; von Bültzingsloewen, 1987; Nakano, 1990; Fegaras & Maier 1995).

In Starburst and DB2, a query is translated into the Query Graph Model (QGM) (Haas et al., 1989). QGM is a query representation that is proprietary to the IBM database products that is based on the idea of the calculus representations above. For

SQL and, as we will see later, also for XQuery, a mapping of query constructs to the QGM is defined (Ozcan et al., 2005), (Nicola & van der Linden, 2005). Unfortunately, only informal descriptions of this mapping are publicly available. Heuristic optimizations, such as the decorrelation of nested queries and the merging of QGM blocks, are performed on this representation.

Translation of XPath 1.0. Path expressions represent an important fragment of XQuery. Many features of the XPath 1.0 standard have become part of the XQuery specification. Thus, translation, optimization, and evaluation techniques proposed for XPath 1.0 should carry over to path expressions in XQuery. (Gottlob et al., 2002) observed that XPath expressions have an exponential worst-case run time when subexpressions are evaluated repeatedly. They propose to use memoization as execution strategy to avoid this redundant work. Along the same line, (Helmer et al., 2002) translate XPath location steps without positional predicates such that creating duplicates is avoided. These ideas were extended in (Hidders & Michiels, 2003), where redundant sort operations are removed when the result of the path expression will still be in document order. (Brantner et.al, 2005) were the first to present a complete translation procedure for XPath 1.0 into algebraic expressions. A comprehensive translation of XPath into SQL statements is proposed in (Grust, 2002).

Normalization and Translation of XQuery. The idea of (Ceri & Gottlob, 1985) to normalize the full query syntax into a core language is also proposed in the XQuery specification (Draper et al., 2007). The formal semantics of XQuery is defined in terms of this core language. Thus, an interpretative view of evaluating XQuery is taken in the formal specification. While some implementations of XQuery implement these semantics literally, it was soon clear that efficient XQuery processing demands a query representation that is easy to optimize. The first proposal to normalize XQuery was proposed by (Manolescu et al.,

2001). Their normalization rules prepare XQuery statements for the translation into SQL statements. Thus, all normalization rules work on the level of XQuery statements, remove nested FLOWR expressions, and establish some normal form that is not formally characterized. Extending previous work (Fegaras & Maier 1995), (Fegaras et al., 2002) translate XQuery statements into monoid comprehensions. Rewrites establish a unique normal form to prepare subsequent optimizations. Monoid comprehensions allow for an elegant integration of different bulk types. Expressions in this calculus can be checked to preserve order or duplicates. Unfortunately, the cited work does not seem to exploit this fact.

The Timber system (Jagadish et al., 2002) follows a different approach. Queries are translated into pattern trees defined in the logical tree algebra TAX. Optimizations are defined as rewrites on this tree algebra. All pattern trees in TAX can be mapped to algebraic operators in the physical algebra.

These early proposals do not fully support the XQuery specification. Some of these efforts included a translation of XQuery into SQL (Krishnamurthy et al., 2003). However, the MonetDB/ Pathfinder project covers a large subset of XQuery. In this system, XML documents are represented in a pre-/post order encoding that maps a unique identifier to each node in the document (Grust, 2002). This allows to construct SQL queries that retrieve all nodes that satisfy a path expression. Later, this translation was extended to larger fragments of XQuery (Grust et al., 2004; Grust & Teubner, 2004).

In the following, as the standardization process of XQuery converged, the focus shifted to a more complete coverage of the XQuery specification. The XQuery engine of the BEA streaming XQuery engine (Florescu et al., 2004) translates XQuery expressions into an internal expression representation. While this representation shares the ideas of the relational algebra, it is specifically designed to represent XQuery expressions. Both normaliza-

Table 1. Comparison of XML translation approaches.

Approach	XPath 1.0	XQuery 1.0	Query Representation
XML TaskForce (Gottlob et al., 2002)	(almost) Full	No	Context value table
XPC (Helmer et. al., 2002; Brantner et. al, 2005)	Full	No	Physical algebra
Natix (Fiebig et. al, 2002; May, 2007)	Full	Partial	Calculus and physical algebra
(Fegaras et al., 2002)		Partial	Monoid comprehension calculus
Timber (Jagadish et al., 2002)	Partial	Partial	Tree algebra
BEA XQuery Processor (Florescu et al., 2004)	Full	Full	Combined logical and physical algebra
Pathfinder and MonetDB/XQuery (Grust et al., 2004; Grust & Teubner, 2004)	Full	Full	Logical algebra and either SQL (Pathfinder) or physical algebra (MonetDB)
MS SQL Server (Pal et al., 2005)	Partial	Partial	Logical and physical algebra
Oracle XML DB (Liu et al., 2005)	Partial	Partial	Logical and physical algebra
IBM DB2 (Ozcan et al., 2005; Nicola & van der Linden, 2005)	Full	Full	Calculus and physical algebra

tion and optimization are carried out as rewrites on this query representation. A similar approach is taken by Galax (Re et al., 2006). This system implements the normalization of the XQuery specification literally. Afterwards, the resulting XQuery core expressions are translated into an extended algebra and optimized using algebraic rewrites.

Commercial relational database products also support XQuery to a varying extent. Microsoft SQL Server (Pal et al., 2005) and Oracle XML DB (Liu et al., 2005) support fragments of the XQuery specification. Queries are translated into algebraic expressions and, if possible, rewriting techniques of the relational optimizer are used for optimizations. To support XQuery in IBM DB2 (Ozcan et al., 2005; Nicola & van der Linden, 2005) the QGM query representation of DB2 was extended. The query representation used in Natix also maps the translated algebraic expression to an internal representation that is similar to the query graph model (Fiebig et. al, 2002; May, 2007). Table 1 summarizes the approaches surveyed in this section.

NAL: THE NATIX A ALGEBRA FOR XQUERY OPTIMIZATION

In the remainder of this chapter, we refer to the logical algebra as defined below when we talk about an algebra or algebraic operator. The logical algebra, NAL, we introduce in this section defines the logical operations executed in a query. This set of operators is sufficient as a target for the translation into an internal query representation as a basis for query optimization.

In contrast to a physical algebra, a logical algebra does not imply any specific implementation. This allows us to investigate the equivalence of two algebraic expressions much more succinctly. Furthermore, query optimization can at least conceptually be split up into a phase with logical optimizations and physical optimization (Chaudhuri, 1998).

The definition of the algebraic operators in NAL requires some notation for our algebra. As noted above, our algebra extends the relational algebra by further operators needed to represent XQuery queries. Furthermore, it is defined over sequences of tuples as detailed below.

We denote sequences by <•>, the empty sequence by ε, and sequence concatenation by ⊕. Note that sequence concatenation is associative but not commutative. For a sequence e we use $\alpha(e)$ to select its first element and $\tau(e)$ to retrieve its tail. We equate sequences containing a single item and the item contained. This implicit conversion is demanded by the XQuery specification.

Tuples are constructed by using brackets ([·]) and concatenated by ∘. The set of attributes of a tuple t is denoted by $A(t)$. The projection of a tuple t on a set of attributes A is denoted by $t_{|A}$. To access a single attribute B in a tuple, $B \in A(t)$, we use $t.B$. For all tuples t_1 and t_2 contained in a sequence of tuples, we demand $A(t_1) = A(t_2)$.

Given that, we can define the set of attributes $A(s)$ provided by a sequence s as the set of attributes of the contained tuples. Let e be an expression whose result is a tuple or a sequence of tuples. Then the set of attributes provided in the result of e is denoted by $A(e)$.

Binding an attribute a of some tuple to a value v is denoted by *[a:v]*. We call an attribute a in an expression e free if it occurs in e and is not bound to a value by e. That is, a value for a has to be provided by some other expression, e.g. an outer query block. We denote the set of free attributes of an expression e by $F(e)$. Note that attributes behave the same way as variables: they are bound to a value by some expression and referenced by another one. From now on, we will use the terms variable and attribute interchangeably.

For an expression e_1 possibly containing free variables, and a tuple e_2, we denote by $e_1(e_2)$ the result of evaluating e_1 where bindings of free variables are taken from variable bindings provided by e_2. Of course this requires $F(e_1) \subseteq A(e_2)$. For a set of attributes, we define the tuple constructor $\perp A$ such that it returns a tuple with attributes in A initialized to *NULL*. Thanks to the *NULL*-value, we can distinguish empty results from unknown values which is not possible in XQuery yet.

Using these notations, we introduce two elementary operations to construct sequences.

The first is #, which returns a singleton sequence consisting of the empty tuple, i.e. a tuple with no attributes. It is used in order to avoid special cases during the translation of XQuery. The second operation, denoted by *e[a]*, constructs a sequence of tuples with attribute a from a sequence of non-tuple values e. For each value c in e, a tuple is constructed containing a single attribute a whose value is c. More formally, we define *e[a]:= ε* if e is empty, and *e[a]:= [a: α(e)] ⊕ τ(e)[a]* else. We use this operation to map sequences of items in the XQuery data model into sequences of tuples in our data model.

We refer to an n-ary function, say f, with $f(e_1, . . ., e_n)$. Sometimes, we will omit the formal parameters in expressions. Then the actual parameters of f must be bound by the enclosing expression. We denote the identity function by *id* and concatenation of functions or operators by ∘.

For result construction we define a function with signature $C(type, name, content)$. It constructs a node of the requested node type, with given tag name, and content. We use the arguments *elem, attr*, etc. to identify the node type. To support computed constructors, the name and content may reference previously bound variables. Not every argument is meaningful for every node type. But for the sake of simplicity, we ignore this fact.

Based on the notation, we are now able to define the algebraic operators in NAL; Table 2 summarizes their definitions. For space reasons we cannot discuss these operators in detail here, and thus we refer to (May, 2007; May et al., 2006) for a detailed discussion of this algebra and possible implementations of the involved operators.

NORMALIZATION OF XQUERY

Prior to the translation of an XQuery statement – or rather transforming its parse tree into the logical algebra – a normalization step is employed to normalize the representation of the query statement. The XQuery specification explicitly defines a core

Table 2. NAL algebra.

Scan Singleton	
$\#$	$:= \langle [] \rangle$
Selection	
$\sigma_p(e)$	$:= \begin{cases} \alpha(e) \oplus \sigma_p(\tau(e)) & if \ p(\alpha(e)) \\ \sigma_p(\tau(e)) & else \end{cases}$
Tid	
$tid_a(e)$	$:= tid_a(e,1)$ where
$tid_a(e,n)$	$:= \alpha(e) \circ [a:n] \oplus tid_a(\tau(e), n+1)$
Projection	
$\Pi_A(e)$	$:= \alpha(e)\mid_A \oplus \Pi_A(\tau(e))$
Tid-Duplicate Elimination	
$\Pi_A^{tid_b}(e)$	$:= \begin{cases} \alpha(e)\mid_A \oplus \Pi_A^{tid_b}(\tau(e)) & if \ \alpha(e).b \notin \Pi_b(\tau(e)) \\ \Pi_A^{tid_b}(\tau(e)) & else \end{cases}$
Map	
$X_{a:e_2}(e_1)$	$:= \alpha(e_1) \circ [a:e_2(\alpha(e_1))] \oplus X_{a:e_2}(\tau(e_1))$
Product	
$e_1 \bar{\times} e_2$	$:= \begin{cases} \varepsilon & if \ e_2 = \varepsilon \\ (e_1 \circ \alpha(e_2)) \oplus (e_1 \bar{\times} \tau(e_2)) & else \end{cases}$
	where e_1 is a singleton
Cross Product	
$e_1 \times e_2$	$:= (\alpha(e_1) \bar{\times} e_2) \oplus (\tau(e_1) \times e_2)$
Join	
$e_1 \times_p e_2$	$:= \sigma_p(e_1 \times e_2)$
D-Join	
$e_1 <e_2>$	$:= \alpha(e_1) \bar{\times} e_2(\alpha(e_1)) \oplus \tau(e_1) < e_2 >$

continued on following page

Table 2. continued

Semijoin	
$e_1 \ltimes_p e_2$	$:= \begin{cases} \alpha(e_1) \oplus (\tau(e_1) \ltimes_p e_2) & \text{if } \exists x \in e_2 : p(\alpha(e_1) \circ x) \\ \tau(e_1) \ltimes_p e_2 & \text{else} \end{cases}$
Antijoin	
$e_1 \rhd_p e_2$	$:= \begin{cases} \alpha(e_1) \oplus (\tau(e_1) \rhd_p e_2) & \text{if } \nexists x \in e_2 : p(\alpha(e_1) \circ x) \\ \tau(e_1) \rhd_p e_2 & \text{else} \end{cases}$
Left Outer Join	
$e_1 \nabla_p^{g:e} e_2$	$:= \begin{cases} (\alpha(e_1) \nabla_p e_2) \oplus (\tau(e_1) \nabla_p^{g:e} e_2) & \text{if } (\alpha(e_1) \nabla_p e_2) \neq \varepsilon \\ (\alpha(e_1) \circ \perp_{A(e_2) \setminus \{g\}} \circ [g:e]) & \text{else} \\ \quad \oplus (\tau(e_1) \nabla_p^{g:e} e_2) \end{cases}$
Union	
$e_1 \,\hat{\cup}\, e_2$	$:= e_1 \oplus e_2$
Intersection	
$e_1 \,\hat{\cap}\, e_2$	$:= e_1 \ltimes_{A(e_1)=A(e_2)} e_2$
Difference	
$e_1 \,\hat{-}\, e_2$	$:= e_1 \rhd_{A(e_1)=A(e_2)} e_2$
Unnest	
$\mu_{A:g}(e)$	$:= (\alpha(e) \times (\Pi_{A:A(g)}(\alpha(e).g))) \oplus \mu_{A:g}(\tau(e))$
Unnest Map	
$\Upsilon_{A:e_2}(e_1)$	$:= \Pi_{\bar{\hat{a}}}(\mu_{A:\hat{a}}(\chi_{\hat{a}:e_2}(e_1)))$
Binary Grouping	
$e_1 \Gamma_{g;A_1 \theta A_2;f} e_2$	$:= \alpha(e_1) \circ [g:G(\alpha(e_1))] \oplus (\tau(e_1) \Gamma_{g;A_1 \theta A_2;f} e_2)$ where
$G(x)$	$:= f(\sigma_{x|_{A_1} \theta A_2}(e_2))$
Unary Grouping	
$\Gamma_{g;\theta A;f}(e)$	$:= \Pi_{A:A'}(\Pi_{A':A}^D(\Pi_A(e))\Gamma_{g;A'\theta A;f} e)$

language of XQuery that is usually much more verbose than the equivalent original statement. But it limits the number of cases to consider, e.g. for describing XQuery's formal semantics or its translation into an optimizer-internal representation. A similar approach is usually taken for SQL (Ceri & Gottlob, 1985).

The rewrites applied to a query during normalization, however, should obey to a number of requirements:

- **Soundness**: Each transformation must preserve the semantics of the given query.
- **Completeness**. Ideally, every query construct should be handled by the normalization and translation step. As XQuery is a query language with many features, we cannot treat every language construct yet. Instead, we concentrate on the XQuery fragment defined below.
- **Uniqueness:** The normalization and translation of equivalent queries should result in the same representation of the query, i.e. a normal form. The application order of rewrite rules should not matter, and it should be ensured that the normal form is reached by the normalization algorithm if the normal form exists.
- **Effectiveness** The normal form should be reached in a finite number of transformations, preferably in a few transformation steps. We will point out how we achieve this.
- **Optimizability**. The normal form should be a good starting point for optimizations applied later during query optimization.

In our presentation of the normalization step, we will first present the XQuery fragment that is currently supported by our approach. We then informally discuss properties of the normalized query. After that we introduce the rewrite rules used to normalize XQuery statements and analyze how they contribute to achieving the desired properties of a normalized query statement. We then illustrate our approach based on a number of examples and conclude this section by enumerating some restrictions of our method.

SUPPORTED XQUERY FRAGMENT

In this chapter, we focus on a subset of XQuery that is expressive enough to formulate complex queries, e.g. nested queries. However, the translation and optimization approach we cover here is general enough to support the missing features. Table 3 presents the subset of the XQuery grammar we currently support. It is a variant of LixQuery grammar (Hidders et al., 2004).

In this grammar, we denote terminals with terminal and non-terminals with nonterminal. Some terminals contain complex regular expressions of tokens. We refer to (Hidders et al., 2004) for their definition and simply use angle brackets instead, i.e. <complex token>. For simplicity, we use a very restrictive set of functions which we all treat as special built-in functions. In particular, we ignore user-defined or recursive functions.

In the grammar, we only give the productions for computed constructors. Since our example queries use direct constructors, we need to normalize them into computed constructors as defined in (Draper et al., 2007). We will use this normalization step in this chapter without repeating the associated rewrites.

We have added flwrExpr to be able to express queries more succinctly and quantExpr because we want to express quantifiers explicitly. Furthermore, we distinguish between general comparison – having existential semantics – and value comparison. All these extensions to LixQuery are syntactic sugar, but are often used in practice. As we will see later, their treatment has several implications on normalization, translation, and optimization of XQuery.

Note that we have simplified the grammar. For example, our grammar does not explicitly

Table 3. Supported XQuery fragment.

mainModule	::=	expr <EOF>
Expr	::=	singleExpr | exprSeq
exprSeq	::=	singleExpr (“,” singleExpr)*
singleExpr	::=	flwrExpr | quantExpr | andExpr
builtIn	::=	(“doc(“ singleExpr “)”
	|	“name(“ singleExpr “)”
	|	“string(“ singleExpr “)”
	|	“integer(“ singleExpr “)”
	|	“contains(“ singleExpr “,” singleExpr “)”
	|	“true()” | “false()”
	|	“not(“ singleExpr “)”
	|	“count(“ singleExpr “)”
	|	“distinct-values(“ singleExpr “)”
flwrExpr	::=	(forExpr | letExpr)+ whereClause? “return” singleExpr
rangeExpr	::=	var “in” singleExpr
bindExpr	::=	var “:=” singleExpr
forExpr	::=	“for” rangeExpr (“,” rangeExpr)*
letExpr	::=	“let” bindExpr (“,” bindExpr)*
whereClause	::=	“where” singleExpr
quantExpr	::=	(“some” | “every”) rangeExpr (“,” rangeExpr)* “satisfies” ExprSingle
andExpr	::=	compExpr ((“or” | “and”) compExpr)?
compExpr	::=	addExpr ((genComp | valComp | nodeComp) addExpr)?

genComp	::=	“=” | “!=” | “<” | “<=” | “>” | “>=”
valComp	::=	“eq” | “ne” | “lt” | “le” | “gt” | “ge”
nodeComp	::=	“<<” | “>>” | “is”
addExpr	::=	multExpr ((“+” | “-”) multExpr)*
multExpr	::=	union ((“*” | “div” | “idiv” | “mod”) union)*
union	::=	path ((“|” | “union” | “intersect” | “except”) union)*
path	::=	filter ((“/” | “//”) path)*
filter	::=	step (“[“ singleExpr “]”)*
step	::=	“.” | “..” | qname | “@” qname | “*” | “@*” | “text()” | primaryExpr
primaryExpr	::=	builtIn | qname | constr | var | literal | empSeq | “(“ expr “)”
literal	::=	string | integer
string	::=	<String>
integer	::=	((<Digits> | “+” <Digits>) | (“-” <Digits>))
var	::=	“$” qname
empSeq	::=	“()”
constr	::=	“element” “{“ singleExpr “}” “{“ expr “}”
	|	“attribute” “{“ singleExpr “}” “{“ expr “}”
	|	“text” “{“ singleExpr “}”
	|	“document” “{“ singleExpr “}”
qname	::=	<NCName> | (<NCName> “:” <NCName>)

enforce any precedence rules for binary operators as it is done in the XQuery specification (Boag et al., 2007). Nevertheless they are still left associative.

A NOTATION FOR NORMALIZATION RULES

Conceptually, the normalization and translation rules we present here match patterns of the textual XQuery representation and transform them, given the bindings of the matched pattern. In this section, we will denote pattern matching with regular expressions on the grammar presented above. We refer to terminal symbols with terminal and to non-terminals with nonterminal. During normalization, some rules introduce new variable names using the expression <$v = newVar()>. Thereby, we create a new variable name to which we can refer by $v. We will also use fun to refer to arbitrary functions including builtIn, andExpr, compExpr, addExpr, multExpr, and constr. In the case of constructors, these arguments refer to the computed node name and the computed content.

As an important preparation step to the translation, we normalize XQuery expressions on the query level. More precisely, all normalization steps work on the abstract syntax tree created by the XQuery parser. Our normalization rewrites transform the XQuery statement into a normal form. The normalized query is easier to translate into our algebra because we have to consider fewer query patterns. Moreover, normalization facilitates common subexpression elimination because we introduce new variables that are bound to complex expressions. In this query representation, it is much easier to detect common subexpressions.

There are many relationships between path expressions embedded into XQuery expressions and equivalent expressions in XQuery (Draper et al., 2007), (Michiels et al., 2006). For example, the transformation of XQuery into the XQuery core breaks location steps into nested FLWOR expressions (Draper et al., 2007). We use several of these techniques and, hence, reuse normalization rules presented there. But we will tailor normalization for our needs. In particular, we will break XPath expressions apart only when a location step contains a filter expression. The reverse step, detecting tree patterns, has been discussed in (Michiels et al., 2006). Our motivation for doing so is that especially for simple path expressions many optimizations are known, e.g. (Amer-Yahia et al., 2001; Helmer et al., 2002; Hidders & Michiels, 2003; Balmin et al., 2004). Several of these optimizations are only tractable or applicable for simple path expressions.

FLWR Expressions

Objectives. The objective of normalizing FLWR expressions consists in obtaining a uniform representation for different formulations of the FLWR expression. As a result, the subsequent steps of query compilation are simplified, most importantly the translation step and several optimizations. For example, during normalization we reduce the number of query patterns which have to be handled during query translation. Our normalization rewrites separate the query into three parts:

- **The binding part** consists of **for** and the **let** clauses. It gathers all queried data, computes intermediate results, and binds them to variables.
- **The modifying part** alters the tuple stream, either by changing the order of items as specified in the **order by** clause or by filtering out items in the **where** clause.
- **The result construction part** consists of the **return** clause, which solely refers to bound variables.

Normalization Rules. In Table 4, the rewriting rules for normalizing FLWR expressions are summarized. We now discuss the idea behind each normalization rule.

N-1 and N-2: We split **for** or **let** clauses that bind multiple variables into individual clauses. Note that, in contrast to the grammar productions for the forExpr and letExpr, the occurrence indicator in both rules is + instead of *. This is necessary for the correctness of the rewrite because it makes sure that the list of for or let clauses contains at least two clauses. After the exhaustive application of this rewrite, each forExpr or letExpr binds at most one variable.

N-3: We split quantified expressions that bind multiple variables into individual quantified expressions. Note that, in contrast to the grammar production for the quantExpr, the occurrence indicator of the RangeExpr in this rule is + instead of *. As for the previous rewrites it is necessary for the correctness of the rewrite. After the exhaustive application of this rewrite, each quantExpr contains at most one RangeExpr.

N-4: When the **where** clause of a FLWR expression contains a complex expression, we introduce a new letExpr and bind the computation of this complex expression to a new variable $p. For this rewrite, we consider $singleExpr_i \in$ {flwrExpr, builtIn, (Expr)} as complex expressions but leave comparisons and quantified expressions as they are. We replace the old complex expression by a reference to the new variable $p. After the exhaus-

Table 4. Normalization of FLWOR expressions.

for rangeExpr$_1$ (, rangeExpr)+	$\rightarrow$	for rangeExpr$_1$ for rangeExpr (, rangeExpr)*	(N-1)
let bindExpr$_1$ (, bindExpr)+	$\rightarrow$	let bindExpr$_1$ let bindExpr (, bindExpr)*	(N-2)
(some|every) rangeExpr$_1$ (, rangeExpr)+ satisfies exprSingle	$\rightarrow$	(some|every) rangeExpr$_1$ satisfies (some|every) rangeExpr (, rangeExpr)* satisfies exprSingle	(N-3)
(forExpr|letExpr)+ where singleExpr$_1$ return singleExpr$_2$	$\rightarrow$	(forExpr|letExpr)+ let < \$p = newVar() >:= singleExpr$_1$ where \$p return singleExpr$_2$	(N-4)
(some|every) rangeExpr$_1$ (, rangeExpr)* satisfies singleExpr	$\rightarrow$	(some|every) rangeExpr$_1$ (, rangeExpr)* let < \$v = newVar() >:= singleExpr satisfies \$v	(N-5)
(forExpr|letExpr)+ whereClause? return singleExpr	$\rightarrow$	(forExpr|letExpr)+ let < \$v = newVar() >:= singleExpr whereClause? return \$v	(N-6)
let var:= (singleExpr$_1$ (, singleExpr)+)	$\rightarrow$	let < \$v = newVar() >:= singleExpr$_1$ let var:= (\$v(, singleExpr)+)	(N-7)
let var:= fun(expr)	$\rightarrow$	let < \$v = newVar() >:= expr let var:= fun(\$v)	(N-8)
singleExpr$_1$ genComp singleExpr2	$\rightarrow$	some < \$v$_1$ = newV ar() > in singleExpr1 let < \$v$_2$ = newV ar() >:= data(\$v1) satisfies some < \$v$_3$ = newV ar() > in singleExpr2 let < \$v$_4$ = newV ar() >:= data(\$v$_3$) satisfies \$v$_2$ = valComp \$v$_4$	(N-9)

tive application of this rewrite the **where** clause contains only references to variables, quantified expressions, or comparison operators.

N-5: We move every complex expression in the range predicate of a quantified expression into a new letExpr. These letExpr are a convenient extension to simplify detection of common subexpressions and during translation. For this rewrite, we consider singleExpr $\in$ {flwrExpr, builtIn, (Expr)} as complex expressions.

N-6: Similar to rule N-4, we move a complex expression from the **return** clause of a FLWR expression into a new letExpr. For this rewrite, we consider singleExpr $\in$ {flwrExpr, builtIn, (Expr), constr, exprSeq} as complex expressions. The exhaustive application of this rewrite leaves only a single variable reference in the **return** clause.

N-7: This rule replaces complex expressions inside a sequence of expressions by variables which are bound to the result of the replaced complex expression. We consider singleExpr $\in$ {flwrExpr, builtIn, (Expr), constr, exprSeq} as complex expressions.

N-8: This rule replaces complex expressions as function arguments by variable references which are bound to the result of the replaced complex expression. We consider singleExpr $\in$ {flwrExpr, builtIn, (Expr), constr, exprSeq} as complex expressions. We also treat built-in functions, constructors, arithmetic expressions, or comparisons as functions and refer to them by fun.

N-9: This rule turns general comparisons denoted by genComp into value comparisons denoted by valComp. The original general comparison

Table 5.

genComp	valComp
=	eq
!=	ne
<	lt
<=	le
>	gt
>=	ge

is replaced by a quantified expression with the corresponding value comparison. The mapping of general comparisons into value comparisons is summarized in the table below (Draper et al., 2007). Note that we introduce the proper type conversion while typing both arguments and, hence, do not introduce them here.

Let us make sure that the rules in Table 4 achieve our goals. First, notice that neither in the **where** clause nor in the **return** clause any of the rewrites introduces complex expressions. Second, notice that the rewrites introduce complex expressions only in new **let** clauses. They possibly create new **for** or **let** clauses containing complex expressions. The exhaustive application of these rewrites eventually results in the normal form discussed at the beginning of this section. Since we only move around complex expressions but do not create ones, we reach this normal form in as many steps as there are complex expressions.

XPath Expressions

When normalizing XPath expressions, our main goal consists in restructuring them such that they are easier to optimize. We attempt this by breaking branching path expressions into simple path expressions. This gives us two important opportunities for optimization:

(1) Predicates become visible. This enables us to detect join predicates, to move them into the **where** clause, and to unnest nested XPath expressions. (2) We assume that indices or ma-

terialized views are available rather for simple path expressions than for complex path expressions. Additionally, the problem of matching view definitions to path expressions in the user query becomes tractable when we extract simple path expressions from complex path expressions.

However, we have to be careful to preserve the semantics of path expressions.

1. In particular, we need to preserve document order, and we need to handle duplicates and position-based functions correctly. Currently, we do not rewrite the XPath expression when its evaluation depends on document order.
2. XPath expressions can contain predicates that correlate the selected node in the current path expression to nodes in another path expression.
3. XPath expressions may contain nested expressions that are interpreted as nested queries.

Our normalization rewrites are summarized in Table 6. They introduce new variables that store the intermediate results of the path expressions. We expect this to be beneficial for factorization of common subexpressions. When we add these variables into the current scope, we have to avoid name clashes.

N-10: This rewrite moves an XPath predicate into the **where** clause of a FLWR expression when the path expression is inside a **for** clause. Note that we ignore several intricate issues here: (1) the result of the XPath predicate is the effective boolean value of expression exprSingle. The computation done for the predicate might depend on actual types returned at runtime. (2) Positional predicates are another source of difficulty we ignore here. (3) Document order must be correct, e.g. when the last axis step before a positional predicate computes a reverse axis.

N-11: This rewrite allows us to break XPath expressions into pieces. Note that in both rewrites

Table 6. Normalization of XPath expressions.

path$_{\$c}$ (/|//) step [singleExpr]	→	for < $v = newVar() > in $c / path (/|//) step where singleExpr return $v	(N-10)
path$_{\$c}$ (/|//) step ([singleExpr])+ path$_2$	→	let < $v1 = newVar() >:= $c / path$_1$ (/|//) step ([singleExpr])+ for < v_2$ = newVar() > in v_1$/path$_2$ return v_2$	(N-11)

we use the variable $c to explicitly refer to the set of context nodes. We also expand abbreviated syntax in path expressions into the corresponding unabbreviated form (Draper et al., 2007), i.e.

1. We treat occurrences of @NodeTest as attribute axis, i.e. attribute::NodeTest.
2. We treat occurrences of .. as parent axis, i.e. parent::node().
3. We expand each occurrence of // in a relative location path to /descendant-or-self::node()/. When the axis step afterwards contains a node test but no positional predicate, we can even replace //NameTest by /descendant::NameTest, which is more efficient to evaluate.
4. We rewrite absolute location paths so that they explicitly use function fn::root, i.e. fn:root(self::node()) treat as document-node()/.
5. When the axis name is omitted from an axis step, the default axis is child unless the axis step contains an attribute test or schema attribute test. Hence, we expand these path expressions by a child step including the node test.

Example Query

In this section, we apply our normalization rules to a concrete query to demonstrate their effectiveness in establishing our normal form. Starting with a query that uses a quantified expression we get existentially quantified expressions, and, thereby

we make implicit computations explicit. Second, we want to rewrite the query such that it is more convenient to optimize. In particular, both types quantified expressions, but also implicit grouping is formulated with nested queries in XQuery 1.0. The resulting normalized query can later be unnested using techniques presented, e.g. in (May et al., 2004; May et al., 2006), realizing performance improvements in orders of magnitude.

```
for $t1 in doc("bib .xml")//
book/ title
where $t1 = doc("reviews.xml")//
entry / title
return $t1
```

Normalization is simple because we only need to turn the general comparison into a quantified expression using rewrite N-9. This rewrite introduces function data to apply atomization to the result of both range expressions.

```
for $t1 in doc("bib .xml")//
book/ title
where some $v1 in $t1
          let $v2:= data ($t1)
        satisfies
          some $v3 in
doc("reviews .xml")// entry /
title
          let $v4:= data ($v3)
          satisfies $v2 eq $v4
return $t1
```

We now have established the desired form:

1. All data retrieval is done in the **for** or **let** clauses.
2. Implicit computations (e.g. the existential nature of general comparison) have become explicit.
3. The **return** clause only contains variable references.
4. Function calls, except function fn:distinct-values, do not contain complex expressions as arguments.

Restrictions

Several of our normalization rewrites are only valid under the assumption that certain information of the involved subexpressions will not be observed in the remainder of the query. This information includes node identity, local namespace declarations, and non-determinism of XQuery expressions. Besides our normalizations, these issues rule out many other optimizations. But for many queries they do not cause any problems, and hence our normalizations will be valuable in many cases.

Node Construction and Node Identity. In some cases, common subexpressions cannot be factorized (Boag et al., 2007). For example:

```
(<a/>, <a/>)
```

is not the same as

```
let $x:= <a/>
return ($x, $x)
```

because the first expression constructs two distinct XML element nodes, whereas the second returns two identical XML nodes. This problem occurs in all rewrites that introduce new **let** clauses containing expressions with constructors. Since most operations do not exploit node identity, this problem is rarely an issue. In most cases, node

construction is only done to construct the final result which is returned to the user.

Namespaces. When moving expressions, we need to be careful because element constructors might introduce new namespaces. When we move expressions out of these scopes, e.g. by introducing a new let expression, we violate these scoping rules as shown in the following example taken from (Florescu & Kossmann, 2004):

```
declare namespace ns="uri1"
for $x in fn:doc("uri ")/ ns:a
where $x/ns:b eq 3
return
    <result xmlns:ns="uri2">
      { for $x in fn:doc("uri ")/
ns:a
            return $x/ns:b }
    </ result>
```

When we apply our normalization rewrites as usual, the FLWOR expression bound to variable $v2 is evaluated using namespace uri1 instead of uri2.

```
declare namespace ns="uri1"
for $x in fn:doc("uri ")/ ns:a
where $x/ns:b eq 3
let $v2:= (for $x in fn:doc("
uri ")/ ns:a
return $x/ns:b)
let $v1:= <result
xmlns:ns="uri2"> { $v2 } </ re-
sult>
return $v1
```

Thus, the rewrites might change the namespace declarations that are defined in the current evaluation context. In principle, one could establish the proper namespace declarations, but in this work we will ignore the problem of namespaces.

Ordering Mode. The result of the following expression is not deterministic. Depending on the order in which the values in the input sequence are applied to the predicate list, the result of this expression can either be an error or the value 3.

```
unordered{
("foo", "bar", 3) [ floor (.) <
5][1]
}
```

Hence, one must be careful when inferring unorderedness in subexpressions of queries, e.g.

```
some $i in ("foo", "bar", 3) [
floor (.) < 5][1]
satisfies true
```

Again, we will ignore these issues in our optimizations and assume deterministic results. We refer to (Grust et al., 2007) for a further discussion on this topic.

TRANSLATION OF XQUERY INTO THE NATIX ALGEBA

The result of normalization, discussed in the previous section, will now turn out to be a convenient starting point for the translation of XQuery queries into our algebra. Let us therefore summarize the structure of normalized queries as they are produced during normalization.

First, path expressions are broken up into simple path expressions. Consequently, we only need to treat simple path expressions without nested path expressions or predicates in our translation function. Second, path expressions are only located in the **for** clause and the **let** clause. This assures uniform results after translation for different formulations of the same query. Third, nested query blocks are explicitly marked by FLWOR expressions or quantified expressions. Fourth, correlation between query blocks is explicitly handled in the **where** clause. Nested query blocks become subject to unnesting in later steps of the optimization process.

The binary T function for FLWOR expressions:

$$T(Q,A) := \begin{cases} T(REST, [tid_x(\mid Y_{x:T_T(e)}(A))[]) & \textit{if } Q = \textit{for } \$x \, [\, at \, \$p\,] \textit{ in } e \textit{ REST or} \\ & \textit{if } Q = \$x \textit{ in } e \textit{ REST} \\ T(REST, X_{x:T_T(e)}(A)) & \textit{if } Q = \textit{let } \$x := e \textit{ REST and e is sequence} - \textit{valued} \\ T(REST, X_{x:T_I(e)}(A)) & \textit{if } Q = \textit{let } \$x := e \textit{ REST and e returns a single item} \\ T(REST, \sigma_{T_I(p)}(A)) & \textit{if } Q = \textit{where } p \textit{ REST} \\ T(REST, Sort_{x_1\cdots x_n}(A)) & \textit{if } Q = \textit{order by } \$x_1 \ldots \$x_n \textit{ REST} \\ \Pi_e(A) & \textit{if } Q = \textit{return } \$e \\ A & \textit{if } Q \textit{ is empty string} \end{cases}$$

The unary functions T_T and T_I for other expressions:

$$T_T(Q) := \begin{cases} \text{translation of Brantner et al.} & \textit{if } Q \textit{ is a simple path expression} \\ \Pi^D(T_T(e)) & \textit{if } Q = \textit{distinct} - \textit{values}(e) \\ T(Q,\#) & \textit{if } Q \textit{ is a FLWOR expression} \\ T_I(Q)[x] & \textit{if } Q \textit{ returns (a sequence of) items} \end{cases}$$

$$T_I(Q) := \begin{cases} \exists t \in T_T(R) : T_I(P) & \textit{if } Q = \textit{some } R \textit{ satisfies } P \\ \forall t \in T_T(R) : T_I(P) & \textit{if } Q = \textit{every } R \textit{ satisfies } P \\ f(T_I(e_1),\ldots,T_I(e_n)) & \textit{if } Q = f(e_1,\ldots,e_n) \\ v & \textit{if } Q \textit{ is a variable reference to variable } \$v \\ c & \textit{if } Q \textit{ is constant } c \end{cases}$$

Translation Function

Based on the properties mentioned above, we specify the translation procedure by means of three mutually recursive procedures T (see Tableequations above). For a given query Q, $T_T(Q)$ translates Q into our algebra. The binary function $T(Q,A)$ is responsible for translating a FLWOR expression Q into the algebra. The first argument of this function is the (remainder of) the query to be translated, and the second argument is the algebraic expression constructed so far. The result of each translation step is a tree of algebraic operators which produce sequences of tuples. For each clause of the FLWOR expression, we give the corresponding translation rule. For non-FLWOR expressions, we use two different unary translation functions. Function $T_I(Q)$ translates a subexpression Q into a function with a simple return type in the XQuery data model, while function $T_T(Q)$ returns an algebraic expression which produces sequences of tuples. Notice that we rely on the translation presented by (Brantner et al., 2005) to translate simple path expressions. However, in contrast to that proposal, we do not fix the implementation of the location steps during translation. This decision is made during cost-based optimization instead. As a consequence, a wider range of optimizations is considered, e.g. using an index.

Since a FLWOR expression can occur within simple expressions and vice versa, these functions are mutually recursive. In the translation rule for the **let** clause we explicitly select the translation function to use: if the expression bound in the **let** clause is sequence-valued, this sequence is turned into a sequence of tuples. Otherwise, we use the translation function that returns single items.

Example Query

Let us consider the quantified query we have discussed above. Below, we repeat the result of normalization:

```
let $d:= doc("bib .xml")
let $v1:= $d //book
for $t in $v1/ title
where some $v2 in $v1/author
        let $v3:= fn: data ($v2)
          satisfies
              some $v4 in $d //
book/ editor
              let $v5:= data ($v4)
              satisfies $v3 eq $v5
return $t
```

We begin with the first **let** clause of the FLWOR expression. The translation results in:

$$X_{d:\,T(\text{doc(\"bib.xml\")})}(\#)$$

After translating the function call in the subscript, we encounter another **let** clause.

$$X_{v1:\,T(\$d//book)}\left(X_{d:X_{d:\text{doc(\"bib.xml\")}}}(\#)\right)$$

We continue with the **for** clause which is mapped to an unnestmap operator by the translation function.

$$Y_{t:\,T(\$v1/title)}\left(X_{v1:Y_{b:d//book}}(\#)\left(X_{d:X_{d:\text{doc(\"bib.xml\")}}}(\#)\right)\right)$$

The **where** clause is translated into a selection operator. We have to translate the predicate recursively.

$$\sigma_{T(...)}\left(Y_{t:Y_{tt:v1/title}}(\#)\left(X_{v1:Y_{b:d//book}}(\#)\left(X_{d:X_{d:\text{doc(\"bib.xml\")}}}(\#)\right)\right)\right)$$

We continue with the first quantified expression.

$$\sigma_{\exists x\in T(...):T)(...)}\left(Y_{t:Y_{tt:v1/title}}(\#)\left(X_{v1:Y_{b:d//book}}(\#)\left(X_{d:X_{d:\text{doc(\"bib.xml\")}}}(\#)\right)\right)\right)$$

To avoid clutter, we will refer to the result of translating the range expression of the first quantified expression by e_1 and to the result of translating the range predicate of this existential quantifier by e_2. Thus, we get:

$$\sigma_{\exists x\in e_1:e_2}\left(Y_{t:Y_{tt:v1/title}}(\#)\left(X_{v1:Y_{b:d//book}}(\#)\left(X_{d:X_{d:\text{doc(\"bib.xml\")}}}(\#)\right)\right)\right)$$

The recursive translation of the range expression is similar to the translation of the **for** clause and **let** clause. The translation of the second quantified expression is also similar to the translation of the first quantifier:

$$e_1 := X_{v2:\text{fn:data}(v1)}\left(Y_{v1:Y_{a:v1/author}}(\#)(\#)\right)$$

$$e_2 := \exists y \in X_{v4:\text{fn:data}(v3)}\left(Y_{v3:Y_{c:c/ediotor}}(Y_{c:d/book}(\#))(\#)\right) : v2 = v4$$

The last translation step consists of translating the **return** clause which introduces a projection.

$$\Pi_t\left(\sigma_{\exists x\in e_1:e_2}\left(Y_{t:Y_{tt:v1/title}}(\#)\left(X_{v1:Y_{b:d//book}}(\#)\left(X_{d:X_{d:\text{doc(\"bib.xml\")}}}(\#)\right)\right)\right)\right)$$

Clearly, the translation is a simple mapping of the normalized XQuery expression into our algebra. The resulting algebraic expression contains nested algebraic expressions – in this example existential quantifiers. In (May et al., 2004; May et al., 2006), we have demonstrated that after unnesting such algebraic expressions the query can be evaluated much more efficiently because the cost-based query optimizer has more choices to evaluate the query. For other algebraic optimizations we can expect similar positive effects.

Mapping to Calculus Representation

In the previous sections, we have presented our normalization steps as rewrites on the abstract syntax tree of the parsed XQuery query. We have also defined a translation function that maps XQuery constructs into our algebra. In Natix we integrate normalization, translation, and factorization of common subexpressions. We also assign a type to all translated constructs and annotate them with cost and cardinality information, see (May, 2007) for details.

The translation presented in the previous section yields a canonical operator tree as it is usually presented in database text books (Garcia-Molina et al., 2001). However, detecting patterns on such an algebraic expression is difficult and inefficient because the argument relationship is directly encoded into the algebraic expression. For many rewrites the exact argument relationship is not important. Such rewrites are more difficult to implement on algebra trees because pattern matching must consider more combinations of argument relationships. For this reason we do not translate the parsed query directly into an algebraic expression. Instead, our internal query representation unifies features of calculus and algebra. It is similar to the query graph model (Haas et al., 1989), (Shanmugasundaram et al., 2001). After the translation step, all steps of the Natix optimizer work on a common query representation. During cost-based optimization, it is turned into

Table 7. Components of a block.

Notation	Description
Π_A	the attributes A specified in the final projection
$P = <p_1 \dots p_k>$	the producers P
$p = l_1 \wedge l_2 \wedge \dots \wedge l_m$	a conjunctive predicate
$C = <c_1 \dots c_n>$	expressions c_i whose result is bound to a variable
$U = <u_1 \dots u_o>$	sequence-valued expressions u_i whose result must be iterated over
$G = <g_1 \dots g_p>$	grouping attributes

a representation closer to an algebraic expression annotated with implementation hints.

Our solution relies on the idea of blocks. Each block is able to capture the semantics of a FLOWR expression. It captures the order of expressions in a FLWOR expression, and at the same time it allows for efficient pattern matching.

As Table 7 shows each block contains a list of producers, P, similar to generators in a calculus expression, a list of AlgChi operators, C, each of which encapsulates the computation of an expression, a list of AlgUnnest operators, U, each of which represents the computation of a sequence-valued function whose result is immediately flattened, and a pointer to the parent block. Additionally it contains a projection list.

To illustrate our idea we first assume a FLWOR expression without **let** or **order by** clauses and with path expressions whose predicates are all moved into the **where** clause if possible. Then the semantics of a simple block is defined as the algebraic expression

$$\Pi_A(\sigma_p(\Upsilon_{pn}(\dots(\Upsilon_{p2}(\Upsilon_{p1}(\#)))))).$$

Thus, the variable in the **return** clause constitutes the projection of the block. The **where** clause is represented by a selection operator, and the **for** clauses are implemented by a sequence of unnest map operators. When the producers p_i

can be evaluated independently, we can turn the unnest map operators into cross products.

Remember that we also denote the concatenation of the application of algebraic operators with ∘. The semantics of the block is defined by the algebraic expression

$$\Pi_A^{(i_1)} \circ$$
$$\sigma_{l_1}^{(i_2)} \circ \quad \sigma_{l_2}^{(i_3)} \circ \ldots \quad \circ \sigma_{l_j}^{(i_j)} \circ$$
$$X_{cn}^{(i_{j+1})} \circ \quad X_{cn}^{(i_{j+2})} \circ \ldots \quad \circ X_{cn}^{(i_k)} \circ$$
$$Y_{p1}^{(i_{k+1})} \circ \quad Y_{p2}^{(i_{k+2})} \circ \ldots \circ Y_{pn}^{(i_{l-1})} \circ$$
$$\#^{(i_l)}.$$

The superscript (i_x) denotes the permutation of these operators that is consistent with the given XQuery expression. For every query, we have $(i_1) = 1$ and $(i_l) = l$, i.e. the projection is the outer-most operator and the singleton scan is the inner-most operator of this expression. The list theApplicationOrder stored in a block represents this permutation of operators that maps positions in the resulting algebraic expressions to pointers of the operator at this position. Thus, after translation, the order of the entries in this list is consistent with the occurrence in the textual query representation. This is too restrictive because a partial order of the expressions would suffice. But later rewrites can simplify these order constraints. The list of grouping attributes is used to implement the distinct and distinct-values functions. Moreover, optimizations like unnesting may introduce grouping operations explicitly.

CONCLUSION AND FUTURE RESEARCH DIRECTIONS

This chapter has presented the approach taken in the native XML database management system Natix to translate XQuery statements into algebraic expressions. As NAL, our algebra, is an extension of the relational algebra, we are able to leverage optimizations that proved useful for relational databases. However, as XQuery is based on a duplicate-aware and order-aware data model care is required. For example, for unnesting nested query blocks we needed to reconsider optimizations known from the relational world.

Such optimizations are much easier to implement if the XQuery statement is normalized prior to the translation into the algebra. In this chapter, we have presented several rewrites we have used to normalize the parsed XQuery statement. However, this set of normalization rewrites is not complete yet, as Natix does not yet cover all features of XQuery. The formal notation of our rewrites allows for formal proofs of correctness of these rewrites – this is part of the future work. Some rewrites may change the semantics of the query statement (e.g. node identity), and thus they cannot be applied in these cases. As a consequence, several optimizations cannot be applied in subsequent steps.

Based on a normalized XQuery statement we perform a translation step into NAL, our algebra over sequences of tuples. Thanks to the prior normalization step, this translation function is rather straight-forward. While this translation function is defined as a mapping of a normalized XQuery statement into an algebraic expression our implementation in Natix performs a translation into a representation closer to a calculus. The advantage of this approach is that optimizations are more efficient and easier to implement. In this chapter, we have outlined how NAL relates to this internal query representation.

Our experience clearly indicates that an algebraic approach to XQuery optimization is useful. First, it allows us to adapt optimization techniques known from relational databases for XML processing. Second, we are able to prove the correctness of optimizations which is part of future work. Finally, our algebraic approach to XML query processing can benefit from experience gained with implementing database systems, i.e. the benefit extends from the XQuery optimizer even to the query execution environment. The techniques introduced in this chapter are the basis for being able to benefit from these advantages.

REFERENCES

Albert, J. (1991). Algebraic properties of bag data types. In *Proceedings of the seventeenth International Conference on Very Large Data Bases,* (pp. 211–219). San Mateo, CA: Morgan Kaufmann.

Amer-Yahia, S., Cho, S. R., Lakshmanan, L. V. S., & Srivastava, D. (2001). Minimization of tree pattern queries. In *Proc. of the ACM SIGMOD Conf. on Management of Data*, (pp. 497–508). New York: ACM press.

Astrahan, M., & Chamberlin, D. (1975). Implementation of a Structured English Query Language. [New York: ACM press.]. *Communications of the ACM, 18*(10), 580–588. doi:10.1145/361020.361215

Balmin, A., Ozcan, F., Beyer, K. S., Cochrane, R., & Pirahesh, H. (2004). A framework for using materialized XPath views in XML query processing. In *Proceedings of the Thirtieth International Conference on Very Large Data Bases*, (pp. 60–71). San Mateo, CA: Morgan Kaufmann.

Beeri, C., & Tzaban, Y. (1999). SAL: An algebra for semistructured data and XML. In *WebDB (Informal Proceedings)*, (pp. 37–42).

Boag, S., Chamberlin, D., Fernández, M.F., Florescu, D., Robie, J., & Siméon, J. (2007). *XQuery 1.0: An XML Query Language*. World Wide Web Consortium (W3C), W3C Recommendation.

Boncz, P., Grust, T., van Keulen, M., Manegold, S., Rittinger, J., & Teubner, J. (2006). MonetDB/XQuery: A fast XQuery processor powered by a relational engine. In *Proc. of the ACM SIGMOD Conf. on Management of Data*, (pp. 479–490). New York: ACM press.

Brantner, M., Kanne, C.-C., Helmer, S., & Moerkotte, G. (2005). Full-fledged algebraic XPath processing in Natix. In *Proc. IEEE Conference on Data Engineering (ICDE)*, (pp. 705–716). Washington, DC: IEEE Computing Society.

Bry, F. (1989). Towards an efficient evaluation of general queries: quantifier and disjunction processing revisited. In *Proc. of the ACM SIGMOD Conf. on Management of Data*, (pp. 193–204). New York: ACM press.

Ceri, S., & Gottlob, G. (1985). Translating SQL into relational algebra: Optimization, semantics, and equivalence of SQL queries. *IEEE Transactions on Software Engineering, 11*(4), 324–345. doi:10.1109/TSE.1985.232223

Chaudhuri, S. (1998). An Overview of Query Optimization in Relational Systems. In *Proceedings of the seventeenth ACM SIGACT-SIGMOD-SIGART symposium on Principles of database systems*, (pp. 34–43). New York: ACM press.

Cluet, S., & Moerkotte, G. (1993). Nested queries in object bases. In *Proceedings of the Fourth International Workshop on Database Programming Languages - Object Models and Language*, (pp. 226–242). Berlin: Springer.

Dayal, U., Goodman, N., & Katz, R. H. (1982). An extended relational algebra with control over duplicate elimination. In *Proc. ACM SIGMOD/SIGACT Conf. on Principles of Database Systems. (PODS)*, (pp. 117–123). New York: ACM press.

Draper, D., Fankhauser, P., Fernandez, M, Malhotra, A, Rose, K., Rys, M., Siméon, J., & Wadler, P (2007). *XQuery 1.0 and XPath 2.0 Formal Semantics*. World Wide Web Consortion (W3C), W3C Recommendation.

Fegaras, L., Levine, D., Bose, S., & Chaluvadi, V. (2002). Query processing of streamed XML data. In *Proceedings of the eleventh international conference on Information and knowledge management*, (pp. 126–133). New York: ACM Press.

Fegaras, L., & Maier, D. (1995) Towards an effective calculus for object query languages. In *Proceedings of the 1995 ACM SIGMOD International Conference on Management of Data*, (pp. 47–58). New York: ACM Press.

Fiebig, T., Helmer, S., Kanne, C.-C., Moerkotte, G., Neumann, J., Schiele, R., & Westmann, T. (2002). Anatomy of a native XML base management system. *The VLDB Journal, 11*(4), 292–314. doi:10.1007/s00778-002-0080-y

Florescu, D., Hillery, C., Kossmann, D., Lucas, P., Riccardi, F., & Westmann, T. (2004). The BEA streaming XQuery processor. *The VLDB Journal, 13*(3), 294–315. doi:10.1007/s00778-004-0137-1

Florescu, D., & Kossmann, D. (2004), XML query processing (tutorial). In *Proceedings of the 20th International Conference on Data Engineering, ICDE 2004, (pg. 874)*. Washington, DC: IEEE Computer Society.

Frasincar, F., Houben, G.-J., & Pau, C. (2002). XAL: An algebra for XML query optimization. In *Proc. Of the Thirteenth Australasian Database Conference (ADC2002)*, (pp. 49–56). Darlinghurst, Australia: Australian Computer Society, Inc.

Garcia-Molina, H., Ullman, J. D., & Widom, J. (2001), *Database Systems: The Complete Book*. Upper Saddle River, NJ: Prentice Hall.

Gottlob, G., Koch, C., & Pichler, R. (2002). Efficient algorithms for processing XPath queries. *In Proceedings of the Twenty- Eighth International Conference on Very Large Data Bases*, (pp. 95–106). San Mateo, CA: Morgan Kaufmann.

Grust, T. (2002), Accelerating XPath location steps. In *Proc. of the ACM SIGMOD Conf. on Management of Data*, (pp. 109–120). New York: ACM press.

Grust, T., Rittinger, J., & Teubner, J. (2007). eXrQuy: Order indifference in XQuery. In *Proceedings of the 23rd IEEE Int'l Conference on Data Engineering (ICDE 2007)*, (pp. 226–235). Washington, DC: IEEE Computer Society.

Grust, T., Sakr, S., & Teubner, J. (2004). XQuery on SQL hosts. In *Proceedings of the Thirtieth International Conference on Very Large Data Bases*. (pp. 252–263). San Mateo, CA: Morgan Kaufmann.

Grust, T., & Teubner, J. (2004). Relational algebra: Mother tongue –XQuery: Fluent. In *Twente Data Management Workshop on XML Databases and Information Retrieval (TDM) 04, (informal proceedings)*.

Haas, L. M., Freytag, J. C., Lohman, G. M., & Pirahesh, H. (1989). Extensive query processing in Starburst. In *Proceedings of the 1989 ACM SIGMOD International Conference on Management of Data*, (pp. 377–388). New York: ACM press.

Helmer, S., Kanne, C.-C., & Moerkotte, G. (2002). Optimized translation of XPath expressions into algebraic expressions parameterized by programs containing navigational primitives. In *Proceedings of the 3nd International Conference on Web Information Systems Engineering (WISE'02)*, (pp. 215–224). Washington, DC: IEEE Computer Society.

Hidders, J., & Michiels, P. (2003). Avoiding unnecessary ordering operations in XPath. In *Database Programming Languages, 9th International Workshop, DBPL 2003*. (pp. 54–74). Berlin: Springer.

Hidders, J., Paredaens, J., Vercammen, R., & Demeyer, S. (2004). A light but formal introduction to XQuery. In *Database and XML Technologies, Second International XML Database Symposium, XSym*, (pp. 5–20). Berlin: Springer.

Hosoya, H., & Pierce, B. (2000). XDuce: A Typed XML Processing Language (Preliminary Report). In *Proc. of WebDB (Selected Papers)*, (pp. 226-244). Berlin: Springer.

Jagadish, H. V., Al-Khalifa, S., Chapman, A., Lakshmanan, L., Nierman, A., & Paparizos, S. (2002). Timber: A native XML database. *The VLDB Journal*, *11*(4), 274–291. doi:10.1007/s00778-002-0081-x

Jarke, M., & Koch, J. (1984). Query optimization in database systems. *ACM Computing Surveys*, *16*(2), 111–152. doi:10.1145/356924.356928

Kay, M. (2008). Ten Reasons Why Saxon is Fast. *IEEE Data Eng. Bull.*, *31*(4), 65–74.

Krishnamurthy, R., Kaushik, R., & Naughton, J. F. (2003). Xmlsql query translation literature: The state of the art and open problems. In *Proc. of the First International XML Database Symposium, XSym 2003*, (pp. 1–18). Berlin: Springer.

Lerner, A., & Shasha, D. (2003). AQuery: Query language for ordered data, optimization techniques, and experiments. In *Proceedings of the 29th international conference on Very large data bases*, (pp. 345–356), VLDB Endowment.

Liu, Z. H., Krishnaprasad, M., & Arora, V. (2005). Native XQuery processing in Oracle XML DB. In *Proceedings of the 2005 ACM SIGMOD International Conference on Management of Data*, (pp. 828–833). New York: ACM press.

Maier, D. (1983). *The Theory of Relational Databases*. Rockville, MD: Computer Science Press.

Manolescu, I., Florescu, D., & Kossmann, D. (2001). Answering XML queries on heterogeneous data sources. In *Proceedings of the 27th International Conference on Very Large Data Bases*, (pp. 241–250). San Mateo, CA: Morgan Kaufmann.

May, N. (2007). *An Algebraic Approach to XQuery Optimization*. Doctoral dissertation, University of Mannheim, Germany.

May, N., Helmer, S., & Moerkotte, G. (2004). Nested queries and quantifiers in an ordered context. In *Proceedings of the 20th International Conference on Data Engineering (ICDE)*, (pp. 239–250). Washington, DC: IEEE Computer Society.

May, N., Helmer, S., & Moerkotte, G. (2006). Strategies for query unnesting in XML databases. *ACM Transactions on Database Systems*, *31*(3), 968–1013. doi:10.1145/1166074.1166081

Michiels, P., Hidders. J. Siméon, J., & Vercammen, R. (2006). *How to recognize different kinds of tree patterns from quite a long way away*. Technical Report TR UA 13-2006, University of Antwerp.

Miklau, G., & Suciu, D. (2002), Containment and equivalence for an XPath fragment. In *Proceedings of the twenty-first ACM SIGMOD-SIGACT-SIGART symposium on Principles of database systems*, (pp. 65–76). New York: ACM press.

Nakano, R. (1990). Translation with optimization from relational calculus to relational algebra having aggregate functions. *ACM Transactions on Database Systems*, *15*(4), 518–557. doi:10.1145/99935.99943

Naughton, J. F., DeWitt, D. J., Maier, D., Aboulnaga, A., Chen, J., & Galanis, L. (2001). The Niagara internet query system. *IEEE Data Eng. Bull.*, *24*(2), 27–33.

Negri, M., M., Pelagatti, G., & Sbattella, L. (1991). Formal semantics of SQL queries. *ACM Transactions on Database Systems*, *16*(3), 513–534. doi:10.1145/111197.111212

Nicola, M., & van der Linden, B. (2005). Native XML support in DB2 universal database. In *Proceedings of the 31st international conference on Very large data bases*, (pp. 1164–1174), VLDB Endowment.

Ozcan, F., Cochrane, R., Pirahesh, H., Kleewein, J., Beyer, K. S., Josifovski, V., & Zhang, C. (2005). System RX: One part relational, one part XML. In *Proc. of the 2005 ACM SIGMOD International Conference on Management of Data*, (pp. 347–358). New York: ACM press.

Pal, S., Cseri, I., Seeliger, O., Rys, M., Schaller, G., Yu, W., et al. (2005). XQuery implementation in a relational database system. In *Proceedings of the 31st international conference on Very large data bases*, (pp. 1175–1186), VLDB Endowment.

Re, C., Siméon, J., & Fernández, M. F. (2006). A complete and efficient algebraic compiler for XQuery. In *Proceedings of the 22nd International Conference on Data Engineering (ICDE)*, (pp 14). Washington, DC: IEEE Computer Society.

Shanmugasundaram, J., Kiernan, G., Shekita, E. J., Fan, C., & Funderburk, J. E. (2001). Querying XML views of relational data. In *Proceedings of the 27th International Conference on Very Large Data Bases*, (pp. 261–270). San Mateo, CA: Morgan Kaufmann.

Slivinskas, G., Jensen, C. S., & Snodgrass, R. T. (2002). Bringing order to query optimization. *SIGMOD Record, 31*(2), 5–14. doi:10.1145/565117.565119

Steenhagen, H. J., Apers, P. M. G., Blanken, H. M., & de By, R. A. (1994), From nested-loop to join queries in OODB. In *Proceedings of the 20th International Conference on Very Large Data Bases*, (pp. 618–629). San Mateo, CA: Morgan Kaufmann.

Suciu, D. (2001). On database theory and XML. *SIGMOD Record, 30*(3), 39–45. doi:10.1145/603867.603874

von Bültzingsloewen, G. (1987). Translating and optimizing sql queries having aggregates. In *Proceedings of the 13th International Conference on Very Large Data Bases*, (pp. 235–243). San Mateo, CA: Morgan Kaufmann.

Wong, E., & Youssefi, K. (1976). Decomposition a strategy for query processing. *ACM Transactions on Database Systems, 1*(3), 223–241. doi:10.1145/320473.320479

ADDITIONAL READING

BOOKS

Chamberlin, D., Draper, D., & Fernández, M. F. Kay. M., Robie, J., Rys, M., Siméon, J, Tivy, J., & Wadler, P. (2004) *XQuery from the Experts – A Guide to the W3C XML Query Language*. Addison Wesley.

Melton, J., & Buxton, S. (2006). *Querying XML: XQuery, XPath, and SQL/XML in Context*, Morgan Kaufmann, San Mateo, CA, USA.

JOURNAL SPECIAL ISSUES

Various Authors (2002). Special Issue on XML Data Management, *VLDB Journal, 11*(4), Springer.

Various Authors (2006). Celebrating 10 Years of XML, *IBM Systems Journal*, 45(2), IBM.

Various Authors (2008). Special Issue on XQuery Processing: Practice and Experience, *Bulletin of the Technical Committee on Data Engineering, 31*(4), IEEE Computer Society.

DOCTORAL DISSERTATION

May, N. (2007). *An Algebraic Approach to XQuery Optimization*. doctoral dissertation, University of Mannheim.

Teubner, J. (2006). *Pathfinder: XQuery Compilation Techniques for Relational Database Targets*. doctoral dissertation. Technische Universität München.

Chapter 14

XML Data Integration:
Schema Extraction and Mapping

Huiping Cao
Arizona State University, USA

Yan Qi
Arizona State University, USA

K. Selçuk Candan
Arizona State University, USA

Maria Luisa Sapino
University Of Torino, Italy

ABSTRACT

Many applications require exchange and integration of data from multiple, heterogeneous sources. eXtensible Markup Language (XML) is a standard developed to satisfy the convenient data exchange needs of these applications. However, XML by itself does not address the data integration requirements. This chapter discusses the challenges and techniques in XML Data Integration. It first presents a four step outline, illustrating the steps involved in the integration of XML data. This chapter, then, focuses on the first two of these steps: schema extraction and data/schema mapping. More specifically, schema extraction presents techniques to extract tree summaries, DTDs, or XML Schemas from XML documents. The discussion on data/schema mapping focuses on techniques for aligning XML data and schemas.

INTRODUCTION

Data integration is the process of combining multiple heterogeneous and autonomous data sources. Its purpose is to provide a logically unified view of the data to the users who need to search or analyze disparate data sources. Data integration is a well studied problem in the data management community (Doan & Halevy, 2005; A. Halevy, Rajaraman, & Ordille, 2006; Lenzerini, 2002). Despite decades of work in the area, however, the problem is still open. In this chapter, we focus on techniques for eXtensible Markup Language (XML) data integration. As we will see, XML provides opportunities in improving compatibilities across data sources; we will however see that XML also introduces unique challenges that require innovative solutions.

DOI: 10.4018/978-1-61520-727-5.ch014

APPLICATIONS

Many applications require effective and efficient data integration and, as the number and diversity of available data sources increase, this requirement gains further significance. In what follows, we briefly introduce a sample of contemporary applications which require data integration solutions.

- *Data warehousing and business intelligence.* A data warehouse is a repository storing large amounts of data collected from different sources (Devlin & Murphy, 1988). The primary goal of a data warehouse is to provide users unified view of (and efficient access to) data collections that were originally located at different sources. Data warehouses are especially useful in enabling large scale data analysis, for example in support of business intelligence applications. Obviously, unless the contributing data sources are identical in structure or are partitions of a single schema, to build the data warehouse, we first need to integrate the data by identifying the correspondences between the data sources and the data warehouse.

- *Peer-to-peer (P2P) systems.* P2P systems leverage autonomous data sources (peers) as if they are part of a single unified data management system (Koloniari & Pitoura, 2005; Pankowski, 2008). Common usage of such systems includes a user initiating a query through one of the autonomous peer system, but getting answers from all relevant peers. Natural challenges include identifying relevant peers across heterogeneous schema and managing the mappings among the schemas of the peers (Anand & Chawathe, 2004; Cherukuri & Candan, 2008). In addition, queries and answers need to be routed within the peers in the system in a way that eliminates redundant query processing (Anand & Chawathe, 2004).

- *Service oriented architectures (SOA) and web information integration.* Service oriented architectures abstract recurring (e.g., business) activity flows, make them available as independent services, and leverage these services as modules within large software systems. This approach reduces costs of developing and deploying new applications and promotes reuse. Consequently, today, the "web" is not only a collection of hyperlinked pages, but rather a collection of dynamic services that one can use to develop web-based applications and mashups (Jhingran, 2006). These web services, with their descriptions, are published so that other people can locate and integrate them into end-to-end information products. Meanwhile, data spaces (Franklin, Halevy, & Maier, 2005; A. Y. Halevy, Franklin, & Maier, 2006) help reduce the cost of managing loosely structured Web data by eliminating the need to impose strict structures on the integrated data. These, however, require resolving potential differences between the data service interfaces and underlying data structures.

- *Scientific data management.* In many scientific domains (e.g., archeology (Kintigh, 2006) and biology (Achard, Vaysseixm, & Barillot, 2001)), individual researchers or communities have different data management conventions, standards, and taxonomies (Qi, Candan, & Sapino, 2007). For example, bioinformatics data have many new data types (e.g., microarrays, interaction maps of proteins, etc.) stored in different databases and in different formats (Achard et al., 2001). In archaeology, there is almost no universally agreed structure or ontology to help support integration and eliminate conflicts that occur due to varying knowledge standards and data interpretations (Kintigh, 2006).

Why XML?

In mid 90's, the growing need for a common platform that can provide uniformity and improve interoperability between businesses and other enterprises led to the wide acceptance of eXtensible Markup Language (XML) as an exchange framework. Today, most of the data interchange is through XML-based data representation standards. XML provides simple, flexible, and self-describing data representation. Its flexibility is due to the fact that alternative schemas can be combined effectively using *disjunctions*. Moreover, it is self-describing in that XML instances carry the structure of the data in the form of human-readable tags that are associated with data elements; consequently XML data can be exchanged without associated schemas. This simplicity and flexibility led to XML's use in many different domains for which ease of data exchange is a primary requirement, these include peer-to-peer (P2P) applications (Pankowski, 2008), bioinformatics (Achard et al., 2001) and semantic web (Decker et al., 2000).

On the other hand, these same properties, especially the flexibility of the structure of the data and the possibility for each user or data contributor to have their own schemas (through Document Type Definitions (DTDs) and XML schemas (E. Rahm, Do, & Massmann, 2004) as opposed to committing to a unique, fixed set of constraints constraining the organization of the data, introduce new challenges in the integration process (Bertino & Ferrari, 2001). In late 90's, Halevy (1999) investigated issues that were then considered critical for XML data integration, including the choice of suitable languages for the description of data sources, the definition of query reformulation algorithms, the translation among different Document Type Definitions

(DTDs) and the formulation of formalisms for source descriptions.

During the past decade, two key complementary challenges to XML data integration emerged: (a) finding alignments, similarities, and compatibilities between different XML data schemas or instances and (b) identifying and resolving conflicts between XML data sources whenever they are not compatible.

OUTLINE OF THE CHAPTER

This chapter will focus on the challenges and solutions in the XML data integration. Figure 1 provides an overview of the underlying process:

- *Schema extraction*: A particular challenge introduced by XML is that not all XML data come with an associated schema. In fact, one of the major differences between XML and its predecessor Standard Generalized Markup Language (SGML) is the relaxation of the requirement of each document having an associated document type definition (DTD), which defines the rules governing the structure. While this enables the use of XML as a flexible messaging and integration medium, in some cases (especially when the integration process is schema-aware), it also necessitates a process to extract a schema from a given collection of schema-less XML documents. We discuss this in Section "SCHEMA EXTRACTION".
- *Matching and mapping*: Finding mappings between data components is a common problem in almost all integration domains. For example, multi-tenant databases, which form the core of many Software and Information as a Service solutions (Aulbach, Grust, Jacobs, & Rittinger, 2008), strive to create integrated/consolidated schemas across similar, but different

Figure 1. Overview of the XML data integration process

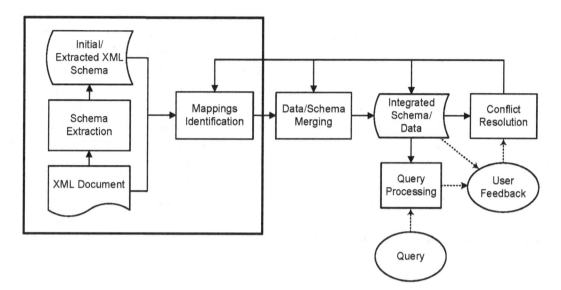

tenant schemas. The mappings from tenant schemas to the consolidated schema help the system manage multiple tenants as a single tenant, thus reducing the overall management and maintenance cost. XML data can often be represented using trees or tree-like graphs (Do & Rahm, 2002; Goldman & Widom, 1997). This impacts solutions for finding mappings between XML data. We discuss XML matching and mapping methodologies in Section "MATCHING AND MAPPING".

- *XML data/metadata merging*: Once the mappings are discovered, the next step in the process is to integrate the XML data or metadata, depending on whether the system is operating on data- or schema-level.
- *Query processing and conflict resolution*: The results of the merge process, however, may not always be a valid XML data or schema. This step uses the resulting merged data to support query processing and apply conflict resolution strategies.

In this chapter, we focus on the first two steps. In a separate chapter, titled "XML Data Integration: Merging, Query Processing and Conflict Resolution", we will discuss the later two steps, merging, query processing over integrated XML data and the strategies that can be used for resolving conflicts. Finally, we conclude the chapter in Section "CONCLUSION".

Running Example

All the examples presented to illustrate the algorithms in this chapter are picked from *universities and research institutes* application domain, where the underlying data includes

- funding organization information, e.g., organization name, organization location, and title of grants (or funds);
- university information, e.g., university name and information about the university president; and
- faculty information, e.g., faculty name and his/her funding information.

SCHEMA EXTRACTION

While in many cases XML documents are created according to a pre-defined structure (e.g., Document Type Definition (DTD) or XML schema (XMLschema)), the existence of a DTD or a schema is not guaranteed. In fact, it has been observed that many XML documents on the web do not follow explicit schemas (Barbosa, Mignet, & Veltri, 2005) (i.e., schemas are unavailable (Barbosa, Mignet, & Veltri, 2006) or the existing schemas are not valid (Bex, Martens, Neven, & Schwentick, 2005). However, during XML data integration (especially when integration needs to be supported by mappings extracted from schemas (E. Rahm & Bernstein, 2001; Shvaiko & Euzenat, 2005), it is critical to have schema information in advance. These lead to research on learning the (implicit) structure of a given XML corpus through various structure extraction techniques (Florescu, 2005).

Intuitively, on one hand, the extracted schema must represent all the input XML documents (this is referred to as the *generalization* property); i.e., each input document must be an instance of the extracted common schema. On the other hand, we do not want to extract an *overly-general* schema, which covers significantly more XML documents than the input data; in other words, the extracted schemas should be specific enough to cover only the input XML documents. This is referred to as the *specification* property. With these properties in mind, we can define the schema extraction problem as follows (Bex, Neven, Schwentick, & Tuyls, 2006; Bex, Neven, & Vansummeren, 2007; Garofalakis, Gionis, Rastogi, Seshadri, & Shim, 2003; Goldman & Widom, 1997):

Definition. The *schema extraction* problem is to identify a schema S from a given set of XML documents D such that S captures the structural information of the documents in D in a minimal way. (I.e., S is general and specific enough at the same time to cover D).

The schema extraction process is also referred to as *schema inference*. The underlying structure of a given collection of XML documents can be described using DTD, XML Schema or in a more general representation such as tree or graph. The structure extraction techniques in the literature target at inferring three kinds of representations: tree or graph summaries (Goldman & Widom, 1997), DTDs (Bex et al., 2005; Bex et al., 2006; Garofalakis et al., 2003) or XML Schemas (Bex et al., 2007; Bex, Neven, & Vansummeren, 2008; Hegewald, Naumann, & Weis, 2006). This section considers these different approaches and discusses representative techniques.

Extraction of Tree and Graph Structures

If one ignores the explicit object references, an XML data/document has a hierarchical structure. OEM (Papakonstantinou, Garcia-Molina, & Widom, 1995) and LORE (McHugh, Abiteboul, Goldman, & Widom, 1997) are two well-known tree-like data models for XML documents that leverage the hierarchical nature of XML data. In OEM, for example, database is a rooted, directed graph, with textual labels on edges and atomic values in leaves. More specifically, each node of the graph corresponds to an element or an attribute of an element in the XML document. A child node corresponds to a sub-element or an attribute of its parent node. For each child of a node, besides the pointer to the child, there is a tag that indicates the name of the child node. If the child is a sub-element, the name is its element tag. If the child is an attribute, the name is the attribute name. In fact, a collection of XML documents can also be viewed as a single large DOM tree, where all the individual documents are rooted at the same node. Figure 2(a) provides an example. Given such an OEM tree, the schema extraction problem can be posed as understanding the common structure governing the root to leaf paths on this tree. Based on this observation, in (Goldman

Figure 2. Example for DataGuide: (a) a database, (b) a tree structured DataGuide, and (c) a graph structured DataGuide

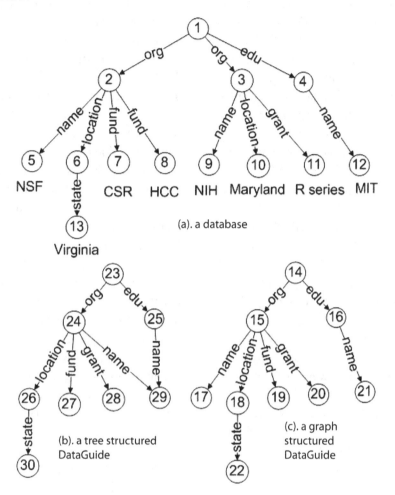

(a). a database

(b). a tree structured DataGuide

(c). a graph structured DataGuide

& Widom, 1997), Goldman and Widom present the *DataGuide* technique for extracting structures as concise summaries of initially schema-free XML databases.

A *DataGuide* of an XML database is a graph, where each object node has a unique identifier and nodes are linked with directed labeled edges. Unlike the graph corresponding to an XML document, each label path (between a given pair of nodes) in the DataGuide is unique. A DataGuide is said to represent a given XML database, if there is one and only one label path for each path in the XML database. More formally, let *DG* be a

DataGuide extracted from a database *D* represented in OEM:

- every label path in the database D exists in the DataGuide *DG* (covers all structural information),
- every label path in the DataGuide *DG* exists in *D* (no redundant information), and
- let *tg(l)* denote the set of target objects one can reach starting from the root and following a label path *l*. In an XML database *tg(l)* may contain more than one object, but the target set of a label path in a DataGuide is a singleton set (minimality).

Figure 2(b) shows a DataGuide for the sample database in Figure 2(a). In the original database, between object nodes '*1*' and '*9*', there is a label path *org.name*; there is a similarly labeled path (between object nodes '*14*' and '*17*' in the DataGuide and this label path is unique.

Note that a given XML data collection may have more than one DataGuide. The graphs in Figures 2(b) and 2(c) are both DataGuides of the database in Figure 2(a). A strong DataGuide (Goldman & Widom, 1997) is a DataGuide such that two label paths l_1 and l_2 point to the same object (i.e., their target sets are identical) if and only if the target sets of l_1 and l_2 are exactly the same in the original database. More formally, given label path l, let $L_{DG}(l)$ be the set of label paths in the DataGuide *DG* which have the same target set as l. Similarly, let $L_D(l)$ be the set of label paths in the Database *D* which have the same target set as l. A *strong DataGuide* refers to a DataGuide such that $\forall_l L_{DG}(l) = L_D(l)$. Consider Figure 2 as an example and let l be *org.name*. The target set of l in *D* is {5, 9} and the set of label paths sharing this target set is $L_D(l) = \{org.name\}$. Consider the same label path in the DataGuide in Figure 2(b); here the target set of l is {17}, the only label path that reaches this target set is *org.name*; thus, we have $L_{DG}(l)=\{org.name\}=L_D(l) = \{org.name\}$. After similar analysis on other label paths, we can see that Figure 2(b) is a strong DataGuide of Figure 2(a). Figure 2(c), however, does not show a strong DataGuide. To see this, consider the same label path *org.name*; in this case, $tg(l)$ in the DataGuide is {29} and $L_{DG}(l)=\{org.name, edu.name\}$, which is different from $L_D(l)$. Thus, the graph is not a strong data guide.

While DataGuides are not unique, Goldman & Widom (1997) show that each XML collection has one and only one strong DataGuide; moreover, given a tree-structured XML collection, construction of the corresponding strong DataGuide is linear in space and time, with respect to the size of the collection. For a more general database (with explicit references, which results in a graph struc-ture), however, the process has exponential cost (intuitively, DataGuide construction is equivalent to conversion of a non-deterministic finite automaton into deterministic one). Strong DataGuides are created by performing a depth-first traversal of the database and recording the target sets of the label paths visited. Since in strong DataGuides there is a one-to-one correspondence between *source target sets* (the target sets of label paths in the source) and DataGuide objects, the algorithm presented in (Goldman & Widom, 1997) maintains a hash table *H* to keep the one-to-one correspondences between the target sets in the source database and the objects in the DataGuide for examined label paths. To begin with, a DataGuide object is created to correspond to the root of the source database. That is, an entry $(\{root_D\}: root_{DG})$ is inserted into *H*. Then, the unexamined source target sets in *H* are expanded in a depth-first order to compute new source target sets and to create corresponding DataGuide objects for them. To expand a source target set *tg* (for an entry (*tg*: *o*) in *H*), the algorithm first gets the labels coming out of any object in *tg*. Then, through different labels, it gets their reachable source target sets. Once a newly computed source target object set *tg'* does not exist in *H*, a new DataGuide object *o'* is created for *tg'* (i.e., a new entry, (*tg'*: *o'*), is added to *H*) and a link from object *o* to *o'* with label *l* is created. Otherwise (i.e., an entry (*tg'*: *o'*) exists in *H*), the algorithm simply links *o* to *o'* using label *l*. Take the database in Figure 2(a) as an example. Initially, $H=\{(\{1\}:14)\}$. Next, the target set {1} is expanded by following two different labels *org* and *edu*. Following the first label *org*, we get source target set {2, 3}. Since this does not exist in *H*, we need to create a corresponding DataGuide object, "*15*", for it and insert this information to *H*, then *H* has one more entry ({2, 3}: *15*). This process is recursively applied to source target set {2, 3} and so on. When every target set is expanded for label paths starting with *org*, the expansion continues to label paths starting with *edu*. Finally, this algorithm would result in the strong DataGuide shown in Figure 2(b).

Since, especially for graph structured databases, strong DataGuide construction can be exponential, Jennifer & Widom (1999) introduce *approximate data guides* that can reduce the construction cost by relying on approximate hash matches. T-Index (Milo & Suciu, 1999) is also similar to DataGuides, but the paths represented in a T-index structure are not limited to those starting from the root. APEX (Chung, Min, & Shim, 2002) is similar to DataGuides and T-Indexes, but it extracts the structure only for frequent paths in the data.

DTD and XML Schema Extraction and Inference

As described above, DataGuides use graphs as the general form to represent the common structures of XML collections. DataGuides, however, are not as expressive as Data Type Definitions (DTDs) (Bex et al., 2005; Bex et al., 2006; Chidlovskii, 2001; Garofalakis et al., 2003; Min, Ahn, & Chung, 2003; Sankey & Wong, 2001) or XML Schema (Bex et al., 2007; Bex et al., 2008; Clark; Hegewald et al., 2006), the two most widely used formats to represent the structure of XML documents.

DTD Extraction

DTD's are most often used for grammar validation, which is the process through which a service verifies the validity of a document against a registered DTD to ensure that it is structurally valid and processable. A DTD can be formally abstracted as quadruple Γ (*I*, *t*, *Rt*, Φ), where *I* is the set of non-terminals, $t = \Sigma \cup \overline{\Sigma}$ is the set of terminals (Σ denotes the alphabet of open-tags and $\overline{\Sigma}$ denotes the set of close-tags), *Rt* is the root, and Φ is a set of production rules which can be used to generate XML documents matching the given DTD. In particular, the strings represented by the right-hand sides of the production rules in Φ are regular expressions and, thus, can be recognized by finite state machines (Hopcroft & Ullman, 1979). Balmin, Papakonstantinou, & Vianu (2004), for example, use this fact to develop an incremental, divide-and-conquer type of validation mechanism for XML documents. Many works (Chitic & Rosu, 2004; Gottlob, Koch, Pichler, & Segoufin, 2005; Segoufin & Vianu, 2002) also show that XML documents can be validated using finite state automata. Based on the observation that DTDs can be abstracted as regular expressions (REs) that can be recognized by finite state automata, a number of works focus on learning these REs. Bex et al. (2006) for example, reduce the DTD extraction problem to learning REs from XML fragments in the XML corpus. Garcia & Vidal (1990) also derive an RE to represent a given XML corpus. Several researchers observed that REs learned through these processes tend to be overly complex to be useful in practical settings (Ehrenfeucht & Zeiger, 1976; Fernau, 2004; Fernau, 2005). Bex, Neven, & Bussche (2004) observe that a significant majority (99% of XSDs or DTDs in practical use) can be represented as single occurrence REs (SOREs), where every element name occurs at most once in the expression. For example, "$((b?(a|c))^+d))$ ^+e" is a SORE while "$a(a|b)^*$" is not ("a" occurs more than once).

Relying on this observation, Bex et al. (2006) provide a scheme to generate SOREs from XML data. A SORE, however, may not be found if the DTD corresponding to the given XML collection cannot be represented using an expressions where each element name occurs only once. In such cases, Bex et al. apply heuristics to find SOREs that are less accurate (i.e., corresponding to a more general DTD than the given XML collection implies). The process is as follows:

- In the first step, the algorithm collects all label paths from root to leaves. In (Bex et al., 2006), these label paths are called strings. For example, from the XML document in

Figure 2(a), we can extract strings *org. name* and *org.location.state*.

- The second step constructs a so called, *single occurrence automaton* for these strings. The automaton has two special states s_{init} as the starting state and s_{end} as the terminal state. All the other states are labeled with element names. There is an edge from one state s_j to another state s_k if (i) $s_j = s_{init}$ and s_k is a starting element name in some XML fragment string, or (ii) $s_k = s_{end}$ and s_j is an ending element name in some XML fragment string, or (iii) $s_j s_k$ is a 2-gram extracted from some XML fragment string. Figure 3(a) shows the automaton we can obtain using the XML fragments in Figure 2(a).

- In the third step, this initial single occurrence automaton is simplified to obtain the SORE (if it exists) by applying four transformation rules:
  - *disjunction rule* merges the states which share the same predecessors and successors disjunctively (using "|"),
  - *concatenation rule* concatenates those adjacent states having only one incoming and outgoing edge,
  - *self-loop rule* removes any self-loop edge on a state "s" and re-labels it as "s^+",
  - *optional rule* removes such edges $s_i \rightarrow s_j$ that there exists another state s_k with $s_i \in prec(s_k)$ and $s_j \in succ(s_k)$. In this case, s_k is re-labeled as $s_k^?$.

Figure 3 gives an example illustrating how these rules are used. When we reach Figure 3(d), the algorithm stops since none of the above rules can be applied. However, Figure 3(d) is not an RE yet.

- If a SORE cannot be derived using the above rules, the algorithm falls back onto repairs

rules that allow some fuzziness in merging the automaton states. For example,
  - an *enable-disjunction rule* is used to add a minimal number of edges to make the predecessors and successors of two states are the same.

In Figure 4, this rule adds the bold line from state "*edu*" to state "*location state?|fund|grant*". Given this new edge, *disjunction* and *concatenation* rules can now be applied to obtain the regular expression in Figure 4(b) and 4(c).

XML Schema Extraction

XML Schema Definitions (XSDs) are more expressive than DTDs. In particular, XSD introduces types, which are essentially regular expressions (Martens, Neven, Schwentick, & Bex, 2006) that can be used to describe elements in the XML schema; each element can take one or more types. The fundamental difference from DTDs, however is that the type (or the corresponding RE) an element will take may be determined by the context (i.e., ancestor elements) in which the elements occur in the XML document. This is in stark contrast to DTDs, where given a disjunctive element definition of the form $A := RE_1|RE_2$, there is absolutely no constraint on whether A can be expressed in a given document using RE_1 or RE_2. In XSD, however, the choice between RE_1 and RE_2 can be tied to the ancestors of A in the given document.

Since DTD extraction techniques do not look for such dependencies, given a set of documents that are created using XSDs (where such dependencies exist), DTD extraction techniques will fail to find them. Bex et al. (2007) argue that in many of the existing XSD extraction approaches, such as Trang (Clark) and XStrut (Hegewald et al., 2006), while the extracted schemas are in XSD syntax, they are equivalent to DTDs in expressive power.

Figure 3. Transformation of a single occurrence automaton in (a) towards a single occurrence RE

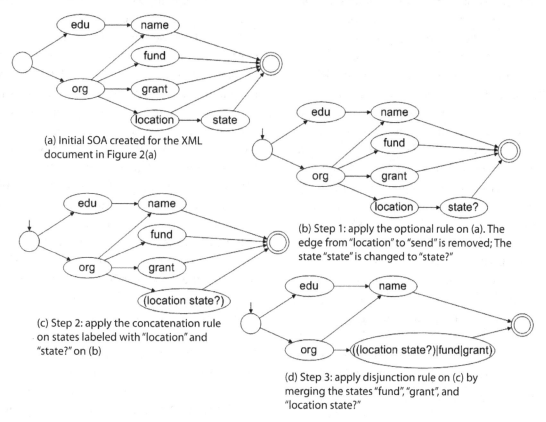

(a) Initial SOA created for the XML document in Figure 2(a)

(b) Step 1: apply the optional rule on (a). The edge from "location" to "send" is removed; The state "state" is changed to "state?"

(c) Step 2: apply the concatenation rule on states labeled with "location" and "state?" on (b)

(d) Step 3: apply disjunction rule on (c) by merging the states "fund", "grant", and "location state?"

Figure 4. SOA repair

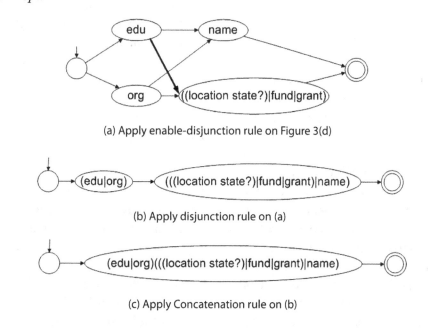

(a) Apply enable-disjunction rule on Figure 3(d)

(b) Apply disjunction rule on (a)

(c) Apply Concatenation rule on (b)

When inferring a DTD, since there is no contextual dependence, the algorithm only needs to distinguish the immediate parent-child relationship among the XML tags to learn the REs corresponding to elements. In learning XSDs, on the other hand, the algorithm also needs to seek to identify whether contexts (i.e., the root-to-element paths in the given set of document) have any impact on the REs corresponding to each element name. This increases the complexity of the analysis. Due to this inherent complexity, Bex et al. (2007) focus on learning a subclass of XSDs commonly used in practice. XSDs in this subclass, named *k-local single occurrence XSDs* (SOXSDs), satisfy the following two properties: First, in these XSDs, determining one element's content model (e.g., *"name"* defined under *"org"*) only depends on a limited number (e.g., *k*) of ancestors of the element -- this is based on the study in (Martens et al., 2006) that, in 98% of the XSDs, one element's content model can be determined based on the label of itself, its parent, or its grandparent (i.e., up to *k=2*); Second, these XSDs only contain elements with different names as in *SORE*s discussed above.

MATCHING AND MAPPING

Matching is a vital step in XML data integration. Given schemas of separate data sources, the matching operation discovers the correspondences or mappings (among constituent objects, such as attributes or values, from different sources) that are not immediately available (for example, due to differences in naming convention) (E. Rahm & Bernstein, 2001). A multitude of approaches (Do & Rahm, 2002; Fuxman et al., 2006; Gal, 2007; Hernández et al., 2007; Hernández, Papotti, & Tan, 2008; Madhavan, Bernstein, & Rahm, 2001) have been developed to perform matching operation for different types of data and metadata. In the context of XML data integration, the term *matching* applies to finding correspondences among XML

schemas (including DTDs) or document instances (XML documents). The techniques focusing on relational database schema matching or ontology matching will not be our focus, but we will refer to them when they are closely related to XML matching. After obtaining the matching results, further processing is needed to translate these correspondences to executable scripts (e.g., SQL, XQuery). Some existing works (Atay, Chebotko, Lu, & Fotouhi, 2007; Fuxman et al., 2006; Hernández et al., 2007; Hernández et al., 2008; Pankowski, Cybulka, & Meissner, 2007; Popa, Velegrakis, Miller, Hernández, & Fagin, 2002) call these scripts *mappings* and call this process *mapping generation*. In order to distinguish the results of the basic matching operation and this one, we call the results of this operation *mapping rules* and call this operation *mapping rule generation*. These mapping rules are used for performing further operations, e.g., data exchange (Hernández et al., 2008), data translation (Milo & Zohar, 1998; Popa et al., 2002), or query evaluation (chapter titled "XML Data Integration: Merging, Query Processing and Conflict Resolution").

In what follows, we first define the terminology in Section "Terminology". Then, in Section "Matching Operation: Identifying Mappings", we detail some main challenges in schema matching and some typical techniques. We cover the problem of mapping rule generation in Section "Mapping Rule Generation"

Terminology

Based on the characteristics of the underlying data and metadata, various types of matching techniques have been developed: these include schema matching (e.g., relational database schemas, catalogs, and XML schemas), ontology matching (Shvaiko & Euzenat, 2005; Shvaiko & Euzenat, 2008), and so forth. Unfortunately, the terminologies used for denoting this operation, such as *matching* (Cupid (Madhavan et al., 2001), COMA (Do & Rahm, 2002)), *match* (Cupid), *alignment* (QOM (Ehrig & Staab, 2004)), *mapping* (QOM (Ehrig & Staab, 2004)), differ from context to context. For clarity, in this chapter, we use the term *matching* to denote the operation, and use *correspondences*, *mapping* or *alignment* to denote the results of this operation.

As stated above, given two data sources S_1 and S_2, the matching operation identifies correspondences between parts (e.g., elements or element sets) of S_1 and S_2. Each such correspondence has an associated confidence value (or probability) $\tau (\in [0,1])$ (the correspondence is more certain when this value is closer to 1). Many works (e.g. (Madhavan et al., 2001)) use the convention that a mapping denotes the matching result as a whole, while a correspondence refers to one pair of matched elements. We also follow this convention. Thus, the set, $M = \{\mu\}$, of correspondences is called a *mapping* (some work (Fuxman et al., 2006) also call the matching results as *matchings*). The *mapping rules*, on the other hand, are pieces of scripts written in specific languages (e.g., SQL, XQuery, etc.) to reflect a mapping between two sources. The mapping rule is sometimes referred to an assertion (Candan, Cao, Qi, & Sapino, 2008; Qi et al., 2007). Each mapping rule from S_1 to S_2 specifies how relevant parts of S_1 can be translated to a form compatible with S_2. Potential uncertainties in mappings (i.e., cases where $\tau < 1.0$) leads to the following observations:

- *Non-singleton mapping sets.* A part of S_1 may match multiple parts of S_2, with different confidence values. Depending on the semantics of the parts being mapped and the integrity constraints governing S_1 and S_2, these mappings might be compatible with each other or conflicting. When only one mapping is allowed, often only the most likely correspondence is maintained (COMA (Do & Rahm, 2002), LSD(Doan, Domingos, & Halevy, 2001), Cupid (Madhavan et al., 2001)). Otherwise, by picking correspondences whose confidence

values exceed some threshold, one-to-many mappings can be preserved (Cupid).
- Matching results are not always symmetric. That is, the results of matching S_1 to S_2 may be different from the results obtained from matching S_2 to S_1 (Do & Rahm, 2002)
- Matching similarity is not necessarily transitive. Let v_1, v_2 and v_3 be three elements in sources S_1, S_2, and S_3. Let $v_i \rightarrow v_j$ denote a correspondence identified from v_i to v_j. If $v_1 \rightarrow v_2$ and $v_2 \rightarrow v_3$, then in general there is no guarantee that $v_1 \rightarrow v_3$.

This of course is a potential problem as it may result in semantically inconsistent scenarios. While it is hard to avoid this problem with mappings identified through pairwise matching operations, composite and hybrid matching techniques may avoid it by considering more than two pairs at a time (COMA (Do & Rahm, 2002)).

For simplicity of the discussion, in the rest of this section, we focus on *mapping*s of the form $\{\mu: v_i \rightarrow v_j (\tau_{ij})\}$, where v_i and v_j are two elements from two different sources S_1 and S_2. However, since during data integration, algorithms may need to take as input more general mappings (Candan et al., 2008; Pottinger & Bernstein, 2003; Qi et al., 2007), in Chapter titled "XML Data Integration: Merging, Query Processing and Conflict Resolution", where we discuss integration based on mappings, we refer to a more general definition of mappings.

Matching Operation: Identifying Mappings

Matching is challenging (Gal, 2006) due to several reasons. First, identical concepts may be named or structured differently. Second, the same or similar words may be used to represent different concepts. To match two sources, one can leverage different types of cues (E. Rahm et al., 2004): (i) schema information such as data types, element names, or structures, (ii) external information such as thesauri, (iii) data instance characteristics, and (iv) previous matching results. Based on how they leverage these, it is possible to classify the available matching techniques using three broad criteria (E. Rahm & Bernstein, 2001; Shvaiko & Euzenat, 2005):

- Element-level vs. structure-level: We can classify matching algorithms based on whether the structural relationship among elements are used or not. Element-level algorithms only analyze elements themselves, but ignoring relationships among them. In contrast, structure-level matching algorithms match elements based on how they are related to each other in the overall structure.

- Instance-based vs. schema-based: The former considers data instances while resolving mappings among schema elements, while the latter only considers schemas during the matching process.

- Syntax-based vs. semantic-based: The syntax-based (or syntactic) approaches only consider syntactic cues (e.g., available thesauri), while the semantic-based methods also leverage available semantics (e.g., integrity constraints).

String-distance based (Cohen, Ravikumar, & Fienberg, 2003; Do, Melnik, & Rahm, 2002; Madhavan et al., 2001; Melnik, Garcia-Molina, & Rahm, 2002; Noy & Musen, 2001), linguistic resource based (Bouquet, Serafini, & Zanobini, 2003; Giunchiglia, Shvaiko, & Yatskevich, 2004; Madhavan et al., 2001; G. A. Miller, 1995; Resnik, 1995), and constraint based (E. Rahm & Bernstein, 2001; Valtchev & Euzenat, 1997) approaches to matching are not specific to XML matching. Thus, we will not focus on them here. Instead, we will focus on techniques that leverage the structure of XML data and schemas as well as *hybrid* and *composite* matching approaches which use multiple (e.g., structure and semantic) techniques.

Structure-Based Techniques

As discussed earlier, the tree-like structure of XML data and schemas renders the structure-based matching techniques play a fundamental role in XML schema matching. Existing structure-based techniques match elements in trees (or graphs) by either computing their similarity in the initial tree structure (Do & Rahm, 2002; Madhavan et al., 2001) or by mapping them to a multi-dimensional space to compute their closeness values (Candan, Kim, Liu, & Suvarna, 2006).

Cupid (Madhavan et al., 2001) is a generic matching approach that can work for both XML and relational databases. This approach considers both structural similarity and non-structural (e.g., linguistics and constraints) information in computing the similarity values of two elements. The similarity value of two elements v_i and v_j is a weighted similarity of all the above factors. In this section, we consider the structure-based bottom-up matching algorithm *TreeMatch*. Given two schema trees S_1 and S_2, the initial similarity value for each leaf element pair is initialized based on an assessment of how compatible the corresponding data types are. Then, *TreeMatch* computes the similarity value *sim* of every element pair (v_1, v_2) $(v_1 \in S_1 \wedge v_2 \in S_2)$ by traversing the two schema trees in post-order. Two cases need to be considered in this computation. In the first case, where the two elements are leaves, their similarity value is the weighted value of their structural similarity value *ssim* and the similarity value *lsim* computed considering other factors (e.g., linguistics). The second case occurs when one element is a non-leaf element. In such a case, the structural similarity of these two elements is measured as the fraction of leaf level element matches. One leaf element *matches* another if their weighted similarity value is higher than some threshold ε. Let v_1 and v_2 be two elements to be matched, *Leaves*(v_1) and *Leaves*(v_2) represent the leaf element sets in sub-trees rooted at v_1 and v_2 respectively. Let $\oplus$ be the union of these two leaf

Figure 5. Two source schemas

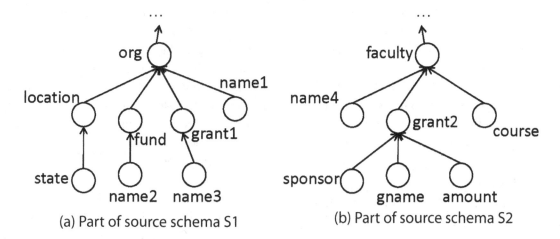

(a) Part of source schema S1

(b) Part of source schema S2

element sets (i.e., $\oplus = Leaves(v_1) \cup Leaves(v_2)$), V_1 represents the set of elements in $Leaves(v_1)$ which matches some element in $Leaves(v_2)$. Similarly, let V_2 represent the set of elements in $Leaves(v_2)$ which matches some element in $Leaves(v_1)$. Then, the $ssim(v_1,v_2)$ is computed as $\dfrac{|V_1 \cup V_2|}{|\oplus|}$.

From the structural similarity value, a weighted similarity value $sim(v_1,v_2)$ over the two elements is computed. Next, this similarity value of two elements is further propagated to the leaf-element pairs in their sub-trees. In particular, given two thresholds ε_h and ε_l, when $sim(v_1,v_2) > \varepsilon_h$, the structural similarity value of every leaf element pair is increased by a factor f_{inc}. On the contrary, when $sim(v_1,v_2) < \varepsilon_l$, $ssim(v_1,v_2)$ is decreased by a factor f_{dec}. This process continues until all the element pairs from both trees are traversed.

We can use the two source schemas in Figure 5 to illustrate this process.

In this figure, to distinguish the different element names in different contexts, we associate with each one a number to make the description easier. Let the matching threshold be $\varepsilon = 0.3$. Let us also assume that initially from the data type compatible matrix, we get that $ssim(name2,gname)=0.5$, $ssim(name1,sponsor)=0.5$, $ssim(name3,gname)=0.5$, ... When we compute $ssim(fund, grant2)$, we

have that element $name2 \in Leaves(fund)$ matches $gname \in Leaves(grant2)$, thus,

$$ssim(fund, grant2) = \frac{|\,\{name2\} \cup \{gname\}\,|}{|\,\{name2, sponsor, gname, amount\}\,|} = \frac{2}{4} = 0.5$$

Next, $ssim(fund,grant2)$ is adjusted to its weighted score $sim(fund,grant2)$. If $sim(fund,grant2)$ is bigger than ε_h, then $ssim(name2,sponsor)=f_{inc} \times ssim(name2,sponsor)$, $ssim(name2,gname)=f_{inc} \times ssim(name2,gname)$, and $ssim(name2, amount) = f_{inc} \times ssim(name2, amount)$.

Milo & Zohar (1998) also use schema graphs for matching; matching is performed node by node starting at the "roots" of the tree-like schema graph. More generally, let $T(V,E)$ be a tree schema. T is called a rooted tree if one of the vertices/nodes is distinguished and called the *root*. T is called a node labeled tree if each node in V is assigned a symbol from an alphabet Σ. T is called an ordered tree if it is rooted and the order among siblings (nodes under the same parent node) is also given. An unordered tree is simply a rooted tree. Given two ordered labeled trees, T_1 and T_2, T_1 is said to *match* T_2 if there is a one-to-one mapping from the nodes of T_1 to the nodes of T_2 such that (a) the roots map to each other, (b) if a tree node v_i maps another tree node v_j, then the children of v_i and

v_j map to each other in left-to-right order and (c) label of v_i is equal to the label of v_j. Note that exact matching can be checked in linear time on ordered trees. T_1 is said to *match* T_2 *at node v* if there is a one-to-one mapping from the nodes of T_1 to the nodes of the sub-tree of T_2 rooted at v. The naive algorithm (which checks for all possible nodes of T_2) takes $O(nm)$ time where n is the size of the T_1 and m is the size of T_2, while there are $O(n\sqrt{m})$ algorithms which leverage special index structures, such as suffix trees for compressed representation and quick access to sub-paths of T_1. While the matching problem is relatively efficient for ordered trees, the problem quickly becomes intractable for unordered trees. In fact, for unordered trees, the matching problem is known to be NP-hard (Kilpeläinen & Mannila, 1995).

As opposed to these potentially expensive approaches, Candan et al. present two approaches in (Candan et al., 2006) and in (Candan, Kim, Liu, & Agarwal, 2007), respectively that use both data instances and hierarchical structures to match two tree-structured schemas, S_1 and S_2. These methods both map the nodes of the tree into a multi-dimensional space (using multi-dimensional scaling in (J. Kruskal, 1964; J. B. Kruskal & Wish, 1978) and using propagation in (Kim & Candan, 2006) and compute the similarity values of the elements in this multi-dimensional space. These approaches work in three steps. First, the nodes in the trees are mapped into two k-dimensional spaces r^k_1 and r^k_2, respectively. Then, these spaces are aligned based on common nodes in the two trees. Finally, once the nodes from both trees are mapped onto a common space, the algorithms use clustering or nearest-neighbor algorithms to find potentially related nodes.

Hybrid and Composite Methods

The difficulty of the matching problem and the different aspects of the data and schema that can be used as cues make pure matching solutions (e.g., solely based on instance, or on structure) inadequate. Due to this, hybrid matching approaches that incorporate multiple information in matching tend to be more effective. Different from the hybrid matching method, which utilizes diverse information but still works as one matcher, the composite matching approaches combine the results of several matching operators. In what follows, we briefly describe some well recognized hybrid and composite methods which work for XML databases.

Onion (Mitra, Wiederhold, & Kersten, 2000) and its predecessor SKAT (Mitra, Wiederhold, & Jannink, 1999) are schema-based matching systems that first perform a linguistic matching and then apply structure-based matching. The structure-based phase, which attempts to match only the unmatched terms, is based on structural isomorphism detection between the subgraphs. Clio (Hernández, Miller, & Haas, 2001; R. J. Miller, Haas, & Hernández, 2000) is a mixed schema-based and instance-based system that proposes a declarative approach to schema matching between either XML or/and relational schemas. After the first phase in which input schemas are translated into an internal representation, the system combines sequentially instance-based attribute classifications (by using a Bayes classifier) with a string matching between elements names (these n-to-m value correspondences can be also entered by the user through a graphical user interface). After that, Clio produces a final mapping. Cupid (Madhavan et al., 2001) also exploits not only structural information, but combines multiple techniques, including linguistic-based, element-based, structure-based and context-dependent matching. It also leverages internal structure, similarity of atomic elements and constraints. In general, to compute the similarity coefficients between elements from two schemas, first, a linguistic matching is performed to match elements based on their names, data types, domains, etc. In this step, a thesaurus is also used to identify synonyms and acronyms. Then, a structural matching is run to match elements based on the similarity of their contexts or vicinities as described earlier.

Next, a final score measuring the similarity of two elements is calculated by combining the two scores obtained in the previous two steps. Finally, the mapping is deduced from these coefficients. In particular, if the adjusted similarity value *sim* of two elements v_i and v_j is no smaller (i.e., equal or bigger) than the given threshold, a correspondence from v_i to v_j (i.e., $\mu=v_i \rightarrow v_j$ (*sim*)) is generated. In the simplest case, only the leaf-level correspondences are returned. The mapping in a general case is one-to-many since a source element may map to many target elements. SF (Melnik et al., 2002) also uses a hybrid combination of different name matchers and SemInt (Li & Clifton, 1994; Li & Clifton, 2000) is a hybrid approach exploiting both schema and instance information. Since they don't specifically deal with XML documents, we omit their descriptions here.

COMA (Do & Rahm, 2002) is a composite matching system working for XML database. Besides using different matching operators, COMA also reuses previous matching results. We briefly introduce the basic ideas of this system:

1. Given two schemas S_i and S_j, COMA finds a set of intermediate schemas, S_k-s, that have some matching results with S_i and S_j: $S_i \leftrightarrow S_k$ (mapping between S_i and S_k) and $S_j \leftrightarrow S_k$.

2. This step computes $S_i \leftrightarrow S_j$ (i.e., mapping between S_i and S_j) by using the previous matching results of other schemas with S_i and S_j (maybe generated by other matchers). Specifically, given l intermediate schemas, for each intermediate schema S_k, COMA uses a *MatchCompose* operation to compute $S_i \leftrightarrow S_j$ from $S_i \leftrightarrow S_k$ and $S_j \leftrightarrow S_k$. The result of *MatchCompose* process using one intermediate schema is a similarity matrix where the similarity value at the i-th row and j-th column is the similarity value for matching $s_i \in S_i$ to $s_j \in S_j$. l is the number of intermediate schemas. The combined result of *MatchCompose* process for all intermediate schema S_k-s is a $m \times n \times l$ similarity cube where each matrix is for one intermediate schema.

3. Next, for each element pair (v_i, v_j) where $v_i \in S_i, v_j \in S_j$, COMA computes their similarity value by aggregating the l similarity values in the similarity cube. This gets a $m \times n$ matrix. The value at the i-th row and j-th column is the aggregated similarity value derived from the matching results (computed using other matchers) with l other schemas.

4. For the elements in one schema, COMA selects its mapping candidates from the other schema using this matrix. The matrix computed in the previous step might imply that one element in a schema may match to many elements in another schema. In this step, COMA finds the best match candidate for each element.

Measuring the Matching Quality

The diversity of the available matching algorithms necessitates objective mechanisms to compare performances of different matching algorithms. Recently, for example, Duchateau et al. (2007) proposed a benchmark to compare the quality of different matching tools. This proposal and others all rely on statistical measures comparing the degrees of false positives (wrongly identified matches) and false negatives (missed matches) against degrees of true positives (correctly identified matches) and true negatives (correctly excluded matches).

Let, as shown in Figure 6, $M=\{(vs_1,vt_1), (vs_2,vt_2),\ldots, (vs_n,vt_n)\}$ denote the matching results returned by a matching algorithm and $M'=\{(vs_1',vt_1'), (vs_2',vt_2'),\ldots, (vs_m',vt_m')\}$ denote the intended matching results (i.e., ground truth). Let the number of correct correspondences be denoted as $c=|M \cap M'|$. Matching accuracy can be quantified by various measures borrowed from the information retrieval field (Do et al., 2002).

These include, $precision = \dfrac{c}{n}$, $recall = \dfrac{c}{m}$, $F - measure = \dfrac{2 \times precision \times recall}{precision + recall}$ .SemInt (Li & Clifton, 2000), for example, uses all three of these measures to evaluate their matching method. *Recall* is used in evaluating the accuracy of LSD (Doan et al., 2001). These standard measures are also used in ontology matching, e.g., QOM (Ehrig & Staab, 2004).

An alternative to *F-measure*, which combines precision and recall, is so called, *overall* measure first proposed in SF (Melnik et al., 2002), and used in COMA (Do & Rahm, 2002). The *overall* measure intends to quantify the user effort that is needed to transform a system returned matching result into the intended one. Given M, M', and c as before, the number of wrongly suggested (false positive) correspondences is $(n-c)$ and the number of missing (false negative) correspondences is $(m-c)$. In total, the amount of corrections (by either deleting false positive results or adding false negative results) that a user has to make is $\dfrac{(n - c) + (m - c)}{m}$. Based on this observation, the overall accuracy can be defined as $overall = 1 - \dfrac{(n - c) + (m - c)}{m}$ (note that this measure can have non-positive values). It is easy to see that $overall = recall - \dfrac{n - c}{m}$; i.e., *overall* refines *recall* by deducting the percentage of the wrongly suggested correspondences. Comparisons between *overall* and *F-Measure* show that, for the same precision and recall values, *overall* tends to provide more pessimistic assessments of the matching quality (Do et al., 2002).

Mapping Rule Generation

The correspondences between source and target elements are inherently ambiguous because they do not contain information on how these elements

Figure 6. Intended matching results and automatically discovered matching results (Adapted from (Do et al., 2002))

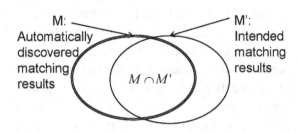

are interpreted in their own schemas, including the contexts and the referential constraints. Therefore, these simple correspondences are not always adequate to retrieve data through one integrated schema from data instances following other schemas, whereas such data retrieval operation is common in applications like data translation, data exchange, or query processing over integrated schema. To make such data retrieval operations possible, more informed mapping rules (assertions) that can semantically connect the elements in one schema to elements in others are needed. More specifically, for a given element $v \in S_1$, an assertion specifies how the instances of v should be translated to instances in S_2. The rule is generally represented as a query q_{S2} in schema S_2 in some specific language, e.g, SQL, XQuery, or XSLT. The process to generate such assertions is called *mapping rule generation*.

In data exchange or data translation, the operation of mapping rule generation happens after the correspondences are identified. The generated rules are used to interpret the data following one schema to comply with another one. In data integration, the mapping rules are generated after schema integration, and are further used during query processing (chapter titled "XML Data Integration: Merging, Query Processing and Conflict Resolution"). To generate mapping rules among relational schemas, there exist various well known techniques, such as source-to-target tuple-generating dependencies (source-to-target tgds (Fagin, Kolaitis, Miller, & Popa, 2005)), GAV (global-as-view (Lenzerini, 2002)), LAV (local-as-view (Lenzerini, 2002)), or GLAV (global-and-local-as-view (Lenzerini, 2002)) assertions. However, the direct application of these techniques to XML database is not trivial due to the hierarchical and nested structures in XML.

Attempts to automatically generate mapping rules for XML schemas include (Fuxman et al., 2006; Hernández et al., 2007; Hernández et al., 2008; Popa et al., 2002; Yu & Popa, 2004) Pankowski et al. (2007) discuss generation of XML schema mapping rules in the presence of key constraints and value dependencies. Atay et al. (2007) present approaches to generate XML to SQL mapping rules for recursive XML schemas. Kementsietsidis, Arenas, & Miller (2003) propose a language which allows specification of alternative semantics for mapping tables and shows that a constraint-based treatment of mappings can lead to efficient mechanisms for inferring new mappings. Arenas & Libkin (2005) propose to use DTDs and source-to-target dependencies together in data translation. Popa et al. (2002) present a *semantic translation* approach to generate mapping rules between hierarchical schemas from simple correspondences between simple elements. In this semantic translation, source-to-target (s-t) dependencies are generated to associate elements in the source schema to elements in the target schema in a certain way by incorporating the semantic constraints in each schema to the element correspondences. The algorithm first computes the primary paths and logical relations for the source and target schemas separately. The primary paths from a nested schema (e.g., XML schema) are a set of elements found on the paths from the root to any non-root element. E.g., $o \in org$, $no \in org.name$, $e \in edu$, $ne \in edu.name$ are all primary paths for the nested schema in Figure 2(b). Then, by taking the referential constraints among elements, the primary paths are combined to logical relations. Each logical relation is of the form "*select * from Ps where Conditions*", where Ps are the primary paths, and *Conditions* are some

equality conditions relating two elements. Then, based on the logical relations from the source and target schema, s-t dependencies are generated. An s-t dependency is in the form of "*for A exists B where C*" where A and B are logical relations in the source and target schemas respectively, and C consists of the equality conditions of the subset of correspondences. To further improve the expressive power of the mapping rules, and the translation/integration performance, Fuxman *et al.* in (2006) extend (Popa et al., 2002) to generate *nested* mapping rules, which allow nesting and correlation of mappings.

Other Considerations

Piazza (A. Y. Halevy, Ives, Suciu, & Tatarinov, 2003), HepToX (Bonifati, Chang, Ho, Lakshmanan, & Pottinger, 2005), QUEST(Qi, Candan, Sapino, & Kintigh, 2006), and FICSR (Candan et al., 2008; Qi et al., 2007) recognize that it is unrealistic to expect an independent data source entering information exchange to agree to a global mediated schema or to perform heavyweight operations to map its schema to every other schema in the group. Piazza presents a mediation language for mapping both the domain and document structures and focuses on *certain answers* that hold for every consistent instance. HepToX, on the other hand, focuses on automated mapping rule generation, without explicitly considering conflicts. FICSR (Candan et al., 2008; Qi et al., 2007) uses a feedback process to incrementally improve mappings through users feedback provided within the context of queries they pose. *Pay-as-you-go* systems (Dong, Halevy, & Yu, 2007; Jeffery, Franklin, & Halevy, 2008; Sarma, Dong, & Halevy, 2008) consider probabilistic mappings, which may improve over time with new evidence, as a way of relaxing the need for enforcing full-, consistent-integration. The idea of applying user feedback to the data integration is not new. In particular, several works (Doan et al., 2001; Jeffery et al., 2008; Wu, Yu, Doan, &

Meng, 2004) explore the role of user feedback in schema matching. TRIO (Benjelloun, Sarma, Halevy, & Widom, 2006) also represents alternatives probabilistically and relies on lineage information for query processing: the lineage information provides the context in which the validity of the various statements about the data and metadata can be assessed.

FUTURE RESEARCH DIRECTIONS

As discussed above, decades of efforts on schema extraction, mapping, and merging have produced a lot of promising techniques. However, there is still a lot of room for improvements. In what follows, we outline several trends that deserve attention.

In this section, we observed that there are many approaches to XML schema matching and integration. Different algorithms use different kinds of information. Thus, often times, they also report results on different testing data sets. This state of affairs raises some critical questions: "how solid are these algorithms?" and "how can one fairly measure the soundness of these techniques?" Gal pointed in (Gal, 2007) that all participating matchers in a benchmark test reported very poor results with only 30-40% precision and even worse, 13-45% recall. On the other hand, "even with such low precision and recall, is it fair to state that these techniques are useless?" "How useful are these matching algorithms after decades of efforts?" Thus benchmarking is a critical research direction in this domain. Recently, there are several efforts (Duchateau et al., 2007) for developing measures for qualities of matching algorithms. At this point, however, there are no benchmarks for measuring the effectiveness of data merging. Moreover, even when such benchmarks exist, they end up relying on statistical measures (like precision and recall), instead of measuring how useful these systems really are in helping problem solving and decision making. Our community

has to answer some tough questions about how to measure the quality of integrated data and how to develop benchmarks that measure the utility of the various algorithms to the end-user.

We also note that most recent applications abhor pre-integration of data and, instead, demand runtime (on-line) integration (E. Rahm, Thor, & Aumueller, 2007). For example, many mashup applications integrate web contents and services on demand based on specific user's input (personalized integration) or the context (context-aware integration). Moreover, some of the new data management frameworks (such as data spaces) assume very limited schema information and are based on very loosely structured data. In such highly dynamic and loosely-structured environments, traditional algorithms may not be efficient. Dynamic (or on-the-fly) data/metadata matching, "pay-as-you-go" integration are some of the proposed solutions to address this challenge. In Chapter titled "XML Data Integration: Merging, Query Processing and Conflict Resolution" we will further discuss these problems and solutions.

CONCLUSION

As shown in Figure 1, XML data integration is a multi-stage process. In this chapter, we focused on the techniques for schema extraction and mapping. We note, however, these are just the starting steps of XML data integration. In order to integrate the data, we need to further perform data/metadata merging. Based on the resulting merged data in query processing, we either need to apply conflict resolution strategies or develop new query processing techniques that can operate on more relaxed data structures, such as graphs. In fact, conflict resolution process can be integrated with query processing to support an incremental approach to cleaning the conflicts: as the user explores the integrated data (and conflicts) within the context of her queries, she can provide more informed conflict resolution feedback to the system. We will discuss merging, query processing over integrated XML data, and cover strategies that can be used for resolving conflicts in a separate chapter, titled "XML Data Integration: Merging, Query Processing and Conflict Resolution".

REFERENCES

Achard, F., Vaysseixm, G., & Barillot, E. (2001). XML, bioinformatics and data integration. *Bioinformatics (Oxford, England)*, *17*(2), 115–125. doi:10.1093/bioinformatics/17.2.115

Anand, A., & Chawathe, S. S. (2004). *Cooperative data dissemination in a serverless environment.* CS-TR-4562, University of Maryland, College Park, MD.

Arenas, M., & Libkin, L. (2005). XML data exchange: Consistency and query answering. *PODS*, (pp. 13-24).

Atay, M., Chebotko, A., Lu, S., & Fotouhi, F. (2007). XML-to-SQL query mapping in the presence of multi-valued schema mappings and recursive XML schemas. *DEXA*, (pp. 603-616).

Aulbach, S., Grust, T., Jacobs, D., & Rittinger, A. K. J. (2008). Multi-tenant databases for software as a service: Schema-mapping techniques. *SIGMOD Conference*, (pp. 1195-1206).

Balmin, A., Papakonstantinou, Y., & Vianu, V. (2004). Incremental validation of XML documents. *ACM Transactions on Database Systems*, *29*(4), 710–751. doi:10.1145/1042046.1042050

Barbosa, D., Mignet, L., & Veltri, P. (2005). Studying the XML web: Gathering statistics from an XML sample. *World Wide Web (Bussum)*, *8*(4), 413–438. doi:10.1007/s11280-005-1544-y

Barbosa, D., Mignet, L., & Veltri, P. (2006). Studying the XML web: Gathering statistics from an XML sample. *World Wide Web (Bussum)*, *9*(2), 187–212. doi:10.1007/s11280-006-8437-6

Benjelloun, O., Sarma, A. D., Halevy, A. Y., & Widom, J. (2006). ULDBs: Databases with uncertainty and lineage. *VLDB*, 953-964.

Bertino, E., & Ferrari, E. (2001). XML and data integration. *IEEE Internet Computing*, *5*(6), 75–76. doi:10.1109/4236.968835

Bex, G. J., Martens, W., Neven, F., & Schwentick, T. (2005). Expressiveness of XSDs: From practice to theory, there and back again. *WWW*, (pp. 712-721).

Bex, G. J., Neven, F., & Bussche, J. V. d. (2004). DTDs versus XML schema: A practical study. *WebDB*, (pp. 79-84).

Bex, G. J., Neven, F., Schwentick, T., & Tuyls, K. (2006). Inference of concise DTDs from XML data. *VLDB*, (pp. 115-126).

Bex, G. J., Neven, F., & Vansummeren, S. (2007). Inferring XML schema definitions from XML data. *VLDB*, (pp. 998-1009).

Bex, G. J., Neven, F., & Vansummeren, S. (2008). SchemaScope: A system for inferring and cleaning XML schemas. *SIGMOD Conference*, (pp. 1259-1262).

Bonifati, A., Chang, E. Q., Ho, T., Lakshmanan, L. V. S., & Pottinger, R. (2005). HePToX: Marrying XML and heterogeneity in your P2P databases. *VLDB*, (pp. 1267-1270).

Bouquet, P., Serafini, L., & Zanobini, S. (2003). Semantic coordination: A new approach and an application. *International Semantic Web Conference*, (pp. 130-145).

Candan, K. S., Cao, H., Qi, Y., & Sapino, M. L. (2008). System support for exploration and expert feedback in resolving conflicts during integration of metadata. *The VLDB Journal*, *17*(6), 1407–1444. doi:10.1007/s00778-008-0109-y

Candan, K. S., Kim, J. W., Liu, H., & Agarwal, R. S. N. (2007). *Multimedia data mining and knowledge discovery*, (pp. 259-290). London: Springer.

Candan, K. S., Kim, J. W., Liu, H., & Suvarna, R. (2006). Discovering mappings in hierarchical data from multiple sources using the inherent structure. *Knowledge and Information Systems, 10*(2), 185–210. doi:10.1007/s10115-005-0230-9

Cherukuri, V. S., & Candan, K. S. (2008). Propagation-vectors for trees (PVT): Concise yet effective summaries for hierarchical data and trees. *LSDS-IR '08: Proceeding of the 2008 ACM Workshop on Large-Scale Distributed Systems for Information Retrieval,* Napa Valley, CA, (pp. 3-10).

Chidlovskii, B. (2001). Schema extraction from XML: A grammatical inference approach. *KRDB,*
Chitic, C., & Rosu, D. (2004). On validation of XML streams using finite state machines. *WebDB,* (pp. 85-90).

Chung, C., Min, J., & Shim, K. (2002). APEX: An adaptive path index for XML data. *SIGMOD Conference,* (pp. 121-132).

Clark, J. (n.d.). *Trang: Multi-format schema converter based on RELAX NG.*

Cohen, W. W., Ravikumar, P., & Fienberg, S. E. (2003). A comparison of string distance metrics for name-matching tasks. *IIWeb,* (pp. 73-78).

Decker, S., Harmelen, F. V., Broekstra, J., Erdmann, M., Fensel, D., Horrocks, I., et al. (2000). The semantic web - on the respective roles of XML and RDF. *IEEE Internet Computing, 4.* Retrieved from http://www.ontoknow

Devlin, B. A., & Murphy, P. T. (1988). An architecture for a business and information system. *IBM Systems Journal, 27*(1), 60–80.

Do, H. H., Melnik, S., & Rahm, E. (2002). Comparison of schema matching evaluations. *Web, Web-Services, and Database Systems,* (pp. 221-237).

Do, H. H., & Rahm, E. (2002). COMA - A system for flexible combination of schema matching approaches. *VLDB,* (pp. 610-621).

Doan, A., Domingos, P., & Halevy, A. Y. (2001). Reconciling schemas of disparate data sources: A machine-learning approach. *SIGMOD Conference,* (pp. 509-520).

Doan, A., & Halevy, A. Y. (2005). Semantic integration research in the database community: A brief survey. *AI Magazine, 26*(1), 83–94.

Dong, X. L., Halevy, A. Y., & Yu, C. (2007). Data integration with uncertainty. *VLDB,* (pp. 687-698).

Duchateau, F., Bellahsene, Z., & Hunt, E. (2007). XBenchMatch: A benchmark for XML schema matching tools. *VLDB,* (pp. 1318-1321).

Ehrenfeucht, A., & Zeiger, H. P. (1976). Complexity measures for regular expressions. *Journal of Computer and System Sciences, 12*(2), 134–146.

Ehrig, M., & Staab, S. (2004). QOM - quick ontology mapping. *International Semantic Web Conference,* (pp. 683-697).

Fagin, R., Kolaitis, P. G., Miller, R. J., & Popa, L. (2005). Data exchange: Semantics and query answering. *Theoretical Computer Science, 336*(1), 89–124. doi:10.1016/j.tcs.2004.10.033

Fernau, H. (2004). Extracting minimum length document type definitions is NP-hard. *ICGI,* (pp. 277-278).

Fernau, H. (2005). Algorithms for learning regular expressions. *ALT,* (pp. 297-311).

Florescu, D. (2005). Managing semi-structured data. *ACM Queue; Tomorrow's Computing Today, 3*(8), 18–24. doi:10.1145/1103822.1103832

Franklin, M. J., Halevy, A. Y., & Maier, D. (2005). From databases to dataspaces: A new abstraction for information management. *SIGMOD Record, 34*(4), 27–33. doi:10.1145/1107499.1107502

Fuxman, A., Hernández, M. A., Ho, C. T. H., Miller, R. J., Papotti, P., & Popa, L. (2006). Nested mappings: Schema mapping reloaded. *VLDB,* (pp. 67-78).

Gal, A. (2006). Why is schema matching tough and what can we do about it? *SIGMOD Record, 35*(4), 2–5. doi:10.1145/1228268.1228269

Gal, A. (2007). The generation Y of XML schema matching panel description. *XSym,* 9pp. 137-139).

Garcia, P., & Vidal, E. (1990). Inference of k-testable languages in the strict sense and application to syntactic pattern recognition. *IEEE Transactions on Pattern Analysis and Machine Intelligence, 12*(9), 920–925. doi:10.1109/34.57687

Garofalakis, M. N., Gionis, A., Rastogi, R., Seshadri, S., & Shim, K. (2003). XTRACT: Learning document type descriptors from XML document collections. *Data Mining and Knowledge Discovery, 7*(1), 23–56. doi:10.1023/A:1021560618289

Giunchiglia, F., Shvaiko, P., & Yatskevich, M. (2004). S-match: An algorithm and an implementation of semantic matching. *ESWS,* (pp. 61-75).

Goldman, R., & Widom, J. (1997). DataGuides: Enabling query formulation and optimization in semistructured databases. *VLDB, 97,* 436–445.

Gottlob, G., Koch, C., Pichler, R., & Segoufin, L. (2005). The complexity of XPath query evaluation and XML typing. *Journal of the ACM, 52*(2), 284–335. doi:10.1145/1059513.1059520

Halevy, A. (1999). *More on data management for XML.* White Paper, available online at http://www.Cs.Washington.edu/homes/alon/widom-Response.html

Halevy, A., Rajaraman, A., & Ordille, J. (2006). Data integration: The teenage years. *VLDB},* 9.

Halevy, A. Y., Franklin, M. J., & Maier, D. (2006). Principles of dataspace systems. *PODS,* (pp. 1-9).

Halevy, A. Y., Ives, Z. G., Suciu, D., & Tatarinov, I. (2003). Schema mediation in peer data management systems. In *ICDE,* (pp. 505-516).

Hegewald, J., Naumann, F., & Weis, M. (2006). XStruct: Efficient schema extraction from multiple and large XML documents. *ICDE Workshops,* 81.

Hernández, M. A., Ho, H., Popa, L., Fuxman, A., Miller, R. J., Fukuda, T., et al. (2007). Creating nested mappings with clio. *ICDE,* (pp. 1487-1488).

Hernández, M. A., Miller, R. J., & Haas, L. M. (2001). Clio: A semi-automatic tool for schema mapping. *SIGMOD Conference,* 607.

Hernández, M. A., Papotti, P., & Tan, W. C. (2008). Data exchange with data-metadata translations. *PVLDB, 1*(1), 260–273.

Hopcroft, J. E., & Ullman, J. D. (1979). *Introduction to automata theory, languages and computation.* Reading, MA: Addison-Wesley Publishing Company.

Jeffery, S. R., Franklin, M. J., & Halevy, A. Y. (2008). Pay-as-you-go user feedback for dataspace systems. In *SIGMOD '08: Proceedings of the 2008 ACM SIGMOD International Conference on Management of Data,* Vancouver, Canada, (pp. 847-860).

Jennifer, R. G., & Widom, J. (1999). Approximate DataGuides. In *Proceedings of the Workshop on Query Processing for Semistructured Data and Non-Standard Data Formats,* (pp. 436-445).

Jhingran, A. (2006). Enterprise information mashups: Integrating information, simply. *VLDB,* (3-4).

Kementsietsidis, A., Arenas, M., & Miller, R. J. (2003). Mapping data in peer-to-peer systems: Semantics and algorithmic issues. In *SIGMOD Conference,* (pp. 325-336).

Kilpeläinen, P., & Mannila, H. (1995). Ordered and unordered tree inclusion. *SIAM Journal on Computing, 24*(2), 340–356. doi:10.1137/S0097539791218202

Kim, J. W., & Candan, K. S. (2006). CP/CV: Concept similarity mining without frequency information from domain describing taxonomies. In *CIKM,* (pp. 483-492).

Kintigh, K. W. (2006). The promise and challenge of archaeological data integration. *American Antiquity.*

Koloniari, G., & Pitoura, E. (2005). Peer-to-peer management of XML data: Issues and research challenges. *SIGMOD Record, 34*(2), 6–17. doi:10.1145/1083784.1083788

Kruskal, J. (1964). Nonmetric multidimensional scaling: A numerical method. *Psychometrika, 29*(2), 115–129. doi:10.1007/BF02289694

Kruskal, J. B., & Wish, M. (1978). *Multidimensional scaling.* Beverly Hills, CA: SAGE publications.

Lenzerini, M. (2002). Data integration: A theoretical perspective. In *PODS '02: Proceedings of the Twenty-First ACM SIGMOD-SIGACT-SIGART Symposium on Principles of Database Systems,* Madison, Wisconsin, (pp. 233-246).

Li, W., & Clifton, C. (1994). Semantic integration in heterogeneous databases using neural networks. In *VLDB,* (pp. 1-12).

Li, W., & Clifton, C. (2000). SEMINT: A tool for identifying attribute correspondences in heterogeneous databases using neural networks. *Data & Knowledge Engineering, 33*(1), 49–84. doi:10.1016/S0169-023X(99)00044-0

Madhavan, J., Bernstein, P. A., & Rahm, E. (2001). Generic schema matching with cupid. In *VLDB,* (pp. 49-58).

Martens, W., Neven, F., Schwentick, T., & Bex, G. J. (2006). Expressiveness and complexity of XML schema. *ACM Transactions on Database Systems, 31*(3), 770–813. doi:10.1145/1166074.1166076

McHugh, J., Abiteboul, S., Goldman, R., & Widom, D. Q. J. (1997). Lore: A database management system for semistructured data. *SIGMOD Record, 26*(3), 54–66. doi:10.1145/262762.262770

Melnik, S., Garcia-Molina, H., & Rahm, E. (2002). Similarity flooding: A versatile graph matching algorithm and its application to schema matching. In *ICDE,* (pp. 117-128).

Miller, G. A. (1995). WordNet: A lexical database for english. *Communications of the ACM, 38*(11), 39–41. doi:10.1145/219717.219748

Miller, R. J., Haas, L. M., & Hernández, M. A. (2000). Schema mapping as query discovery. In *VLDB,* (pp. 77-88).

Milo, T., & Suciu, D. (1999). Index structures for path expressions. In *Proceedings Database Theory - ICDT '99, 7th International Conference, Jerusalem, Israel, January 10-12, 1999,* (LNCS Vol. 1540, pp. 277-295).

Milo, T., & Zohar, S. (1998). Using schema matching to simplify heterogeneous data translation. In *VLDB,* (pp. 122-133).

Min, J., Ahn, J., & Chung, C. (2003). Efficient extraction of schemas for XML documents. *Information Processing Letters, 85*(1), 7–12. doi:10.1016/S0020-0190(02)00345-9

Mitra, P., Wiederhold, G., & Jannink, J. (1999). Semi-automatic integration of knowledge sources. In *Proc. 2nd International Conference on Information Fusion,* (pp. 572–581).

Mitra, P., Wiederhold, G., & Kersten, M. L. (2000). A graph-oriented model for articulation of ontology interdependencies. In *EDBT,* (pp. 86-100).

Noy, N., & Musen, M. (2001). Anchor-PROMPT: Using non-local context for semantic matching. In *Proceedings of the Workshop on Ontologies and Information Sharing at the International Joint Conference on Artificial Intelligence (IJCAI),* (pp. 63-70).

Pankowski, T. (2008). XML data integration in SixP2P: A theoretical framework. In *Intl. Workshop on Data Management in Peer-to-Peer Systems,* (pp. 11-18).

Pankowski, T., Cybulka, J., & Meissner, A. (2007). XML schema mappings in the presence of key constraints and value dependencies. *EROW.*

Papakonstantinou, Y., Garcia-Molina, H., & Widom, J. (1995). Object exchange across heterogeneous information sources. In *ICDE,* (pp. 251-260).

Popa, L., Velegrakis, Y., Miller, R. J., Hernández, M. A., & Fagin, R. (2002). Translating web data. In *VLDB,* (pp. 598-609).

Pottinger, R. A., & Bernstein, P. A. (2003). Merging models based on given correspondences. In *VLDB.*

Qi, Y., Candan, K. S., & Sapino, M. L. (2007). FICSR: Feedback-based inconsistency resolution and query processing on misaligned data sources. In *SIGMOD,* (pp. 151-162).

Qi, Y., Candan, K. S., Sapino, M. L., & Kintigh, K. W. (2006). QUEST: QUery-driven exploration of semistructured data with ConflicTs and partial knowledge. *CleanDB.*

Rahm, E., & Bernstein, P. A. (2001). A survey of approaches to automatic schema matching. *The VLDB Journal, 10*(4), 334–350. doi:10.1007/s007780100057

Rahm, E., Do, H. H., & Massmann, S. (2004). Matching large XML schemas. *SIGMOD Record, 33*(4), 26–31. doi:10.1145/1041410.1041415

Rahm, E., Thor, A., & Aumueller, D. (2007). Dynamic fusion of web data. In *XSym,* (pp. 14-16).

Resnik, P. (1995). Using information content to evaluate semantic similarity in a taxonomy. *IJCAI,* 448-453.

Sankey, J., & Wong, R. K. (2001). Structural inference for semistructured data. In *CIKM,* (pp. 159-166).

Sarma, A. D., Dong, X., & Halevy, A. (2008). Bootstrapping pay-as-you-go data integration systems. In *SIGMOD '08: Proceedings of the 2008 ACM SIGMOD International Conference on Management of Data,* Vancouver, Canada, (pp. 861-874).

Segoufin, L., & Vianu, V. (2002). Validating streaming XML documents. In *PODS,* (pp. 53-64).

SGML. (n.d.). *Standard generalized markup language.* Retrieved from http://www.w3.org/MarkUp/SGML/

Shvaiko, P., & Euzenat, J. (2005). A survey of schema-based matching approaches. *J. Data Semantics, 4,* 146–171.

Shvaiko, P., & Euzenat, J. (2008). Ten challenges for ontology matching. *OTM Conferences,* (2), 1164-1182.

Valtchev, P., & Euzenat, J. (1997). Dissimilarity measure for collections of objects and values. *IDA*, 259-272.

Wu, W., Yu, C., Doan, A., & Meng, W. (2004). An interactive clustering-based approach to integrating source query interfaces on the deep web. *SIGMOD '04: Proceedings of the 2004 ACM SIGMOD International Conference on Management of Data*, Paris, France, (pp. 95-106).

XML. (n.d.). *Extensible markup language*. Retrieved from http://www.w3.org/XML/

XMLschema. (n.d.). Retrieved from http://www.w3.org/XML/Schema

Yu, C., & Popa, L. (2004). Constraint-based XML query rewriting for data integration. *SIGMOD*, (pp. 371).

Chapter 15
XML Data Integration:
Merging, Query Processing and Conflict Resolution

Yan Qi
Arizona State University, Tempe, USA

Huiping Cao
Arizona State University, Tempe, USA

K. Selçuk Candan
Arizona State University, Tempe, USA

Maria Luisa Sapino
University of Torino, Italy

ABSTRACT

In XML Data Integration, data/metadata merging and query processing are indispensable. Specifically, merging integrates multiple disparate (heterogeneous and autonomous) input data sources together for further usage, while query processing is one main reason why the data need to be integrated in the first place. Besides, when supported with appropriate user feedback techniques, queries can also provide contexts in which conflicts among the input sources can be interpreted and resolved. The flexibility of XML structure provides opportunities for alleviating some of the difficulties that other less flexible data types face in the presence of uncertainty; yet, this flexibility also introduces new challenges in merging multiple sources and query processing over integrated data. In this chapter, the authors discuss two alternative ways XML data/schema can be integrated: conflict-eliminating (where the result is cleaned from any conflicts that the different sources might have with each other) and conflict-preserving (where the resulting XML data or XML schema captures the alternative interpretations of the data). They also present techniques for query processing over integrated, possibly imprecise, XML data, and cover strategies that can be used for resolving underlying conflicts.

DOI: 10.4018/978-1-61520-727-5.ch015

INTRODUCTION

One of the primary motivations behind the development of eXtensible Markup Language (XML) is to create a framework that can support interoperability between businesses and other enterprises. In short time, the simplicity and flexibility of XML leads to many new applications, including peer-to-peer (P2P) applications (Koloniari & Pitoura, 2005; Pankowski, 2008), bioinformatics (Achard, Vaysseixm, & Barillot, 2001), and semantic web (Decker et al., 2000). As we have seen in Chapter titled "XML Data Integration: Schema Extraction and Mapping", the simple, flexible and self-describing data representation of XML provides unique opportunities to support data integration. On the other hand, these same properties, especially the flexibility of the structure of the data and the possibility for each data contributor and user to have their own schemas also introduce many new challenges in the integration process. Figure 1 provides an overview of the major steps underlying the XML data integration process:

- *Schema extraction*: A particular challenge introduced by XML is that not all XML data come with an associated schema. While this enables the use of XML as a flexible messaging and integration medium, when the integration process is schema-aware, it also necessitates a process to extract schemas that can be used during integration.
- *Matching and mapping*: Finding mappings between data components is a common problem in almost all integration domains. XML data can often be represented using trees or tree-like graphs (Goldman & Widom, 1997). This impacts solutions for finding mappings between XML data.
- *XML data/metadata merging*: Once the mappings are discovered, the next step in the process is to integrate the XML data or metadata, depending on whether the system

is operating on data- or schema-level. This is often done through a transform-and-merge process.

- *Query processing and conflict resolution*: The results of the merge process, however, may not always be a valid XML data or schema. In these cases, in order to be able to use the resulting merged data in query processing, we either need to apply conflict resolution strategies or develop new query processing techniques that can operate on more relaxed data structures, such as graphs.

In fact, conflict resolution process can be integrated with query processing to support an incremental approach to cleaning the conflicts: as the user explores the integrated data (and conflicts) within the context of her queries, she can provide more informed conflict resolution feedback to the system.

In Chapter "XML Data Integration: Schema Extraction and Mapping" we have discussed the first two bullets in detail. In this chapter, we focus on merging and query processing over integrated XML data, and cover strategies that can be used for resolving conflicts with the user's help. The running example we use in this chapter is from the same domain (*universities and research institutes*) as Chapter "XML Data Integration: Schema Extraction and Mapping".

MERGING

Once the mappings between the sources are discovered through the matching process, the input sources can be merged into a logical "global" view for further use in integrated data processing. The merge process takes as input (a) a set of sources and (b) the mappings among them, and generates an integrated (target) data or schema.

Figure 1. Overview of the XML data integration process

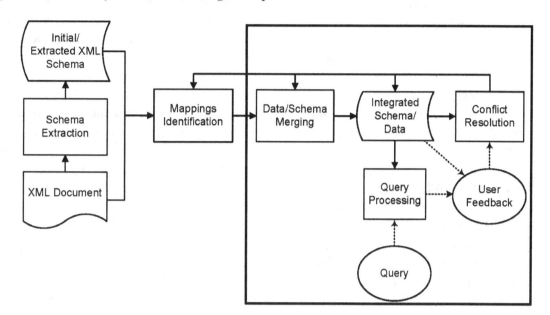

Handling Conflicts during the Merge Process

Due to the imperfectness of the matching process and possible incompatibilities among the input sources, inputs cannot always be merged perfectly. According to the ways that conflicts are handled, we can classify the merging algorithms into two broad categories:

- Conflict-elimination strategies: conflicts are resolved during the integration process and one unified target schema is generated (Pottinger & Bernstein, 2003).
- Conflict-preserving strategies: all interpretations of the data are preserved in one unified representation (Candan, Cao, Qi, & Sapino, 2008; Qi, Candan, & Sapino, 2007a) and conflicts are left to be resolved through user feedback during query processing.

Generalized Mappings

In this section, we will use a more general form of mappings than the one we have used in Chapter titled "XML Data Integration: Schema Extraction and Mapping". Without loss of generality, let us denote each source as a node and edge labeled directed graph, $S(V,E)$, where each node, $v \in V$, corresponds to a labeled element, attribute or value, and each edge, $e \in E$ between two nodes corresponds to a named relationship between the corresponding data elements. Given this, a mapping over two sources $S_1 (V_1, E_1)$ and $S_2 (V_2, E_2)$ is a pair $M(C, M)$ where

- $C (C_M, E_M)$ describes any knowledge that is not directly obtainable from the input sources, such as elements not covered in either source but needed to properly unify the input sources; and
- each element $\mu \in M$ is in the form of $\langle V_i, V_j, map\_name, \tau \rangle$ where $V_i \subseteq V_1 \cup C.C_M$, $V_j \subseteq V_2 \cup C.C_M$, and map_name denotes the type of the correspondence (e.g. "*equality*", "*subsumption*", or "*similarity*") between V_i

and V_j, and τ is the confidence value associated to this mapping element.

Note that this general mapping definition corresponds to the basic mapping rules defined in the previous section when (a) $C.C_M$ and $C.E_M$ are all empty and (b) for $\mu \in M$, both V_i and V_j contain one element respectively and *map_name* is always "*equality*".

Conflict-Elimination Strategies

In (Pottinger & Bernstein, 2003), Pottinger and Bernstein analyze generic merge requirements for schema integration (or merging), including preserving the elements, relationships, constraints and properties. More specifically, they present a *Merge* operator for schema integration which satisfies these requirements. The operator works for schemas conforming to a general model, thus can be adapted to XML schemas as well. The algorithm takes as input two source schemas S_1, S_2, and the mapping M_{12} between them. The output is a unified schema S which keeps all the elements and relationships in the input models and the input mapping.

M_{12} is a general mapping as described above, with some limitations:

- First, no confidence value is attached to mapping elements.
- Secondly, V_i and V_j are singleton; i.e., the mapping rules are defined over element pairs.
- The correspondence types are limited to "*equality*" and "*similarity*". "*Equality*" means that two elements are semantically equal, whereas, "*similarity*" denotes that two elements are related but not completely equal.

As discussed in Section "Generalized Mappings", given a correspondence μ: $\langle v_1, v_2 \rangle$, both v_1 and v_2 do not have to belong to S_1 or S_2; but they

may be some new concept/element defined in M_{12}. This is, for instance, very useful in representing a mapping correspondence where an element in one schema equals to a combination of several elements in another. As an example, let us consider a scenario where a *name* element in one model refers to two elements *firstName* and *lastName* in another model. This can be represented using three correspondences μ_1: $\langle c, name \rangle$, μ_2: $\langle c_1, firstName \rangle$, and μ_3: $\langle c_2, lastName \rangle$, where c, c_1, and c_2 are new elements introduced, such that c has *parent-child* relationships with c_1 and c_2.

Given S_1, S_2, and M_{12}, the outline of the *Merge* process is as follows:

1. First, the *Merge* operator initializes the integrated schema S with an empty schema.
2. Then, elements are created and added to S. To do this, the elements in S_1, S_2, and M_{12} are grouped, in such a way that there is one group for each mapping condition μ:$\langle v_i, v_j \rangle$.
3. For each group, a new element is created in S to represent this group of elements. The properties of each new element "c" are the union of the properties of the group that c represents.
4. Next, new relationships are inserted into S. Two cases need to be considered in inserting relationships between two elements c_i and c_j in S, where c_i and c_j represent two distinct groups g_i and g_j, respectively.
   - First case is when g_i and g_j do not contain elements with "*similarity*" type of correspondence. In this case, if there is a correspondence μ: $\langle v_i', v_j' \rangle$ ($v_i' \in g_i$, $v_j' \in g_j$) of type T and with cardinality l, a new relationship $Rel(c_i, c_j)$ with the same type and same cardinality is created in S for c_i and c_j.
   - If some elements in g_i and g_j have "*similarity*" type correspondence, then a new similarity mapping element, c, is created and every mapping

Figure 2. Example of the Merge process. (a) Two source schemas and the mapping between them (b) The integrated schema (Pottinger & Bernstein, 2003). Note the edge between two elements denotes the parent-child relationship between them. They are implicit in the graphs

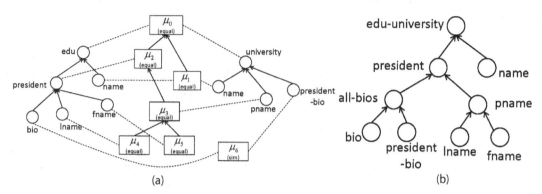

(a)   (b)

relationship originating from *c* is replaced by a *"parent-child"* relationship.

Figure 2 shows an example execution of the *Merge* operator. In this example, the element *'edu-university'* in Figure 2(b) merges the nodes *'edu'*, *'university'*, and *'μ_0'* in the source schemas and the mapping. Similarly, *'pname'* in Figure 2(b) incorporates the nodes *'pname'* and *'μ_3'* in Figure 2(a). The mapping μ_6 is reflected by creating a new node *'all-bios'* with two children in the original schemas.

Different from (Pottinger & Bernstein, 2003), which eliminates the conflicts and maintains only one merged consistent schema, (Chiticariu, Kolaitis, & Popa, 2008) creates multiple such schemas while one is to be selected in later stages through user interaction. The algorithm first creates a unified representation, where correspondences between elements are represented by mapping-edges. In the second phase, for each compatible subset of mapping-edges, a different merge result is obtained. To cope with the inherent cost of enumerating different mapping strategies, the algorithm uses several heuristics to identify and eliminate redundant strategies.

Conflict-Preserving Strategies

Attempting to resolve conflicts at the merging time may limit the future usage of data: if only one integrated schema is generated by enforcing only some constraints, this integrated target schema obviously misses some of the information in the input sources. In contrast, Candan *et al.* (Candan et al., 2008; Qi, Candan, Sapino, & Kintigh, 2006; Qi, Candan, & Sapino, 2007a) propose to merge sources (schemas or data instances) by preserving the possible different interpretations in the integrated target graph (schema or data instance) and attempt to resolve conflicts only when needed (e.g., in query processing).

A value-null in databases is said to occur when the value cannot be determined for certain. A value-null can be of type *"existential"* (the value exists, but is not known), *"maybe"* (the value may or may not exist), *"place holder"* (the value is known not to exist, so a dummy symbol is used as a place holder), or *"partial"* (the value is known to be in a given set) (Candan, Grant, & Subrahmanian, 1997). For example,

- *"Node &5's tag can be 4, 6, or 9."*

is a value null.

337

Qi et al. (2006) introduce structure-nulls, which occur when the structural relationship between the data nodes cannot be determined in certain. For example,

- *"Node &5 is a child of node &3 or &4"*.
- *"Either node &5 or &6 is a child of node &3"*.

are structure nulls. A structure-null can also be of type *"existential"* (the structural relationship exists, but is not known), *"maybe"* (structural relationship may or may not exist), *"place holder"* (the structural relationship is known not to exist), or *"partial"* (the structural relationship is known to be in a given set of alternatives). An early attempt at modeling semi-structured data with missing and partial data is presented in (Liu & Ling, 2000); authors use an object-based model, where *null, or-valued,* and *partial set* objects are used to handle partial and missing knowledge in semi-structured data. Although it is richer than standard semi-structured data models, such as Object Exchange Model (OEM) (Buneman, Fan, & Weinstein, 1999; McHugh, Abiteboul, Goldman, & Widom, 1997), and Document Object Model (DOM), this model is more focused on *value* nulls and does not capture inconsistencies and missing knowledge in the structure of the data. Qi et al. (2006) present an assertion-based data model, **QUEST**, which captures both *value*-based and *structure*-based "nulls" in data.

Candan *et al.* in (2008) extend this framework to capture more general relationships (e.g., *WORKS-AT*) in addition to XML parent-child relationships. They also extend the assertions with trust values describing how *trustable* each assertion is. The trust value represents the user's source preference, assessment of mapping certainty, and the amount of agreement among different sources on this assertion. Candan et al. (Candan et al., 2008; Qi, Candan, & Sapino, 2007a) also introduce new *coordination* constructs that represent constraints that the integration process imposes on the various source relationships. The six basic constructs introduced in (Candan et al., 2008; Qi, Candan, & Sapino, 2007a), as part of their FICSR framework, are shown in Figure 3. Constructs (a)-(c) coordinate multiple relationships *from* a single element, while constructs (d)-(f) coordinate relationships from multiple elements *to* a single one. Candan et al. (2008) also show how to combine these constructs to obtain more complex and richer coordination semantics among a set of elements. Enriching the integrated graph with these *coordination* constructs (used along with the original source relationships) allows FICSR to preserve the multiple possible worlds (i.e., different interpretations) in the integrated graph. Thus, instead of having to enforce these constraints during the integration time, FICSR is able to defer the resolution process to a later stage in processing. In what follows, we roughly present FICSR's integration process. This work differs in several ways from other integration algorithms, which generally take as input only the source graphs and a mapping. FICSR takes as input, in addition to the source graphs, the following rules:

- *mapping rules*: FICSR uses a general mapping rule format; each mapping rule μ: $\langle V_i, V_j, map\_name, \tau \rangle$ consists of subsets, $V_i \subseteq V_1$ and $V_j \subseteq V_2$, of elements from the sources S_1 and S_2, a correspondence name *map_name*, and a confidence τ.

- *embedding rules*: embedding rules of the form ρ:$\langle c_1, c_2, rel\_name, \tau \rangle$ describe how elements that do not belong to any of the sources (but might be created during the integration process) relate to each other. Here, c_1 or c_2 can be either an element created during the integration process or an element in $V_1 \cup V_2$ (but at least one of them is a new element).

- *co-validity rules*: co-validity rules of the form γ:$\langle E, \tau \rangle$ represent the inter-dependence of various relationships in the source

Figure 3. Choice and coordination constructs with (a) Negatively coordinate the destinations of w: either Rel(w,u) or Rel(w,v) holds, but not both, (b) Positively coordinate the destinations of w: both Rel(w,u) and Rel(w,v) needs to hold, (c) Implication of the destinations of w: if Rel(w,v) holds, then Rel(w,u) must hold (destination coordination) (d) Negatively coordinate the sources of w: either Rel(u,w) or Rel(v,w) holds, but not both, (e) Positively coordinate the sources of w: both Rel(u,w) and Rel(v,w) holds together, (f) Implication of the sources of w: if Rel(v,w) holds, then Rel(u,w) must hold (source coordination) (Adapted from (Candan et al., 2008; Qi, Candan, & Sapino, 2007a))

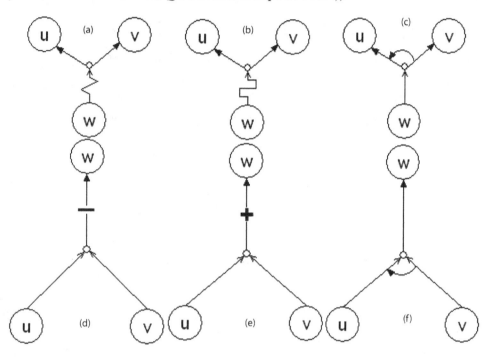

graphs; i.e., the relationships in E either all hold together or none holds.

Given mappings and above rules, the merge algorithm integrates the sources by incorporating these mappings and rules:

- For each mapping rule μ: $\langle V_i, V_j, map\_name, \tau \rangle$, a new element c_k with the name *map_name* is created. Then, each element in V_i, V_j is linked to c_k with positively coordinated edges. During this process, the edges to c_k from the elements in V_i (or V_j) are positively coordinated with each other;
- When incorporating an embedding rule ρ: $\langle c_1, c_2, rel\_name, \tau \rangle$ into the integrated graph, if the relationship *rel_name* has no

arity constraint, an edge with label *rel_name* is created from the concept c_1 to c_2. Otherwise, the edge may need to be negatively coordinated with other edges. For example, if the edge describes the parent-child relationship where an element can have only one parent, the edge from c_1 to c_2 with label "*parent*" needs to be coordinated with the other edges coming out of c_1 and going to other concepts.

- To incorporate a co-validity rule of the form γ:$\langle E, \tau \rangle$, all the maximal subsets $E' \subseteq E$ with the same source and destinations are detected and all these subsets are positively coordinated. The remaining co-validity requirements are recorded as integrity constraints to be enforced separately.

Figure 4. Example of the FICSR integration process. (a) First source graph, (b) Second source graph, (c) Integrated full graph

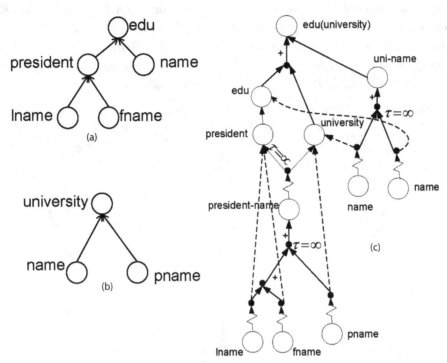

We use Figure 4 as an example to illustrate the integration algorithm.

Let us consider the following integration rules:

- mapping rules:

  μ_1: $\langle\{lname, fname\}, \{pname\}, president\text{-}name, \infty\rangle$

  μ_2: $\langle\{edu\}, \{university\}, edu(university), \infty\rangle$

  μ_3: $\langle\{name\}, \{name\}, uni\text{-}name, \infty\rangle$

- embedding rules:

  ρ_1: $\langle president\text{-}name, president, parent\text{-}child, \infty\rangle$

  ρ_2: $\langle president\text{-}name, university, parent\text{-}child, 1\rangle$

  ρ_3: $\langle uni\text{-}name, edu(university), parent\text{-}child, 1\rangle$

- no co-validity rules.

While incorporating the three mapping rules, FICSR introduces positive coordinate constructs to connect the source elements to the new concepts.

For example, for μ_1, before coordinating the elements in $\{lname, fname\}$ $\{pname\}$, they are first positively coordinated among themselves. For the embedding rules, FICSR incorporates three corresponding edges in the graph (from *president-name* to *president*, from *president-name* to *university*, from *uni-name* to *edu(university)*).

Figure 4(c) shows the full integrated graph.

Note that in the resulting graph, potential conflicts among the input schemas have not been resolved; the identification and resolution of any such conflict is deferred to query processing phase.

While, FICSR data model can capture more general relationships, rich conflicts, and coordination semantics, Kimelfeld & Sagiv (2008) focus on tree structured data. In particular, (Kimelfeld & Sagiv, 2008) introduces probabilistic XML data representation, where XML data are represented in the form of tree structures composed of two types of nodes: ordinary nodes and distributional nodes. Ordinary nodes follow the definition of nodes in the traditional XML model; distributional nodes, however, specify the probabilistic process of generating a random document. Depending upon the semantics indicated by its distribution, a distributional node can be one of the following five types (Kimelfeld & Sagiv, 2008):

- **ind** - the probability of choosing one of its children is independent of that of choosing any other;
- **det** - all of its children are deterministically chosen;
- **mux** - the probabilities of choosing different children are mutually exclusive;
- **exp** - the probability of choosing any of its children is explicitly given;
- **cie** - the probability of choosing a child is determined by the conjunction of a set of independent random Boolean variables, called events.

Kimelfeld et al. (2008) classify probabilistic XML models based on the types of distributional nodes they contain. For instance, $PrXML^{\{ind\}}$ represents probabilistic XML models which use only **ind** distributional nodes. An example of $PrXML^{\{ind,mux\}}$ is shown in Figure 5. There are three distributional nodes: two of them are of type **ind** and the third is of type **mux**. Note that, since they are exclusive with each other, the sum of the probabilities of the two choices under the third distributional node is 1.0.

QUERY PROCESSING

Query processing over integrated XML data shares many of the key difficulties, which other types of integrated data also pose. For instance, often some form of XML query reformulation is necessary in order to process queries over local

Figure 5. An Example of Probabilistic XML Document

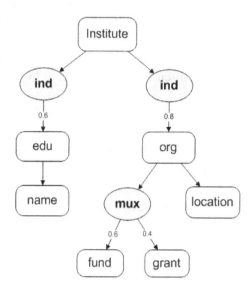

data sources. Similarly, when data sources in the XML integration system are autonomous, query processing (even routing (Zhuge, Liu, Feng, & He, 2004)) needs to be performed without the support of a central mechanism, completely through peer-to-peer interaction. Since uncertainty and imperfections can be introduced during source matching and merging, special mechanisms that can handle inconsistency during query processing may be needed. While the special, relatively more flexible structure of XML provides opportunities for alleviating some of the difficulties that other less flexible data types face during integration, it also poses new challenges in that existing XML query processing techniques are often not directly applicable.

As in any integration system, there are two major ways to execute an XML query over data that initially exist in different sources. The first approach is to reformulate the query for each source, execute them independently at these sources, collect results, and integrate these results into a single unified answer. The second approach is to use mappings discovered in the previous steps to integrate the data in a common form and process the query over this integrated data. In this chapter, we discuss both of these two approaches. But, first we provide a brief overview of how queries over XML data are formulated. In Section "XML Query Processing with Local Sources", we discuss major approaches to XML query processing across local sources. Then, in Section "Query Processing over uncertain XML data" we discuss challenges associated to query processing with uncertain data due to imprecise integration.

Querying XML Data

XPath (1999) and XQuery (2006), two popular query languages for querying XML documents, rely on *path expressions* -- which express the desired characteristics of the paths on the underlying data graph -- as building blocks. These path expressions combine requirements about values (such as the element tags of an XML document) with requirements about the structural organization of the elements of interest. Path expressions of type, $P^{\{/,//,*\}}$, are composed of query steps, each consisting of an axis (parent/child "/" or ancestor/descendant "//") test between data elements and a label test (including "*" wildcard which can match any element or tag). Often, multiple path expressions are combined into twigs (i.e., tree patterns (Amer-Yahia, Cho, Lakshmanan, & Srivastava, 2001; Jagadish et al., 2002)) by using path expressions of type $P^{\{[],/,//,*\}}$, where "[]" denotes any predicate including sub-path expressions; as illustrated in Figure 6), such tree patterns can be visualized as trees, where nodes correspond to tag-predicates and edges correspond to a parent-child or ancestor-descendant axis. Thus, a twig query, q, can be represented in the form of a node- and edge-labeled tree, $T_q(V_q, E_q)$. The query q may be attached with tag and edge predicates *tag_pred(qv)* and *axis_pred(qe)*, where *tag_pred(qv)* denotes the tag predicate corresponding to the vertex $qv \in V_q$ and *axis_pred(qe)* denotes the axis predicate

associated with the edge $qe \in E_q$. An answer to q over data graph G is a pair, $r = \langle \mu_{node}, \mu_{edge} \rangle$, of mappings:

- μ_{node} is a mapping from the nodes of the query tree to the nodes of the data graph, such that given $qv \in V_q$ and the corresponding data node, $\mu_{node}(q, v)$, $tag(\mu_{node}(q, v))$ satisfies *tag_pred(qv)*.
- M_{edge} is a mapping from the edges of the query tree to *simple paths* in the data graph, such that given $qe = \langle qv_i, qv_j \rangle \in E_q$, the path μ_{qe}, from $\mu_{node}(qv_i)$ to $\mu_{node}(qv_j)$, satisfies *axis_pred(qe)*. Note that a path consisting of a single edge can satisfy both parent-child and ancestor-descendant axis, while a multi-edge path can satisfy only ancestor-descendant axis.

In XPath semantics, for each result instance, $r = \langle \mu_{node}, \mu_{edge} \rangle$, only the matches for the right most query element are included in the final result (e.g., for the query shown in Figure 6, only the matches for the query element "grant" are returned).

XML Query Processing with Local Sources

In this section, we discuss major alternatives for XML query processing across local sources. We also present techniques used for XML query reformulation as well as source selection and query routing.

Alternative Architectures for Query Processing with Local Sources

Broadly speaking, there are two alternative architectures for query processing over local sources: the architecture shown in Figure 7(a) makes use of a global (and integrated) XML schema for query reformulation, while the alternative in Figure 7(b)

Figure 6. An example query twig

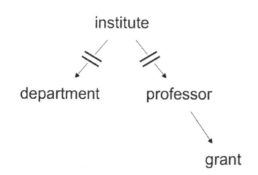

institute[//department]//professor/grant

rewrites queries purely, based on peer-to-peer mappings (Cruz, Xiao, & Hsu, 2004; Lenzerini, 2004; McBrien & Poulovassilis, 2003).

- *Query processing with global schema.* The process of query processing with a global schema is illustrated in Figure 7(a). Through a unique interface, or application, an initial query, usually in the form of XPath or XQuery, is constructed on the basis of the global schema (obtained through a priori schema matching and merging). This initial query is reformulated according to the correspondences between the global schema and local schemas. Note that, due to the flexibilities afforded by XML, local schema is often described in XML (through schema extraction in Chapter "XML Data Integration: Schema Extraction and Mapping") even for non-XML data sources. Next, a source selection manager helps identify the data sources over which the reformulated query should be processed. Query optimization and query execution are performed locally on the selected data sources. Finally, all results are collected from local data sources and combined. Systems exploiting

this architecture include MARS (Deutsch & Tannen, 2003a), PEPSINT (Cruz et al., 2004) and Agora (Manolescu, Florescu, Kossmann, Xhumari, & Olteanu, 2000).

- *Query processing through peer-to-peer interactions.* In the peer-to-peer integration approach to XML query processing, mapping rules are created between local schemas using the techniques presented in Chapter "XML Data Integration: Schema Extraction and Mapping", but a global schema does not exist (Figure 7(b)). Again, the local schema is represented in XML. Therefore, the initial query is in the form of XPath or XQuery, described in terms of its corresponding (*target*) schema. A source selection manager helps identify the peers (*sources*) on which the remote query processing should be made. Then, according to mapping rules between target and sources, the initial query is translated into the query formulated in terms of the various source schemas. Systems that follow this approach include Piazza (A. Y. Halevy, Ives, Suciu, & Tatarinov, 2003; A. Y. Halevy et al., 2004), HePToX (Bonifati, Chang, Ho, Lakshmanan, & Pottinger, 2005) and SixP2P (Pankowski, 2008).

Query processing in a peer-to-peer setting can be treated as a special case of processing with global schema, if we think of the target schema as the global schema to which all other local (source) schemas are mapped. This, however, requires $O(N^2)$ source-to-target mappings, where N is the number of peers, against $O(N)$ for the case of the former approach. The advantage of the peer-to-peer setting, however, is that (unlike the global schema which may be overly lossy to accommodate all source schemas) the query reformulations may be more precise since it leverages pairwise mappings between peers.

Figure 7. Alternative architectures of query processing with local sources. (a) Integration with a Global Schema, (b) Peer-to-Peer Integration

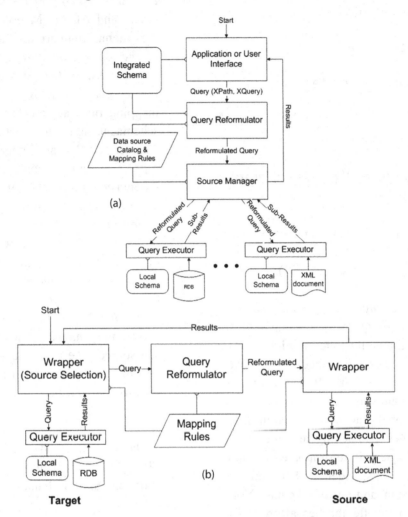

XML Query Reformulation

In order to process a user's query over local sources, we need to reformulate this query into queries which can be understood by individual data sources: Given a source schema S_S, target schema S_t, a set of mapping rules, M, between S_S and S_t, and a query q_t which is defined in terms of S_t, the goal of query reformulation is to find a query q_s formulated in terms of S_S such that it is equivalent to q_t according to M. Within the context of XML query processing, the initial query q_t, can be in the form of a tree pattern (Arion, Benzaken, &

Manolescu, 2007; Calvanese, Giacomo, Lenzerini, & Vardi, 1999; Gao, Wang, & Yang, 2007; Gu, Xu, & Chen, 2008; Lakshmanan, Wang, & Zhao, 2006; Xu & Özsoyoglu, 2005), XPath (Afrati et al., 2009; Balmin, Özcan, Beyer, Cochrane, & Pirahesh, 2004; Cautis, Deutsch, & Onose, 2008; Tang, Yu, Özsu, Choi, & Wong, 2008) or XQuery (Deutsch & Tannen, 2003b; Lenzerini, 2002; Onose, Deutsch, Papakonstantinou, & Curtmola, 2006) statement. Query rewriting schemes differ from each other based on the underlying restrictions on schemas, summaries and other applicable constraints (such as conjunctive queries only)

Figure 8. An example of query rewriting in the GAV. (a) Local schema S_1, (b) Local schema S_2, (c) A global schema S_g (d) A twig query in terms of S_g, and its reformulated queries corresponding to S_1 and S_2 respectively

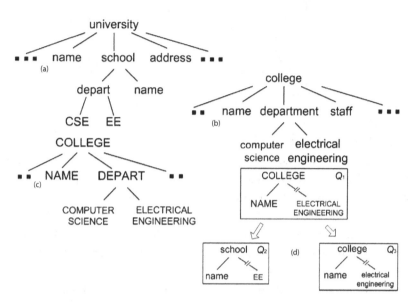

(Arion et al., 2007; Deutsch & Tannen, 2003b; Lakshmanan et al., 2006). Most generally, we can classify approaches into two major classes based on the way the mapping rules, *M*, are leveraged: global-as-view (GAV, where the global schema is described in terms of the local schemas) and local-as-view (LAV, where each local schema is described as a view over the global schema).

- In GAV, the initial query, stated in terms of the integrated schema *S*, is translated into queries for local schemas through "view unfolding", where references in the input query to the target schema *S* are eliminated and replaced by the corresponding references to the local schemas (Gu et al., 2008; Lenzerini, 2002). Consider Figure 8 which presents two local schemas (S_1 and S_2) and a global schema (S_g). The correspondences among these schemas are presented in Table 3(d). Given these and a twig query, "Q_1 = //COLLEGE[NAME]// ELECTRICAL ENGINEERING", the re-

formulated queries Q_2 and Q_3 are shown in Figure 8(e).

- In LAV, all sources are described as views over the global schema; thus query reformulation can be seen as answering the query using a set of views (A. Y. Halevy, 2001). Most current work on query reformulation for XML integration belongs to this category (Afrati et al., 2009; Arion et al., 2007; Balmin, Özcan et al., 2004; Calvanese et al., 1999; Cautis et al., 2008; Deutsch & Tannen, 2003b; Gao et al., 2007; Lakshmanan et al., 2006; Onose et al., 2006; Tang et al., 2008; Xu & Özsoyoglu, 2005).

Query reformulation schemes can also be classified into two types based on the *qualities* of the resulting reformulations:

- An equivalent rewriting scheme aims to find a rewriting of the initial query *q* with regard to a given view, in a way that preserves the semantics of *q* (Arion et al., 2007; Balmin,

Table 1. Mapping table: each entity in S_g has a view on local schemas

S_1	S_2	S_g
...	...	...
university	college	COLLEGE
(university.)name	(college.)name	NAME
depart	department	DEPART
CSE	computer science	COMPUTER SCIENCE
EE	electrical engineering	ELECTRICAL ENGINEERING
...	...	...

Özcan et al., 2004; Cautis et al., 2008; Deutsch & Tannen, 2003b; Onose et al., 2006; Tang et al., 2008; Xu & Özsoyoglu, 2005). Generally, these approaches follow a "generate-and-test" strategy: the initial step produces candidate rewritings, which are then tested to see if they are equivalent to the initial query. A common approach for generating candidate rewritings for conjunctive queries is the "bucket algorithm" (A. Y. Halevy, 2001), which first enumerates possible rewritings for each entity in the query as partial rewritings, then combines these partial rewritings into candidate rewritings for the whole query. Equivalences between the initial query and its rewritings are validated through an unfolding process: (a) first the views in the reformulation are unfolded to express these rewritings in terms of source data and (b) the equivalence between the initial query and these unfoldings are evaluated (Levy, Mendelzon, Sagiv, & Srivastava, 1995).

- Equivalent rewritings may not always exist or may be expensive to identify. An alternative is the *maximally-contained rewriting*, where the reformulated queries do not return all answers, but miss as few of the results as possible. The approaches presented in (Gao et al., 2007; Lakshmanan et al., 2006) fall under this category. (Lakshmanan et al., 2006), for example, first identifies embeddings (i.e., partial matching from the query to a view in a

way preserving node tags and structural relationships) and uses these embeddings to formulate queries on the views. Since the embeddings are potentially more general than the original query, the result set is likely to contain more results than what an equivalent rewriting would return.

In general, even maximally-contained rewritings are not guaranteed to exist. More recently Afrati et al.(2009) propose *minimally-containing rewritings*, where the results are supersets of those of equivalent reformulations, with only few false additions.

Source Selection and XML Query Routing

Peer-to-peer (P2P) data management systems are gaining in popularity because of their decentralized and distributed nature, which provides a number of advantages, such as high robustness, better use of the resources, better scalability and the lack of need for integrated-administration (Koloniari & Pitoura, 2005). In peer-to-peer settings, where the search needs to be done in a distributed fashion on multiple peers, being able to quickly locate peers which can help answer a given query is critical for efficiency. This is usually performed in one of the two ways:

- *Source selection*: In this case, each source peer registers its metadata (e.g. schemas), describing its content, into the directory service of the P2P network. In most cases, the registered source description is a summary of the original data or metadata (Cherukuri & Candan, 2008; Tajima & Fukui, 2004). Peers that have queries, then, use these source descriptions to identify peers in the network that have the most relevant schemas or data sets. Source selection approaches include centralized directories (Katsis, Deutsch, & Papakonstantinou, 2008; Mihaila, Raschid, & Tomasic, 2002) as well as distributed directory approaches (Bouchou, Alves, & Musicante, 2003; Cooper, 2004; Nguyen, Yee, & Frieder, 2008).

- *Query routing: A*lternatively, queries are injected into the system and these queries are routed towards peers that have relevant schema/data by the network. The local peers execute queries on their local data and forward the results back to the query originator. Query routing approaches include (Koloniari, Petrakis, & Pitoura, 2003; Koudas, Rabinovich, Srivastava, & Yu, 2004; Peng & Chawathe, 2003; Suciu, 2002; Tatarinov & Halevy, 2004). These often rely on text- or XML-message filtering schemes (Altinel & Franklin, 2000; Candan, Dönderler, Qi, & Kim, 2006; Candan, Hsiung, Chen, & Agrawal, 2006; Diao, Altinel, Franklin, Zhang, & Fischer, 2003; Ives, Halevy, & Weld, 2002) that can quickly route query messages towards relevant peers based on registered source descriptions.

Distributed directory based source selection approaches are generally built on query routing schemes: first, the *source selection query* is routed in the network towards peers that can answer this source selection query. These peers respond back with IDs of peers that are able to answer the main query. Once this phase is over, the initiating peer sends the query to these peers.

Query Processing over uncertain XML Data

Uncertainties and conflicts may be introduced during the integration of XML data and metadata. Therefore, processing queries over integrated XML data may require more expressive query processing infrastructures than basic XML frameworks provide. For instance, the mapping rules can be probabilistic in nature and this may lead to integrated XML data which itself is probabilistic. Moreover, conflicts in data sources may render it harder to represent integrated data in tree-like forms which are common to XML; instead, it may be more suitable to leverage graph-based models that are able to describe the inherently more complex structural uncertainty due to integration.

Data Pre-cleaning vs. Pay-as-you-Go

Traditionally, a consistent interpretation (i.e. a "model") of the data or metadata with conflicts is defined as a maximal, self-consistent subset of the data (Bertossi, 2006; Mercer & Risch, 2003). Intuitively, each model is a *possible world*, where there are no conflicts. Data cleaning approaches aim to identify a maximal possible world, which keeps as many of the original assertions about the data (Pottinger & Bernstein, 2003). Restoration of consistency through a model-based interpretation leads to loss of information; thus, identifying a possible world in advance of query processing may be disadvantageous. In such cases, delaying possible-worlds analysis until after query processing might provide context within which conflicts might be eliminated in an informed manner. (Bonifati et al., 2005; Candan et al., 2008; A. Y. Halevy et al., 2003; Qi, Candan, & Sapino, 2007a) and dataspace and pay-as-you-go systems (Dong, Halevy, & Yu, 2007; Franklin, Halevy, & Maier, 2005; A. Halevy, Rajaraman, & Ordille, 2006; Jeffery, Franklin, & Halevy, 2008; Sarma, Dong, & Halevy, 2008) keep alternative plausible interpretations during query processing and assist the user in observing alternatives through a data exploration process at query time.

Data and Result Compatibility

Given an uncertain XML document all results satisfying a query might not be compatible. One way to resolve this problem is to include in the result only those instances that are in all models of the data. This set is often referred to as the set of *certain answers*. (Arenas & Libkin, 2008) shows that computing the set of certain answers for a give query is coNP-complete, except for some special cases. In addition to being expensive to compute, limiting the result to the set of certain answers is often overly cautious. Instead, the *quality* of a result instance can be evaluated based on the amount of conflicts in the data from which it is extracted or based on how compatible it is with the other results to the given query.

Data Compatibility Analysis

As described earlier, (Kimelfeld & Sagiv, 2008) introduces probabilistic XML documents, where each document P indicates a set, D, of XML documents, called *possible worlds*. Each document d in D is associated with a probability, $p(d)$, where p is a function to specify the probability distribution of XML documents in D. Given a twig query q, and a probabilistic XML document P, the evaluation of q over P leads to a set of results, R. For each answer $r \in R$, it can be an answer to evaluating q over multiple documents in D, and its probability (or degree of certainty in terms of possible worlds) is the combination of probabilities of possible worlds related to q. Therefore, one way to perform query processing on probabilistic XML document P is to enumerate all possible worlds according to P, evaluate the twig query q over each possible world one by one, and finally compute the probability of each answer. Enumeration however is often intractable, because it is NP-complete to determine if there is a match of q in some possible worlds of P. Fortunately,

the user usually does not need all matches and the top-K matches, which have largest probabilities, may be sufficient.

Result Compatibility Analysis

QUEST (Qi, Candan, Sapino, & Kintigh, 2007) captures the compatibility among result instances, a result instance and a set of results or among sets of result, using a reflexive and symmetric "≈" relation:

- Given two result instances r_i and r_j, $r_i \approx r_j$ if and only if the result instances considered together do not violate any structural constraints inherent in XML.
- Given a result instance r' and a set of result instances $R = \{r_1, r_2, \ldots, r_N\}$, $r' \approx R$, if and only if $\forall r_i \in R$, $r' \approx r_i$.
- Given two sets of result instances $R = \{r_1, r_2, \ldots, r_N\}$ and $U = \{u_1, u_2, \ldots, u_M\}$, $R \approx U$ if and only if $\forall r_i \in R$, $\forall u_j \in U$, $r_i \approx u_j$.

Instead of defining the *model* on the data itself, **QUEST** focuses on models of the query results. Given a set of results, R, a compatibility graph, G_c, is used by **QUEST** to capture all pairwise compatibility relationships. (Qi et al., 2006), then defines a *model*, composed of compatible result paths, as a maximal clique in the compatibility graph. For each pair of nodes (representing result paths), an edge is included between them if they are compatible. **QUEST** provides various result exploration options to the user to enable her to obtain a high level understanding of the available data related to her query

The maximal cliques in a graph can be exponential in the number of vertices (Moon & Moser, 1965). There are polynomial time delay algorithms for enumeration of cliques (i.e., if the graph of size n contains C cliques, the time to output all cliques is bounded by $O(n^k C)$ for some constant k) (1988), but in general graphs, C can be exponential in n; for example as many as $3^{n/3}$ in Moon-Moser's graphs (Moon & Moser, 1965).

(Qi et al., 2006) also observes that it is possible to avoid enumeration of cliques or finding of the maximal cliques in the entire compatibility graph, when supporting many of the relevant exploration tasks. For instance, the task of counting the number of maximal cliques a path occurs in can be performed by counting those maximal cliques containing only its neighbors. Also defining the models on the query results as opposed to the data itself, (Qi, Candan, & Sapino, 2007a) is able to significantly reduce the complexity of model-based analysis.

Data and Result Compatibility Analysis

FICSR (Candan et al., 2008; Qi, Candan, & Sapino, 2007a) performs *model*-based analysis to compute *trust* (or *agreement*) values associated with assertions that make up an integrated data representation. To efficiently compute the agreement values, during an initial off-line analysis process, *FICSR* partitions the integrated relationship graph into small-sized constraint *zones*, each consisting of a mutually-dependent set of relationship constraints. Given a zone, trust value associated with an assertion in this zone is defined in terms of the alternative *models* in which the assertion is valid versus the total number *models* of the zone. Figure 9 illustrates this process with an example. Figure 9(a) is a simplified version of the integrated relationship graph shown in Figure 4(c). In Figure 9(b) this integrated graph is split into six zones; note that the relationship constraints contained in each zone are mutually-dependent. For example, in zone 6, there are two mutually-dependent relationships both of which must exist concurrently in any model. *FICSR* first analyzes each zone individually to obtain an *agreement* score for each relationship alternative. Figure 9(c) shows an example of this zone analysis process: in this example, the agreement value of the relationship between nodes "lname" and "president-name" in zone 6 is computed as 0.5, because this relationship is valid only in one of the two possible models of this zone (see Figure 9(d)). While the agreement

analysis process is still NP-complete, the initial zone-partitioning of the graph and the per-zone nature of the agreement analysis prevent this off-line process from becoming unacceptably costly. In *FICSR*, the agreement score of each result is computed based on the agreement scores of the relationships involved in the result; more specifically, given agreement values associated to the underlying assertions, the agreement of a result, r, consisting of assertions, $A(r)$, is computed as

$$agr(r) = \prod_{a_i \in A(r)} agr(a_i).$$

FICSR relies on ranked query processing techniques in (Qi, Candan, & Sapino, 2007b) to identify top-K high-agreement results to present to the user. While assertions and result agreement values are based on the initial off-line analysis of the integrated data representation, *FICSR* also performs a **QUEST**-like run-time analysis on the results of a given query. In particular, given two results r_1 and r_2 and their assertions $A(r_1)$ and $A(r_2)$, the compatibility between the results are measures in terms of conflicts that assertions in $A(r_1)$ and $A(r_2)$ cause when considered together. If the results identified are found to imply conflicts when considered together, then this leads to the reduction of the *validity* assessments of these results when presented to the user. In particular, when the highest-agreement results are mutually conflicting and thus resulting in low validity, it triggers a feedback process that calls for inputs from the user. The results of the user feedback are reflected on the trust values associated with the assertions in the integrated data as well as the mappings that lead to these trust values to be computed in the first place.

Twig Query Processing on Graphs

A structural summary or a merged XML document is often a directed (and weighted) graph instead of being a simple tree. On the other hand, in XML

Figure 9. An example of the zone analysis process of FICSR. (a) A simplified version of the integrated relationship graph in Figure 4(c), (b) The zone-graph: individual zones in the graph are highlighted with different shades. Note that zones are linked to each other through data/concept nodes, (c) After zone analysis, each edge in the integrated relationship graph has a corresponding agreement value, (d) The two models of zone 6

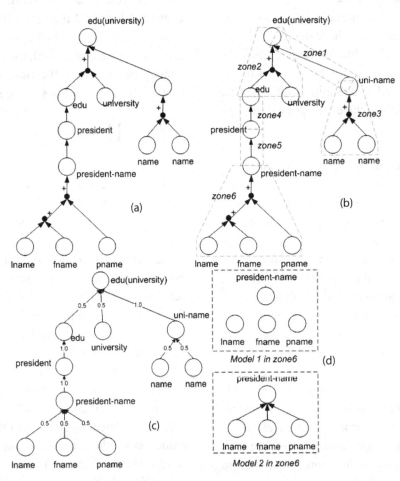

databases, query processors are often designed to exploit the tree-like structure of the XML data. In fact, many existing (binary or holistic) structural join operators, including TwigStack/PathStack (Bruno, Koudas, & Srivastava, 2002), iTwigJoin (Chen, Lu, & Ling, 2005) and Stack-Tree-Desc/ Anc (Al-Khalifa et al., 2002) are structurally-informed variants of the standard sort-merge join algorithm: they require that the data nodes are available in a *structurally sorted* order before the join operation can be performed. To implement structural join operations efficiently, most XML query processors rely on index structures based on structurally-informed node labeling schemes (such as Dietz's labeling (Dietz, 1982), which assigns interval-labels to nodes in such a way that descendant nodes have intervals that are contained within the intervals of their ancestors). This enables checking the ancestor-descendant relationships quickly. Such structural labeling and sorting are especially feasible when the underlying data has a tree-structure, but becomes non-trivial when the queries have to be evaluated on graph-data. When data is graph structured, however, these techniques are not directly applicable. (Computer & Vagena, 2004) proposes techniques for evaluating twig queries over graph-structured data. Authors observe that, in a directed graph, the ancestor-descendant relationship of a tree pattern edge is satisfied if there is a path from the ancestor node to the descendant node. Thus, the authors rephrase the ancestor-descendant search in terms of checking *reachability* in the graph and propose a 2-hop cover based labeling scheme (based on (E. Cohen, Halperin, Kaplan, & Zwick, 2002)) to help answer ancestor-descendant queries efficiently (especially on directed acyclic graphs).

When data have weights, not all results are equally desirable: results need to be ranked according to the underlying cost model. For instance, (Fuhr & Großjohann, 2001) presents an XML query language extended with IR-related features, including weighting and ranking. XRANK (Guo, Shao, Botev, & Shanmugasundaram, 2003) and ObjectRank (Balmin, Hristidis, & Papakonstantinou, 2004) compute PageRank (Brin & Page, 1998) style ranking results for keyword-based (IR-style) database queries. XSEarch (S. Cohen, Mamou, Kanza, & Sagiv, 2003), a search engine for XML data, relies on extended information retrieval techniques for ranking. *Retrieval by information unit* (RIU) (W. Li, Candan, Vu, & Agrawal, 2001), BANKS-I (Bhalotia, Hulgeri, Nakhe, & Sudarshan, 2002), BANKS-II (Kacholia et al., 2005), and DPBF (Ding, Yu, Wang, Qin, & Lin, 2007), on the other hand, recognize that in many cases a single node is not sufficient to answer user queries. Instead, given a query consisting of a set of keywords, these algorithms try to find *small* sub-trees (in a given weighted graph) containing all the query keywords. An example is shown in Figure 10. In this example, the user provides three query keywords, {department, grant, professor} to be searched on weighted graph fragment in Figure 10(a); here edge weights indicate the cost or penalty of the corresponding edges. In this example, document "a" contains keyword "grant", document "b" contains "department" and document

"c" contains "professor". Figure 10(b) shows two results of this query: The result in Figure 10(b) has one more document than that in Figure 10(c), but a smaller total edge cost. Finding minimal trees to answer keyword queries on weighted graphs is shown to be computationally expensive (W. Li et al., 2001). Since users are usually interested in not all but top-K results, (Bhalotia et al., 2002; Ding et al., 2007; Kacholia et al., 2005; W. Li et al., 2001) rely on efficient heuristics and approximations for progressively identifying the smallest K trees covering the given keywords. As we mentioned above, however, while answering keyword-based queries on graph data is useful in various application domains (such as XML source selection (Aboulnaga & Gebaly, 2007)), for twig query processing, structural relationships between the data elements need to be considered along with keywords and tags (Qi, Candan, & Sapino, 2007b). Thus, using the notation in Section "Querying XML Data", we can define the problem of top-K query processing over a given weighted graph G as follows:

- Given a weighted graph G, a query $q=T_q(V_q, E_q)$ and a positive integer K, top-K query processing over G is to obtain a set, R, of answers to q over G, in decreasing order of agreement or trust, such that (a) the size of R is K, (b) the i-th answer has higher agreement than the $(i+1)$-th answer, and (c) there are no other answers to q over G having higher agreement value than any answer in R.

(Qi, Candan, & Sapino, 2007a) shows that ranked ancestor-descendant relationships (i.e., reachability problem) can be enumerated by applying Yen's top-K shortest loopless path algorithm (Yen, 1971). Executing twig queries on the weighted graph, however, requires combining multiple such ancestor-descendant and parent-child results. In the literature, there are a number of ranked-join algorithms for top-K queries (Can-

Figure 10. A keyword query, {department, grant, professor}, and two matches on a sample weighted graph. (a) A weighted graph fragment, (b) One result of the query, (c) A second result of the query

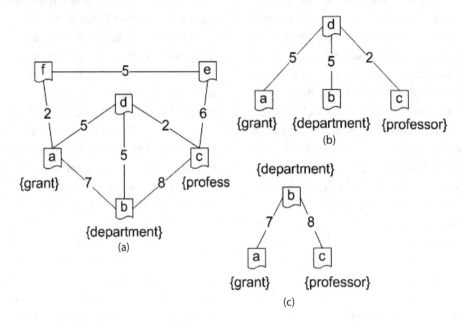

dan, Li, & Priya, 2000; Chaudhuri, Gravano, & Marian, 2004; Fagin, 1996; C. Li, Chang, Ilyas, & Song, 2005). These rely on weight-sorted input streams for pruning unpromising matches. In particular, (Fagin, Lotem, & Naor, 2003; 2003) presents an NRA algorithm which (a) considers data sources which can provide results only in (progressively) descending order of desirability and which (b) enumerates top-*K* desirable join results without having to access all the data from these sources. A common assumption behind all these algorithms, including (Fagin, Lotem et al., 2003), is that the function which evaluates the score of combined results is monotonic. (Qi, Candan, & Sapino, 2007b) develops top-*K* twig query evaluation algorithms for weighted data graphs. In particular, authors present a cost model for the query answers and prove that answering twig queries on weighted graphs is NP-hard. In particular, they show that, while the problem can be viewed as *ranked structural-joins* along query axises, the monotonicity property, necessary for

ranked-join algorithms (Candan et al., 2000; Chaudhuri et al., 2004; Fagin, 1996; Fagin, Lotem et al., 2003; Ilyas, Aref, & Elmagarmid, 2003; C. Li, Chang, & Ilyas, 2006), is violated. This is illustrated by the example in Figure 11. The twig query in Figure 6 is first split into sub-queries: "institute//department" and "institute//professor/ grant". A match "institute/school/department" to "institute//department" is displayed in Figure 11(a), with cost 12; two matches "institute/school/ professor/grant" and "institute/professor/grant" to "institute//professor/grant" are in Figure 11(b), with cost 10 and 9 respectively. The result in Figure 11(c), obtained by combining "institute/school/ department" (cost=12) and "institute/school/ professor/grant" (cost=10) has smaller overall cost (i.e., 17) than the result shown in Figure 11(d), obtained by combining "institute/school/ department" (cost=12) and "institute/professor/ grant" (cost=9). The failure of monotonicity in this example is due to the overlapping path fragment "institute/school" between the sub-results that are

Figure 11. An example for ranked structural-join, where the monotonicity property is not satisfied. (a) A match for sub-query "institute//department" (cost = 12), (b) Two matches for sub-query "institute// professor/grant" (cost = 10 and 9), (c) A match for query "institute[//department]//professor/grant" (cost = 17), (d) A match for query "institute[//department]//professor/grant" (cost = 21)

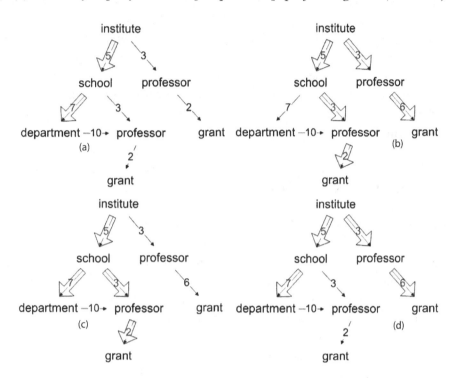

FUTURE RESEARCH DIRECTIONS

being combined. Consequently, when processing twig queries, the very common strategy of splitting the twig query into separated path queries, evaluating each path query independently, and then combining sub-results (i.e., results of path queries) with ranked join algorithm cannot be implemented using traditional ranked join algorithms. Instead, authors present a *sum-max monotonicity* property that holds top-*K* twig query evaluation and they develop a new HR-Join algorithm for performing ranked joins efficiently to compute answers to twig queries. (Kimelfeld & Sagiv, 2006) also considers the problem of executing twig-patterns over weighted graphs and proposes polynomial delay (i.e., the time between two consecutive results is polynomial in the size of the input) execution strategies for ranked enumeration of results.

The existing works in this area have provided promising solutions, but more challenges lay ahead. Pay-as-you-go is a promising strategy towards avoiding the cost of conflict resolution in XML integration. Still, cost of query processing is one of the most significant challenges in XML integration. When the number of involved data sources becomes large or when they are highly conflicting, query processing requires more efficient support at the levels of hardware or software. Parallelizing architectures can be exploited to speed up the query processing through data-partitioned parallel evaluation. New computing frameworks, such as MapReduce (Dean & Ghemawat, 2004) will certainly help in this direction.

Another issue to be considered here can be summarized as the "too-many-answers" problem (Amer-Yahia et al., 2001). When the size of the integrated relationship graph is large, there may be too many results of a given query. It is not possible to display all of them to the user from a practical point of view. Unfortunately, the top-K strategy may not help with this problem, in that not all results are comparable if they do not have scores associated with. Two thoughts can lead to solutions to this problem: Firstly, sampling techniques, where a properly selected sample of the results is presented to the user, can help. Secondly, supported by relevance feedback techniques, query refinement can help user achieve more precise queries to quickly locate information of interest. (Candan et al., 2008; Qi, Candan, & Sapino, 2007a), for example, leverage user feedback for eliminating conflicts identified during query processing. After the system processes the query over data with conflicts and provides a ranked list of results along with highlights showing the conflicts identified within these results, the user is allowed to assess these results and conflicts. The user assessment can be absolute (e.g., "result X is wrong and should be eliminated") or relative (e.g., "I think result X agrees more with my domain knowledge than result Y"). These assessments are used not only to re-rank query results, but also to re-assess (a) importance of constraints that lead to these conflicts, (b) the trust/agreement values associated with the merged data representation (used in computing the query results), and (c) the qualities of mapping rules (which are used for creating the merged data representation in the first place). Feedback driven XML query processing requires further research into (a) the design of easy-to-use interfaces for capturing the user's feedback and (b) algorithms for reflecting the user feedback effectively and efficiently into the conflict resolution and query processing stages of the XML integration workflow.

CONCLUSION

Today, XML is the backbone of all contemporary Web standards and it is increasingly serving as the most ubiquitous data exchange format. While, due to its structural flexibility, in 90's XML gained acceptance as a potential solution to the data interoperability problem, this more flexible nature also implies that there are fewer cues and constraints to inform the integration process. In other words, from one hand, having fewer constraints to deal with implies easier compatibility across data sources; from the other hand, this also implies that there are many more ways to put data together and effective integration requires support from the user. Pay-as-you-go integration, which is becoming more common, is a step in this direction and future research will increasingly focus on techniques that enable context- and user-support to eliminate uncertainties for more effective integration solutions.

REFERENCES

Aboulnaga, A., & Gebaly, K. E. (2007). μBE: User guided source selection and schema mediation for internet scale data integration. *ICDE,* 186-195.

Achard, F., Vaysseixm, G., & Barillot, E. (2001). XML, bioinformatics and data integration. *Bioinformatics (Oxford, England), 17*(2), 115–125. doi:10.1093/bioinformatics/17.2.115

Afrati, F., Chirkova, R., Gergatsoulis, M., Kimelfeld, B., Pavlaki, V., & Sagiv, Y. (2009). On rewriting XPath queries using views. In *EDBT '09: Proceedings of the 12th International Conference on Extending Database Technology,* Saint Petersburg, Russia, (pp. 168-179).

Al-Khalifa, S., Jagadish, H. V., Patel, J. M., Wu, Y., Koudas, N., & Srivastava, D. (2002). Structural joins: A primitive for efficient XML query pattern matching. *ICDE,* (pp. 141).

Altinel, M., & Franklin, M. J. (2000). Efficient filtering of XML documents for selective dissemination of information. In *VLDB '00: Proceedings of the 26th International Conference on very Large Data Bases,* (pp. 53-64).

Amer-Yahia, S., Cho, S., Lakshmanan, L. V. S., & Srivastava, D. (2001). Minimization of tree pattern queries. *SIGMOD Conference,* (pp. 497-508).

Arenas, M., & Libkin, L. (2008). XML data exchange: Consistency and query answering. [JACM]. *Journal of the ACM, 55*(2). doi:10.1145/1346330.1346332

Arion, A., Benzaken, V., & Manolescu, I. P. Yannis. (2007). Structured materialized views for XML queries. In *VLDB '07: Proceedings of the 33rd International Conference on very Large Data Bases,* Vienna, Austria, (pp. 87-98).

Balmin, A., Hristidis, V., & Papakonstantinou, Y. (2004). ObjectRank: Authority-based keyword search in databases. *VLDB,* (pp. 564-575).

Balmin, A., Özcan, F., Beyer, K. S., Cochrane, R. J., & Pirahesh, H. (2004). A framework for using materialized XPath views in XML query processing. *VLDB '04: Proceedings of the Thirtieth International Conference on very Large Data Bases,* Toronto, Canada, (pp. 60-71).

Bertossi, L. E. (2006). Consistent query answering in databases. *SIGMOD Record, 35*(2), 68–76. doi:10.1145/1147376.1147391

Bhalotia, G., Hulgeri, A., Nakhe, C., & Sudarshan, S. C. S. (2002). Keyword searching and browsing in databases using BANKS. *ICDE,* (pp. 431-440).

Bonifati, A., Chang, E. Q., Ho, T., Lakshmanan, L. V. S., & Pottinger, R. (2005). HePToX: Marrying XML and heterogeneity in your P2P databases. In *VLDB,* (pp. 1267-1270).

Bouchou, B., Alves, M. H. F., & Musicante, M. A. (2003). Tree automata to verify XML key constraints. *WebDB,* (pp. 37-42).

Brin, S., & Page, L. (1998). The anatomy of a large-scale hypertextual web search engine. *Computer Networks, 30*(1-7), 107-117.

Bruno, N., Koudas, N., & Srivastava, D. (2002). Holistic twig joins: Optimal XML pattern matching. *SIGMOD Conference,* (pp. 310-321).

Buneman, P., Fan, W., & Weinstein, S. (1999). Query optimization for semistructured data using path constraints in a deterministic data model. In *DBPL,* (pp. 208-223).

Calvanese, D., Giacomo, G. D., Lenzerini, M., & Vardi, M. Y. (1999). Answering regular path queries using views. In *Proc. of the 16th IEEE Int. Conf. on Data Engineering (ICDE 2000,* (pp. 389-398).

Candan, K. S., Cao, H., Qi, Y., & Sapino, M. L. (2008). System support for exploration and expert feedback in resolving conflicts during integration of metadata. *The VLDB Journal, 17*(6), 1407–1444. doi:10.1007/s00778-008-0109-y

Candan, K. S., Dönderler, M. E., & Qi, Y. R. Jaikannan, & Kim, J. W. (2006). FMware: Middleware for efficient filtering and matching of XML messages with local data. *Middleware '06: Proceedings of the ACM/IFIP/USENIX 2006 International Conference on Middleware,* Melbourne, Australia, (pp. 301-321).

Candan, K. S., Grant, J., & Subrahmanian, V. S. (1997). A unified treatment of null values using constraints. *Inf.Sci., 98*(1-4), 99–156.

Candan, K. S., Hsiung, W., & Chen, S. T. Junichi, & Agrawal, D. (2006). AFilter: Adaptable XML filtering with prefix-caching suffix-clustering. *VLDB '06: Proceedings of the 32nd International Conference on very Large Data Bases,* Seoul, Korea, (pp. 559-570).

Candan, K. S., Li, W., & Priya, M. L. (2000). Similarity-based ranking and query processing in multimedia databases. *Data & Knowledge Engineering, 35*(3), 259–298. doi:10.1016/S0169-023X(00)00025-2

Cautis, B., Deutsch, A., & Onose, N. (2008). XPath rewriting using multiple views: Achieving completeness and efficiency. *WebDB.*

Chaudhuri, S., Gravano, L., & Marian, A. (2004). Optimizing top-k selection queries over multimedia repositories. *IEEE Transactions on Knowledge and Data Engineering, 16*(8), 992–1009. doi:10.1109/TKDE.2004.30

Chen, T., Lu, J., & Ling, T. W. (2005). On boosting holism in XML twig pattern matching using structural indexing techniques. In *SIGMOD Conference,* (pp. 455-466).

Cherukuri, V. S., & Candan, K. S. (2008). Propagation-vectors for trees (PVT): Concise yet effective summaries for hierarchical data and trees. In *LSDS-IR '08: Proceeding of the 2008 ACM Workshop on Large-Scale Distributed Systems for Information Retrieval,* Napa Valley, CA, (pp. 3-10).

Chiticariu, L., Kolaitis, P. G., & Popa, L. (2008). Interactive generation of integrated schemas. In *SIGMOD Conference,* (pp. 833-846).

Cohen, E., Halperin, E., Kaplan, H., & Zwick, U. (2002). Reachability and distance queries via 2-hop labels. In *SODA,* (pp. 937-946).

Cohen, S., Mamou, J., Kanza, Y., & Sagiv, Y. (2003). XSEarch: A semantic search engine for XML. In *VLDB,* (pp. 45-56).

Computer, Z. V., & Vagena, Z. (2004). Twig query processing over graph-structured XML data. In *WEBDB, Paris, Frence,* (pp. 43-48).

Cooper, B. F. (2004). Guiding queries to information sources with InfoBeacons. In *Middleware '04: Proceedings of the 5th ACM/IFIP/USENIX International Conference on Middleware,* Toronto, Canada, (pp. 59-78).

Cruz, I. F., Xiao, H., & Hsu, F. (2004). Peer-to-peer semantic integration of XML and RDF data sources. In *AP2PC,* (pp. 108-119).

Dean, J., & Ghemawat, S. (2004). MapReduce: Simplified data processing on large clusters. In *OSDI'04: Proceedings of the 6th Conference on Symposium on Opearting Systems Design \& Implementation,* San Francisco, CA, (pp. 10-10).

Decker, S., Harmelen, F. V., Broekstra, J., Erdmann, M., Fensel, D., Horrocks, I., et al. (2000). The semantic web - on the respective roles of XML and RDF. *IEEE Internet Computing, 4,* Retrieved from http://www.ontoknow

Deutsch, A., & Tannen, V. (2003a). MARS: A system for publishing XML from mixed and redundant storage. *VLDB '2003: Proceedings of the 29th International Conference on very Large Data Bases,* Berlin, Germany, (pp. 201-212).

Deutsch, A., & Tannen, V. (2003b). Reformulation of XML queries and constraints. *ICDT,* (pp. 225-241).

Diao, Y., Altinel, M., Franklin, M. J., Zhang, H., & Fischer, P. (2003). Path sharing and predicate evaluation for high-performance XML filtering. *ACM Transactions on Database Systems, 28*(4), 467–516. doi:10.1145/958942.958947

Dietz, P. F. (1982). Maintaining order in a linked list. In *STOC,* (pp. 122-127).

Ding, B., Yu, J. X., Wang, S., Qin, L., & Lin, X. Z. X. (2007). Finding top-k min-cost connected trees in databases. In *ICDE,* (pp. 836-845).

DOM. (n.d.) Retrieved from Http://www.w3.org/DOM

Dong, X. L., Halevy, A. Y., & Yu, C. (2007). Data integration with uncertainty. In *VLDB*, (pp. 687-698).

Fagin, R. (1996). Combining fuzzy information from multiple systems. In *PODS*, (pp. 216-226).

Fagin, R., Kolaitis, P. G., & Popa, L. (2003). Data exchange: Getting to the core. In *PODS*, (pp. 90-101).

Fagin, R., Lotem, A., & Naor, M. (2003). Optimal aggregation algorithms for middleware. *Journal of Computer and System Sciences*, *66*(4), 614–656. doi:10.1016/S0022-0000(03)00026-6

Franklin, M. J., Halevy, A. Y., & Maier, D. (2005). From databases to dataspaces: A new abstraction for information management. *SIGMOD Record*, *34*(4), 27–33. doi:10.1145/1107499.1107502

Fuhr, N., & Großjohann, K. (2001). XIRQL: A query language for information retrieval in XML documents. In *SIGIR*, (pp. 172-180).

Gao, J., Wang, T., & Yang, D. (2007). MQTree based query rewriting over multiple XML views. In *DEXA*, (pp. 562-571).

Goldman, R., & Widom, J. (1997). DataGuides: Enabling query formulation and optimization in semistructured databases. In *VLDB}'97*, (pp. 436-445).

Gu, J., Xu, B., & Chen, X. (2008). An XML query rewriting mechanism with multiple ontologies integration based on complex semantic mapping. *Information Fusion*, *9*(4), 512–522. doi:10.1016/j.inffus.2007.04.002

Guo, L., Shao, F., Botev, C., & Shanmugasundaram, J. (2003). XRANK: Ranked keyword search over XML documents. In *SIGMOD Conference*, (pp. 16-27).

Halevy, A., Rajaraman, A., & Ordille, J. (2006). Data integration: The teenage years. *VLDB}*, 9.

Halevy, A. Y. (2001). Answering queries using views: A survey. *The VLDB Journal*, *10*(4), 270–294. doi:10.1007/s007780100054

Halevy, A. Y., Ives, Z. G., Madhavan, J., Mork, P., Suciu, D., & Tatarinov, I. (2004). The piazza peer data management system. *IEEE Transactions on Knowledge and Data Engineering*, *16*(7), 787–798. doi:10.1109/TKDE.2004.1318562

Halevy, A. Y., Ives, Z. G., Suciu, D., & Tatarinov, I. (2003). Schema mediation in peer data management systems. *In ICDE*, (pp. 505-516).

Ilyas, I. F., Aref, W. G., & Elmagarmid, A. K. (2003). Supporting top-k join queries in relational databases. In *VLDB*, (pp. 754-765).

Ives, Z. G., Halevy, A. Y., & Weld, D. S. (2002). An XML query engine for network-bound data. *The VLDB Journal*, *11*(4), 380–402. doi:10.1007/s00778-002-0078-5

Jagadish, H. V., Al-Khalifa, S., Chapman, A., Lakshmanan, L. V. S., Nierman, A., & Paparizos, S. (2002). TIMBER: A native XML database. *The VLDB Journal*, *11*(4), 274–291. doi:10.1007/s00778-002-0081-x

Jeffery, S. R., Franklin, M. J., & Halevy, A. Y. (2008). Pay-as-you-go user feedback for dataspace systems. In *SIGMOD '08: Proceedings of the 2008 ACM SIGMOD International Conference on Management of Data*, Vancouver, Canada, (pp. 847-860).

Johnson, D. S., Papadimitriou, C. H., & Yannakakis, M. (1988). On generating all maximal independent sets. *Information Processing Letters*, *27*(3), 119–123. doi:10.1016/0020-0190(88)90065-8

Kacholia, V., Pandit, S., Chakrabarti, S., Sudarshan, S., Desai, R., & Karambelkar, H. (2005). Bidirectional expansion for keyword search on graph databases. In *VLDB*, (pp. 505-516).

Katsis, Y., Deutsch, A., & Papakonstantinou, Y. (2008). Interactive source registration in community-oriented information integration. *Proc. VLDB Endow., 1*(1), 245-259.

Kimelfeld, B., & Sagiv, Y. (2006). Twig patterns: From XML trees to graphs. In *WebDB*.

Kimelfeld, B., & Sagiv, Y. (2008). Modeling and querying probabilistic XML data. *SIGMOD Record, 37*(4), 69–77. doi:10.1145/1519103.1519115

Koloniari, G., Petrakis, Y., & Pitoura, E. (2003). Content-based overlay networks for XML peers based on multi-level bloom filters. In *DBISP2P*, (pp. 232-247).

Koloniari, G., & Pitoura, E. (2005). Peer-to-peer management of XML data: Issues and research challenges. *SIGMOD Record, 34*(2), 6–17. doi:10.1145/1083784.1083788

Koudas, N., Rabinovich, M., Srivastava, D., & Yu, T. (2004). Routing XML queries. *ICDE*, 844.

Lakshmanan, L. V. S., Wang, H., & Zhao, Z. (2006). Answering tree pattern queries using views. *VLDB '06: Proceedings of the 32nd International Conference on very Large Data Bases*, Seoul, Korea, (pp. 571-582).

Lenzerini, M. (2002). Data integration: A theoretical perspective. *PODS '02: Proceedings of the Twenty-First ACM SIGMOD-SIGACT-SIGART Symposium on Principles of Database Systems*, Madison, Wisconsin, (pp. 233-246).

Lenzerini, M. (2004). Principles of P2P data integration. In *DIWeb*, (pp. 7-21).

Levy, A. Y., Mendelzon, A. O., Sagiv, Y., & Srivastava, D. (1995). Answering queries using views. In *PODS*, (pp. 95-104).

Li, C., Chang, K. C., & Ilyas, I. F. (2006). Supporting ad-hoc ranking aggregates. In *SIGMOD Conference*, (pp. 61-72).

Li, C., Chang, K. C., Ilyas, I. F., & Song, S. (2005). RankSQL: Query algebra and optimization for relational top-k queries. In *SIGMOD Conference*, (pp. 131-142).

Li, W., Candan, K. S., Vu, Q., & Agrawal, D. (2001). Retrieving and organizing web pages by ``information unit''. In *WWW*, (pp. 230-244).

Liu, M., & Ling, T. W. (2000). A data model for semistructured data with partial and inconsistent information. In *EDBT*, (pp. 317-331).

Manolescu, I., Florescu, D., Kossmann, D., Xhumari, F., & Olteanu, D. (2000). Agora: Living with XML and relational. In *VLDB '00: Proceedings of the 26th International Conference on very Large Data Bases*, (pp. 623-626).

McBrien, P., & Poulovassilis, A. (2003). Defining peer-to-peer data integration using both as view rules. In *DBISP2P*, (pp. 91-107).

McHugh, J., Abiteboul, S., Goldman, R., & Widom, D. Q. J. (1997). Lore: A database management system for semistructured data. *SIGMOD Record, 26*(3), 54–66. doi:10.1145/262762.262770

Mercer, R. E., & Risch, V. (2003). Properties of maximal cliques of a pair-wise compatibility graph for three nonmonotonic reasoning system. In *Answer Set Programming*.

Mihaila, G. A., Raschid, L., & Tomasic, A. (2002). Locating and accessing data repositories with WebSemantics. *The VLDB Journal, 11*(1), 47–57. doi:10.1007/s007780200061

Moon, J. W., & Moser, L. (1965). On cliques in graphs. *Israel Journal of Mathematics, 3*(1), 23–28. doi:10.1007/BF02760024

Nguyen, L. T., Yee, W. G., & Frieder, O. (2008). Adaptive distributed indexing for structured peer-to-peer networks. In *CIKM '08: Proceeding of the 17th ACM Conference on Information and Knowledge Management*, Napa Valley, CA, (pp. 1241-1250).

Onose, N., Deutsch, A., Papakonstantinou, Y., & Curtmola, E. (2006). Rewriting nested XML queries using nested views. In *SIGMOD '06: Proceedings of the 2006 ACM SIGMOD International Conference on Management of Data,* Chicago, IL (pp. 443-454).

Pankowski, T. (2008). XML data integration in SixP2P: A theoretical framework. In *Intl. Workshop on Data Management in Peer-to-Peer Systems,* (pp. 11-18).

Peng, F., & Chawathe, S. S. (2003). Streaming XPath queries in XSQ. In *ICDE,* (pp. 780-782).

Pottinger, R. A., & Bernstein, P. A. (2003). Merging models based on given correspondences. *VLDB.*

Qi, Y., Candan, K. S., & Sapino, M. L. (2007a). FICSR: Feedback-based inconsistency resolution and query processing on misaligned data sources. In *SIGMOD,* (pp. 151-162).

Qi, Y., Candan, K. S., & Sapino, M. L. (2007b). Sum-max monotonic ranked joins for evaluating top-K twig queries on weighted data graphs. In *VLDB,* (pp. 507-518).

Qi, Y., Candan, K. S., Sapino, M. L., & Kintigh, K. W. (2006). QUEST: QUery-driven exploration of semistructured data with ConflicTs and partial knowledge. *CleanDB.*

Qi, Y., Candan, K. S., Sapino, M. L., & Kintigh, K. W. (2007). Integrating and querying taxonomies with quest in the presence of conflicts. In *SIGMOD '07: Proceedings of the 2007 ACM SIGMOD International Conference on Management of Data,* Beijing, China, (pp. 1153-1155).

Sarma, A. D., Dong, X., & Halevy, A. (2008). Bootstrapping pay-as-you-go data integration systems. In *SIGMOD '08: Proceedings of the 2008 ACM SIGMOD International Conference on Management of Data,* Vancouver, Canada, (pp. 861-874).

Suciu, D. (2002). Distributed query evaluation on semistructured data. *ACM Transactions on Database Systems, 27*(1), 1–62. doi:10.1145/507234.507235

Tajima, K., & Fukui, Y. (2004). Answering XPath queries over networks by sending minimal views. In *VLDB,* (pp. 48-59).

Tang, N., Yu, J. X., Özsu, M. T., Choi, B., & Wong, K. (2008). Multiple materialized view selection for XPath query rewriting. In *ICDE,* (pp. 873-882).

Tatarinov, I., & Halevy, A. (2004). Efficient query reformulation in peer data management systems. In *SIGMOD '04: Proceedings of the 2004 ACM SIGMOD International Conference on Management of Data,* Paris, France, (pp. 539-550).

XML. (n.d.). *Extensible markup language.* Retrieved from http://www.w3.org/XML/

Xpath. (1999). Retrieved from http://www.w3.org/TR/xpath

Xquery. (2006).

Xu, W., & Özsoyoglu, Z. M. (2005). Rewriting XPath queries using materialized views. In *VLDB '05: Proceedings of the 31st International Conference on very Large Data Bases,* Trondheim, Norway, (pp. 121-132).

Yen, J. Y. (1971). Finding the K shortest loopless paths in a network. *Management Science, 17*(11), 712–716. doi:10.1287/mnsc.17.11.712

Zhuge, H., Liu, J., Feng, L., & He, C. (2004). Semantic-based query routing and heterogeneous data integration in peer-to-peer semantic link networks. In *ICSNW,* (pp. 91-107).

Section 5
XML Semantics Utilization and Advanced Application

Chapter 16
Document and Schema XML Updates

Dario Colazzo
Laboratoire de Recherche en Informatique (LRI-CNRS), Université de Paris-Sud, France

Giovanna Guerrini
DISI – Università degli Studi di Genova, Italy

Marco Mesiti
DICo – Università degli Studi di Milano, Italy

Barbara Oliboni
DI – Università degli Studi di Verona, Italy

Emmanuel Waller
Laboratoire de Recherche en Informatique (LRI-CNRS), Universite de Paris-Sud, France

ABSTRACT

Purpose of this chapter is to describe the different research proposals and the facilities of main enabled and native XML DBMSs to handle XML updates at document and schema level, and their versions. Specifically, the chapter will provide a review of various proposals for XML document updates, their different semantics and their handling of update sequences, with a focus on the XQuery Update proposal. Approaches and specific issues concerned with schema updates will then be reviewed. Document and schema versioning will be considered. Finally, a review of the degree and limitations of update support in existing DBMSs will be discussed.

INTRODUCTION

XML (W3C, 1998) is nowadays everywhere employed for the representation and exchange of information on the Web. The document structure is often described through a DTD or an XML schema

DOI: 10.4018/978-1-61520-727-5.ch016

(W3C, 2004). Both XML native (e.g., Tamino, eXist, TIMBER) and enabled (e.g., Oracle, IBM DB2, SQL Server) DBMSs have been so far proposed (Bourret, 2007) for storing and querying XML documents. Some enabled DBMSs support XML schema for the specification of a mapping between the XML schema and internal relational or object-relational representation of XML documents (Florescu &

Kossman, 1999). Relevant, from many points of view, is the use of XML schemas in data management. They can be used for the optimization of query execution, for the specification of access control policies and indexing structures.

Despite the high dynamicity of the contexts where XML documents are employed, XML updates have received less attention than XML queries and the W3C proposal for XML document updates has appeared as a recommendation only recently (W3C, 2008). Different alternative proposals for XML updates have been elaborated in the meantime; among the most recent let us mention XQuery! (Ghelli et al., 2006) and FLUX (Cheney, 2007, 2008). A subtle issue in XQueryUpdate and XQuery! is bound to the two-phase semantics of updates that first collects updates into a *pending update list* by evaluating an expression without altering the data, and then performs all of the updates at once. An additional *snap* operator provides programmer control over when to apply pending updates. The issues of determining whether updates commute (Ghelli et al., 2008) have then been investigated. Motivated by the need of detecting data dependencies between reads and updates of XML documents, so to optimize the execution of update operations, approaches for detecting conflicts among updates (Raghavachari & Shmueli, 2006) have also been investigated.

Updates on XML schemas have received even less attention despite the great impact they may have in the database organization. Indeed, a schema change may affect the data structures developed for the organization, as well as the efficient retrieval and protection of the documents within contained. Even if commercial tools (e.g. Stylus Studio, XML Spy) have been developed for graphically designing XML Schema Definitions (XSDs), they do not support the specification of schema updates nor the semi-automatic revalidation of documents within contained. Commercial DBMSs, like Oracle 11g, Tamino, DB2 v.9, support XSDs at different levels, but the support for schema

evolution is quite limited (actually, a simplified version of adaptation is supported only by Oracle 11g through the *copyEvolve* function).

Given an XML database, updates both to documents and to the schema can lead to *evolution* or to *versioning*. With evolution the original data and schema are replaced by the updated ones upon some update primitives are applied on it. With versioning the original documents and schema are preserved and a new updated version of the document/schema created. This raises the problem of handling different versions of the same document/schema. Specifically, query execution needs to consider mappings among versions and update compositions.

Purpose of this chapter is to describe the different research proposals and the facilities of existing systems to handle XML updates at document and schema level, and their versions. Specifically, the chapter will provide a review of various language proposals for the specification of XML document updates, their different semantics and their handling of update sequences, with a focus on the XQuery Update proposal. Approaches and specific issues concerned with schema updates will then be reviewed along with document and schema versioning issues. Finally, we will discuss the current support of major DBMSs to handle updates on XML documents and schema.

LANGUAGES FOR DOCUMENT UPDATES

In this section we overview the main current proposals for XML update languages. Before getting into details of their main and distinguishing features, we first enumerate and discuss the fundamental update operations that are generally supported by every current XML update language. Then, we discuss the characteristics that every language should present and we get into details of the four most complete and interesting proposals: the W3C proposal XQuery Update Facility

Algorithm 1. The ebay.xml document

```
<?xml version='1.0' ?>
<root>
  <listing>
   <seller_info>
      <name> cubsfantony</name>
     <rating> 848</rating>
   </seller_info>
   <auction_info>
     <current_bid>620.00</current_bid>
     <time_left> 4 days, 14 hours +  </time_left>
     <high_bidder>
        <name> gosha555@excite.com </name>
        <rating>-2 </rating>
     </high_bidder>
      <status><closed>2009-10-12</closed></status>
   </auction_info>
   <item_info>
     <memory> 256MB PC133 SDram</memory>
     <hard_drive> 30 GB 7200 RPM IDE Hard Drive</hard_drive>
     <cpu>Pentium III 933 System  </cpu>
     <description> NEW Pentium III 933 System
                  - 133 MHz BUS Speed Pentium Motherboard,...
     </description>
   </item_info>
  </listing>
</root>
```

(called XQuery UF in the following) (W3C, 2008), XQuery! (read XQuery bang) (Ghelli et al., 2006), FLux (Cheney, 2008), and XUpdate (XUpdate, 2000). When discussing each single language we will outline its distinctive features and updating mechanisms. Language expressions will be specified on the XML document in Algorithm 1. The document contains information about auctions in ebay. Each listing element contains information about an auction: information about the seller, the item(s) object of the auction, and on the auction itself (current bid, time left, the highest bidder, and the status – open or closed – of the auction).

Document Update Operations

By exploiting the (W3C, 2008) terminology, here we describe the basic data update operations. In the following, the term *node* is used to indicate an XML node (e.g., an element, attribute, or text node).

Insert: this operation consists of inserting one or more nodes into a given position of the *target XML document*. The node(s) to be inserted can be the result of a query expression, usually called *source expression*, while the inserting position is established in terms of a target node, which is determined by a *target expression*. The inserting position can be, for example, just after (before) the target node, or just after (before) the last (first) child of the target node.

Delete: this operation consists of deleting one or more nodes, determined by the evaluation of a target expression.

Replace: this operation replaces one node, determined by a target expression, with one or more nodes, determined by a source expression.

Rename: this operation is used to rename a node, which is the result of a target expression. In general, the new name can also be the result of a query expression.

Distinguished Features of Document Update Languages

Before starting the discussion about the main language proposals, we first introduce some distinguished characteristics of an update language, around which we will organize the discussion itself:

- *Handling of nondeterminism.* Nondeterministic behaviour can arise since in general the list of simple update operations accumulated during query execution may be applied in several orders, which may differ from the order in which operations have been added to the list, and not necessarily yield the same final result.
- *Grammatical restrictions on single update constructs.* Each language poses its own restrictions on the way an update expression can be nested into other query expressions, on the kind of allowed queries to determine target and sources nodes, and so on.
- *Degree of exhaustiveness of semantics specification.* This depends on how many parts of the semantics are not specified, and therefore left as implementation-dependant.
- *Adopted notion of snapshot.* A snapshot is the scope inside which update operations are kept pending, and outside which update operations are considered as applied.

XQuery-UF

This language, extension of XQuery, is currently a candidate W3C recommendation and supports the document update operations previously presented,

plus a new one called *transform* (discussed later in the section). The language semantics is based on the *XDM model* that is a tree representation of nodes contained within a document.

One of the guidelines in this language design has been to minimize the impact on the current semantics specification of XQuery (W3C, 2007), so to have a (almost) conservative extension of this last one. For this reason, in XQuery-UF only the *return, then* and *else* branches of *if-then–else* clauses are allowed to contain update expressions, while in *for, let, where,* and *order by* clauses they are forbidden. The following query update illustrates the syntax for deletion.

```
delete node fn:doc("ebay.xml")/
root/listing[1]
```

The query deletes the first listing element. Note that the fact that only one node must be deleted is explicitly declared. To delete multiple nodes, nodes should be used in the place of node; the same holds for other update operations.

The current specification of XQuery-UF states that the result of an XQuery-UF statement is an XDM instance (the result of the truly query part) plus a list of simple update operations (update list) created during query execution.

```
for $x in fn:doc("ebay.xml")//
seller_info
  where $x/mail
  return (delete node $x/mail,
$x/mail)
```

This query deletes mail elements, if present as children of the seller_info element, and returns the deleted elements as a query result. The update list produced by the above expression is the sequence of all deletions produced by the iteration.

In XQuery-UF the update list is applied by respecting the following priority: insertions first, then replacements, and finally deletions (actually a further priority order is imposed among operations of the same kind, see (W3C, 2008) for details).

Another guideline in the definition of XQuery-FU has been ensuring simplicity of programming and maximizing query optimization based on logical equivalences. Hence the language designers have established that each XQuery-UF query has only *one global* snapshot, coinciding with the whole query itself. This means that update operations are accumulated in the update list, kept pending during query evaluation, and materialized *just before* ending. So, the following statement returns the number of email elements present in the *input* document, even though new email elements can be inserted by the query itself.

```
let $c=count(fn:doc("ebay.
xml")//seller_info/mail)
return (
    for $x in node fn:doc("ebay.
xml")//seller_info
    where not($x/mail)
    return (inset node <mail> no
email </mail> into $x),$c
)
```

The insert into operation supports several options, like for example the possibility of inserting an element before (after) the first child of the target node. This can be achieved by specifying the as first (as last) option just before into (see the details in (W3C, 2008)).

Under the point of view of exhaustiveness of semantics specification, XQuery-UF leaves several choices to the language implementation, like, for instance, deciding the actual positions of inserted nodes when inserted into is used without specifying neither as first nor as last option. The only imposed requirement is that chosen positions must not interfere with inserted nodes whose positions have been specified by either as first or as last. Therefore, in the following example it is never the case that in the updated document the element bound to $a is inserted as last element.

```
let $a=<item_info>iia</item_
info>
let $b=<item_info>iib</item_
info>
let $x= fn:doc("ebay.xml")/root/
listing[1]
return (insert node $b as last
into $x,
        insert node $a into $x)
```

It is also left to language implementation the choice of node identifiers for text nodes obtained by collapsing multiple text nodes that become adjacent due to update operations. Finally, it is also left to language implementation the possibility of performing static type analysis in order to statically raise type errors that otherwise would be raised at run time. Other minor issues are implementation dependent, whose description we omit since this is beyond the scope of this chapter.

XQuery-UF also provides a mechanism to copy (by creating new node identifiers) a fragment of an XDM instance, to modify it, and use the modified copy in the return clause. The following is an example taken from the W3C draft. The update expression requires copying a node, modifying the copy, and returning both the original node and the modified copy:

```
let $oldx:= /a/b/x
return
    copy $newx:= $oldx
    modify (rename node $newx as
"newx",
            replace value of node
$newx by $newx * 2)
    return ($oldx, $newx)
```

This example also shows the use of the rename and the replace update operations; it is worth noticing that this statement does not update the input document, but only a copy of a fragment of its. These kinds of expressions are named *transform* expressions.

The current XQuery-FU specification also contains type rules to enforce some constraints on update expressions, by using type information about input data. Typically, these rules are able to *statically* check that some required properties about source and target expressions are always addressed at *run time*. For example, for expressions like replace node Expr1 with Expr2, the type rules are able to infer the type of Expr1 and check that the type is either an element, text, comment or processing instruction type. In the case that the Expr1 inferred type is rather an element *sequence* type, then a static type error is raised (since in this case Expr1 can evaluate to multiple nodes).

Current W3C type rules are not able to infer either the type of newly updated documents or to check that updates preserve document validity with respect to an XML schema.

XQuery!

XQuery! (Ghelli et al., 2006) is a conservative extension of XQuery-UF and introduces three main novelties: i) the possibility of anticipating the execution of the update list to subexpressions, ii) update expressions may occur in function definition, and iii) the programmer has control on the order in which update lists are applied.

A first example of XQuery! statement is the following, showing that it can be useful to apply updates before the end of the query. As illustrated by the example, update list materialization is expressed by the new operator snap, delimiting a local snapshot. The statement below deletes the last mail element of each seller_info element if the number of mail element is greater than 7, applies the updates by using snap, and then counts the remaining number of mail elements.

```
for $x fn:doc("ebay.xml")//sell-
er_info
return (if count($x/mail)>7 then
snap(delete node
```

```
$x/email[last()]) else (),
count($x/mail))
```

Thanks to the presence of snap, the query for each seller_info element returns the number of mail elements after the last one has been (possibly) eliminated. To express the same query in XQuery UF, two different query expressions are needed, the first one performing the deletion, and the second one counting the mail elements.

As shown in (Ghelli et al., 2008) the introduction of snap requires small modification to the XQuery-UF semantics specification. On the other hand, the snap can complicate logical optimizations since logical equivalences are harder to detect. To deal with this problem some recent papers have introduced techniques to detect commutative updates in a query, in order to recover standard logical equivalences leading to logical optimizations (see (Ghelli et al., 2008) and papers therein cited).

As previously said, XQuery! allows the use of update operations and snap inside function definition. This implies that some function calls can cause some side-effects, which can be the desired effects in several situations. For example, as illustrated by the following function (Ghelli et al., 2008), one can define a function nextid to increment the integer value inside a counter element and return the new counter value:

```
declare variable $d:= element
counter { 0 };
declare function nextid() as
xs:integer {
snap { replace { $d/text() }
with { $d + 1 },
$d } };
```

A third distinctive feature of XQuery! is the availability of mechanisms to control the execution order of update lists created by the code embodied by a snap. A user can choose three possible semantics of update list application: *ordered, non-deterministic,* and *conflict-detection.* This can be done by specifying an optional keyword after each snap. The ordered semantics entails that update operations are executed in the order specified by the update list. The non-deterministic option entails that the implementation is free to choose an arbitrary execution order. The conflict-free detection implies a two-phase treatment of the update list. First, absence of conflicts among single update operations is checked. Second, if this check succeeds the update list is executed in some order chosen by the implementation.

Each approach has pros and cons. The ordered semantics is deterministic and therefore easy to be managed by the user; on the other hand, the strict control on execution order leaves few optimization possibilities to the optimizer. The non-deterministic semantics, by contrast, leaves more optimization possibilities, since the optimizer can commute update operations to improve efficiency; on the other hand, the user has low control on program behaviour, and development and testing phases may become rather hard. The conflict-free semantics joins the advantages of the two previous ones, but has the inconvenient that the presence of conflicts may raise errors difficult to understand by the user.

Currently, XQuery! has no type system. Specifically, the multiple-snapshot semantics seems to make type inference rather complex. Another problem that makes type analysis difficult is aliasing (also present in XQuery-UF): when several variables are bound to a node and one of the variables is the target of an update, then it is difficult to propagate type changes to all variables during type analysis.

FLux

The only existing XML update language with a rich type system is Flux (Cheney, 2008). In order to make type analysis feasible, this language is based on some simplified design choices: elements have no node identity (like in XDuce (Hosoya and

Pierce, 2000) and microXQ (Colazzo et al., 2006)), source and target nodes can be selected by only using simple XPath expressions (only the child axis is allowed). To show how this assumption simplifies things, consider the following example, taken by (Cheney, 2008) and violating this assumption. Suppose, we wish to update the document <a><b/></a> with the following statement

```
UPDATE //* BY {DELETE a/b; RE-
NAME * TO c}
```

Since the first target expression is //node(), the two update operations are in conflict (they can act on the same node), and then the final result actually depends on the order in which the two updates are executed. The two possible results can be <a/> and <a><c/></a>. Besides complicating semantics specification, this also makes type analysis difficult. The problem is overcome by only allowing child navigation for selecting nodes involved in update operation.

The main distinctive feature of FLux lies in its powerful type system. It allows to check that update operations meet several type constraints, and, even more importantly, to infer the type of the result of an update. This is very important because, when the update statement is applied to a valid document with respect to an XML schema, by checking inclusion between the statement inferred type and the document schema, the property that the update *always* (for each input instance of the document schema) preserves validation can be statically checked. Finally, another important distinctive feature of Flux is that its semantics is completely specified.

XUpdate

An early proposal is (XUpdate, 2000). It provides all basic document update operations, on element, attribute, text, processing instruction and comment nodes. Source expressions are full XPath expressions (XQuery was not published at that

Table 1. Characteristics of document update languages

	Insert, delete, replace, rename	Semantics	Non-determinism	Semantics specification	Typing
XQuery-UF	All +transform	Global Snapshot	Controlled, and some issues left to implementations	Almost exhaustive	Weak form
XQuery!	All + transform	Local Snapshot	User controlled, and some issues left to implementations	Almost exhaustive	No
Flux	All	One-pass: updates are immediately applied.	Controlled	Exhaustive	Strong and exhaustive
XUpdate	All	Left to implementation	Left to implementation	Rather exhaustive	No

time, and is not used in XUpdate).

Target expressions are syntactically restricted to text, names and variables. However, complex expressions can be obtained by combining several basic update operations, or through variables. Variables allow target expressions to be related to the result of source expressions. This mechanism is necessary for allowing, for instance, to move a fragment specified by a source expression from one place to another within the input document. Basic update operations can then be grouped in sequences. With respect to the syntax, such a program is itself an XML document (as, e.g., in XSLT).

The emphasis, in XUpdate, is on providing a simple and intuitive language, with several implementations (e.g., in Java, Python). Typing issues or snapshots are not considered. From the point of view of exhaustiveness of semantics specification, XUpdate leaves several choices open, including in case of conflicts within or between basic update operations.

In Table 1, we report for each presented language, the set of supported update operations, the assumed semantics, how the language addresses the non-determinism, the presence of a semantics specgification, and the form of supported typing.

LANGUAGES FOR SCHEMA UPDATES

XML document collections are often associated with a DTD or an XML schema describing the structure of document in a collection. An example of XML schema containing the most significant constructs of the language is reported in Algorithm 2 and 3. Since also the structure, and not only the content, of a document evolves over time a first, basic, issue is the identification of a suitable set of evolution primitives to express the changes that may occur on the schema of an XML document collection.

Such primitives are more complex than those for altering an XML document because they have to handle a greater variety of constructs occurring in a schema. Specifically, primitives should include those for altering the internal structure of a schema (such as, the insertion of new element declarations and type definitions, altering the structure of a complex type). Note that, since XSDs are XML documents as well, updates on schemas can be expressed as document updates on the corresponding documents. Since, however, each schema must satisfy some consistency notions and updates also impact the associated documents (as discussed in the next session) schema updates pose some specific issues and ad-hoc languages for updating schemas allows a much more convenient

Algorithm 2. The ebay.xsd schema (part I)

```xml
<?xml version="1.0" encoding="utf-8"?>
<xs:schema elementFormDefault="qualified"
           xmlns:xs="http://www.w3.org/2001/XMLSchema">
   <xs:element name="root">
      <xs:complexType>
         <xs:sequence minOccurs="0" maxOccurs="unbounded">
            <xs:element name="listing">
               <xs:complexType>
                  <xs:sequence>
                     <xs:element name="seller_info"
                     type="person_info_type"/>
                     <xs:element ref="auction_info"/>
                     <xs:element minOccurs="0"
                     maxOccurs="unbounded"
                  ref="item_info"/>
                  </xs:sequence>
               </xs:complexType>
            </xs:element>
         </xs:sequence>
      </xs:complexType>
   </xs:element>
   <xs:complexType name="person_info_type">
      <xs:sequence>
         <xs:element name="name" type="xs:string"/>
         <xs:element name="mail" type="xs:string" minOccurs="0"
            maxOccurs="unbounded"/>
         <xs:element name="rating" type="xs:string"/>
      </xs:sequence>
   </xs:complexType>
   <xs:element name="auction_info">
      <xs:complexType>
         <xs:sequence>
            <xs:element name="current_bid" type="dollars"/>
            <xs:element name="time_left" type="xs:string"/>
            <xs:element name="high_bidder" type="person_info_type"/>
            <xs:element ref="status"/>
         </xs:sequence>
      </xs:complexType>
   </xs:element>
```

Algorithm 3. The ebay.xsd schema (part II)

```
    <xs:element name="status">
        <xs:complexType>
            <xs:choice>
                    <xs:element name="opened" type="xs:date"/>
                    <xs:element name="closed" type="xs:date"/>
            </xs:choice>
        </xs:complexType>
    </xs:element>
    <xs:element name="item_info">
        <xs:complexType>
            <xs:sequence>
                    <xs:element name="memory" type="xs:string"/>
                    <xs:element name="hard_drive" type="xs:string"/>
                    <xs:element name="cpu" type="xs:string"/>
                    <xs:choice>
                        <xs:element name="brand" type="xs:string"/>
                        <xs:element name="description"
                        type="xs:string"/>
                    </xs:choice>
            </xs:sequence>
        </xs:complexType>
    </xs:element>
    <xs:simpleType name="dollars">
        <xs:restriction base-"xs:decimal">
            <xs:minExclusive value="0"/>
            <xs:maxExclusive value="1000"/>
        </xs:restriction>
    </xs:simpleType>
</xs:schema>
```

schema manipulation. XML schema updates have mainly been investigated in the context of the X-Evolution system (Mesiti et al., 2006), where two specific languages supporting schema modifications have been proposed: a graphical language and the XSchemaUpdate language (Cavalieri et al., 2008b). In what follows we first briefly present the basic primitives for schema evolution and then those two languages.

Primitives for Schema Evolution

Schema evolution has firstly been investigated for schemas expressed by DTDs in (Kramer & Rundensteiner, 2001), that proposed and discussed in detail a set of evolution operators. The set of elementary internal operators includes: the creation of a new element, the deletion of an element, the addition and the deletion of a subelement and of an attribute to an element, the modification of quantifiers, attribute types, attribute values, and

Table 2. Modification primitives for an XML Schema

	Insert	Update	Delete
Simple Types	insert global type insert new member type	change restriction change base type rename type change member type make global a local type make local a global type	remove type remove member type
Complex types	insert global type insert local element insert ref element insert operator	rename local element rename global type change type local element change cardinality change operator make global a local type make local a global type	remove local element remove substructure remove type
Elements	insert global element	rename global element change type global element make reference a local element make local a reference element	remove global element

modifications to *groups* of elements. A notion of completeness of the proposed set of operators is provided and requirements of consistency and minimality are formulated. However, since DTDs are considerably simpler than XSDs the proposed operators do not cover all the kinds of schema changes that can occur on an XSD.

Tan & Goh (2004) focus on the use of XML Schema for specifying (domain-specific) standards and categorize the possible changes that may occur between revisions of standards. They identify three different categories of changes:

- *Migratory changes*, dealing with the movement of elements or attributes to other parts of the documents. Examples of changes in this category are morphing of an element to an attribute, migration of a subelement from one element to another.
- *Structural changes*, affecting the structure of the documents through the addition or removal of attributes or elements. Examples of changes in this category are additions/removals of elements, subelements, and attributes.

- *Sedentary changes*, which involve no movement and have no effect on the structure of the documents. Examples of changes in this category are renaming of elements and attributes and changes in simple data types.

Moreover, they identify one category of change that is difficult to model, i.e., *semantic changes*. This category may not affect the structure of the schema at all. Such changes involve a change in the interpretation or the meaning of a term or terms used within the specification. For example, the name element in the person_info_type complex type of the ebay.xsd schema in Algorithm 2 will contain only the last name of a person instead of the entire name.

Guerrini et al. (2005) introduce the kinds of modifications at the vocabulary, content model, and data type levels that can be applied on an XSD classified according to the main components that can appear in a schema specification (elements, complex types, and simple types) and the main types of change (insertion, update, and deletion). The identified modifications are summarized in Table 2.

Figure 1. Graphical representation of the ebay.xsd schema

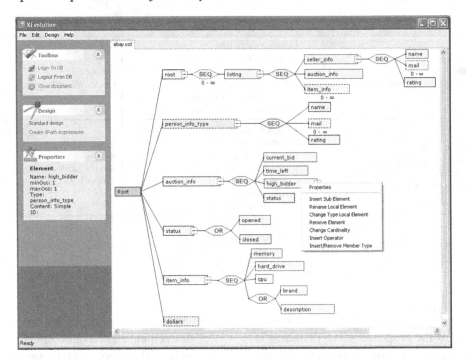

Schema modifications are associated with applicability conditions that must hold before their application in order to guarantee that the updated schema is still consistent. For example, global types/elements can be removed only if elements in the schema of such a type or referring to it do not exist. Moreover, when renaming an element in a complex type T, an element with the same tag should not occur in T.

A Graphical Language for Schema Evolution

A tree-based representation of an XSD schema is provided in X-Evolution. Figure 1 contains the graphical representation of the XSD schema in Algorithm 2 and 3. A Root node is introduced to aggregate all the global element declarations and global type definitions. Nodes SEQ, ALL, and OR are introduced to represent sequence, all, and choice groups. Repeatability of nodes is reported below the nodes.

In X-Evolution, by graphically selecting a node of the tree representation of a schema, the schema evolution operations that can be applied on such a node are visualized. For example, by clicking on the element high_bidder of Figure 1, the primitives for a local element are shown. When the user invokes an evolution primitive, a graphical menu for setting primitive parameters is shown to the user. For example, suppose that a sibling element is to be inserted into the high_bidder element in Figure 1. The menu in Figure 2 is shown. The user can specify whether the subelement should be positioned above (i.e., before in the document order) or below (i.e., after in the document order) the element high_bidder, its data type, and its cardinality. Once the parameters have been inserted, X-Evolution checks whether the applicability conditions of the primitive are met and, if they are, the operation is executed and the evolved schema visualized.

XSchemaUpdate

The XSchemaUpdate language supports schema update statements of the format:

```
UPDATE SCHEMA ObjectSpec
Update Spec
```

where *ObjectSpec* is the specification of the *update object*, that is, the set of nodes belonging to an XSD that needs to be updated. The update operation is executed on each node belonging to the update object. An update object is specified by the location of the schema and an *XSPath* expression (Cavalieri et al., 2008a) on such a schema. XSPath has been tailored for specifying path expressions on XSD schemas because the use of XPath over a schema would result in the specification of complex expressions that do not reflect the user expectations in query formulation. Moreover, the possibilities of specifying references to element declarations and of defining an element type as global require facilities for navigating internal links that are not supported in XPath. An XSPath expression identifies the components of a schema: types and elements, being them local or global, named or anonymous, along with attributes and operators.

Once the component to be updated has been identified, through an *Update Spec* statement it is possible to specify the modification operation to be applied on the schema. A user-friendly syntax has been developed for the specification of the modification primitives presented. The following statement specifies to insert a new optional local element logo (the URI of an image representing an item to be sold) of type xs:string after the brand element.

```
UPDATE SCHEMA ("ebay.xsd")/item_
info!sequence!choice
INSERT ELEMENT logo OF TYPE
xs:string (0,1)
```

Figure 2. Parameters for element insertion

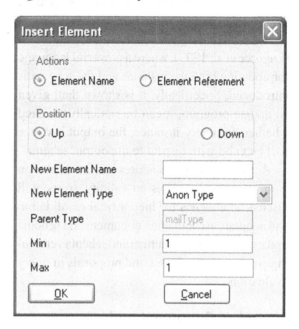

```
AFTER !brand
```

where */item_info!sequence!choice* is an XS-Path expression identifying the choice group operator in the global element item_info.

EVOLUTION AND VERSIONING: IMPLICATIONS ON DOCUMENT VALIDATION, ORGANIZATION AND RETRIEVAL

The executions of updates at document and schema level have implication in the organization and management of information. XML documents and schemas change over time: an XML document and/or its structure could be modified; design errors could be fixed, and schema could be refined. This means that documents and schemas evolve with respect to time. Approaches have been developed to manage the consequences of substituting the old document/schema with a new one (named *evolution*) or to create a new updated copy (named *versioning*).

Several of those issues are very similar in the context of object-oriented databases. Some of them, including revalidation, are studied in (Lagorce et al, 1997), where a powerful language for updating both the instance and the schema is introduced. Specifically, it is shown that, given an update program, it can be statically checked whether, for every instance, the output instance will be valid with respect to the output schema.

A first issue to be addressed for evolution is the impact of updates on validity, so we will discuss approaches for incremental revalidation and adaptation (both upon document and schema updates). Then, for document and schema versioning we present the issues and proposals in query evaluation.

Impact of Document and Schema Evolution

When considering updates to documents, there are two main issues concerning validity: (i) how to check the validity of the updated document with respect to its schema *incrementally*, that is, taking advantage of its validity for the schema before the update; (ii) in case the updated document is no longer valid for the schema, the possibility of *adapting* the schema to include the new document structure can be considered.

Incremental validation of XML documents, represented as trees, upon document updates, has been investigated for atomic (Balmin et al., 2004, Barbosa et al., 2004, Bouchou & Ferrari Alves, 2003) and composite (Barbosa et al., 2006) XML updates. Given an update operation on a document, it is simulated, and only after verifying that the updated document is still valid for its schema the update is executed. The key idea of these approaches is to take advantage of the knowledge of the validity of the document prior to the update, together with the update specified on the document, to avoid whole document revalidation thus checking only the conditions that the update may invalidate. Efficiency of those

proposals is bound to the *conflict-free* schema property. A schema is said to be conflict-free when in type definitions subelement names appear only once. This property is assumed as well by proposals addressing revalidation and adaptation of documents upon schema evolution, both for what concerns the original schema and the evolved one. Most schemas employed on the Web do exhibit this property (Choi, 2002). An extension of the incremental validation process to document correction is proposed in (Bouchou et al., 2006) where upon validation failure local corrections to the document are proposed to the user.

Schema adaptation has been investigated, for schemas expressed as DTDs, by Bouchou et al. (2004), and for XML Schemas by Klettke et al. (2005). In (Bouchou et al., 2004) document updates invalidating some documents can lead to changes in the DTD. Specifically, updates resulting in invalid XML documents are treated in different ways, according to the kind of user performing them. Invalid updates performed by ordinary users are rejected, whereas invalid updates performed by administrators can be accepted, thus resulting in a change on the schema. The validity of a document after such an update is enforced by changing the schema. The rationale for this approach is the increasing demand for tools specifically designed for administrators not belonging to the computer science community, but capable of making decisions on the evolution of the applicative domain. Klettke et al. (2005) address the same problem in the context of XML Schema. Specifically, they distinguish four possible outcomes of update operations on documents: *ignore* the schema (all update operations are accepted); *reject* the updates that produce documents not valid for the schema; *redo* after an invalidating document update, the user is requested to explicitly modify the schema; automatically *evolve* the schema after an invalidating document update, which corresponds to what is proposed in (Bouchou et al., 2004). They discuss how the schema constraints can be relaxed upon deletion, insertion, renaming, and replacing of elements and attributes.

When considering updates to schema, in a schema evolution rather than a schema versioning approach according to Roddick (1995), documents that were valid for the original schema could not be valid for the new one, thus the XML document should be revised and adapted to the updated XML Schema and revalidated. The incremental validation of XML documents upon schema evolution is supported by X-Evolution (Guerrini et al., 2007). A number of schema evolution operations actually preserve validity like introducing an optional element, renaming a type, increasing the number of repetitions of an element. Intuitively, whenever a validity preserving primitive is invoked, the documents are valid without the documents having to be checked; whenever other primitives are invoked on a type, all the document elements of that type should be retrieved for checking whether they are still valid for the new type. Depending on the primitive, different checks need to be performed. For example, when renaming a global element, the algorithm extracts elements tagged with the original global name from the documents. If no element is identified, it means that the documents are still valid.

Upon schema evolution, when documents are no longer valid for the new schema, they need to be adapted to the new schema to be still usable. In X-Evolution, both automatic and query-based approaches have been devised to face this issue. The adapt algorithm, detailed in Guerrini et al. (2007), has been developed to automatically adapt documents to the new schema by a minimal set of operations. Depending on the adopted primitives invoked on the structure of an element *e*, the adaptation process may require the insertion of new subelements into *e*, to remove subelements, or both. As another example, suppose that the OR operator in the *item_info* element is modified in the SEQ operator. In this case, new elements should be added to the elements of this type in order to be valid for the new schema.

A key issue in the adaptation process is the determination of the values to assign when new elements should be inserted into the documents to make them valid. In X-Evolution, two approaches can be followed. According to the automatic approach the default values are assigned to new elements depending on their types (for simple types, default primitive values are assigned, whereas, for complex types, the simplest structure of that type is extracted and associated with the element). By contrast, according to the query-based approach a schema modification statement is coupled with a document update statement that specifies the new content depending on the context where it is invoked. Specifically, in XSchemaUpdate the schema update statement includes an optional *AdaptSpec* clause allowing the specification of an adaptation statement for documents that are instances of the original schema. Each node belonging to the update object has a counterpart in valid documents. Given a node *n* in the update object and a document *D*, the set of document nodes (elements, attributes or values) corresponding to *n* are identified as context for the specification of an XQuery Update expression. The expressions associated with such nodes are evaluated and the new version of the document is generated.

Impact of Document and Schema Versioning

In the versioning context, different approaches were proposed in the literature, to handle both schema and document versions.

In (Chien et al., 2002), the authors deal with issues related to the management of multiversion XML documents. In particular, they propose efficient techniques for storing, retrieving, viewing, exchanging, and querying multiversion XML documents. The main solutions they propose are the edit-based and the reference-based approaches. The former focuses on the representation of changes, while the latter focuses on the representation of the document parts that remains unchanged. The edit-based approach represents updates to XML documents, and is based on the use of edit scripts for evaluating the differences between two subsequent versions of a given document. The main advantage of this approach is its incremental nature: new document versions are added to the repository, without modifying the information previously stored. The main limitations of the edit-based approach are related to the fact that information is split between the actual database and the scripts, and to the fact that edit scripts are not XML objects. The reference-based approach preserves the logical structure of the evolving document, and uses of object references. A version is represented as a list of objects: the first kind of objects are "reference records" representing document parts that remained unchanged from a version to another one, i.e., they represent common part between two versions. The other kinds of objects are actual document object records. XML documents are represented as ordered trees, and thus multiple versions can be considered as a forest of ordered trees, where each tree represents a version.

In (Snodgrass et al., 2008), the authors extend their previous approach, for supporting the creation and validation of time-varying documents without changing the related XML Schema, to support also the versioning of the schema. In particular, they focus on the representation of a time-varying schema and the validation of XML documents with respect to such schema. The proposal is based on a non-temporal schema (bundle) that can be considered as a base schema, and on temporal and physical annotations. Temporal annotations describe how the document can change, while physical annotations describe where timestamps are placed. The base schema, temporal annotations, and physical annotations are XML documents that can be time-varying as the versioned schema.

In (Wang & Zaniolo, 2008), the authors propose an approach to represent, in a concise way, the versions of an XML document, and to query them by using XML query languages. In this proposal, the different versions of a given XML document are managed as a unit (i.e., as an XML document), by storing only the delta changes to the document itself. The XML document representing the successive versions is called *V-Document* and contains annotated elements. In a V-Document, each element is related to the two attributes *v-start* and *v-end* representing the valid version interval of the element: *v-start* represents the initial version when the element is first added to the XML document, and *v-end* represents the last version in which such an element is valid. *v-start* and *v-end* attributes can be version numbers or timestamps. For example, a portion of the *V-Document* related to versioned document for the example considered in this work, could be the following:

```
...
<seller_info vstart="2009-04-10"
vend="now">
   <name vstart="2009-04-10"
vend="now">cubsfantony</name>
   <rating vstart="2009-04-10"
vend="2009-04-15">848</rating>
   <rating vstart="2009-04-16"
vend="now">850</rating>
</seller_info>
...
```

In this simple example, the rating of the seller is 848 in version valid in the interval from 2009-04-10 to 2009-04-15 and 850 in version valid from 2009-04-16 until now.

This V-Document portion describes an UPDATE operation related to the fact that the rating of the sellers passes from 848 to 850 in these two versions of the considered document:

```
<document> <!-- Version 1 on
2009-04-10 -->
...
<seller_info>
  <name>cubsfantony</name>
  <rating>848</rating>
```

```
</seller_info>
...
</document>
<document> <!-- Version 2 on
2009-04-16 -->
...
<seller_info>
  <name>cubsfantony</name>
  <rating>850</rating>
</seller_info>
...
</document>
```

The main advantage of this approach is that there is no storage redundancy: the nodes which do not change over time are representing in the V-Document as a single node timestamped with its validity interval. In this example the nodes for the <seller_info> and the <name> are reported as single nodes in the V-Document, while the updated node, related to the <rating>, is reported twice.

In the context of document versioning, an approach for supporting branch versioning is proposed in (Rosado et al., 2006). This paper focuses on collaborative scenarios, where new versions can be generated from any past version, and represent relationships between versions by means of a version tree. In this work, the authors represent the different versions of an XML document in a single XML document. In particular, they use versionstamp instead of timestamp, i.e., they do not consider temporal validity information related to each version, but represent only relationships between versions. A step forward with respect this approach is described in (Rosado et al., 2007), where the authors add temporal information to each version included in the document.

DBMS SUPPORT FOR UPDATES AT DOCUMENT AND SCHEMA LEVEL

In this section we examine the support of most relevant commercial DBMSs in the treatment of document/schema modification and versioning. For each DBMS we briefly report their support to XML and then move into the details of document/schema modification and versioning. A comparison among the presented systems is finally presented.

SQL Server 2008

In SQL Server (Malcom, 2008), XML data can be generated from standard relational tables and query results by using a FOR XML clause in a SELECT statement. The converse of FOR XML is a relational rowset generator function named OpenXML; it extracts values from the XML data into columns of a rowset by evaluating XPath expressions. OpenXML is used by applications that shred incoming XML data into tables or for querying by using the Transact-SQL language. Moreover, in SQL Server the XML type has been included for natively storing XML documents in columns of tables.

Beside the support for querying XML documents through XQuery, SQL Server allows the modification of XML documents through the proprietary method modify(), which operates on instances of the XML type (Vithanala, 2005). This method is invoked in the SET clause of an UPDATE statement. The SQL Server data manipulation language uses the insert, delete, and replace value of keywords to support insert, delete, and update operations on XML documents (the rename operation is not supported). The keyword is followed by an XQuery expression that identifies one or more nodes object of the operation. Modification of a typed XML instance is subjected to validation checks according to the schema constraints defined on the XML data type.

SQL Server supports a subset of W3C XML Schema specification and maintains a container of XSD files, named *XML schema collection,* that may be related or unrelated to another one (Pal et al., 2006). Each schema in an XML schema collection *C* is identified using its target namespace.

Columns of type XML constrained to C can be declared in the creation of tables. The constraint imposed by C is the collective set of the schema constraints imposed by the individual XSDs in C. When a value is inserted into a column of type XML constrained to C or a pre-existing value is updated, the value is validated against C.

A new version of an XSD with a new target namespace can be added to C and is treated like a new schema. Suppose that within the schema collection C, two target namespaces, named EBAY-V1 and EBAY-V2 respectively, are present. Whenever EBAY-V2 is obtained from EBAY-V1 by adding optional elements and attributes, and global elements and type definitions, no re-validation is required. An XML column of type C can store instances of both EBAY-V1 and EBAY-V2 schemas. Since queries can be posed both on documents conforming to the old and the new versions of the schema, it ensures that a search can distinguish between a <root> element within the target namespace EBAY-V1 from one within the target namespace EBAY-V2 and thus improving the performance of query evaluation.

No specific support for XML document versioning is provided by SQL Server.

DB2 Version 9.5

DB2 supports the XML type for storing XML documents in columns of a table. Moreover, it allows the shredding of XML documents in relational tables, query processing through both SQL/XML and XQuery (details on the support of XML in DB2 can be found in (Steegmans et al., 2004)).

XQuery-UF, previously described in this document, is completely supported by DB2 (Nicola et al., 2007). DB2 uses the conventional syntax of the SQL UPDATE statement and its SET clause to assign a new value to the corresponding XML column. An application can locally load a document, modify it, and send the updated version to the DB2 server to replace the old one or, by exploiting

the transform operation, can simply send a SQL UPDATE statement. This last option allows the server to modify single elements/attributes of a document instead of replacing the entire document. Updates at document level preserve well-formness of the modified document. This means that updates that do not lead to well-formed documents are rejected. The possibility to check validity with respect to a schema is supported.

XML Schema is mainly employed for the validation of documents. DB2 has an XSD schema repository (named XSR) that maintains a copy of the schema that might be used during validation (named *object schema*s). Schema needs to be registered in order to be used for validation. Validation is performed during insertion or using the XMLValidate function, which is part of the SQL/XML standard.

DB2 has built-in support for a simple form of schema evolution. If the new schema is backward-compatible with the old schema (i.e. validity is preserved with respect to the old schema), then the old schema can be replaced with the new schema repository (Nicola et al., 2005).

This form of schema evolution limits the type of changes one can make on schema and also the effects on document validity. Indeed, since backward compatibility is required, there is no need to perform re-validation. Indeed, only the update operations on the schema that do not alter validity are allowed.

Also for schema versioning DB2 offers limited facilities. It offers the possibility to maintain the old and new versions of the schemas, under different names.

Since validation is not performed on a column basis, in the same column of a table a mix of documents that conform to the old schema and to the new schema can appear. Query statements can be specified on documents valid for the old, the new or both schema versions. To enable version-aware operations, DB2 supplies the function xmlxsrobjectid for determining the version to be used in validating a document. No specific support for XML document versioning is provided by DB2.

Oracle 11g

Oracle supports the XMLType type for the representation of XML documents in columns of relational tables. Three storage models are available: *structured* (by shredding documents in object-relational tables), *unstructured* (by storing documents as CLOB files), and *binary* (by storing documents in a binary format specifically tailored for XML). Oracle supports the last version of the W3C XQuery specification and is fully complaint with the SQL/XML standard.

For updating XML documents, Oracle introduces a set of update functions, such as deleteXML(), updateXML(), insertXML(), as extensions to SQL/XML functions for declaratively updating XML at the node level (Liu et al., 2007). These operations share the following commonalities: they all accept an XML instance as input an return a new instance as output; they can be used to return in a SELECT query a modified version of the stored document or to persistently update in an UPDATE statement a document stored in the database; the identification of the nodes target of the operation is expressed through an XPath expression (XQuery expressions are not allowed). These operations provide transactional, snapshot semantics for updating XML. The rename operation is not supported.

An XSD schema to be useful should be registered. Once a schema has been registered, it can be used for validating XML documents through functions isSchemaValid() and schemaValidate() and for creating XMLTYPE tables and columns bound to the XSD. Full and partial validation procedures are supported in Oracle. Partial validation ensures only that all of the mandatory elements and attributes are present, and that no unexpected elements or attributes occur in the document. Partial validation does not ensure that the instance document is fully compliant with

the XSD schema. Full validation can always be enforced through CHECK constraints and PL/SQL BEFORE INSERT triggers. Oracle XML DB supports two kinds of schema evolution:

- *Copy-based schema evolution*, in which all instance documents that conform to the schema are copied to a temporary location in the database, the old schema is deleted, the modified schema is registered, and the instance documents are inserted into their new locations from the temporary area. The PL/SQL procedure DBMS_XMLSCHEMA.copyEvolve is employed for this purpose.

- *In-place schema evolution*, which does not require copying, deleting, and inserting existing data and thus is much faster than copy-based evolution, but can be applied only when there is backward compatibility of the new schema. That is, it is permitted if no changes to the storage model are required and if the changes do not invalidate existing documents. DBMS_XMLSCHEMA.inPlaceEvolve is the PL/SQL procedure employed for this purpose.

Oracle provides a way to create and manage different versions of a resource. When a resource, such as a table or column, is updated, Oracle stores the pre-update contents as a separate resource version. Oracle provides PL/SQL package DBMS_XDB_VERSION to put a resource under version-control (VCR) and retrieve different versions of the resource. Through this features it is thus possible to handle different versions of an XML document. A document is registered as a VCR and the system always resolves to the latest version of the target resource, or the selected version within the current workspace. It is, however, possible to explicitly refer to any specific version, by identifying the target resource by its OID-based path.

Table 3. Evolution and versioning support in commercial systems

DBMS	Type of schema	validation	document modification	schema modification	document versioning	schema versioning	schema evolution
SQL Server	subset XSD	total	Yes, proprietary extension	no	no	yes	no
DB2	XSD	total	Yes, XQuery-UF	no	no	partially	partially
Oracle 11g	XSD	partial and total	Yes, proprietary extension	no	yes	no	yes
Tamino	subset XSD	total	Yes, proprietary extension	yes	yes	no	partially

Tamino

Tamino (Software AG, 2008) is a DBMS develop for storing and querying XML documents directly in their native type. A database consists of multiple *collections,* that is containers of XML documents. A collection can have an associated set of XSDs. Documents in the collection need to be validated against them.

Updates at document node level can be performed through the insert, delete, replace and rename operations specifically developed. Users can either specify directly one of the update operations or can construct more complex expressions by using FLWU expressions. These expressions are variants of the FLWOR expressions that can contain update operations. The result of applying update operations should be a well-formed document. Whenever a document with an associated schema is modified, the validity of the updated document is checked. When more than one update is requested for the same document, the order of the operation is irrelevant.

Tamino uses a simplified version of XSD, named TSD -- Tamino Schema Definition, and through its schema editor it is possible to modify schemas in different way. Moreover, it allows to automatically convert DTDs, XSDs into TSDs. Schema modifications should guarantee that documents contained in a collection should remain

valid against the new representation of the schema, otherwise the schema modification operation is not permitted. In this extent, Tamino thus supports schema evolution (backward compatibility should be guaranteed). In the current version there is no support for schema versioning.

Tamino relied on webDAV versioning system to handle several versions of the same resource. In order to track the history of the content and deleted properties of a versionable resource, an author can put the resource under version control with a VERSION-CONTROL request. Additionally, in order to support access by simple clients such as an HTTP 1.1 client, auto-versioning is supported. Ideally, as a document is edited using a WebDAV-capable client, the DeltaV server will automatically version its contents.

Comparison

Table 3 summarises the support of the presented commercial DBMSs for document/schema evolution/versioning. Specifically, the table reports the kind of schema specification adopted (entirely the XML Schema specification or a subset), the type of validation algorithms supported, whether they provide operators for the specification of document and schema modification, schema evolution and document/schema versioning. We remark that where the support is "partial" it means that it requires backward compatibility. Oracle is the only that supports schema evolution without requiring backward compatibility.

CONCLUSION AND FUTURE TRENDS

In this chapter we have discussed the current efforts of the academic and industrial researchers in facing updates on XML documents and schema. Starting from the primitives that are required for documents and schemas, we have presented the current language proposals for the specification of updates. Then, we moved to consider, from a data management point of view, the current proposals for handling the implications of updates both in the case of evolution (i.e., previous version is discarded) and versioning (i.e., all previous versions are maintained). We have shown as different issues arise in these situations, and provided ideas on how to face them. Finally, we presented the current equipments of major database systems to handle updates on XML documents and schemas.

As emerged from the discussion, many issues still need to be addressed in the field. For what concern schema evolution, a first issue is the introduction of a snap operator for set of schema update primitives. Therefore, validity checking and document adaptation can be executed for the entire set of primitives. However, the presence of conflicting statements within the set should be properly handled. Conflicts can arise both at schema and instance level. At schema level, a statement can request the insertion of a subelement in the declaration of an element removed by a previous statement. At data level, an adaptation primitive can be specified considering the original document, and not the document obtained by applying the preceding adaptation statements. Static safety conditions should thus be determined to avoid both kinds of conflicts: conditions for performing

a single document adaptation at the invocation of the snap operator; conditions under which the set of primitives will never commit. The same issues of (safely) composing document adaptation operations arise if the adaptation process is performed lazily, that is, when documents are accessed the first time after their schema has evolved, which is reasonable in some situations.

Concerning schema versioning, the proliferation of versions can create the need for developing approaches for handling and efficiently accessing the different versions of the same XSD. Moreover, relying on a direct graph model for representing the different versions, manipulation operations should be developed (remove old versions, delete corresponding document, move /transform documents of a version into another version, and so on). Moreover, the idea to develop a snap operator also in the field of versioning should be evaluated (in order to minimize the number of versions to be created and also for checking whether different sequences of update operations can lead to the same version).

REFERENCES

W3C. (1998). *Extensible Markup Language (XML)*.

W3C. (2004). *XML Schema Part 0: Primer. Second Edition*

W3C. (2007). *XQuery 1.0 and XPath 2.0 Formal Semantics, recommendation. XUpdate*. (2000). Retrieved from http://xmldb-org.sourceforge.net/xupdate

W3C. (2008). XQuery Update Facility 1.0, candidate recommendation.

Balmin, A., Papakonstantinou, Y., & Vianu, V. (2004). Incremental Validation of XML Documents. *ACM Transactions on Database Systems, 29*(4), 710–751. doi:10.1145/1042046.1042050

Barbosa, D., Leighton, G., & Smith, A. (2006). Efficient Incremental Validation of XML Documents After Composite Updates. In *Database and XML Technologies, 4th International XML Database Symposium*, (LNCS Vol. 4516, pp. 107-121).

Barbosa, D., Mendelzon, A., Libkin, L., & Mignet, L. (2004). Efficient Incremental Validation of XML Documents. In *International Conference on Data Engineering*, (pp. 671-682).

Bouchou, B., Cheriat, A., Ferrari, M. H., & Savary, A. (2006). XML Document Correction: Incremental Approach Activated by Schema Validation. In *Tenth International Database Engineering and Applications Symposium*, (pp. 228-238).

Bouchou, B., Duarte, D., Ferrari Alves, M. H., Laurent, D., & Musicante, M. A. (2004). Schema Evolution for XML: A Consistency-preserving Approach. In *International Conference on Mathematical Foundations of Computer Science* (LNCS vol. 3153, pp. 876-888).

Bouchou, B., & Ferrari Alves, M. H. (2003). Updates and Incremental Validation of XML Documents. In *Database Programming Languages, 9th International Workshop*, (LNCS Vol. 2921, pp. 216-232).

Bourret, R. (2007). *XML Database Products*. Available at http://www.rpbourret.com/xml/XMLDatabaseProds.htm

Cavalieri, F., Guerrini, G., & Mesiti, M. (2008a). Navigational Path Expression on XML Schemas. In *International Conference on Database and Expert Systems Applications*, (LNCS Vol. 5181, pp. 718-726).

Cavalieri, F., Guerrini, G., & Mesiti, M. (2008b). *XSchemaUpdate: Schema Evolution and Document Adaptation*. Technical report, University of Genova, Switzerland.

Cheney, J. (2007). Lux: A Lightweight, Statically Typed XML Update Language. In *PLAN-X 2007*, (pp. 25-36).

Cheney, J. (2008). Flux: FunctionaL Updates for XML. In *ACM International Conference on Functional Programming*.

Chien, S.-Y., Tsotras, V. J., & Zaniolo, C. (2001). XML Document Versioning. *SIGMOD Record*, *30*(3), 46–53. doi:10.1145/603867.603875

Chien, S.-Y., Tsotras, V. J., & Zaniolo, C. (2002). Efficient schemes for managing multiversion XML documents. *The VLDB Journal*, *11*(4), 332–353. doi:10.1007/s00778-002-0079-4

Choi, B. (2002). What are Real DTDs Like? In *Fifth International Workshop on the Web and Databases*, (pp. 43-48).

Colazzo, D., Ghelli, G., Manghi, P., & Sartiani, C. (2006). Static analysis for path correctness of XML queries. [JFP]. *Journal of Functional Programming*, *16*(4-5), 621–661. doi:10.1017/S0956796806005983

Florescu, D., & Kossmann, D. (1999). Storing and Querying XML Data using an RDMBS. *IEEE Data Eng. Bull.*, *22*(3), 27–34.

Ghelli, G., Ré, C., & Simon, J. (2006). XQuery!: An XML Query Language with Side Effects. In *EDBT Workshops 2006*, (pp. 178-191).

Ghelli, G., Rose, K. H., & Simon, J. (2008). Commutativity Analysis in XML Update Languages. *ACM Transactions on Database Systems*, *33*(4). doi:10.1145/1412331.1412341

Guerrini, G., Mesiti, M., & Rossi, D. (2005). Impact of XML schema evolution on valid documents. In *ACM International Workshop on Web Information and Data Management*, (pp. 39-44).

Guerrini, G., Mesiti, M., & Sorrenti, M. A. (2007). XML Schema Evolution: Incremental Validation and Efficient Document Adaptation. In *Database and XML Technologies, 5th International XML Database Symposium*, (LNCS Vol. 4704, pp. 92-106).

Hosoya, H. H. & Pierce, B. C. (2000). XDuce: A typed XML processing language (preliminary report). In *Proceedings of Third International Workshop on the Web and Databases (WebDB2000)*, (LNCS Vol. 1997, pp. 226-244).

Klettke, M., Meyer, H., & Hänsel, B. (2005). Evolution: The Other Side of the XML Update Coin. In *International Workshop on XML Schema and Data Management.*

Kramer, D. K., & Rundensteiner, E. A. (2001). Xem: XML Evolution Management. In *Eleventh International Workshop on Research Issues in Data Engineering: Document Management for Data Intensive Business and Scientific Applications*, (pp. 103-110).

Lagorce, J.-B., Stockus, A., & Waller, E. (1997). Object-Oriented Database Evolution. In *Sixth International Conference on Database Theory*, (pp. 379-393).

Liu, Z. H., Krishnaprasad, M., Warner, J. W., Angrish, R., & Arora, V. (2007). Effective and efficient update of xml in RDBMS. In *Proceedings of ACM SIGMOD international Conference on Management of Data*, (pp. 925-936).

Malcolm, G. (2008). *What's New for XML in SQL Server 2008.* In Microsoft SQL Server 2008 white papers.

Melton, J., & Buxton, S. (2006). Querying XML – Xquery, XPath, and SQL/XML in Context. Morgan-Kaufmann.

Mesiti, M., Celle, R., Sorrenti, M. A., & Guerrini, G. (2006). X-Evolution: A System for XML Schema Evolution and Document Adaptation. In *EDBT*, (pp 1143-1146).

Nicola, M., & Jain, U. (2007). *Update XML in DB2 9.5.* Retrieved from www.ibm.com/developerworks/db2/library/techarticle/dm-0710nicola/

Nicola, M. & van der Linden, B. (2005). *Native XML Support in DB2 Universal Database.*

Pal, S., Tomic, D., Berg, B., & Xavier, J. (2006). Managing Collections of XML Schemas in Microsoft SQL Server 2005. In *Proc. Of the 10th Int'l Conference on Extending Database Technology*, (pp. 1102-1105).

Raghavachari, M., & Shmueli, O. (2006). Conflicting XML Updates. In *EDBT 2006*, (pp. 552-569).

Roddick, J. F. (1995). A Survey of Schema Versioning Issues for Database Systems. *Information and Software Technology, 37*(7), 383–393. doi:10.1016/0950-5849(95)91494-K

Rosado, L. A., Márquez, A. P., & Gil, J. M. (2007). Managing Branch Versioning in Versioned/Temporal XML Documents. In *5th International XML Database Symposium (XSym)*, (pp. 107-121).

Rosado, L. A., Márquez, A. P., & González, J. M. F. (2006): Representing Versions in XML Documents Using Versionstamp. In *4th International Workshop on Evolution and Change in Data Management – (ER Workshop)*, (pp. 257-267).

Snodgrass, R.T, Dyreson, Currim, F., Currim, S., Joshi, S. (2008). Validating quicksand: Temporal schema versioning in τXSchema. *Data & Knowledge Engineering, 65*, 223–242. doi:10.1016/j.datak.2007.09.003

Software AG. (2008). *Tamino Schema Editor.* On-line Documentation.

Steegmans, B., et al. (2004). *XML for DB2 Information Integration*. Redmond, WA: IBM Redbook Series.

Tan, M., & Goh, A. (2004). Keeping Pace with Evolving XML-Based Specifications. In *Current Trends in Database Technology – EDBT Workshops*, (LNCS Vol. 3268, pp. 280-288).

Vithanala, P. (2005). *Introduction to XQuery in SQL Server 2005*. Retrieved from http://msdn.microsoft.com

Wang, F., & Zaniolo, C. (2008). Temporal Queries and Version Management for XML Document Archives. [DKE]. *Journal of Data and Knowledge Engineering*, *65*, 304–324. doi:10.1016/j.datak.2007.08.002

Chapter 17
Integration of Relational and Native Approaches to XML Query Processing

Huayu Wu
National University of Singapore, Singapore

Tok Wang Ling
National University of Singapore, Singapore

ABSTRACT

Existing XML twig pattern query processing algorithms fall into two classes: the relational approach and the native approach. Both kinds of approaches have their advantages and limitations. Particularly, the relational approach can search for data values (content search) efficiently using tables, but it is not efficient to match query structure to documents (structural search). The native approach processes structural search efficiently, but it has problem dealing with values. In this chapter, a hybrid approach for XML query processing is introduced. In this approach, the content search and the structural search in a twig pattern query are performed separately using the data structures in the relational approach and the native approach, i.e. relational tables and inverted lists. The authors show that this hybrid style technique can process both structural search and content search efficiently, and then improve the query processing performance comparing to the existing approaches. Furthermore, when more semantic information on object class and relationship between objects in the XML document is known, the relational tables used can be optimized according to such semantic information to achieve a better performance. Finally after performing twig pattern matching, value results can be extracted easily using relational tables, rather than navigating the document again in many other approaches.

INTRODUCTION

XML is emerging as a standard format for data representation and exchange over the Internet. As a result, there is a compelling need of developing

DOI: 10.4018/978-1-61520-727-5.ch017

efficient algorithms to query XML data. An XML document is normally modeled as a tree, without considering ID references. In an XML tree, the nodes represent the elements, attributes and values in the document and the edges reflect the nested relationships between elements, attributes and values. Figure 1 shows a small XML document with

Figure 1. An XML document with tree model representation.

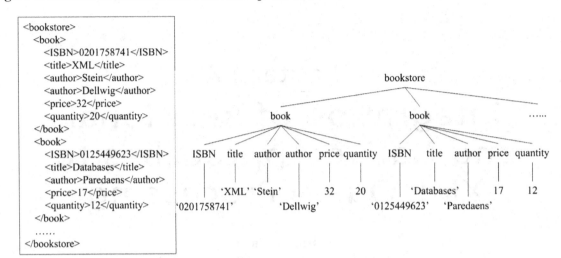

its tree model representation. In most standard XML query languages, e.g. XPath and XQuery recommended by W3C, the core pattern of a query is also a tree structure (or a set of tree structures). We call such a tree-structured query pattern a *twig pattern*. Finding all occurrences of a twig pattern query in an XML document is considered as an essential operation for XML query processing. Consider a query to find the titles of all books written by Paredaens in the bookstore document shown in Figure 1, the corresponding XPath expression is *//book[author="Paredaens"]/title*, and the twig pattern representation of this XPath query is shown in Figure 2.

Normally, an XML query consists of structural search and content search. The structural search in a query aims to find all matches that satisfy the structural constraints between query nodes in the document. Whereas the content search filters the query result based on the value comparison in query predicates. For the above XPath query, *//book[author]/title* is a structural search and *author="Paredaens"* is a content search. How to efficiently process structural search and content search are equivalently important to achieve a good query processing performance.

Figure 2. Example twig pattern query.

The XML query processing algorithms are categorized into two classes: the relational approach and the native approach. In the early stage, many research works focus on using relational databases to store and query semi-structured XML data. The main idea of the relational approach is to shred XML documents into relational tables, and transform XML queries into SQL queries to query the database. During query transformation, an XML query structure is normally expressed by multiple selections and joins in the corresponding SQL statement, thus the overhead on these table operations, especially join, may seriously affect the efficiency of the structural search. Later how to process XML queries natively becomes a hot research topic, because the native approach does not use relational database and avoids the overhead on relational operations. The structural join based approach is an important native approach widely accepted by researchers. In this approach, inverted lists are used to store the occurrences of each type of document node, in terms of their positional labels, and the queries are processed by performing structural joins between query nodes using corresponding inverted lists. The structural join based approach is proven very efficient to process structural search, in contrast with the relational approach. However, the inverted list could not perform value comparison in content search efficiently. Furthermore, after finding the occurrences of a query pattern in a given document, inverted list is not feasible to extract child values to answer the query based on positional labels. Value extraction has to be done by navigating the original document, which is obviously not efficient.

In this chapter, we integrate the ideas of the relational approach and the native approach to process XML twig pattern queries. In more details, both relational tables and inverted lists are used to perform content search and structural search separately in a query. With this hybrid approach, problems in the relational approach and the native approach are avoided and the advantages are inherited. Furthermore, the relational tables used in this approach can be optimized when more semantics on object is known in XML documents. These semantic optimizations will further enhance the query processing efficiency. Before we move to the details, some background knowledge and related work are introduced in advance.

BACKGROUND

Twig Pattern Query and Document Labeling

As mentioned earlier, an XML document is normally modeled as a tree, without considering ID references. In an XML tree, two nodes connected by a tree edge are in parent-child (PC) relationship, and the two nodes on the same path are in ancestor-descendant (AD) relationship. A twig pattern query is also in tree structure, but different from document tree, the edge in a twig pattern query can be either single lined ('/') or double lined ('//'). The '/' (or '//') edge specifies that the two document nodes which match the two query nodes at the ends of the edge must be in parent-child (or ancestor-descendant) relationship. To process a twig pattern query means to find the occurrences of the query pattern in a given document tree, in such a way that (1) the query nodes have the identical names as the corresponding document nodes and (2) the relationships indicated by '/' and '//' edges in the query are satisfied between the corresponding document nodes. Checking the condition (1) can be simply done by comparing the string names between query nodes and document nodes, whereas checking the PC or AC relationship between two document nodes in the condition (2) is normally processed by assigning *positional labels* (or *labels* if no confusion arises) to each document node and comparing the labels of the two nodes. Thus, the basic requirement of document labeling is that the PC or AD relationship between two document nodes must be easily determined by their labels.

There are multiple labeling schemes for static XML documents, which are seldom updated, as well as dynamic XML documents with frequent updates. For example, the containment labeling scheme (Zhang, Naughton, DeWitt, Luo & Lohman, 2001) can be used for static documents, and the QED scheme (Li & Ling, 2005) can be used for dynamic documents. In this chapter, we adopt the containment labeling scheme for illustrations. In the containment labeling scheme, each positional label contains three numbers: *pre*, *post* and *level*. *Pre* and *post* are the pre-order and post-order traversal position of the associated node in the document tree, and *level* is the depth of the associated node in the document tree. The PC or AD relationship between two nodes can be determined by checking their labels based on the following properties:

Figure 3. The bookstore document with containment labeling

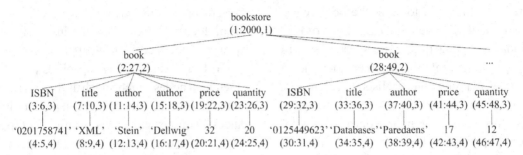

(i) Node *a* is an ancestor of node *b* in an XML tree, if and only if the interval (*a.pre, a.post*) contains the interval (*b.pre, b.post*), or say

a.pre < *b.pre* < *b.post* < *a.post*

(ii) Node *a* is the parent of node *b* in an XML tree, if and only if the interval (*a.pre, a.post*) contains the interval (*b.pre, b.post*) and *a* is one level higher than *b*, or say

a.pre < *b.pre* < *b.post* < *a.post* and *a.level* + *1* = *b.level*

The labeled document tree for the bookstore document shown in Figure 1 using containment labeling scheme is shown in Figure 3.

Semantic Information on Object, Property and Value

Object, or entity, is a unit to model a person, place, thing, concept, or event about which a system needs to manage information. Each object has a number of properties, which are also referred as attributes, to describe the object from different aspects. In database area, object with properties is also an important information unit for data management. For example, the ER model in relational databases basically designs a database with the information of object and relationship between objects. Queries, no matter in relational databases or in XML databases, are normally object oriented too, because most queries are either to find certain property values of a particular object or to find the relationships between several objects.

In an XML document tree, value and property can be easily identified. We consider each leaf text node as a value node, and the parent of each value node as a property node. For example, in the document tree in Figure 3, the *'XML'* node is a value node, and its parent node *title* is a property node. This inference always holds for any types of documents, regardless of whether there is other semantic information known or not. The relational table built in our approach is based on inferred property and value, as discussed later.

However, to identify an object or a relationship between two or more objects is not so trivial. Intuitively, we can consider the parent of each property node as an object node, e.g. in Figure 3, the parent node *book* of each property *title* is an object node. Due to the heterogeneity of XML data, this inference rule does not hold sometimes. Consider two different designs of book data in Figure 4, which contains similar information as the document shown in Figure 3. In these two designs, the parents of each *author* property are *authors* and *basic_info*. Obviously they are not objects. There are many works trying to identify object in XML data. Liu et al. (2007) infer an object by its cardinality in DTD. Ling et al. (2005) design a semantic rich schema for XML data in which objects are explicitly specified. Chen et al. (2003) and Yu et al. (2006) discover semantics like key and functional dependency in XML data, which can help to identify object. Spink (2002) and Doan et al. (2006) identify object by

Figure 4. Two different designs for book information.

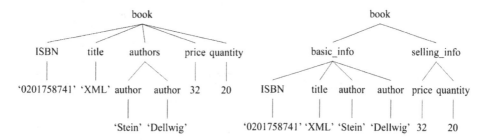

interacting with the user. For many public XML data, the object information is normally declared by the document owner or even can be captured by common sense.

The hybrid approach introduced in this chapter constructs relational tables based on the default property information. Once the semantic information about object is available, we can optimize the tables to be object based. Using the object-based tables the query processing performance can be further improved. Details about the semantic optimization are introduced later.

EXISTING WORK

Relational Approach

Relational model is a dominant model for structured data. Over decades, relational database management systems (RDBMS) have been well developed to store and query structured data. As XML becomes more and more popular, many researchers and organizations put more efforts into designing algorithms to store and query semistructured XML data using the mature RDBMS. Generally, those relational approaches shred XML documents into relational tables and transform XML queries into SQL statements to query the database. The advantage of the relational approach is that the existing query optimizer in relational databases can be directly used to optimize the transformed queries. Especially for the queries

with content search, the RDBMS can not only process the value comparisons efficiently, but also push the value predicates ahead of table joins using the optimizer.

There are multiple shredding methods proposed for the relational approach, which are classified into structure-based method and schema-based method. The structure-based method decomposes an XML document tree based on different tree components. For example, the node approach (Zhang et al, 2001) stores each document node with its positional label into relational tables, as shown in Figure 5(a). A twig pattern query, under the node approach, is decomposed into separate nodes, and the structural joins between nodes in the twig pattern query are transformed into θ-joins on labels between tables in SQL. The twig pattern query shown in Figure 2 is transformed as:

select*title.value*

from*Node book, Node title, Node author*

where*book.pre<title.pre and book.post>title. post and book.level=title.level-1 and*

book.pre<author.pre and book.post>author. post and book.level=author.level-1 and

author.value= 'Paredaens'

We can see that when the query is complex, the node approach may involve too many θ-joins for structural search, which is not as efficient as equi-join to process using most RDBMS. The edge approach (Florescu & Kossmann, 1999) is quite similar to the node approach, except the edge approach puts each edge into tables. Thus it suffers the same efficiency problem as the node

Figure 5. Example tables in relational approaches. (a) Node table, (b) Path table

tag_name	pre	end	level	value
book	2	27	2	null
ISBN	3	6	3	0201758741
title	7	10	3	XML
...	...	...	...	...
book	28	49	2	null
...	...	...	...	...

path	pre	end	level	value
/bookstore	1	2000	1	null
/bookstore/book	2	27	2	null
/bookstore/book/ISBN	3	6	3	0201758741
...	...	...	...	...
/bookstore/book	28	49	2	null
...	...	...	...	...

Figure 6. Example DTD, hierarchical structural between DTD elements, and the relations

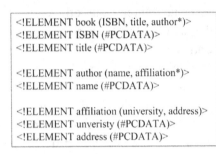

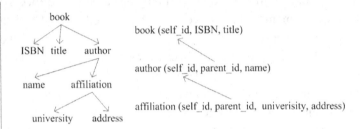

approach for structural search. The path approach (Yoshikawa, Amagasa, Shimura & Uemura, 2001; Pal et al, 2004) is another kind of structure-based method in the relational approach, which stores each path wholly without decomposition. One example path table is shown in Figure 5(b). The path approach saves table joins between different nodes or edges along the same path, however, to perform a structural search involving "//"-axis, the path based approach has to do a string pattern matching ("LIKE" in SQL) on the *path* column, which is also an expensive operation for relational database systems.

The other class of shredding methods in the relational approach is the schema-based method (Shanmugasundaram et al, 1999; Shanmugasundaram et al, 2001). By this method, XML documents are shredded based on schematic information, e.g. DTD. As a result, different from the structure-based method, the relational tables in the schema-based method vary for documents with different schemas. Consider the example shown in

Figure 6. Based on the DTD, we can get a hierarchical structure between elements. Then from the hierarchical structure, a set of relational tables are built. The *self_id* and *parent_id* are the primary key and the foreign key of each table, which play as join attributes during query processing.

The schema-based approach is efficient for XML documents without recursive tags and the queries without "//"-axis, such as the document in Figure 3 and the query in Figure 2. However, when dealing with "//"-axis in a deep document with recursive tags, the schema-based approach may have difficulty in determining which relational tables should be joined and how many times to join them. Consider a fragment <VP><NP><VP><NP><PP>...</PP></NP></VP></NP></VP> in the TreeBank data (TreeBank, 2002) with many recursively nested elements. When we process a query VP//NP, the schema-based approach can hardly determine what tables between VP and NP should be joined and how many times to join those tables.

To meet the illustration of semantic optimizations, the example document shown in this chapter is rather flat and cannot reflect the problems in structural search for all relational approaches. However, when we also consider a deep and recursive document, such as the TreeBank, we can see that all these relational approaches suffer from problems in structural search.

Native Approach

To improve the performance of structural search in twig pattern queries, many native approaches are proposed. In a native approach, documents are not stored using relational tables, thus the overhead on table joins can be avoided. One direct native approach is the navigational approach, which traverses tree-structured XML document to find the occurrences of each query pattern. To facilitate the document traversal, some APIs, e.g. SAX parser (http://www.saxproject.org), are normal used in the navigational approach. Similar to the navigational approach, some works (Wang, Park, Fan & Yu, 2003; Rao & Moon, 2004) transform XML documents and twig pattern queries into sequences, and perform subsequence matching to find the query occurrences in the documents. Both the navigational approach and the subsequence matching based approach may cause a high I/O cost, as the whole document will be considered during query processing. The structural join based approach is an important class of the native approach and has attracted a lot of research interest. In the structural join based approach, an inverted list for each type of document node is adopted to organize all the node occurrences of that node type, in terms of the positional labels of each corresponding node, in document order. To process a twig pattern query, only the inverted lists for the relevant node types are scanned. Structural joins between any pair of connected query nodes are performed by comparing the labels in the inverted lists of the two nodes, to determine whether the

positional relationship (PC or AD relationship) specified by the query edge is satisfied. The hybrid approach proposed in this chapter incorporate relational tables into the structural join based native approach to process XML queries, thus we mainly discuss the existing structural join based algorithms.

In the early stage, Zhang et al. (2001) proposed a *multi-predicate merge join* algorithm based on the containment labeling scheme, and showed the superiority over several relational approaches. Later Al-Khalifa et al. (2002) pointed out an efficiency problem of Zhang's work, and proposed an improved stack-based algorithm. Both of the two algorithms are called binary join based approaches, because they decompose the twig pattern queries into binary relationships, i.e. "/" or "//" between two query nodes, and then match each binary relationship and combine the binary matches. The major problem of this binary join based approach is that many binary matches are useless intermediate results. A holistic twig join algorithm, *TwigStack*, was proposed later (Bruno, Koudas & Srivastava, 2002) to avoid the large size of useless intermediate results. The idea of TwigStack is introducing multiple stacks to perform structural joins for each query path, without decomposing it into binary relationships, and then merge the paths to get final result. TwigStack is proven optimal for twig pattern queries with only "//"-axis. There are many subsequent works to optimize TwigStack to improve performance, or extend it to solve different problems. In particular, Lu et al. (2004) introduced a list structure to make TwigStack optimal for queries containing parent-child relationships. *TSGeneric* (Jiang, Wang, Lu & Yu, 2003) improved the query performance based on indexing each inverted list and skipping labels within one list. Chen et al. (2005) divided one inverted list into several sub-lists associated to each prefix path or each (tag, level) pair and pruned some sub-lists before evaluating a twig pattern. Lu et al. (2005) used Extended Dewey labeling scheme and scanned only the labels of leaf nodes in a twig query. Jiang et al. (2004) and Yu et al. (2006) extended twig pattern query to support OR-predicate and NOT-predicate separately.

Also there are different graphic indexes proposed to improve the query evaluation efficiency of the structural join based algorithms. *DataGuides* (Goldman & Widom, 1999) is an early path index which could cover all path information. Later *1-index* (Milo & Suciu, 1999) and *A(k)-index* (Kaushik, Shenoy, Bohannon & Gudes, 2002) were proposed to reduce the index size based on backward bisimilarity and k-bisimilarity. F&B index (Kaushik, Rohannon, Naughton & Korth, 2002; Wang et al, 2005) is proven to be the smallest index to cover all twig patterns for any XML document, though its size is normally too large. Generally these graphic indexes can aid the structural join based twig pattern matching algorithms by saving structural joins in partial path or twig in the query pattern. A recent work, TwigX-Guide (Haw & Lee, 2008) also showed that the performance of a structural join based approach can be improved by incorporating graphic index into query processing. These graphic indexes can also be used for structural search in the hybrid approach introduced in this chapter.

The efficient processing of structural search makes the structural join based algorithms a good choice for XML twig pattern query processing. However, most structural join based algorithms do not differentiate content search from structural search. Using structural join techniques to process content search may cause several problems (Wu, Ling & Chen, 2007), e.g. treating content nodes as structural nodes will produce tremendous number of inverted lists due to the large variety of contents, structural search is inefficient to process range search such as *age>30*, etc. Also because inverted list can only be used to retrieve labels by node names, but not available to get child values based on node labels, additional document navigation

is necessary to extract actual values to answer a query. The relational approach does not have such problems in content search and value extraction, as both the retrieval of labels by node names and the retrieval of values by labels can be done in relational tables.

Hybrid Management of Relational Data and XML

To meet the increasing needs of the semi-structured XML data, many database systems extend their relational implementation to support XML format. Most database systems, e.g. IBM System RX (Beyer et al, 2005), Oracle 11g (Zhang, et al, 2009) and Microsoft SQL Server 2005 (O'Neil, O'Neil, Pal, Cseri, Schaller & Westbury, 2004), claim that their systems are hybrid for both relational data and native XML data. However, the term "hybrid" in their systems is different from the "hybrid" we refer to in query processing. In System RX and Oracle 11g, XML data is not shredded into tables, but stored wholly as either a tree structure or a binary stream on disk. They allow queries to mix SQL syntax and XQuery syntax, but when they execute an XML query over the native XML data, actually they use the navigational native approach, which scans the whole document to return the found matches. Similarly, SQL Server 2005 also indicates their XML storage is native. However, to process an XML query, their approach is pure relational approach. For each XML document, they have a table in which each tuple corresponds to an XML node with OrdPath label (O'Neil, O'Neil, Pal, Cseri, Schaller & Westbury, 2004). XML queries are eventually transformed into SQL and processed over the relational tables. As we see, in those database systems, the "hybrid" means they support both relational format and XML format on a unique platform. However, when they process an XML query, they either use a relational approach or a native approach.

A Summary on Relational Approach and Native Approach

Both the relational approach and the native approach to process XML queries have their own advantages and disadvantages. In the relational approach, the values in an XML document can be efficiently managed using relational tables, and both content search and content extraction can be easily performed by SQL selection. However, though there are different methods to shred XML data into tables, all of them suffer from problems in performing structural search. The native approach is a good choice for structural search, especially for "//"-axis queries. However, the native approach cannot perform content search efficiently, and cannot extract values to answer a query from the inverted list index.

It is not easy to generally comment on which kind of approach is better in query processing performance, because both approaches have a number of variants, and both approaches may employ different indexes to speed up query processing. In some preliminary reports, Zhang et al. (2001) conducted experiments to show a binary structural join method is better than the node based relational approach, Chaudhri et al. (2003) concluded that the native approach is suitable for large data sets and the relational approach is good for smaller data sets. However, all the comparisons are done by particular implementations of the relational approach and the native approach. As mentioned by Serna et al. (2005), there is no tool feasible to analyze whether XML data should be queried natively or using RDBMS, for a better performance.

Although it is hard to compare the two approaches, the advantages and limitations of the two approaches are obvious. It will be interesting to find a way to combine the advantages of the relational approach and the native approach, and avoid the limitations. Motivated on this, in this chapter we introduce a hybrid approach, which integrates relational tables into structural join based native approach to process twig pattern queries.

HYBRID APPROACH IN XML QUERY PROCESSING

An Overview

We have seen that both the relational approach and the native approach have their advantages and limitations. An interesting attempt is to design a hybrid algorithm that integrates the relational approach and the native approach to process XML queries. In the hybrid algorithm, the structural search can be simply performed by structural joins using inverted lists, but how to design relational tables for content search and final answer extraction becomes a question. The relational tables can be designed based on the semantic information including object, relationship between objects, property and value. In general cases, we assume no object information is available and build relational tables based on the default semantics on property: the parent node of each value is a property node, which is always correct for all documents. Once we have more information on object, the tables can be optimized to be object-based tables, which can process queries more efficiently as shown later.

The system maintains two sets of data structures when loading and parsing an XML document: inverted lists and relational tables. Inverted lists store the node labels of each type of document node, and relational tables store each value with the label of its associated property (or object, in optimizations). There are three steps to process a twig pattern query. . First the system performs content search for the value comparisons in query predicates using relational tables, and rewrites the query by removing the value comparisons. In the second step, the rewritten query, which contains only structural constraints, is processed by any structural join based algorithm, e.g. TwigStack, using inverted lists. The last step is to extract the

Figure 7. General steps of twig pattern processing using the semantic approach.

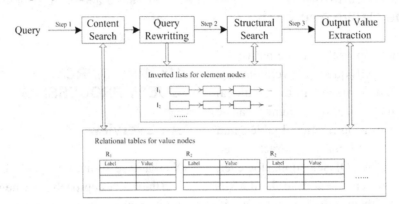

values to answer the query from the relational tables. The general process is shown in Figure 7. We perform content search before structural search because similar to the selection operation in SQL queries, content search normally leads high selectivity. Next we discuss how to construct inverted lists and relational tables, and how to process an XML twig pattern query.

Data Structure Construction

In this section, we discuss how to construct different data structures when the system loads an XML document and makes it ready to answer twig pattern queries. As a hybrid approach, there are two important data structures to maintain: inverted list and relational table. Inverted list is applicable to perform structural search in a query, which is commonly used in many structural join based twig pattern query processing algorithms,

as well as many XML keyword search algorithms. After assigning positional labels to each document node, we put the labels for each type of node into one inverted list, in document order. Different from many other algorithms, we do not maintain inverted lists for value nodes. Instead, we store each value with the label of its associated property or object node into a relational table. Next, we describe the new document labeling and the relational tables in more details.

When we label the document, value nodes are not labeled. Then different from the document labeling in Figure 3, the new labeled tree for the bookstore document is shown in Figure 8.

As mentioned earlier, the relational tables are built based on semantics such as object, relationship between objects, property and value. Without additional information, we can only infer the semantics of property and value. Based on this information, we construct relational tables for

Figure 8. New labeled tree for the bookstore document, with value nodes unlabeled.

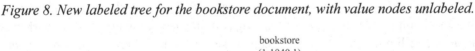
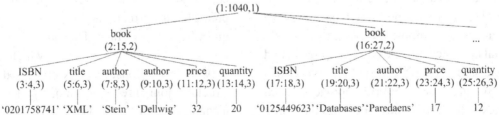

Figure 9. Example property tables for properties title, author and price.

R_title

label	value
(5:6,3)	XML
(19:20,3)	Databases
...	...

R_author

label	value
(7:8,3)	Stein
(9:10,3)	Dellwig
(21:22,3)	Paredaens
...	...

R_price

label	value
(11:12,3)	32
(23:24,3)	17
...	...

each type of property in such a way that the value under each property of this type is stored in one tuple, together with the label of the corresponding property node. The relational tables for the properties *title*, *author* and *price* are shown in Figure 9. We call them property tables.

The relational tables to store data values and the corresponding property labels have the following advantages for query processing:

- Bi-directional selection. From the table, we could not only select the property labels from a given value, but also select the value based on a property label. This is essential for query processing because when we perform content search we need to find relevant labels from values, whereas to answer the query, we need to extract values based on labels.

- Easy maintenance. Since the tuples in each table are not necessarily ordered by label or value, any insertion or deletion does not affect existing tuples. Some systems, e.g. System RX (Beyer et al, 2005), build value based index for structural paths or nodes to aid content search. Every time the document is updated, their index has to be updated as well.

- Advanced content search support. With the powerful SQL for table selection, twig pattern queries with range comparisons, or even *contains* functions in query predicates can be processed. More on *contains* func-

tion can be found in the XPath specification (http://www.w3.org/TR/xpath).

Query Processing

As shown in Figure 7, query processing in our approach contains three steps: content search and query rewriting, structural search, and value extraction. Now we describe the steps in details.

Content Search and Query Rewriting

In many native twig pattern query processing algorithms, content search is generally not differentiated from structural search. Besides the drawbacks mentioned in the previous sections, to mix content search with structural search also affects a good query plan generation, in which content search should be performed before structural search for the similar reason as selection 'push ahead' in relational optimizers.

In this hybrid approach, content search and structural search are performed separately. As a result, we can perform content search for the value comparisons in predicates first. After that the inverted lists for the relevant query nodes are reduced, and the query is simplified by removing the value comparisons correspondingly. To perform structural search for a simplified query with smaller inverted list on certain query nodes could significantly improve the performance. Also, using relational table to perform content search can efficiently support range search.

Figure 10. The rewritten query of the query shown in Figure 2.

The inverted list for the query node *author*_{Paredaens} contains only the labels of property *author* whose child value is 'Paredaens', e.g. the lable (21:22,3); wheares in the original query, the inverted list for the query node *author* contains all the *author* labels, including (7:8,3), (9:10.3), etc.

Given a twig pattern query, we can identify all the value comparisons in predicates. A value comparison can be formulated as *property operator 'value'*. For example, in the query shown in Figure 2, the value comparison is *author = 'Paredaens'*. For each value comparison, we perform content search by accessing the corresponding property table to execute a SQL selection, to find all the labels satisfying the value comparison. The selected results are put into a temporary inverted list for the corresponding property. Since the content search has been performed, the original twig pattern query can be rewritten by removing the value comparisons, and probably renaming the corresponding property nodes so that the system knows the new inverted lists for these properties should take effect.

We take the twig pattern query in Figure 2 as an example to illustrate the content search process. The predicate *author = 'Paredaens'* is the only value comparison requiring content search. We use the table R_{author}, which is shown in Figure 9, to perform this content search by selecting labels based on the value of 'Paredaens'. Then we put the selected labels into a new inverted list for the property *author*. After processing the content search, the original query can be rewritten by removing the value comparison on the property *author*, as shown in Figure 10. We rename the *author* node as *author*_{paredaens}, so that the structural search algorithm knows the new inverted list should be used for this query node.

The reason that we can simplify the original query by removing the value comparison is we actually have already solve this content search and the labels in the new inverted list for *author*_{Paredaens} all correspond to the author nodes with child value

of 'Paredaens'. Then we can perform structural search for the simplified query with the reduced inverted list for author node.

Structural Search and Value Extraction

There are many structural join based algorithms to perform structural search, e.g. TwigStack. They scan the inverted lists for the relevant query nodes, and perform structural joins for each pair of query nodes in "/" or "//" relationship in the twig pattern query. We can adopt any of them to perform structural search in our hybrid approach. Note that after performing structural search for the rewritten query, the newly created inverted lists for some property nodes are deleted because they are particularly for the current query only. The details of how to perform structural join using those algorithms are not presented in this chapter.

The results of structural search (twig pattern matching) are all the occurrences of the query structure in the document tree, in terms of labels. However, these labels are meaningless to users. We have to extract the actual data values based on the labels of the output query nodes. The property table again performs a role. For the same query example, after finding the label (19:20,3) for the title node, we can access the table R_{title} to extract the value of 'Databases' for that label, and return this value to the user.

A Summary

The introduced hybrid approach performs content search and structural search of a twig pattern query separately using relational tables and inverted lists. By performing content search first, the query can be simplified and the relevant inverted lists are reduced, to achieve a better performance in pattern matching. The trade-off of query simplification and inverted list reduction is the table selection during content search. In most RDBMS, selection can be executed very efficiently; it will not affect the benefit we gain from query simplification and inverted list reduction, as shown in experimental studies (Wu, Ling & Chen, 2007).

The hybrid approach effectively solves problems in the relational approach and the native approach. The problems in content management, content search and content extraction appearing in the native approach are covered by relational tables; while the inefficiency of performing structural search, e.g. "//"-axis joins, in the relational approach is solved by native structural joins using inverted lists.

We conducted experiments to validate the efficiency of the hybird approach. First, we compare it to a proven efficient relational approach (Grust, van Keulen & Teubner, 2004). This relational approach is an optimized node based approach, which is much more efficient than the traditional node approach, the edge approach, and a native approach (though the author did not mention the exact implementation of the native approach) by their reports. For all queries, the hybrid approach outperforms the optimized node approach. In more details, with relational index built for the optimized node approach, the hybrid approach is 2-3 times faster. If there is no index built, it is 6-8 times faster than the optimized node approach.

Then we compare the hybrid approach to a well known native approach, TwigStack. We do not use any graphic index (e.g. DataGuides, F&B index) to aim structural joins in both approaches. When the queries do not contain value comparisons as predicates, the hybrid approach is the same as TwigStack because only structural search is involved during query processing. If the queries have value comparisons, it is 10%-70% better than TwigStack, depending on the number of value predicates and the selectivity of the predicates.

SEMANTIC OPTIMZATIONS

The approach introduced in the previous section is based on property tables. As stated earlier, the semantics on property and value is default for all XML documents, so the approach is a general approach for any document and any twig pattern query. When other semantics, such as object and relationship between objects, is known for a particular document, the relational tables can be optimized based on such information, to achieve a better performance. The motivation of the object-based optimization is that the object is an important information unit for most queries. By building relational tables based on object, we can not only save the structural join between an object and its properties, but also avoid affecting "//"-axis join between the object and other internal elements, which is a serious problem in the path-based relational approach (to illustrate the semantic optimization, we did not use a deep document with recursive tags as example and then the drawbacks of relational tables in "//"-axis search is not reflected in our example document). In this section, we introduce three semantic optimizations.

Optimization 1: Object/ Property Table

The use of the property table to perform content search improves the query processing performance in two aspects: the reduction of labels in the inverted lists for the corresponding property query node, and the reduction of number of query nodes and the number of structural joins. If we have knowledge on objects, we can further reduce the inverted lists, query nodes and structural joins.

Consider the twig pattern query in Figure 2 again. Suppose the author Paredaens only appears once in the bookstore document, then after performing content search using the property table, the inverted list for *author* contains only one label. However, the inverted list for the query

Figure 11. Example object/property tables for the bookstore document.

$R_{book/title}$

label	value
(2:15,2)	XML
(16:27,2)	Databases
...	...

$R_{book/author}$

label	value
(2:15,2)	Stein
(2:15,2)	Dellwig
(16:27,2)	Paredaens
...	...

$R_{book/price}$

label	value
(2:15,2)	32
(16:27,2)	17
...	...

Figure 12. The rewritten query of the query shown in Figure 2, under Optimization 1.

The inverted list for the query node $book_{author=Paredaens}$ contains only the labels of object *book* whose property *author* has a value of 'Paredaens', e.g. the lable (16:27,2); wheares in the original query, the inverted list for the query node *book* contains all the *book* labels, including (2:15,2), etc.

node *book* still contains quite a lot of labels, though we know only one of them satisfies the condition that *author = 'Paredaens'*. If we know *book* is an object for the property *author*, we can optimize the property table to be object/property table, and reduce the labels of *book* directly from the constraints on *author*. Several example object/property tables for the bookstore document are shown in Figure 11.

Comparing the object/property tables in Figure 11 to the property tables in Figure 9, we can find that the name of each object/property table indicates both the object and the property, and the labels in each object/property table are the labels of the corresponding object, instead of property. Now the content search of the twig pattern query in Figure 2 can be performed in the table $R_{book/author}$ to directly reduce the labels in the inverted list for *book*, and the original query can be rewritten as shown in Figure 12. The renamed node $book_{author=Paredaens}$ in the rewritten query is to indicate that the new inverted list, generated during content search processing, should take effect for this new *book* node.

We can see now the rewritten query contains fewer query nodes and requires fewer structural joins, comparing to the rewritten query using property tables in Figure 10. Furthermore, the inverted list for book in the rewritten query contains only a few labels, which makes the only structural join quite efficient.

The problem of this optimization is that the order information of the multi-valued properties cannot be kept using object/property tables. For example, author is a multi-valued property and the order of authors of a certain book may be important, but using the book/author table, we cannot tell the order of two authors with the same book label. To solve this problem, we can simply put an additional column containing ordinal number of each property value under the same object.

Optimization 2: Object Table

It is very common that a query contains multiple predicates on different properties of the same object. In this case, using Optimization 1, we need to join multiple object/property tables for the different properties to get the object labels. If we can merge the object/property tables for the same object, we can do the selection based on multiple predicates in one table. This motivates a second optimization.

Figure 13. Book tables for the bookstore document under Optimization 2.

R_{book}

label	ISBN	title	price	quantity
(2:15,2)	0201758741	XML	32	20
(16:27,2)	0125449623	Databases	17	12
...	...	...	...	...

$R_{book/author}$

label	value
(2:15,2)	Stein
(2:15,2)	Dellwig
(16:27,2)	Paredaens
...	...

Figure 14. An example query and query rewriting under Optimization 2.

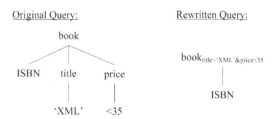

In Optimization 2, we merge the object/property tables for the same object and single-valued properties, to get object tables. For multi-valued properties, we just keep the object/property tables. The tables for the bookstore document under Optimization 2 are shown in Figure 13.

The table R_{book} is an object table containing all the single-valued properties for book. Using this table, queries with multiple predicates could be executed more efficiently. For example, consider a query to find the ISBN of the books with title of XML and price less than 35. The original twig pattern for this query, and the rewritten query using object table under Optimization 2 are shown in Figure 14.

With the object table for book, the original query can be significantly simplified, and the performance is improved undoubtedly. If the multiple predicates on the same object involve both single-valued properties and multi-valued properties, we can perform selection for all single-valued properties in the object table, and then join with the selection results from the object/property tables for the multi-valued properties.

The object table itself has several potential problems. We discuss two problems of the object table, with proposed solutions.

Rare Property

Properties may optionally appear under the belonging objects. Some of them even appear quite rarely. We call these properties *rare properties*. In an object table, if we keep a column for each rare property, the table may contain too many NULL entries. For example in the bookstore document, if we create an additional column of *second_title* in the book table, but actually only a few books have a second title, then for most tuples that field will be NULL. Many RDBMS can deal with this case in their physical storage. In case some systems do not have this function, we can maintain a rare property table to store all such rare properties. The rare property table contains several fields: the object label, the object name, the rare property name and the property value. Suppose in the bookstore document, *second_title* and *sale_region* are two rare properties, the rare property table for this

Figure 15. Rare property table for the bookstore document.

$R_{rare\_property}$

label	object	property	value
(76:89,2)	book	second_title	A first course
(126:141,2)	book	sale_region	Singapore
(252:269,2)	book	second_title	An introduction to data mining
...	...	...	...

Figure 16. Vertical partitioning for the book table.

R_{book_p1}

label	title
(2:15,2)	XML
(16:27,2)	Databases
...	...

R_{book_p2}

label	ISBN	price	quantity
(2:15,2)	0201758741	32	20
(16:27,2)	0125449623	17	12
...	...	...	...

document is shown in Figure 15. Queries involving rare properties are processed by accessing the rare property table with the object name and the property name.

Vertical Partitioning

Another problem of the object table is about the tuple size. Since the object table stores values of all single-valued properties, the size of each tuple may be large. When we perform a selection based on only a few properties, all other properties are also loaded. This results a high I/O cost.

A common way in RDBMS design to reduce such I/O cost is the vertical partitioning of a table (Navathe, Ceri, Wiederhold & Dou, 1984). Vertical partitioning means the attributes in a physical table are divided into several groups and to create separate tables for every group of attributes. When we perform a selection, only the smaller table containing the relevant attributes is loaded. In practice, a similar vertical partitioning technique can be adopted to avoid high I/O cost of loading all property values in an object table. For example, in the bookstore document, suppose many twig pattern queries contain the predicates

on book titles. To perform such a content search, we need to select book labels based on titles. Now we can split the original book table into two smaller tables, one of which contains labels and titles and the other one contains labels and the rest properties. The partitioning results are shown in Figure 16. To answer such queries, we only need to access the table R_{book_p1}, in which the tuple sizes are much smaller.

Optimization 3: Relationship Table

XML document tree cannot reflect the relationships between objects, though such relationships do exist and sometimes are very useful to interpret queries and to improve query processing performance. Consider another bookstore document with information about branches, as shown in Figure 17. In this document, the property *quantity* is actually not a property of *book*, but a property of the *relationship* between branch and book.

When we have such relationship information, we can build a relationship table to store the property values of the corresponding relationship, and the labels of the participating objects. This relationship table is quite similar to the relation-

Figure 17. The bookstore document with branch information.

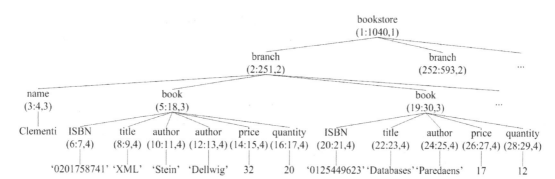

ship table in ER design in RDBMS. The table for the relationship between branch and book is shown in Figure 18. Note that in this example, the relationship is a binary relationship between two objects. The relationship table can also be constructed based on ternary or n-ary relationships in the document.

Consider a query to find the branch which has some book with a low quantity that less than 15, without caring which book exactly. For this query, the original twig pattern expression and the rewritten expression under the help of the relationship table are shown in Figure 19. The content search is performed by selecting branch labels based on the value comparison on quantity from the relationship table. As a result, in the rewritten query we can remove the book node without affecting the query results. In the simplified rewritten query, there are fewer query nodes and the inverted list for branch contains fewer labels, so the execution performance can be improved.

When a query involves predicates on both an object and a relationship between several objects, content search for different predicates can be performed separately, and thus the inverted lists for the different involved nodes are all reduced. If a certain object is involved in both an object predicate and a relationship predicate, after selecting labels from both the object table and the relationship table we also need to take the intersection to

Figure 18. Relationship table for the relationship between branch and book.

$R_{branch\text{-}book}$

branch_label	book_label	quantity
(2:251,2)	(5:18,3)	20
(2:251,2)	(19:30,3)	12
...	...	...

construct the temporary inverted list for this object node to process the rewritten query.

Summary on Semantic Optimizations

The original hybrid approach without optimization is proposed based on the general semantic information that the parent of each value node must be its property node. With more semantics on objects and their properties, and relationship between objects known, we can choose different optimization methods to change the semantic tables. Generally, more semantics known, we can further optimize the tables, to achieve better query processing performance. The attempt that uses semantic information to accelerate XML query processing can be incorporated with the state-of-the-art semantic rich document describing models and semantics discovery techniques.

Figure 19. An example query and query rewriting under Optimization 3.

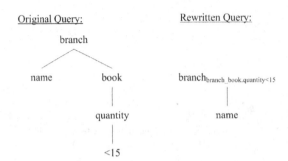

FUTURE RESEARCH DIRECTIONS

The approach introduced in this chapter integrates the relational and the native approaches to XML query processing. This attempt also opens a new window to processing queries with ID references in one XML document or queries across multiple XML documents.

XML document with ID references are normally modeled as a graph, instead of a tree. To process a query involving ID references over an XML graph, traditional labeling schemes are no longer applicable to check the positional relationship between each pair of query nodes. A graph-based labeling scheme (Wang, Li, Luo & Gao, 2008) is proposed recently to aid structural join, but it considers ID reference as a random link between document nodes. In fact, an ID reference is not a random link. It is a reference from an ID value to the object with the same value on its IDREF attribute. It will be interesting to combine such semantic information into the query processing to make it more efficient.

Some queries may be issued across multiple XML documents. Different documents are related by the predicates that compare path values between those documents. Existing structural join algorithms have difficulty in joining paths across multiple documents; however, the relational tables have such capability. Joining the tables for different objects or properties in different documents based on the value comparison, we can easily solve the predicate to link the documents.

When we use table join to handle queries involving several sub-structures, e.g. the sub-structures on both sides of an ID reference or a link between documents, we need to generate a better query plan to decide whether the structural joins for each sub-structure, or table joins linking the sub-structures should be performed first.

CONCLUSION

The existing XML query processing approaches, i.e. the relational approach and the native approach, have their advantages and limitations. Typically, the relational approach is good for content management, content search and content extraction, but it suffers from inefficiency in performing structural search, especially for "//"-axis join between query nodes. While the native approach can efficiently process structural joins, but they have problems dealing with contents. In this chapter, we introduce a hybrid approach to process XML twig pattern query. The main technique of the hybrid approach is to use both inverted lists and relational tables to process a twig pattern query. In more details, the structural search in the query is performed by structural joins using inverted lists, and the content search is performed by SQL selection in relational tables.

Initially, when there is no semantic information on object is known, we can at least infer that the parent of each value node must be the corresponding property node. Then the relational tables (i.e. property tables) are constructed based on property and value. Using such property tables, content search can be efficiently performed, and furthermore, the number of query nodes, the number of structural joins and the size of relevant inverted lists are all reduced by rewriting the original query, to result a better performance on structural search. We also discuss three optimization methods when more semantic information on object and relationship between objects is known. If we know the object of each property, we can change property tables to object/property tables, and if we could identify the common object of a set of properties, we can merge the object/property tables for those single-valued properties under the same object to an object table, and keep the object/property tables for the multi-valued properties. Furthermore, if we know some properties belong to a relationship between several objects, we can additionally introduce a relationship table. Using the optimized tables, the content search can be performed more efficiently, the query structure can be further simplified, and the inverted lists for the relevant objects can be further reduced. Thus, with these optimizations, the query processing performance can be further improved.

Finally, after finding the occurrences of a query pattern in a given XML document, the hybrid approach could easily extract actual values from relational tables to answer the query, without accessing the original document again.

REFERENCES

Al-Khalifa, S., & Jagadish, H. V., Koudas, N., Patel, J., M., Srivastava, D., & Wu, Y. (2002). Structural joins: a primitive for efficient XML query pattern matching. In *18th International Conference on Data Engineering* (pp. 141-154). Washington, DC: IEEE Computer Society.

Beyer, K., & Cochrane, R. J., Josifovski, V., Kleewein, J., Lapis, G., Lohman, G., et al. (2005). System RX: one part relational, one part XML. In *2005 ACM SIGMOD International Conference on Management of Data* (pp. 347-358). New York: ACM.

Bruno, N., Koudas, N., & Srivastava, D. (2002). Holistic twig joins: optimal XML pattern matching. In *2002 ACM SIGMOD International Conference on Management of Data,* (pp. 310-321). New York: ACM.

Chaudhri, A. B., Rashid, A. & Zicari, R. (2003). *XML data management: native XML and XML-enabled database systems.* Reading, MA: Addison-Wesley.

Chen, T., Lu, J., & Ling, T. W. (2005). On boosting holism in XML twig pattern matching using structural indexing techniques. In *2005 ACM SIGMOD International Conference on Management of Data* (pp. 455-466). New York: ACM.

Chen. Y., Davidson, S., B., Hara, C., S., & Zheng, Y. (2003). RRXS: Redundancy reducing XML storage in relations. In *29th International Conference on Very Large Data Bases* (pp. 189-200). Ohio: VLDB Endowment.

Doan, A., Ramakrishnan, R., Chen, F., DeRose, P., Lee, Y., & McCann, R. (2006). Community information management. *A Quarterly Bulletin of the Computer Society of the IEEE Technical Committee on Data Engineering, 29*(1), 64–72.

Florescu, D., & Kossmann, D. (1999). Storing and querying XML data using an RDBMS. *A Quarterly Bulletin of the Computer Society of the IEEE Technical Committee on Data Engineering, 22*(3), 27–34.

Goldman, R., & Widom, J. (1997). DataGuides: enabling query formulation and optimization in semistructured databases. In *23rd International Conference on Very Large Data Bases* (pp. 436-445). San Francisco: Morgan Kaufmann Publishers Inc.

Grust, T., van Keulen, M., & Teubner, J. (2004). Accelerating XPath evaluation in any RDBMS. *ACM Transactions on Database Systems, 29*(1), 91–131. doi:10.1145/974750.974754

Haw, S., & Lee, C. (2008). TwigX-Guide: twig query pattern matching for XML trees. *American Journal of Applied Science, 5*(9), 1212–1218. doi:10.3844/ajassp.2008.1212.1218

Jiang, H., Lu, H., & Wang, W. (2004). Efficient processing of XML twig queries with OR-predicates. In *2004 ACM SIGMOD International Conference on Management of Data* (pp. 59-70). New York: ACM.

Jiang, H., Wang, W., Lu, H., & Yu, J. (2003). Holistic twig joins on indexed XML documents. In *29th International Conference on Very Large Data Bases* (pp. 273-284). Ohio: VLDB Endowment.

Kaushik, R., Rohannon, P., & Naughton, J. F., & Korth, H., F. (2002). Covering indexes for branching path queries. In *2002 ACM SIGMOD International Conference on Management of Data* (pp. 133-144). New York: ACM.

Kaushik, R., Shenoy, P., Bohannon, P., & Gudes, E. (2002). Exploiting local similarity for indexing paths in graph-structured data. In *18th International Conference on Data Engineering* (pp. 129-140). Washington, DC: IEEE Computer Society.

Li, C., & Ling, T. W. (2005). QED: a novel quaternary encoding to completely avoid re-labeling in XML updates. In *14th ACM International Conference on Information and Knowledge Management* (pp. 501-508). New York: ACM.

Ling, T. W., Lee, M., L., & Dobbie, G. (2005). *Semistructured database design*. Berlin: Springer.

Liu, Z., & Chen, Y. (2007). Identifying meaningful return information for XML keyword search. In *16th ACM SIGMOD International Conference on Management of Data* (pp. 329-340). New York: ACM.

Lu, J., Chen, T., & Ling, T. W. (2004). Efficient processing of XML twig patterns with parent child edges: a look-ahead approach. In *13th ACM International Conference on Information and Knowledge Management* (pp. 533-542). New York: ACM.

Lu, J., & Ling, T. W., Chan, C., Y., & Chen, T. (2005). From region encoding to extended Dewey: on efficient processing of XML twig pattern matching. In *31th International Conference on Very Large Data Bases* (pp. 193-204). Ohio: VLDB Endowment.

Milo, T., & Suciu, D. (1999). Index structures for path expressions. In *7th International Conference on Database Theory,* (pp. 277-295). Berlin: Springer.

Navathe, S., Ceri, S., Wiederhold, G., & Dou, J. (1984). Vertical partitioning algorithms for database design. *ACM Transactions on Database Systems, 9*(4), 680–710. doi:10.1145/1994.2209

O'Neil, P. E., O'Neil, E., J., Pal, S., Cseri, I., Schaller, G., & Westbury, N. (2004). ORDPATHs: Insert-Friendly XML Node Labels. *2004 ACM SIGMOD International Conference on Management of Data,* (pp. 903-908). New York: ACM.

Pal, S., Cseri, I., Schaller, G., Seeliger, O., Giakoumakis, L., & Zolotov, V. (2004). Indexing XML data stored in a relational database. In *30th International Conference on Very Large Data Bases,* (pp. 1146-1157). Ohio: VLDB Endowment.

Shanmugasundaram, J., & Shekita, E., J., Kiernan, J., Krishnamurthy, R., Viglas, S., Naughton, J., F., & Tatarinov, I. (2001). A general technique for querying XML documents using a relational database system. *SIGMOD Record, 30*(3), 20–26. doi:10.1145/603867.603871

Shanmugasundaram, J., Tufte, K., Zhang, C., He, G., & DeWitt, D. J., & Naughton, J., F. (1999). Relational databases for querying XML documents: limitations and opportunities. In *25th International Conference on Very Large Data Bases* (pp. 302-314). San Francisco: Morgan Kaufmann Publishers, Inc.

Spink, A. (2002). A user-centered approach to evaluating human interaction with web search engines: an exploratory study. *Information Processing & Management*, *38*(3), 401–426. doi:10.1016/S0306-4573(01)00036-X

TreeBank. (2002). Retrieved from University of Washington Database Group. Retrieved from http://www.cs.washington.edu/research/xmldatasets/www/repository.html#treebank

Wang, H., Li, J., Luo, J., & Gao, H. (2008). Hash-based subgraph query processing method for graph-structured XML documents. In *34th International Conference on Very Large Data Bases,* (pp. 478-489). Ohio: VLDB Endowment.

Wang, W., Wang, H., Lu, H., Jiang, H., Lin, X., & Li, J. (2005). Efficient processing of XML path queries using the disk-based F&B index. In *31th International Conference on Very Large Data Bases* (pp. 145-156). Ohio: VLDB Endowment.

Wu, H., & Ling, T. W., & Chen, B. (2007). VERT: a semantic approach for content search and content extraction in XML query processing. In *26th International Conference on Conceptual Modeling* (pp. 534-549). Berlin: Springer.

Yoshikawa, M., Amagasa, T., Shimura, T., & Uemura, S. (2001). XRel: a path-based approach to storage and retrieval of XML documents using relational databases. *ACM Transactions on Internet Technology*, *1*(1), 110–141. doi:10.1145/383034.383038

Yu, C., & Jagadish, H. V. (2006) Efficient discovery of XML data redundancies. In *32th International Conference on Very Large Data Bases* (pp. 103-114). Ohio: VLDB Endowment.

Yu, T., & Ling, T. W., & Lu, J. (2006). Twig-StackList¬: A holistic twig join algorithm for twig query with NOT-predicates on XML data. In *11th International Conference on Database Systems for Advanced Applications* (249-263). Berlin: Springer.

Zhang, C., & Naughton, J., F., DeWitt, D., J., Luo, Q., & Lohman, G., M. (2001). On supporting containment queries in relational database management systems. *SIGMOD Record*, *30*(2), 425–436. doi:10.1145/376284.375722

Zhang, N., Agarwal, N., Chandrasekar, S., Idicula, S., Medi, V., Petride, S., & Sthanikam, B. (2009). Binary XML storage and query processing in Oracle 11g. In *35th International Conference on Very Large Data Bases,* (pp. 1354-1365). Ohio: VLDB Endowment.

Chapter 18
XML Query Evaluation in Validation and Monitoring of Web Service Interface Contracts

Sylvain Hallé
University of California, Santa Barbara, USA

Roger Villemaire
Université du Québec à Montréal, Canada

ABSTRACT

Web service interface contracts define constraints on the patterns of XML messages exchanged between cooperating peers. The authors provide a translation between Linear Temporal Logic (LTL) and a subset of the XML Query Language XQuery, and show that an efficient validation of LTL formulae can be achieved through the evaluation of XQuery expressions on message traces. Moreover, the runtime monitoring of interface constraints is possible by feeding the trace of messages to a streaming XQuery processor. This shows how advanced XML query processing technologies can be leveraged to perform trace validation and runtime monitoring in web service production environments.

INTRODUCTION

Service-oriented architectures (SOA) have become an important concept in systems development with the advent of web services (Alonso et al., 2004). Because of their flexible nature, web services can be dynamically discovered and orchestrated together to form value-added composite applications. However, this appealing modularity is also the source of one major issue: by dynamically combining heterogeneous, cross-business services, how can one ensure the interaction between each of

them proceeds as was intended by their respective providers? Whether for specifying performance or interoperability constraints, business policies or legal guidelines, a good web service has to have a well-defined and enforceable *interface contract* (Meredith & Bjorg, 2003).

While not strictly an XML technology, a web service depends heavily on XML for both its definition language, the Web Service Description Language (WSDL) (Christensen et al., 2001) and its messaging protocol, the Simple Object Access Protocol (SOAP). Specification languages such as DTD, RELAX NG, Schematron and XML Schema (XSD) have become natural candidates for express-

DOI: 10.4018/978-1-61520-727-5.ch018

ing so-called *data contracts*, specifying the shape of each message sent or received by a service. However, while data contracts are relatively straightforward to specify and verify, interface contracts go beyond such static requirements and also include a temporal aspect. For example, the online documentation for the popular Amazon E-Commerce Service (Amazon, 2009) elicits constraints on possible *sequences* of operations that must be fulfilled to avoid error messages and transaction failures (Hughes et al., 2008).

Compliance to interface these contracts can be checked in two different and complementary ways. First, an interaction can be recorded by some observer into a trace (or log) file, which can then be analyzed *a posteriori* to discover violations: this is called *trace validation* or *log analysis*. The same validation can also be performed on-the-fly, intercepting and analyzing messages as they are received or sent and warning of violations in real time: this is called *runtime monitoring*.

Although it is widely believed that interface contracts should, *in theory*, be verified or monitored in various ways, these tasks are often dismissed in execution environments on the grounds that: 1) they will cause an overhead sacrificing performance; 2) they require the development of new algorithms and the use of new, possibly untrusted software components.

The goal of this chapter is to challenge these two beliefs by showing how advanced XML query processing technologies can be leveraged to perform trace validation and runtime monitoring. The key idea consists in representing message exchanges as the progressive construction of a global XML "trace" document. Since contracts impose restrictions on the content and sequence of messages, validating and enforcing them simply becomes appropriately querying this document —harnessing the available computing capabilities of readily-available XML query engines in web service environments.

BACKGROUND

In layman's terms, a web service can be described as an independent software system providing its functionality through the exchange of messages. Generally, a service resides on a remote, public server accessible through the Internet using standard protocols. For example, when using the Simple Object Access Protocol (SOAP) over HTTP, communications to and from a web service are realized through the sending of XML documents to an endpoint URL. Among popular web service providers, we mention Amazon and Google. Figure 1 shows how, for example, one can send a request to a map service to obtain the geographical coordinates of a street address.

An Example: The Online Trading Company

Although some web services, like the previous example, require *stateless* request/response patterns, many web services allow for long-running, *stateful* transactions spanning multiple messages. Examples of such services abound in the literature; the reader is referred to Ghezzi & Guinea (2007), Hughes et al. (2008), Mahbub & Spanoudakis (2005), Hallé et al. (2009c), IBM (2002).

Let us consider the case of an online trading company, adapted from Josephraj (2005). A trading company is responsible for selling and buying stocks for its customers; it exposes its functionalities through a web service interface. An external buyer (which can be a human interfacing through a web portal, or another web service acting on behalf of some customer) can communicate through a set of XML messages, each representing a business operation performed by the trading company.

A client service first logs into the system by providing a user name. The shop offers a discount if a user connects with the commitment to buy at least one product, which is signalled with the commitToBuy XML element. The shop responds

Figure 1. Communications with a web service are carried through the exchange of XML messages in sequence.

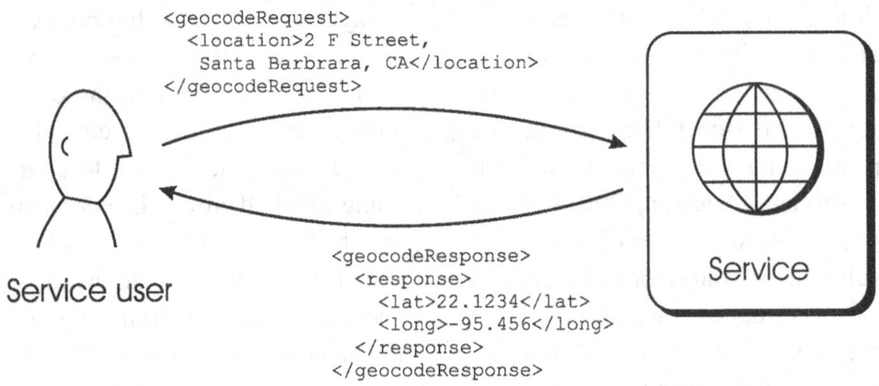

to the login with a loginConfirmation, providing a unique ID for the session. Additionally, if the user's commitment to buy a product has been accepted by the shop, a maximum delay in minutes before which the first transaction must take place is given in the expiration element.

A customer can ask for the list of available products through the exchange of a getAllStocks message, to which the company replies with a stockList message. The customer can also buy or sell stock products. In the case of a buy, this is done by first sending a placeBuyOrder message listing the name and desired amount of each product to be bought. The trading company checks the availability of each product and returns a confirmation of the transaction giving a bill identifier. The last step is for the customer to complete the transaction by proceeding to a cash transfer. This is achieved by providing an account number. The transfer can be done for multiple buy orders at the same time. Alternatively, instead of a cash transfer, a cancelTransaction message listing some bill-ids can be sent to revoke these transactions before payment. A sell operation works similarly.

All these operations can be intertwined. At any moment, we suppose that a customer can ask information about particular products, place concurrent buy/sell orders, complete or cancel any number of pending transactions. This general context is appropriate to represent the requirements of e-commerce applications.

Interface Contracts

In order to interact with the trading company, a service consumer must be informed of how the "conversation" is expected to take place. Even though it is not explicitly documented, a web service always imposes an *interface contract*. The first obvious aspect of such a contract covers the structure and content of each possible message. To this end, a standardized language called the Web Service Description Language (WSDL) allows a web service developer to give the list of accepted operations (and hence possible message types) and the shape of each message, using either the DTD or the Schema syntax. For example, it might require that an order request be placed through a placeBuyOrder message following this template:

<message>
<action>placeBuyOrder</action>
<stock>
<name>s_1</name>
<amount>a_1</amount>
</stock>
...
<stock>

Table 1. Temporal constraints for the online trading company's interface contract.

1. A user whose commitment to buy has been accepted by the shop will eventually send a placeBuyOrder message.
2. No placeBuyOrder can be sent before first receiving a product list.
3. The same unique ID must be present in all confirmation messages.
4. The first placeBuyOrder of a client whose commitToBuy has been accepted by the shop must occur within x minutes of the login, with x the timeout value sent when the session was opened.

```
<name>s_n</name>
<amount>a_n</amount>
</stock>
</message>
```

WSDL, however, was designed for stateless services; the specification for the online trading company, hence, does not prevent messages from being called in any sequence. Yet, as was pointed out by Josephraj (2005), it is well-known that not all message exchanges represent valid transactions, i.e. interactions between services that lead to the successful completion of the cooperation. Conditions ensuring a safe and sound interaction between services must also include specification of valid *message traces*. In the case of the trading company, possible contract properties are listed in Table 1.

It is important to note the varied nature of these properties. Some involve simple precedence relations; some state invariants that must be fulfilled at all times. Some go even further: by referring to "every buy and sell order", constraint 4 requires that the delay between some future message be specified by some data value given in the second message of the conversation. This specification is called "data-aware", because the sequence of messages and their content are interdependent. The reader is referred to Hallé et al. (2009c) for a deeper exposition of data-aware constraints.

The notion of interface contract is not new or specific to web services. The Interface Description Language (IDL) (Snodgrass, 1989) was developed for distributed systems communicating through Remote Procedure Calls (RPC). By defining each component's procedure names and input-output arguments in a language-independent fashion, IDL allowed systems developed using various technologies to properly invoke each other. To this end, WSDL can be seen as a web service "cousin" to IDL.

In many scenarios, additional constraints can complexify the monitoring process: asynchronous communications, lost, delayed or out-of-order messages can distort an otherwise valid interaction, without it being any of the services' "fault". In this chapter, a focus has been placed on providing means of *detecting* that an assumption on the communication has been violated for one of the collaborating services, and not on repairing an invalid transaction or determining the actual cause of the violation.

Enforcing Interface Contracts

Although expressed in plain English, we shall see that the previous constraints can be formalized in a very large variety of specification languages. However, no matter the chosen language, a question remains: how can one verify that a completed transaction complied with the contract, and how does one enforce this contract at runtime? Several solutions have been proposed, which can be condensed into three categories.

Static Analysis. The first such category involves the static analysis of a model of the actual pair consumer-service before any interaction takes place; this is called *model checking* (Huth & Ryan, 2000). This method provides the highest level of certainty by exhaustively exploring all possible execution paths with the aid of a tool called a model checker (Ghose & Koliadis, 2007; Gover-natori et al., 2006, Fu et al., 2004). However, this exhaustiveness comes at a price: static analysis requires a specification of the client and service processes, called a *transition system*, in order to check their possible interactions. Moreover, due to the sheer complexity of the problem, these models abstract away the actual messages by representing them by single letters. Since they require specific tools to be realized, static analysis methods are not considered in this chapter.

Trace Validation. A second possibility is to collect a trace of messages for later analysis. During a transaction between web services, several message traces can be obtained:

- An external observer can record the global pattern of messages sent by each service and align them in the order in which they are intercepted. This global trace has been called by Bultan et al. (2003) a *conversation*.
- A service can record the messages that are received or sent from its interface. There exists one such local message trace for each service cooperating in a transaction.

In trace validation (also called *trace checking* or *log analysis*), the idea is to mine such traces to find violations of contracts (van der Aalst & Verbeek, 2008). One reason for doing so might be to check accountability: in the case a business contract has been violated, one might be interested to dig the circumstances of that violation, identify the guilty party and engage in compensation measures (Wang et al., 2008).

From a syntactical point of view, validating the format of each message in the trace against its WSDL Schema specification is a rather mature and well-accepted methodology, and is supported by commercial tools like the .NET or the IBM Web Service Validation Tools. However, most major service providers, such as Amazon or Google, also offer development frameworks in a

variety of programming languages; through the use of front-end classes standing for the various available operations, these frameworks actually spare an application developer from manually creating XML messages and thereby ensure that these messages are correct by construction. This makes validation of XML Schemata unnecessary in many cases.

Trace validation of *temporal* properties, on the other hand, has been much less studied. It has been attempted by Howard et al. (2003), where a trace of messages is converted into a transition system producing exactly that trace; contract properties are verified using the SPIN model checker. With Specifications using XQuery on traces (SXQT) (Venzke, 2004), a trace of XML messages is analyzed by means of formulæ converted into XQuery expressions. Temporal trace validation has also been applied outside the web service context: instead of traces of messages, some other works concentrate on traces of *events* generated by an arbitrary system. Regular expressions (Garavel & Mateescu, 2004), SQL queries (Lencevicius et al., 2000) and temporal logic (Havelund & Rosu, 2001) can be used to mine a trace for sequences of undesirable events.

Runtime Monitoring. In trace validation, one has to wait for a trace to be complete before analyzing it; therefore, this method needs adaptations to be used in a context where the monitoring should occur in parallel with the execution of the workflow. This leads to a third solution called *runtime monitoring*, where the state of "validity" of a trace is updated at every new message sent or received. Violations can then be caught immediately, seconds after they have occurred, as exemplified by the ASTRO and Dynamo projects (Baresi et al., 2008).

Several arguments in favour of runtime monitoring approaches have been put forward (Ghezzi & Guinea, 2007). First, the satisfaction of requirements sometimes depends on assumptions on the partners that cannot be verified prior to the actual implementation of the system. In the particular case of service-oriented architectures, partners can be discovered dynamically and can even change drastically during execution. In some occasions, a static, *a priori* model checking of the intended process is simply impossible or intractable when modelling channels of potentially infinite length or very large data domains (Mahbub & Spanoudakis, 2005). Finally, there also exist situations at runtime which, although they do not constitute strict violations of a specification, must be addressed as soon as they are discovered: Barbon et al. (2006) give the example of an online shop being refused a money transfer by its partner bank, or of a client repeatedly asking for products that are no longer in stock. Independent of these technical aspects, the runtime monitoring of a process is also sound business-wise. Robinson (2003) remarks that monitoring can increase trust in an electronic marketplace by providing the consumer of a service with the ability to check by itself the transaction that takes place.

A number of approaches to the runtime monitoring of systems in general have been suggested over the years. Propositional runtime monitoring was used by Gan et al. (2007), where patterns of messages exchanged by a web service are specified using UML 2.0 Sequence Diagrams, and then transformed into classical finite-state automata. Krüger et al. (2007) use UML Message Sequence Charts with the same intent, using aspect-oriented programming to call monitoring methods with the use Java *pointcuts*. In Barbon et al. (2006) an elegant framework for the automatic synthesis of monitors is presented, using the Run-Time Monitor specification Language (RTML). Barringer et al. (2004) describe an algorithm for rule-based runtime monitoring, where the rules are temporal fixpoint functions that can include data arguments. Stolz (2007) makes a similar use of data parameterization for a quantified variant of linear temporal logic (LTL). The BeepBeep runtime monitor (Hallé & Villemaire, 2009a) processes messages sent by a web application on-the-fly and takes as input the same extension to

LTL as in this chapter. Input-Output State Transition Systems (IOSTS) can be used to specify and monitor properties (Constant et al., 2007). Ghezzi & Guinea (2007) suggest a framework in which correlations between data in multiple messages are expressed and can be checked at runtime. Execution traces are stored into a database by Baazizi et al. (2008); contract properties are then converted into SQL queries into that database and re-evaluated on every new message. Finally, inferences on Event Calculus (EC) expressions have also been attempted to discover contract violations (Mahbub & Spanoudakis, 2007).

A CASE FOR XML QUERY PROCESSING

Since the message traces considered are formed of XML documents, it is natural to think that properties on such traces can be validated using XML methods. However, with the notable exception of Venzke (2004), none of the aforementioned works use XML query engines to perform validation or monitoring of traces of XML messages. Most even abstract away the XML nature of the messages by representing them by single symbols.

Remark that a message trace $\sigma = \sigma_1 \sigma_2 \ldots$ can be seen as an XML document by itself. It suffices to encapsulate each message sequentially into a global *trace* "document" as follows:

```
<trace>
<message>
σ₁
<message>
σ₂
...
</message>
</message>
</trace>
```

The sequential ordering of the messages in σ is carried through the children nesting of the <message> elements. (Although placing each message side by side seems more natural, we shall see later why this nested representation is preferable.) This property can be used to map properties on sequences of messages in a trace into a form of query on an XML document using descendant-axis operands. For example, consider the following expression *Q*:

```
every $x in /trace/message[1]
satisfies
   every $y in $x/message[1]
satisfies
      (not($y/commitAccepted =
"true") or
         some $z in $y//mes-
sage[1] satisfies
            $z/name =
"placeBuyOrder" (1)
```

An XQuery engine computing *Q* on the above document will return true if the second message of the trace does not contain an element commitAccepted with a value of "true", or otherwise when a placeBuyOrder message is encountered; otherwise, the processor will return "false". Therefore, the previous XQuery expression returns "true" exactly when a trace fulfils Temporal Specification 1 in Table 1.

Based upon that observation, an XQuery processor can be used as a web service trace validator (Hallé & Villemaire, 2008b):

1. From a constraint, build an XQuery query *Q* such that *Q* returns false if and only if the constraint is violated
2. Compute the result of *Q* with an XQuery engine on a "document" formed by aggregating all exchanged messages with the service, as shown above

We list a few advantages of doing so. First, XML query processors are common. First, virtually all existing solutions for trace validation and runtime monitoring require changes to the web service execution environments. In contrast, most (if not all) web service execution environments provide XML processing capabilities natively; hence, translating contract specifications into XML queries allows to perform trace validation without any new technology. Using XML query engines to perform trace validation is a powerful way of leveraging existing resources available in production environments while minimizing the modifications required to a service.

Second, XML query languages are standardized. Although, as we shall see later, there exists a very wide variety of specification languages, any production environment equipped with an XML processing engine can process these constraints.

Finally, XML query processors are efficient. Experimental results shown later in this chapter indicate that, in contexts where data domains of 100 elements and transactions formed of up to 1,500 messages, the validation of a trace requires less than 10 ms per message.

XML QUERY PROCESSING FOR TRACE VALIDATION

We now systematize the approach suggested above by rephrasing it into a formal model. In recent years, the importance of specifying patterns of interaction manifested itself in the development and use of numerous languages to define cooperations between services. Among them, we find the Web Service Choreography Description Language (WS-CDL) developed by the W3C (Kavantas et al. 2005), the re-use of UML Sequence Diagrams (OMG, 1997) in a web service context (Gan et al., 2007), SSDL Message Exchange Patterns (MEP) (Parastatidis et al., 2005), the *Let's Dance* choreography description language (Decker et al., 2006), and the Web Service Choreography Interface (WSCI) (Arkin et al., 2002). Multi-agent web services are modelled in Walton et al. (2004) using a custom protocol language called MAP; Kazhamiakin et al. (2006) model web service compositions by finite-state systems, akin to the conversation specifications of Bultan et al. (2003).

In the following, we stop our choice on a logical formalism called Linear Temporal Logic (LTL) and show how any LTL formula can be translated into an equivalent XQuery expression. LTL has already been suggested for the expression of web service interface contracts (Nakajima, 2005; Fu et al., 2004; Robinson, 2006). Although we concentrate on LTL, our approach is general: most, if not all previous languages can be mapped into equivalent LTL expressions, or extensions thereof; this includes, among others, UML Sequence Diagrams (or more specifically Message Sequence Charts) (Caporuscio et al., 2004, Gan et al., 2007), SSDL's Message Exchange Patterns (MEP) and Rules protocol frameworks (Parastatidis et al., 2005), and the *Let's Dance* choreography description language (Decker et al., 2006). Hence, any result valid for LTL applies to these notations as well, and the translation can be straightforwardly adapted to them.

LTL has been introduced to express properties about sequences of states in systems called Kripke structures (Clarke et al., 2000). In the present case, the states to be considered are messages inside a conversation. Formally, let us denote by M the set of XML messages. A sequence of messages $\sigma_1 \sigma_2$ ..., where $\sigma_i \in M$ for every $i \geq 1$, is called a message trace. We write σ_i to denote the i-th message of the trace σ, and σ^i to denote the trace obtained from σ by starting at the i-th message.

A domain function is used to fetch and compare values inside a message; it receives an argument π representing a *path* from the root to some element of the message. This path is defined using standard, XPath 1.0 notation. Formally, if we let D be a domain of values, and Π be the set of XPath expressions, the domain function Dom is an application $M \times \Pi \rightarrow 2^D$ which, given a message $m \in M$ and a path $\pi \in \Pi$, returns a subset $Dom_m(\pi)$ of D, representing the set of values appearing in message m at the end of the path π. For example, if we let Π be the set of XPath formulæ, $\pi \in \Pi$

be the particular formula "/message/stock/name", and $m \in M$ be the following message:

```
<message>
<action>placeBuyOrder</action>
<stock>
<name>stock-1</name>
<amount>123</amount>
</stock>
<stock>
<name>stock-2</name>
<amount>456</amount>
</stock>
</message>
```

then $Dom_m(\pi) = \{$stock-1, stock-2$\}$.

LTL's syntax is based on classical propositional logic, using the connectives $\neg$ ("not"), $\vee$ ("or"), $\wedge$ ("and"), $\rightarrow$ ("implies"), to which four temporal operators have been added. An LTL formula is a well-formed combination of these operators and connectives, according to the usual construction rules:

Definition 1 (LTL Syntax). Let π be a path formula in some language, and $S \subseteq D$ be a subset of some data domain D. The set of LTL formulæ φ is given by the following BNF grammar:

$$\varphi \equiv \pi = S \mid \neg\varphi \mid \varphi \wedge \varphi \mid \varphi \vee \varphi \mid \varphi \rightarrow \varphi \mid \mathbf{G}\,\varphi \mid \mathbf{F}\,\varphi \mid \mathbf{X}\,\varphi \mid \varphi\,\mathbf{U}\,\varphi$$

Boolean connectives have their usual meaning. The temporal operator $\mathbf{G}$ means "globally". For example, the formula $\mathbf{G}\,\varphi$ means that formula φ is true in every message of the trace. The operator $\mathbf{F}$ means "eventually"; the formula $\mathbf{F}\,\varphi$ is true if φ holds for some future message of the trace. The operator $\mathbf{X}$ means "next"; it is true whenever φ holds in the next message of the trace. Finally, the $\mathbf{U}$ operator means "until"; the formula $\varphi\,\mathbf{U}\,\psi$ is true if φ holds for all messages until some message satisfies ψ. The semantics below formalizes these definitions:

Definition 2 (LTL Semantics). Let φ be a LTL formula, π and S be defined as previously. We say that a message trace σ *satisfies* φ, and write $\sigma \square \varphi$, if and only if it respects the following rules:

$$\sigma \models \pi = S \Leftrightarrow Dom_{\sigma 1}(\pi) \text{ is equal to } S$$

$$\sigma \models \neg\varphi \Leftrightarrow \sigma \nvDash \varphi$$

$$\sigma \models \varphi \wedge \psi \Leftrightarrow \sigma \models \varphi \text{ and } \sigma \models \psi$$

$$\sigma \models \varphi \vee \psi \Leftrightarrow \sigma \models \varphi \text{ or } \sigma \models \psi$$

$$\sigma \models \mathbf{X} \varphi \Leftrightarrow \sigma^2 \models \varphi$$

$$\sigma \models \mathbf{G} \varphi \Leftrightarrow \sigma^i \models \varphi \text{ for every } i \geq 1$$

$$\sigma \models \mathbf{F} \varphi \Leftrightarrow \sigma^i \models \varphi \text{ for some } i \geq 1$$

$$\sigma \models \varphi \mathbf{U} \psi \Leftrightarrow \text{ there exists } k \text{ such that } \sigma^k \models \psi \text{ and } \sigma^i \models \varphi \text{ for every } i < k$$

As usual, we define $\varphi \rightarrow \psi \equiv \neg\varphi \vee \psi$. We also extend the notation and allow to write $\pi = d$ when $Dom_m(\pi) = \{d\}$.

Equipped with LTL, our interface contracts can be revisited and expressed in this formal language. For example, Temporal Property 1 in Table 1 becomes the following LTL Property:

$$(\mathbf{X} \text{ message/commitAccepted = true}) \rightarrow (\mathbf{F} \text{ message/name = placeBuyOrder}) \quad (2)$$

This formula explains that if the second message of the trace has a commitAccepted element with value "true", then eventually, a placeBuyOrder message will be sent.

Translation to XQuery

Intuitively, the LTL formula (2) on a message trace σ and the XQuery expression (1) on a document are equivalent: they express the same thing, albeit using different notations. It seems reasonable to think that every LTL formula can be transformed, by hand, into an XQuery expression. Our goal is to devise a systematic way of transforming the former into the latter.

To this end, we develop a recursive translation function ω_ρ, which takes as input an LTL formula and produces an equivalent XQuery expression. The function also carries a parameter ρ, which is a pointer to the current message of the trace. When starting the translation, ρ must point to the first message of the trace document. The XPath expression /trace/message[1] can be used to designate this first message.

It suffices to define ω_ρ for each of the constructs given previously. The translation of XML path expressions is direct: for π a path in a message and $d \in D$ a value at the end of that path, the following FLWOR expression gives an equivalent Boolean result:

$$\omega_\rho(\pi = d) \equiv \text{for } \$x \text{ in } \rho/\pi \text{ return } \$x = \text{``}d\text{''}$$

It is important to remark that the path π is *relative* to the current message of the trace; hence π must be appended to ρ. XQuery allows all logical connectors, therefore, the translation of $\neg$, $\vee$ and $\wedge$ is also straightforward; it has, though, to be encapsulated within a FLWOR expression.

$$\omega_\rho(\varphi \vee \psi) \equiv \text{for } \$x \text{ in } \rho \text{ return } (\omega_{\$x}(\varphi) \text{ or } \omega_{\$x}(\psi))$$

$$\omega_\rho(\varphi \wedge \psi) \equiv \text{for } \$x \text{ in } \rho \text{ return } (\omega_{\$x}(\varphi) \text{ and } \omega_{\$x}(\psi))$$

$$\omega_\rho(\neg\varphi) \equiv \text{for } \$x \text{ in } \rho \text{ return } not(\omega_{\$x}(\varphi))$$

In this translation, $\$x$ is a fresh XQuery variable, bound to the for statement. By construction, there is only one candidate for $\$x$; hence the FLWOR expression returns only one Boolean value, and not a sequence of Booleans.

It remains to translate the temporal operators into equivalent XQuery code. We consider first the case of the $\mathbf{G}$ operator. According to the semantics of LTL, a formula of the form $\mathbf{G} \varphi$ is true on the trace which starts at the current message, if and only if all subsequent messages (including the current one), satisfy φ. Since ρ is a pointer to the current message, and that all subsequent messages are nested children, then the path expression ρ// message[1] denotes all the messages starting from ρ and following it. The XQuery formula must then express that each message in this set satisfies the remaining formula φ, or more precisely, the translation of φ into XQuery. We obtain the following expression:

$\omega_\rho(\mathbf{G}\ \varphi) \equiv$ every x in ρ//message[1] satisfies $\omega_{\$x}(\varphi)$)

Remark that since φ must be true on each such message, the root on which φ is evaluated is $x.

The translation of the "next" **X** operator, can be seen as a special case of **G**, where the set of desired messages contains only the immediate successor to ρ:

$\omega_\rho(\mathbf{X}\ \varphi) \equiv$ every x in ρ/message[1] satisfies $\omega_{\$x}(\varphi)$)

The translation of **F** φ states that some message in the future satisfies φ:

$\omega_\rho(\mathbf{F}\ \varphi) \equiv$ some x in ρ//message[1] satisfies $\omega_{\$x}(\varphi)$)

We postpone the translation of the remaining LTL operator, **U**. A simple proof by induction (which we omit) can then show that this transformation preserves the equivalence between LTL and XQuery.

As an example, applying ω to LTL Specification 1 yields the following XQuery expression:

```
every $x in /trace/message[1]
satisfies
   every $y in $x/message[1]
satisfies
      (not($y/commitAccepted =
"true") or
```

```
            some $z in $y//mes-
sage[1] satisfies
                $z/name =
"placeBuyOrder"
```

This is exactly the XQuery expression obtained from our intuitive observation earlier in this chapter; however, this time the formula has been obtained using a systematic translation of an LTL formula into XQuery.

Extensions to LTL

The mapping provided above covers a subset of XQuery: there exist valid XQuery expressions which do not correspond to any LTL formula. We can take advantage of the greater expressive power of XQuery to introduce a few extensions to classical LTL, which can be verified by an XQuery engine at no additional cost.

Data Correlations Between Messages. Temporal Specifications 3 and 4 require a correlation between data content of multiple messages in the trace and have been dubbed "data-aware" for that reason (Hallé et al., 2009c). An extension to LTL called LTL-FO+ is required to take care of them. This extension allows a first-order quantification on the content of messages; it was introduced in Hallé & Villemaire (2009b) and is defined as follows:

Definition 3 (LTL-FO+ Syntax). Let $\pi \in \Pi$ be defined as previously. We have the following:

- Any LTL formula is an LTL-FO+ formula
- If φ is an LTL-FO+ formula, x_i is a free variable in φ, $\pi \in \Pi$ is a path expression, then $\exists_\pi x_i$: φ and $\forall_\pi x_i$: φ are LTL-FO+ formulæ.

It allows the expression of statements such as "for all x in π, φ(x)", where φ(x) is a formula where x appears as a free variable. It indicates that all values at the end of π in the current message satisfy φ.

Definition 4 (LTL-FO+ Semantics). Let φ be a LTL-FO+ formula, π and S be defined as previously. Denote by $\varphi[x/k]$ the formula φ' obtained from φ by replacing x by k. We say that a message trace σ *satisfies* φ, and write $\sigma \vDash \varphi$, if and only if it respects the rules in Definition 2, plus the following rules:

$$\sigma \vDash \exists_\pi x_i: \varphi \Leftrightarrow \sigma \vDash \varphi[x/k] \text{ for some } k \in Dom_{\sigma 1}(\pi)$$

$$\sigma \vDash \forall_\pi x_i: \varphi \Leftrightarrow \sigma \vDash \varphi[x/k] \text{ for every } k \in Dom_{\sigma 1}(\pi)$$

It suffices to add the following two mapping rules to the original ω to support LTL-FO+'s quantifiers on data:

$$\omega_\rho(\exists_\pi x_i: \varphi) \equiv \text{some \$x in } \rho/\pi \text{ satisfies } \omega_\rho(\varphi))$$

$$\omega_\rho(\forall_\pi x_i: \varphi) \equiv \text{some \$x in } \rho/\pi \text{ satisfies } \omega_\rho(\varphi))$$

Metric Temporal Logic. Metric temporal logic (MTL) is an extension of regular temporal logic for expressing time delays in business contracts (Governatori et al., 2006; Artho et al., 2003). Such constraints can be handled by allowing formulæ to access the value of a global clock τ provided by the execution environment. A quantification on τ simply amounts to fetching the current timestamp from that internal clock; metric temporal logic then becomes a particular case of data parameterization, and is already covered by our previous extension. For example, temporal property 4 in Table 1 can be expressed as follows:

$$\mathbf{X} (\forall_{message/timeout} x: \forall\tau\, t_1: \mathbf{F} \text{ (message/name =}$$
$$\text{placeBuyOrder} \wedge \forall\tau\, t_2: t_2 - t_1 < x))$$

This property reads as follows: if the second message of the trace provides a timeout value x at some time point t_1, then some placeBuyOrder message will be sent in the future at a time point t_2, such that $t_2 - t_1$ falls within the time range x. This indeed expresses the requirement that at least one buy order will appear within the delay specified by the service.

This translation of LTL into XQuery performs well on existing engines. In experiments detailed in Hallé & Villemaire (2008b), a set of 100 trace files of length ranging from 10 to approximately 1,500 messages was produced. Each of these traces was then sent to an XQuery engine, which evaluated the XQuery translation of each of Specifications 1-4. Barring exceptional cases, the average time required to process one message does not exceed 5 milliseconds. An interesting point is that the total processing time remains similar between the group of Constraints 1-2, which are plain LTL formulæ, and the group of Constraints 3-4, which require LTL-FO+'s first-order quantification mechanism to be expressed. This indicates that, for the Interface Specifications studied in these experiments, extending trace validation to temporal first-order properties added no noticeable load on the XML query engine, and can therefore be performed "for free", using the same XML technologies that are required for the more traditional LTL.

XML QUERY PROCESSING FOR RUNTIME MONITORING

Given these positive experimental results, it seems sensible to apply the same technique used for trace validation to runtime monitoring. However, our previous method operates in a *post mortem* fashion: the trace is assumed complete before feeding it to the XML query engine. In runtime monitoring, we are not interested in waiting for the end of the trace, but rather wish to discover violations as the execution progresses, in real time. Therefore, the previous technique must be adapted to runtime monitoring.

There exist two main modes of representing and processing XML documents by XPath and XQuery engines. In the *Document Object Model* (DOM) (Apparao et al., 1998), the nested tag structure of the original document is translated in memory into a tree model; to process a query, the engine can retrieve arbitrary parts of the document by specifying the path to the desired nodes. Although relatively straightforward, this method suffers from the fact that the whole document must be loaded in memory in order to be processed. An alternate approach consists of representing an XML document as a sequence of events generated as it is parsed. Only this sequence of events is fed to the engine, which consumes them in their order of arrival and updates its state to compute the desired query result. *Streaming* XML (Brownell, 2002) shifts the processing burden from the parser, which is relieved from building a tree structure from XML code, to the query engine, which is forced to update its state based on a linearized version of the document where backtracking is not permitted. A crucial advantage of streaming XML is that the query results are also streamed: whenever possible, the engine sends its results progressively to an output pipe, as the input document is being read, and without having to wait until the end of document has been reached.

This feature of streaming XML can be put to good use to perform basic monitoring of web services at runtime. It suffices to remark that an XQuery engine computing query (1) on an XML stream will send true on its output pipe if the second message of the trace does not contain an element commitAccepted with a value of "true", or otherwise as soon as a placeBuyOrder message is encountered. If the stream is closed by reading the </trace> element, false will be sent on the output pipe. Based upon that observation, a *streaming* XQuery processor can be used as a web service runtime monitor using the same translation we provided for trace validation (Hallé & Villemaire, 2009b).

Available Streaming Capabilities

This idea is mitigated by the fact that the efficient evaluation of XQuery on streaming XML is still an open problem subject to a large amount of research; the reader is referred to Li & Agrawal (2005), Park & Kang (2007), and Koch et al. (2004) for a sample of relevant works on that topic. Consequently, the support for XQuery in streaming mode is still partial and varies greatly from tool to tool.

For example, our choice of a recursive nesting of the messages within each other is voluntary. Putting messages side-by-side under the root element is not an appropriate choice, although it seems more natural: no XQuery tool currently supports the following-sibling and previous-sibling axes in streaming mode, and these axes would be necessary to translate the LTL operators.

The W3C maintains a list of XQuery implementations[1] which can be classified into three categories with respect to streaming support.

Insufficient streaming support. In this category fall all XQuery engines that must be discarded for various reasons:

- Some do not support streaming XML processing at all: these include Galax (Fernández et al., 2009) and XMLTaskForce (Gottlob et al., 2002)
- Some XQuery engines support only XPath 1.0 in streaming mode, such as TwigM (Chen et al. 2006), XSQ (Peng & Chawathe, 2003), TurboXPath (Bar-Yossef et al., 2004) and XAOS (Barton et al., 2003).
- Some streaming XQuery engines only support a fragment of the language: GCX (Schmidt et al., 2007) does not support the quantifiers every and some, Nux[2] forbids the use of the descendant axis.

Sufficient streaming support. In this category, we find the XQuery engines that provide full streaming support for all the language features required by our translation. Tools in this category are mostly academic and experimental, such as XQPull (Fegaras et al. 2006) and MXQuery (Botan et al., 2007).

Partial streaming support. Although they support streaming processing of XQuery expressions with quantifiers and descendant axes, the tools in this category impose restrictions on the way in which they can be used. Notable proponents include Saxon[3] and DataDirect XQuery[4] (DDXQ), two commercial products that we tested under an evaluation license.[5]

Although a few tools fully support our translation of LTL to XQuery, engines with partial support are more representative of the streaming capabilities likely to be found in an actual web service execution environment. The remainder of this chapter therefore concentrates on tools from this category.

The Forward-Only Fragment of LTL

By definition, a streaming XML source can only be read in the forward direction, and this can be done only once. This entails that any XQuery result that requires some form of backtracking in the source document cannot be handled. Fully streaming engines circumvent this problem by carefully memorizing the parts of the stream which will need to be used later in the computation of a result, so that rewinding in the source is not required. On the contrary, "partial" engines perform only partial memorization and cannot evaluate some queries in streaming mode, even though they are formed of language constructs supported by the streaming engine.

We study in this section the fragment of LTL that can be supported within the limits of XQuery engines with partial streaming support. We call it the *forward-only fragment* of LTL, noted $LTL^{\rightarrow}$, since it corresponds to formulæ which can be evaluated without backtracking in the message trace.

We shall first identify a set of syntactical conditions on the structure of an LTL formula which are sufficient to prevent backtracking.

We first remark that no temporal operator can be in the scope of **G**. Indeed, evaluating a formula of the form **G** $\spadesuit$ φ, with $\spadesuit \in \{\mathbf{G}, \mathbf{F}, \mathbf{U}, \mathbf{X}\}$ on a message trace $\sigma_1, \sigma_2, ...$ requires first evaluating $\spadesuit \varphi$ on σ_1. However, evaluating the temporal operator $\spadesuit$ will require reading σ_2 and possibly σ_3, σ_4, and so on. Once $\spadesuit \varphi$ has been decided for σ_1, it needs to be evaluated again starting at σ_2, yet due to the previous evaluation of $\spadesuit \varphi$ on σ_1, we can no longer guarantee that the source has not been read past σ_2.[6] By a similar reasoning, no temporal operator can be in the scope of **F** or **U**.

Since temporal operators express properties about the sequence of messages, it is natural that some restrictions apply when a trace can only be read in one direction. More surprisingly however, the forward-only consumption of a message trace also restricts the use of the Boolean connectives.

In a formula of the form $\varphi \wedge \psi$, no temporal operator can be in the scope of φ. It suffices to realize that both φ and ψ must be evaluated from the same starting point; therefore, the presence of a temporal operator in φ can possibly consume messages which will need to be rewound when the evaluation of ψ takes places. No temporal operator can be in the scope of a universal quantifier either. Indeed, evaluating $\forall_{\pi} x: \varphi$ on a message trace $\sigma_1, \sigma_2, ...$ requires checking that φ is respected for all values of x admissible for π. When a first value for x is picked, if φ is contains a temporal operator, then messages $\sigma_1, \sigma_2, ...$ might be consumed before deciding on the value (true or false) of φ. Once this is done, a second value for x must be chosen, and φ must be checked again, starting from σ_1.

We can, however, introduce a weaker version of the quantifiers, noted $\exists_{\pi}^{1}$ and $\forall_{\pi}^{1}$, that assume that, in every message, there exists at most one possible value for the variable. Hence, the quantifier $\exists_{p} 1\ x: \varphi$ is true when the value of the single element p in the current message satisfies φ. Since no backtracking is involved to decide the quantifier, temporal operators can be present in its scope, provided they respect the above rules.

By using this weakened quantifier, we can observe that all the temporal properties shown in Table 1 belong to LTL⁻. Although restrictive, the forward-only fragment of LTL presents two advantages:

- The logic is *bottom-up*: it is defined from the streaming capabilities of existing engines and therefore constitutes a least common denominator for runtime monitors.
- The logic is *simple*: since no memorization of the document is required, it can be monitored by an XQuery engine in a small and *constant* memory space.

Mapping the "Until" Operator

Up to now, the translation of the LTL U operator in XQuery has not been covered. Unlike the other LTL operators, $\varphi\ U\ \psi$ is more complex, since it asserts two different things: 1) ψ eventually occurs for some message, and 2) for every preceding message, φ holds. A classical result in temporal logic shows that G and F are particular cases of until; more specifically, $F\ \varphi \equiv \text{true}\ U\ \varphi$ and $G\ \varphi \equiv \neg(\text{true}\ U\ \neg\varphi)$.

There exist two possible ways of translating $\varphi\ U\ \psi$ into XQuery. The first one consists in giving an equivalent XQuery expression:

```
some $x in ρ/descendant::*/mes-
sage satisfies ω_ρ(φ) and
    every $y in (ρ/descendant::*/
message intersect
    $x/ancestor::*/message)
satisfies ω_ρ(ψ)
```

However, the function explicitly requires computing a set of messages by reading backwards because of the ancestor axis on the second line. Although the ancestor axis could be evaluated in a streaming fashion by carefully memorizing appropriate pieces of the source, we found no tool capable of doing so.

A second possibility is to define a recursive, user-defined function that computes the Boolean value of the operator, as follows:

```
declare function local:until(ρ)
{
    if (ω_ρ(ψ)) then true else
    if (ω_ρ(φ)) then
local:until(ρ/message)
    else false};
```

The translation of an LTL formula using this version of the "until" does not require any backward computation. The translation method becomes a little more involved: one new until$_i$ function must be declared for every occurrence of U in the formula, since ψ and φ, which both translate as XQuery expressions, cannot be passed as arguments to an XQuery function and must therefore be translated directly into the body of the function. Yet again, we found no tool capable of handling *recursive* user-defined functions.

The only reasonable compromise we can suggest is to support the "until" operator at the top level of a formula only. When the LTL-FO+ formula to evaluate is of the form $\varphi\ U\ \psi$, we monitor two formulæ separately: $G\ \varphi$ on one side, and $F\ \psi$ on the other. It suffices to keep the monitors running until either $F\ \psi$ announces true (in which case $\varphi\ U\ \psi$ is fulfilled), or $G\ \varphi$ announces false (in which case $\varphi\ U\ \psi$ is violated).

Experimental Results

In experiments detailed in Hallé & Villemaire (2009b), 100 trace files of length ranging from 10 to approximately 800 messages we produced. Each of these traces was then sent to two commercial XQuery engines with partial streaming support (Saxon and DataDirect XQuery) and one academic engine with full streaming support (MXQuery). These engines evaluated the XQuery translation of Interaction Specifications 1-4 in streaming mode. It took in average 1 to 4 milliseconds, and never more than 32 milliseconds, to process one message of a trace. This tends to show that monitoring web service interface contracts through streaming XML engines can actually be done in real time.

As a fully streaming engine, MXQuery performed reasonably well on most properties, especially compared with commercial engines with partial streaming support. One notable exception is Specification 3, where the engine failed to complete the evaluation of the query for some of the traces. These results show that, for the moment, fully streaming engines are more experimental and fragile in nature than commercial-grade products with limited streaming support. The forward-only fragment of LTL can therefore be seen as a "safe zone" where more stable tools can be used to perform runtime monitoring.

CONCLUSION

In retrospect, we have shown how representative web service constraints can be checked on traces of messages using XML methods. In particular, we showed how any formula in the Linear Temporal Logic LTL can be translated into an equivalent XQuery expression on a message trace. This allows standard, off-the-shelf XML query processors such as Saxon to validate interface contracts. Finally, we showed how the validation of representative constraints, expressed both in LTL and LTL-FO+, can be done efficiently using an XQuery processor. We hope these results will open the way to other works leveraging the power of XML query processors available in web service execution environments for the formal validation of collaborations between peers.

REFERENCES

Alonso, G., Casati, F., Kuno, H., & Machiraju, V. (2004). *Web Services, Concepts, Architectures and Applications*. Berlin: Springer Verlag.

Amazon e-commerce service, (2009). Retrieved on April 20th, 2009 from http://docs.amazonwebservices.com/AWSEcommerceService/2005-03-23/

Apparao, V., Byrne, S., Champion, M., Isaacs, S., Jacobs, I., Hors, A. L., et al. (1998). *Document object model (DOM), W3C Recommendation*. Retrieved on April 20th, 2009 from http://www.w3.org/TR/REC-DOM-Level-1/

Arkin, A., Askary, S., Fordin, S., Jekeli, W., Kawaguchi, K., Orchard, D., et al. (2002). *Web service choreography interface (WSCI) 1.0*. Retrieved on April 20th, 2009 from http://www.w3.org/TR/wsci

Artho, C., Drusinsky, D., Goldberg, A., Havelund, K., Lowry, M. R., Pasareanu, C. S., et al. (2003). Experiments with test case generation and runtime analysis. In E. Börger, A. Gargantini, & E. Riccobene (Eds.), *Abstract State Machines*, (LNCS vol. 2589, pp. 87-107). Berlin: Springer.

Baazizi, M. A., Sebahi, S., Hacid, M.-S., Benbernou, S., & Papazoglou, M. P. (2008). Monitoring web services: A database approach. In Mähönen et al. (2008), *Proceedings of ServiceWave 2008*, (pp. 98-109).

Bar-Yossef, Z., Fontoura, M., & Josifovski, V. (2004). On the memory requirements of XPath evaluation over XML streams. In A. Deutsch (Ed.) *PODS*, (pp. 177-188). New York: ACM.

Barbon, F., Traverso, P., Pistore, M., & Trainotti, M. (2006). Run-time monitoring of instances and classes of web service compositions. In *ICWS*, (pp. 63-71). Washington, DC: IEEE Computer Society.

Baresi, L., Guinea, S., Kazhamiakin, R., & Pistore, M. (2008). An integrated approach for the run-time monitoring of BPEL orchestrations. In Mähönen, et al. (2008), *Proceedings of ServiceWave 2008*, (pp. 1-12).

Barringer, H., Goldberg, A., Havelund, K., & Sen, K. (2004). Rule-based runtime verification. In B. Steffen, & G. Levi (Eds.) *VMCAI*, (LNCS Vol. 2937, pp. 44-57). Berlin: Springer.

Barton, C., Charles, P., Goyal, D., Raghavachari, M., Fontoura, M., & Josifovski, V. (2003). Streaming XPath processing with forward and backward axes. In U. Dayal, K. Ramamritham, & T. M. Vijayaraman (Eds.) *ICDE*, (pp. 455-466). Washington, DC: IEEE Computer Society.

Botan, I., Fischer, P. M., Florescu, D., Kossmann, D., Kraska, T., & Tamosevicius, R. (2007). Extending XQuery with window functions. In C. Koch, J. Gehrke, M. N. Garofalakis, D. Srivastava, K. Aberer, A. Deshpande, etal. (Eds.), *VLDB*, (pp. 75-86). New York: ACM.

Bravetti, M., Núñez, M., & Zavattaro, G. (Eds.). (2006). *Web Services and Formal Methods, Third International Workshop, WS-FM 2006 Vienna, Austria, September 8-9, 2006, Proceedings*, (LNCS Vol. 4184). Berlin: Springer.

Brownell, D. (2002). *SAX2*. Cambridge: O'Reilly.

Bultan, T., Fu, X., Hull, R., & Su, J. (2003). Conversation specification: a new approach to design and analysis of e-service composition. In *WWW*, (pp. 403-410).

Caporuscio, M., Inverardi, P., & Pelliccione, P. (2004). Compositional verification of middleware-based software architecture descriptions. In *ICSE*, (pp. 221-230). Washington, DC: IEEE Computer Society.

Chen, Y., Davidson, S. B., & Zheng, Y. (2006). An efficient XPath query processor for XML streams. In *ICDE*, (p. 79). Washington, DC: IEEE Computer Society.

Christensen, E., Curbera, F., Meredith, G., & Weerawarana, S. (2001). *Web services description language (WSDL) 1.1, W3C note*.

Clarke, E. M., Grumberg, O., & Peled, D. A. (2000). *Model Checking*. Cambridge, MA: MIT Press.

Constant, C., Jéron, T., Marchand, H., & Rusu, V. (2007). Integrating formal verification and conformance testing for reactive systems. *IEEE Transactions on Software Engineering*, *33*(8), 558–574. doi:10.1109/TSE.2007.70707

Decker, G., Zaha, J. M., & Dumas, M. (2006). Execution semantics for service choreographies. In Bravetti et al. (eds.), WS-FM, (pp. 163-177).

Fegaras, L., Dash, R. K., & Wang, Y. (2006). A fully pipelined XQuery processor. In *XIME-P*.

Fernández, M., Siméon, M. F. J., Chen, C., Choi, B., Gapeyev, V., Marian, A., et al. (2009). *Galax, an XQuery implementation*. Retrieved on April 20th, 2009 from http://www.galaxquery.org

Fu, X., Bultan, T., & Su, J. (2004). Analysis of interacting BPEL web services. In S. I. Feldman, M. Uretsky, M. Najork, & C. E. Wills (Eds.) *WWW*, (pp. 621-630). New York: ACM.

Gan, Y., Chechik, M., Nejati, S., Bennett, J., O'Farrell, B., & Waterhouse, J. (2007). Runtime monitoring of web service conversations. In *CASCON '07: Proceedings of the 2007 conference of the center for advanced studies on Collaborative research*, (pp. 42-57). New York: ACM.

Garavel, H., & Mateescu, R. (2004). SEQ.OPEN: A Tool for Efficient Trace-Based Verification. In S. Graf & L. Mounier (Eds.) *Model Checking Software, 11th International SPIN Workshop, Barcelona, Spain, April 1-3, 2004, Proceedings*, (LNCS vol. 2989, pp. 151-157). Berlin: Springer.

Ghezzi, C., & Guinea, S. (2007). *Run-Time Monitoring in Service-Oriented Architectures*, (pp. 237-264). Berlin: Springer.

Ghose, A., & Koliadis, G. (2007). Auditing business process compliance. In Krämer et al. (2007), *Proceedings of the International Conference on Service-Oriented Computing (ICSOC-2007)*, (LNCS Vol. 4749, pp. 169-180).

Gottlob, G., Koch, C., & Pichler, R. (2002). Efficient algorithms for processing XPath queries. In *VLDB*, (pp. 95-106). San Francisco: Morgan Kaufmann.

Governatori, G., Milosevic, Z., & Sadiq, S. W. (2006). Compliance checking between business processes and business contracts. In *EDOC*, (pp. 221-232). Washington, DC: IEEE Computer Society.

Hallé, S., & Villemaire, R. (2008a). Runtime monitoring of message-based workflows with data. In *EDOC*, (pp. 63-72). Washington, DC: IEEE Computer Society.

Hallé, S., & Villemaire, R. (2008b). XML methods for validation of temporal properties on message traces with data. In Meersman & Tari (2004), Proceedings of the OTM 2008 Confederated International Conferences, CoopIS, DOA, GADA, IS, and ODBASE 2008. Part I on On the Move to Meaningful Internet Systems, (LNCS Vol. 5331, pp. 337-353).

Hallé, S., & Villemaire, R. (2009a). Browser-Based Enforcement of Interface Contracts in Web Applications with BeepBeep. In A. Bouajjani & O. Maler (Eds.), *Computer Aided Verification, 21st International Conference, CAV 2009, Grenoble, France, June 26 – July 2, 2009, Proceedings*, (LNCS vol. 5643, pp. 648-653). Berlin: Springer.

Hallé, S., & Villemaire, R. (2009b). Runtime monitoring of web service choreographies using streaming XML. In *SAC*, (pp. 1851-1858). New York: ACM.

Hallé, S., Villemaire, R., & Cherkaoui, O. (2009c). Specifying and Validating Data-Aware Temporal Web Service Properties. In *IEEE Trans. Software Eng.,* (to be published in 2009).

Havelund, K., Rosu, G. (2001). *Testing Linear Temporal Logic Formulæ on Finite Execution Traces*. RIACS Technical Report TR 01-08.

Howard, Y., Gruner, S., Gravell, A. M., Ferreira, C., & Augusto, J. C. (2003). Model-based trace-checking. In *SoftTest: UK Software Testing Research Workshop II*.

Hughes, G., Bultan, T., & Alkhalaf, M. (2008). Client and server verification for web services using interface grammars. In T. Bultan, & T. Xie (Eds.) *TAV-WEB*, (pp. 40-46). New York: ACM.

Huth, M. R. A., & Ryan, M. D. (2000). *Logic in Computer Science: Modelling and Reasoning about Systems*. Cambridge, UK: Cambridge University Press.

IBM conversation support project, (2002). Retrieved on April 20th, 2009 from http://www.research.ibm.com/convsupport

Josephraj, J. (2005). *Web services choreography in practice*. Retrieved on April 20th, 2009 from http://www.128.ibm.com/developerworks/web-services/library/ws-choreography/

Kavantzas, N., Burdett, D., Ritzinger, G., Fletcher, T., & Lafon, Y. (2005). *Web services choreography description language version 1.0*. Retrieved on April 20th, 2009 from http://www.w3.org/TR/ws-cdl-10/

Kazhamiakin, R., Pistore, M., & Santuari, L. (2006). Analysis of communication models in web service compositions. In L. Carr, D. D. Roure, A. Iyengar, C. A. Goble, & M. Dahlin (Eds.), *WWW*, (pp. 267-276). New York: ACM.

Koch, C., Scherzinger, S., Schweikardt, N., & Stegmaier, B. (2004). FluXQuery: An optimizing XQuery processor for streaming XML data. In M. A. Nascimento, M. T. Özsu, D. Kossmann, R. J. Miller, J. A. Blakeley, & K. B. Schiefer (Eds.) *VLDB*, (pp. 1309-1312). San Francisco: Morgan Kaufmann.

Krämer, B. J., Lin, K.-J., & Narasimhan, P. (Eds.). (2007). *Service-Oriented Computing - ICSOC 2007, Fifth International Conference, Vienna, Austria, September 17-20, 2007, Proceedings,* (LNCS Vol. 4749). Berlin: Springer.

Krüger, I. H., Meisinger, M., & Menarini, M. (2007). Runtime verification of interactions: From MSCs to aspects. In Sokolsky & Tasiran (2007), *Runtime Verification,* (LNCS Vol. 4839, pp. 63-74).

Lencevicius, R. Ran., A, Yairi, R. (2000). Apache Web Server Execution Tracing Using Third Eye. In M. Ducassé, (Ed.) *Proceedings of the Fourth International Workshop on Automated Debugging, AADEBUG 2000, Munich, Germany.* Retrieved on June 20th, 2009 from http://arxiv.org/abs/cs.SE/0011022

Li, X., & Agrawal, G. (2005). Efficient evaluation of XQuery over streaming data. In K. Böhm, C. S. Jensen, L. M. Haas, M. L. Kersten, P.-Å. Larson, & B. C. Ooi (Eds.) *VLDB*, (pp. 265-276). New York: ACM.

Mahbub, K., & Spanoudakis, G. (2005). Run-time monitoring of requirements for systems composed of web-services: Initial implementation and evaluation experience. In *ICWS*, (pp. 257-265). Wasington, DC: IEEE Computer Society.

Mahbub, K., & Spanoudakis, G. (2007). *Monitoring WS-Agreements: An Event Calculus-Based Approach,* (pp. 265-306). Berlin: Springer.

Mähönen, P., Pohl, K., & Priol, T. (Eds.). (2008). Towards a Service-Based Internet. *In Proceedings of the First European Conference, ServiceWave 2008, Madrid, Spain, December 10-13,* (LNCS Vol. 5377). Berlin: Springer.

Meersman, R., & Tari, Z. (Eds.). (2008). *On the Move to Meaningful Internet Systems 2008: CoopIS, DOA, and ODBASE, OTM Confederated International Conferences, Monterrey, Mexico, October 10-14, 2008, Proceedings, Part I,* (LNCS vol. 5331). Berlin: Springer.

Meredith, G., & Bjorg, S. (2003). Contracts and types. *Communications of the ACM, 46*(10), 41–47. doi:10.1145/944217.944236

Nakajima, S. (2005). Lightweight formal analysis of web service flows. *Progress in Informatics,* (2), 57-76.

Object Management Group. (1997). *UML specification version 1.1, OMG document ad/97-08-11.* Retrieved on April 20th, 2009 from http://www.omg.org/cgi-bin/doc?ad/97-08-11

Parastatidis, S., Webber, J., Woodman, S., Kuo, D., & Greenfield, P. (2005). *SOAP service description language (SSDL).* Tech. Rep. CS-TR-899, University of Newcastle, Newcastle upon Tyne.

Park, J. H., & Kang, J.-H. (2007). Optimization of XQuery queries including for clauses. In *ICIW,* (p. 37). Washington, DC: IEEE Computer Society.

Peng, F., & Chawathe, S. S. (2003). XPath queries on streaming data. In A. Y. Halevy, Z. G. Ives, & A. Doan (Eds.) *SIGMOD Conference,* (pp. 431-442). New York: ACM.

Robinson, W. (2006). A requirements monitoring framework for enterprise systems. *Requir. Eng., 11*(1), 17–41. doi:10.1007/s00766-005-0016-3

Robinson, W. N. (2003). Monitoring web service requirements. In *RE,* (pp. 65-74). Washington, DC: IEEE Computer Society.

Schmidt, M., Scherzinger, S., & Koch, C. (2007). Combined static and dynamic analysis for effective buffer minimization in streaming xquery evaluation. In *ICDE*, (pp. 236-245). Washignton, DC: IEEE.

Snodgrass, R. (1989). *The Interface Description Language: Definition and Use.* London: W.H. Freeman.

Sokolsky, O., & Tasiran, S. (Eds.). (2007). *Runtime Verification, 7th International Workshop, RV 2007*, Vancover, Canada, March 13, 2007, *Revised Selected Papers,* (LNCS Vol. 4839). Berlin: Springer.

Stolz, V. (2007). Temporal assertions with parametrised propositions. In Sokolsky & Tasiran (2007), *Runtime Verification,* (pp. 176-187).

van der Aalst, W. M., & Verbeek, H. M. (2008). Process mining in web services: The WebSphere case. *Bulletin of the IEEE Computer Society Technical Committee on Data Engineering,* (pp. 45-48).

Venzke, M. (2004). Specifications using XQuery expressions on traces. *Electronic Notes in Theoretical Computer Science, 105,* 109–118. doi:10.1016/j.entcs.2004.05.004

Wang, C., Nepal, S., Chen, S., & Zic, J. (2008). Cooperative data management services based on accountable contract. In Meersman & Tari (2004), *On the Move to Meaningful Internet Systems: OTM 2008,* (pp. 301-318).

ENDNOTES

[1]   http://www.w3.org/XML/Query/#implementations

[2]   http://dsd.lbl.gov/nux

[3]   http://www.saxonica.com

[4]   http://www.datadirect.com

[5]   An open source version of Saxon is also available, but as of July 2008, it did not allow streaming XML processing.

[6]   These conditions are sufficient, but not necessary. For example, $\mathbf{G}\ (\mathbf{G}\ \varphi) \equiv \mathbf{G}\ \varphi$ and $\mathbf{G}\ (\mathbf{X}\ \varphi) \equiv \mathbf{X}\ (\mathbf{G}\ \varphi)$.

Compilation of References

Aberer, K., Cudre-Mauroux, P., Datta, A., Despotovic, Z., Hauswirth, M., Punceva, M., & Schmidt, R. (2003). P-Grid: A Self-Organizing Structured P2P System. *SIGMOD Record, 32*(3), 29–33. doi:10.1145/945721.945729

Abiteboul, S., Alexe, B., Benjelloun, O., Cautis, B., Fundulaki, I., Milo, T., & Sahuguet, A. (2004). An Electronic Patient Record "On Steroids": Distributed, Peer-to-Peer, Secure and Privacy-Conscious (demo). In *Proceedings of VLDB* (pp. 1273–1276).

Abiteboul, S., Alstrup, S., Kaplan, H., Milo, T., & Rauhe, T. (2006). Compact Labeling Scheme for Ancestor Queries. *SIAM Journal on Computing, 35*(6), 1295–1309. doi:10.1137/S0097539703437211

Abiteboul, S., Baumgarten, J., Bonifati, A., & Cobena, G. Cremarenco, Dragan, C.F., Manolescu, I., Milo, T., & Preda, N. (2003). Managing Distributed Workspaces with Active XML (demo). In *Proceedings of VLDB* (pp. 1061–1064).

Abiteboul, S., Bonifati, A., Cobena, G., Manolescu, I., & Milo, T. (2003). Dynamic XML Documents with Distribution and Replication. In *Proceedings of ACM SIGMOD* (pp. 527–538).

Abiteboul, S., Buneman, P., & Suciu, D. (2002). *Data on the Web: From Relations to Semistructured Data and XML.* San Francisco, CA: Morgan Kaufmann Publishers.

Abiteboul, S., Manolescu, I., Polyzotis, N., Preda, N., & Sun, C. (2008). XML Processing in DHT Networks. In *Proceedings of IEEE ICDE* (pp. 606–615).

Aboulnaga, A., & Gebaly, K. E. (2007). μBE: User guided source selection and schema mediation for internet scale data integration. *ICDE,* 186-195.

Aboulnaga, A., Naughton, J. F., & Zhang, C. (2001). *Generating Synthetic Complex-structured XML Data.* Paper presented at the Fourth International Workshop on the Web and Database (WebDB), Santa Barbara, USA.

Achard, F., Vaysseixm, G., & Barillot, E. (2001). XML, bioinformatics and data integration. *Bioinformatics (Oxford, England), 17*(2), 115–125. doi:10.1093/bioinformatics/17.2.115

Afanasiev, L., Manolescu, I., & Michiels, P. (2005). *MemBeR: A Micro-benchmark Repository for XQuery.* Paper presented at Third International XML Database Symposium (XSym), Trondheim, Norway. Afanasiev, L., Manolescu, I., & Michiels, P. (n.d.). *MemBeR: XQuery Micro-Benchmark Repository.* Retrieved April 1, 2009, from http://lips.science.uva.nl/Resources/MemBeR/index.html

Afrati, F., Chirkova, R., Gergatsoulis, M., Kimelfeld, B., Pavlaki, V., & Sagiv, Y. (2009). On rewriting XPath queries using views. In *EDBT '09: Proceedings of the 12th International Conference on Extending Database Technology,* Saint Petersburg, Russia, (pp. 168-179).

Agrawal, R., Somani, A., & Xu, Y. (2001). Storage and querying of e-commerce data. *VLDB,* 149-158

Aguiar Moraes Filho, J., & Härder, T. (2008, September 10–12). EXsum—An XML summarization framework. In *Proceedings of the 12th International Database Engineering and Applications Symposium, Coimbra, Portugal, 2008,* (pp. 139–148). New York: ACM Press.

Albert, J. (1991). Algebraic properties of bag data types. In *Proceedings of the seventeenth International Conference on Very Large Data Bases,* (pp. 211–219). San Mateo, CA: Morgan Kaufmann.

Al-Khalifa, S., Jagadish, H. V., Koudas, N., Patel, J. M., Srivastava, D., & Wu, Y. (2002). Structural joins: A primitive for efficient XML query pattern matching. In *Proceedings of the 18th International Conference on Data Engineering* (pp. 141-152). San Jose, CA: IEEE Computer Society.

Alonso, G., Casati, F., Kuno, H., & Machiraju, V. (2004). *Web Services, Concepts, Architectures and Applications.* Berlin: Springer Verlag.

Altinel, M., & Franklin, M. J. (2000). Efficient filtering of XML documents for selective dissemination of information. In *Proceedings of the 26th International Conference on Very Large Data Bases (VLDB'00),* (pp. 53–64), San Francisco, CA.

Amagasa, T., Yoshikawa, M., & Uemura, S. (2003). QRS: a robust numbering scheme for XML documents. In *Proceedings of the 19th International Conference on Data Engineering* (5-8 March 2003), (pp. 705 – 707).

Amazon e-commerce service, (2009). Retrieved on April 20th, 2009 from http://docs.amazonwebservices.com/AWSEcommerceService/2005-03-23/

Amer-Yahia, S., & Lalmas, M. (2006). XML Search: Languages, INEX and Scoring. *SIGMOD Record, 35*(4). doi:10.1145/1228268.1228271

Amer-Yahia, S., Cho, S. R., Lakshmanan, L. V. S., & Srivastava, D. (2001). Minimization of tree pattern queries. In *Proc. of the ACM SIGMOD Conf. on Management of Data,* (pp. 497–508). New York: ACM press.

Amer-Yahia, S., Cho, S., Lakshmanan, L. V. S., & Srivastava, D. (2002). Tree pattern query minimization. *The VLDB Journal, 11*(4), 315–331. doi:10.1007/s00778-002-0076-7

Amer-Yahia, S., Laksmanan, L. V. S., & Pandit, S. (2004). FlexPath: Flexible Structure and Full-Text Querying for XML. In *Proceedings of ACM SIGMOD* (pp. 83–94).

Anand, A., & Chawathe, S. S. (2004). *Cooperative data dissemination in a serverless environment.* CS-TR-4562, University of Maryland, College Park, MD.

Antoshenkov, G. (1997). Dictionary-based order-preserving string compression. *The VLDB Journal, 6*(1), 26–39. doi:10.1007/s007780050031

Apparao, V., Byrne, S., Champion, M., Isaacs, S., Jacobs, I., Hors, A. L., et al. (1998). *Document object model (DOM), W3C Recommendation.* Retrieved on April 20th, 2009 from http://www.w3.org/TR/REC-DOM-Level-1/

Arenas, M., & Libkin, L. (2008). XML data exchange: Consistency and query answering. [JACM]. *Journal of the ACM, 55*(2). doi:10.1145/1346330.1346332

Arion, A., Benzaken, V., & Manolescu, I. P. Yannis. (2007). Structured materialized views for XML queries. In *VLDB '07: Proceedings of the 33rd International Conference on very Large Data Bases,* Vienna, Austria, (pp. 87-98).

Arion, A., Bonifati, A., Manolescu, I., & Pugliese, A. (2007). XQueC: A query-conscious compressed XML database. *ACM Transactions on Internet Technology, 7*(2), 1–35. doi:10.1145/1239971.1239974

Arkin, A., Askary, S., Fordin, S., Jekeli, W., Kawaguchi, K., Orchard, D., et al. (2002). *Web service choreography interface (WSCI) 1.0.* Retrieved on April 20th, 2009 from http://www.w3.org/TR/wsci

Artho, C., Drusinsky, D., Goldberg, A., Havelund, K., Lowry, M. R., Pasareanu, C. S., et al. (2003). Experiments with test case generation and runtime analysis. In E. Börger, A. Gargantini, & E. Riccobene (Eds.), *Abstract State Machines,* (LNCS vol. 2589, pp. 87-107). Berlin: Springer.

Astrahan, M., & Chamberlin, D. (1975). Implementation of a Structured English Query Language. [New York: ACM press.]. *Communications of the ACM, 18*(10), 580–588. doi:10.1145/361020.361215

Atay, M., Chebotko, A., Lu, S., & Fotouhi, F. (2007). XML-to-SQL query mapping in the presence of multi-valued schema mappings and recursive XML schemas. *DEXA*, (pp. 603-616).

Aulbach, S., Grust, T., Jacobs, D., & Rittinger, A. K. J. (2008). Multi-tenant databases for software as a service: Schema-mapping techniques. *SIGMOD Conference*, (pp. 1195-1206).

Baazizi, M. A., Sebahi, S., Hacid, M.-S., Benbernou, S., & Papazoglou, M. P. (2008). Monitoring web services: A database approach. In Mähönen et al. (2008), *Proceedings of ServiceWave 2008*, (pp. 98-109).

Balmin, A., Eliaz, T., Hornibrook, J., Lim, L., Lohman, G. M., & Simmen, D. E. (2006). Cost-based optimization in DB2 XML. *IBM Systems Journal, 45*(2), 299–320.

Balmin, A., Hristidis, V., & Papakonstantinou, Y. (2004). ObjectRank: Authority-based keyword search in databases. *VLDB,* (pp. 564-575).

Balmin, A., Özcan, F., Beyer, K. S., Cochrane, R. J., & Pirahesh, H. (2004). A framework for using materialized XPath views in XML query processing. *VLDB '04: Proceedings of the Thirtieth International Conference on very Large Data Bases,* Toronto, Canada, (pp. 60-71).

Balmin, A., Papakonstantinou, Y., & Vianu, V. (2004). Incremental Validation of XML Documents. *ACM Transactions on Database Systems, 29*(4), 710–751. doi:10.1145/1042046.1042050

Banavar, G., Chandra, T., Mukherjee, B., & Nagarajarao, J. (1999). An efficient multicast protocol for content-based publish-subscribe systems. In *Proceedings of the 19th International Conference of Distributed Computing Systems,* (pp. 262-271).

Bao, Z., Ling, T. W., Chen, B., & Lu, J. (2009). Effective XML Keyword Search with Relevance Oriented Ranking. In *Proceedings of ICDE.*

Barbon, F., Traverso, P., Pistore, M., & Trainotti, M. (2006). Run-time monitoring of instances and classes of web service compositions. In *ICWS,* (pp. 63-71). Washington, DC: IEEE Computer Society.

Barbosa, D., Leighton, G., & Smith, A. (2006). Efficient Incremental Validation of XML Documents After Composite Updates. In *Database and XML Technologies, 4th International XML Database Symposium,* (LNCS Vol. 4516, pp. 107-121).

Barbosa, D., Mendelzon, A. O., Keenleyside, J., & Lyons, K. (2002). *Toxgene: An extensible template-based data generator for XML.* Paper presented at the Fifth International Workshop on the Web and Database, Madison, WI.

Barbosa, D., Mendelzon, A., Libkin, L., & Mignet, L. (2004). Efficient Incremental Validation of XML Documents. In *International Conference on Data Engineering,* (pp. 671-682).

Barbosa, D., Mignet, L., & Veltri, P. (2005). Studying the XML web: Gathering statistics from an XML sample. *World Wide Web (Bussum), 8*(4), 413–438. doi:10.1007/s11280-005-1544-y

Baresi, L., Guinea, S., Kazhamiakin, R., & Pistore, M. (2008). An integrated approach for the run-time monitoring of BPEL orchestrations. In Mähönen, et al. (2008), *Proceedings of ServiceWave 2008,* (pp. 1-12).

Barg, M., & Wong, R. K. (2001). Structural proximity searching for large collections of semistructured data. In *Proceedings of CIKM.* 175-182.

Barringer, H., Goldberg, A., Havelund, K., & Sen, K. (2004). Rule-based runtime verification. In B. Steffen, & G. Levi (Eds.) *VMCAI,* (LNCS Vol. 2937, pp. 44-57). Berlin: Springer.

Barton, C., Charles, P., Goyal, D., Raghavachari, M., Fontoura, M., & Josifovski, V. (2003). Streaming XPath processing with forward and backward axes. In *Proceedings of the 19th International Conference on Data Engineering* (pp. 455-466). Banglore, India: IEEE Computer Society.

Bary, T., Paoli, J., & Sperberg-McQueen, C. M. (Eds.). (1998, February 10). *Extensible Markup language (XML) 1.0.* Retrieved January 22, 2009, from http://www.w3.org/TR/1998/REC-xml-19980210.html

Bar-Yossef, Z., Fontoura, M., & Josifovski, V. (2004). On the memory requirements of xpath evaluation over xml streams. In *PODS '04: Proceedings of the twenty-third ACM SIGMOD-SIGACT-SIGART symposium on Principles of database systems* (pp. 177-188). New York: ACM Press.

Bar-Yossef, Z., Fontoura, M., & Josifovski, V. (2005). Buffering in query evaluation over xml streams. In *PODS '05: Proceedings of the twenty-fourth ACM SIGMOD-SIGACT-SIGART symposium on Principles of database systems* (pp. 216-227). New York: ACM.

Beckett, D., & McBride, B. (2004). *RDF/XML Syntax Specification (Revised) W3C Recommendation.* Retrieved February 10, 2004, from http://www.w3.org/TR/rdf-syntax-grammar

Beeri, C., & Tzaban, Y. (1999). SAL: An algebra for semistructured data and XML. In *WebDB (Informal Proceedings)*, (pp. 37–42).

Benjelloun, O., Sarma, A. D., Halevy, A. Y., & Widom, J. (2006). ULDBs: Databases with uncertainty and lineage. *VLDB*, 953-964.

Berglund, A., Boag, S., Chamberlin, D., Fernández, M. F., Kay, M., Robie, J., & Siméon, J. (2007, January 23). *XML Path Language (XPath) 2.0.* W3C Recommendation. Available at http://www.w3.org/TR/xpath20/

Berkeley DB Data Store. (2006). Retrieved from http://www.sleepycat.com/products/data.shtml

Bernstein, P. A., Giunchiglia, F., Kementsietsidis, A., Mylopoulos, J., Serafini, L., & Zaihrayeu, I. (2002). Data Management for Peer-to-Peer Computing: a Vision. In *Proceedings of ACM WebDB* (pp. 89–94).

Bertino, E., & Ferrari, E. (2001). XML and data integration. *IEEE Internet Computing, 5*(6), 75–76. doi:10.1109/4236.968835

Bertossi, L. E. (2006). Consistent query answering in databases. *SIGMOD Record, 35*(2), 68–76. doi:10.1145/1147376.1147391

Bex, G. J., Martens, W., Neven, F., & Schwentick, T. (2005). Expressiveness of XSDs: From practice to theory, there and back again. *WWW,* (pp. 712-721).

Bex, G. J., Neven, F., & Bussche, J. V. d. (2004). DTDs versus XML schema: A practical study. *WebDB,* (pp. 79-84).

Bex, G. J., Neven, F., & Vansummeren, S. (2007). Inferring XML schema definitions from XML data. *VLDB,* (pp. 998-1009).

Bex, G. J., Neven, F., & Vansummeren, S. (2008). SchemaScope: A system for inferring and cleaning XML schemas. *SIGMOD Conference,* (pp. 1259-1262).

Bex, G. J., Neven, F., Schwentick, T., & Tuyls, K. (2006). Inference of concise DTDs from XML data. *VLDB,* (pp. 115-126).

Beyer, K., & Cochrane, R. J., Josifovski, V., Kleewein, J., Lapis, G., Lohman, G., et al. (2005). System RX: one part relational, one part XML. In *2005 ACM SIGMOD International Conference on Management of Data* (pp. 347-358). New York: ACM.

Bhalotia, G., Hulgeri, A., Nakhe, C., & Sudarshan, S. C. S. (2002). Keyword searching and browsing in databases using BANKS. *ICDE,* (pp. 431-440).

Bloom, B. H. (1970). Space/time trade-offs in hash coding with allowable errors. *Communications of the ACM, 13*(7), 422–426. doi:10.1145/362686.362692

Boag, S., Chamberlin, D., Fernández, M. F., Florescu, D., Robie, J., & Siméon, J. (2007). *XQuery 1.0: An XML Query Language.* Retrieved March 25, 2006. from http://www.w3.org/TR/xquery/

Böhme, T., & Rahm, E. (2001). *XMach-1: a benchmark for XML data management.* Paper presented in the German Database Conference BTW2001, Berlin, Germany.

Boncz, P. A., Grust, T., van Keulen, M., Manegold, S., Rittinger, J., & Teubner, J. (2006). MonetDB/XQuery: A fast XQuery processor powered by a relational engine. In *Proceedings of the ACM SIGMOD International Conference on Management of Data* (pp. 479-490). Chicago: ACM.

Bonifati, A., Chang, E. Q., Ho, T., Lakshmanan, L. V. S., & Pottinger, R. (2005). HePToX: Marrying XML and heterogeneity in your P2P databases. In *VLDB*, (pp. 1267-1270).

Bonifati, A., Cuzzocrea, A., Matrangolo, U., & Jain, M. (2004). XPath Lookup Queries in P2P Networks. In *Proceedings of ACM WIDM* (pp. 48–55).

Borkar, V. R., Carey, M. J., Lychagin, D., Westmann, T., Engovatov, D., & Onose, N. (2006). Query processing in the AquaLogic data services platform. *VLDB*, (pp. 1037-1048).

Botan, I., Fischer, P. M., Florescu, D., Kossmann, D., Kraska, T., & Tamosevicius, R. (2007). Extending XQuery with window functions. In C. Koch, J. Gehrke, M. N. Garofalakis, D. Srivastava, K. Aberer, A. Deshpande, etal. (Eds.), *VLDB*, (pp. 75-86). New York: ACM.

Bouchou, B., & Ferrari Alves, M. H. (2003). Updates and Incremental Validation of XML Documents. In *Database Programming Languages, 9th International Workshop*, (LNCS Vol. 2921, pp. 216-232).

Bouchou, B., Alves, M. H. F., & Musicante, M. A. (2003). Tree automata to verify XML key constraints. *WebDB*, (pp. 37-42).

Bouchou, B., Cheriat, A., Ferrari, M. H., & Savary, A. (2006). XML Document Correction: Incremental Approach Activated by Schema Validation. In *Tenth International Database Engineering and Applications Symposium*, (pp. 228-238).

Bouchou, B., Duarte, D., Ferrari Alves, M. H., Laurent, D., & Musicante, M. A. (2004). Schema Evolution for XML: A Consistency-preserving Approach. In *International Conference on Mathematical Foundations of Computer Science* (LNCS vol. 3153, pp. 876-888).

Bouquet, P., Serafini, L., & Zanobini, S. (2003). Semantic coordination: A new approach and an application. *International Semantic Web Conference,* (pp. 130-145).

Bourret, R. (2007). *XML Database Products*. Available at http://www.rpbourret.com/xml/XMLDatabaseProds.htm

Brantner, M., Helmer, S., Kanne, C. C., & Moerkotte, G. (2005). Full-fledged algebraic XPath processing in Natix. In *Proceedings of the 21st International Conference on Data Engineering*, ICDE 2005 (pp. 705-716). Tokyo, Japan: IEEE Computer Society.

Bravetti, M., Núñez, M., & Zavattaro, G. (Eds.). (2006). *Web Services and Formal Methods, Third International Workshop, WS-FM 2006 Vienna, Austria, September 8-9, 2006, Proceedings*, (LNCS Vol. 4184). Berlin: Springer.

Bray, T., Hollander, D., Layman, A., & Tobin, R. (2006). *Namespaces in XML 1.0* (2nd Ed.). Retrieved April 24, 2009, from http://www.w3.org/TR/REC-xml-names/

Bray, T., Paoli, J., Sperberg-McQueen, C. M., Maler, E., & Yergeau, F. (2008). *Extensible Markup Language (XML) 1.0 (Fifth Edition) W3C Recommendation*. Retrieved November 26, 2008, from http://www.w3c.org/TR/2008/REC-xml-20081126/

Bremer, J.-M., & Gertz, M. (2003). On Distributing XML Repositories. In *Proceedings of ACM WebDB*, (pp. 73–78).

Bressan, S., Dobbie, G., Lacroix, Z., Lee, M. L., Li, Y. G., Nambiar, U., & Wadhwa, B. (2001). *XOO7: Applying OO7 Benchmark to XML Query Processing Tools*. Paper presented at the 10th ACM International Conference on Information and Knowledge Management (CIKM), Atlanta, GA.

Bressan. S., Lee, M. L., Li, Y. G., Lacroix, Z. & Nambiar, U. (2001). *The XOO7 XML management system benchmark*. Retrieved March 12, 2009, from http://www.comp.nus.edu.sg/~ebh/XOO7/download/XOO7_TechReport.pdf

Brin, S., & Page, L. (1998). The anatomy of a large-scale hypertextual web search engine. *Computer Networks, 30*(1-7), 107-117.

Broder, A. Z. (1993). *Some Applications of Rabin's Fingerprinting Method*. Berlin: Springer-Verlag.

Broder, A. Z., Najork, M., & Wiener, J. L. (2003). Efficient URL Caching for World Wide Web Crawling. In *Proceedings of ACM WWW* (pp. 679–689).

Brownell, D. (2002). *SAX2*. Cambridge: O'Reilly.

Bruno, N., Gravano, L., & Doudas, N. (2003). Navigation-vs. index-based XML multi-query processing. In *Proceedings of the 19nd International Conference on Data Engineering (ICDE'03)*, (pp. 139–150), Washington, DC.

Bruno, N., Gravano, L., Koudas, N., & Srivastava, D. (2003). Navigation- vs. index-based XML multi-query processing. In *Proceedings. 19th International Conference on Data Engineering, 2003*, (pp. 139-150).

Bruno, N., Koudas, N., & Srivastava, D. (2002). Holistic twig joins: Optimal XML pattern matching. In *Proceedings of the ACM SIGMOD International Conference on Management of Data* (pp. 310-322). Madison, WI: ACM.

Brunskill, E. (2001). Building Peer-to-Peer Systems with Chord, a Distributed Lookup Service. In *Proceedings of IEEE HotOS*, (pp. 81–86).

Bry, F. (1989). Towards an efficient evaluation of general queries: quantifier and disjunction processing revisited. In *Proc. of the ACM SIGMOD Conf. on Management of Data*, (pp. 193–204). New York: ACM press.

Bultan, T., Fu, X., Hull, R., & Su, J. (2003). Conversation specification: a new approach to design and analysis of e-service composition. In *WWW*, (pp. 403-410).

Buneman, P., Fan, W., & Weinstein, S. (1999). Query optimization for semistructured data using path constraints in a deterministic data model. In *DBPL*, (pp. 208-223).

Calvanese, D., Giacomo, G. D., Lenzerini, M., & Vardi, M. Y. (1999). Answering regular path queries using views. In *Proc. of the 16th IEEE Int. Conf. on Data Engineering (ICDE 2000*, (pp. 389-398).

Candan, K. S., Cao, H., Qi, Y., & Sapino, M. L. (2008). System support for exploration and expert feedback in resolving conflicts during integration of metadata. *The VLDB Journal, 17*(6), 1407–1444. doi:10.1007/s00778-008-0109-y

Candan, K. S., Dönderler, M. E., & Qi, Y. R. Jaikannan, & Kim, J. W. (2006). FMware: Middleware for efficient filtering and matching of XML messages with local data. *Middleware '06: Proceedings of the ACM/IFIP/USENIX 2006 International Conference on Middleware*, Melbourne, Australia, (pp. 301-321).

Candan, K. S., Grant, J., & Subrahmanian, V. S. (1997). A unified treatment of null values using constraints. *Inf. Sci., 98*(1-4), 99–156.

Candan, K. S., Hsiung, W., & Chen, S. T. Junichi, & Agrawal, D. (2006). AFilter: Adaptable XML filtering with prefix-caching suffix-clustering. *VLDB '06: Proceedings of the 32nd International Conference on very Large Data Bases*, Seoul, Korea, (pp. 559-570).

Candan, K. S., Kim, J. W., Liu, H., & Agarwal, R. S. N. (2007). *Multimedia data mining and knowledge discovery*, (pp. 259-290). London: Springer.

Candan, K. S., Kim, J. W., Liu, H., & Suvarna, R. (2006). Discovering mappings in hierarchical data from multiple sources using the inherent structure. *Knowledge and Information Systems, 10*(2), 185–210. doi:10.1007/s10115-005-0230-9

Candan, K. S., Li, W., & Priya, M. L. (2000). Similarity-based ranking and query processing in multimedia databases. *Data & Knowledge Engineering, 35*(3), 259–298. doi:10.1016/S0169-023X(00)00025-2

Candan, S. K., & Hsiung, P. W., Chen, S., Tatemura, J., & Agrawal, D. (2006). AFilter: adaptable XML filtering with prefix-caching suffix-clustering. In *VLDB '06: Proceedings of the 32nd international conference on Very large data bases* (pp. 559-570). VLDB Endowment.

Caporuscio, M., Inverardi, P., & Pelliccione, P. (2004). Compositional verification of middleware-based software architecture descriptions. In *ICSE*, (pp. 221-230). Washington, DC: IEEE Computer Society.

Carey, M. J., DeWitt, D. J., & Naughton, J. F. (2003). The OO7 Benchmark. *SIGMOD Record, 22*(2), 12–21. doi:10.1145/170036.170041

Carzaniga, A., Roseblum, D. S., & Wolf, A. L. (2000). Archieving scalability and expressiveness in an internet-scale event notification services. In *Proceedings of the 19th ACM Symposium on Principles of Distributed Computing*, (pp. 219-227).

Carzaniga, A., Rutherford, M. J., & Wolf, A. L. (2004). A routing scheme for content-based networking. In *Proceedings of IEEE Conference on Computer Communications (INFOCOM '04)*, Hong Kong, China.

Cautis, B., Deutsch, A., & Onose, N. (2008). XPath rewriting using multiple views: Achieving completeness and efficiency. *WebDB.*

Cavalieri, F., Guerrini, G., & Mesiti, M. (2008). Navigational Path Expression on XML Schemas. In *International Conference on Database and Expert Systems Applications*, (LNCS Vol. 5181, pp. 718-726).

Cavalieri, F., Guerrini, G., & Mesiti, M. (2008). *XSchemaUpdate: Schema Evolution and Document Adaptation.* Technical report, University of Genova, Switzerland.

Ceri, S., & Gottlob, G. (1985). Translating SQL into relational algebra: Optimization, semantics, and equivalence of SQL queries. *IEEE Transactions on Software Engineering, 11*(4), 324–345. doi:10.1109/TSE.1985.232223

Chamberlin, D. Florescu, D., et al. (2008). *XQuery update facility.* Retrieved from http://www.w3.org/TR/xquery-update-10/

Chamberlin, D., & Robie, J. (2008). *XQuery 1.1.* Retrieved from http://www.w3.org/TR/xquery-11/

Chamberlin, D., Carey, M. J., Florescu, D., Kossmann, D., & Robie, J. (2006). Programming with XQuery. *XIME-P.*

Chamberlin, D., Engovatov, D., Florescu, D., & Melton, J. (2008). *XQuery scripting extension 1.0.* Retrieved from http://www.w3.org/TR/xquery-sx-10/

Chan, C.-Y., & Ni, Y. (2006). Content-based dissemination of fragmented XML data. In *Proceedings of the 26th International Conference on Distributed Computing Systems (ICDCS)*, (pp. 44-53).

Chan, C.-Y., & Ni, Y. (2007). Efficient XML data dissemination with piggybacking. In *Proceedings of the ACM International Conference on Management of Data (SIGMOD).*

Chan, C.-Y., Fan, W., Felber, P., Garofalakis, M., & Rastogi, R. (2002a). Tree pattern aggregation for scalable XML data dissemination. In *Proceedings of the 28th international conference on Very Large Data Bases (VLDB'02)*, (pp. 826–837), Hong Kong, China.

Chan, C.-Y., Felber, P., Garofalakis, M., & Rastogi, R. (2002). Efficient filtering of xml documents with xpath expressions. *The VLDB Journal, 11*(4), 354–379. doi:10.1007/s00778-002-0077-6

Chand, R., & Felber, P. (2003). A scalable protocol for contentbased routing in overlay networks. In *Technical Report RR-03-074, Institut EURECOM, Feb.*

Chau, T., Muthusamy, V., Jacobsen, H. A., Litani, E., Chan, A., & Coulthard, P. (2008). Automating SLA modeling. In *Proceedings of the 2008 conference of the Centre for Advanced Studies on Collaborative Research*, Richmond Hill, Ontario, Canada.

Chaudhri, A. B., Rashid, A. & Zicari, R. (2003). *XML data management: native XML and XML-enabled database systems.* Reading, MA: Addison-Wesley.

Chaudhuri, S. (1998). An Overview of Query Optimization in Relational Systems. In *Proceedings of the seventeenth ACM SIGACT-SIGMOD-SIGART symposium on Principles of database systems*, (pp. 34–43). New York: ACM press.

Chaudhuri, S., Gravano, L., & Marian, A. (2004). Optimizing top-k selection queries over multimedia repositories. *IEEE Transactions on Knowledge and Data Engineering, 16*(8), 992–1009. doi:10.1109/TKDE.2004.30

Chen, L., Gupta, A., & Kurul, E. M. (2005). Stack-based algorithms for pattern matching on DAGs. In *VLDB '05: Proceedings of the 31st international conference on Very large data bases*, (pp. 493-504).

Chen, Q., Lim, A., & Ong, K. (2003, June 9-12). D(k)-Index: An adaptive Structural summary for graph-structured data. In *Proceedings of the ACM SIGMOD International Conference on Management of Data*, San Diego, CA (pp.134-144). New York: ACM Press.

Chen, S., Li, H. G., Tatemura, J., Hsiung, W. P., Agrawal, D., & Candan, S. K. (2006). Twig2Stack: bottom-up processing of generalized-tree-pattern queries over XML documents. In *VLDB '06: Proceedings of the 32nd international conference on Very large data bases* (pp. 283-294). VLDB Endowment.

Chen, S., Li, H.-G., Tatemura, J., Hsiung, W.-P., Agrawal, D., & Candan, S. K. (2008). Scalable filtering of multiple generalized-tree-pattern queries over xml streams. *IEEE Transactions on Knowledge and Data Engineering, 20*(12), 1627–1640. doi:10.1109/TKDE.2008.83

Chen, T., Lu, J., & Ling, T. W. (2005). On boosting holism in XML twig pattern matching using structural indexing techniques. In *2005 ACM SIGMOD International Conference on Management of Data* (pp. 455-466). New York: ACM.

Chen, Y., Davidson, S. B., & Zheng, Y. (2004). BLAS: An efficient XPath processing system. *ACM SIGMOD International Conference on Management of Data* (pp. 47-58). New York: ACM.

Chen, Y., Davidson, S. B., & Zheng, Y. (2006). An Efficient XPath Query Processor for XML Streams. In *ICDE '06: Proceedings of the 22nd International Conference on Data Engineering.* Washington, DC: IEEE Computer Society.

Chen, Z., Jagadish, H. V., Lakshmanan, L. V., & Paparizos, S. (2003). From tree patterns to generalized tree patterns: on efficient evaluation of XQuery. In *VLDB '2003: Proceedings of the 29th international conference on Very large data bases* (pp. 237-248). VLDB Endowment.

Cheney, J. (2001). Compressing XML with multiplexed hierarchical PPM models. *Data Compression Conference* (pp. 163-172). Washington, DC: IEEE.

Cheney, J. (2007). Lux: A Lightweight, Statically Typed XML Update Language. In *PLAN-X 2007*, (pp. 25-36).

Cheney, J. (2008). Flux: FunctionaL Updates for XML. In *ACM International Conference on Functional Programming.*

Cherukuri, V. S., & Candan, K. S. (2008). Propagation-vectors for trees (PVT): Concise yet effective summaries for hierarchical data and trees. *LSDS-IR '08: Proceeding of the 2008 ACM Workshop on Large-Scale Distributed Systems for Information Retrieval*, Napa Valley, CA, (pp. 3-10).

Cheung, A. K., & Jacobsen, H.-A. (2006). Dynamic load balancing in distributed content-based publish/subscribe. In *Proceedings of the ACM/IFIP/USENIX 2006 International Conference on Middleware (Middleware'06)*, (pp. 141–161), New York.

Cheung, A., & Jacobsen, H.-A. (2008). Efficient Load Distribution in Publish/Subscribe. Technical report, Middleware Systems Research Group, University of Toronto.

Chidlovskii, B. (2001). Schema extraction from XML: A grammatical inference approach. *KRDB*, Chitic, C., & Rosu, D. (2004). On validation of XML streams using finite state machines. *WebDB*, (pp. 85-90).

Chien, S.-Y., Tsotras, V. J., & Zaniolo, C. (2001). XML Document Versioning. *SIGMOD Record, 30*(3), 46–53. doi:10.1145/603867.603875

Chien, S.-Y., Tsotras, V. J., & Zaniolo, C. (2002). Efficient schemes for managing multiversion XML documents. *The VLDB Journal, 11*(4), 332–353. doi:10.1007/s00778-002-0079-4

Chiticariu, L., Kolaitis, P. G., & Popa, L. (2008). Interactive generation of integrated schemas. In *SIGMOD Conference,* (pp. 833-846).

Choi, B. (2002).What are Real DTDs Like? In *Fifth International Workshop on the Web and Databases*, (pp. 43-48).

Christensen, E., Curbera, F., Meredith, G., & Weerawarana, S. (2001). *Web services description language (WSDL) 1.1, W3C note*.

Christopher, R., Siméon, J., & Fernández, M. (2006). *A complete and efficient algebraic compiler for XQuery.* ICDE.

Chung, C., Min, J., & Shim, K. (2002, June 3-6). APEX: An Adaptive Path Index for XML data. In *Proceedings of the ACM SIGMOD International Conference on Management of Data*, Madison, WI, (pp.121-132). New York: ACM Press.

Clark, J., & DeRose, S. (Eds.). (1999, November 16). *XML Path Language (XPath) Version 1.0.* Retrieved January 22, 2009, from http://www.w3.org/TR/xpath

Clarke, E. M., Grumberg, O., & Peled, D. A. (2000). *Model Checking.* Cambridge, MA: MIT Press.

Cluet, S., & Moerkotte, G. (1993). Nested queries in object bases. In *Proceedings of the Fourth International Workshop on Database Programming Languages - Object Models and Language*, (pp. 226–242). Berlin: Springer.

Cohen, E., Halperin, E., Kaplan, H., & Zwick, U. (2002). Reachability and distance queries via 2-hop labels. In *SODA,* (pp. 937-946).

Cohen, E., Kaplan, H., & Milo, T. (2002). Labeling dynamic XML trees. In *Proceedings of the Twenty-First ACM SIGMOD-SIGACT-SIGART Symposium on Principles of Database Systems,* Madison, Wisconsin, June 03 - 05, (pp. 271-281). New York: ACM.

Cohen, S., Mamou, J., Kanza, Y., & Sagiv, Y. (2003). XSEarch: A semantic search engine for XML. In *VLDB,* (pp. 45-56).

Cohen, W. W., Ravikumar, P., & Fienberg, S. E. (2003). A comparison of string distance metrics for name-matching tasks. *IIWeb,* (pp. 73-78).

Colazzo, D., Ghelli, G., Manghi, P., & Sartiani, C. (2006). Static analysis for path correctness of XML queries. [JFP]. *Journal of Functional Programming, 16*(4-5), 621–661. doi:10.1017/S0956796806005983

Computer, Z. V., & Vagena, Z. (2004). Twig query processing over graph-structured XML data. In *WEBDB, Paris, Frence,* (pp. 43-48).

Constant, C., Jéron, T., Marchand, H., & Rusu, V. (2007). Integrating formal verification and conformance testing for reactive systems. *IEEE Transactions on Software Engineering, 33*(8), 558–574. doi:10.1109/TSE.2007.70707

Cooper, B. F. (2004). Guiding queries to information sources with InfoBeacons. In *Middleware '04: Proceedings of the 5th ACM/IFIP/USENIX International Conference on Middleware,* Toronto, Canada, (pp. 59-78).

Cooper, B., Sample, N., Franklin, M., Hjaltason, G., & Shadmon, M. (2001, September 11-14). A Fast Index for Semistructured Data. In P.M.G. Apers, P. Atzeni, S. Ceri, S. Paraboschi, K. Ramamohanarao, & R.T. Snodgrass (Eds.), *Proceedings of 27th International Conference on Very Large Data Bases VLDB,* Roma, Italy (pp.341-350). San Francisco, CA: Morgan Kaufmann Publishers Inc.

Cover, R. (2000). *NASA Goddard Astronomical Data Center (ADC) 'Scientific Dataset' XML.* Retrieved June 17, 2009, from http://xml.coverpages.org/nasa-adc.html

Crainiceanu, A., Linga, P., Gehrke, J., & Shanmugasundaram, J. (2004). Querying Peer-to-Peer Networks using P-Trees. In *Proceedings of ACM WebDB,* (pp. 25–30).

Crainiceanu, A., Linga, P., Machanavajjhala, A., Gehrke, J., & Shanmugasundaram, J. (2007). P-Ring: An Efficient and Robust P2P Range Index Structure. In *Proceedings of ACM SIGMOD,* (pp. 223–234).

Cruz, I. F., Xiao, H., & Hsu, F. (2004). Peer-to-peer semantic integration of XML and RDF data sources. In *AP2PC,* (pp. 108-119).

Cugola, G., Nitto, E. D., & Fuggetta, A. (2001). The JEDI event-based infrastructure and its application to the development of the OPSS WFMS. *IEEE Transactions on Software Engineering, 27*(9), 827–850. doi:10.1109/32.950318

Cugola, G., Nitto, E. D., & Picco, G. P. (2000). Content-based dispatching in a mobile environment. In *Proceedings of the Workshop su Sistemi Distribuiti: Algoritmi, Architetture e Linguaggi.*

Cuzzocrea, A., Darmont, J., & Mahboubi, H. (2009). (to appear). Fragmenting Very Large XML Data Warehouses via K-Means Clustering Algorithm. *Journal of Business Intelligence and Data Mining, 4*(3).

Data Repository, X. M. L. (n.d.). Retrieved June 17, 2009, from http://www.cs.washington.edu/research/xml datasets/www/repository.html

Database Group Leipzig. (n.d.). *XMach-1: A benchmark for XML Data Management.* Retrieved Febrary 20, 2009, from http://dbs.uni.leipzig.de/en/projeket/XML/XmlBenchmarking.html

Date, C. J. (1990). *An introduction to database systems,* (Vol. I, 5th Ed.). Reading, MA: Addison-Wesley.

Dayal, U., Goodman, N., & Katz, R. H. (1982). An extended relational algebra with control over duplicate elimination. In *Proc. ACM SIGMOD/SIGACT Conf. on Principles of Database Systems. (PODS),* (pp. 117–123). New York: ACM press.

Dean, J., & Ghemawat, S. (2004). MapReduce: Simplified data processing on large clusters. In *OSDI'04: Proceedings of the 6th Conference on Symposium on Opearting Systems Design \& Implementation,* San Francisco, CA, (pp. 10-10).

Decker, G., Zaha, J. M., & Dumas, M. (2006). Execution semantics for service choreographies. In Bravetti et al. (eds.), WS-FM, (pp. 163-177).

Decker, S., Harmelen, F. V., Broekstra, J., Erdmann, M., Fensel, D., Horrocks, I., et al. (2000). The semantic web - on the respective roles of XML and RDF. *IEEE Internet Computing, 4,* Retrieved from http://www.ontoknow

DeHaan, D., Toman, D., Consens, M. P., & Özsu, M. T. (2003). A Comprehensive XQuery to SQL translation using dynamic interval encoding. *SIGMOD Conference,* (pp. 623-634).

Demers, A., Gehrke, J., Hong, M. S., Riedewald, M., & White, W. (2006). Towards expressive publish/subscribe systems. In *Proceedings of the 10th International Conference on Extending Database Technology (EDBT),* (pp. 627-644).

Deutsch, A., & Tannen, V. (2003a). MARS: A system for publishing XML from mixed and redundant storage. *VLDB '2003: Proceedings of the 29th International Conference on very Large Data Bases,* Berlin, Germany, (pp. 201-212).

Deutsch, A., & Tannen, V. (2003b). Reformulation of XML queries and constraints. *ICDT,* (pp. 225-241).

Devlin, B. A., & Murphy, P. T. (1988). An architecture for a business and information system. *IBM Systems Journal, 27*(1), 60–80.

Diao, Y., & Franklin, M. (2003). Query processing for high-volume XML message brokering. In *VLDB '2003: Proceedings of the 29th international conference on Very large data bases* (pp. 261-272). VLDB Endowment.

Diao, Y., Altinel, M., Franklin, M. J., Zhang, H., & Fischer, P. (2003). Path sharing and predicate evaluation for high-performance XML filtering. *ACM Transactions on Database Systems, 28*(4), 467–516. doi:10.1145/958942.958947

Diao, Y., Rizvi, S., & Franklin, M. (2004). Towards an Internet-scale XML dissemination service. In *Proceedings of the 30ᵗʰ International Conference on Very Large Data Base,* (pp. 612-623).

Diaz, A. L., & Lovell, D. (2003). *XML generator.* Retrieved from http://www.alphaworks.ibm.com/tech/xmlgenerator

Dietz, P. (1982, May 5-7). Maintaining order in a linked list. In *Proceedings of the fourteenth annual ACM symposium on Theory of Computing,* San Francisco, California, USA (pp.122 –127). New York: ACM Press.

Ding, B., Yu, J. X., Wang, S., Qin, L., & Lin, X. Z. X. (2007). Finding top-k min-cost connected trees in databases. In *ICDE,* (pp. 836-845).

Do, H. H., & Rahm, E. (2002). COMA - A system for flexible combination of schema matching approaches. *VLDB,* (pp. 610-621).

Do, H. H., Melnik, S., & Rahm, E. (2002). Comparison of schema matching evaluations. *Web, Web-Services, and Database Systems,* (pp. 221-237).

Doan, A., & Halevy, A. Y. (2005). Semantic integration research in the database community: A brief survey. *AI Magazine, 26*(1), 83–94.

Doan, A., Domingos, P., & Halevy, A. Y. (2001). Reconciling schemas of disparate data sources: A machine-learning approach. *SIGMOD Conference,* (pp. 509-520).

Doan, A., Ramakrishnan, R., Chen, F., DeRose, P., Lee, Y., & McCann, R. (2006). Community information management. *A Quarterly Bulletin of the Computer Society of the IEEE Technical Committee on Data Engineering, 29*(1), 64–72.

Dong, X. L., Halevy, A. Y., & Yu, C. (2007). Data integration with uncertainty. *VLDB,* (pp. 687-698).

Dong, X., Halevy, A., & Tatarinov, I. (2003). *Containment of nested XML queries.* Tech. Rep. UW-CSE-03-12-05, University of Washington.

Draper, D., Fankhauser, P., Fernandez, M, Malhotra, A, Rose, K., Rys, M., Siméon, J., & Wadler, P (2007). *XQuery 1.0 and XPath 2.0 Formal Semantics.* World Wide Web Consortion (W3C), W3C Recommendation.

Duchateau, F., Bellahsene, Z., & Hunt, E. (2007). XBench-Match: A benchmark for XML schema matching tools. *VLDB,* (pp. 1318-1321).

Ehrenfeucht, A., & Zeiger, H. P. (1976). Complexity measures for regular expressions. *Journal of Computer and System Sciences, 12*(2), 134–146.

Ehrig, M., & Staab, S. (2004). QOM - quick ontology mapping. *International Semantic Web Conference,* (pp. 683-697).

Espil, M. M., & Vaisman, A. A. (2007). Aggregate Queries in Peer-To-Peer OLAP. In *Proceedings of ACM DOLAP* (pp. 102–111).

Fagin, R. (1996). Combining fuzzy information from multiple systems. In *PODS,* (pp. 216-226).

Fagin, R., Kolaitis, P. G., Miller, R. J., & Popa, L. (2005). Data exchange: Semantics and query answering. *Theoretical Computer Science, 336*(1), 89–124. doi:10.1016/j.tcs.2004.10.033

Fagin, R., Lotem, A., & Naor, M. (2003). Optimal aggregation algorithms for middleware. *Journal of Computer and System Sciences, 66*(4), 614–656. doi:10.1016/S0022-0000(03)00026-6

Fallside, D. C., & Walmsley, P. (2004). *XML Schema Part 0: Primer Second Edition.* Retrieved March 14, 2009. From http://www.w3.org/TR/xmlschema-0/

Fegaras, L., & Maier, D. (1995) Towards an effective calculus for object query languages. In *Proceedings of the 1995 ACM SIGMOD International Conference on Management of Data,* (pp. 47–58). New York: ACM Press.

Fegaras, L., Dash, R. K., & Wang, Y. (2006). A fully pipelined XQuery processor. In *XIME-P.*

Fegaras, L., Levine, D., Bose, S., & Chaluvadi, V. (2002). Query processing of streamed XML data. In *Proceedings of the eleventh international conference on Information and knowledge management,* (pp. 126–133). New York: ACM Press.

Fenner, W., Rabinovich, M., Ramakrishnan, K. K., Srivastava, D., & Zhang, Y. (2005). XTreeNet: Scalable overlay networks for XML content dissemination and querying (synopsis). In *Proceedings of the 10th International Workshop on Web Content Catching and Distribution,* French Riviera, France.

Fernandez, M. F., Morishima, A., & Suciu, D. (2001). Efficient evaluation of XML middle-ware queries. *SIGMOD Conference,* (pp. 103-114).

Fernández, M., Siméon, M. F. J., Chen, C., Choi, B., Gapeyev, V., Marian, A., et al. (2009). *Galax, an XQuery implementation*. Retrieved on April 20th, 2009 from http://www.galaxquery.org

Fernau, H. (2004). Extracting minimum length document type definitions is NP-hard. *ICGI*, (pp. 277-278).

Fernau, H. (2005). Algorithms for learning regular expressions. *ALT*, (pp. 297-311).

Ferragina, P. Luccio, & F., Muthukrishna, S. (2006). Compressing and searching XML data via two zips. *International World Wide Web Conference* (pp. 751-760). New York: ACM.

Fidler, E., Jacobsen, H.-A., Li, G., & Mankovski, S. (2005). The PADRES distributed publish/subscribe system. In *International Conference on Feature Interactions in Telecommunications and Software Systems (ICFI'05)*, (pp. 12–30), Leicester, UK.

Fiebig, T., Helmer, S., Kanne, C.-C., Moerkotte, G., Neumann, J., Schiele, R., & Westmann, T. (2002). Anatomy of a native XML base management system. *The VLDB Journal, 11*(4), 292–314. doi:10.1007/s00778-002-0080-y

Fisher, D. K., Lam, F., Shui, W. M., & Wong, R. K. (2006, January 16-19). Dynamic Labeling Schemes for Ordered XML Based on Type Information. In G. Dobbie, & J. Bailey (Eds.), *Proceedings of the 17th Australasian Database Conference*, Hobart, Australia (Vol. 49, pp. 59-68). Darlinghurst, Australia: Australian computer Society, Inc.

Florescu, D. (2005). Managing semi-structured data. *ACM Queue; Tomorrow's Computing Today, 3*(8), 18–24. doi:10.1145/1103822.1103832

Florescu, D., & Kossmann, D. (1999). Storing and querying XML data using an RDBMS. *A Quarterly Bulletin of the Computer Society of the IEEE Technical Committee on Data Engineering, 22*(3), 27–34.

Florescu, D., & Kossmann, D. (2004), XML query processing (tutorial). In *Proceedings of the 20th International Conference on Data Engineering, ICDE 2004, (pg. 874)*. Washington, DC: IEEE Computer Society.

Florescu, D., Hillery, C., Kossmann, D., Lucas, P., Riccardi, F., & Westmann, T. (2004). The BEA streaming XQuery processor. *The VLDB Journal, 13*(3), 294–315. doi:10.1007/s00778-004-0137-1

Fontoura, M., Josifovski, V., Shekita, E., & Yang, B. (2005, October 31-November 5). Optimizing Cursor Movement in Holistic Twig Joins. In *Proceedings of the 14th ACM International Conference on Information and Knowledge Management, Bremen, Germany* (pp. 784–791). New York: ACM Press.

Franceschet, M. (2005, August 28-29). XPathMark: An XPath Benchmark for XMark Generated Data. In S. Bressan, S. Ceri, E. Hunt, Z. G. Ives, Z. Bellahsene, M. Rys, & R. Unland (Eds.), *Database and XML Technologies, Third International XML Database Symposium, XSym, Trondheim, Norway* (LNCS Vol. 3671, pp. 129-143). Berlin: Springer.

Franklin, M. J., Halevy, A. Y., & Maier, D. (2005). From databases to dataspaces: A new abstraction for information management. *SIGMOD Record, 34*(4), 27–33. doi:10.1145/1107499.1107502

Frasincar, F., Houben, G.-J., & Pau, C. (2002). XAL: An algebra for XML query optimization. In *Proc. Of the Thirteenth Australasian Database Conference (ADC2002)*, (pp. 49–56). Darlinghurst, Australia: Australian Computer Society, Inc.

Fu, X., Bultan, T., & Su, J. (2004). Analysis of interacting BPEL web services. In S. I. Feldman, M. Uretsky, M. Najork, & C. E. Wills (Eds.) *WWW*, (pp. 621-630). New York: ACM.

Fuhr, N., & Großjohann, K. (2001). XIRQL: A query language for information retrieval in XML documents. In *SIGIR*, (pp. 172-180).

Fuxman, A., Hernández, M. A., Ho, C. T. H., Miller, R. J., Papotti, P., & Popa, L. (2006). Nested mappings: Schema mapping reloaded. *VLDB*, (pp. 67-78).

Gailly, J., & Adler, M. (2007). *gzip (GNU zip) compression utility.* Retrieved from http://www.gnu.org/software/gzip

Gal, A. (2006). Why is schema matching tough and what can we do about it? *SIGMOD Record, 35*(4), 2–5. doi:10.1145/1228268.1228269

Gal, A. (2007). The generation Y of XML schema matching panel description. *XSym,* 9pp. 137-139).

Galanis, L., Wang, Y., Jeffery, S. R., & DeWitt, D. J. (2003). Locating data sources in large distributed systems. In *Proceedings of the 29th international conference on Very Large Data Bases (VLDB'03),* (pp. 874–885), Berlin, Germany.

Gan, Y., Chechik, M., Nejati, S., Bennett, J., O'Farrell, B., & Waterhouse, J. (2007). Runtime monitoring of web service conversations. In *CASCON '07: Proceedings of the 2007 conference of the center for advanced studies on Collaborative research,* (pp. 42-57). New York: ACM.

Gao, J., Wang, T., & Yang, D. (2007). MQTree based query rewriting over multiple XML views. In *DEXA,* (pp. 562-571).

Garavel, H., & Mateescu, R. (2004). SEQ.OPEN: A Tool for Efficient Trace-Based Verification. In S. Graf & L. Mounier (Eds.) *Model Checking Software, 11th International SPIN Workshop, Barcelona, Spain, April 1-3, 2004, Proceedings,* (LNCS vol. 2989, pp. 151-157). Berlin: Springer.

Garcia, P., & Vidal, E. (1990). Inference of k-testable languages in the strict sense and application to syntactic pattern recognition. *IEEE Transactions on Pattern Analysis and Machine Intelligence, 12*(9), 920–925. doi:10.1109/34.57687

Garcia-Molina, H., Ullman, J. D., & Widom, J. (2001), *Database Systems: The Complete Book.* Upper Saddle River, NJ: Prentice Hall.

Garofalakis, M. N., Gionis, A., Rastogi, R., Seshadri, S., & Shim, K. (2003). XTRACT: Learning document type descriptors from XML document collections. *Data Mining and Knowledge Discovery, 7*(1), 23–56. doi:10.1023/A:1021560618289

Geng, K., & Dobbie, G. (2006). *An XML document generator for semantic query optimization experimentation.* Paper presented at the 8th International Conference on Information Integration and Web-based Application & Services, Yogyakarta, Indonesia.

Ghelli, G., Ré, C., & Simon, J. (2006). XQuery!: An XML Query Language with Side Effects. In *EDBT Workshops 2006,* (pp. 178-191).

Ghelli, G., Rose, K. H., & Simon, J. (2008). Commutativity Analysis in XML Update Languages. *ACM Transactions on Database Systems, 33*(4). doi:10.1145/1412331.1412341

Ghezzi, C., & Guinea, S. (2007). *Run-Time Monitoring in Service-Oriented Architectures,* (pp. 237-264). Berlin: Springer.

Ghose, A., & Koliadis, G. (2007). Auditing business process compliance. In Krämer et al. (2007), *Proceedings of the International Conference on Service-Oriented Computing (ICSOC-2007),* (LNCS Vol. 4749, pp. 169-180).

Gibbons, P. B., Karp, B., Ke, Y., Nath, S., & Seshan, S. (2003). IrisNet: an Architecture for a World-Wide Sensor Web. *IEEE Pervasive Computing / IEEE Computer Society [and] IEEE Communications Society, 2*(4), 22–33. doi:10.1109/MPRV.2003.1251166

Giunchiglia, F., Shvaiko, P., & Yatskevich, M. (2004). S-match: An algorithm and an implementation of semantic matching. *ESWS,* (pp. 61-75).

Gnome Libxml2. (2000). Retrieved from http://xmlsoft.org/

Goldman, R., & Widom, J. (1997). DataGuides: Enabling query formulation and optimization in semistructured databases. In *Proceedings of 23rd International Conference on Very Large Data Bases* (pp. 436-445). Athens, Greece: ACM.

Goldman, R., & Widom, J. (1999, January 13). Approximate Data Guide. In *Proceedings of the Workshop on Query Processing for Semistructured Data and Non-Standard Data Formats*, Jerusalem, Israel.

Goldman, R., McHugh, J., & Widom, J. (1999, June 3-4). From semistructured data to XML: Migrating the Lore data model and query language. In S. Cluet, & T. Milo (Eds.), *Proceedings of the 2nd International Workshop on the Web and Databases, ACM SIGMOD Workshop*, Philadelphia, PA (pp. 25-30).

Gong, X. Q., Qian, W. N., Yan, Y., & Zhou, A. Y. (2005). Bloom filter-based XML packets filtering for millions of path queries. In *Proceedings of the 21st International Conference on Data Engineering*, (pp. 890-901).

Gottlob, G., Koch, C., & Pichler, R. (2002). Efficient Algorithms for Processing XPath Queries. In *Proceedings of VLDB*, (pp. 95–106).

Gottlob, G., Koch, C., Pichler, R., & Segoufin, L. (2005). The complexity of XPath query evaluation and XML typing. *Journal of the ACM, 52*(2), 284–335. doi:10.1145/1059513.1059520

Gou, G., & Chirkova, R. (2007). Efficient algorithms for evaluating xpath over streams. In *SIGMOD '07: Proceedings of the 2007 ACM SIGMOD international conference on Management of data* (pp. 269-280). New York: ACM Press.

Governatori, G., Milosevic, Z., & Sadiq, S. W. (2006). Compliance checking between business processes and business contracts. In *EDOC*, (pp. 221-232). Washington, DC: IEEE Computer Society.

Graefe, G. (1993). Query evaluation techniques for large databases. *ACM Computing Surveys, 25*(2), 73–170. doi:10.1145/152610.152611

Graefe, G. (1995). The Cascades framework for query optimization. *A Quarterly Bulletin of the Computer Society of the IEEE Technical Committee on Data Engineering, 18*(3), 19–29.

Graefe, G., & DeWitt, D. J. (1987, May 27–29). The EXODUS optimizer generator. In U. Dayal (Ed.), *Proceedings of the 1987 ACM SIGMOD International Conference on Management of Data, San Francisco, California* (pp. 160-172). New York: ACM Press.

Graefe, G., & McKenna, W. J. (1993, April 19-23). The volcano optimizer generator: Extensibility and efficient search. In *Proceedings of the Ninth International Conference on Data Engineering, Vienna, Austria* (pp. 209–218). Washington, DC: IEEE Computer Society.

Gray, J. (1993). *The Benchmark Handbook (2nd ed.)*. San Francisco, USA: Morgan Kaufmann Publishers, Inc.

Green, T. J., Gupta, A., Miklau, G., Onizuka, M., & Suciu, D. (2004). Processing XML streams with deterministic automata and stream indexes. *ACM Transactions on Database Systems, 29*(4), 752–788. doi:10.1145/1042046.1042051

Gribble, S. D., Halevy, A. Y., Ives, Z. G., Rodrig, M., & Suciu, D. (2001). What can Database do for Peer-to-Peer? In *Proceedings of ACM WebDB*, (pp. 31–36).

Grust, T. (2002), Accelerating XPath location steps. In *Proc. of the ACM SIGMOD Conf. on Management of Data*, (pp. 109–120). New York: ACM press.

Grust, T., & Teubner, J. (2004). Relational algebra: Mother tongue –XQuery: Fluent. In *Twente Data Management Workshop on XML Databases and Information Retrieval (TDM) 04, (informal proceedings)*.

Grust, T., Mayr, M., Rittinger, J., Sakr, S., & Teubner, J. (2007). A SQL: 1999 code generator for the pathfinder xquery compiler. *SIGMOD Conference*, (pp. 1162-1164).

Grust, T., Rittinger, J., & Teubner, J. (2007). eXrQuy: Order indifference in XQuery. In *Proceedings of the 23rd IEEE Int'l Conference on Data Engineering (ICDE 2007)*, (pp. 226–235). Washington, DC: IEEE Computer Society.

Grust, T., Rittinger, J., & Teubner, J. (2007). Why off-the-shelf RDBMSs are better at XPath than you might expect. *SIGMOD Conference*, (pp. 949-958).

Grust, T., Rittinger, J., & Teubner, J. (2008). Pathfinder: XQuery off the relational shelf. *IEEE Data Eng. Bull.*, *31*(4), 7–12.

Grust, T., Sakr, S., & Teubner, J. (2004). XQuery on SQL hosts. In *Proceedings of the Thirtieth International Conference on Very Large Data Bases*. (pp. 252–263). San Mateo, CA: Morgan Kaufmann.

Grust, T., van Keulen, M., & Teubner, J. (2004). Accelerating XPath evaluation in any RDBMS. *ACM Transactions on Database Systems*, *29*(1), 91–131. doi:10.1145/974750.974754

Gu, J., Xu, B., & Chen, X. (2008). An XML query rewriting mechanism with multiple ontologies integration based on complex semantic mapping. *Information Fusion, 9*(4), 512–522. doi:10.1016/j.inffus.2007.04.002

Guerrini, G., Mesiti, M., & Rossi, D. (2005). Impact of XML schema evolution on valid documents. In *ACM International Workshop on Web Information and Data Management*, (pp. 39-44).

Guerrini, G., Mesiti, M., & Sorrenti, M. A. (2007). XML Schema Evolution: Incremental Validation and Efficient Document Adaptation. In *Database and XML Technologies, 5th International XML Database Symposium*, (LNCS Vol. 4704, pp. 92-106).

Guo, L., Shao, F., Botev, C., & Shanmugasundaram, J. (2003). XRANK: Ranked Keyword Search over XML Documents. In *Proceedings of SIGMOD*, (pp. 16-27).

Gupta, A. K., & Suciu, D. (2003). Stream processing of xpath queries with predicates. In *SIGMOD '03: Proceedings of the 2003 ACM SIGMOD international conference on Management of data* (pp. 419-430). New York: ACM Press.

Gupta, A., & Agarwal, S. (2008). A review on XML compressors and future trends. *International Journal of Computer Sciences and Engineering Systems*, *2*(4), 227–234.

Gupta, A., Agrawal, D., & El Abbadi, A. (2003). Approximate Range Selection Queries in Peer-to-Peer Systems. In *Proceedings of CIDR*. Retrieved from http://www-db.cs.wisc.edu/cidr/cidr2003/program/p13.pdf

Gupta, A., Halevy, A., & Suicu, D. (2002). View selection for XML stream processing. In *Proceedings of the 5th International Workshop on the Web & Database,* (pp. 83-88).

Gupta, A., Suicu, D., & Halevy, A. (2003). The view selection problem for XML content based routing. In *Proceedings of the 22nd International Conference on Principles of Database System*, (pp. 68-77).

Haas, L. M., Freytag, J. C., Lohman, G. M., & Pirahesh, H. (1989). Extensive query processing in Starburst. In *Proceedings of the 1989 ACM SIGMOD International Conference on Management of Data*, (pp. 377–388). New York: ACM press.

Halevy, A. (1999). *More on data management for XML*. White Paper, available online at http://www.Cs.Washington.edu/homes/alon/widom-Response.html

Halevy, A. Y. (2001). Answering queries using views: A survey. *The VLDB Journal, 10*(4), 270–294. doi:10.1007/s007780100054

Halevy, A. Y., Franklin, M. J., & Maier, D. (2006). Principles of dataspace systems. *PODS,* (pp. 1-9).

Halevy, A. Y., Ives, Z. G., Madhavan, J., Mork, P., Suciu, D., & Tatarinov, I. (2004). The piazza peer data management system. *IEEE Transactions on Knowledge and Data Engineering, 16*(7), 787–798. doi:10.1109/TKDE.2004.1318562

Halevy, A. Y., Ives, Z. G., Suciu, D., & Tatarinov, I. (2003). Schema mediation in peer data management systems. In *ICDE,* (pp. 505-516).

Hallé, S., & Villemaire, R. (2008). Runtime monitoring of message-based workflows with data. In *EDOC*, (pp. 63-72). Washington, DC: IEEE Computer Society.

Hallé, S., & Villemaire, R. (2008). XML methods for validation of temporal properties on message traces with data. In Meersman & Tari (2004), Proceedings of the OTM 2008 Confederated International Conferences, CoopIS, DOA, GADA, IS, and ODBASE 2008. Part I on On the Move to Meaningful Internet Systems, (LNCS Vol. 5331, pp. 337-353).

Hallé, S., & Villemaire, R. (2009). Browser-Based Enforcement of Interface Contracts in Web Applications with BeepBeep. In A. Bouajjani & O. Maler (Eds.), *Computer Aided Verification, 21st International Conference, CAV 2009, Grenoble, France, June 26 – July 2, 2009, Proceedings*, (LNCS vol. 5643, pp. 648-653). Berlin: Springer.

Hallé, S., & Villemaire, R. (2009). Runtime monitoring of web service choreographies using streaming XML. In *SAC*, (pp. 1851-1858). New York: ACM.

Han, W. S., Jiang, H., Ho, H., & Li, Q. (2008). StreamTX: extracting tuples from streaming XML data. *Proc. VLDB Endow., 1*(1), 289-300.

Hansen, P., & Roberts, F. S. (1996). An Impossibility Result in Axiomatic Location Theory. In *Mathematics of Operations Research*.

Härder, T., Haustein, M., Mathis, C., & Wagner, M. (2007). Node labeling schemes for dynamic XML documents reconsidered. *Data & Knowledge Engineering, 60*, 126–149. doi:10.1016/j.datak.2005.11.008

Hariharan, S., & Shankar, P. (2006). Evaluating the role of context in syntax directed compression of XML documents. *Data Compression Conference* (pp. 453). Washington, DC: IEEE.

Haustein, M., & Härder, T. (2007). An efficient infrastructure of native transactional XML processing. *Data & Knowledge Engineering, 61*, 500–523. doi:10.1016/j.datak.2006.06.015

Havelund, K., Rosu, G. (2001). *Testing Linear Temporal Logic Formulæ on Finite Execution Traces*. RIACS Technical Report TR 01-08.

Haw, S., & Lee, C. (2008). TwigX-Guide: twig query pattern matching for XML trees. *American Journal of Applied Science, 5*(9), 1212–1218. doi:10.3844/ajassp.2008.1212.1218

He, H., Wang, H., Yang, J., & Yu, P. S. (2007). BLINKS: Ranked Keyword Searches on Graphs. In *Proceedings of SIGMOD*.

He, J., Ng, W., Wang, X., & Zhou, A. (2006). An efficient co-operative framework for multi-query processing over compressed XML data. *International Conference on Database Systems for Advanced Applications*, (LNCS Vol. 3882, pp. 218-258).

Hegewald, J., Naumann, F., & Weis, M. (2006). XStruct: Efficient schema extraction from multiple and large XML documents. *ICDE Workshops*, 81.

Helmer, S., Kanne, C.-C., & Moerkotte, G. (2002). Optimized translation of XPath expressions into algebraic expressions parameterized by programs containing navigational primitives. In *Proceedings of the 3nd International Conference on Web Information Systems Engineering (WISE'02)*, (pp. 215–224). Washington, DC: IEEE Computer Society.

Henzinger, M. R., Henzinger, T. A., & Kopke, P. W. (1995). Computing simulation on finite and infinite graphs. In *Proceedings of 36th Annual Symposium on Foundations of Computer Science* (pp. 453-462). Milwaukee, Wisconsin: IEEE Computer Society.

Hernández, M. A., Ho, H., Popa, L., Fuxman, A., Miller, R. J., Fukuda, T., et al. (2007). Creating nested mappings with clio. *ICDE*, (pp. 1487-1488).

Hernández, M. A., Miller, R. J., & Haas, L. M. (2001). Clio: A semi-automatic tool for schema mapping. *SIGMOD Conference*, 607.

Hernández, M. A., Papotti, P., & Tan, W. C. (2008). Data exchange with data-metadata translations. *PVLDB, 1*(1), 260–273.

Hidders, J., & Michiels, P. (2003). Avoiding unnecessary ordering operations in XPath. In *Database Programming Languages, 9th International Workshop, DBPL 2003.* (pp. 54–74). Berlin: Springer.

Hidders, J., Paredaens, J., Vercammen, R., & Demeyer, S. (2004). A light but formal introduction to XQuery. In *Database and XML Technologies, Second International XML Database Symposium, XSym,* (pp. 5–20). Berlin: Springer.

Hopcroft, J. E., & Ullman, J. D. (1979). *Introduction to automata theory, languages and computation.* Reading, MA: Addison-Wesley Publishing Company.

Hosoya, H. H. & Pierce, B. C. (2000). XDuce: A typed XML processing language (preliminary report). In *Proceedings of Third International Workshop on the Web and Databases (WebDB2000),* (LNCS Vol. 1997, pp. 226-244).

Hou, S., & Jacobsen, H.-A. (2006). Predicate-based filtering of XPath expressions. In *Proceedings of the 22nd International Conference on Data Engineering (ICDE'06),* (p. 53), Washington, DC.

Howard, Y., Gruner, S., Gravell, A. M., Ferreira, C., & Augusto, J. C. (2003). Model-based trace-checking. In *SoftTest: UK Software Testing Research Workshop II.*

Hristidis, V., Koudas, N., Papakonstantinou, Y., & Srivastava, D. (2006). Keyword Proximity Search in XML Trees. *IEEE Transactions on Knowledge and Data Engineering, 18*(4). doi:10.1109/TKDE.2006.1599390

Hristidis, V., Papakonstantinou, Y., & Balmin, A. (2003). Keyword Proximity Search on XML Graphs. In *ICDE.*

Hu, S., Muthusamy, V., Li, G., & Jacobsen, H.-A. (2008). Distributed Automatic Service Composition in Large-Scale Systems. In *Proceedings of the second international conference on Distributed event-based systems* (pp 233-244), ACM: New York.

Huang, Y. Q. & Molina, H. G. (2004). Publish/subscribe in a mobile environment. *Wireless Networks. Special Issue: Pervasive computing and communications, 10*(6), 643-652.

Huang, Yu., Liu, Z., & Chen, Y. (2008). Query Biased Snippet Generation in XML Search. In *SIGMOD.*

Huebsch, R., Hellerstein, J. M., Lanham, N., Loo, B. T., Shenker, S., & Stoica, I. (2003). Querying the Internet with Pier. In *Proceedings of VLDB,* (pp. 321–332).

Huffman, D. A. (1952). A method for the construction of minimum redundancy codes. *The Institute of Radio Engineers, 9*(40), 1098–1101.

Hughes, G., Bultan, T., & Alkhalaf, M. (2008). Client and server verification for web services using interface grammars. In T. Bultan, & T. Xie (Eds.) *TAV-WEB,* (pp. 40-46). New York: ACM.

Huth, M. R. A., & Ryan, M. D. (2000). *Logic in Computer Science: Modelling and Reasoning about Systems.* Cambridge, UK: Cambridge University Press.

IBM conversation support project, (2002). Retrieved on April 20th, 2009 from http://www.research.ibm.com/convsupport

IBM XML Generator. (n.d.). Retrieved from http://www.alphaworks.ibm.com/tech/xmlgenerator

Ilyas, I. F., Aref, W. G., & Elmagarmid, A. K. (2003). Supporting top-k join queries in relational databases. In *VLDB,* (pp. 754-765).

Ioannidis, Y. E., & Kang, Y. (1990, May 23–26). Randomized algorithms for optimizing large join queries. In *Proceedings of the 1990 ACM SIGMOD International Conference on Management of Data,* Atlantic City, NJ, (pp. 312–321). New York: ACM Press.

Ives, Z. G., Halevy, A. Y., & Weld, D. S. (2002). An XML query engine for network-bound data. *The VLDB Journal, 11*(4), 380–402. doi:10.1007/s00778-002-0078-5

Jacobsen, H.-A. (2006). *The PADRES content-based publish/subscribe system web site.* Retrieved http://padres.msrg.toronto.edu/Padres/

Jagadish, H. V., Al-Khalifa, S., Chapman, A., Lakshmanan, L. V. S., Nierman, A., & Paparizos, S. (2002). TIMBER: A native XML database. *The VLDB Journal, 11*(4), 274–291. doi:10.1007/s00778-002-0081-x

Jagadish, H. V., Lakshmanan, L. V. S., Scannapieco, M., Srivastava, D., & Wiwatwattana, N. (2004). Colorful XML: One hierarchy isn't enough. *SIGMOD Conference*, (pp. 251-262).

Jagadish, H. V., Lakshmanan, L. V. S., Srivastava, D., & Thompson, K. (2001). TAX: A tree algebra for XML. *DBPL*, (pp. 149-164).

Jarke, M., & Koch, J. (1984). Query optimization in database systems. *ACM Computing Surveys, 16*(2), 111–152. doi:10.1145/356924.356928

Jeffery, S. R., Franklin, M. J., & Halevy, A. Y. (2008). Pay-as-you-go user feedback for dataspace systems. In *SIGMOD '08: Proceedings of the 2008 ACM SIGMOD International Conference on Management of Data,* Vancouver, Canada, (pp. 847-860).

Jennifer, R. G., & Widom, J. (1999). Approximate DataGuides. In *Proceedings of the Workshop on Query Processing for Semistructured Data and Non-Standard Data Formats,* (pp. 436-445).

Jhingran, A. (2006). Enterprise information mashups: Integrating information, simply. *VLDB,* (3-4).

Jiang, H., Lu, H., & Wang, W. (2004). Efficient processing of XML twig queries with OR-predicates. In *2004 ACM SIGMOD International Conference on Management of Data* (pp. 59-70). New York: ACM.

Jiang, H., Lu, H., Wang, W., & Yu, J. X. (2002). Path materialization revisited: An efficient storage model for XML data. *Australasian Database Conference.*

Jiang, H., Wang, W., Lu, H., & Yu, J. (2003). Holistic twig joins on indexed XML documents. In *29th International Conference on Very Large Data Bases* (pp. 273-284). Ohio: VLDB Endowment.

Johnson, D. S., Papadimitriou, C. H., & Yannakakis, M. (1988). On generating all maximal independent sets. *Information Processing Letters, 27*(3), 119–123. doi:10.1016/0020-0190(88)90065-8

Josephraj, J. (2005). *Web services choreography in practice.* Retrieved on April 20th, 2009 from http://www.128.ibm.com/developerworks/webservices/library/ws-choreography/

Josifovski, V., Fontoura, M., & Barta, A. (2005). Querying XML streams. *The VLDB Journal, 14*(2), 197–210. doi:10.1007/s00778-004-0123-7

Kabra, N., & DeWitt, D. (1999, April). OPT++: An object-oriented implementation for extensible database query optimization. *The VLDB Journal, 8*(1), 55–78. doi:10.1007/s007780050074

Kacholia, V., Pandit, S., Chakrabarti, S., Sudarshan, S., Desai, R., & Karambelkar, H. (2005). Bidirectional expansion for keyword search on graph databases. In *VLDB,* (pp. 505-516).

Kanne, C-C.,& Moerkotte, G. (2000). Efficient storage of XML data. *ICDE,* 198.

Kantere, V., Tsoumakos, D., & Roussopoulos, N. (2004). Querying Structured Data in an Unstructured P2P System. In *Proceedings of ACM WIDM,* (pp. 64–71).

Katsis, Y., Deutsch, A., & Papakonstantinou, Y. (2008). Interactive source registration in community-oriented information integration. *Proc.VLDB Endow., 1*(1), 245-259.

Kaushik, R., Bohannon, P., Naughton, J. F., & Korth, H. F. (2002). Covering indexing for branching path queries. In *Proceedings of the ACM SIGMOD International Conference on Management of Data* (pp. 133-144). Madison, Wisconsin: ACM.

Kaushik, R., Bohannon, P., Naughton, J., & Shenoy, P. (2002, August 20-23). Updates for Structure Indexes. In P.A. Bernstein, Y.E. Ioannidis, R. Ramakrishnan, & D. Papadias (Eds.), *Proceedings of 28th International Conference on Very Large Data Bases,* Hong Kong, China (pp.239-250). San Francisco, CA: Morgan Kaufmann.

Kaushik, R., Shenoy, P., Bohannon, P., & Gudes, E. (2002). Exploiting local similarity for indexing paths in graph-structured data. In *18th International Conference on Data Engineering* (pp. 129-140). Washington, DC: IEEE Computer Society.

Kavantzas, N., Burdett, D., Ritzinger, G., Fletcher, T., & Lafon, Y. (2005). *Web services choreography description language version 1.0*. Retrieved on April 20th, 2009 from http://www.w3.org/TR/ws-cdl-10/

Kay, M. (2008). Ten reasons why Saxon XQuery is fast. *IEEE Data Eng. Bull., 31*(4), 65–74.

Kazhamiakin, R., Pistore, M., & Santuari, L. (2006). Analysis of communication models in web service compositions. In L. Carr, D. D. Roure, A. Iyengar, C. A. Goble, & M. Dahlin (Eds.), *WWW*, (pp. 267-276). New York: ACM.

Kementsietsidis, A., Arenas, M., & Miller, R. J. (2003). Mapping data in peer-to-peer systems: Semantics and algorithmic issues. In *SIGMOD Conference,* (pp. 325-336).

Kilpeläinen, P., & Mannila, H. (1995). Ordered and unordered tree inclusion. *SIAM Journal on Computing, 24*(2), 340–356. doi:10.1137/S0097539791218202

Kim, J. W., & Candan, K. S. (2006). CP/CV: Concept similarity mining without frequency information from domain describing taxonomies. In *CIKM,* (pp. 483-492).

Kim, W. (1982, Sep 7). On optimizing an SQL-like nested query. *ACM TODS.*

Kimelfeld, B., & Sagiv, Y. (2006). Twig patterns: From XML trees to graphs. In *WebDB.*

Kimelfeld, B., & Sagiv, Y. (2008). Modeling and querying probabilistic XML data. *SIGMOD Record, 37*(4), 69–77. doi:10.1145/1519103.1519115

Kintigh, K. W. (2006). The promise and challenge of archaeological data integration. *American Antiquity.*

Kleinberg, J. (2002). An Impossibility Theorem for Clustering. In *NIPS.*

Klettke, M., Meyer, H., & Hänsel, B. (2005). Evolution: The Other Side of the XML Update Coin. In *International Workshop on XML Schema and Data Management.*

Knuth, D. E. (1973). *The Art of Computer Programming III: Sorting and Searching*, (2nd Ed.). Reading, MA: Addison-Wesley.

Knuth, D. E., Morris, J. H., & Pratt, V. R. (1977). Fast pattern matching in strings. *SIAM Journal on Computing, 6*(2), 323–350. doi:10.1137/0206024

Koch, C., Scherzinger, S., Schweikardt, N., & Stegmaier, B. (2004). FluXQuery: An optimizing XQuery processor for streaming XML data. In M. A. Nascimento, M. T. Özsu, D. Kossmann, R. J. Miller, J. A. Blakeley, & K. B. Schiefer (Eds.) *VLDB*, (pp. 1309-1312). San Francisco: Morgan Kaufmann.

Koloniari, G., & Pitoura, E. (2004). Content-based routing of path queries in peer-to-peer systems. In *Proceedings of the 7th International Conference on Extending Database Technology (EDBT'04)*, (pp. 29–47).

Koloniari, G., & Pitoura, E. (2005). Peer-to-peer management of XML data: Issues and research challenges. *SIGMOD Record, 34*(2), 6–17. doi:10.1145/1083784.1083788

Koloniari, G., Petrakis, Y., & Pitoura, E. (2003). Content-based overlay networks for XML peers based on multi-level bloom filters. In *DBISP2P*, (pp. 232-247).

Koudas, N., Rabinovich, M., Srivastava, D., & Yu, T. (2004). Routing xml queries. In *Proceedings of the 20th International Conference on Data Engineering (ICDE'04)*, (p. 844), Washington, DC.

Koutrika, G., Simitsis, A., & Ioannidis, Y. E. (2006). Pr'ecis: The Essence of a Query Answer. In *ICDE.*

Krämer, B. J., Lin, K.-J., & Narasimhan, P. (Eds.). (2007). *Service-Oriented Computing - ICSOC 2007, Fifth International Conference, Vienna, Austria, September 17-20, 2007, Proceedings*, (LNCS Vol. 4749). Berlin: Springer.

Kramer, D. K., & Rundensteiner, E. A. (2001). Xem: XML Evolution Management. In *Eleventh International Workshop on Research Issues in Data Engineering: Document Management for Data Intensive Business and Scientific Applications*, (pp. 103-110).

Krishnamurthy, R., Kaushik, R., & Naughton, J. F. (2003). Xmlsql query translation literature: The state of the art and open problems. In *Proc. of the First International XML Database Symposium, XSym 2003*, (pp. 1–18). Berlin: Springer.

Krishnaprasad, M., Liu, Z. H., Manikutty, A., Warner, J. W., & Arora, V. (2005). Towards an industrial strength SQL/XML Infrastructure. In *Proceedings of the 21st International Conference on Data Engineering*, ICDE 2005 (pp. 991-1000). Tokyo, Japan: IEEE Computer Society.

Krishnaprasad, M., Liu, Z. H., Manikutty, A., Warner, J. W., Arora, V., & Kotsovolos, S. (2004). Query rewrite for XML in Oracle XML DB. *VLDB*, (pp. 1122-1133).

Krüger, I. H., Meisinger, M., & Menarini, M. (2007). Runtime verification of interactions: From MSCs to aspects. In Sokolsky & Tasiran (2007), *Runtime Verification*, (LNCS Vol. 4839, pp. 63-74).

Kruskal, J. (1964). Nonmetric multidimensional scaling: A numerical method. *Psychometrika, 29*(2), 115–129. doi:10.1007/BF02289694

Kruskal, J. B., & Wish, M. (1978). *Multidimensional scaling.* Beverly Hills, CA: SAGE publications.

Kwon, J., Rao, P., Moon, B., & Lee, S. (2005). FiST: scalable xml document filtering by sequencing twig patterns. In *VLDB '05: Proceedings of the 31st international conference on Very large data bases* (pp. 217-228). VLDB Endowment.

Lagorce, J.-B., Stockus, A., & Waller, E. (1997). Object-Oriented Database Evolution. In *Sixth International Conference on Database Theory*, (pp. 379-393).

Lakshmanan, L. V. S., Wang, H., & Zhao, Z. (2006). Answering tree pattern queries using views. *VLDB '06: Proceedings of the 32nd International Conference on very Large Data Bases*, Seoul, Korea, (pp. 571-582).

Lakshmanan, L. V., & Parthasarathy, S. (2002). On Efficient Matching of Streaming XML Documents and Queries. In *EDBT '02: Proceedings of the 8th International Conference on Extending Database Technology*, (pp. 142-160).

Lanzelotte, R. S., & Valduriez, P. (1991, September 3–6). Extending the Search Strategy in a Query Optimizer. In G. M. Lohman, A. Sernadas, & R. Camps (Eds.), *Proceedings of the 17th International Conference on Very Large Data Bases, Barcelona, Spain* (pp. 363–373). San Francisco: Morgan Kaufmann Publishers.

Lencevicius, R. Ran., A, Yairi, R. (2000). Apache Web Server Execution Tracing Using Third Eye. In M. Ducassé, (Ed.) *Proceedings of the Fourth International Workshop on Automated Debugging, AADEBUG 2000, Munich, Germany.* Retrieved on June 20th, 2009 from http://arxiv.org/abs/cs.SE/0011022

Lenzerini, M. (2002). Data integration: A theoretical perspective. In *PODS '02: Proceedings of the Twenty-First ACM SIGMOD-SIGACT-SIGART Symposium on Principles of Database Systems*, Madison, Wisconsin, (pp. 233-246).

Lenzerini, M. (2004). Principles of P2P data integration. In *DIWeb*, (pp. 7-21).

Lerner, A., & Shasha, D. (2003). AQuery: Query language for ordered data, optimization techniques, and experiments. In *Proceedings of the 29th international conference on Very large data bases*, (pp. 345–356), VLDB Endowment.

Levy, A. Y., Mendelzon, A. O., Sagiv, Y., & Srivastava, D. (1995). Answering queries using views. In *PODS*, (pp. 95-104).

Ley, M. (2009). *DBLP—Some lessons learned.* Paper presented at the VLDB' 09, Lyon, France.

Li, C., & Ling, T. W. (2005). QED: A novel quaternary encoding to completely avoid re-labeling in XML updates. *CIKM*, (pp. 501-508).

Li, C., Chang, K. C., & Ilyas, I. F. (2006). Supporting ad-hoc ranking aggregates. In *SIGMOD Conference*, (pp. 61-72).

Li, C., Chang, K. C., Ilyas, I. F., & Song, S. (2005). Rank-SQL: Query algebra and optimization for relational top-k queries. In *SIGMOD Conference*, (pp. 131-142).

Li, C., Ling, T. W., & Hu, M. (2006). Efficient Processing of Updates in Dynamic XML Data. In *Proceedings of the 22nd international Conference on Data Engineering*, April 03 - 07, ICDE (pp. 13). Washington, DC: IEEE Computer Society.

Li, G. L., & Jacobsen, H.-A. (2005). Composite subscriptions in content-based publish/subscribe systems. In *Proceedings of ACM/IFIP/USENIX International Middleware Conference*, (pp. 249-269).

Li, G. L., Hou, S., & Jacobsen, H. A. (2009). Routing of XML and XPath queries in data dissemination network. In *Proceedings of the 29th International Conference of Distributed Computing Systems*, (pp. 627-638).

Li, G., Cheung, A., Hou, S., Hu, S., Muthusamy, V., Sherafat, R., et al. (2007). Historic data access in publish/subscribe. In *Proceedings of the 2007 inaugural international conference on Distributed event-based systems* (pp 80-84), Toronto, Ontario, Canada.

Li, G., Hou, S., & Jacobsen, H.-A. (2005). A unified approach to routing, covering and merging in publish/subscribe systems based on modified binary decision diagrams. In *Proceedings of the 25th International Conference on Distributed Computing Systems (ICDCS'05)*, (pp. 447–457), Columbus, OH.

Li, G., Hou, S., & Jacobsen, H.-A. (2008). Routing of XML and XPath queries in data dissemination networks. In *Proceedings of The 28th International Conference on Distributed Computing Systems (ICDCS'08)*, (pp. 627–638), Washington, DC.

Li, G., Muthusamy, V. & Jacobsen, H- A. (2007). *NIÑOS: A Distributed Service Oriented Architecture for Business Process Execution*. The Journal of ACM Transactions on Computational Logics, 4(1), Article 2, Jan 2010.

Li, G., Muthusamy, V., & Jacobsen, H.-A. (2008). Adpative content-based routing in general overlay topologies. In *Proceedings of the 9th ACM/IFIP/USENIX International Middleware Conference* (pp 249-269). Berlin: Springer.

Li, G., Muthusamy, V., & Jacobsen, H.-A. (2008). Subscribing to the past in content-based publish/subscribe. Technical report, Middleware Systems Research Group, University of Toronto.

Li, G., Ooi, B. C., Feng, J., Wang, J., & Zhou, L. (2008). EASE: an Effective 3-in-1 Keyword Search Method for Unstructured, Semi-structured and Structured data. In *SIGMOD*.

Li, Q., & Moon, B. (2001). Indexing and Querying XML Data for Regular Path Expressions. In P. M. Apers, P. Atzeni, S. Ceri, S. Paraboschi, K. Ramamohanarao, and R. T. Snodgrass, (Eds.), *Proceedings of the 27th international Conference on Very Large Data Bases*, September 11 - 14, Very Large Data Bases, (pp. 361-370). San Francisco, CA: Morgan Kaufmann Publishers.

Li, W., & Clifton, C. (1994). Semantic integration in heterogeneous databases using neural networks. In *VLDB*, (pp. 1-12).

Li, W., & Clifton, C. (2000). SEMINT: A tool for identifying attribute correspondences in heterogeneous databases using neural networks. *Data & Knowledge Engineering*, 33(1), 49–84. doi:10.1016/S0169-023X(99)00044-0

Li, W., Candan, K. S., Vu, Q., & Agrawal, D. (2001). Retrieving and organizing web pages by ``information unit''. In *WWW*, (pp. 230-244).

Li, X., & Agrawal, G. (2005). Efficient evaluation of XQuery over streaming data. In K. Böhm, C. S. Jensen, L. M. Haas, M. L. Kersten, P.-Å. Larson, & B. C. Ooi (Eds.) *VLDB*, (pp. 265-276). NewYork: ACM.

Li, Y. G. (n.d.). *The XOO7 benchmark*. Retrieved Febrary 28, 2009, from http://www.comp.nus.edu.sg/~ebh/XOO7.html

Li, Y., Yu, C., & Jagadish, H. V. (2004). Schema-free XQuery. In *Proceedings of VLDB* (pp. 72–83).

Liefke, H., & Suciu, D. (2000). XMill: An efficient compressor for XML data. In *Proceedings of the ACM SIGMOD International Conference on Management of Data* (pp. 153-164). Dallas, TX: ACM.

Ling, T. W., Lee, M., L., & Dobbie, G. (2005). *Semistructured database design*. Berlin: Springer.

Liu, H., & Jacobsen, H.-A. (2002). A-ToPSS: A Publish/Subscribe System Supporting Approximate Matching. In *Proceedings of 28th International Conference on Very Large Data Bases* (pp 1107-1110), Hong Kong, China.

Liu, H., & Jacobsen, H.-A. (2004). Modeling uncertainties in publish/subscribe systems. In *Proceedings of the 20th International conference on Data Engineering* (pp 510-522), Boston.

Liu, H., Muthusamy, V., & Jacobsen, H.-A. (2009). Predictive Publish/Subscribe Matching. Technical report, Middleware Systems Research Group, University of Toronto.

Liu, M., & Ling, T. W. (2000). A data model for semistructured data with partial and inconsistent information. In *EDBT,* (pp. 317-331).

Liu, Z. H., & Murthy, R. (2009). A decade of XML data management: An industrial experience report from Oracle. *ICDE,* (pp. 1351-1362).

Liu, Z. H., Chandrasekar, S., Baby, T., & Chang, H. J. (2008). Towards a physical XML independent XQuery/SQL/XML engine. *PVLDB, 1*(2), 1356–1367.

Liu, Z. H., Krishnaprasad, M., & Arora, V. (2005). Native XQuery processing in Oracle XML DB. In *Proceedings of the 2005 ACM SIGMOD International Conference on Management of Data*, (pp. 828–833). New York: ACM press.

Liu, Z. H., Krishnaprasad, M., Chang, H. J., & Arora, V. (2007). *XMLTable index An efficient way of indexing and querying XML property data*. ICDE, (pp. 1194-1203).

Liu, Z. H., Krishnaprasad, M., Warner, J. W., Angrish, R., & Arora, V. (2007). Effective and efficient update of xml in RDBMS. *SIGMOD Conference,* (pp. 925-936).

Liu, Z. H., Krishnaprasad, M., Warner, J. W., Angrish, R., & Arora, V. (2007). Effective and efficient update of xml in RDBMS. In *Proceedings of ACM SIGMOD international Conference on Management of Data,* (pp. 925-936).

Liu, Z. H., Novoselsky, A., & Arora, V. (2008). Towards a unified declarative and imperative XQuery processor. *IEEE Data Eng. Bull., 31*(4), 33–40.

Liu, Z., & Chen, Y. (2007). Identifying meaningful return information for XML keyword search. In *16th ACM SIGMOD International Conference on Management of Data* (pp. 329-340). New York: ACM.

Liu, Z., & Chen, Y. (2008). Reasoning and Identifying Relevant Matches for XML Keyword Search. In *VLDB*.

Loo, B. T., Huebsch, R., Hellerstein, J. M., Stoica, I., & Shenker, S. (2004). Enhancing P2P File-Sharing with an Internet-Scale Query Processor. In *Proceedings of VLDB* (pp. 432–443).

Lu, J., & Ling, T. W. (2004). Labeling and querying dynamic XML trees, In *Proceedings of the Sixth Asia Pacific Web Conference,* Hangzhou, China, April 14-17, APWeb, (pp. 180–189).

Lu, J., & Ling, T. W., Chan, C., Y., & Chen, T. (2005). From region encoding to extended Dewey: on efficient processing of XML twig pattern matching. In *31th International Conference on Very Large Data Bases* (pp. 193-204). Ohio: VLDB Endowment.

Lu, J., Chen, T., & Ling, T. W. (2004). Efficient processing of XML twig patterns with parent child edges: a lookahead approach. In *Proceedings of 2004 International Conference on Information and Knowledge Management (CIKM)*, Washington, DC, November 8-13, (pp. 533–542).

Ludäscher, B., Mukhopadhyay, P., & Papakonstantinou, Y. (2002). A transducer-based xml query processor. In *Proceedings of the 28th international conference on Very Large Data Bases VLDB 2002* (pp. 227-238). VLDB Endowment.

Madhavan, J., Bernstein, P. A., & Rahm, E. (2001). Generic schema matching with cupid. In *VLDB*, (pp. 49-58).

Mahbub, K., & Spanoudakis, G. (2005). Run-time monitoring of requirements for systems composed of web-services: Initial implementation and evaluation experience. In *ICWS*, (pp. 257-265). Wasington, DC: IEEE Computer Society.

Mahbub, K., & Spanoudakis, G. (2007). *Monitoring WS-Agreements: An Event Calculus-Based Approach*, (pp. 265-306). Berlin: Springer.

Mähönen, P., Pohl, K., & Priol, T. (Eds.). (2008). Towards a Service-Based Internet. *In Proceedings of the First European Conference, ServiceWave 2008, Madrid, Spain, December 10-13,* (LNCS Vol. 5377). Berlin: Springer.

Maier, D. (1983). *The Theory of Relational Databases.* Rockville, MD: Computer Science Press.

Malcolm, G. (2008). *What's New for XML in SQL Server 2008.* In Microsoft SQL Server 2008 white papers.

Mandhani, B., & Suciu, D. (2005). Query Caching and View Selection for XML Databases. In *Proceedings of VLDB* (pp. 469–480).

Manolescu, I., Florescu, D., & Kossmann, D. (2001). Answering XML queries on heterogeneous data sources. In *Proceedings of the 27th International Conference on Very Large Data Bases*, (pp. 241– 250). San Mateo, CA: Morgan Kaufmann.

Manolescu, I., Florescu, D., Kossmann, D., Xhumari, F., & Olteanu, D. (2000). Agora: Living with XML and relational. In *VLDB '00: Proceedings of the 26th International Conference on very Large Data Bases,* (pp. 623-626).

Manolescu, I., Miachon, C., & Michiels, P. (2006). *Towards micro-benchmarking XQuery.* Paper presented at the first International Workshop on Performance and Evaluation of Data Management Systems (EXPDB), Chicago, IL.

Martens, W., Neven, F., Schwentick, T., & Bex, G. J. (2006). Expressiveness and complexity of XML schema. *ACM Transactions on Database Systems, 31*(3), 770–813. doi:10.1145/1166074.1166076

Mathis, C. (2009). *Storing, indexing, and querying XML documents in native XML database management systems.* Doctoral Dissertation, Dept. of Computer Science, University of Kaiserslautern, Germany.

Mathis, C., Weiner, A. M., Härder, T., & Hoppen, C. R. F. (2008). XTCcmp: XQuery compilation on XTC. In . *Proceedings of the VLDB Endowment, 1*(2), 1400–1403.

May, N. (2007). *An Algebraic Approach to XQuery Optimization.* Doctoral dissertation, University of Mannheim, Germany.

May, N., Helmer, S., & Moerkotte, G. (2004). Nested queries and quantifiers in an ordered context. In *Proceedings of the 20th International Conference on Data Engineering (ICDE),* (pp. 239–250). Washington, DC: IEEE Computer Society.

May, N., Helmer, S., & Moerkotte, G. (2006). Strategies for query unnesting in XML databases. *ACM Transactions on Database Systems, 31*(3), 968–1013. doi:10.1145/1166074.1166081

McBrien, P., & Poulovassilis, A. (2003). Defining peer-to-peer data integration using both as view rules. In *DBISP2P*, (pp. 91-107).

McGuinness, D. L., & Harmelen, F. V. (2004). OWL Web Ontology Language Overview WC3 Recommendation. Retrieved February 10, 2004, from http://www.w3.org/TR/owl-features

McHugh, J., & Widom, J. (1999). *Query optimization for XML.* Paper presented in the 25th International Conference on Very Large Data Bases, Edinburgh, Scotland.

McHugh, J., Abiteboul, S., Goldman, R., Quass, D., & Widom, J. (1997, September). Lore: A database management system for semistructured data. *SIGMOD Record, 26*(3), 54–66. doi:10.1145/262762.262770

Meersman, R., & Tari, Z. (Eds.). (2008). *On the Move to Meaningful Internet Systems 2008: CoopIS, DOA, and ODBASE, OTM Confederated International Conferences, Monterrey, Mexico, October 10-14, 2008, Proceedings, Part I*, (LNCS vol. 5331). Berlin: Springer.

Megginson, D., & Brownell, D. (2004, April 27). *Simple API for XML (SAX)*. Retrieved January 22, 2009, from http://www.saxproject.org/

Melnik, S., Garcia-Molina, H., & Rahm, E. (2002). Similarity flooding: A versatile graph matching algorithm and its application to schema matching. In *ICDE*, (pp. 117-128).

Melton, J., & Buxton, S. (2006). Querying XML – Xquery, XPath, and SQL/XML in Context. Morgan-Kaufmann.

MemBeR XML Generator. (n.d.). Retrieved April 3, 2009, from http://ilps.science.uva.nl/Resources/MemBeR/member-generator.html

Menezes, A. J., van Oorschot, P. C., & Vanstone, S. A. (1996). *Handbook of Applied Cryptography*. Boca Raton, FL: CRC Press.

Mercer, R. E., & Risch, V. (2003). Properties of maximal cliques of a pair-wise compatibility graph for three nonmonotonic reasoning system. In *Answer Set Programming*.

Meredith, G., & Bjorg, S. (2003). Contracts and types. *Communications of the ACM, 46*(10), 41–47. doi:10.1145/944217.944236

Mesiti, M., Celle, R., Sorrenti, M. A., & Guerrini, G. (2006). X-Evolution: A System for XML Schema Evolution and Document Adaptation. In *EDBT*, (pp 1143-1146).

Michiels, P., Hidders. J. Siméon, J., & Vercammen, R. (2006). *How to recognize different kinds of tree patterns from quite a long way away*. Technical Report TR UA 13-2006, University of Antwerp.

Mihaila, G. A., Raschid, L., & Tomasic, A. (2002). Locating and accessing data repositories with WebSemantics. *The VLDB Journal, 11*(1), 47–57. doi:10.1007/s007780200061

Miklau, G., & Suciu, D. (2002), Containment and equivalence for an XPath fragment. In *Proceedings of the twenty-first ACM SIGMOD-SIGACT-SIGART symposium on Principles of database systems*, (pp. 65–76). New York: ACM press.

Miklau, G., & Suciu, D. (2004). Containment and equivalence for a fragment of XPath. *Journal of the ACM, 51*(1), 2–45. doi:10.1145/962446.962448

Miller, G. A. (1995). WordNet: A lexical database for english. *Communications of the ACM, 38*(11), 39–41. doi:10.1145/219717.219748

Miller, R. J., Haas, L. M., & Hernández, M. A. (2000). Schema mapping as query discovery. In *VLDB*, (pp. 77-88).

Milo, T., & Suciu, D. (1999). Index structures for path expressions. In *Proceedings of 7th International Conference on Database Theory*, (pp. 277-295). Jerusalem, Israel: Springer.

Milo, T., & Zohar, S. (1998). Using schema matching to simplify heterogeneous data translation. In *VLDB*, (pp. 122-133).

Min, J., Ahn, J., & Chung, C. (2003). Efficient extraction of schemas for XML documents. *Information Processing Letters, 85*(1), 7–12. doi:10.1016/S0020-0190(02)00345-9

Min, J., Park, M., & Chung, C. W. (2003). XPRESS: A queriable compression for XML data. *ACM SIGMOD International Conference on Management of Data* (pp. 122-133). New York: ACM.

Min, J., Park, M., & Chung, C. W. (2006). A compressor for effective archiving, retrieval, and update of XML documents. *ACM Transactions on Internet Technology, 6*(3), 223–258. doi:10.1145/1151087.1151088

Min, J., Park, M., & Chung, C. W. (2007). XTREAM: An efficient multi-query evaluation on streaming XML data. *Information Sciences, 177*(17), 3519–3538. doi:10.1016/j.ins.2007.03.009

Mitra, P., Wiederhold, G., & Jannink, J. (1999). Semi-automatic integration of knowledge sources. In *Proc. 2nd International Conference on Information Fusion,* (pp. 572–581).

Mitra, P., Wiederhold, G., & Kersten, M. L. (2000). A graph-oriented model for articulation of ontology inter-dependencies. In *EDBT,* (pp. 86-100).

Mohammad, S., & Martin, P. (2009). *XML Structural Indexes* (Technical Report No. 2009-560). Kinston, Ontario, Canada: Queen's University.

Moon, J. W., & Moser, L. (1965). On cliques in graphs. *Israel Journal of Mathematics, 3*(1), 23–28. doi:10.1007/BF02760024

Moro, M. M., Bakalov, P., & Tsotras, V. J. (2007). Early profile pruning on xml-aware publish-subscribe systems. In *Proceedings of the 33rd international conference on Very large data bases (VLDB'07),* (pp. 866–877), Vienna, Austria.

Mühl, G. (2001). Generic constraints for content-based publish/subscribe systems. In *Proceedings of the 6th International Conference on Cooperative Information Systems (CoopIS'01),* (LNCS vol. 2172, pp. 211–225), Trento, Italy.

Murthy, R., & Banerjee, S. (2003). XML schemas in Oracle XML DB. *VLDB,* (pp. 1009-1018).

Murthy, R., Liu, Z. H., Krishnaprasad, M., Chandrasekar, S., Tran, A., & Sedlar, E. (2005). Towards an enterprise XML architecture. In *SIGMOD Conference* (pp. 953-957).

Muthusamy, V., & Jacobsen, H.-A. (2005). Small-scale Peer-to-peer Publish/Subscribe. In *Proceedings of the MobiQuitous Conference* (pp 109-119). New York: ACM.

Muthusamy, V., & Jacobsen, H.-A. (2007). Infrastructure-less Content-Based Pub. Technical report, Middleware Systems Research Group, University of Toronto.

Muthusamy, V., & Jacobsen, H.-A. (2008). SLA-driven distributed application development. In *Proceedings of the 3rd Workshop on Middleare for Service Oriented Computing* (pp. 31-36), Leuven, Belgium.

Muthusamy, V., Jacobsen, H.-A., Coulthard, P., Chan, A., Waterhouse, J., & Litani, E. (2007). SLA-Driven Business Process Management in SOA. In *Proceedings of the 2007 conference of the center for advanced studies on Collaborative research* (pp 264-267), Richmond Hill, Ontario, Canada.

Nakajima, S. (2005). Lightweight formal analysis of web service flows. *Progress in Informatics,* (2), 57-76.

Nakano, R. (1990). Translation with optimization from relational calculus to relational algebra having aggregate functions. *ACM Transactions on Database Systems, 15*(4), 518–557. doi:10.1145/99935.99943

Natchetoi, Y., Wu, H., & Dagtas, S. (2007). EXEM: Efficient XML data exchange management for mobile applications. *Information Systems Frontiers, 9*(4), 439–448. doi:10.1007/s10796-007-9045-4

Naughton, J. F., DeWitt, D. J., Maier, D., Aboulnaga, A., Chen, J., & Galanis, L. (2001). The Niagara internet query system. *IEEE Data Eng. Bull., 24*(2), 27–33.

Navathe, S., Ceri, S., Wiederhold, G., & Dou, J. (1984). Vertical partitioning algorithms for database design. *ACM Transactions on Database Systems, 9*(4), 680–710. doi:10.1145/1994.2209

Negri, M., M., Pelagatti, G., & Sbattella, L. (1991). Formal semantics of SQL queries. *ACM Transactions on Database Systems, 16*(3), 513–534. doi:10.1145/111197.111212

Ng, W., & Cheng, J. (2004). XQzip: Querying compressed XML using structural indexing. *International Conference on Extending Database Technology* (pp. 219-236). New York: ACM.

Ng, W., Lam, W., & Cheng, J. (2006). Comparative Analysis of XML Compression Technologies. *World Wide Web: Internet and Web Information Systems, 9,* 5–33.

Ng, W., Lam, W., Wood, P. T., & Levene, M. (2006). XCQ: A queriable XML compression system. *Knowledge and Information Systems, 10*(4), 421–452. doi:10.1007/s10115-006-0012-z

Nguyen, L. T., Yee, W. G., & Frieder, O. (2008). Adaptive distributed indexing for structured peer-to-peer networks. In *CIKM '08: Proceeding of the 17th ACM Conference on Information and Knowledge Management,* Napa Valley, CA, (pp. 1241-1250).

Ni, Y., & Chan, C.-Y. (2008). Dissemination of heterogeneous XML data (Poster Paper). In *Proceedings of the 17th International World Wide Web Conference,* (pp. 1059-1060).

Nicola, M. & van der Linden, B. (2005). *Native XML Support in DB2 Universal Database.*

Nicola, M., & Jain, U. (2007). *Update XML in DB2 9.5.* Retrieved from www.ibm.com/developerworks/db2/library/techarticle/dm-0710nicola/

Nicola, M., & Van der Linden, B. (2005). Native XML support in DB2 universal database. In *Proceedings of the 31st International Conference on Very Large Data Bases* (pp. 1164–1174). Trondheim, Norway: ACM.

Nicola, M., Kogan, I., & Schiefer, B. (2007). *An XML transaction processing benchmark.* Paper presented at SIGMOD'07, Beijing, China.

NITF. (2005). NITF DTD. Retrieved from http://www.nitf.org/IPTC/NITF/3.3/documentation/nitf.html

Novoselsky, A., & Liu, Z. H. (2008). XVM - *A hybrid sequential-query virtual machine for processing XML languages.* PLAN-X.

Noy, N., & Musen, M. (2001). Anchor-PROMPT: Using non-local context for semantic matching. In *Proceedings of the Workshop on Ontologies and Information Sharing at the International Joint Conference on Artificial Intelligence (IJCAI),* (pp. 63-70).

O'Neil, P. E., O'Neil, E., J., Pal, S., Cseri, I., Schaller, G., & Westbury, N. (2004). ORDPATHs: Insert-Friendly XML Node Labels. *2004 ACM SIGMOD International Conference on Management of Data,* (pp. 903-908). New York: ACM.

Object Management Group. (1997). *UML specification version 1.1, OMG document ad/97-08-11.* Retrieved on April 20th, 2009 from http://www.omg.org/cgi-bin/doc?ad/97-08-11

Olteanu, D. (2007). SPEX: Streamed and Progressive Evaluation of XPath. *IEEE Transactions on Knowledge and Data Engineering, 19*(7), 934–949. doi:10.1109/TKDE.2007.1063

Olteanu, D., Meuss, H., Furche, T., & Bry, F. (2002). XPath: Looking Forward. *XML-Based Data Management and Multimedia Engineering — EDBT 2002 Workshops,* (pp. 892-896).

Online Computer Library Center. (2008). *Dewey decimal classification.* Retrieved January 13, 2009, from http://www.oclc.org/dewey/versions/ddc22print/intro.pdf

Onose, N., Deutsch, A., Papakonstantinou, Y., & Curtmola, E. (2006). Rewriting nested XML queries using nested views. In *SIGMOD '06: Proceedings of the 2006 ACM SIGMOD International Conference on Management of Data,* Chicago, IL (pp. 443-454).

Ooi, B. C., Tan, K. L., Zhou, A. Y., Goh, C. H., Li, Y. G., Liau, C. Y., et al. (2003). PeerDB: Peering into Personal Databases. In *Proceedings of ACM SIGMOD,* (pp. 659–659).

Osborne, M. J., & Rubinstein, A. (1994). *A Course in Game Theory.* Cambridge, MA: MIT Press.

Ozcan, F., Cochrane, R., Pirahesh, H., Kleewein, J., Beyer, K. S., Josifovski, V., & Zhang, C. (2005). System RX: One part relational, one part XML. In *Proc. of the 2005 ACM SIGMOD International Conference on Management of Data,* (pp. 347–358). New York: ACM press.

Ozsu, M. T., & Valduriez, P. (1999). *Principles of Distributed Database Systems.* Upper Saddle River, NJ: Prentice-Hall.

Pal, S., Cseri, I., Schaller, G., Seeliger, O., Giakoumakis, L., & Zolotov, V. (2004). Indexing XML data stored in a relational database. In *30th International Conference on Very Large Data Bases,* (pp. 1146-1157). Ohio: VLDB Endowment.

Pal, S., Cseri, I., Seeliger, O., Rys, M., Schaller, G., Yu, W., et al. (2005). XQuery implementation in a relational database system. In *Proceedings of the 31st international conference on Very large data bases,* (pp. 1175–1186), VLDB Endowment.

Pal, S., Tomic, D., Berg, B., & Xavier, J. (2006). Managing Collections of XML Schemas in Microsoft SQL Server 2005. In *Proc. Of the 10th Int'l Conference on Extending Database Technology,* (pp. 1102-1105).

Pang, X., Catania, B., & Tan, K. (2003). Securing your Data in Agent-based P2P Systems. In *Proceedings of IEEE DASFAA* (pp. 55–62).

Pankowski, T. (2008). XML data integration in SixP2P: A theoretical framework. In *Intl. Workshop on Data Management in Peer-to-Peer Systems,* (pp. 11-18).

Pankowski, T., Cybulka, J., & Meissner, A. (2007). XML schema mappings in the presence of key constraints and value dependencies. *EROW.*

Papaemmanouil, O., & Cetintemel, U. (2005). SemCast: semantic multicast for content-based data dissemination. In *Proceedings of the 21st International Conference on Data Engineering,* (pp. 242-253).

Papakonstantinou, Y., Garcia-Molina, H., & Widom, J. (1995). Object exchange across heterogeneous information sources. In *ICDE,* (pp. 251-260).

Paparizos, S., Wu, Y., Lakshmanan, L. V., & Jagadish, H. V. (2004, June 13–18). Tree Logical Classes for Efficient Evaluation of XQuery. In *Proceedings of the 2004 ACM SIGMOD International Conference on Management of Data, Paris, France* (pp. 71–82). New York: ACM Press.

Parastatidis, S., Webber, J., Woodman, S., Kuo, D., & Greenfield, P. (2005). *SOAP service description language (SSDL).* Tech. Rep. CS-TR-899, University of Newcastle, Newcastle upon Tyne.

Park, J. H., & Kang, J.-H. (2007). Optimization of XQuery queries including for clauses. In *ICIW,* (p. 37). Washington, DC: IEEE Computer Society.

Peng, F., & Chawathe, S. S. (2003). Streaming XPath queries in XSQ. In *ICDE,* (pp. 780-782).

Peng, F., & Chawathe, S. S. (2003). Xpath queries on streaming data. *SIGMOD '03: Proceedings of the 2003 ACM SIGMOD international conference on Management of data* (pp. 431-442). New York: ACM Press.

Pennock, D. M., Horvitz, E., & Giles, C. L. 2000. An Impossibility Theorem for Clustering. In *AAAI.*

Petrovic, M., Muthusamy, V., & Jacobsen, H.-A. (2005). Content-based routing in mobile ad hoc networks. In *Proceedings of the Second Annual International Conference on Mobile and Ubiquitous Systems: Networking and Services* (pp 45-55), San Diego, CA.

Pirahesh, H., Hellerstein, J. M., & Hasan, W. (1992, June 2–5). Extensible/Rule Based Query Rewrite Optimization in Starburst. In M. Stonebraker (Ed.), *Proceedings of the 1992 ACM SIGMOD International Conference on Management of Data, San Diego, California* (pp. 39–48). New York: ACM Press.

Polyzotis, N., Garofalakis, M., & Ioannidis, Y. (2004, June 13-18). Approximate XML Query Answers. In G. Welkum, A.C. Konig, & S. Dessloch (Eds.), *Proceedings of the ACM SIGMOD International Conference on Management of Data,* Paris, France (pp.263-274). New York: ACM Press.

Popa, L., Velegrakis, Y., Miller, R. J., Hernández, M. A., & Fagin, R. (2002). Translating web data. In *VLDB*, (pp. 598-609).

Pottinger, R. A., & Bernstein, P. A. (2003). Merging models based on given correspondences. In *VLDB*.

PSD. (2005). *PSD DTD*. Retrieved from http://matra. sourceforge.net/dtdtree/bio/psdml_dtdtree.php

Qi, Y., Candan, K. S., & Sapino, M. L. (2007). FICSR: Feedback-based inconsistency resolution and query processing on misaligned data sources. In *SIGMOD*, (pp. 151-162).

Qi, Y., Candan, K. S., & Sapino, M. L. (2007). Sum-max monotonic ranked joins for evaluating top-K twig queries on weighted data graphs. In *VLDB*, (pp. 507-518).

Qi, Y., Candan, K. S., Sapino, M. L., & Kintigh, K. W. (2006). QUEST: QUery-driven exploration of semi-structured data with ConflicTs and partial knowledge. *CleanDB*.

Qi, Y., Candan, K. S., Sapino, M. L., & Kintigh, K. W. (2007). Integrating and querying taxonomies with quest in the presence of conflicts. In *SIGMOD '07: Proceedings of the 2007 ACM SIGMOD International Conference on Management of Data,* Beijing, China, (pp. 1153-1155).

Qin, L., Yu, J., & Ding, B. (2007). TwigList: Make Twig Pattern Matching Fast. *DASFAA 2007,* (LNCS Vol. 4443, pp. 850-862). Berlin: Springer.

Rabin, M. O. (1981). *Fingerprinting by Random Polynomials.* CRCT TR-15-81, Harvard University, Cambridge, MA.

Raghavachari, M., & Shmueli, O. (2006). Conflicting XML Updates. In *EDBT 2006*, (pp. 552-569).

Rahm, E., & Bernstein, P. A. (2001). A survey of approaches to automatic schema matching. *The VLDB Journal, 10*(4), 334–350. doi:10.1007/s007780100057

Rahm, E., Do, H. H., & Massmann, S. (2004). Matching large XML schemas. *SIGMOD Record, 33*(4), 26–31. doi:10.1145/1041410.1041415

Rahm, E., Thor, A., & Aumueller, D. (2007). Dynamic fusion of web data. In *XSym,* (pp. 14-16).

Rao, P., & Moon, B. (2004). PRIX: Indexing and querying XML using Prufer sequences. In *Proceedings of the 20th International Conference on Data Engineering* (pp. 288-300). Boston: IEEE Computer Society.

Ratnasamy, S., Francis, P., Handley, M., Karp, R., & Shenker, S. (2001). A Scalable Content-Addressable Network. In *Proceedings of ACM SIGCOMM* (pp. 161–172).

Re, C., Siméon, J., & Fernández, M. F. (2006). A complete and efficient algebraic compiler for XQuery. In *Proceedings of the 22nd International Conference on Data Engineering (ICDE),* (pp 14). Washington, DC: IEEE Computer Society.

Resnik, P. (1995). Using information content to evaluate semantic similarity in a taxonomy. *IJCAI, 448-453.*

Robinson, W. (2006). A requirements monitoring framework for enterprise systems. *Requir. Eng., 11*(1), 17–41. doi:10.1007/s00766-005-0016-3

Robinson, W. N. (2003). Monitoring web service requirements. In *RE,* (pp. 65-74). Washington, DC: IEEE Computer Society.

Roddick, J. F. (1995). A Survey of Schema Versioning Issues for Database Systems. *Information and Software Technology, 37*(7), 383–393. doi:10.1016/0950-5849(95)91494-K

Rosado, L. A., Márquez, A. P., & Gil, J. M. (2007). Managing Branch Versioning in Versioned/Temporal XML Documents. In *5th International XML Database Symposium (XSym),* (pp. 107-121).

Rosado, L. A., Márquez, A. P., & González, J. M. F. (2006): Representing Versions in XML Documents Using Versionstamp. In *4th International Workshop on Evolution and Change in Data Management – (ER Workshop),* (pp. 257-267).

Runapongsa, K., Patel, J. M., Jagadish, H. V., Chen, Y., & Al-Khalifa, S. (2003). *The Michigan benchmark: towards XML query performance diagnostics.* Paper presented at the 29th VLDB Conference, Berlin, Germany.

Sahuguet, A. (2001). *Kweelt: More than just "yet another framework to query XML!* Paper presented at ACM SIGMOD, Santa Barbara, CA.

Sakr, S. (2008). *XSelMark: A micro-benchmark for selectivity estimation approaches of XML queries.* Paper presented at the 19th International Conference on Database and Expert Systems Applications (DEXA 2008), Turin, Italy.

Salomon, D. (1998). *Data compression, The complete reference.* New York: Springer-Verlag, Inc.

Sankey, J., & Wong, R. K. (2001). Structural inference for semistructured data. In *CIKM,* (pp. 159-166).

Sarma, A. D., Dong, X., & Halevy, A. (2008). Bootstrapping pay-as-you-go data integration systems. In *SIGMOD '08: Proceedings of the 2008 ACM SIGMOD International Conference on Management of Data,* Vancouver, Canada, (pp. 861-874).

Sartiani, C., Manghi, P., Ghelli, G., & Conforti, G. (2004). XPeer: A Self-Organizing XML P2P Database System. In . *Proceedings of P, 2PDB,* 456–465.

Schenkl, R., & Theobald, M. (2006). Structural Feedback for Keyword-Based XML Retrieval. In *ECIR.*

Schkolnick, M. (1977). A clustering algorithm for hierarchical structures. [TODS]. *ACM Transactions on Database Systems, 2*(1), 27–44. doi:10.1145/320521.320531

Schmidt, A. (2003). *XMark-An XML Benchmark project.* Retrieved Febrary 25, 2009, from http://monetdb.cwi.nl/xml/

Schmidt, A., Waas, F., Kersten, M., Carey, M. J., Manolescu, I., & Busse, R. (2002). *XMark: A benchmark for XML data management.* Paper presented at the 28th Very Large Data Base (VLDB), Hong Kong, China.

Schmidt, A., Waas, F., Kersten, M., Florescu, D., Manolescu, I., & Carey, M. J. & Busse, R. (2001). *The XML Benchmark Project.* (Tech. rep. INS-R0103). Amsterdam, The Netherlands, CWI.

Schmidt, M., Scherzinger, S., & Koch, C. (2007). Combined static and dynamic analysis for effective buffer minimization in streaming xquery evaluation. In *ICDE,* (pp. 236-245). Washignton, DC: IEEE.

Segall, B., Aronld, D., Boot, J., Henderson, M., & Phelps, T. (2000). Content-based routing with Elvin4. In *Proceedings of the Australian UNIX and Open Systems User group Conference.*

Segoufin, L., & Vianu, V. (2002). Validating streaming XML documents. In *PODS,* (pp. 53-64).

Selcuk Candan, K., Hsiung, W.-P., Chen, S., Tatemura, J., & Agrawal, D. (2006). AFilter: adaptive XML filtering with prefix-caching and suffix-clustering. In *Proceedings of the 32nd International Conference on Very Large Data Bases,* (pp. 559-570).

Selinger, P. G., Astrahan, M. M., Chamberlin, D. D., Lorie, R. A., & Price, T. G. (1979). Access Path Selection in a Relational Database Management System. In *Proceedings of the 1979 ACM SIGMOD International Conference on Management of Data, Boston, Massachusetts,* (pp. 23–34). New York: ACM Press.

Seward, J. (2008). *bzip2 and libbzip2, version 1.0.5 A program and library for data compression.* Retrieved from http://bzip.org/1.0.5/bzip2-manual-1.0.5.html

Shanmugasundaram, J., & Shekita, E., J., Kiernan, J., Krishnamurthy, R., Viglas, S., Naughton, J., F., & Tatarinov, I. (2001). A general technique for querying XML documents using a relational database system. *SIGMOD Record, 30*(3), 20–26. doi:10.1145/603867.603871

Shanmugasundaram, J., Kiernan, G., Shekita, E. J., Fan, C., & Funderburk, J. E. (2001). Querying XML views of relational data. In *Proceedings of the 27th International Conference on Very Large Data Bases,* (pp. 261–270). San Mateo, CA: Morgan Kaufmann.

Shanmugasundaram, J., Tufte, K., Zhang, C., He, G., & DeWitt, D. J., & Naughton, J., F. (1999). Relational databases for querying XML documents: limitations and opportunities. In *25th International Conference on Very Large Data Bases* (pp. 302-314). San Francisco: Morgan Kaufmann Publishers, Inc.

Shaya, E., Gass, J., Blackwell, J., Thomas, B., Holmes, B., Cheung, C., et al. (2000). *XML at the ADC: Steps to a Next Generation Data Repository.* Retrieved June 17, 2009, from http://www.adass.org/adass/proceedings/adass99/O9-05/

Sherafat Kazemzadeh, R., & Jacobsen, H.-A. (2007). δ-Fault-Tolerant Publish/Subscribe systems. Technical report, Middleware Systems Research Group, University of Toronto.

Sherafat Kazemzadeh, R., & Jacobsen, H.-A. (2008). Highly Available Distributed Publish/Subscribe Systems. Technical report, Middleware Systems Research Group, University of Toronto.

Shvaiko, P., & Euzenat, J. (2005). A survey of schema-based matching approaches. *J. Data Semantics, 4,* 146–171.

Shvaiko, P., & Euzenat, J. (2008). Ten challenges for ontology matching. *OTM Conferences, (2),* 1164-1182.

Silberstein, A., & He, H. nd Yi, K. & Yang J. (2005). Boxes: Efficient maintenance of order-based labeling for dynamic XML data, In *Proceedings of the 21st International Conference on Data Engineering,* 5-8 April, Tokyo, Japan, (pp. 285–296).

Silberstein, A., He, H., Yi, K., & Yang, J. (2005, April 5-8). BOXes: Efficient Maintenance of Order-Based Labeling for Dynamic XML Data. In *Proceeding of the 21st International Conference on Data Engineering, ICDE 2005,* Tokyo, Japan (pp.285-296). Washington, DC: IEEE Computer Society.

Skeen, D. (1998). *Publish-subscribe architecture: publish-subscribe overview.* Retrieved from http://www.vitria.com

Slivinskas, G., Jensen, C. S., & Snodgrass, R. T. (2002). Bringing order to query optimization. *SIGMOD Record, 31*(2), 5–14. doi:10.1145/565117.565119

Snodgrass, R. (1989). *The Interface Description Language: Definition and Use.* London: W.H. Freeman.

Snodgrass, R.T, Dyreson, Currim, F., Currim, S., Joshi, S. (2008). Validating quicksand: Temporal schema versioning in τXSchema. *Data & Knowledge Engineering, 65,* 223–242. doi:10.1016/j.datak.2007.09.003

Snoeren, A. C., Conley, K., & Gifford, D. K. (2001). Mesh-based content routing using XML. *ACM SIGOPS Operating Systems Review, 35*(5), 160–173. doi:10.1145/502059.502050

Software AG. (2008). *Tamino Schema Editor.* On-line Documentation.

Sokolsky, O., & Tasiran, S. (Eds.). (2007). *Runtime Verification, 7th International Workshop, RV 2007,* Vancover, Canada, March 13, 2007, *Revised Selected Papers,* (LNCS Vol. 4839). Berlin: Springer.

Spink, A. (2002). A user-centered approach to evaluating human interaction with web search engines: an exploratory study. *Information Processing & Management, 38*(3), 401–426. doi:10.1016/S0306-4573(01)00036-X

Srivastava, D., Al-Khalifa, S., Jagadish, H. V., Koudas, N., Patel, J. M., & Wu, Y. (2002). Structural Joins: A Primitive for Efficient XML Query Pattern Matching. In *Proceedings of IEEE ICDE,* (pp. 141–152).

Steegmans, B., et al. (2004). *XML for DB2 Information Integration.* Redmond, WA: IBM Redbook Series.

Steenhagen, H. J., Apers, P. M. G., Blanken, H. M., & de By, R. A. (1994), From nested-loop to join queries in OODB. In *Proceedings of the 20th International Conference on Very Large Data Bases,* (pp. 618–629). San Mateo, CA: Morgan Kaufmann.

Stoica, I., Morris, R., Karger, D., Kaashoek, M. F., & Balakrishnan, H. (2001). Chord: A scalable Peer-to-Peer Lookup Service for Internet Applications. In *Proceedings of ACM SIGCOMM,* (pp. 149–160).

Stolz, V. (2007). Temporal assertions with parametrised propositions. In Sokolsky & Tasiran (2007), *Runtime Verification,* (pp. 176-187).

Stonebraker, M. (1975). Implementation of integrity constraints and views by query modification. In *SIGMOD Conference,* (pp. 65-78).

Stonebraker, M., & Hellerstein, J. M. (2005). *What goes around comes around. Readings in database systems,* (4ᵗʰ Ed.). San Francisco: Morgan Kaufmann.

Stonebraker, M., Brown, P., & Moore, D. (1999). *Object-relational DBMSs: Tracking the next great wave.* San Francisco: Morgan-Kauffman Publishers.

Su, H., Rundensteiner, E. A., & Mani, M. (2005). Semantic query optimization for XQuery over XML streams. In *VLDB '05: Proceedings of the 31st international conference on Very large data bases,* (pp. 277-288).

Suciu, D. (2001). On database theory and XML. *SIGMOD Record, 30*(3), 39–45. doi:10.1145/603867.603874

Suciu, D. (2002). Distributed query evaluation on semi-structured data. *ACM Transactions on Database Systems, 27*(1), 1–62. doi:10.1145/507234.507235

Tajima, K., & Fukui, Y. (2004). Answering XPath queries over networks by sending minimal views. In *VLDB,* (pp. 48-59).

Tan, M., & Goh, A. (2004). Keeping Pace with Evolving XML-Based Specifications. In *Current Trends in Database Technology – EDBT Workshops,* (LNCS Vol. 3268, pp. 280-288).

Tang, N., Yu, J. X., Özsu, M. T., Choi, B., & Wong, K. (2008). Multiple materialized view selection for XPath query rewriting. In *ICDE,* (pp. 873-882).

Tatarinov, I., & Halevy, A. (2004). Efficient query reformulation in peer data management systems. In *SIGMOD '04: Proceedings of the 2004 ACM SIGMOD International Conference on Management of Data,* Paris, France, (pp. 539-550).

Tatarinov, I., Viglas, S. D., Beyer, K., Shanmugasundaram, J., Shekita, E., & Zhang, C. (2002). Storing and querying ordered XML using a relational database system. In *Proceedings of the 2002 ACM SIGMOD international Conference on Management of Data,* Madison, WI, June 03 - 06, *SIGMOD '02* (pp. 204-215). New York: ACM.

The DBLP Computer Science Bibliography. (2009, January). *DBLP XML records* [Data file]. Retrieved January 22, 2009, from http://www.informatik.uni-trier.de/~ley/db/

TheKaZaA Homepage. (2006). Retrieved from http://www.kazaa.com

Tian, F., DeWitt, D. J., Chen, J., & Zhang, C. (2002). The design and performance evaluation of alternative XML storage strategies. *SIGMOD Record, 31*(1), 5–10. doi:10.1145/507338.507341

TIBCO. (1999). *TIB/Rendezvous.* Retrieved from http://www.tibco.com

Tolani, P. M., & Haritsa, J. R. (2002). XGRIND: A query-friendly XML compressor. In *Proceedings of the 18th International Conference on Data Engineering* (pp. 225-234). San Jose, CA: IEEE Computer Society.

TreeBank. (2002). Retrieved from University of Washington Database Group. Retrieved from http://www.cs.washington.edu/research/xmldatasets/www/repository.html#treebank

Tsoumakos, D., & Roussopoulos, N. (2003). A Comparison of Peer-to-Peer Search Methods. In *Proceedings of ACM WebDB,* (pp. 61–66).

University of Washington XML Repository. (2006). Retrieved from http://www.cs.washington.edu/research/xmldatasets/

Vakali, A., Catania, B., & Maddalena, A. (2005, March-April). XML Data Stores: Emerging Practices. *Internet Computing, IEEE, 9*(2), 62–69. doi:10.1109/MIC.2005.48

Valtchev, P., & Euzenat, J. (1997). Dissimilarity measure for collections of objects and values. *IDA, 259-272.*

van der Aalst, W. M., & Verbeek, H. M. (2008). Process mining in web services: The WebSphere case. *Bulletin of the IEEE Computer Society Technical Committee on Data Engineering,* (pp. 45-48).

Venzke, M. (2004). Specifications using XQuery expressions on traces. *Electronic Notes in Theoretical Computer Science, 105*, 109–118. doi:10.1016/j.entcs.2004.05.004

Vithanala, P. (2005). *Introduction to XQuery in SQL Server 2005*. Retrieved from http://msdn.microsoft.com

von Bültzingsloewen, G. (1987). Translating and optimizing sql queries having aggregates. In *Proceedings of the 13th International Conference on Very Large Data Bases*, (pp. 235–243). San Mateo, CA: Morgan Kaufmann.

W3C (1999). *XML Path Language (XPath) 1.0*. Retrieved from http://www.w3.org/TR/xpath

W3C (2006). *XQuery 1.0*. Retrieved from http://www.w3.org/TR/xquery

W3C. (1998). *Extensible Markup Language (XML)*.

W3C. (2004). *XML Schema Part 0: Primer. Second Edition*

W3C. (2007). *XQuery 1.0 and XPath 2.0 Formal Semantics, recommendation. XUpdate*. (2000). Retrieved from http://xmldb-org.sourceforge.net/xupdate

W3C. (2008). XQuery Update Facility 1.0, candidate recommendation.

Wang, C., Nepal, S., Chen, S., & Zic, J. (2008). Cooperative data management services based on accountable contract. In Meersman & Tari (2004), *On the Move to Meaningful Internet Systems: OTM 2008,* (pp. 301-318).

Wang, F., & Zaniolo, C. (2008). Temporal Queries and Version Management for XML Document Archives. [DKE]. *Journal of Data and Knowledge Engineering, 65*, 304–324. doi:10.1016/j.datak.2007.08.002

Wang, H., Li, J., Luo, J., & Gao, H. (2008). Hash-based subgraph query processing method for graph-structured XML documents. In *34th International Conference on Very Large Data Bases,* (pp. 478-489). Ohio: VLDB Endowment.

Wang, H., Park, S., Fan, W., & Yu, P. (2003). ViST: A dynamic index method for querying XML data by tree structures. In *Proceedings of the ACM SIGMOD International Conference on Management of Data* (pp. 110-121). San Diego, California: ACM.

Wang, W., Wang, H., Lu, H., Jiang, H., Lin, X., & Li, J. (2005). Efficient processing of XML path queries using the disk-based FB index. In *Proceedings of the 31st International Conference on Very Large Data Bases* (pp. 145–156). Trondheim, Norway: ACM.

Weiner, A. M., & Härder, T. (2009, September 7–10). Using Structural Joins and Holistic Twig Joins for Native XML Query Optimization. In *Proceedings of the 13ᵗʰ East European Conference on Advances in Databases and Information Systems, Riga, Latvia*. Berlin: Springer.

Weiner, A. M., Mathis, C., & Härder, T. (2008, March 25). Rules for Query Rewrite in Native XML Databases. In *Proceedings of the 2008 EDBT Workshop on Database Technologies for Handling XML Information on the Web, Nantes, France,* (pp. 21–26). New York: ACM Press.

Weis, M., Naumann, F., & Brosy, F. (2006). *A duplicate detection benchmark for XML (and relational) data*. Paper presented at the SIGMOD workshop on Information Quality for Information Systems (IQIS), Chicago, IL.

Witten, I. H., Neal, R. M., & Cleary, J. G. (1987). Arithmetic coding for data compression. *ACM Communication, 30*(6), 520–540. doi:10.1145/214762.214771

Wong, E., & Youssefi, K. (1976). Decomposition a strategy for query processing. *ACM Transactions on Database Systems, 1*(3), 223–241. doi:10.1145/320473.320479

Wong, R. K., & Lam, F. Shui, & W. M. (2007). Querying and maintaining a compact XML storage. *International World Wide Web Conference,* (pp. 1073-1082). New York: ACM.

Wu, H., & Ling, T. W., & Chen, B. (2007). VERT: a semantic approach for content search and content extraction in XML query processing. In *26th International Conference on Conceptual Modeling* (pp. 534-549). Berlin: Springer.

Wu, W., Yu, C., Doan, A., & Meng, W. (2004). An interactive clustering-based approach to integrating source query interfaces on the deep web. *SIGMOD '04: Proceedings of the 2004 ACM SIGMOD International Conference on Management of Data,* Paris, France, (pp. 95-106).

Wu, X., Lee, M. L., & Hsu, W. (2004). A Prime Number Labeling Scheme for Dynamic Ordered XML Trees. In *Proceedings of the 20th international Conference on Data Engineering,* March 30 - April 02, *ICDE* (pp. 66). Washington, DC: IEEE Computer Society.

Wu, X., Souldatos, S., Theodoratos, D., Dalamagas, T., & Sellis, T. (2008). Efficient evaluation of generalized path pattern queries on XML data. In *WWW '08: Proceeding of the 17th international conference on World Wide Web* (pp. 835-844). New York: ACM.

Wu, Y., Patel, J. M., & Jagadish, H. V. (2003, March 5–8). Structural Join Order Selection for XML Query Optimization. In U. Dayal, K. Ramamritham, & T. M. Vijayaraman (Eds.), *Proceedings of the 19ᵗʰ International Conference on Data Engineering, Bangalore, India* (pp. 443–454). Washington, DC: IEEE Computer Society.

XML Path Language. (2006). Retrieved from http://www.w3.org/TR/xpath

XML. (n.d.). *Extensible markup language.* Retrieved from http://www.w3.org/XML/

XMLschema. (n.d.). Retrieved from http://www.w3.org/XML/Schema

Xpath. (1999). Retrieved from http://www.w3.org/TR/xpath

XQuery 1.0 and XPath 2.0 Full-Text. (2006). Retrieved from http://www.w3.org/TR/2005/WD-xquery-full-text-20050404/

Xu, L., Bao, Z., & Ling, T. W. (2007). A Dynamic Labeling Scheme Using Vectors. In R. Wagner, N. Revell, & G. Pernul, (Eds.), *Proceedings of the 18th international Conference on Database and Expert Systems Applications,* Regensburg, Germany, September 03 - 07, (LNCS Vol. 4653, pp. 130-140). Berlin: Springer-Verlag.

Xu, L., Ling, T. W., Wu, H., & Bao, Z. (2009). DDE: From Dewey to a Fully Dynamic XML Labeling. To appear in *Proceedings of the 2009 ACM SIGMOD international Conference on Management of Data* Providence, Rhode Island, United States, June 29 – July 2, 2009.

Xu, W., & Özsoyoglu, Z. M. (2005). Rewriting XPath queries using materialized views. In *VLDB '05: Proceedings of the 31st International Conference on very Large Data Bases,* Trondheim, Norway, (pp. 121-132).

Xu, Y., & Papakonstantinou, Y. (2005). Efficient Keyword Search for Smallest LCAs in XML Databases. In *Proceedings of SIGMOD.*f

Yan, W., Hu, S., Muthusamy, V., Jacobsen, H.-A., & Zha, L. (2009). Efficient event-based resource discovery. In *Proceedings of the 2009 inaugural international conference on Distributed event-based systems*, Nashville, TN.

Yao, B. B. (2003). *XBench- A family of benchmarks for XML DBMSs.* Retrieved February 15, 2009, from http://se.uwaterloo.ca/~ddbms/projects/xbench/

Yao, B. B., Özsu, M. T., & Keenleyside, J. (2002). *XBench—A family of benchmarks for XML DBMSs.* Paper presented at Efficiency and Effectiveness of XML Tools and Techniques and Data Integration over the Web, (EEXTT), Hong Kong, China.

Yao, B. B., Özsu, M. T., & Khandelwal, N. (2004). *XBench benchmark and performance testing of XML DBMSs.* Paper presented at the 20ᵗʰ International Conference on Data Engineering, Boston, MA.

Yen, J. Y. (1971). Finding the K shortest loopless paths in a network. *Management Science, 17*(11), 712–716. doi:10.1287/mnsc.17.11.712

Yoshikawa, M., Amagasa, T., Shimura, T., & Uemura, S. (2001). XRel: A path-based approach to storage and retrieval of XML documents using relational databases. *ACM Transactions on Internet Technology, 1*(1), 110–141. doi:10.1145/383034.383038

Yu, C., & Jagadish, H. V. (2006) Efficient discovery of XML data redundancies. In *32th International Conference on Very Large Data Bases* (pp. 103-114). Ohio: VLDB Endowment.

Yu, C., & Popa, L. (2004). Constraint-based XML query rewriting for data integration. *SIGMOD,* (pp. 371).

Yu, T., & Ling, T. W., & Lu, J. (2006). TwigStackList¬: A holistic twig join algorithm for twig query with NOT-predicates on XML data. In *11th International Conference on Database Systems for Advanced Applications* (249-263). Berlin: Springer.

Zhang, C., Naughton, J. F., DeWitt, D. J., Luo, Q., & Lohman, G. M. (2001). On supporting containment queries in relational database management systems. In *Proceedings of the 2001 ACM SIGMOD International Conference on Management of Data* (pp. 425-436). Santa Barbara, CA: ACM.

Zhang, N., Agarwal, N., Chandrasekar, S., Idicula, S., Medi, V., Petride, S., & Sthanikam, B. (2009). Binary XML storage and query processing in Oracle 11g. In *35th International Conference on Very Large Data Bases,* (pp. 1354-1365). Ohio: VLDB Endowment.

Zhang, N., Haas, P. J., Josifovski, V., Lohman, G. M., & Zhang, C. (2005, August 30–September 2). Statistical Learning Techniques for Costing XML Queries. In K. Boehm, C. S. Jensen, L. M. Haas, M. L. Kersten, P. Larson, & B. C. Ooi (Eds.), *Proceedings of the 31ˢᵗ International Conference on Very Large Data Bases, Trondheim, Norway* (pp. 289–300). New York: ACM Press.

Zhang, N., Kacholia, V., & Özsu, M. T. (2004). A succinct physical storage scheme for efficient evaluation of path queries in XML. In *Proceedings of the 20th International Conference on Data Engineering* (pp. 54-65). Boston: IEEE Computer Society.

Zhang, N., Özsu, M. T., Ilyas, I. F., & Aboulnaga, A. (2006). FIX: A feature-based indexing technique for XML documents. In *Proceedings of the 32nd International Conference on Very Large Data Bases* (pp. 259-271). Seoul, Korea: ACM.

Zhang, X., Yang, L. H., Lee, M. L., & Hsu, W. (2004). Scaling SDI systems via query clustering and aggregation. In *Proceedings of the 9th International Conference on Database Systems for Advanced Applications,* (pp. 21-23).

Zhuge, H., Liu, J., Feng, L., & He, C. (2004). Semantic-based query routing and heterogeneous data integration in peer-to-peer semantic link networks. In *ICSNW,* (pp. 91-107).

Ziv, J., & Lempel, A. (1977). An universal algorithm for sequential data compression. *IEEE Transactions on Information Theory, 30*(6), 520–540.

Ziv, J., & Lempel, A. (1978). Compression of Individual Sequences via Variable-rate Coding. *IEEE Transactions on Information Theory, IT-24*(5), 530–536. doi:10.1109/TIT.1978.1055934

Zorba – The XQuery processor (n.d.). Retrieved from http://www.zorba-xquery.com/f

Zou, Q., Liu, S., & Chu, W. (2004, November 12-13). Ctree: A Compact Tree for Indexing XML Data. In A.H.F. Laender, D. Lee, & M. Ronthaler (Eds.), *Proceedings of the 6th annual ACM international workshop on Web Information and Data Management, WIDM 2004,* Washington, DC, (pp.39-46). New York: ACM Press.

About the Contributors

Changqing Li is currently a Postdoctoral Associate in Duke University, U.S.A. He received his Ph.D. Degree in Computer Science from National University of Singapore, and Master Degree from Peking University. Dr. Li has been working on XML query and update processing, and text processing and search. He has published 20 papers. He is an editor of this book, and his publications also appear in top international database journals and conferences. Particularly his paper was one of the two candidates for the Best Student Paper Award in a top international database conference ICDE'06. Dr. Li was a member of the Program Committees of International Conferences CIKM, DEXA, and KDIR. He was also a reviewer of journals and conferences TKDE, ACM SIGMOD, VLDB, ICDE, WWW, ACM GIS, etc.

Tok Wang Ling is a professor of the Department of Computer Science at National University of Singapore. His research interests include Data Modeling, ER approach, Normalization Theory, and Semistructured Data Model and XML query processing. He published over 190 papers, co-authored a book and co-edited 9 conference proceedings. He organized and served as Conference Co-chair of 8 conferences including SIGMOD'2007 and VLDB'2010. He served as PC Co-chair of 5 conferences including ER'2003. He served on the PC of more than 130 database conferences. He is a steering committee member of ER Conference. He was an Advisor of the steering committee of DASFAA, chair and vice chair of the steering committee of ER and DASFAA conference, a steering committee member of DOOD and HSI. He is an editor of 5 journals including Data & Knowledge Engineering. He is a senior member of ACM, IEEE, and Singapore Computer Society.

***

Vikas Arora is a software engineer with more than 15 years experience in the industry in both development and management roles. His work has focussed on data management technologies including query processing, XML/XQuery, language interoperability, web services. He has several patents and publications in these areas, and has contributed to the development of standards and products based on these technologies. He holds a B.Tech. in Computer Science from the Indian Institute of Technology Kharagpur and M.S. in Computer Science from the University of California Santa Barbara.

Angela Bonifati is a researcher in Computer Science at Icar CNR, National Research Council (Italy). She received her Laurea degree in Computer Science Engineering from University of Calabria (Italy) in 1997, and her Ph.D. degree in Computer Science Engineering from Politecnico di Milano (Italy) in

2001. She has been a Post-Doc student at Inria (France) during 2002–2003 and a visiting researcher at University of British Columbia (Canada) since 2004. Her research interests cover several aspects of data management and web technologies, and include (but are not limited to) XML query and update languages and processing, XML data integration and distribution, data warehouses and web services.

K. Selçuk Candan is a professor at the School of Computing and Informatics (Department of Computer Science and Engineering) at the Arizona State University. He joined the department in August 1997, after receiving his Ph.D. from the Computer Science Department at the University of Maryland at College Park. Prof. Candan's primary research interest is in the area of management of non-traditional, heterogeneous, and imprecise (such as multimedia, web, and scientific) data. He has published over 130 articles and many book chapters. He has also authored 9 patents. Currently, Prof. Candan is an editorial board member of the Very Large Databases (VLDB) journal. He has also served in the organization and program committees of many conferences. In 2006, he served as an organization committee member for SIGMOD'06, the flagship database conference of the ACM. In 2008, he served as a PC Chair for another leading, flagship conference of the ACM, this time focusing on multimedia research (SIGMM'08). He received his B.S. degree in computer science from Bilkent University in Turkey in 1993.

Huiping Cao is a postdoctoral research associate in the Department of Computer Science and Engineering, School of Computing and Informatics, at Arizona State University (ASU). Before joining ASU in June 2007, she received her Ph.D. in Computer Science from The University of Hong Kong. Dr. Cao's research interests include data mining (such as spatio-temporal data analysis) and databases (e.g., integrating heterogeneous data). She has served as a program committee member for Workshop on Real Time Business Intelligence (RTBI09) and Workshop on Multimedia Data Mining conjunction with SDM09. She has also served as a reviewer for IEEE Transactions on Knowledge and Data Engineering, Data & Knowledge Engineering, Geoinformatica, Knowledge and Information Systems, etc.

Chee-Yong Chan is an Associate Professor in the Computer Science Department at the National University of Singapore. He received his B.Sc. (Hons) and M.Sc. degrees in Computer Science from the National University of Singapore, and his Ph.D. degree in Computer Science from the University of Wisconsin-Madison. His current research interests include XML databases, query processing and optimization, indexing techniques, and data warehousing systems. He is a member of the ACM and the IEEE Computer Society.

Yi Chen is an Assistant Professor in the Department of Computer Science and Engineering at Arizona State University, USA. She received Ph.D. degree in Computer Science from the University of Pennsylvania in 2005. She is a recipient of the NSF CAREER award. Her current research interests focus on empowering non-expert users to easily access diverse structured data, in particular, searching and optimization in the context of databases, information integration, workflows, and social network (http://www.public.asu.edu/~ychen127/).

Chin-Wan Chung received a Ph.D. degree from the University of Michigan, Ann Arbor in 1983. He was a Senior Research Scientist and a Staff Research Scientist in the Computer Science Department at the General Motors Research Laboratories (GMR). While at GMR, he developed Dataplex, a heterogeneous distributed database management system integrating different types of databases. Since

1993, he has been a professor in the Department of Computer Science at the Korea Advanced Institute of Science and Technology (KAIST), Korea. At KAIST, he developed a full-scale object-oriented spatial database management system called OMEGA, which supports ODMG standards. His current research interests include the semantic Web, the mobile Web, sensor networks and stream data management, and multimedia databases.

Dario Colazzo received his PhD degree at the University of Pisa (Italy), in 2004, and is currently assistant professor at the University of Paris South at Orsay. His main research interests are on type and programming language theory for the optimization and correctness checking of programs manipulating XML data. Hi is also interested on modal logic and process calculi theory. He co-organized the ECOOP XOODB workshop 2009, and served as PC member of EDBT DataX workshop 2009, and as a reviewer for international conferences and journals.

Alfredo Cuzzocrea is actually a Researcher at the Institute of High Performance Computing and Networking of the Italian National Research Council, Italy, and an Adjunct Professor at the Department of Electronics, Computer Science and Systems of the University of Calabria, Italy. His research interests include multidimensional data modelling and querying, data stream modelling and querying, data warehousing and OLAP, OLAM, XML data management, Web information systems modelling and engineering, knowledge representation and management models and techniques, Grid and P2P computing. He is author or co-author of more than 105 papers in referred international conferences (including EDBT, SSDBM, ISMIS, ADBIS, DEXA, DaWaK, DOLAP, IDEAS, SEKE, WISE, FQAS, SAC) and international journals (including DKE, JIIS, IJDWM, WIAS). He serves as program committee member of referred international conferences (including ICDM, SDM, PKDD, PAKDD, CIKM, ICDCS, ER, WISE, DASFAA, FQAS, SAC) and as review board member of referred international journals (including TODS, TKDE, TSMC, IS, DKE, JIIS, IPL, TPLP, COMPJ, DPDB, KAIS, INS, IJSEKE, FGCS). He also serves as PC Chair in several international conferences and as Guest Editor in international journals like JCSS, DKE, KAIS, IJBIDM, IJDMMM and JDIM.

Gillian Dobbie is a Professor in the Department of Computer Science at the University of Auckland. She received a Ph.D. from the University of Melbourne, held lecturing positions at the University of Melbourne and Victoria University of Wellington, and visiting research positions at Griffith University and the National University of Singapore. She has published over 70 international refereed journal and conference papers in areas as diverse as formal foundations for databases, object oriented databases, semistructured databases, logic and databases, data warehousing, data mining, access control, e-commerce and data modeling.

Ke Geng got his first Masters degree of Computer Networks in China. When he moved to New Zealand, he changed his major to database management and gained a Masters degree from the University of Auckland in 2006. Then he began his PhD research with his supervisor Professor Gillian Dobbie. His research area is XML semantic query optimization. His interests include database management, XML, data classification, benchmarks and networks.

Giovanna Guerrini is associate professor at the Department of Computer and Information Sciences of the University of Genova, Italy. She received the MS and PhD degrees in Computer Science from the University of Genova, Italy, in 1993 and 1998, respectively. She had been assistant professor at the University of Genova (1996-2001) and associate professor at the University of Pisa (2001-2005). Her research interests include object-oriented, active, and temporal databases as well as semi-structured and XML data handling. She served as Program Committee member of international conferences, like EDBT, ECOOP, ACM OOPSLA, ACM CIKM and she is currently serving as Conference Co-chair for ECOOP 2009.

Sylvain Hallé received the BS degree in mathematics from Université Laval in 2002 and the MSc in mathematics and PhD in computer science from Université du Québec à Montréal in 2004 and 2008, respectively. He is currently a postdoctoral research fellow at University of California, Santa Barbara. He received fellowships from the Natural Sciences and Engineering Research Council of Canada (NSERC) in 2005 and Quebec's Research Fund on Nature and Technologies (FQRNT) in 2008. His major research interests include Web applications and formal verification. He is a member of the ACM, the Association for Symbolic Logic, the IEEE, and the IEEE Computer Society. He was co-chair of DDBP 2008, TIME 2008 and DDBP 2009.

Theo Härder obtained his Ph.D. degree in Computer Science from the TU Darmstadt, Germany in 1975. In 1976, he spent a post-doctoral year at the IBM Research Lab in San Jose and joined the project System R. In 1978, he was associate professor for Computer Science at the TU Darmstadt. As a full professor, he is leading the research group Databases and Information Systems (DBIS) at the TU Kaiserslautern since 1980. He is the recipient of the Konrad Zuse Medal (2001) and the Alwin Walther Medal (2004) and obtained the Honorary Doctoral Degree from the Computer Science Dept. of the University of Oldenburg in 2002. His research interests are in many DBIS areas, in particular, DBMS architecture, transaction systems, information integration, and XML databases. He is author/coauthor of 7 textbooks and of more than 250 scientific contributions with >140 peer-reviewed conference papers and >60 journal publications. His professional services include numerous positions as chairman of DBIS in the German Computer Society, conference/program chairs and program committee member, editor-in-chief of Computer Science – Research and Development (Springer), associate editor of Information Systems (Elsevier), World Wide Web (Kluver), and Transactions on Database Systems (ACM).

Shuang Hou has worked at Middleware Systems Research Group in the Department of Electrical and Computer Engineering at University of Toronto from 2004 to 2007. She received B.S. degree in Computer Engineering at Harbin Institute of Technology and M.S. degree in Computer Science from the University of Toronto. She has been active in the area of content-based Publish/Subscribe distributed system, matching and routing of XML and XPath Queries in Data Dissemination Networks.

Hans-Arno Jacobsen holds the Bell University Laboratories Chair in Software, and he is a faculty member in the Department of Electrical and Computer Engineering and the Department of Computer Science at the University of Toronto, where he leads the Middleware Systems Research Group. His principal areas of research include the design and the development of middleware systems, distributed systems, and information systems. Arno's current research focus lies on publish/subscribe, content-based routing, event processing, and aspect-orientation.

Jihyun Lee is a Ph.D student in the Department of Computer Science at Korea Advanced Instituted of Science and Technology (KAIST), South Korea. Her research interests include XML data management, the semantic Web, ontology data management, and information retrieval on the Web.

Guoli Li is a Ph.d candidate at Computer Science department in University of Toronto. Her research focus on "historic data access in Publish/Subscribe". Guoli received her master degree in computer science from University of Toronto in 2005. She also received her Master degree in electronic engineering from Xi'an jiaotong university in 2002. Guoli finished her bachelor's degree in Information Techniques from Xi'an Jiaotong University in 1999.

Zhen Hua Liu is a veteran of industrial strength database system kernel developer and data architect in DBMS industry for 18 years. He has worked extensively in the area of SQL query processing for RDBMS, type, function and index extensibility for Object Relational DBMS, XQuery, SQL/XML processing, XML storage and indexing for XML DBMS. He has patents and publications in these areas and has contributed to the development of SQL/XML standard and XQuery Java API. His primary interest is in Data Space search, mining and knowledge discovery. He holds degree of Computer Science from University of California at Berkeley and is a member of ACM/SIGMOD and IEEE Computer Society.

Ziyang Liu is a Ph.D. candidate and an SFAz (Science Foundation Arizona) Graduate Fellowship recipient in the Department of Computer Science and Engineering at Arizona State University. He joined Arizona State University in August 2006 and received M.S. degree in Computer Science in May 2008. His current research focuses on keyword search on structured and semi-structured data and workflow management (http://www.public.asu.edu/~zliu41/).

Jiaheng Lu is an Associate professor of the Department of Computer Science at Renmin University of China. He received his Ph.D. Degree in Computer Science from National University of Singapore. His advisor is Prof. Ling Tok Wang. His research interests include semi-structured Data Model, XML query processing, cloud computing and spatial database. He published over 10 papers at top conferences and journals, including SIGMOD, VLDB, ICDE et al. He served as PC member of more than 10 conferences.

Patrick Martin is a Professor of the School of Computing at Queen's University in Kingston, Ontario, Canada. He received his PhD degree from the University of Toronto in 1984. He is the leader of the Database Systems Laboratory. His research interests are in the areas of web services, data management for pervasive computing and self-managing database management systems. He is also a Visiting Scientist with IBM's Centre for Advanced Studies.

Norman May is a graduate of the University of Mannheim and University of Waterloo, Canada, where he has studied Business Administration and Computer Science. He received his doctoral degree from the University of Mannheim in Germany. This research focused on query optimization and query execution for analytical queries and XML queries. He contributed to the Natix XML database developed at the University of Mannheim. Dr. May joined SAP Research in May 2007. His research results were published in international conferences and journals.

Marco Mesiti is assistant professor at University of Milan, Italy. He received the MS and PhD degrees in Computer Science from the University of Genova, Italy, in 1998 and 2003, respectively. His main research interests include the management of XML documents, XML schema evolution, and access control mechanisms for XML. He has been a visiting researcher at the applied research center of Telcordia Technologies, Morristown, New Jersey. He co-organized the three editions of the EDBT DataX workshop and served as PC member of EDBT PhD workshop 2006 and 2008, ADBIS Conference 2006, IEEE SAINT 2005, IEEE SAINT 2006, EDBT Workshop ClustWeb 2004, and as reviewer for international conferences and journals.

Guido Moerkotte is a full professor at the University of Mannheim. He earned his doctoral degree and habilitation from University of Karlsruhe in the group of Prof. Lockemann. Before coming to the University of Mannheim he held a professorship at RWTH Aachen. His research also includes collaborations with IBM Research in Almaden or Microsoft Research. He made significant research contributions in the area of databases which were published in over 100 research publications in international conferences, journals, and books. He served as reviewer for various conferences and scientific journals. His major research interests are in the area of query processing and query optimization but also transaction processing and storage structures. His research results were applied to various database management systems including GOM, an object oriented database, Natix, an XML database, and Demaq, a system for declarative messaging and queuing.

Samir Mohammad received the BSc and the MSc degrees in Computer Science from Al-Zaytoonah University, and the University of Jordan, respectively. He is a fourth-year PhD candidate in the School of Computing at Queen's University, Canada. He is a member of the Database research group, and is advised by Dr. Patrick Martin. His research interest is database systems and pervasive computing, with specialization in designing structural indexes for XML data that can be used to efficiently query XML databases. He is a recipient of Grace L. Boileau Graduate Award.

Yuan Ni is a Staff Researcher at IBM China Research Laboratory. She received her B.Sc degree in Computer Science from the Fudan University in 2003, and her Ph.D. degree in Computer Science from the National University of Singapore in 2008. Her current research interests include XML query processing, RDF data management, Semantic Technology.

Anguel Novoselsky has been working in the area of compiler and language design for more than 20 years with companies in USA, Canada and Bulgaria. Currently, he is a consulting member developing XML components including XQuery, XSLT, XMLSchema and other XML processors. He holds M.S. of Computer Science from Technical Institute of Sofia, Bulgaria.

Barbara Oliboni is assistant professor at the Department of Computer Science of the University of Verona. In 1998 she received the Master Degree in Computer Science by the University of Verona, and in 2003 she received the Ph.D. degree in Computer Engineering by the Politecnico of Milan with the dissertation "Blind queries and constraints: representing flexibility and time in semistructured data". From April 2003 to October 2005 she was a Post-Doc fellow at the Department of Computer Science of the University of Verona. He has been reviewer for national and international conferences, journals and magazines. She is involved since some years as a member of the program committee of international conferences.

M. Tamer Özsu is Professor of Computer Science and University Research Chair at the University of Waterloo and Director of the David R. Cheriton School of Computer Science. Dr. Özsu's current research focuses on Internet-scale data distribution, multimedia data management, and XML query processing and optimization. He is a Fellow of ACM, a Senior Member of IEEE, and a member of Sigma Xi.

Myung-Jae Park is a Ph.D. student in the Department of Computer Science at the Korea Advanced Institute of Science and Technology (KAIST), Korea. His research interests include XML, ontology and the semantic Web, and publish/subscribe systems.

Yan Qi is a PhD candidate at the School of Computing and Informatics (Department of Computer Science and Engineering) at Arizona State University. He received his Bachelor's and Master's degree on Computer Science from the University of Science and Technology of China. His research interests include conflict identification and resolution in data integration, XML query processing, and table summarization in relational database. Currently, he is working on the extension of RDF model and SPARQL query language to support the rank-aware query processing over ontology information.

Maria Luisa Sapino is Full Professor at the Computer Science Department of the University of Torino, and adjunct professor at Arizona State University. Her initial contributions to computer science were in the area of logic programming and artificial intelligence, specifically in the semantics of negation in logic programming, and in the abductive extensions of logic programs. Since mid-90s she has been applying these techniques to the challenges associated with database access control, and with heterogeneous and multimedia data management. In particular, she developed novel techniques and algorithms for similarity based information retrieval, content based image retrieval, and web accessibility for users who are visually impaired. She also focused on temporal and synchronization aspects of distributed multimedia presentations in the presence of resource constraints. Her current research interests are mostly addressed toward the integration of heterogeneous information sources (in particular, integration of taxonomic information) and toward the definition of innovative navigation methods within rich multimedia archives, such as newspaper archives, television archives, or archives containing big quantities of heterogeneous scientific data, for example in the archaeology domain (the archaeological domain is the focus of the NSF funded project "AOC: Archaeological Data Integration for the Study of Long-Term Human and Social Dynamics" at ASU) Maria Luisa Sapino's active collaborations include national and international Universities and Research Centers: RAI- Centro Ricerche e Innovazioni Tecnologiche, Telecom Italia Lab, University of Napoli Federico II (prof. Antonio Picariello), Arizona State University (Prof. K. Selcuk Candan), and Rensselaer Polytechnic Institute (Prof. Sibel Adali).

Junichi Tatemura received the BE degree in electrical engineering and the ME and PhD degrees in information engineering from the University of Tokyo. He was an assistant professor in the Institute of Industrial Science, University of Tokyo from 1994 to 2001. He is currently a senior research staff member in NEC Laboratories America, Inc., Cupertino, California. His current research interests include service-oriented data management (such as web services, XML, data stream, and data-centric cloud computing) and web data management (such as data extraction and mining from the web).

Roger Villemaire received the PhD degree from the University of Tübingen in 1988. He was a postdoctoral fellow at McGill University and later at Université du Québec à Montréal (UQAM). He is a professor in the Department of Computer Science at UQAM, which he joined in 1993. His research interests include applications of logic in computer science, in particular formalisms, methods and algorithms which can help to realize reliable computing systems. He was co-chair of TIME 2008 and served on its program committee in 2009. He is a member of the ACM, the Association for Symbolic Logic and the IEEE Computer Society.

Emmanuel Waller received his PhD in Computer Science from the University of Paris South at Orsay in 1993. He is assistant professor at the University of Paris South at Orsay, and was part-time assistant professor at Ecole Polytechnique from 1999 to 2007. His main research interests include updates, schema evolution, views, polymorphic type inference, document publication, in XML, object or relational databases. He published articles in JCSS, PODS, SIGMOD, ICDT, etc. He co-organized the ECOOP XOODB workshop 2009, and served as PC member of EDBT DataX workshop 2009, VLDB PhD workshop 2009, VLDB XSym workshop 2009, and as a reviewer for international conferences and journals.

Andreas Matthias Weiner studied Computer Science at the University of Kaiserslautern from 2002 to 2007. In July 2007, he joined the research group Databases and Information Systems (DBIS) lead by Prof. Härder. Since that time, he has been working on his doctoral dissertation. His research interests are in the following areas: XML databases, cost-based query optimization, and XQuery. In the XTC (XML Transaction Coordinator) project, he explores cost-based native XML query optimization techniques.

Huayu Wu is a third-year PhD student in the Department of Computer Science, School of Computing at the National University of Singapore. He received his B.Sc. (Honors) degree in the School of Computing at the National University of Singapore in 2006. His research interest is database technologies, with specification in XML twig pattern query processing, XML keyword search, semantic approach in XML query processing and XML document labeling, and he is advised by Professor Dr. Tok Wang Ling. He has published papers on leading database conferences, including the ACM SIGMOD Conference, the International World Wide Web Conferences (WWW) and the International Conference on Conceptual Modeling (ER).

Liang Xu joined National University of Singapore in 2002. After an undergraduate degree in Compute science, he is now a PhD candidate and a Graduate Fellowship recipient at School of Computing, National University of Singapore. His current research focuses on XML labeling and query processing.

Ning Zhang obtained his Ph.D. degree from the University of Waterloo. His dissertation was titled "Query Processing and Optimization in Native XML Databases". He had worked in Oracle XML database group before he joined Facebook recently. At Oracle, he has worked on the Oracle XML Index and Binary XML storage and processing. Dr. Ning Zhang's research interests span database storage, query processing, indexing, and query optimization.

Index

A

access control policies 362

acyclic graphs 100

advertisement-based routing algorithms 227, 231

algebraic optimizations 283, 284, 285, 286, 301

algebra representation 283

algebras 285

algorithms 227, 228, 230, 231, 232, 234, 236, 238, 240, 243, 246, 247, 252

Amazon E-Commerce Service 407

ancestor-descendant (AD) relationships 125, 126, 133, 134, 135, 139, 387

Apache Xerces 210, 225

application benchmarks 66, 67, 68, 77, 78, 79, 80, 93, 94

application program interfaces (API) 100, 123

archiving 48, 51, 59, 60, 62, 64

arithmetic encoding 49, 50, 51, 52, 54, 55, 56, 57, 59, 60, 61

Atom Web syndication format 1

autonomous peer systems 309

B

bag semantics 285

benchmarks 66, 67, 68, 69, 70, 71, 72, 73, 74, 75, 77, 78, 79, 80, 81, 83, 85, 87, 88, 93, 94, 95, 96

benchmarks, traditional 67

binary large object (BLOB) 18, 32, 34

bioinformatics 309, 310, 327, 334, 354

bioinformatics data 309

blogs 1

B

bloom-filters 258, 260, 277

Boolean value 185, 187

brokers 227, 247, 248, 249

buffer memory optimality 184, 185

business intelligence applications 309

business intelligence (BI) 309

bzip2 48, 51, 53, 58, 61, 65

C

calculus representations 285, 286

cardinality estimates 284

catalog information 258

centralized publish/subscribe system 228

character large object (CLOB) 18, 32, 34

child axis 285

child values 387, 392

Chord 256, 257, 259, 260, 265, 266, 267, 269, 270, 272, 275, 277, 278, 280

Chord's DHT 256

client services 407

commitToBuy XML element 407

complex twig query 100, 101

composite applications, value-added 406

compression ratios 47, 48, 51, 52, 53, 58, 60, 61, 62, 63

conflict-eliminating integration 333, 335

conflict-preserving integration 333, 335

conflict resolution 333, 334, 353, 354

conflicts 333, 334, 335, 337, 340, 347, 348, 349, 354, 355, 359

coNP complexity class 285

containment 126, 127, 131, 132, 135, 139, 140, 141, 142

Containment labeling 125, 126, 139